ALSO BY BERNARD CLAYTON

The Breads of France
The Complete Book of Pastry
The Complete Book of Soups and Stews
Cooking Across America
Complete Book of Small Breads

Bernard Clayton's New

COMPLETE BOOK
OF BREADS

Bernard Clayton, Jr.

Working drawings by Donnie Cameron

SIMON & SCHUSTER

New York London Toronto Sydney

SIMON & SCHUSTER
Rockefeller Center
1230 Avenue of the Americas
New York, NY 10020

This Simon & Schuster edition 2003

SIMON & SCHUSTER and colophon are registered trademarks
of Simon & Schuster, Inc.

For information regarding special discounts for bulk purchases,
please contact Simon & Schuster Special Sales:
1-800-456-6798 or business@simonandschuster.com

Designed by Katy Riegel

Manufactured in the United States of America

10   9   8   7   6   5

Library of Congress Cataloging-in-Publication Data
Clayton, Bernard.
    Bernard Clayton's new complete book of breads / Bernard Clayton, Jr. ;
working drawings by Donnie Cameron.—[Rev. version].
        p.   cm.
    Includes index.
    1. Bread.   I. Title.
TX769.C5328   2003
641.8'15—dc21   2003045473
ISBN-13: 978-0-7432-3472-6
ISBN-10:   0-7432-3472-3

WITH THANKS

Since writing the first edition of *The Complete Book of Breads* I have talked with and written to several thousand home bakers on several continents about recipes, techniques, problems, successes, and a dozen and one other things that bakers talk about when they get together. It has been an exciting period and I wish to thank them all for their understanding when I didn't have an answer, and their letters of appreciation when I did.

My appreciation, too, to those in the United States and Canada who have sent me bags of flour, packets of yeast, slices of bread, whole loaves of bread, a new kind of rolling pin, a different spatula, favorite recipes, and on and on, to my great delight.

I remain indebted to those who helped me write the first book and whose names appear in its pages. Here are several more who have been particularly helpful and supportive and should be added to that special group:

Craig Claiborne, celebrated food authority and author, who early on visited my kitchen studio and assured me the volume had merit.

Wendy and Michael London, who have made their bake shop in Saratoga Springs, New York, one of the finest in the country, and who have helped me time and again with their knowledge of the art of baking.

Julia Child, with whom I have talked and corresponded for a decade about what makes a good loaf of French bread and where in this country and France it could be found.

Bernard Bruinsma, Tacoma, Washington, an outstanding authority on yeast and flour who never failed to have an answer when I had a question. His help is reflected throughout the book.

Random House, for permission to quote from *The Laurel Kitchen Bread Book* by Laurel Robertson.

Henry Holt and Company, Inc., for permission to reprint the recipe for Feta Biscuits from *Cooking and Baking the Greek Way* by Anne Theoharous. Copyright © 1977 by Anne Theoharous.

Carl G. Sontheimer, head of Cuisinarts, who urged me to give the food processor equal time in my kitchen, and whose belief in its ability to make fine bread, I now fully share. I thank him, too, for permission to use recipes from his fine magazine, *The Pleasures of Cooking*.

Jep Morgan, who sent fresh herbs from the Morgan Herb Farm in Acworth, Georgia, when I did the many recipes that called for herbs.

Barbara St. Amand, an outstanding cook and teacher, who flew from her home in Atlanta to work in my kitchen to help develop new recipes.

Sunset magazine, which contributed much to my first book, for permission to adapt the recipes for Italian Olive Bread, Golden Beehive, and Italian Mother Loaf.

Shirley O. Corriher, Atlanta, for permission to use her grandmother's recipe for "touch-of-grace" Southern Biscuits.

The staff of Red Star Yeast (Universal Foods Corporation), Milwaukee, Wisconsin, who several times explained the complexities of yeast so that I could understand this incredible fungus—no small task. I thank them too, for permission to use recipes from the excellent Red Star cookbooks—Sauerkraut Rye, Hearty White, and Buttermilk Rye.

The Pillsbury Company, for permission to adapt the winning recipes of Kayleen Sloboden (Cheese Bread Ring) and Bonnie Komlos (Familia-Raisin Bread) in the 1984 Pillsbury Bake-Off® Contest.

Reader's Digest Association, Ltd., London, for its help.

Carole Lalli, my editor and friend. Together we share this book.

And, finally, *un grand merci* to the *boulangers* and food people on the Continent, especially France, who have been my teachers and with whom I have spent many rewarding hours.

To my wife,
who let me write the first
Complete Book of Breads
in her kitchen and then
suggested I build my own.
Which I did.

CONTENTS

INTRODUCTION

"THIS IS A working cookbook."

Those words were written more than thirty years ago as the preamble to *The Complete Book of Breads*. The aim of the book then, as it is now, was to encourage anyone to make a loaf of delicious bread and enjoy doing it, as well as serving bread at the table.

It has succeeded far more than I could have dreamed. (I thought at the time I would be happy if the publisher would print at least enough copies so that I could give them to my family.) Little did I realize that it would become a classic among cookbooks. It would lead a revolution in bread-baking at home, and encourage a rebirth of traditional artisan bakeries.

My words of encouragement thirty years ago are unchanged.

Baking bread is a relaxed art. Unlike the precise steps in making pastries, bread baking allows a comforting margin of error. There is no step in the bread-making process that cannot, in some way, be delayed or moved ahead just a bit to make it more convenient to fit into a busy schedule. If the dough you are kneading gets stubborn, pulls back, and refuses to be shaped, as is its wont—walk away from it for a few minutes. It will relax, and so will you.

Many wondrous things happen in bread baking, and some not so wondrous.

The most wondrous is infusing life, literally, into the dough with tiny grains of yeast, and watching the dough grow and mature before your eyes. A miracle.

On the other hand, a less-wondrous thing is forgetting to add yeast, as the dough just sits there waiting for you to do something to help (which, at this point, can't be much).

I have been asked by many how the son of a country newspaper editor who had many careers in writing got into cookbooks, especially one about bread. I grew up in a family of dedicated butter-and-cream cooks, and married one. I knew my way around a kitchen and I knew what pots and pans and skillets were for.

Moving to Indiana from the West Coast changed all that. It was a particularly cold and miserable winter—especially so after living in California and Hawaii. I felt trapped in my apartment which, fortunately, had a kitchen with all of the requisite tools.

One day, I read in *Time* magazine about a cookbook by three women, including one named Julia Child, on mastering the art of French cooking. I bought the book. I even remember my first endeavor: a slice of ham with mustard sauce. Across the top of the recipe I wrote the date—March 16, 1967—and what I thought of the results. I gave myself an A. Before that moment, it never occurred to me that I could do well in the kitchen beyond frying an egg or grilling a steak.

Breads intrigued me. We had just returned from a lengthy bicycle, canal boat, and gypsy-wagon trip across Ireland, England, and the Continent, and were enamored with the wonderful country breads we ate along the way.

I could bake them at home. Or so I thought.

When I started to look for recipes for these breads, as well as the necessary ingredients, I found almost nothing. The few books on breads were not well written and were difficult to follow.

I had to drive a hundred miles to a big-city flour mill for bread flour and rye and whole wheat flours, which came only in 50-pound bags. Some of my baking pans I made from black-metal stove pipe I got from Honey Jones at his country trading post south of town. (I still use them.) Honey and I traded (because Honey had no teeth, for a length of pipe I baked a whole-wheat loaf with a soft crust).

Since then, there have been literally hundred of cookbooks on baking.

Ingredients and equipment abound, in catalogues and in kitchenware shops. A variety of flours is only minutes away in the market across town. In a recent King Arthur Flour catalogue (one of the best), I could order not only every kind of American and Canadian hard, soft, and in-between wheat flours, but also flours from France, Ireland, and Italy, not to mention a flour that borders on overkill—a blend of eight grains: wheat, triticale, rye, millet, oat, buckwheat, barley, and soy.

New equipment, yeasts, and techniques have been introduced to make home bread-making easier and faster with no loss of quality. Equipment ranges from baking stones, clay baking domes, and a huge array of special baking tins to mixers, and food processors powerful enough to take over kneading. New and larger food processors cut down kneading time impressively. The most surprising development in bread-baking was an import from Japan, the bread machine; greeted by skeptics at first (I among them), it has developed a coterie of devoted admirers around the world.

Thirty years ago, commercial white bread, much of it squeezing soft, had three-quarters of the market; the balance was made up of a smattering of whole-wheat and rye breads and a few others. There were few hand-crafted, hearth-baked loaves by artisan bakers.

Imagine the puzzled look you might have been given thirty years ago in almost any bakery, if you were to ask for a loaf of hoska or anise kuchen or challah or walnut onion or focaccia or semolina sourdough or pumpernickel, not to mention beer bread. Or if you told the baker you preferred his Russian rye over his Swedish rye!

For new bakers, a final word.

Bread-baking, a relaxed discipline, is also a forgiving one. A few grains more or less of sugar or salt or yeast will make little difference in the results. I seldom scrape a knife across a measuring cup to get *exactly* one cup of flour. I eyeball it, which saves time and gives me the feeling that I am the one who's in control. I know it will all balance out in the end and be a great loaf of bread.

Bread making is not a gentle art, especially when you are kneading by hand. Don't baby the dough! Break the kneading rhythm by occasionally throwing the ball of dough down hard against the table top. *Wham! Bam!* Don't be gentle with it. Smack it down hard. Let it sound all the way to the living room. Let them know something great is going on! The dough loves it!

For the new baker (and to freshen the skills of a more knowledgeable one) I suggest first reading the "Thrill of Discovery" chapter, which gives the sense of adventure to be found in bread-making, then baking The First Loaf (page 17). Return to the Discovery recipes later after you have made the first loaf. You will do so with confidence!

Good baking!

EQUIPMENT
THAT CONTRIBUTES
TO A PERFECT LOAF

A LOAF OF BREAD can be made in two ways, by hand or in a machine.

BY HAND:

Work space is perhaps the most important consideration in making dough by hand, but the space need not be overlarge. An area 2 feet square is adequate for almost all bread-making—assembling the ingredients, the mixing, the kneading, and the shaping.

All the loaves in my first bread book were made on a 2-foot-square Formica counter-top between the stove and the sink, and on an 18-inch-square board in our trailer while traveling the United States. Later, when I built a new kitchen with two 12-foot work tables, I found that I still centered my work on a small space on one countertop.

Formica is a good surface, but it can be scratched with a knife or dough scraper. A table of maple is my preference, but it must be cleaned thoroughly after each batch of dough. And never allow a knife to get near it. It is not a cutting block!

Stainless steel is very good. While it looks cold and unyielding, for sanitary reasons it is the only surface allowed in commercial kitchens by the health departments of most cities.

The height of the countertop or table is more important than its composition. It should be high enough to allow the palms of the hands, arms extended, to rest on the top surface. If it is too low, it will tire your back; too high, you cannot push *with force* down on the dough.

By Electric Mixer:

An electric mixer with a dough hook attachment will take all the toil out of bread-making. And it does it just as well as by hand.

I have used the large-model KitchenAid (K5A) on medium batches of dough with great success. However, a large batch of dough may climb up the dough hook and work its way into the gears. Nothing stops it unless I force the dough with a rubber scraper to remain below the wide metal collar.

In the first steps of making dough, when it is nothing more than a batter, I use the flat paddle-type beater at medium speed and then attach the dough hook only after the batter or dough is thick enough to move with the revolving arm. The KitchenAid people suggest the dough hook for the entire process but I like to start with the flat beater.

A second machine in my kitchen is a Bosch Universal Kitchen Machine, a powerful mixer with an extra-large bowl and a clawlike kneading arm that effectively rolls and tumbles the dough. There is sometimes a point in the mixing process when the dough is slick and slides around the bowl rather than tumbling, but a little additional flour will correct this.

There are many other good mixers with kneading devices; however, don't attempt to mix heavy doughs in a machine that is not guaranteed by the company to handle it. Mixing and kneading puts a strain on small motors, and even my large machines will get hot during the few minutes it takes to knead a batch of dough. Do not use light-weight or portable or hand-held mixers because the danger of damage is too great. They are fine for batters no thicker than pancake mixes, but that is all.

By Food Processor:

In all the years that I have baked bread nothing has surprised me more than the ability of the food processor to knead dough in 60 *seconds* or less. I was late accepting the processor as a viable machine because I believed that only a long period of kneading would make a good loaf of bread. I was wrong.

I am not familiar with the dynamics involved but I do know that the force of the whirling blade, steel or plastic, is tremendous and can accomplish in a moment or two what otherwise would take long minutes.

The recipes in the book have been tested on one of the larger Cuisinart models, the DLC-7 Super Pro. It is a rugged model for the home kitchen and I know a number of chefs and caterers who use it as well.

There are a number of other food processors now on the market that knead dough. Some are small and underpowered and should not be used for volumes larger than suggested by the manufacturer. I also have one of the early Cuisinarts, a smaller model in which I prepare only one medium loaf at a time.

In my large machine I use a steel blade for 4 cups of flour or less, and a special stubby plastic blade for up to 7 or 8 cups of flour.

The sequence begins with some of the flour and other dry ingredients, including the yeast, processed with the liquid to make a heavy batter. As more flour is added, the batter becomes dough that is spun around the bowl by the blade. When the dough cleans the sides of the bowl, it is processed from 45 to 60 seconds. The finished dough should have a soft, pliable texture and it should feel slightly sticky. Stretch the dough with your hands to test it. If it feels hard, lumpy, or uneven, continue processing until it feels uniformly soft and pliable.

Food processor instructions for the recipes in this book have been adapted to work with fast-rising yeasts by adding the dry yeast to the flour *before* the liquid is added, rather than proofing the yeast separately.

There is one problem related to making dough in the food processor that can be exasperating, but is easily overcome. On occasion the blade will stick to the center shaft, held there by a film of dough that has worked its way under the blade and onto the shaft. Once there, the heat generated by the whirling blade creates a bond that is difficult to break. If this happens, take out the dough and pulse the blade in the empty bowl several times. The blade should lift out. If not, pour boiling hot water into the bowl and turn the processor on for a few seconds. Voila!

Note: After having written so glowingly of both the mixer and food processor, I must explain that many of the batter breads in the book are done in a bowl by hand because it is hardly worth the bother of cleaning the blades and hooks and odd-shaped bowls of the machines. I like the bowl-hand method because mixing the batters is so easily done and washing up after is minimal.

BREAD MACHINE

The bread machine can be used for mixing and kneading most of the doughs in this book.

Whether a recipe can be adapted for the machine depends on the size of the machine and the number of cups of flour it can knead. The 1½ pound machine will take 3 cups of flour. The 1 pound machine will knead 2 cups. Recipes calling for more flour must be scaled down.

Follow the manufacturer's instructions for operation and add ingredients in the order suggested by the bread-machine manual.

DOUGH KNIFE OR SCRAPER

One of the handiest implements in the baker's hands is a dough knife or dough blade. The French call it a *coupe-pâte*. It is a rectangular piece of steel (about 4 by 5 inches) with a wooden handhold that quickly becomes an extension of the arm when you work and knead dough by hand. It is great for lifting and working doughs that are sticky during the early part of kneading. A thin, flexible blade is better than a heavy, stiff one—a 4-inch putty knife is a good substitute.

ROLLING PIN

There are only a few doughs that need a rolling pin. My favorite weighs 6 pounds, has ball bearings in the handles, and rolls an 18-inch-wide swath. The graceful French rolling pin is marvelous for pastry and some bread doughs but too light for others.

CONVENTIONAL BREAD PANS

Don't discard your shiny aluminum bread pan because it doesn't brown bread as well on the bottom and sides as the dark metal or Pyrex pans. When you turn out the loaf and find it less brown than you wanted, put it back in the oven—without the pan—for an additional 5 to 10 minutes. The crust will brown nicely.

The silicone-coated (Teflon) pans are excellent—they will produce a deep brown crust with no sticking. Equally good are those of black steel and stoneware.

SPECIAL BREAD PANS

French bread in the classic shapes of the *baguette, ficelle, flûte,* or *bâtard* is baked in special pans or raised in baskets or between cloths and baked directly on the hot oven floor.

Manufactured in France and now widely available in the United States, the pans are for two to six loaves and pressed out of a single piece of metal. I make my own double pans from black stovepipe that I buy at a country store near my home. The pipe costs about one dollar.

The French *banneton* is a woven basket, cloth-lined, in which the dough rises and is then turned out directly onto a baking sheet or, as in France, the hot oven floor. It can be duplicated by shopping for a selection among round and rectangular wicker baskets sold in kitchenware departments. Shape a piece of tightly woven cloth to fit into the basket; tie the cloth to the bottom of the basket so it will stay in place when the dough is turned out. Dust the cloth liberally with flour each time you use it.

A pastry cloth or a length of duck or light canvas can become the *couche* to shape long loaves that will be baked directly on baking sheets, on a baking stone, or on the oven floor. The shaped dough for the final rising is held between folds of the cloth. The ends of the *couche* are held in place by pieces of wood (to act like bookends) to force the dough up, not out.

To shape the tall cylindrical loaves such as panettone, use a coffee can. It costs nothing extra and the printing on the metal absorbs the heat to give the loaf a handsome deep-brown crust. The can is expendable, so if the bread should stick cut the bottom and push out the obstinate loaf.

For a yeast bread, fill the can a little more than halfway. Cover it with plastic wrap and let it rise to the edge of the can—no more. "Oven-spring"—the action of the heat on the yeast dough—will blossom it up, out, and over the edge like a mushroom.

Place the can on a lower rack so that the rising dough will not push its way against the roof of the oven.

BAKING SHEET

A heavy baking or cookie sheet, silicone-coated, such as Teflon, is the best because it does not have to be brushed with oil or sprinkled with cornmeal each time before using. Get the heaviest and largest your oven will accommodate, allowing a 1-inch clearance on all sides to facilitate the flow of hot air around it. The heavier the baking sheet the better it will retain heat when preheated, and the better it will duplicate baking on an oven floor. Some heavy-gauge dark steel baking sheets (26 by 17 inches) weigh more than 6 pounds! Excellent.

PARCHMENT PAPER

There will seldom be a sticking problem if baking sheets and tins are lined with parchment paper. It can be bought in gourmet cookware shops and housewares departments in rolls 15 inches wide by 16 feet long. Large 16-by-24-inch flat sheets can be bought, but only in large quantities, at bakery supply houses.

BAKING STONE

A baking stone placed on the lower shelf of the oven is as close as most home bakers can get to baking thick-crusted loaves on the oven floor as bakers have been doing for centuries. The stones are manufactured of heat-retaining composition stone in two shapes—a 16-inch round plate or a 14-by-16-inch rectangle. A stone weighs about 10 pounds and is heavy enough to closely duplicate the baking qualities of the brick floor of a wood-fired oven.

Unlike a baking sheet that can be moved in and out of the oven to receive the dough, the preheated stone is better left in place in the oven and the bread taken to it. Pans or baking sheets with dough can be placed on the heavy stone to produce a thicker bottom crust.

Pizzas and pastries, especially those with moist fillings, can also be baked on the hot stone to get a thrust of heat from the bottom that ambient air can never give.

THE OVEN

Assume that the oven thermostat is not accurate until proven otherwise. A good oven thermometer, the mercury-filled columnar by Taylor, for example, is a good investment when you consider just the cost of ingredients, to say nothing of your time. Even though the utility company will usually adjust your oven at no cost, continue to use the thermometer to check the thermostat.

A too-cool oven will not bake bread. A too-hot oven may scorch it. An oven that is just right will produce a masterpiece.

The heat in an oven varies in intensity from side to side, front to back, and top to bottom. Move the pans and turn them at least once during the baking period to compensate for these variations.

I have seven ovens in my studio-kitchen—gas, electric (including one convection oven), and one wood-fired. With the conventional ovens I have found almost no difference between electricity and gas as to the appearance and quality of breads or pastries.

My countertop convection oven works on the same principle of convection cooking that many restaurant and bakery ovens utilize. Heat from a conventional electric element is fan-driven to swirl and circulate around foods. It is unnecessary to preheat this oven. Loaves bake uniformly and at temperatures about 50° lower than those of other ovens and need not be shifted during the bake period.

I like the convection oven but I find the so-called portable model limited in capacity when compared with my other ovens.

My wood-fired oven, in which I bake directly on the stone floor after it is swept clean, produces a thick bottom crust on bread and pizza that is hard to duplicate except with a baking stone (see above). My first wood-fired oven was built of adobe in my backyard. My second one was built of firebrick into the stone fireplace of the studio-kitchen.

Plans for the outdoor adobe oven are in the chapter "Homemade Oven."

I have not found a need for a microwave oven in my kitchen to do my kind of baking.

THERMOMETER

The liquid mixed with the dry ingredients (including the yeast) should be within the range of 120° and 130°. Too hot, the yeast is killed. Too cool, the dough will be slow to rise. An accurate thermometer that can test the temperature of the liquid (usually water) is essential.

An excellent thermometer is the small Bi-Therm from Taylor. It has a stainless steel stem with a 1-inch dial protected by an unbreakable crystal. There are many other uses for it in the kitchen, ranging from testing the doneness of a pork roast to gauging the temperature of the interior of a freezer.

Candy and meat thermometers can also be used if they register low enough.

TIMER

A timer is as essential to the baking process as an accurate thermometer. There are many good timers on the market and usually one comes as part of the home range. My favorite, however, is a timer about the size of a yo-yo that I hang around my neck. It goes with me to other parts of the house or out into the yard to remind me that something is rising in a bowl or baking in the oven. It is made by Terraillon and sold in most gourmet cookware shops and by catalogue.

KNIFE

A sharp knife adds a touch of professionalism that a good loaf of bread deserves. A slice of bread is only as attractive as a knife will permit it to be. A dull knife can torture and wreck the most beautiful bread while a sharp knife can do wonders with a less-than-perfect loaf.

There are a number of excellent knives on the market. I use a stainless steel Swiss knife with a long serrated blade that allows me to cut with a rhythmic sawing motion. Now about fifteen years old, the knife has cut hundreds of loaves and pastries and is still sharp as a razor. The secret is that I respect the blade and use it *only* for bread.

TO MAKE STEAM

Steam has a multiple role in baking thin-crusted, crispy loaves of peasant breads: it softens and protects the dough as it rises for a longer period than would be possible without the added moisture, and it favors the growth of the *jet*, the slash down the top of the loaf. The moist oven also helps caramelize the sugar in the dough to give the crust a golden yellow color and an overall glossy appearance.

Steam is made by introducing water into the oven just before the bread is put in. A pan placed on the bottom of the oven before the oven is turned on will be sizzling hot when a cup of water is poured into it about 3 minutes before putting in the loaves. (Be careful—the steam erupting out of the pan can burn.) A fine spray of water into the hot oven from an atomizer (an empty, washed window-cleaner bottle or plant sprayer) is a substitute for the pan of water. I prefer the pan because a spray of cool water directly toward the oven light bulb can be a shattering experience.

INGREDIENTS
AND HOW
THEY ARE COMBINED

ALL RECIPES in this book can be reduced by dividing the ingredients in half. But don't bother to divide a packet of yeast—the action will be slightly more vigorous but this presents no problem. One caution: always be certain there is sufficient dough to fill the appropriate pan in the amount called for in the recipe or a less-than-attractive loaf may result. (See Dough Volume chart, page 16.)

The instructions in all of the recipes are divided into timed steps so that at no point are you left to guess what should be done next.

Bread-making may sound complicated and some lists of ingredients appear formidable. They are not. Many students in my baking classes and many readers of my other cookbooks had never baked before. Yet they learned quickly to make a variety of breads.

The only surprise in this book is the pleasant and rewarding and recurring one that it was you who baked the handsome loaf of bread just taken from the oven.

INGREDIENTS
Flour

The cornerstone of all bread-making is flour—white, whole-wheat, barley, buckwheat, corn, oat, rye, and rice. Only the last has no collection of its own in the book.

There are essentially two kinds of wheat grown by farmers and ranchers: hard and soft. A third wheat, important to the American diet but not in breads and pastries, is a hard wheat variety called "durum," which is used in making pastas such as macaroni, spaghetti, and noodles as well as feed for poultry and livestock.

All three wheats share in varying degrees an important element that makes wheat unique among the cereal flours. This element is gluten—a plant protein prized by bakers because when mixed with water it forms an elastic network that catches the gas generated by the yeast—and raises and expands the dough.

Hard wheat, grown in the Great Plains and our western prairie lands, has a high gluten content and is milled into "bread" flour. Bread flour, happily, has now returned to the shelves of the neighborhood market after an absence of two generations; if it is scarce in your markets, you may substitute "unbleached" flour. Despite its name, the flour is bleached in an aging rather than a chemical process, and is milled from a blend of hard wheats. It can be substituted for bread flours with good results.

Bread flour is favored by commercial bakers not only for its taste and texture but because it can withstand punishing treatment from heavy machinery.

Soft wheat, grown in the milder regions of middle and eastern America, produces a flour lower in gluten, one that is ideal for baking such products as pastries, crackers, cookies, and cakes. At the bottom of the gluten scale is cake flour, which has only enough of the protein to hold the cake together in the oven while a delicate and tender structure of cells is formed. A little higher up the gluten scale is pastry flour, ideal for pie and tart dough because it can tolerate a considerable amount of shortening without becoming tough.

At mid-range is the versatile all-purpose flour, a blend of hard and soft wheat flours that has been developed by the nation's millers to take care of a wide range of home baking needs with one flour—from breads and biscuits to pies and doughnuts.

All-purpose flour can be substituted for most other wheat flours called for in recipes. It will not rise as high as bread flour but it is a worthy substitute nevertheless.

I have been asked many times about the flour used by French bakers in producing their famous loaves. A combination of three parts all-purpose to one part bread flour is very close in characteristics to French bread flour. However, French flour gets no chemical treatment whatsoever except for minute additions of ascorbic acid, which strengthens the dough and gives the loaf more volume. U.S. unbleached flour has perhaps the closest affinity to French flour.

It is easy to check the protein, or gluten, content of a flour—beyond the sales description on the sack—by looking at the small panel of nutritional information on the side of the package. Although figures vary somewhat from brand to brand and mill to mill, here is the protein range: bread flour, 12.5 percent; unbleached, 11 percent; all-purpose, 9 percent; pastry, 8 percent; and cake, 7 percent or less.

Bromated white flour is used primarily by commercial bakers. The flour is treated with potassium bromate to toughen the dough for the rigors of kneading.

Whole-wheat flour, which is made from the whole kernel, is relatively easy to work and knead because of its full quota of gluten. While any whole-wheat flour may be used in these recipes, I often use stone-ground whole-wheat because it gives the bread a rougher texture. Graham and pumpernickel are similar to stone-ground.

Whole-wheat flour contains the entire germ or fat portion of the wheat kernel. If it is to be stored for any length of time, whole-wheat flour should be kept in the refrigerator or freezer to prevent rancidity.

Rye is a grain with little gluten in its makeup. Hence, most of the time rye flour must be mixed with white or whole-wheat flour to give the dough its necessary gluten network. Rye flour may be graded white, medium, dark, rye meal, or pumpernickel; the one most commonly used is medium rye flour. Dark pumpernickel flours are coarsely ground with bran particles left in. White rye, for a rye bread light in color, is seldom used in home baking.

For most of the recipes in this book, flour is not sifted. The amount of flour given is only approximate because flour varies greatly in its ability to absorb moisture due to differences from harvest to harvest, sack to sack, as well as month to month as the humidity changes and the flour absorbs or releases moisture. For instance, flour kept in a warm kitchen in wintertime will be dry and more receptive to liquid than flour stored in a humid room in summertime.

In the latter stages of mixing dough, add flour sparingly. It is better to slowly add the last bit of flour to be certain the texture of the dough is just right rather than to overwhelm the dough with flour. If you do go beyond the point where the dough is soft and elastic, and it becomes hard, add water. The dough will accept it, though reluctantly.

In many recipes alternate flours are listed. The first is preferred but the second can be substituted with good results.

I don't think it is necessary to buy the more expensive nationally advertised flours when one can get less well known but equally good flour from local mills or packaged under a supermarket name. Milling standards are so high in this country that you can be certain the sacks contain what the labels claim they do.

Flour freezes and keeps well for a year or more. If you have extra freezer space at 0° F., watch supermarket shelves for bargains and for those flours that appear seasonally and briefly and then are gone for long periods. Buy the bargain and freeze it.

Wheat Substitutes

Many people are allergic to wheat in any form. While there are breads made without wheat flour, the recipes that follow have some general guidelines for substitutions.

As a substitute for 1 cup wheat flour, the American Dietetic Association suggests *one* of the following:

>   I cup barley flour
>   I cup corn flour

> ³/₄ cup coarse cornmeal
> 1 cup fine cornmeal
> ⁷/₈ cup rice flour
> 1¹/₄ cups rye flour
> 1¹/₃ cups oat flour
> ⁷/₈ cup potato starch flour

When substituting for wheat flour, a product of better flavor and texture is generally obtained by a combination of flours rather than using a single one. Here is a nonwheat flour mixture for general use:

> 1 cup cornstarch
> 2 cups rice flour
> 1 cup soy flour
> 3 cups potato starch flour

When using this combination of flours, lower baking temperatures by 25° and use a little less shortening. Substitute cup for cup in recipes that call for wheat flour.

The texture of quick (nonyeast) breads is improved if the dough is allowed to stand in the pan for 20 minutes before baking. Finished quick breads will hold their shape better if left in the pan for 5 minutes before removing, and they are generally most successful made in small quantities.

Yeast and Other Leavenings

Almost all breads are leavened in one or more ways. Without leavening, bread would come out of the ovens as flat as Swedish *knäckebröd,* a rye wafer.

Yeast is the most important of the leaveners, followed by chemicals such as baking powder and baking soda. Yeast cells, wild or cultivated, feasting on the sugars in the mixture, produce carbon dioxide to raise the dough and make it light. The Egyptians used it. Pasteur discovered it. Americans packaged it.

In the late twentieth century, genetic engineers developed new and different yeast cultures that have dramatically changed the baking process. Two brands of the new yeast are available: Red Star's Quick-Rise and Fleischmann's RapidRise. The names are a clue to what they do. Ordinarily dough for white bread made with conventional yeast takes about 2 hours to make—two risings, kneading, and shaping. The new yeasts cut the rising time in half.

Warmth is a sine qua non for using the new yeast. The temperature of the liquid added to the yeast is higher than most home bakers are accustomed to—between 120° and 130°. This is not the tepid 100° to 120° that is called for in conventional recipes; this liquid is hot to the touch. I recommend always using a kitchen thermometer to measure water temperature to be sure it is in the 120° to 130° range. (See the preceding chapter on equipment.)

Have all ingredients at room temperature when you begin. The addition of two or three ice-cold eggs or a stick of butter taken directly from the refrigerator can throw a deep chill into the dough and reduce its ability to perform as expected. It is even worthwhile to heat the mixing bowl before starting to work.

The ingredients need to be warm and so does the dough when it is put aside to rise if it is to fulfill its promise. For the dough, the best temperature is between 90° and 100°, which is warm compared to the lower temperatures usually recommended. I find that the pilot light in my gas oven, with the door slightly ajar, provides an ideal climate. So does an electric oven—turned on for 1 minute—and then turned off.

A convection oven can also be used for rising. Set the temperature control knob to the lowest reading. Turn the timer to 1 hour. The air should feel warm (about 90°), not hot.

Dough will rise just as well at room temperature; it will simply take longer.

One important difference between working with quick-rising and conventional yeasts is that the new yeasts should *not* be proofed. Repeat—should *not* be proofed. This is a hard habit to break. Grandma did it, why not me? Nevertheless, the new yeasts have been designed to be mixed with the flour and not separated out. They do better when sheltered by the other ingredients, which protect them from the high temperatures now recommended.

If all of these conditions are met, the dough will behave as promised. However, if not, no great harm is done. The dough will still rise but it will take a little more time.

In tests in my kitchen, with neighbors on a tasting panel, we found little or no difference in taste between loaves made with the different yeasts, new or old. Also, there was no change in texture.

While commercial bakers and some home bakers use large 1-pound bricks of fresh yeast, most home bakers will find dry yeast (conventional or fast) packets and the small fresh compressed cakes more convenient. I use only dry yeast because the packets are so readily available and may be stored unrefrigerated. However, if yeast is to be used infrequently it is best to store it in the refrigerator or, for long periods, in the freezer.

Brewer's yeast is not a leavening agent. Known also as "nutritional" or "primary" yeast, it has been heat-treated and cannot be substituted for live yeast. It is, however, an excellent source of biologically complete and digestible protein and is often used in baking.

Baking soda, the first chemical leavener to be used, reacts with acids, such as sour cream or buttermilk, to produce carbon dioxide. The reaction is almost instantaneous, requiring fast assembly of ingredients and immediate baking. Baking powder has a multiple action that releases a small amount of gas while the ingredients are put together. The main thrust comes from the heat of the oven.

Self-rising flour and cornmeal mix contain baking powder and salt.

Fat

Fat is the generic term for one of the most important and essential ingredients used in baking, whether it be butter, lard, margarine, or oil, or a combination. Fat imparts richness and tenderness. Fats, especially butter and lard, contribute a unique flavor, and fat also lubricates the gluten in the dough so that it is free to rise.

Because of its delicious flavor and rich aroma, butter is one of the most highly regarded fats for baking. Sweet or unsalted butter is preferred because it indicates a fresher, sweeter product than salted butter, which has a longer shelf life.

Lard is frequently used for bread-making, especially in country loaves. It is readily available on the market, as it has been since pigs first ran loose down village streets in colonial America, and it has an attractive low price.

Solid vegetable and animal fats are made with oils through which hydrogen gas has been forced under pressure to produce a creamy solid—hence the word *hydrogenated*. Vegetable shortening is a good-tasting compromise without a pronounced taste. It is less expensive than butter and a good choice for those who eschew animal fat because of dietary or religious considerations.

Salad or cooking oil may be substituted in recipes when melted shortening is specified.

MILK AND BUTTERMILK

Milk

A loaf made with milk has a velvety grain, a browner crust, and a creamy-white crumb. The loaf is softer and stays that way longer than bread made without milk. Milk also complements the nutrients of many doughs.

Most of the recipes in this book specify nonfat dry milk because it is easy and convenient to use. All one adds is water. When warming or heating this reconstituted milk, there is no danger of scorching—a common hazard with whole milk. And it is nonfat!

But use whole milk if that is your choice. I had written so much about dry milk in earlier recipes that the mother superior of a New Jersey convent was prompted to write and ask if the sisters who baked with my books might not use milk from their own herd of dairy cows. I hastened to assure her they could!

Buttermilk

If fresh buttermilk is not a staple in your refrigerator you might wish to keep a can of cultured buttermilk powder on hand. A cup of water and 4 tablespoons of the powder is equivalent to 1 cup of liquid buttermilk. A 1-pound can will make a total of 5 quarts of buttermilk. When making a recipe, the powder is mixed in with the other dry ingredients plus an appropriate amount of liquid. It is available in the dry milk sections of most large supermarkets and health food stores.

Salt

Salt controls the action of the yeast in doughs and strengthens the gluten, and salt accents the flavor of other ingredients.

Sugar

Granulated sugar imparts a rich brown color to the crust through caramelization. In moderate amounts sugar increases yeast fermentation, while sugar in the high concentration typical of raised sweet breads will inhibit it.

The fineness of confectioners' sugar, which contains cornstarch to retard lumping and crystallization, makes it easy to blend with other ingredients; it is used primarily in decorating festive breads.

KNEADING AND RISING

Kneading

When the dough is kneaded, gluten—a plant protein found chiefly in wheat flour—forms an elastic network to trap the carbon dioxide produced by the yeast.

Kneading by hand should be done at a comfortable height that allows the arms to be fully extended, palms resting on the work surface. The rough mass is turned out of the bowl onto a work surface which has been sprinkled lightly with flour. If the dough is sticky, begin by lifting and turning it with a dough scraper or dough blade. Add sprinkles of flour as needed. Fold the dough in half; push down hard against it with your hands, away from the body. As you pull back, give the dough a quarter of a turn. Fold it. Push. Repeat the sequence—push-turn-fold.

Break the rhythmic pattern frequently by lifting the ball of dough above the table and bringing it crashing down against the work surface. *Wham!* This is a wholly satisfying action that signals to the household that bread is being made. Don't be gentle with the dough. Pummel and push it! Return to the cadence of push-turn-fold.

Vigorous action gives the dough body and suppleness. It will be elastic when stretched between the hands. When fully kneaded the dough can be stretched paper-thin.

If the dough is too firm or inelastic after the first kneading, water may be added; if the dough is soft and slack, add more flour.

Here is another test to indicate when the dough has enough flour. Hit the ball of dough with an open hand. Hold the hand on the dough for a count of ten. Lift off the hand. If the hand is clean—no dough particles clinging—the dough is about ready to be put aside to rise, depending on the kneading time prescribed by the recipe. If the dough sticks to the hand, add flour.

When sufficient flour has been added to dough kneaded by a dough hook, the dough will form a soft, elastic ball around the revolving arm and completely clean the sides of the bowl.

In a food processor, the dough has sufficient flour when the dough forms a rough mass and rides with the blade—and cleans (somewhat) the sides of the bowl. Dough kneaded in a food processor will be slightly sticky when turned from the bowl but can be adjusted with light sprinkles of flour.

Rising (Proofing)

Dough comes of age when it rises. It has been pushed and shoved by hand or twisted under the dough hook or pummeled by the processor blade, and now comes the quiet time when it grows and matures. Now is the time for the yeast cells to give off carbon dioxide to expand and puff the dough.

A heavy stoneware bowl is ideal for raising, or proofing, most doughs because it keeps a constant temperature during the period of time when the dough is expanding. For the first rising, cover the bowl with plastic wrap. Pull it tightly across the top to contain the moisture.

Some home bakers like to drop the dough into a plastic bag and let it rise there. The bag must be of sufficient volume, of course, to allow the dough to expand.

There are two ways to determine if the dough has risen sufficiently. One is by watching it move up the side of the bowl to a place you have earlier determined is twice or three times the volume, depending on the recipe. The other is to press one or two fingers in the dough near the edge. If the indentations remain, the dough has risen sufficiently.

After the dough has been punched down, formed into whatever shape and size loaves you want, and placed in a bread pan or on a baking sheet, the dough is allowed to rise

again—expanding to at least double its volume. Most peasant breads and country loaves are allowed to triple in volume.

If the final rising of the loaves has been allowed to go on too long the expanded dough may collapse in the heat of the oven. If this happens (it rarely does) turn the dough back onto the work surface. Knead briefly and reshape. The dough will double or triple in volume in about two-thirds of the usual time.

Dough Volume

If the dough is to yield an attractive loaf it must be baked in a pan of the proper size. Too little dough will produce a stunted loaf, while too much can create a misshapen loaf that seems to be all top and no body.

Determine the total amount of the dough by weight or measure, then decide how many loaves, and of what size, you wish to bake. Follow this chart:

PAN SIZE	(INCHES)	VOLUME	WEIGHT
Large	9 x 5 x 3	3 cups	2 pounds
Medium	8 x 4 x 2	2½ cups	1½ pounds
Small	7 x 3 x 2	1½ cups	1 pound
Miniature	5 x 3 x 2	¾ cup	½ pound
Sub-mini	4 x 2 x 1	½ cup	5 to 6 ounces

Note: Some pans may be ½ inch larger in their dimensions.

THE FIRST LOAF

THIS MAY BE your first loaf of yeast-raised bread.

You want it to be picture-perfect when it comes from the oven—wrapped in a golden brown crust and, when cut with the knife, a creamy white slice that demands to be eaten.

Such a loaf is one that I use in teaching—developed over a number of years to best demonstrate how easy it is to make a loaf of bread. I like this loaf so much for sandwiches and toast that there is almost always a loaf, fresh or frozen, in the house.

Blend the dry yeast with the other dry ingredients—some of the flour, all of the sugar, salt, and nonfat dry milk—pour in the warm liquids, and the new bread-making process begins.

This loaf is not exclusively for beginners, I hasten to add, for many longtime home bakers have made it a tradition in their kitchens. It is also versatile. While the recipe below is for an all-white bread, it is a basic loaf that can be made into a dozen different breads. There are variations of this recipe throughout the book, including Kulich, Buttermilk Bread, and others.

For the first edition of *The Complete Book of Breads* I developed and wrote several recipes for the new baker, to introduce the more than 300 recipes to follow. I have put the best of each of those together in this one recipe. It is a valuable introduction to the basic ingredients that the home baker will use time and again.

The beginning baker is encouraged to read the preceding chapters on techniques, ingredients, and equipment leading up to this, the first loaf. To adjust this recipe and other recipes in the book for the bread machine, see p. 3.

The First Loaf   [two medium or three small loaves]

INGREDIENTS

5 to 6 cups bread or all-purpose flour, approximately
3 tablespoons sugar
2 teaspoons salt
1 package dry yeast
1/4 cup nonfat dry milk
2 cups hot water (120°–130°)
3 tablespoons shortening, room temperature

BAKING PANS

2 medium (8"-x-4") or 3 small (7"-x-3") loaf pans, greased or Teflon. Refer to the Dough Volume chart (page 16) for other pan combinations.

BY HAND
OR MIXER
15 mins.

In a large mixing bowl measure 2 cups flour, sugar, salt, yeast, and dry milk. Pour the hot water into the dry ingredients and beat by hand or with mixer flat beater to blend thoroughly. Add the shortening; continue beating. Add 1 cup flour and with a wooden spoon beat 100 vigorous strokes, or for 3 minutes at medium speed in the mixer.

If by hand, continue adding flour, 1/4 cup at a time, and stirring with a wooden spoon until it becomes a shaggy mass. Work more flour into the dough with your hands if it is sticky.

If by mixer, attach the dough hook and add flour, 1/4 cup at a time, until the dough forms a soft, elastic ball around the revolving hook.

KNEADING
10 mins.

If by hand, turn the dough out onto a floured work surface and begin to knead with a strong push-turn-fold motion. Occasionally bring the dough down hard against the work surface with a sharp *whack!* Do this several times during the process. If the dough continues to be sticky, add light sprinkles of flour.

If using the dough hook, continue to knead for 10 minutes. If the ball of dough sticks to the sides of the bowl, add sprinkles of flour. Should the dough try to climb over the protective collar at the top of the hook as it turns, hold it back with the edge of a rubber spatula.

When properly kneaded the dough will be soft and elastic. It can be pulled into a thin sheet when stretched between the hands.

A caution: too much flour will make a hard ball that will behave poorly. Work 1 or 2 teaspoons water into the dough. By the same token, if the dough is wet and slack and difficult to handle, add 1 or 2 tablespoons flour.

BY PROCESSOR
5 mins.

Attach the short plastic dough blade.

Measure 3 cups flour into the work bowl and add the sugar, salt, yeast, and nonfat dry milk. Pulse to blend. In a small bowl or saucepan pour the hot water over the shortening to soften.

With the processor running, pour the liquid through the feed tube to make a heavy batter. Add flour, ¼ cup at a time, until a soft mass forms and is spun around the bowl by the force of the blade. The dough will clean the sides of the bowl. With the short blade some flour may cling to the bottom of the bowl. If so, stop the machine and scrape the dry ingredients into the center and continue processing.

KNEADING
60 secs.

Process to knead for 60 seconds. Stop the machine; pinch the ball of dough. If it is dry, add a small portion of water and continue kneading. If it seems wet, add flour by tablespoons. The dough, when kneaded, will be somewhat sticky and very elastic. Light sprinkles of flour will make the dough manageable. Pull and stretch the dough between your hands to test elasticity; if necessary, process for a few seconds more.

FIRST RISING
1 hour

Place the dough in a lightly greased bowl, cover tightly with plastic wrap to retain the moisture, and leave at room temperature until the dough has doubled in bulk, about 1 hour.

SHAPING
10 mins.

Turn back the plastic wrap and punch down the dough. Turn it onto the floured work surface and knead for a moment or so to force out any bubbles. Divide the dough into 2 or 3 pieces with a sharp knife.

Shape each piece into a ball and let it rest on the work surface for 2 or 3 minutes. Form a loaf by pressing the ball of dough into a flat oval roughly the length of the baking pan. Fold the oval in half, pinch the seam tightly to seal, tuck under the ends, and place seam down in the pan.

SECOND RISING
45 mins.

Cover the pans with wax or parchment paper and leave until the dough has doubled in volume, about 45 minutes at room temperature.

PREHEAT

Preheat the oven to 400° about 20 minutes before baking.

BAKING
400°
10 mins.
350°
25–30 mins.

Place the loaves in the hot oven for 10 minutes, then lower the heat to 350° for an additional 25 to 30 minutes. Midway through baking and again at the end turn the pans end for end so the loaves are uniformly exposed to the heat.

(If using convection oven, reduce heat 50°.)

When the loaves are a golden brown and sound hollow when thumped on the bottom crust, they are done.

FINAL STEP   Turn out onto wire racks to cool. If you want a soft, tender crust, brush the hot loaves with melted butter or margarine.

This bread may be frozen for a later presentation—up to 6 months at 0°. Toasts beautifully.

Finally, if this is your first loaf, stand back and admire your creation.

WHITE BREADS

WHITE FLOUR is the dominant flour in bread-making and the breads made with it have a variety of textures that add delight to meals and snacks. In this chapter they range from Frisian Sugar Loaf, Feather Bread, and Home Roman Meal to Salt-Free and Sally Lunn.

White flour, as will be seen in later chapters, is also an important ingredient in many dark breads that would not rise sufficiently without the gluten contributed by the white flour.

Thirty-Minute White Bread   [two loaves]

The panned dough for this light and airy loaf is placed in a cold oven, the heat is turned on for 60 seconds and turned off, and then the dough is allowed to rise for exactly 30 minutes (hence, the name) before the oven heat is turned on. The dough rises only once (in the pan) before it is baked.

KitchenAid home economists created this loaf to demonstrate the ease of kneading with a dough hook. It can be done by hand, of course.

INGREDIENTS

1 cup milk

2 tablespoons vegetable shortening or butter

3 teaspoons salt

1 cup lukewarm water (105°–115°)

2 packages dry yeast

2 tablespoons sugar

6 to 7 cups bread or all-purpose flour, approximately

1 tablespoon butter, melted

BAKING PANS	2 medium (8½"-x-4½") loaf pans, greased or Teflon
BY HAND OR MIXER 8 mins.	Warm the milk in a saucepan to soften the shortening or butter for a few moments. Add the salt and the lukewarm water. Add the yeast and sugar and stir to dissolve.

Stir in 2 cups flour and beat for 3 minutes at medium speed in an electric mixer or 150 strong strokes with a wooden spoon. Gradually add 2 more cups flour, and continue beating for 3 minutes—or 150 strokes.

Note: While the entire mixing and kneading operation can be done in the electric mixer, I like to judge the feel of the dough by hand before turning the job over to a dough hook.

Turn off the mixer and add about 2 more cups flour. Work it in with a spoon, and when it becomes stiff, with your hands. When the dough has a rough form and is cleaning the sides of the mixing bowl, turn it out on the floured work surface.

KNEADING 8 mins.	Knead for about 8 minutes with a strong push-turn-fold motion. Occasionally throw the dough hard against the work surface (stimulates the gluten). Or replace the dough in the mixer bowl and put under the dough hook for an equal length of time.
BY PROCESSOR 10 mins.	Place 2 cups flour in the work bowl and then add the other ingredients, as above. Pulse several times to thoroughly mix. Remove the cover and add 2 more cups flour. Replace the cover and pulse to blend.

Add the remaining flour through the feed tube, pulsing after each addition, until the dough begins to form and is carried around the bowl by the force of the blade.

KNEADING 45 secs.	Turn on the machine to knead for 45 seconds.
SHAPING 10 mins.	Divide the dough in half, and shape the balls. Let rest under a cloth for 5 minutes.

Form the loaves by pressing each (with your palm or rolling pin) into an oval, roughly the length of the baking pan. Fold the oval in half, pinch the seam tightly to seal, tuck under the ends, and place seam down in the pan. Brush the loaves with the melted butter.

RISING 30 mins.	Place the pans in a cold oven and turn heat to 400° for 60 seconds—1 minute, no more. Turn it off!

BAKING **400°** **45 mins.**	About 30 minutes later turn the oven to 400° and bake for 45 minutes, or until the loaves are brown. When done, they will sound hollow when tapped on the bottom crust with the forefinger. If the crust is soft, return to the oven, without the pans, for 10 minutes. (If using a convection oven, reduce heat 50°.)
FINAL STEP	Place the loaves on a metal rack to cool. The bread is fine for sandwiches and toast. It also freezes very well.

Cuban Bread   [two plump loaves]

This loaf is a beginner's dream. Often I have used it in baking classes to demonstrate the ease with which good bread can be made. Cuban bread is close kin to the traditional French bread made with only yeast, flour, water, salt, and a little sugar. The top is cut with a sharp knife or razor blade before it goes into the oven to allow it to open in the heat like a giant blossom.

It is a spectacular loaf to present to family and guests.

INGREDIENTS	5 to 6 cups of bread or all-purpose flour, approximately 2 packages dry yeast 1 tablespoon salt 2 tablespoons sugar 2 cups hot water (120°–130°) Sesame or poppy seeds (optional)
BAKING SHEET	1 baking sheet, Teflon, greased, or sprinkled with cornmeal, or lined with parchment paper
BY HAND **OR MIXER** **15 mins.**	Place 4 cups flour in a large mixing bowl and add the yeast, salt, and sugar. Stir until they are well blended. Pour in the hot water and beat with 100 strong strokes, or for 3 minutes with a mixer flat beater. Gradually work in the remaining flour (using fingers if necessary), ½ cup at a time, until the dough takes shape and is no longer sticky.
KNEADING **8 mins.**	Sprinkle the work surface with flour. Work in the flour as you knead, keeping a dusting of it between the dough and the work surface. Knead for 8 minutes by hand or with a dough hook until the dough is smooth, elastic, and feels alive under your hands.
BY PROCESSOR **5 mins.**	Attach the short plastic blade. Place 2 cups flour in the work bowl and add the other ingredients, as

above. Pulse several times to thoroughly mix. Remove the cover and add 2 more cups flour. Replace the cover and pulse to blend.

Add the remaining flour through the feed tube, pulsing after each addition, until the dough begins to form and is carried around the bowl by the force of the blade.

KNEADING
45 secs.

Turn on the machine to knead for 45 seconds.

RISING
15 mins.

Place the dough in a greased bowl, cover with plastic wrap, and put in a warm place (80°–100°) until double in bulk, about 15 minutes.

SHAPING
4 mins.

Punch down the dough, turn it out on the work surface, and cut into 2 pieces. Shape each into a round. Place on the baking sheet. With a sharp knife or razor, slash an **X** on each of the loaves, brush with water, and, if desired, sprinkle with sesame or poppy seeds.

BAKING
400°
45–50 mins.

Place the baking sheet on the middle shelf of a *cold oven.* Place a large pan of hot water on the shelf below, and heat the oven to 400°. The bread, of course, will continue to rise while the oven is heating. Bake for about 50 minutes, or until the loaves are a deep golden brown. Thump on the bottom crusts to test for doneness. If they sound hard and hollow, they are baked.

(If using a convection oven, reduce heat 50°.)

FINAL STEP

Turn the loaves out onto metal racks and cool before slicing.

Since the bread has no shortening it will not keep beyond a day or so. Even though it may begin to stale, it will make excellent toast for several days. It freezes well.

Egg Harbor Bread   [two medium loaves]

This delicious Amish white bread was brought to the village of Egg Harbor, on the shores of Lake Michigan, by Kathryn Zeller when she came from Ohio to start Butter and Eggs, a fine bakery-deli in this Door County resort community.

The bakery is in an old granary building, and is run solely by the Zellers— Kathryn, her husband, and three children. The entire family pitches in during the summer vacations, and then it is back to school in Athens, Ohio, where some teach and some attend. As with so many French boulangers who live over the family-run bakery, the Zellers live in an apartment above Butter and Eggs. "At least it's close when I go downstairs at two in the morning to begin my day," Kathryn says.

*Vacationers returning home take with them baskets of the Egg Harbor loaf
to freeze and to please the family during the winter months.*

*While most breads rise (or proof) only 2 times, this bread gets its texture
and lightness from 5 risings in a covered bowl plus one in the loaf pans.*

*While the Butter and Eggs bakery uses margarine in this recipe, the dairy
farmers in Wisconsin would probably suggest butter instead, and some Amish
ladies would substitute home-rendered lard.*

INGREDIENTS	3 tablespoons sugar
	1 tablespoon salt
	2½ cups hot water (120°–130°)
	2 tablespoons margarine, room temperature
	5 to 6 cups bread flour, approximately
	2 packages dry yeast
	1 egg, beaten, mixed with 1 tablespoon milk

BAKING PANS

2 medium (8"-x-4") loaf pans, Teflon or greased

BY HAND
OR MIXER
6 mins.

In a bowl dissolve the sugar and salt in the hot water. Stir in the
margarine and set aside.

Measure 3 cups flour into the mixing or mixer bowl and add the
yeast. Blend. Slowly pour in the liquid, stirring with a wooden spoon
or mixer flat beater. Beat the heavy batter 100 times with the spoon, or
for 2 minutes with the flat beater.

Add flour, ½ cup at a time. If by hand, stir with the wooden spoon
and then work by hand to form a heavy rough mass that can be lifted
from the bowl to the work surface. If using a mixer, attach the dough
hook and add the flour to form a soft mass.

KNEADING
10 mins.

With the dough on the work surface, knead with a strong push-turn-
fold motion, adding sprinkles of flour if the dough is sticky. The
dough will be elastic and can be stretched between the hands without
breaking apart. Knead for 10 minutes.

If using a mixer, add flour if necessary to make a soft, elastic ball
that will form around the revolving dough hook and, at the same time,
clean the sides of the bowl. Knead for 10 minutes.

BY PROCESSOR
5 mins.

Attach the short plastic dough blade.

Prepare the sugar, salt, water, and shortening liquid as above.

Measure 3½ cups flour into the work bowl and add the yeast. Pulse
to blend. With the machine on, slowly pour the liquid through the
feed tube. Add flour, ¼ cup at a time, until the batter forms a rough

mass that rides with the blade and cleans the sides of the bowl. Stop the machine to pinch the dough to determine if it needs more flour (if slack) or teaspoons of water (if dry).

KNEADING
60 secs.

Process to knead for 60 seconds. The dough should be slightly sticky when it comes from the work bowl but, when dusted with flour, it will be easy to handle.

SERIES OF
RISINGS
1½ hours:
(1) 30 mins.
(4) 15 mins.

The dough has *5 risings* before it is made into loaves—the first time for 30 minutes, and 15 minutes each for the remaining 4.

Place the dough in a greased bowl, cover with plastic wrap, and set aside until the dough doubles in volume, about 30 minutes.

Turn back the plastic cover and punch down the dough with extended fingers. Turn the dough over. Replace the plastic wrap and set aside for 15 minutes.

At 15-minute intervals, punch down the dough 3 more times.

SHAPING
8 mins.

Turn the dough from the bowl and allow it to rest for 4 or 5 minutes before dividing into 2 pieces.

Shape each piece into a ball. Flatten with the palm into an oblong roughly the length of the loaf pan. Fold lengthwise, pinch the seam together, tuck in the ends, and drop into the prepared tin. Press down with the hand to force the dough into the corners.

PAN RISING
50 mins.

Cover the pans with greased wax or parchment paper and put aside to almost triple in volume. The dough should rise 1½" to 2" above the rim of the tin in about 50 minutes.

PREHEAT

Preheat the oven to 400° about 15 minutes before baking.

BAKING
400°
30–40 mins.

Brush the loaves with the egg-milk wash, and place the pans on the middle or lower shelf of the oven. Bake until the loaves are a golden brown, 30 to 40 minutes, and test done when rapped on the bottom crust with a forefinger. For a deeper overall brown, remove from the pans and return to the oven for an additional 10 minutes.

(If using a convection oven, reduce heat 50°.)

FINAL STEP

Remove from the oven and allow to cool on a metal rack before slicing.

This loaf makes great toast. Try it also for French toast. It freezes beautifully, and will keep for 6 months at 0°.

Scottish Buttermilk Bread   [one loaf]

On a trip that took me first to Scotland and then Ireland, I found the Scots' buttermilk bread to be closely akin to Irish soda bread. Both are delicious, though there are no raisins or currants in this loaf as may be found in the Irish.

There is no baking powder in this recipe; it relies entirely on the buttermilk and soda for the leavening. Buttermilk powder, which may be substituted for the milk itself, can be found in most supermarkets and specialty food stores.

INGREDIENTS

2 cups all-purpose flour, approximately
1/2 teaspoon *each* baking soda and cream of tartar
1/4 teaspoon salt
1 teaspoon sugar
1 tablespoon butter, room temperature
3/4 cup buttermilk (or 3 tablespoons buttermilk powder
    in 3/4 cup water), room temperature

BAKING SHEET

1 baking sheet, Teflon or sprinkled with cornmeal or flour

PREHEAT

Preheat the oven to 375°.

**BY HAND
OR MIXER
10 mins.**

Measure the flour into a medium bowl and add the baking soda, cream of tartar, salt, and sugar. With your fingers or a mixer flat beater work the butter into the flour until it resembles rice or small peas. Slowly add the buttermilk. If the dough is too moist to handle without sticking, dust with additional flour. There is no kneading, only mixing to thoroughly blend the ingredients.

**BY PROCESSOR
5 mins.**

Attach the steel blade.

Measure the flour, the other dry ingredients, and the butter into the work bowl. Pulse to cut the mixture into coarse meal. Slowly pour the buttermilk down the feed tube with the machine running. The dough should be taken out of the machine just *before* it forms a ball and rides on the blade, so add liquid with care. If the mixture is obviously too wet to handle, add 1/4 cup or so more of flour. Pulse. The dough will be moist and perhaps sticky when taken from the bowl but can be fashioned into a ball with the help of sprinkles of flour.

**SHAPING
4 mins.**

Pat into a round loaf about 8" across and flatten slightly. With a razor, cut an X about 1/2" deep in the top. Place on the prepared sheet.

**BAKING
375°
35–40 mins.**

Place on the middle shelf of the hot oven and bake for 35 to 40 minutes, or until the loaf is a lovely golden brown. To test for doneness, turn the loaf on its side and tap the bottom crust with a forefinger. If it has a hard, hollow sound it is done.

(If using a convection oven, reduce heat 50°.)

FINAL STEP

Place on a rack to cool before cutting.

While this loaf can be frozen, it is best when it is fresh out of the oven.

Frisian Sugar Loaf   [two loaves]

A slice of bread with pockets of melted sugar, flavored and tinted with cinnamon, stays in my mind with a force equal to the occasion on which it was eaten. With the wind at our backs, we had just bicycled our way across the great Zuider Zee dike in the Netherlands. For days we had cycled into the strong wind off the North Sea and suddenly it was behind us, pushing the bikes across the 18-mile dike and into the province of Friesland in less than 90 minutes.

The occasion called for a typically Dutch breakfast—cold cuts, slices of delicious cheeses, and an assortment of breads. And among the breads was the Frisian Sugar Loaf with its pockets of sweet, sticky goodness, flavored with cinnamon. Memorable.

INGREDIENTS

1 cup sugar cubes
1 tablespoon ground cinnamon
6 cups all-purpose or bread flour, approximately
$^1/_3$ cup nonfat dry milk
1 package dry yeast
2 teaspoons salt
2 cups hot water (120°–130°)
3 tablespoons shortening

BAKING PANS

2 medium (8½"-x-4½") loaf pans, greased or Teflon, lined with wax or parchment paper

PREPARATION
5 mins.

With the handle of kitchen shears, an ice cracker, or a tack hammer, crack the sugar cubes. Don't crush them. Try to break them into halves or quarters. Place them in a small bowl and sprinkle with the cinnamon. Turn with a spoon or fingers until all of the broken pieces are well dusted.

BY HAND
OR MIXER
10 mins.

In a mixing bowl place 2 cups flour, the dry milk, yeast, and salt. Pour in the hot water and add the shortening. With an electric mixer beat for 2 minutes at medium speed, or 150 strong strokes with a wooden spoon. Stir in the balance of the flour, ½ cup at a time, until the dough is a rough mass.

KNEADING
8 mins.

The sugar cubes are added gradually during the kneading process whether by hand or under a dough hook.

Turn the dough onto a lightly floured work surface and knead for 2 minutes with the rhythmic motion of push-turn-fold. Flatten the dough and sprinkle with about ¼ cup sugar cube mixture. Fold the dough over the cubes and continue kneading. When the cubes have disappeared into the dough, add another ¼ cup. Again work the sugar into the dough with a kneading motion or under the dough hook. Repeat with the balance of the sugar cubes. Knead for 8 minutes by hand or dough hook.

The dough will have taken on some of the cinnamon color, but this is desirable. If some of the sugar bits work their way out of the dough during the kneading process, press them in again. If the surface of the dough becomes sticky with sugar, dust with flour.

BY PROCESSOR
5 mins.

Attach the plastic dough blade.

Place 3 cups flour in the work bowl; add the dry milk, yeast, salt, and shortening. Pour in the hot water. Pulse the processor 3 or 4 times, until all the ingredients are well blended. Add additional flour, ¼ cup at a time, until the dough is no longer wet but soft and slightly sticky. Process until the dough forms a ball and cleans the sides of the bowl.

KNEADING
50 secs.

Let the dough knead for 50 seconds.

The broken sugar cubes are added to the dough *after* it is taken from the work bowl. The spinning blade would simply pulverize the cubes if they were put in the bowl with the dough. See the kneading instructions above for working the sugar bits in the dough.

FIRST RISING
1 hour

Place the dough in a greased bowl. Turn to coat the dough completely. Cover the bowl with plastic wrap and move to a warm place (80°–100°) until the dough has doubled in bulk, about 45 minutes to 1 hour.

To proof the dough in a convection oven, place the bowl on a rack. Turn the dial to a low setting. The oven should be warm, about 90°. Leave the oven on. Proof for 45 minutes.

SHAPING
15 mins.

Turn the dough onto the work surface and divide with a sharp knife. When the dough is cut, moist pockets of sugar will be exposed. Carefully close the cut edges, pinching the seams tightly. Shape the pieces into balls, and let them rest for 3 or 4 minutes.

Form a loaf by pressing or rolling each into an oval—roughly the length of the pan. Fold the oval in half, pinch the seam to seal, tuck under the ends, and place in the loaf pan, seam down.

SECOND RISING
45 mins.

Place the pans in a warm place, cover with wax or parchment paper, and leave until the center of the dough has risen ½" above the edge of the pan, about 45 minutes.

PREHEAT

Preheat the oven to 400° about 20 minutes before baking.

BAKING
400°
15 mins.
350°
40 mins.

If desired, cut a pattern in the top of the loaf with a razor blade or sharp knife. Place the loaves in the hot oven for 15 minutes, reduce heat to 350°, and bake for an additional 40 minutes. Midway during baking shift the position of the tins so the bread is exposed equally to temperature variations in the oven.

(If using a convection oven, no preheating is necessary. Bake at 325° for 45 minutes, or until golden brown.)

FINAL STEP

Carefully turn the pans on their sides on a cooling rack. Tug gently on the paper lining to loosen the breads and pull them out. Allow the breads to cool before serving.

These loaves make exceptionally fine toast but must be watched so the sugar does not burn.

English Muffin Bread   [two small loaves]

While it will win few awards for beauty or delicate crust, English Muffin Bread has a coarse, bubble-filled texture and is delicious when toasted. Serve as one would a regular English muffin. This recipe came from a small bakery on the Oregon coast that used baking soda rather than baking powder stirred into the soft batter to produce the bread's unique texture and taste. An equal amount of baking powder undissolved can be substituted for baking soda in this recipe because soda sometimes leaves light brown streaks through the loaf, which some might not find attractive. I like it either way.

Try it under a poached egg or for the more elaborate eggs Benedict.

INGREDIENTS

1 package dry yeast
½ cup nonfat dry milk
2 teaspoons salt
4 cups bread flour, approximately
2 cups hot water (120°–130°)
½ teaspoon baking soda dissolved in 1 tablespoon warm water

BAKING PANS

2 small (7½"-x-3½") loaf pans, greased or Teflon

BY HAND
OR MIXER
15 mins.

Note: The batter mixture will be allowed to proof until it has risen double in volume before the baking soda is added.

In a bowl combine the yeast, dry milk, salt, and 2 cups flour.

Pour in the hot water and stir to blend thoroughly. Stir in additional flour, ½ cup at a time, until the batter is thick. Stir the batter about 200 strokes by hand, or for 3 minutes with a flat beater in the mixer. The dough will pull away from the sides of the bowl in thick ribbons.

BY PROCESSOR
5 mins.

Attach the steel blade.

Place 3 cups flour, the yeast, dry milk, and salt in the work bowl. Pulse to mix. With the machine running, add the hot water to the dry ingredients. Add the remaining flour. Process for 1 minute. The thick batter will be elastic and stringy.

The baking soda dissolved in water is added by hand after the first rising.

FIRST RISING
1 hour

Cover the bowl with plastic wrap and put in a warm place (80°–100°) for about 1 hour, or until the batter has doubled in volume—it will be quite bubbly.

SHAPING
5 mins.

Stir down the batterlike dough and add the dissolved baking powder. Be certain it is well blended.

Spoon or pour into the pans, pushing the dough into the corners with a rubber spatula. The pans will be about two-thirds full.

SECOND RISING
1 hour

Lay plastic wrap or wax paper over the pans and return to a warm place. The dough will rise to the edge of the pans, about 1 hour.

PREHEAT

Preheat the oven to 375° 20 minutes before baking.

BAKING
375°
1 hour

Bake the loaves for about 1 hour. The loaves will be well browned and pull away from the sides of the pan when done.

(If using a convection oven, reduce heat 50°.)

FINAL STEP

Turn the bread out from the pans. Allow to cool on a wire rack before cutting.

The loaves can be kept for several months in a 0° freezer.

Sally Lunn   [one large tube loaf]

Sally Lunn is a sweet bread rich in eggs and butter. A yeast batter bread, it is not to be kneaded—beaten only. There is also a quick bread version with almost identical ingredients, which is leavened with baking powder rather than yeast.

There are two explanations of the name. One is that it is from soleil et lune, *French for "sun and moon." At one time, the dough was shaped into buns and, to many, the golden top crust and the white bottom evoked an image of the two heavenly bodies. The other points to a Sally Lunn, who was born and lived in Bath in England in the eighteenth century and is reputed to have made the breads. She baked them for all the important tea parties in Bath.*

A special round Sally Lunn pan, 2½ inches deep, is still used in England. When baked, the bread is cut into horizontal slices and the slices toasted and buttered; then the slices are put together again and the Sally Lunn is served hot reshaped in its original form.

INGREDIENTS	3½ to 4 cups all-purpose flour
	⅓ cup sugar
	1 teaspoon salt
	1 package dry yeast
	½ cup *each* milk and water
	½ cup (1 stick) butter
	3 eggs, room temperature

BAKING PAN

One 9" tube pan, greased or Teflon

BY HAND
OR MIXER
20 mins.

In a large bowl mix 1½ cups flour, the sugar, salt, and yeast. In a saucepan combine the milk, water, and butter. Place over low heat until the liquid is warm and the butter soft (the butter need not completely melt). Gradually pour the liquid into the dry ingredients and beat for 3 minutes with a wooden spoon, or for 2 minutes with the mixer flat beater at medium speed. Add the eggs and 1 cup flour—or enough to make a thick batter. Continue to beat for 2 minutes with the spoon or at high speed with the mixer. Stop beating and stir in enough additional flour to make a stiff batter.

BY PROCESSOR
5 mins.

Attach the plastic dough blade.

Place 2 cups flour in the work bowl and add the other ingredients, as above. Pulse several times to thoroughly mix. Remove the cover and add ½ cup more flour. Replace the cover and pulse to blend.

Add the remaining flour through the feed tube, pulsing after each addition, until the batter becomes stiff, about 30 seconds.

FIRST RISING
1 hour

Cover the bowl with plastic wrap and leave at room temperature until the dough has doubled in bulk, about 1 hour.

SHAPING
4 mins.

Stir the batter down and beat well for about 30 seconds. Pour or spoon into the pan.

SECOND RISING 50 mins.	Cover the pan with wax paper and let rise until the dough has doubled in volume, about 50 minutes.
PREHEAT	Preheat the oven to 325° 20 minutes before baking.
BAKING 325° 50 mins.	Bake for 50 minutes or until the loaf is golden brown. When done, a wooden toothpick or metal skewer stuck in the center of the loaf will come out clean and dry. (If using a convection oven, reduce heat 40°.)
FINAL STEP	Carefully remove the loaf from the pan. To cool, place on a wire rack. It will be somewhat fragile while it is hot. It is best served while still warm.

Buttermilk Bread   [two loaves]

The name Buttermilk Bread has a country-kitchen lilt, and this loaf has a country-kitchen taste. It is light and of good texture, with a golden brown crust and creamy insides.

*   This bread makes delicious toast and sandwiches, and may be baked either in loaf pans or rolled by hand into long tapered loaves. For variety, I sprinkle one with sesame and the other with poppy seeds.*

INGREDIENTS	5 to 5¹/₂ cups bread or all-purpose flour 3 tablespoons sugar 2 teaspoons salt ¹/₄ teaspoon baking soda I package dry yeast I cup water I cup buttermilk (or 4 tablespoons buttermilk powder plus I cup water) ¹/₃ cup shortening I egg, beaten Sesame and/or poppy seeds
BAKING PANS	2 medium (8½"-x-4½") loaf pans, greased or Teflon, or 1 baking sheet, greased, Teflon, or sprinkled with cornmeal
BY HAND OR MIXER 20 mins.	In a large mixing or mixer bowl stir together 2 cups flour, the sugar, salt, baking soda, and yeast. In a saucepan combine the water, buttermilk, and shortening and place over low heat to warm. (The shortening does not need to melt, and, because of the buttermilk, the mixture may appear curdled, but no matter.) Gradually add the liquid to the dry

ingredients and beat for 2 minutes by hand or with a mixer flat beater. Add 1 cup flour to make a thick batter, and beat for another 2 minutes.

From this point forward, use a wooden spoon and fingers to work in the additional flour—or use a dough hook. Add flour gradually, until the mass of dough is soft and not sticky. Then turn out onto a lightly floured work surface.

KNEADING
8 mins.

Knead until the ball of dough is smooth and elastic—about 8 minutes by hand or dough hook. If the dough is slack and soft and has a tendency to stick, add sprinkles of flour. It will pull away cleanly from the sides of the bowl when it has enough flour.

BY PROCESSOR
10 mins.

Attach the plastic dough blade.

Place 2 cups flour in the work bowl and add the other dry ingredients, as above. Pulse several times to thoroughly mix. With the machine running, gradually add the warmed liquid through the feed tube. Remove the cover and add the shortening and 2 more cups flour. Replace the cover and pulse to blend.

Add the remaining flour through the feed tube, pulsing after each addition, until the dough takes shape and is carried around the bowl by the force of the blade.

KNEADING
45 secs.

With the machine running, knead for 45 seconds.

FIRST RISING
1 hour

Place the dough in a greased bowl, cover tightly with plastic wrap, and put in a warm place (80°–100°) until the dough has doubled in bulk, about 1 hour.

SHAPING
5 mins.

Punch down the dough and cut into 2 pieces. Turn the cut side under and gently press and pat the dough into an oblong shape that will fit tightly into the pan.

For a long loaf, roll each ball of dough back and forth under the palms until it is of the desired length.

SECOND RISING
45 mins.

Cover with wax paper and return to a warm place for about 45 minutes, or until the dough has risen about 1" above the edge of the pan. The long loaves should double in size.

PREHEAT

Preheat the oven to 375° 20 minutes before baking.

BAKING
375°
40 mins.

Brush the loaves with the egg and, if desired, sprinkle with seeds. Bake for about 40 minutes, or until the crust is a golden brown and a loaf sounds hollow when thumped on the bottom. If the bottom is soft and the bread does not seem brown enough, return the loaf to the oven without the pan for another 5 or 10 minutes.

(If using a convection oven, reduce heat 50°.)

FINAL STEP

Place the loaves on wire racks to cool.

Turnipseed Sisters' White Loaf   [two loaves]

Ola and Minnie Turnipseed, two elderly spinster sisters, legends as cooks in northern Indiana (RFD, Monticello), cooked and served dinners for guests in their kerosene-lit farm home for more than thirty years.

I had taken my family, including grandsons, to the home for one of the Turnipseed noontime dinners, and to get this recipe. When the meal had been served on platters down the center of the table, the sisters pulled up chairs to talk. The old dining room was quite dark at midday and one of the sisters was quite deaf and both spoke in rather loud voices. For the two little boys the excellence of the food was overshadowed by the strange and loud voices in a dark Victorian dining room and I could see tears coming. I quickly got them into the sunshine out by the barn and the moment passed.

This is an adaptation of the big loaf of white bread they had baked in a wood-and-corncob–burning stove.

The Turnipseed loaf is leavened with a starter fermented with hops. If for some reason the hops starter is not viable, use another starter from the "Starters" chapter.

INGREDIENTS

Sponge:
1 cup Hops Starter (page 243)
2 cups warm water (105°–115°)
3 cups bread or all-purpose flour
2 teaspoons sugar

Dough:
$^1/_2$ cup lard or other shortening, room temperature
1 tablespoon salt
3$^1/_2$ to 4 cups bread or all-purpose flour, approximately
1 teaspoon butter, melted

BAKING PANS

2 medium (8½"-x-4½") baking pans, greased or Teflon

PREPARATION
8 hours

To make the sponge, in a large bowl stir together the hops starter, water, flour, and sugar.

Cover with plastic wrap and put in a warm place (80°–90°) for 8 hours or overnight, until the sponge has bubbled and is light and frothy. It will about double in volume in this time.

BY HAND
OR MIXER
15 mins.

To make the dough, remove the plastic wrap, stir down the sponge, add the lard or other shortening, salt, and 2 cups flour. Stir vigorously with a wooden spoon for 3 minutes, or with a mixer flat beater at medium speed for the same length of time. Stop the mixer. Stir in the balance of the flour, ½ cup at a time. The dough will be a rough, shaggy mass that will clean the sides of the bowl. Add sprinkles of flour if the dough continues to stick.

KNEADING
10 mins.

Turn the dough onto a lightly floured work surface and knead with the rhythmic motion of push-turn-fold. The dough will become smooth and elastic. If the dough should continue to stick and is moist, sprinkle on additional flour. Break the kneading rhythm by occasionally throwing the dough down hard against the countertop. Knead for 8 minutes by hand or under the dough hook.

BY PROCESSOR
5 mins.

Prepare the sponge as above.
    Attach the short plastic blade.
    The order of ingredients is different from above.
    Pour the sponge into the work bowl and add 2 cups flour, shortening, and salt. Pulse to blend. Pulse while adding additional flour through the feed tube, ¼ cup at a time, until the batter becomes dough and forms a ball that is whipped around the bowl by the blade.

KNEADING
45 secs.

When the dough cleans the sides of the bowl, turn on the machine to knead for 45 seconds.

FIRST RISING
2 hours

Place the dough in a greased bowl, cover with plastic wrap, and leave at room temperature until the dough has risen to twice its original size. This is a somewhat longer process than with yeast dough, so allow 2 hours.

SHAPING
8 mins.

Punch down the dough and knead for a moment to press out the air bubbles. Divide the dough into 2 pieces. Shape into balls. Let them rest for 3 or 4 minutes. Form a loaf by pressing the ball of dough into a flat oval, roughly the length of the bread pan. Fold the oval in half, pinch the seam tightly to seal, tuck under the ends, and place in the pan, seam down. Repeat for the second loaf.

SECOND RISING
I hour

Cover the pans with wax paper and leave until the dough has risen above the level of the pan, about 1 hour.

PREHEAT	Preheat the oven to 425° 20 minutes before baking.

BAKING
425°
15 mins.
350°
15 mins.

Bake the loaves in the hot oven for 15 minutes, reduce heat to 350°, and continue baking for an additional 15 minutes, or until the loaves are a light golden color. Turn 1 loaf out of the pan and test for doneness by tapping the bottom crust with a forefinger. A hard, hollow sound means the bread is done. If it is not, return the loaf in its pan to the oven for an additional 10 minutes.

If the loaf seems slow to brown (due to the chemical makeup of the hops-raised dough), brush with milk halfway through baking. At the same time, shift the pans in the oven so the loaves are exposed equally to temperature variations in the oven.

(If using a convection oven, bake at 375° for 15 minutes. Reduce heat to 300° and continue baking for an additional 30 minutes, or until the bread is brown and tests done, as above.)

FINAL STEP

Remove the bread from the oven. Turn from the pans and place on a metal rack to cool. Brush the crusts with the melted butter.

When the bread has cooled, slice, taste, and praise the memory of the Turnipseed sisters of Indiana.

Swedish Caraway Bread   [one loaf]

The zest of orange, a little brown sugar, a dollop of butter, and a sprinkle of caraway seeds are boiled together in water to begin a Swedish caraway bread made with white flour only. Usually a dark grain is used with caraway by Swedish bakers. The inside is speckled with orange flecks and somewhat shaded because of the brown sugar.

INGREDIENTS

³/₄ cup water
2 tablespoons brown sugar
Zest (peel) of 1 orange, grated
1 tablespoon butter
1 teaspoon caraway seeds
1 teaspoon salt
1 package dry yeast
2 cups bread or all-purpose flour, approximately

BAKING PAN

1 small (7½"-x-3½") baking pan, greased or Teflon

PREPARATION
15 mins.

In a small saucepan boil the water, brown sugar, orange zest, butter, and caraway seeds for 3 minutes. Pour into a large mixing bowl to cool to lukewarm (105°–115°).

BY HAND OR MIXER 15 mins.	When cooled to lukewarm, add the salt, yeast, and 1 cup flour. Stir together. Beat for 2 minutes with a mixer flat beater at medium-high speed, or for an equal length of time with a wooden spoon.
FIRST RISING 1½ hours	More flour will be added later. For now, scrape down the sides of the bowl, cover with plastic wrap, and put in a warm place for 1½ hours.
KNEADING 8 mins.	Stir down the raised batterlike dough with a wooden spoon. Add the balance of the flour, ½ cup at a time, blending in first with the spoon and then by hand. The dough will be a shaggy mass that will clean the sides of the bowl. If it does not and is sticky, sprinkle with additional flour.
	Turn the dough onto a lightly floured work surface and knead with the rhythmic motion of push-turn-fold. The dough will become smooth and elastic and bubbles will rise beneath the surface. Occasionally break the kneading rhythm by throwing the dough down hard against the work surface.
	Knead by hand for about 8 minutes, or under a dough hook for an equal length of time.
BY PROCESSOR 5 mins.	Place the steel blade in the processor.
	Measure 1 cup flour, the salt, and yeast into the work bowl. When the liquid (above) has cooled, add to the dry ingredients. Close the cover and pulse to blend. Pour the remaining flour, ¼ cup at a time, through the feed tube while the machine is running. Carefully add the last bit of flour. The dough will form a mass and begin to clean the bowl as it whirls around.
KNEADING 45 secs.	Keep the machine running and knead for 45 seconds.
SHAPING 10 mins.	Shape the dough into a ball and let rest on the work surface for 3 or 4 minutes. Form the loaf by pressing the ball into a flat oval, roughly the length of the bread pan. Fold the oval in half, pinch the seam tightly to seal, tuck under the ends, and place in the pan, seam down.
SECOND RISING 1 hour	Cover the pan with wax paper. Leave at room temperature (70°) for 1 hour, or until the dough has doubled in bulk.
PREHEAT	Preheat the oven to 350° 20 minutes before baking.
BAKING 350° 1 hour	Place the pan on the middle rack of the oven and bake for 1 hour, or until the loaf is brown and crusty. Midway during baking, turn the pan around so the loaf will be uniformly exposed to temperature variations

in the oven. Turn the loaf out of its pan and tap the bottom crust with the forefinger. It should feel hard and sound hollow. If not, return to the oven in its pan for an additional 5 to 10 minutes.

(If using a convection oven, reduce heat 40°.)

FINAL STEP

Remove from the pan and place on a metal rack to cool before slicing. This loaf freezes beautifully.

Sister Virginia's Daily Loaf   [two loaves]

The Shakers, a peaceful and industrious people who founded one of their religious colonies in central Kentucky in 1805, today are remembered chiefly for the simple, fine lines of their furniture. Unexcelled cooks and bakers, they could and did set a tidy and tasty table. The "daily loaf" of fine white bread was always present.

Sister Virginia, who created this loaf, was one of the Kentucky community's members. As that was a celibate order, all members were gone by the mid-1920s, but Sister Virginia earned for herself a certain immortality for creating this fine bread.

INGREDIENTS

1 package dry yeast
1/4 cup warm water (105°–115°), plus 1 cup water
1 cup milk
2 tablespoons sugar
2 teaspoons salt
4 tablespoons lard or vegetable shortening
7 cups bread or all-purpose flour, approximately
1/2 tablespoon butter, melted

BAKING PANS

2 medium (8½"-x-4½") loaf pans, greased or Teflon

PREPARATION
20 mins.

In a small bowl or cup dissolve the yeast in the ¼ cup warm water. Stir to dissolve, and set aside. Warm the milk in a large saucepan and add the sugar, salt, and lard. The lard need only soften, not melt. Add the 1 cup water. Pour in the yeast mixture and stir together with a large wooden spoon.

BY HAND
OR MIXER
10 mins.

Pour in 3 cups flour and beat 100 strong strokes by hand, or for 3 minutes with a mixer flat beater, until the batter is smooth. Continue adding flour, ½ cup at a time, working the dough, first with the spoon and then with the fingers until it cleans the sides and bottom of the bowl.

KNEADING
8 mins.

Turn the dough onto a floured work surface and begin the kneading process—push and turn, fold, push and turn. If the moist dough breaks through the skin of the dough, sprinkle with flour and continue kneading. Knead for 8 minutes by hand, or an equal length of time with a dough hook. The dough will gradually become smooth and elastic.

BY PROCESSOR
5 mins.

The order of ingredients differs for the processor.

Heat the milk, sugar, salt, and lard in the saucepan. Cool with the 1 cup water. Add the dissolved yeast (prepared as above) and stir to blend.

Attach the plastic dough blade. Place 3 cups flour in the work bowl. Add the liquid and pulse to mix. Add the remaining flour, ¼ cup at a time, through the feed tube, pulsing after each addition, until the dough is carried in a ball by the blade. The dough will clean the sides of the bowl.

KNEADING
45 secs.

Keep the machine running and process for 45 seconds to knead.

FIRST RISING
1 hour

Place the dough in a greased bowl, cover tightly with plastic wrap, and leave at room temperature until it has doubled in bulk, about 1 hour.

SHAPING
10 mins.

Turn out the dough, knead briefly to press out any gas bubbles, and divide into 2 equal pieces.

With your hands, press the ball of dough into an oblong piece the length of the pan. Fold lengthwise; pinch the seam together. Turn the dough over, seam down, and tuck in the ends. Drop into the prepared pan and push down with the fingers to fill the corners. Repeat with the second piece.

SECOND RISING
1 hour

Cover the pans and leave until the dough has doubled in bulk, the center slightly above the edge of the pan, about 1 hour.

PREHEAT

Preheat the oven to 350° 20 minutes before baking.

BAKING
350°
40 mins.

Brush the dough with the melted butter, and place on the lower oven shelf. Bake until the crust is a golden brown and the loaves are loose in their pans, about 40 minutes. Thump the bottom crust with the forefinger. A hard hollow sound means the bread is baked. The bottom crust also will be nicely browned.

(If using a convection oven, reduce heat 40°.)

FINAL STEP	Remove the bread from the oven and turn the loaves onto a metal cooling rack.

Remove the bread from the oven and turn the loaves onto a metal cooling rack.

This bread makes excellent toast and will keep in a paper sack (not in the refrigerator!) for several days. It freezes well.

Thank you, Sister Virginia.

Rich White Bread   [two plump loaves]

Rich in milk, lard (or butter), sugar, and eggs, it is deserving of its name. The loaf is big and plump. A slice is white and nicely textured. Toasts beautifully. Great sandwich bread, as well.

INGREDIENTS

1½ cups hot water (120°–130°)
½ cup nonfat dry milk
2 tablespoons sugar
2 teaspoons salt
2 packages dry yeast
5½ to 6 cups bread or all-purpose flour, approximately
2 tablespoons lard or butter, room temperature
2 eggs, room temperature

BAKING PANS

2 large (9"-x-5") loaf pans, greased or Teflon

BY HAND OR MIXER 15 mins.

Pour the hot water into a mixer bowl and stir in the milk, sugar, salt, yeast, and 3 cups flour. Blend. Add the lard or butter and eggs. Beat with a spoon until the batter is smooth and sheets off the spoon, or at medium speed with the mixer flat beater for 2 minutes.

Stir in the balance of the flour, ½ cup at a time, first with the spoon and then by hand. The dough will be a rough, shaggy mass that will clean the sides of the bowl. Scrape down the sides of the bowl with your fingertips or with a plastic scraper.

KNEADING 8 mins.

Turn the dough onto a lightly floured work surface and knead with the rhythmic motion of push-turn-fold for about 8 minutes. Or work under a dough hook of an electric mixer for 8 minutes.

The dough will become smooth and elastic. Sprinkle more flour on the dough if it sticks to your hands (or the sides of the mixer bowl).

BY PROCESSOR 4 mins.

Attach the short dough blade.

Pour the hot water, dry milk, sugar, salt, and yeast into the work bowl. Stir to mix and allow the yeast to dissolve. Add 3 cups flour. Pulse to mix. Scrape along the bottom edge with a spatula if necessary to moisten all of the flour. Add the lard or butter and eggs. Pulse to blend.

Add the balance of the flour, ½ cup at a time, through the feed tube, pulsing after each addition. When the batter thickens and becomes dough, the mass will whirl around the work bowl and clean the sides.

KNEADING
45 secs.

Keep the machine running and knead for 45 seconds.

FIRST RISING
1½ hours

Place the dough in the bowl and pat with buttered fingers to keep the surface from forming a crust. Cover the bowl with plastic wrap and leave at room temperature until the dough has doubled in bulk, about 1½ hours.

SECOND RISING
30 mins.

Turn back the plastic wrap and punch down the dough with fingers. Fold toward the center and turn over. Re-cover and let it rise until three-quarters doubled in bulk, about 30 minutes.

SHAPING
10 mins.

Knead the dough for a few moments to press out the bubbles. Divide the dough into 2 pieces. Shape into balls, and let rest for 3 or 4 minutes.

Form each loaf by pressing a dough ball into a flat oval, roughly the length of the baking pan. Fold the oval in half, pinch the seam tightly to seal, tuck under the ends, and place in the pan, seam down.

THIRD RISING
50 mins.

Cover the loaves with wax or parchment paper and leave until the center of the dough has risen to 1" above the edge of the pan, about 50 minutes.

PREHEAT

Preheat the oven to 400° 20 minutes before baking.

BAKING
400°
35 mins.

Bake the loaves until the crusts are golden brown and loose in their pans, about 35 minutes. Midway during baking and again near the end of it, shift the pans so the loaves are equally exposed to temperature variations. When done, remove the loaves from the pans and thump the bottom crust with the forefinger. A hard hollow sound indicates the bread is baked.

(If using a convection oven, reduce heat 40°.)

FINAL STEP

Cool the loaves on a metal rack before slicing.

This bread will stay fresh for several days because of the high butter-fat content. Freezes well.

Note: For a soft crust, brush the loaves with melted butter while they're cooling and cover with a tea towel for 30 minutes.

Feather Bread   [two long loaves]

Feather Bread is feather light. Weighing only a pound, each loaf comes out of the oven about 20 inches long, with a girth of 10 inches. Bread flour is the key to this hefty growth although all-purpose will make a perfectly respectable loaf.

While it looks like a French baguette, with the same open texture when cut, it is a little richer and sweeter. The bread has a golden crust, brushed before-hand with nothing but slightly beaten egg white.

INGREDIENTS	4 to 4¹/₂ cups bread flour (or all-purpose flour) 2 packages dry yeast 1 tablespoon *each* sugar and salt 1¹/₂ cups hot water (120°–130°) ¹/₃ cup butter or other shortening, room temperature 1 egg white, slightly beaten, mixed with 1 tablespoon water
BAKING SHEET	1 baking sheet, Teflon, or greased, or sprinkled with cornmeal
BY HAND OR MIXER 6 mins.	In a mixing bowl place 3 cups flour and the yeast, sugar, and salt. Stir to blend. Pour in the hot water. Stir with a heavy spoon or a mixer flat beater for 2 minutes, until the batterlike dough is smooth. Cut the butter into 2 or 3 pieces and drop into the bowl. Stir until the butter has been absorbed into the mixture. Add the balance of the flour, ¼ cup at a time, stirring vigorously after each addition. When the dough is a shaggy mass and can be lifted from the bowl, place on a floured work surface. Or, if in the mixer, insert the dough hook.
KNEADING 8 mins.	Knead until the dough is smooth and elastic, about 8 minutes by hand or with the dough hook. Add sprinkles of flour if the dough is sticky. The dough should clean the bowl when sufficient flour has been added. The dough will be soft and warm—like a baby's bottom.
BY PROCESSOR 6 mins.	Insert the metal blade. Pour 3 cups flour into the work bowl and add the remaining ingredients, except the egg white glaze. Pulse to blend, and let rest for 1 minute. Add the balance of the flour, ¼ cup at a time, through the feed tube. Pulse until the dough forms a rough ball that is carried around the bowl by the blade.
KNEADING 45 secs.	With the machine running knead for 45 seconds.
FIRST RISING 1 hour	Place the dough in a greased bowl, cover with plastic wrap, and leave at room temperature until it doubles in volume, about 1 hour.

SHAPING 8 mins.	Knead for 30 seconds to flatten the dough and press out the bubbles. Divide into 2 pieces. Under the palms of your hands, roll each into an 18"- or 20"-long *baguette*. Place on the baking sheet, with the seam under.
SECOND RISING 45 mins.	Cover the loaves with wax paper and leave at room temperature until the loaves double in volume, about 45 minutes.
PREHEAT	Preheat the oven to 425° 20 minutes before baking.
BAKING 425° 25 mins.	Make a ½"-deep slash down the top of the loaf with a razor blade or sharp knife. In the oven the crust will open along this line. Or, cut diagonal slashes as you would for a French loaf. Brush the loaves with the egg white mixture, and bake until they are light and shiny brown, about 25 minutes. Turn a loaf over and tap the bottom with a forefinger. A hard hollow sound means the bread is baked. (If using a convection oven, reduce heat by 50°.)
FINAL STEP	Remove from the oven and place on a metal rack to cool. These loaves are best eaten fresh, although they can be frozen as soon as they cool and put away in the deep freeze for a party occasion months hence with admirable results. This is a great barbecue bread.

Poppy Seed Bubble Loaf or Monkey Bread
[one large tube loaf]

It is a Poppy Seed Bubble Loaf to some and, to others, Monkey Bread. Jim Beard saw no reason for the nonsensical name except that it stuck because of the bread's silly shape. Whichever name it goes by, it is a handsome and spectacular bread made with yeast dough from which small pieces are pinched or cut, then dipped into melted butter and poppy seeds or currants. They rise in a tube pan to triple their original height and resemble a tall, studded crown.

Serve warm to guests and let them pick their own irregularly shaped piece, each with its crown of poppy seeds or currants. The loaf can also be sliced.

INGREDIENTS	6 cups bread or all-purpose flour, approximately 1 package dry yeast 2 cups hot water (120°–130°) ⅔ cup nonfat dry milk 2 tablespoons vegetable shortening, room temperature

2 teaspoons salt
2 tablespoons sugar
2 cups (4 sticks) butter

Bubble Loaf:
$^1/_4$ cup poppy seeds

Monkey Bread:
$^1/_2$ cup brown sugar
$^1/_2$ cup presoaked currants (see Note)

BAKING PAN	One 10" tube pan, lightly greased, or Teflon

BY HAND
OR MIXER
20 mins.

In a large mixing or mixer bowl pour 3 cups flour, the yeast, and water, and stir to dissolve the yeast into the mixture. Add the dry milk, shortening, salt, and sugar. Stir briskly with a wooden spoon about 150 strokes, or for 2 minutes with a mixer flat beater. Add the balance of the flour, ½ cup at a time, and work into the moist batterlike dough with a wooden spoon and then by hand. When the dough is soft but not sticky, turn it out onto a lightly floured work surface.

KNEADING
8 mins.

Dust the dough with a sprinkle of flour and begin to knead with a push-turn-fold movement. If the moisture breaks through the skin and the dough begins to stick, sprinkle with flour. Soon it will become elastic and lose its stickiness. Knead for a total of 8 minutes by hand or under the dough hook.

BY PROCESSOR
4 mins.

Attach the plastic dough blade.

Pour 2 cups flour, the yeast, and water into the work bowl, cover, and pulse to mix. Let stand for a moment to dissolve the yeast. Add the dry milk, shortening, salt, and sugar. Turn on the machine for 30 seconds to form a smooth batterlike dough. Add additional flour, ¼ cup at a time, pulsing after each addition, until the dough becomes a unified mass and spins around the bowl, cleaning the sides.

KNEADING
45 secs.

Keep the machine running and knead for 45 seconds. Remove the cover and test the dough with the fingers. It may be somewhat sticky. Turn from the bowl, sprinkle with flour, and work into a ball.

FIRST RISING
1 hour

Put the dough in a greased bowl, cover tightly with plastic wrap, and set aside at room temperature until it has doubled in bulk and become puffy, about 1 hour.

SHAPING
20 mins.

In a small saucepan melt the butter. If making a Bubble Loaf, pour the poppy seeds into a shallow saucer. If making Monkey Bread, add the brown sugar to the butter. Pour the currants into the butter-brown sugar mixture and heat.

Punch down the dough and force out the bubbles with your palms.

To make the Bubble Bread, pinch off pieces of the dough that will make tiny balls about 1" in diameter. The size need not be exact since they will rise in different shapes, but some uniformity is desirable. Pinch off a dozen or so; dip them, one at a time, first in the butter and then in the poppy seeds. Place them on the bottom of the pan, seed side up. Continue on, one batch after another, placing them close together. When the bottom is filled, begin a second row by stacking it on top of the first. The balls usually fill 2 rows comfortably.

For Monkey Bread, roll the dough into a rectangle ¼" thick. Cut lengthwise into ¾" strips and cut the strips into 3"-long strips. Dip each piece into the butter-currant mixture and toss haphazardly into the tube pan. Fill the pan to a uniform depth.

SECOND RISING
40 mins.

Cover the pan with wax paper and leave at room temperature until the balls or pieces have risen two-thirds of the way up the sides of the container, about 40 minutes.

PREHEAT

Preheat the oven to 375° about 20 minutes before baking.

BAKING
375°
1 hour

Bake until the loaf tests done, about 1 hour. A slender metal skewer inserted in the loaf will come out dry and clean. Also, after it has been turned out of the pan, tap on the bottom with a forefinger. A hard, hollow sound means the bread is baked.

(If using a convection oven, reduce heat 40°.)

FINAL STEP

This handsome loaf can come apart if handled roughly while still hot. Be careful. Allow it to cool for 10 minutes and then unmold onto a metal cooling rack. Set it on a plate to take to the table.

Let guests have the fun of pulling off their own pieces of warm bread. After it is cooled, the loaf can be sliced and served—or toasted. *Note:* The currants are soaked for about 1 hour in water or, if you wish, rum, brandy, or wine. Drain, then pat dry with paper towels.

Weissbrot mit Kümmel   [one large round loaf]
(German White Bread with Caraway Seeds)

Weissbrot mit Kümmel is a fine white bread, made with wheat flour, and with just a hint of caraway. In the fifteenth century, a Nuremberg baker sat for his portrait surrounded by big loaves of white bread and small loaves of dark ones. This loaf is a descendant of the white.

Brushed or sprayed with water during baking, it produces a deep golden crust with a satisfying crackle.

INGREDIENTS	4 cups bread or all-purpose flour, approximately
	2 packages dry yeast
	2 teaspoons sugar
	$3/4$ cup hot milk (120°–130°)
	2 eggs, room temperature
	$1/2$ cup (1 stick) butter or margarine, room temperature
	2 teaspoons salt
	1 tablespoon caraway seeds

BAKING SHEET

1 baking sheet, Teflon, or greased, or sprinkled with cornmeal

BY HAND
OR MIXER
18 mins.

In a large mixing or mixer bowl combine 3 cups flour, the yeast, and sugar and form a well in the center. Pour in the hot milk. With a large wooden spoon or mixer flat beater pull the flour into the liquid to form a batter. Beat in the eggs, one at a time, then the butter or margarine and salt. Work the dough by hand or under the dough hook and add flour until it forms a rough mass.

Form a rough ball and rest it on the bottom of the bowl.

FIRST RISING
15 mins.

Fill the bowl with water (70°) to cover the dough by 2". The dough will slowly rise to the surface of the water as it ferments (and creates gas), about 15 minutes.

Remove the dough from the water and pat dry with paper toweling.

KNEADING
10–12 mins.

Place the dough on a floured work surface, punch down, and knead out the bubbles. Work in the caraway seeds. Keep the dough sprinkled with flour to control the stickiness. Continue to work and knead the dough by hand or under a dough hook until it is smooth and elastic, about 10 minutes.

BY PROCESSOR
10 mins.

Attach the plastic blade.

Place 2 cups flour in the work bowl and add the other ingredients, as above. Pulse several times to blend into a batter. Remove the cover and add 1 more cup flour. Replace the cover. Pulse.

Add the remaining flour through the feed tube, ¼ cup at a time, pulsing after each addition, until the dough forms a rough mass and is carried around the bowl by the force of the blade.

KNEADING
45 secs.

Keep the machine running and knead for 45 seconds. Work in caraway seeds by hand.

SHAPING
2 mins.

Place the dough on the work surface and pat into a round loaf, slightly mounded in the center, about 8" in diameter. Place on the prepared baking sheet.

SECOND RISING
35 mins.

Cover the dough with a tent of foil so that it does not touch the ball. It will double in bulk in about 35 minutes.

PREHEAT

Preheat the oven to 375° about 20 minutes before baking.

BAKING
375°
I hour

Place the loaf in the middle shelf of the oven. Brush or spray with water twice during the 1-hour bake period. The crust will be a golden brown, but if it appears to be browning too quickly, cover with a piece of foil or brown sack paper the last 10 or 15 minutes. Midway during baking, turn the loaf on the baking sheet to expose it equally to the vagaries of the oven.

Turn over the loaf and tap the bottom crust with a forefinger. A hard, hollow sound means the bread is baked. If not, return to the oven for an additional 10 minutes.

(If using a convection oven, reduce heat 40°.)

FINAL STEP

Turn the loaf onto a metal rack to cool before slicing.

This is a handsome loaf that deserves a special presentation at the table—carried in as one would a suckling pig (with which it goes very well).

Old Order Amish Bread   [two loaves]

This loaf, prized among the Old Order Amish families in northern Indiana, came to me from my wife's grandmother, a member of the order. The women bake it only with a premium bread flour milled from hard spring wheat, which now can be found as "bread flour" in most supermarkets. This loaf can be made with all-purpose flour, but to bake it as these farm women do, use bread flour made from spring or winter wheat.

INGREDIENTS

5 to 6 cups bread flour, approximately
I package dry yeast

⅓ cup sugar
2 teaspoons salt
1½ cups hot water (120°–130°)
⅓ cup cooking oil

BAKING PANS

2 medium (8½"-x-4½") baking pans, greased or Teflon, or any desired combination of pans, according to Dough Volume chart (page 16)

BY HAND
OR MIXER
20 mins.

In a large mixing or mixer bowl measure 2 cups flour, the yeast, sugar, salt, water, and oil. Stir with a wooden spoon or beat with a mixer flat beater until it is well blended. Add additional flour, ½ cup at a time, working it together first with the spoon and then with your hands, or if in the mixer, the flat beater and then the dough hook, until a rough mass has formed and the dough has cleaned the sides of the bowl. The dough will be elastic but not sticky. If the moisture breaks through the surface, dust with flour.

KNEADING
8 mins.

Turn the dough onto a generously floured work surface and knead with a strong push-turn-fold motion or under the dough hook for about 8 minutes. If the dough seems slack and doesn't hold its shape, add additional flour and work into the mass.

BY PROCESSOR
4 mins.

Attach the short plastic blade.
    Place 2 cups flour in the work bowl and add the other ingredients, as above. Pulse several times to thoroughly mix. Remove the cover and add 1 more cup flour. Replace the cover and pulse to blend.
    Add the remaining flour through the feed tube, ¼ cup at a time, pulsing after each addition, until the dough begins to form and is carried around the bowl by the force of the blade.

KNEADING
45 secs.

Keep the machine running and knead for 45 seconds.

FIRST RISING
1 hour

Wash and grease the work bowl, then return the dough to it. Cover tightly with plastic wrap. Leave the bowl at room temperature until the dough has doubled in bulk, about 1 hour.

SECOND RISING
45 mins.

Turn back the plastic wrap and punch down the dough. Replace the plastic wrap and leave the dough until it has risen again, about 45 minutes.

SHAPING
10 mins.

Turn the dough onto the work surface, punch down, and knead briefly to work out the bubbles. Divide the dough into 2 pieces, form loaves, and place in the pans.

THIRD RISING **40 mins.**	Cover the loaves with wax paper and leave at room temperature until the dough has risen about 1" above the edge of the pans, 40 minutes.
PREHEAT	Preheat the oven to 400° 20 minutes before baking.
BAKING **400°** **10 mins.** **350°** **30 mins.**	Put the loaves in the hot oven for 10 minutes, reduce heat to 350°, and bake for an additional 30 minutes, until the loaves are a golden brown. They will be done when a toothpick inserted in the center of the loaf comes out dry and clean. (If using a convection oven, reduce heat 40°.)
FINAL STEP	Remove the bread from the oven, turn out from the pans immediately, and leave on a metal rack to cool. This bread makes excellent toast and keeps well in the freezer for 6 to 8 months.

Zeppelin   [three long loaves]

This Viennese bâton *resembles one of Count von Zeppelin's famous lighter-than-air machines, hence the name given to it by the bakers.*

*   There are several touches in the preparation of the loaves that lift the Zeppelin above the ordinary. A sponge, sprinkled with a layer of flour, is set aside for 3 hours before the actual preparation begins. To give an authentic baked-on-the-hearth flavor to the bread, a can of wood ashes—from the fireplace or the barbecue pit—is placed in the back of the hot oven.*

INGREDIENTS	4 to 5 cups bread or all-purpose flour, approximately 2 packages dry yeast 2$^{1}/_{2}$ cups hot water (120°–130°) 2 tablespoons nonfat dry milk 2 teaspoons salt 1 tablespoon vegetable oil, plus extra 1 tablespoon salt mixed with $^{1}/_{4}$ cup water
BAKING SHEET	1 baking sheet, greased or Teflon
SPECIAL EQUIPMENT	1 cup ashes, from fireplace or barbecue, in a can
PREPARATION **3 hours**	In a large mixing or mixer bowl measure 2 cups flour and stir in the dry yeast. Add 2 cups hot water and stir with a wooden spoon until mixture becomes a heavy batter or sponge. Sprinkle the surface with a thin

layer of flour, cover the bowl with plastic wrap, and let the dough rise at room temperature for 3 hours.

If using a processor, in the work bowl measure 2 cups flour and stir in the yeast. Pulse to blend. Add 2 cups hot water; pulse. Sprinkle the surface with a thin layer of flour, cover, and leave for 3 hours while the sponge ferments.

Holes will appear in the top and the sponge may drop or sink in the center. All the better.

BY HAND OR MIXER 15 mins.

In a small bowl mix the dry milk, ½ cup hot water, and salt and pour this over the sponge. Work it into the batter by hand or with the mixer flat beater. Add the oil. Work in additional flour until the dough forms a shaggy mass that can be lifted from the bowl and placed on the work surface or left in the bowl under the dough hook.

KNEADING 8 mins.

Knead under your palms or with a dough hook for 8 minutes, or until the dough becomes elastic and silky. It will feel alive under your hands.

BY PROCESSOR 4 mins.

Attach the short plastic blade.

Mix the dry milk, ½ cup water, and salt together and pour into the sponge; pulse. Add the oil. Then add the remaining flour, ¼ cup at a time, pulsing after each addition—until the dough cleans the sides of the bowl.

KNEADING 45 secs.

Keep the machine running and knead for 45 seconds.

FIRST RISING 1 hour

Pat the ball of dough lightly with vegetable oil and drop into the large bowl. Cover tightly with plastic wrap and leave at room temperature until the dough doubles in bulk, 1 hour.

SECOND RISING 20 mins.

Punch down the dough, and let it rise again, about 20 minutes.

SHAPING 6 mins.

Turn the dough out onto the work surface and cut into 3 pieces. To give the loaves a zeppelin shape, roll the ends under the palms while leaving the center fairly fat. Then pat it into a shape roughly the size of a slender football. Point the ends. Place on the baking sheet.

THIRD RISING 20 mins.

Cover the loaves with wax paper and put aside to rise for about 20 minutes.

PREHEAT

Place the small can of ashes in the back of the oven. Preheat the oven to 400° about 20 minutes before baking.

BAKING
400°
45 mins.

Just before placing the loaves in the oven, cut 3 diagonal slashes across the top of each with a sharp knife or razor blade. Brush the loaves with the salt water. During baking brush the loaves every 10 minutes with the solution. Bake for about 45 minutes, until golden brown and tapping the bottom crust with a forefinger yields a hard, hollow sound.

(If using a convection oven, reduce heat 50°.)

FINAL STEP

Remove the bread from the oven, lift the loaves off the baking sheet, and place them on a metal rack to cool.

Methodist White Bread   [one large loaf]

In 1907 the Ladies of the Trinity M.E. Church of Delphi, Indiana, printed a cookbook of favorite community recipes, and one of the most popular was and has been for many years a creamy white loaf of bread made with a 3-day-old fermented cooked Potato Starter. The leavening had the improbable name of "Witch Yeast." Dry yeast can be substituted for the starter with good results.

The taste and aroma of this bread will carry one back to Hoosier wood-fired bake stoves of a century ago.

INGREDIENTS

3 medium potatoes, peeled and cut into pieces
2 cups water
2 teaspoons salt
2 tablespoons sugar
1 cup hot potato water (from the boiled potatoes)
4 to 5 cups bread or all-purpose flour, approximately
$\frac{1}{2}$ cup Cooked Potato Starter (page 241), or 1 package dry yeast

BAKING PAN

1 large (9"-x-5") loaf pan, greased or Teflon

PREPARATION
6$\frac{1}{2}$ hours

Six hours beforehand, in a saucepan cover the potato pieces with the 2 cups water; boil covered until soft, about 25 minutes. Pour off the water; reserve, but keep hot. Mash the potatoes.

In a large bowl mix the mashed potatoes, salt, sugar, hot potato water, and ½ cup flour. Stir until thoroughly blended. The mixture should be lukewarm to the touch. Mix in ½ cup starter (or sprinkle in dry yeast if it is to be used instead). Cover with plastic wrap and set in a warm place for at least 6 hours. Stir once or twice during this period.

BY HAND
OR MIXER
15 mins.

Remove the plastic wrap, stir again, and add 1 cup flour. Beat about 50 times by hand or with the mixer flat beater, and add an additional 2 cups flour, one at a time, until the mixture is too thick to beat with a spoon.

(The use of potato starter will require about 1 additional cup flour to offset the added moisture.)

Work and blend by hand or the dough hook. When the dough cleans the bowl and is no longer sticky, turn the ball out onto a floured work surface.

KNEADING
8 mins.

Knead by hand or with the dough hook for 8 minutes. The dough will be smooth and elastic.

BY PROCESSOR
5 mins.

Prepare the first ingredients, as above.

Attach the plastic blade.

After the 6-hour period during which time the batterlike dough is fermenting, pour the mixture into the work bowl. Add flour, a small portion at a time, through the feed tube. Pulse each time to blend.

KNEADING
45 secs.

When the dough cleans the sides of the bowl and is whirled by the blade, knead for 45 seconds.

FIRST RISING
1 hour

Place the dough back in the bowl (washed and greased), cover with plastic wrap, and leave in a warm place to double in volume, about 1 hour.

SHAPING
10 mins.

Punch down the dough and round into a ball. Let rest for 3 or 4 minutes.

Form the loaf by pressing the ball of dough into a flat oval, roughly the length of the baking pan. Fold the oval in half, pinch the seam tightly to seal, tuck under the ends, and place in the pan, seam down.

SECOND RISING
50 mins.

Cover the pan with wax paper and leave at room temperature until the dough has doubled in bulk and rises 1" above the edge of the pan, about 50 minutes.

PREHEAT

Preheat the oven to 400° 20 minutes before baking.

BAKING
400°
10 mins.
350°
40 mins.

Bake the loaf in the hot oven for 10 minutes, then reduce heat to moderately hot—350°—and bake for 40 minutes more. Turn the loaf from its pan and tap with the forefinger. If the finger strikes a soft, dull thud, return the bread in its pan to the oven. Bake for an additional 5 to 10 minutes. Test again.

(If using a convection oven, reduce heat 40°.)

FINAL STEP

Remove the bread from the oven and turn the loaf out onto a wire cooling rack.

Especially good when served warm (not hot) from the oven, or toasted. Freezes well at 0° for up to 6 months—less time, of course, in freezers that don't get that cold.

Pusstabrot   [one large or two medium loaves]
(Hungarian White Bread)

A golden flaky crust sprinkled liberally with fennel seed, this Hungarian white bread is fine with any meal; its tender, moist slices make noteworthy sandwiches.

The sponge is started an hour or so beforehand by pouring the yeast mixture into a deep well in the center of the flour—and allowing a thin batter to bubble up and over the rest of the flour.

I had baked this bread in my kitchen many years before I visited Hungary, and I was delighted to find the same bread served at the stylish but elderly Grand Hotel Margitsziget on the island between Buda and Pest.

INGREDIENTS	4¹/₂ to 5 cups bread or all-purpose flour, approximately
	2 teaspoons salt
	2 tablespoons sugar
	¹/₂ teaspoon fennel seeds, plus extra for sprinkling
	1¹/₂ cups hot water (120°–130°)
	2 packages dry yeast
	2 tablespoons vegetable oil
	1 egg white, beaten, mixed with 1 teaspoon water and pinch of salt

BAKING SHEET   1 baking sheet, greased or Teflon

PREPARATION
1¹/₂ hours

Roast the fennel seeds in a small saucepan, and grind or pound with a pestle.

In a large mixing or mixer bowl measure 3 cups flour. Add the salt, sugar, and ground fennel seeds. Mix with a large wooden spoon and form a well in the center. Pour in the hot water, yeast, and oil. With the spoon carefully draw in enough flour from the sides to form a thin batter (and dissolve the yeast).

If using a processor, measure 3 cups flour, the salt, sugar, and ground fennel into the work bowl. Pulse to mix. Push the flour up against the sides of the bowl with a rubber spatula, creating a well in the center. Pour in the water and yeast and add the oil; stir. With a spoon carefully draw in enough flour from the sides to form a thin batter.

Cover the bowl with plastic and leave until the sponge in the center has risen and flowed over the flour along the sides of the bowl, about 1 hour.

BY HAND
OR MIXER
5 mins.

With the spoon, and then your hands, work the flour into the sponge, pulling it from the sides with the spoon. Mix with your hands or the mixer flat beater until the dough is firm but elastic. If necessary, add another cup flour, in small portions, to control the stickiness.

KNEADING **8 mins.**	Sprinkle the work surface with flour and turn out the dough. Knead under the heel of the hand or with the dough hook until the dough is light, elastic, soft, and feels alive, about 8 minutes.
BY PROCESSOR **I hour**	Attach the steel blade. Turn the machine on and thoroughly blend the wet mixture with the dry flour. Add enough of the remaining flour through the feed tube, pulsing after each addition, until the dough is formed and is carried around the bowl by the force of the blade.
KNEADING **45 secs.**	With the machine running knead for 45 seconds.
FIRST RISING **I hour**	Return the dough to the work bowl and pat lightly with a little vegetable oil spread over the hands. Cover tightly with plastic wrap. Let the dough double in bulk, about 1 hour.
SHAPING **5 mins.**	Turn the dough back onto the work space and knead briefly to work out the bubbles. If for 1 loaf, shape the dough into a ball, flatten the top slightly, and place on the baking sheet. If for 2 loaves, divide the dough and shape.
SECOND RISING **40 mins.**	Cover the loaf or loaves with wax paper and leave at room temperature until double in bulk, about 40 minutes.
PREHEAT	Preheat the oven to 350° 20 minutes before baking and place a shallow pan of hot water on the lower shelf. The oven broiling pan is good for this.

BAKING
350°
50 mins.
	Cut a ½" slash down the center of each loaf. Brush with the egg white mixture and sprinkle with a little fennel seed.
	    Put the loaf or loaves in the middle rack of the oven and bake for 50 minutes. Midway during baking and again near the end, shift the loaves. When the loaves are golden brown and tapping the bottom crust yields a hard, hollow sound, they are done. If not, return to the oven for 5 to 10 minutes.
	    (If using a convection oven, place water in the bottom pan. Reduce heat 50° and bake for 45 minutes, or until the loaf sounds hollow when tapped.)

FINAL STEP	Remove from the oven and place the bread on a metal rack to cool before serving or packaging to freeze.

White Bread with Chocolate   [two small loaves]

This is a delicious white bread—with a core of chocolate—that is much like the wonderful petit pain au chocolat *beloved by French schoolchildren who clutch it in hot little hands to melt the chocolate into sweet dark pools of goodness.*

These loaves are small so they may be torn apart with forks or by hand rather than cut (which smears the chocolate). Without the chocolate, this is a fine bread for toasting. Perhaps bake one loaf with and one without.

The boulanger *uses finger-size rectangles of chocolate, called* barres *or "logs." They are available in gourmet shops and fine food stores.*

INGREDIENTS	1¼ cups hot water (120°–130°)
	1 package dry yeast
	¼ teaspoon ground ginger
	3½ to 4 cups bread or all-purpose flour, approximately
	¼ cup nonfat dry milk
	1 tablespoon sugar
	2 teaspoons salt
	2 tablespoons shortening
	4 1-ounce sweet or semisweet chocolate squares, broken in half

BAKING PANS   2 small (7½"-x-3½") loaf pans, greased or Teflon

PREPARATION
Overnight   The night before, prepare the sponge. In a medium bowl measure ¾ cup hot water, the yeast, and ginger. Stir well. Blend in 1 cup flour with a wooden spoon to make a thin batter. Cover with plastic wrap and set aside to work overnight.

BY HAND
OR MIXER
15 mins.   In the morning turn back the plastic wrap and stir down the sponge, which will have risen and fallen during the night. Add ½ cup hot water, the dry milk, sugar, salt, and shortening. Stir in the balance of the flour, ¼ cup at a time, first with the spoon and then by hand or mixer, until the dough is a rough, shaggy mass that cleans the sides of the bowl. If the dough is slack and moisture breaks through, add sprinkles of flour.

KNEADING
8 mins.   Put the dough under a mixer dough hook, or turn onto a lightly floured work surface and knead by hand with the rhythmic motion of push-turn-fold. Add sprinkles of flour if needed. The dough will become smooth and elastic. Continue kneading for 8 minutes by hand or with the dough hook.

BY PROCESSOR
5 mins.   Prepare the sponge, as above. The following morning pour the sponge into the processor work bowl.

Attach the steel blade.

Measure in the ½ cup hot water, dry milk, sugar, salt, shortening and 1 cup of the remaining flour. Close the cover and turn the machine on for 5 seconds to thoroughly blend. Add the remaining flour through the feed tube, pulsing after each addition, until the dough begins to form and is carried around the bowl by the force of the blade.

KNEADING
45 secs.

Keep the machine running and knead for 45 seconds.

FIRST RISING
1 hour

Place the dough in a greased bowl and cover tightly. Leave at room temperature until the dough doubles in bulk and is puffy, about 1 hour.

SHAPING
15 mins.

Now the chocolate is added.

First, punch down the dough and knead for a moment to press out the bubbles. With a sharp knife, divide the loaf. Shape into balls, and let rest under a towel for 5 minutes.

Form each loaf by pressing a ball under the palms into a flat oval, roughly the length of the baking pan. Lay half the chocolate pieces down the center of the oval. Fold the oval in half, pinch the seam tightly to seal, tuck under the ends, and place in the pan, seam down. Repeat with the second ball of dough.

SECOND RISING
40 mins.

Cover the pans with wax paper and leave until the center of the dough has risen ½" to 1" above the edge, about 40 minutes.

PREHEAT

Preheat the oven to 375° 20 minutes before baking.

BAKING
375°
35 mins.

Bake the loaves for about 35 minutes, until the loaves are a golden brown. Tapping the bottom of each loaf should yield a hard, hollow sound when done. If not done, return to the oven in their pans for up to an additional 10 minutes. Midway during baking and again near the end of it, shift the loaves so they are exposed equally to the oven's temperature variations.

(If using a convection oven, reduce heat 40°.)

FINAL STEP

Remove the bread from the oven. Turn the loaves onto a metal rack to cool.

This bread is absolutely delicious served warm, but expect to smear the chocolate if you cut the slices with a knife. To tear by hand is best.

Lee's Rich Loaf   [two loaves]

This white bread can be made with a grand swirl of nuts, sugar, raisins, and cinnamon through its heart or made simply as a no-frills loaf.

Naomi Lee does it both ways with a recipe that has been fine-tuned in her southern Indiana kitchen for a number of years. It began as a different recipe but she began to tailor it in response to family comments and judgments, such as using butter instead of margarine, two eggs rather than one, a bit less salt and a bit more sugar. And so it went for two decades, but now she believes it is exactly as she wants it—rich in taste, well textured, and delicious.

Naomi Lee makes a 2-loaf batch of dough. Half of the dough is rolled around a nut-raisin-cinnamon mixture while the other half is left as is.

INGREDIENTS

Dough:
1 teaspoon salt
¹/₄ cup sugar
¹/₄ cup (½ stick) butter, room temperature
1¹/₄ cups hot water (120°–130°)
¹/₃ cup nonfat dry milk
5 cups bread or unbleached flour, approximately
1 package dry yeast
2 eggs, room temperature

Filling (for 1 loaf):
¹/₄ cup chopped walnuts
¹/₄ cup presoaked raisins (see Notes)
1 teaspoon ground cinnamon
2 tablespoons sugar
2 teaspoons grated orange zest
1 tablespoon butter, softened or melted

BAKING PANS

2 medium (8½"-x-4½") loaf pans, greased or Teflon

BY HAND
OR MIXER
15 mins.

In a small saucepan measure the salt, sugar, butter, and hot water. Add the dry milk and stir together. Heat over low flame until the butter is melted, but don't bring to a boil.

Measure 2 cups flour into a mixing or mixer bowl and pour in the liquid. Blend into a light batter. Add the yeast (the flour will have cooled the water, hence won't hurt the yeast). Stir the eggs into the mixture, and beat by hand with 50 strong strokes, or under a mixer flat beater for 2 minutes, until the batter is thoroughly mixed.

Add the balance of the flour, ¼ cup at a time, blending first with the wooden spoon and then by hand or with the dough hook. When the dough has formed a rough, shaggy mass, place on the floured work surface or leave in the mixer to be kneaded. If the dough is sticky, add sprinkles of flour. Don't overload the dough with flour or it will become a hard cannonball! It must be soft and elastic.

KNEADING
10 mins.

Knead the dough with a strong push-turn-fold motion, occasionally lifting the dough off the work surface and sending it crashing back. Or place under the dough hook of an electric mixer. If the dough remains slack and moisture pushes its way through the surface, add small quantities of flour. When sufficient flour has been added, the dough under the hook will clean the sides of the bowl and not stick. The dough kneaded by hand will be soft and elastic. Knead for 10 minutes.

BY PROCESSOR
4 mins.

Insert the short plastic blade.

Heat the water-butter mixture, as above. Measure 2 cups flour and yeast into the work bowl. Pulse to blend. Pour in the liquid and pulse several times to make a thin batter. Add the eggs. Pulse.

Remove the cover to add 1 cup flour. Pulse. With the machine running, add the balance of the flour, ¼ cup at a time, through the feed tube.

KNEADING
50 secs.

When the dough has formed a ball and is riding on the blade and cleaning the sides of the bowl, knead with the machine running for 50 seconds.

FIRST RISING
1 hour

Place the dough in a greased bowl, cover tightly with plastic wrap, and set aside at room temperature to double in volume, about 1 hour.

SHAPING
15 mins.

Turn back the plastic wrap and punch down the dough. Lift to the work surface and divide the dough into 2 pieces.

For a plain loaf, form the dough into a ball. Let it rest for 3 or 4 minutes and then press into an oval roughly the length of the bread pan. Fold lengthwise, pinch the seam tightly to close, and drop in the prepared pan, seam under.

For a swirl loaf, form the dough into a ball and let rest for a few minutes. Meanwhile, in a small bowl mix together the nuts, raisins, cinnamon, sugar, and orange zest. With the fingers and rolling pin, push, stretch, and roll the dough into a rectangle slightly larger than the width of the pan and about 14" long. The dough will be about ½" thick.

Spread the butter over the dough with a brush or your fingers—taking care not to butter the narrow top edge where the seam will be made. Spread the nut mixture over the butter. Carefully roll to the top, and pinch the edge into the body. Tuck under the ends, and place the loaf in the prepared pan.

SECOND RISING
50–60 mins.

Cover the 2 pans with wax paper and put aside until doubled in volume, to the edge of the baking pan, about 50 minutes to 1 hour.

PREHEAT

Preheat the oven to 400° 20 minutes before baking.

BAKING
400°
35–40 mins.

Bake on the lower shelf of the oven for 35 to 40 minutes or until the loaves test done when the bottom crust is tapped with the forefinger.
    (If using a convection oven, bake at 350°.)

FINAL STEP

Remove from the oven and place on a metal rack to cool before serving.

Notes: Beforehand soak the raisins in water or, if you wish, rum, brandy, or wine for about 1 hour. Drain and press dry on paper towels.

For a delicious and colorful alternative, frost the loaves with confectioners' sugar, a few drops of vanilla, and just enough milk to make a smooth mixture.

Portuguese Sweet Bread
[two round, braided, or coiled loaves]

When the Portuguese came to Hawaii to work in the sugarcane fields in the 1880s, they brought with them not only their traditions but their cuisine. This bread is but one of the many good things that have been handed down from generation to generation.

I have eaten it in Hawaii as well as in Portugal, and this recipe reflects the best qualities of both. It is adapted from a recipe brought to the Islands by Maria Concecas de Souza, the great-grandmother of Genevieve Rodrigues, a fine home baker and a friend.

The dough can be fashioned in different ways. One is to simply press out a flattened round loaf to bake in a pie plate. Another is to braid the dough, brush with beaten egg, and sprinkle with coarsely granulated decorating sugar. Or, work half the dough into a long rope, about 30 inches in length and 1½ inches in diameter, and coil inside a cake pan. Brush with egg, and sprinkle with a dozen or so raisins. My own preference is the colorful coil.

The loaf is made with condensed rather than whole fresh milk because the latter was scarce on islands given over wholly to fields of cane, not to pasture. It adds its own unique flavor to the loaf but fresh milk can be substituted, of course, and not diluted with water.

INGREDIENTS	5¹/₂ to 6 cups bread or all-purpose flour, approximately
	2 packages dry yeast
	¹/₂ cup granulated sugar
	2 teaspoons salt
	¹/₂ cup condensed milk diluted with ¹/₂ cup water (120°–130°)
	¹/₈ teaspoon vanilla extract
	1 teaspoon lemon juice
	3 eggs, room temperature, plus 1 egg, beaten
	¹/₄ cup currants or raisins, plus 12 more for garnish
	¹/₂ cup (1 stick) butter, room temperature
	2 tablespoons granulated sugar or coarsely granulated decorating sugar

BAKING SHEET OR PIE PANS

1 baking sheet (for braids), greased or Teflon, or two 9" pie pans (for round loaves or coils), greased.

BY HAND OR MIXER 18 mins.

In a large mixing or mixer bowl combine 3 cups flour, the yeast, sugar, and salt. Make a well in the center of the flour, pour in the diluted milk and add the vanilla extract and lemon juice. Break the 3 eggs into the mixture, and gently stir with a large wooden spoon or mixer flat beater until all the ingredients are combined. Add the ¼ cup currants or raisins. Beat in the butter; add more flour, ¼ cup at a time. When the dough becomes difficult to stir by hand or with the beater, work in the flour with your fingers or dough hook until it can be gathered in a rough, soft ball.

KNEADING 10 mins.

Turn out the dough onto a floured work surface and knead with the heel of your hand or under a dough hook until it is smooth and elastic, about 10 minutes. If currants or raisins fall out, push them back in.

BY PROCESSOR 10 mins.

Attach the plastic dough blade.

Place 2 cups flour in the work bowl and add the yeast, sugar, and salt. Pulse to blend. Pour in the diluted milk and add the vanilla extract and lemon juice. With the machine running, add the 3 eggs through the feed tube, one at a time, and, when they are absorbed into the mixture, add the butter.

Add the remaining flour through the feed tube, pulsing after each addition, until the dough begins to form and is carried around the bowl by the force of the blade.

KNEADING 45 secs.

Keep the machine running and knead for 45 seconds.

Turn the dough from the bowl. It will be sticky. Work in currants or raisins by hand. Dust with sprinkles of flour.

FIRST RISING 1½ hours	Drop the dough into a bowl, pat with greased fingers, cover the bowl with plastic wrap, and put aside in a warm place (80°–90°) until the dough has doubled, about 1½ hours.
REST 10 mins.	Punch down the dough, divide in half, and put aside to rest for 10 minutes.
SHAPING 20 mins.	Each piece can be shaped in one of the following ways: • Pat the dough into a flattened round, about 8" across, and place in a greased pie pan. • The Portuguese call the coiled loaf *caracois*. Roll the piece into a 30"-long rope and coil it in a 9" pie pan. • The braid is a *tranca a tricana*. Divide the dough into 3 equal pieces; roll each into a 14"-long rope. Lay them side by side and weave into a thick braid. Pinch ends together and turn under slightly. Place on the baking sheet.
SECOND RISING 1 hour	Cover the loaves with wax paper and put them in a warm place to double in volume, about 1 hour.
PREHEAT	Preheat the oven to 350° 20 minutes before baking.
BAKING 350° 1 hour	Brush the flat loaf with the beaten egg. Brush the coil with the beaten egg and dot it with a dozen or so currants or raisins. Brush the braid with the egg, and sprinkle with sugar or coarsely granulated decorating sugar. Place the loaf or loaves in the oven. They will be baked when they are a golden brown and a wooden toothpick or skewer inserted in the loaf comes out clean and dry, about 1 hour. (If using a convection oven, reduce heat 50°.)
FINAL STEP	Handle the loaves with care when removing them from the baking sheet or pie pan to place on the wire cooling rack. A spatula will help in lifting the coils and braids.

Home Roman Meal Bread   [two loaves]

Home Roman Meal Bread is a solid, rough-textured loaf that many feel is superior to one of the best commercial breads on the market, Roman Meal. It is made with 1 cup Roman Meal cereal plus ½ cup wheat germ.

The cereal, a blend of whole wheat, whole rye, bran, and defatted flaxseed meal, was fed to the Roman legions, according to the box top. The cereal can be ordered by mail from Roman Meal Company, P.O. Box 11126, Tacoma, WA 98411, or www.romanmeal.com.

INGREDIENTS	5½ to 6 cups bread or all-purpose flour, approximately
	2 packages dry yeast
	1 cup Roman Meal cereal
	¼ cup nonfat dry milk
	½ cup wheat germ
	2 teaspoons salt
	¼ cup vegetable oil
	2½ cups hot water (120°–130°)

BAKING PANS

2 medium (8"-x-4") loaf pans, greased or Teflon

BY HAND OR MIXER 15 mins.

In a large mixing or mixer bowl measure 3 cups flour and stir in the yeast, cereal, dry milk, wheat germ, salt, oil, and water. Beat briskly by hand or at medium speed with a mixer flat beater. Turn to high for 2 minutes, or beat for an equal length of time by hand.

Stir in the balance of the flour, ½ cup at a time, by hand or using a dough hook in the mixer, until the dough is a rough, shaggy mass that cleans the sides of the bowl. If the dough continues to be slack and sticky, add sprinkles of flour.

KNEADING 10 mins.

If by hand, turn the dough onto a lightly floured work surface and knead with a rhythmic motion of push-turn-fold. The dough will become smooth and elastic, and feel alive under your hands. Break the kneading rhythm occasionally by throwing the dough down hard against the work surface. In the mixer, the dough will clean the sides of the bowl and cling to the dough hook. If it does not, and remains moist, add sprinkles of flour.

BY PROCESSOR 6 mins.

Attach the short dough blade.

Measure 3 cups flour into the processor work bowl and add the yeast, cereal, dry milk, wheat germ, and salt. Pulse several times to blend well. With the machine running, pour in the oil and hot water. Stop the machine for a minute to allow the wheat particles to absorb the moisture.

Add flour, ¼ cup at a time, to form a rough mass that spins with the blade and, at the same time, cleans the sides of the bowl.

KNEADING 1 min.

Turn on the processor and knead for 1 minute.

FIRST RISING 50 mins.	Place the dough in a bowl and pat with buttered or greased fingers. Cover the bowl tightly with plastic wrap and leave at room temperature until the dough has risen to twice its original size, about 50 minutes. You can test if it has risen by poking a finger in it; the dent will remain.
SHAPING 12 mins.	Punch down the dough and knead for 30 seconds to press out the bubbles. Divide the dough into 2 pieces. Shape into balls, and let rest under a towel for 3 minutes. Form each loaf by pressing a ball into a flat oval, roughly the length of the baking pan. Fold the oval in half, pinch the seam tightly to seal, tuck under the ends, and place in the pan, seam down.
SECOND RISING 45 mins.	Cover the pans with wax or parchment paper and leave until the center of the dough has risen about 1" above the level of the pan, about 45 minutes.
PREHEAT	Preheat the oven to 350° 20 minutes before baking.
BAKING **350°** 45 mins.	Bake the loaves until golden brown, about 45 minutes. Tapping the bottom of the loaf should yield a hard, hollow sound. Midway during baking and again near the end, shift the pans so the loaves are exposed equally to the temperature variations in the oven. (If using a convection oven, reduce heat 50°.)
FINAL STEP	Remove the bread from the oven and turn onto a metal rack to cool before slicing. The slice is moist and chewy. It toasts beautifully and can be kept frozen at 0° for several months.

Hearty White Bread   [one large or two small loaves]

Three hearty ingredients—wheat germ, potato flakes, and dry milk solids—make a loaf that is as healthy as it is delicious.

INGREDIENTS	3$^1/_2$ cups bread or all-purpose flour, approximately 2 eggs, room temperature 1 cup hot water (120°–130°) 2 tablespoons vegetable oil 2 packages dry yeast $^1/_2$ cup wheat germ $^1/_2$ cup instant potato flakes $^1/_4$ cup nonfat dry milk 2 tablespoons sugar 2 teaspoons salt

BAKING PANS	1 large (9"-x-5") or 2 small (7"-x-3") baking pans, greased or Teflon
BY HAND OR MIXER 8 mins.	Measure 2 cups flour into a mixing or mixer bowl and add the eggs, hot water, oil, yeast, wheat germ, potato flakes, dry milk, sugar, and salt. Stir with a wooden spoon or mixer flat beater to blend. Add flour, ¼ cup at a time, to form a rough mass by hand or in the mixer. Continue to work the mass by hand or with a dough hook until it has absorbed sufficient flour to make a dough that is not sticky.
KNEADING 10 mins.	If by hand, turn the dough out of the bowl onto a floured work surface. Knead with a push-turn-fold rhythm. Add sprinkles of flour if the dough is sticky. Occasionally raise the dough high above the work surface and bring it crashing down to stimulate the gluten even more. Knead until the dough is soft and elastic and a piece can be stretched between the hands into a thin sheet. If under the dough hook, knead at low speed until the dough has absorbed all of the flour and has formed a soft ball around the rotating arm. If the dough sticks to the sides of the bowl, add small portions of flour.
BY PROCESSOR 5 mins.	Attach the steel blade. The order of ingredients differs from above. In a small bowl mix together the eggs, hot water, and oil; set aside. Measure 2½ cups flour into the work bowl and add the yeast, wheat germ, potato flakes, dry milk, sugar, and salt. Pulse to blend. With the processor running, pour the liquid slowly through the feed tube to form a heavy batter. Add flour, ¼ cup at a time, until the dough becomes a mass that rides with the blade and cleans the sides of the bowl.
KNEADING 1½ mins.	Once the dough forms a ball, process for 1½ minutes. If the dough is wet and sticks to the sides of the work bowl, add flour by the tablespoon, with the machine running; if the dough is too dry and hard, add water by the teaspoon. The dough should be soft, smooth, elastic, and slightly sticky when kneading is complete.
FIRST RISING 1 hour	Place the ball of dough in a greased bowl, cover tightly with plastic wrap, and set aside to double in bulk, about 1 hour.
SHAPING 10 mins.	Turn back the plastic wrap and deflate the dough with a thrust of your fingers. Lift the dough from the bowl and place on a floured work surface. Form into a ball, then let rest for 3 or 4 minutes to relax the dough.

Press the dough into a flat oval roughly the length of the bread pan. (Divide into 2 pieces if for small tins.) Fold the oval lengthwise, pinch the seam tightly, tuck in the ends, and drop the loaf into the prepared pan, seam down.

SECOND RISING
30 mins.

Cover the dough with parchment paper or a piece of greased sack paper and set aside to rise to double in volume, about 30 minutes.

PREHEAT

Preheat the oven to 400° 20 minutes before baking.

BAKING
400°
15 mins.
375°
25 mins.

Place the pan on the lower shelf of the oven and bake for 15 minutes. Reduce heat to 375° and continue baking for 25 minutes. The loaf will be a golden brown when baked. If it seems to be browning too quickly, cover with a piece of sack paper or foil.

(If using a convection oven, reduce heat 50° for each of the 2 bake periods.)

FINAL STEP

Place on a metal rack to cool.

Slice and enjoy! And try it toasted.

Salt-Free White Bread [one large loaf]

Without the control salt has over yeast, the leavening action is dramatic. Don't let it rise above the level of the pan, however, or it may collapse just as grandly as it rose.

This bread has a flat taste that I enjoy as do many other people, but those who don't and who are not on a restricted diet can sprinkle a little salt on the slice if they wish.

Monsieur Raymond Calvel, the noted French baking authority, suggests the addition of ¹/₃ cup mashed potatoes and 2 tablespoons nonfat dry milk to this recipe to give the bread more flavor. With the addition of the potato, the bread will not dry out as quickly as it might otherwise.

The addition of 2 tablespoons finely processed zest or rind of grapefruit, lime, or orange is a substitute for salt in delicious loaves baked by Joe Howard, a friend who has an outstanding small bakery in Farmington, Connecticut. It works in this recipe also.

INGREDIENTS

1 package dry yeast
1 tablespoon sugar
3 to 3¹/₂ cups bread or all-purpose flour, approximately
1 cup hot water (120°–130°)
2 tablespoons vegetable oil

BAKING PAN	1 large (9"-x-5") baking pan, greased or Teflon
BY HAND OR MIXER 15 mins.	In a large mixing or mixer bowl stir the yeast and sugar into 1 cup flour. Pour in the hot water and oil. Beat for 2 minutes with the flat beater at medium, or equal time with a wooden spoon. Add another ½ cup flour. Beat for 2 minutes at high speed in the mixer or vigorously with the spoon. If using a mixer, attach a dough hook and stir in the balance of the flour, ½ cup at a time, until the dough forms a ball around the revolving arm. If by hand, stir in the flour with the wooden spoon and then by hand. The dough will be a rough, shaggy mass that will clean the sides of the bowl. If the dough is moist and sticky, add small sprinkles of flour.
KNEADING 10 mins.	If by hand, turn the dough onto a lightly floured work surface and knead with the rhythmic motion of push-turn-fold. The dough will become smooth and elastic, and bubbles will form under the surface. Vary the kneading rhythm occasionally by raising the dough above the table and banging it down hard. If using a mixer, continue kneading with the dough hook for 10 minutes. The dough should form a smooth, soft ball around the dough hook and completely clean the sides of the bowl. If it does not, add sprinkles of flour.
BY PROCESSOR 5 mins.	Attach the metal blade. Measure the yeast, sugar, and 2 cups flour into the work bowl. Pulse to blend. With the processor running, pour in the hot water and oil. Add flour, ¼ cup at a time, through the feed tube to form a rough mass that will ride with the blade and clean the sides of the bowl.
KNEADING 1 min.	Knead with the processor running for 1 minute.
FIRST RISING 1 hour	Drop the dough into the mixing bowl and pat with buttered fingers. Cover the bowl tightly with plastic wrap and leave until the dough has risen to about twice its original size, 1 hour.
SHAPING 10 mins.	Punch down the dough and knead for 30 seconds to press out the bubbles. Shape into a ball and let rest for 3 to 4 minutes to relax the dough. Form the loaf by pressing the ball into a flat oval roughly the length of the pan. Fold the oval in half, pinch the seam to seal, tuck under the ends, and place in the pan, seam down.

SECOND RISING
45 mins.

Cover the pan with wax paper and set aside to rise until the loaf has risen to the level of the pan, or about doubled, 45 minutes.

PREHEAT

Preheat the oven to 400° about 20 minutes before baking.

BAKING
400°
30 mins.

Bake the loaf in the hot oven until it has a lovely light brown crust, about 30 minutes. Midway during baking and again near the end, shift the loaf so it is exposed equally to the temperature variations in the oven. To test for doneness, turn the loaf out of the pan and tap the bottom crust with a forefinger. If it gives a hollow, hard sound, the bread is done. If not, return the loaf to the oven out of the pan for an additional 5 to 10 minutes.

(If using a convection oven, reduce heat 50°.)

FINAL STEP

Remove from the pan and cool on a metal rack.

BRAN BREADS

BRAN IS THE BROWN, flaky outer covering of the wheat kernel. It has a nutlike flavor and is often mistaken for one of several breakfast cereals that have much the same name. Those are bran, too, but of different texture and form. They may be substituted if real bran is not available. Bran flakes are available in the specialty food departments of most supermarkets and in health food stores.

Because it is so easy to beat together the ingredients by hand in a mixing bowl, I have not indicated either a mixer or food processor in three of the four bran recipes. It is a simple mixing process that leaves only a bowl and a wooden spoon to wash later.

Bran-Nut Bread   [one loaf]

A crusty loaf with a broken ridge down the center that complements the coarseness of the crumb, this bread is delicious thinly sliced and served with a soft cheese. Nuts give this rough-textured loaf a special richness.

I made this loaf with white flour for my first book but I later chose whole wheat for the fiber.

INGREDIENTS
2 cups whole-wheat flour
3 teaspoons baking powder
1 teaspoon salt
2 cups bran flakes
1 1/3 cups milk
1 egg, room temperature
2 tablespoons shortening, melted
2 tablespoons molasses
1 cup chopped walnuts

BAKING PAN	1 medium (8½"-x-4½") loaf pan, greased or Teflon, lined with buttered wax paper to cover sides and bottom
PREHEAT	Preheat the oven to 375°.
BY HAND 25 mins.	In a medium bowl measure the flour and sprinkle in the baking powder and salt. Blend well with a wooden spoon or spatula. Add the bran. In another bowl combine the milk and egg. Stir this into the flour, and add the shortening, molasses, and nuts. Mix to blend, but don't beat. Pour the batter into the baking pan and allow it to stand for 15 minutes before putting in the oven.
BAKING 375° 1 hour	Place the batter in the hot oven and bake until the loaf tests done, about 1 hour. It is baked when a wooden toothpick or metal skewer inserted in the center of the loaf comes out dry and clean. (If using a convection oven, reduce heat 50° and bake for 50 minutes, or until it tests done.)
FINAL STEP	Turn the loaf from the pan with care and place on a metal cooking rack. It will be a crusty loaf unless it is brushed with butter and covered with a towel. Most like it crisp. Regardless, it is better if allowed to age overnight before slicing.

Hilo Bran Bread

[three small loaves, two medium loaves, or six muffins]

This bread, from the recipe by a member of the Hilo Women's Club on the Big Island of Hawaii, is a good, straightforward bran loaf. The mixture is easy to work, and is light and fluffy when it is spooned or poured into the pans. I lived a number of years in the Islands and knew firsthand about the good food prepared in the kitchens of the big sugar plantations along the Hamakua Coast. I knew also that the molasses for this recipe came from a nearby sugar refinery; the bran came by ships from flour mills more than 2,000 miles away.

INGREDIENTS	3 cups all-purpose flour 3 cups bran flakes 4 teaspoons baking powder ½ cup sugar 1 teaspoon *each* salt and baking soda 2½ cups milk 6 tablespoons molasses

| BAKING PANS | 3 small (7"-x-3") or 2 medium (8"-x-4") baking pans, greased or Teflon, lined with buttered wax paper along sides and bottom. Leave the tabs of paper sticking out about ½" so the loaf can be pulled from the pan. Or 1 muffin pan, greased. |

PREHEAT — Preheat the oven to 350°.

BY HAND
20 mins.

In a large mixing bowl measure the flour, bran, baking powder, sugar, salt, and baking soda. Into a small bowl pour the milk and molasses. Stir well. Pour this into the dry ingredients and mix thoroughly.

Pour the batter into the prepared pans and let the mixture rest for 10 minutes.

BAKING
350°
30–50 mins.

Bake for about 50 minutes, or until the bread tests done when a wooden toothpick inserted in the loaf comes out clean and dry. If you are making muffins, bake for about 30 minutes and test, as above.

(If using a convection oven, reduce heat 50° and bake loaves for about 45 minutes, or until they test done, as above. Muffins should be baked in 30 minutes.)

FINAL STEP

Remove the bread from the oven. Hot quick bread is fragile when taken from the pan, so do so with care.

It is delicious served warm with butter.

Butter Bran Bread   [two small loaves or one large loaf]

Butter Bran Bread tastes like bran, which it is made with, but it also has butter, eggs, cornmeal, raisins, and nuts. I found the recipe in an old church cookbook under a rather prosaic name—Bran Cornmeal Bread. I changed the name to capture the richness of its dark, crisp crust and coarse-textured slice.

The first word I wrote about this loaf is still on the corner of the recipe card: "tremendous."

INGREDIENTS

¹/₂ cup (1 stick) butter, room temperature
¹/₂ cup sugar
2 eggs, room temperature
2 cups bran flakes
²/₃ cup all-purpose flour
1¹/₃ teaspoons baking powder
¹/₂ teaspoon salt
5 tablespoons yellow or white cornmeal
1 cup milk
1 cup raisins, nuts, or dates or a mixture of all

BAKING PANS	2 small (7½"-x-3½") loaf pans or 1 large (9"-x-5") pan, greased or Teflon, lined with buttered wax paper along the sides and bottom. Leave paper tabs projecting so the loaf can be pulled from the pan.
PREHEAT	Preheat the oven to 375°.
BY HAND 18 mins.	In a large bowl cream together the butter and sugar. Beat in the eggs, one at a time, and add the bran.
	On a length of wax paper sift the flour, then resift with the baking powder and salt. Add the cornmeal. Alternately, beat the dry ingredients and milk into the bran mixture. Add the raisins and/or dates and nuts. Mix thoroughly into the batter.
	Spread the batter in the pans. Make a slight depression down the center of the batter to compensate for the expansion in the oven.
BAKING 375° 45 mins.	Bake the bread for about 45 minutes, or until the loaves test done when a toothpick or metal skewer inserted in the center of a loaf comes out dry and clean.
	(If using a convection oven, place the pans on the lower shelf, reduce heat 50°, and bake for about 40 minutes, or until the loaves test done, as above.)
FINAL STEP	Remove the pans from the oven. Turn on their sides and gently slip the loaves out by pulling the wax paper. Place on a wire rack to cool.
	This loaf will keep for several days wrapped in foil, and can be kept frozen for several months.

High-Fiber Bran Loaf   [two medium loaves]

Calling it "dietary as well as delicious because of its high fiber content," a doctor of internal medicine and an enthusiastic home baker from Columbus, Ohio, bakes and recommends this loaf developed by one of his patients, Mrs. T. V. Dickens. She has been baking a loaf of this fine bread for her family each week for years. Dr. Martin Derrow says the various proportions of cereal, bran, and whole-wheat flour can be varied according to taste and availability. And other shortenings may be substituted for the butter.

Seven Grain Cereal is difficult to find in my markets so I substitute lightly sweetened granola.

INGREDIENTS	2 cups whole-wheat flour
	1 package dry yeast
	2 teaspoons salt

2 cups hot water (120°–130°)
$^1/_4$ cup ($^1/_2$ stick) butter, room temperature
2 tablespoons honey
$^1/_2$ cup 7 Grain Cereal or sweetened granola
$^1/_2$ cup wheat germ
1 cup bran flakes
Rind of 1 orange, grated
2 cups bread or unbleached flour, approximately

BAKING PANS

2 medium (8½"-x-4½") loaf pans, greased or Teflon

BY HAND
OR MIXER
10 mins.

Measure the whole-wheat flour into a mixing or mixer bowl and add the yeast and salt. Pour in the hot water. Stir to blend. Add the butter, honey, cereal or granola, wheat germ, bran flakes, and orange zest. Mix thoroughly with a wooden spoon or with a mixer flat beater.

Add the white flour, ½ cup at a time, until the soft batter becomes a shaggy mass that can be lifted from the bowl and dropped on the work surface. Or leave in the mixer bowl to be kneaded with the dough hook.

KNEADING
8 mins.

If the dough is sticky and moist, add sprinkles of flour. Knead the dough with the rhythmic motion of push-turn-fold. Use a dough blade (as an extension of your arm) to help lift and turn the dough. Knead for 8 minutes by hand or dough hook.

BY PROCESSOR
5 mins.

Attach the dough blade. Measure the whole-wheat flour, yeast, salt, and hot water into the work bowl, and pulse several times to blend. Remove the cover and add the butter, honey, cereal or granola, wheat germ, bran flakes, and orange zest. Turn the machine on for 10 seconds to blend. Add the white flour, ¼ cup at a time, until the dough becomes a mass and cleans the sides of the bowl as it whirls on the blade.

KNEADING
45 secs.

Keep the machine running to knead for 45 seconds.

FIRST RISING
50 mins.

Drop the dough into a greased bowl, cover tightly with plastic wrap, and leave at room temperature to double in bulk, about 50 minutes.

SHAPING
8 mins.

Turn the dough from the bowl onto a floured surface and divide in half. Shape each half into a ball and press into an oval roughly the length of the pan. Fold lengthwise in half, pinch the seam together, and place in the pan, seam under. Push the dough into the corners.

SECOND RISING 40 mins.	Cover the pans with plastic wrap. Allow the dough to double in bulk, about 1" above the edge of the pan, 40 minutes.
PREHEAT	Preheat the oven to 400° 20 minutes before baking.
BAKING 400° 20 mins. 350° 20 mins.	Bake the loaves for about 20 minutes; reduce heat to 350°, and bake for an additional 20 minutes, until the crust is a deep brown. If the crust is browning too rapidly, cover with foil or brown paper. Turn a loaf out of its pan, and tap the bottom crust with the forefinger. It is baked when it sounds hollow and hard. (If using a convection oven, reduce heat 50°.)
FINAL STEP	Turn the loaves out onto a metal rack to cool. Allow the loaves to cool completely before slicing. This may be hard to do since the bread, while it is baking and then cooling, issues forth a wonderful aroma that demands investigation—immediately.

WHOLE-WHEAT BREADS

ONE OF THE MOST VERSATILE of the dark flours the home baker can use, whole wheat is called "whole meal" or "wheatmeal" by the English and Irish, and "graham flour," after Dr. Sylvester Graham, who in 1837 advocated flour milled from the whole grain.

Because it does have a full quota of gluten, whole wheat is relatively easy to work and knead.

Stone-ground whole-wheat flour, which is ground between stones, the top one weighing more than one ton and revolving all the while, is coarser than whole wheat from a modern mill where the wheat is ground between steel rollers.

Whole wheat is a great source of fiber.

Honey-Lemon Whole-Wheat Bread   [two loaves]

After a few hours or overnight to rise slowly in the refrigerator, Honey-Lemon Whole-Wheat Bread, when baking, will fill the house with a wonderful aroma, and a taste to match—especially when toasted.

The dough is taken out of the refrigerator and slipped into the hot oven, carrying with it a moist coating that gives a different color and texture to the finished crust.

INGREDIENTS

3 cups bread or all-purpose flour
2 packages dry yeast
2 teaspoons salt
2¼ cups hot water (120°–130°)
¼ cup honey
3 tablespoons shortening, room temperature
1 tablespoon grated or diced lemon peel
2 to 3 cups whole-wheat flour, approximately
Vegetable oil

BAKING PANS	2 large (9"-x-5") baking pans, greased or Teflon
BY HAND OR MIXER 15 mins.	In a large mixing or mixer bowl combine the white flour, yeast, and salt. Pour in the hot water. Add the honey, shortening, and lemon peel. Stir briskly with a wooden spoon to blend, or for 2 minutes at medium speed with the mixer flat beater. Scrape the bowl occasionally.

In a large mixing or mixer bowl combine the white flour, yeast, and salt. Pour in the hot water. Add the honey, shortening, and lemon peel. Stir briskly with a wooden spoon to blend, or for 2 minutes at medium speed with the mixer flat beater. Scrape the bowl occasionally.

Add 1 cup whole-wheat flour. Beat at high speed or by hand for 1 minute. The batter will be thick and rubberlike, and pull away from the bowl in strands.

Stop beating. Stir in an additional 1 to 2 cups whole-wheat flour, depending on the moistness of the developing dough. The dough should be elastic, soft, and, at this stage, not overly sticky. If the dough continues to be slack and moist, add sprinkles of white flour.

KNEADING
10 mins.

If by hand, turn the dough out onto a lightly floured work surface and knead with the rhythmic motion of push-turn-fold. The dough will slowly become smooth and elastic. Occasionally change the kneading rhythm by throwing the dough down hard against the countertop. Knead for about 10 minutes. If using a dough hook, knead for 10 minutes, adding sprinkles of flour if the dough sticks to the sides of the bowl.

BY PROCESSOR
8 mins.

Attach the short plastic dough blade.

Place all of the above ingredients except the whole-wheat flour in the work bowl. Pulse to make a batterlike dough. With the machine running, measure in 1 to 1½ cups whole-wheat flour. Blend well. Turn off the machine and let the heavy batter rest for 3 minutes, until the whole-wheat flour has been absorbed into the batter. Turn on the machine, and add 1 to 1½ cups whole-wheat flour through the feed tube gradually. Turn off the machine, remove the cover, and feel the dough. It should be soft, perhaps a bit sticky, but a solid—not hard—mass.

KNEADING
45 secs.

Turn on the machine and knead for 45 seconds while the dough is whipped around the work bowl by the blade—and the dough cleans the sides of the bowl. If the dough is too heavy and the processor should stall, remove and continue by hand.

REST
20 mins.

Cover the dough with a towel or a length of wax paper and allow it to rest for 20 minutes.

SHAPING
8 mins.

Knead the dough for 30 seconds to press out the bubbles, and divide into 2 pieces. Shape into balls and let rest for 3 to 4 minutes.

Form each loaf by pressing a ball under your palms or with a rolling pin into a flat oval, roughly the length of the baking pan. Fold the oval in half, pinch the seam tightly to seal, tuck under the ends, and place in the pan, seam down.

Brush the surface of the dough with vegetable oil. Cover the pans loosely with wax paper, and then with plastic wrap. The loose covering allows the dough to rise above the level of the pan.

REFRIGERATION
2–24 hours

Place the pans in the refrigerator for 2 to 24 hours to double the volume.

PREHEAT

Remove the pans from the refrigerator and let stand while the oven heats to 400°, about 20 minutes.

BAKING
400°
30–40 mins.

Uncover the loaves. Prick any surface bubbles with a toothpick just before slipping the loaves into the oven. Bake on the lower rack of the hot oven for 30 to 40 minutes. When the loaves are brown and tapping the bottom crust yields a hard, hollow sound, they are done. If not, return them in their pans to the oven for up to an additional 10 minutes.

(If using a convection oven, reduce heat 50° and bake for 40 minutes, or until the loaves test done, as above.)

FINAL STEP

Remove the bread from the oven, turn from the pan immediately, and place on a metal rack to cool.

Note: For a soft crust, brush with melted butter or margarine as soon as bread comes out of the oven.

Buttermilk Whole-Wheat Bread
[one large or two medium loaves]

There is only one rising of the dough in this even-textured loaf leavened with yeast and baking powder. Both interact with buttermilk to give the loaf a different but delicious flavor.

INGREDIENTS

2 packages dry yeast
³/₄ cup warm water (105°–115°)
1¹/₄ cups buttermilk, room temperature (or 1¹/₄ cups water and
    4 tablespoons buttermilk powder)
1¹/₂ cups bread flour, approximately
3 cups whole-wheat flour, stone-ground preferred
¹/₄ cup shortening, room temperature
2 tablespoons brown sugar or molasses
2 teaspoons baking powder
2 teaspoons salt

BAKING PANS	1 large (9"-x-5") or 2 medium (8½"-x-4½") loaf pans, greased or Teflon
PREPARATION 15 mins.	In a large mixing bowl sprinkle the yeast over the warm water and stir briefly to dissolve. Set aside while allowing the buttermilk to reach room temperature, about 15 minutes.
BY HAND OR MIXER 12 mins.	When at room temperature, pour the buttermilk, white flour, 1 cup whole-wheat flour, shortening, brown sugar or molasses, baking powder, and salt into the yeast mixture. Blend with 50 strong strokes of a wooden spoon, or at low speed in a mixer until the flour and dry ingredients are absorbed.

With a wooden spoon or mixer flat beater stir in the remaining whole-wheat flour, ½ cup at a time, and, when it becomes thick, work with the fingers. Allow 4 or 5 minutes for the whole-wheat flour to fully absorb the liquid before adding more flour. The dough will be slightly sticky and soft. You may wish to add more white flour to help control the stickiness.

KNEADING 8 mins.	Sprinkle flour on the work surface and turn out the soft dough. In the early stages of kneading, a metal spatula or a dough blade will help turn and fold the dough. It will also scrape up the film of dough on the work surface. Knead with a strong push-turn-fold action, occasionally lifting the dough above the counter and banging it down hard. Knead for 8 minutes, by hand or with a dough hook.
BY PROCESSOR 6 mins.	Prepare the yeast mixture as above.

The order in which the ingredients are added differs from above.

Attach the short plastic dough blade.

Measure the white flour into the work bowl and add the yeast mixture. Pulse to blend. Remove the cover and add 2 cups whole-wheat flour, and *all* of the other ingredients. Close and turn machine on to thoroughly blend. Add the remaining flour through the feed tube, pulsing after each addition, until the dough begins to form and is carried around the bowl by the force of the blade.

KNEADING 45 secs.	Keep the machine running and knead for 45 seconds.
SHAPING 10 mins.	There is no "first" rising—the dough is put in the pans and set aside to rise.

Divide the dough into 2 pieces, if desired, and allow to rest for 5 minutes. Shape into balls; press the balls into ovals the length of the pans. Fold in half lengthwise, pinch the seam, and place in the pans with the seam under. Push the dough into the corners of the pans.

RISING
1 hour

Cover the pans with wax paper and leave at room temperature until the dough has risen 1" to 2" above the level of the pan, about 50 minutes.

PREHEAT

Preheat the oven to 425° 20 minutes before baking.

BAKING
425°
30–35 mins.

Bake the loaf or loaves in the oven until they are golden brown and loose in the pans, about 30 to 35 minutes. Cover with foil or brown paper if the crusts are browning too rapidly. The loaves are baked if the sound is hard and hollow when thumped on the bottom crust.

(If using a convection oven, reduce heat 40°.)

FINAL STEP

Remove the loaves from the oven and place on wire racks to cool before slicing.

Chopped Wheat Bread   [two loaves]

This is a fine-tasting wheat bread that begins 2 or 3 days prior to baking when the wheat kernels are covered with water and left to soften, and, sometimes, sprout. The soaked wheat kernels are then ground and, along with soy and whole-wheat flours and brewer's yeast, baked into a highly nutritional loaf.

This is one of the best-tasting whole-wheat breads to come from my kitchen and certainly deserved a better name than the soggy one it had—Soaked Wheat Bread.

The whole unmilled wheat kernel can be found in most health food stores and specialty food departments in supermarkets—or on the farm.

INGREDIENTS

2 cups wheat kernels
1 1/2 cups hot water (120°–130°)
2 packages dry yeast
1/4 cup oil (corn, peanut, safflower, etc.), plus 1/3 cup for kneading
1/4 cup molasses, unsulphured preferred
1 tablespoon salt
1/4 cup brewer's yeast
2 tablespoons soy flour, if available
3 cups whole-wheat flour, approximately

BAKING PANS

2 medium (8"-x-4") loaf pans, greased or Teflon

PREPARATION
2 or 3 days
ahead

Soak the wheat kernels in a bowl with water to cover 2 or 3 days beforehand.

On baking day, drain the kernels and grind in a food grinder, using the finest blade, or process with the steel blade briefly, 1 or 2 pulses. Do not cream the wheat. Leave it in fine particles.

BY HAND
OR MIXER
20 mins.

Place the chopped wheat in a large mixing or mixer bowl. Stir in the hot water, dry yeast, ¼ cup oil, molasses, salt, brewer's yeast, soy flour, and 1½ cups whole-wheat flour. Add the balance of the flour gradually, ¼ cup at a time, stirring it into the mixture thoroughly after each addition.

KNEADING
10 mins.

This is a heavy, dense dough that will require your hands—and much patience. Pour ⅓ cup oil in a small bowl and dip your fingers into this during the kneading process, about 10 minutes. It will also be helpful to have a dough blade or a wide putty knife to flip the dough over during the kneading. It will never have the live and elastic feel of white dough.

The dough is difficult to knead under a mixer dough hook. The hook will just push a hole into the dough without ever kneading it.

BY PROCESSOR
5 mins.

This is a heavy dough that is likely to stop the motors of most processors. Try it if you wish, but I suggest proceeding by hand and saving the machine.

FIRST RISING
1½ hours

Place the dough in a bowl, cover with plastic wrap, and leave at room temperature until doubled in bulk, about 1½ hours.

SHAPING
10 mins.

Punch down the dough and knead for 30 seconds to press out the bubbles. Divide the dough in half. Shape each half into a ball. Form each loaf by pressing a ball into a flat oval, roughly the length of the baking pan. Fold the oval in half, pinch to seal, and place in the pan, seam down.

SECOND RISING
1 hour

Cover the pans with wax paper and allow the dough to rise to the level of the edge of the pans, about 1 hour.

PREHEAT

Preheat the oven to 325° 20 minutes before baking.

BAKING
325°
1 hour

Place the pans on the lower shelf of the moderate oven for 1 hour. When the loaves are a crusty brown and sound hard and hollow when tapped on the bottom, they are baked. If not, return to the oven in their pans for an additional 5 to 10 minutes. Midway through baking and again near the end, shift the loaves so they are exposed equally to temperature variations in the oven.

(If using a convection oven, reduce heat 25°.)

FINAL STEP

Remove the bread from the oven, turn from the pans, and cool on a metal rack before serving.

Chopped Wheat Bread keeps well for 2 weeks or more if wrapped in foil. It also freezes well.

Max's Loaf   [one loaf]

What better way for a baker to celebrate the birth of a son than to create a loaf in his name? The Max of Max's Loaf is the son of two bakers/chefs in Saratoga Springs, New York—Michael and Wendy London, who own and operate one of this country's finest bakery/delicatessens. When I need to be inspired to be creative in baking I drive to that lovely city in upstate New York just to watch the two Londons at work.

Craig Claiborne has compared the outpouring of their baked riches to Demel's in Vienna, Wittamer's in Brussels, Peltier's in Paris, and Zauner's in Bad Ischl, Austria.

At the time this was written, Max was 5 years old, and thousands of loaves had been baked in his name. Shortly after his arrival, his parents had decided to develop a supremely healthy bread, and created this loaf of whole-wheat flour and pure honey as well as sunflower seeds in and on top of the loaf. It has an uncommonly interesting texture.

INGREDIENTS

¹/₄ cup honey, clover preferred
¹/₂ cup buttermilk
1¹/₄ cups hot water (120°–130°)
2 teaspoons salt (optional)
2 packages dry yeast
4 cups whole-wheat flour, approximately
¹/₂ cup toasted sunflower seeds, plus 1 cup untoasted for crust
1 egg yolk, beaten, mixed with 1 tablespoon milk

BAKING PAN

1 large (9"-x-5") baking pan, greased or Teflon

BY HAND
OR MIXER
10 mins.

In a mixing or mixer bowl combine the honey, buttermilk, water, and salt. Stir to dissolve the honey. Add the yeast, 2 cups flour, and the toasted sunflower seeds. Beat to blend with a wooden spoon or a mixer flat beater. Add the balance of the flour, ½ cup at a time, working it into the dough with the blade or by hand. *Don't* overload the dough with flour too quickly, but give it time to be absorbed into the dough, otherwise it may turn into a hard ball. When the dough is a rough mass, lift to the floured work surface, or leave in the mixer bowl if using the dough hook.

KNEADING **8 mins.**	The dough will become less sticky and more elastic as the kneading continues, but it will never have the elasticity of a white flour dough. If by hand, use a dough blade to help turn and work the dough. Knead by hand or in the machine for 8 minutes.
BY PROCESSOR **5 mins.**	This is a dense dough that some processors cannot prepare successfully. Try it with the plastic dough blade, but if the machine labors under the load, finish it by hand. Place 2 cups whole-wheat flour in the bowl and add the honey, buttermilk, water, salt, and yeast. Pulse to blend and dissolve the yeast. Add the toasted sunflower seeds, and the balance of the whole-wheat flour, ¼ cup at a time, until the dough forms a ball that is carried around the bowl by the blade.
KNEADING **40 secs.**	Process to knead for 40 seconds.
FIRST RISING **20 mins.**	Drop the dough into a greased bowl, cover tightly with plastic wrap, and leave at room temperature to rise for 20 minutes.
SECOND RISING **40 mins.**	Remove the plastic wrap, punch down the dough with the fingers, turn the dough over, and replace the plastic cover. Leave to rise a second time for 40 minutes.
SHAPING **10 mins.**	Turn the dough onto a lightly floured work surface and press it into an oval roughly the length of the bread pan. Fold in half and pinch the seam together. Let rest for a moment. Spread the untoasted sunflower seeds on the work surface. Brush the top and sides of the loaf with the egg-milk mixture. Carefully hold the loaf in both hands, invert it over the seeds, and roll it gently back and forth to pick up the seeds. Place the shaped loaf in the prepared pan. Tuck in the ends, and press down with the flat of the hand.
THIRD RISING **45 mins.**	Cover the pan with wax paper or a clean towel and leave until risen about 1" above the top of the pan, about 45 minutes.
PREHEAT	Preheat the oven to 375° about 20 minutes before baking.
BAKING **375°** **40 mins.**	Place the loaf in the oven and bake for about 40 minutes, or until the loaf is a deep brown and sounds hard and hollow when bottom crust is tapped with a forefinger. (If using a convection oven, reduce heat 40°.)
FINAL STEP	Unmold the loaf and let it stand, seed side up, on a rack until cool.

Gugelhupf Complet Biologique   [one large loaf]
(Whole-Wheat Gugelhupf)

A gugelhupf made with whole-wheat flour is the inspiration of one of Stras-bourg's finest boulangers, Monsieur Jean Pierre Scholler, whom I watched as he baked one spring morning when dawn was just breaking over the city's Place Broglie.

Whole wheat is a revered flour in this famous French bakery which was started 100 years ago by M. Scholler's great-great-grandfather, M. Jacques Zimper. It was he who went against the trend of baking everything with white flour and, at the urging of a physician friend, baked a dark, rough loaf of whole-wheat bread. It became the cornerstone of the Scholler bakery which today is the city's premier boulangerie de régime.

Flour used for festive loaves like gugelhupf has traditionally been white. But in keeping with the family's love affair with whole wheat, M. Scholler broke tra-dition to make a delicious gugelhupf with whole wheat. Unrefined cane sugar is in M. Scholler's original recipe, but I have substituted dark brown sugar, which is more easily obtained.

INGREDIENTS

$1/4$ cup hazelnuts (measured after grinding)
$1/3$ cup raisins
3 cups whole-wheat flour, approximately
$1/4$ cup dark brown sugar
1 teaspoon salt
1 package dry yeast
$1^3/4$ cups milk, heated (120°–130°)
1 egg, room temperature
2 tablespoons vegetable oil
$1/2$ cup bread or all-purpose flour
2 teaspoons butter, room temperature
Whole and slivered almonds
Confectioners' sugar

BAKING PAN

1 large (9") pan—a gugelhupf pan is best; angel food cake pan or bundt mold are satisfactory substitutes.

PREPARATION
15 mins.

Coarsely grind the nuts, and soak the raisins in a small bowl of water for 15 minutes. Drain the raisins and dry them on a paper towel.

BY HAND
OR MIXER
15 mins.

In a large mixing or mixer bowl pour 2 cups whole-wheat flour, the sugar, salt, and yeast. Stir to blend well, and add the hot milk. Break the egg into the batter, add the oil, and beat rapidly 40 to 50 strokes with a wooden spoon, or for 2 minutes with a mixer flat beater. Add the nuts and raisins. Blend.

Add the white flour, and continue beating. Slowly add the balance of the whole-wheat flour. Mix well to be certain the whole-wheat flour has absorbed its fill of moisture before adding final sprinkles of flour to make a solid but elastic mass that can be lifted from the bowl.

KNEADING
8 mins.

Dough that is largely whole wheat is more sticky than all-white dough, and it is helpful to have a dough blade or putty knife at hand to help work the dough and to keep the work surface scraped clean of film. Or knead with a mixer dough hook. Sprinkles of white flour will more quickly control stickiness than will whole-wheat flour. A small addition of white flour will not affect proportions. Knead the dough vigorously by hand or dough hook for 8 minutes. The dough will become smooth and elastic.

BY PROCESSOR
4 mins.

Use the steel blade.

Prepare the nuts and fruit as above; however, they are added *after* the dough is kneaded, not during.

Measure 1½ cups whole-wheat flour into the work bowl and add the brown sugar, salt, and dry yeast. Pulse to blend. Pour in the milk and add the egg and vegetable oil. With the machine running, add the balance of the whole-wheat and then the white flour to make a dough that forms a mass on the whirling blade and cleans the sides of the bowl.

KNEADING
2 mins.

Keep the machine running and knead the dough for 45 seconds.

Take the dough from the machine, press into an oval, and spread the hazelnuts and raisins over the surface. Work and knead the mixture thoroughly into the dough.

FIRST RISING
1½–2 hours

Clean the bowl and grease. Return the dough to the bowl, cover tightly with plastic wrap, and leave at room temperature until double in volume, 1½ to 2 hours.

SECOND RISING
30 mins.

Turn back the plastic wrap. Punch down the dough with extended fingers; turn it over. Re-cover the bowl and leave to rise again, about 30 minutes.

SHAPING
8 mins.

Butter the pan with the 2 teaspoons butter to which the almonds will stick. Place the whole almonds uniformly along the bottom, and the slivered almonds against the sides.

Flatten the ball of dough into an oval roughly the diameter of the pan. With your fingers, tear and fashion a hole in the center through which the pan's tube will slip. Drop the dough into place in the pan and push down with the fingers.

For pans without tubes, lay the ball of dough in the center of the pan and push into the form with your fingers.

THIRD RISING 1 hour	Cover the pan with wax paper and leave at room temperature until the dough reaches the edge of the pan, 1 hour.
PREHEAT	Preheat the oven to 375° about 20 minutes before baking.
BAKING 375° 50 mins.	Place the pans on the middle shelf of the oven. Midway during baking, turn the pan around to expose it to the different heat variations. When the top is a deep brown, remove the pan from the oven and test for doneness with a cake-testing pin or metal skewer. If particles cling to the pin when inserted into the bread, return to the oven for an additional 10 minutes. Turn the loaf out of its pan. If the crust is not a deep golden brown, return to the oven without the pan for an additional 8 to 10 minutes. (If using a convection oven, reduce heat 50°.)
FINAL STEP	Place on a metal rack to cool. When completely cool, sprinkle with confectioners' sugar and serve.

Vollkornbrot   [two loaves]

Made with only whole wheat, this Viennese loaf, as expected, has abundant wheat flavor. The dough will not be as easy to work as those made with white or blended flours, but the result is worthwhile—a delicious heavy slice, fairly dense in texture, that is clearly of peasant origin.

INGREDIENTS	3 cups whole-wheat flour, approximately 2 packages dry yeast $1/4$ cup nonfat dry milk 2 teaspoons salt 1 cup hot water (120°–130°) 2 tablespoons molasses, dark preferred 1 tablespoon butter, room temperature 1 egg white mixed with $1/4$ cup water and $1/2$ teaspoon salt
BAKING PANS	2 medium (8½"-x-4½") loaf tins, greased or Teflon
BY HAND OR MIXER 8 mins.	In a large mixing bowl measure 1½ cups whole-wheat flour, the yeast, dry milk, and salt. Stir to blend. Pour in the hot water and molasses. Add the butter. Stir vigorously with 50 strokes with a wooden spoon, or 2 minutes under the mixer flat beater.

Add the balance of the flour, ¼ cup at a time, until the dough is a soft mass. It is easy to add too much flour to the mixture, so carefully measure the final portions. Let the dough stand for 5 minutes at this stage so you can be certain the flour has absorbed the liquid, else the dough may suddenly become dry and solid.

KNEADING
8 mins.

Turn the dough onto a work surface sprinkled with white flour. Knead under the heel of the hand, or under a mixer dough hook for 8 minutes. Add liberal sprinkles of flour if the dough continues to be tacky; this dough calls for more patience than a white dough or blend. If using a dough hook, the dough will clean the sides of the bowl.

BY PROCESSOR
5 mins.

Use the steel blade.

Measure 1½ cups whole-wheat flour into the work bowl with the other dry ingredients. Pulse to blend. Add the hot water, molasses, and butter. Turn the machine on for 10 seconds to blend thoroughly. Add flour, ¼ cup at a time, until the soft batter becomes a rough, shaggy mass of dough that will ride around the bowl on the steel blade.

KNEADING
50 secs.

Keep the machine running and knead for 50 seconds. The dough will clean the sides of the bowl.

FIRST RISING
1½ hours

Shape the dough into a ball, put in a warm greased bowl, turning to film all sides, and cover the bowl tightly with plastic wrap. Leave at room temperature until doubled in volume, about 1½ hours.

SHAPING
5 mins.

Punch down with the fingers and turn from the bowl onto the floured work surface. Cut the dough in 2 pieces and shape into loaves. Place them in the prepared tins.

SECOND RISING
1 hour

Cover the tins with wax paper and leave until the dough expands to a height level with the edge of the pan, about 1 hour.

PREHEAT

Preheat the oven to 375° 20 minutes before baking.

BAKING
375°
45 mins.

Uncover the loaves and brush with the egg white glaze. Bake until the loaves test done, when tapping the bottom crust yields a hard and hollow sound, about 45 minutes. When they come from the oven the loaves will be a deep brown thanks to the whole-wheat flour and dark molasses.

(If using a convection oven, reduce heat 50°.)

FINAL STEP

Remove the bread from the oven and turn out onto a metal rack.

These loaves freeze well.

Fruit-Nut Graham Bread   [two loaves]

Nuts and fruit peek from every surface of this bread and pop out when the dough is being kneaded. Despite its rough, unkempt appearance, it makes a delicious whole-wheat loaf, with pieces of glacéed fruits adding a pleasant bite. It is the kind of loaf that disappears during the course of one meal.

INGREDIENTS

Dough:
3 cups bread or all-purpose flour, approximately
3 cups whole-wheat flour
2 packages dry yeast
$^3/_4$ cup nonfat dry milk
1 tablespoon salt
2 tablespoons packed brown sugar
2 cups hot water (120°–130°)
2 tablespoons shortening, room temperature
1 cup glacéed fruit
1 cup chopped walnuts

Topping:
$^1/_2$ cup confectioners' sugar
2 teaspoons milk
$^1/_8$ teaspoon vanilla extract
1 tablespoon chopped walnuts

BAKING PANS

2 medium (8½"-x-4½") baking pans, greased or Teflon

BY HAND
OR MIXER
8 mins.

In a large mixing or mixer bowl measure 1½ cups *each* white and whole-wheat flours, and stir in the yeast, milk, salt, and brown sugar. Pour in the hot water and stir by hand or at medium speed in the mixer for 1 minute, or until fully absorbed. Add the balance of the whole-wheat flour, and the shortening. Beat at medium-high speed for 3 minutes, or by hand.

Add the white flour, ¼ cup at a time, starting first with a wooden spoon and then mixing by hand or with a flat beater.

KNEADING
8 mins.

Sprinkle the work surface liberally with flour and turn the ball of dough onto it. Or leave in the mixer bowl under the dough hook. If the dough is slack, or moist and sticky, work sprinkles of flour into it. Soon it will become elastic and springy, and will no longer stick to the fingers or the work surface. Knead with a strong push-turn-fold motion for about 8 minutes, or with the dough hook.

BY PROCESSOR 5 mins.	Use the plastic dough blade. Measure 1½ cups *each* white and whole-wheat flours into the work bowl. Pulse. Add the yeast, dry milk, salt, and brown sugar. Pulse to blend. Add the hot water and the shortening. With the processor on, add ½ cup of each of the flours, alternating between the two.
KNEADING 45 secs.	Keep the machine running and knead the dough for 45 seconds. The dough will form a ball and ride the blade, cleaning the sides of the bowl as it swishes around. Stop the processor, remove the cover, and feel the dough. It will be slightly sticky but a sprinkle of flour should dry the surface.
FIRST RISING 1¼ hours	Return the dough to the mixing bowl, pat all over with greased fingertips and cover the bowl with plastic wrap to keep in the moisture. Leave at room temperature until the dough has doubled in bulk and is puffy to the touch, about 1¼ hours.
SHAPING 10 mins.	Dredge the sticky fruit and nuts in a tablespoon of flour spread on the work surface. Punch down the dough, and begin to work in the fruit and nuts. This will take about 4 minutes. With a knife cut the dough into 2 pieces. Form each into a round ball, flatten into an oval the length of the pan, fold in half, and seal the seam by pinching with your fingers. Pat into shape and place the loaf, seam down, in the pan.
SECOND RISING 45 mins.	Cover the pans with wax paper and leave to rise until the center of the dough has risen about 1" above the edge of the pan, about 45 minutes.
PREHEAT	Preheat the oven to 375° 20 minutes before baking.
BAKING 375° 45 mins.	Slip the pans into the oven and bake until the crusts are a dark brown and the loaves have pulled away from the sides, about 45 minutes. If the crusts brown too quickly, place a piece of foil or brown paper over them. When tapping on the bottom crust yields a hard and hollow sound, they are done. (If using a convection oven, reduce heat 50°.)
FINAL STEP	Remove the bread from the oven and place on a wire rack to cool. Meanwhile, in a small bowl mix the confectioners' sugar, milk, and vanilla. While the loaves are still warm drizzle the tops with the confectioners' icing and sprinkle with the chopped walnuts.

Wheat Germ Bread   [two loaves]

One cup of wheat germ—milled from the heart of the wheat berry—joins with whole-wheat flour, molasses, and butter to make a dark brown loaf, moist and wheaty in taste.

INGREDIENTS	1³/₄ cups water
	3 teaspoons sugar
	2 teaspoons salt
	¹/₃ cup butter or margarine, room temperature
	¹/₃ cup molasses, unsulphured preferred
	2 packages dry yeast
	1 cup wheat germ
	³/₄ cup milk, heated (120°–130°)
	4 cups whole-wheat flour
	1 to 2 cups bread or all-purpose flour, approximately

BAKING PANS   2 medium (8½"-x-4½") loaf pans, greased or Teflon

PREPARATION
15 mins.

In a saucepan heat the water, sugar, salt, butter, and molasses. The water should be sufficiently hot to warm the mixture and soften the butter. Allow the mixture to cool to lukewarm (105°–115°). Add the yeast.

Meanwhile, measure the wheat germ into a small bowl and pour the milk over it. Let it stand until the liquid has been absorbed by the wheat germ, and is only warm to the touch.

BY HAND
OR MIXER
15 mins.

In a large mixing or mixer bowl stir the molasses and wheat-germ mixtures together. Add 2 cups whole-wheat flour and 1 cup bread flour; stir together with a wooden spoon for 150 strong strokes or with the mixer flat beater. Stir in the remaining whole-wheat flour and sufficient white flour to form a rough ball of dough. If the ball is sticky, add liberal sprinkles of flour.

KNEADING
8 mins.

Turn the dough onto a floured work surface and with a strong push-turn-fold motion knead the dough until it is smooth and elastic. Or knead with the mixer dough hook until the dough cleans the sides of the bowl, 8 minutes in either case.

BY PROCESSOR
5 mins.

Prepare the molasses and wheat-germ mixture, as above.

Attach the plastic dough blade.

Measure 2 cups whole-wheat and 1 cup bread flour into the processor work bowl. Pulse. With the machine running, pour the 2 mixtures through the feed tube. Add whole-wheat flour, ¼ cup at a time, to form a rough mass that will clean the sides of the bowl. Add small amounts of white flour, if needed, to form the dough.

KNEADING
50 secs.

Keep the machine running and knead the dough for 50 seconds.

FIRST RISING
1½ hours

Place the dough in a greased bowl, cover tightly with plastic wrap, and leave at room temperature until the dough has doubled in bulk, about 1½ hours. The dough will be puffy to the touch.

SHAPING
5 mins.

Punch down the dough, work it briefly under the hands, and divide into 2 pieces. Shape these into loaves and place in the pans.

SECOND RISING
1¼ hours

Cover the pans with wax paper and leave until the dough has risen above the edge of the pan or doubled in bulk, about 1¼ hours.

PREHEAT

Preheat the oven to 375° 20 minutes before baking.

BAKING
375°
50 mins.

Place the loaves on the middle shelf of the oven and bake for about 50 minutes. When tapping the bottom crust yields a hard and hollow sound and the loaves are brown, they are done.
(If using a convection oven, reduce heat 50°.)

FINAL STEP

Remove the bread from the oven and turn the loaves out onto a metal rack to cool.

It is fine toasted, and will keep for a long time in the freezer tightly wrapped in foil or plastic.

Walnut Wheat Bread   [two loaves]

Butter, honey, and walnuts are the heart and soul of this 100 percent whole-wheat bread. It is a large loaf, with nuts peeking through the crusts—top, bottom, and sides. Inside, it is moist, open textured, and rich with nuts.

The bread is fine for any meal or occasion but especially good for breakfast or brunch—thinly sliced and served with sweet butter.

INGREDIENTS

5 to 6 cups whole-wheat flour, approximately
2 packages dry yeast
2 teaspoons salt
½ cup nonfat dry milk
2¼ cups hot water (120°–130°)
¼ cup honey
2 tablespoons butter, room temperature
1 cup coarsely chopped English walnuts

BAKING PANS	2 medium (8½"-x-4½") loaf pans, greased or Teflon

BY HAND
OR MIXER
15 mins.

In a large mixing or mixer bowl measure 3 cups whole-wheat flour, the yeast, salt, and dry milk. Stir to blend. Pour in the hot water and add the honey and butter. Stir the thick batterlike dough vigorously 75 strokes with a wooden spoon or under a mixer flat beater.

Add 1 cup whole-wheat flour, working it into the batter with a spoon or the beater. Add the balance of the flour, ¼ cup at a time, until the batter forms a moist and sticky mass. (More flour will be added momentarily.) Let the dough rest for 4 or 5 minutes to allow the wheat particles to absorb their full quota of moisture.

Replace the flat beater with a dough hook. Continue adding flour, a small portion at a time, until the dough is a shaggy mass that can be lifted out of the bowl onto the work surface—or left in the mixer bowl to work with the dough hook.

KNEADING
8 mins.

Turn the dough onto a lightly floured work surface and knead with a strong push-turn-fold motion for about 8 minutes, or until the dough is soft, elastic, and feels alive under your hands. Or knead for 8 minutes in the bowl with a dough hook.

BY PROCESSOR
7 mins.

Use the plastic dough blade.

Measure 3 cups flour into the work bowl and add all of the ingredients in the order above, except the walnuts. Pulse several times to blend. Allow to rest for 3 minutes before proceeding.

Add the balance of the flour, ¼ cup at a time, until the batter becomes dough and the ball rides on the blade. Add the last of the flour with care—don't create a cannonball. Lift the cover and feel the dough. It should be moist and somewhat sticky but not stiff.

KNEADING
2 mins.

With the machine running process for 45 seconds to knead.

Turn from the bowl, add sprinkles of flour, and knead by hand for a few moments to make a ball that is smooth and elastic.

FIRST RISING
1 hour

Place the dough in a bowl, cover tightly with plastic wrap, and leave at room temperature until it has doubled in bulk, about 1 hour. It will be puffy.

SHAPING
15 mins.

Turn back the plastic wrap, punch down the dough, and transfer it to the work surface. Flatten the dough into a large oval and place the walnuts in the center. Fold in the sides to enclose the nuts. Knead them into the dough. This will take about 5 minutes. Let the dough rest for a few minutes before shaping the loaves.

Divide the dough into 2 pieces. Press each piece into an oval, fold in half lengthwise, pinch seam closed, and drop into the pan, seam side down.

SECOND RISING
45 mins.

Cover the pans with wax paper and let rise until approximately doubled in volume, about 45 minutes.

PREHEAT

Preheat the oven to 375° about 20 minutes before baking.

BAKING
375°
45 mins.

Bake the loaves in the moderately hot oven for 45 minutes. The loaves will be a deep brown and will pull away from the sides of the pan when done. They can also be tested with a wooden toothpick inserted in the center of the loaf. If it comes out dry, the bread is done.
(If using a convection oven, reduce heat 50°.)

FINAL STEP

Remove the bread from the oven and turn the loaves onto a wire rack to cool before serving.
The bread keeps well in a plastic bag for at least a fortnight.

Rudi's Stone-Ground Wheat   [two loaves]

In the early seventies a group of young and enthusiastic university students in my small Midwest city opened a vegetarian restaurant, The Tao, and a bakery. The bakery became part of a religious order named for Swami Rudrananda (Rudi). Rudi's has since moved to larger pastures in Boston. It is sadly missed in my town but it did leave behind a legacy of fine food and delicious baked goods. It also left behind one of its best bakers, Trent Ripley, who helped me with this recipe.

Stone-Ground has 4 wheat ingredients—whole-wheat flour, bread flour, cracked wheat, and wheat germ. But it also has honey, molasses, sunflower seeds, and sesame seeds.

Outstanding!

INGREDIENTS

¹/₂ cup cracked wheat (bulgur), soaked and drained
3 cups whole-wheat flour, stone-ground preferred
2 cups bread or all-purpose flour, approximately
2 packages dry yeast
2 teaspoons salt
2 cups hot water (120°–130°)
¹/₃ cup honey
2 tablespoons molasses
¹/₂ cup wheat germ

¹/₃ cup *each* sunflower and sesame seeds, plus extra for topping
3 tablespoons shortening (of choice)
I egg, beaten, mixed with I tablespoon milk

BAKING PANS

2 medium (8"-x-4") loaf pans, greased or Teflon

PREPARATION
45–60 mins.

Soak the cracked wheat in tap water for 45 minutes to 1 hour, depending on the size of the grains. The larger takes longer. Test by biting one grain. It should be *al dente*—firm but not hard. Drain.

BY HAND
OR MIXER
8 mins.

In a large mixing or mixer bowl measure all of the whole-wheat flour and 1 cup white flour. Stir in the yeast and salt. Pour in the hot water and blend with 30 strong strokes with a wooden spoon, or for 3 minutes with the mixer flat beater. Add the cracked wheat, honey, molasses, wheat germ, sunflower and sesame seeds. Stir briskly to blend into a heavy but smooth batter. If using a mixer, remove the flat beater now and attach the dough hook.

Drop in the shortening, and stir into the mixture. With the wooden spoon or under the dough hook, add flour, ½ cup at a time, to form a soft dough that cleans the sides of the bowl. If the dough remains wet and sticky, add liberal sprinkles of flour but don't overload and make it into a cannonball.

KNEADING
8–10 mins.

If by hand, turn the dough out of the bowl onto a floured work surface. Vigorously knead the dough for 8 minutes with a rhythmic push-turn-fold motion. Add flour as needed to control the stickiness. If using a mixer, knead under the dough hook (adding flour if needed) for 10 minutes. The dough will clean the sides of the bowl and form a ball around the revolving hook. Again, don't overload with flour—leave a bit on the slack side and control with light sprinkles of flour.

BY PROCESSOR
5 mins.

Prepare the cracked wheat, as above.

Attach the plastic dough blade.

Measure 2 cups *each* whole-wheat and white flour into the processor work bowl. Add the yeast and salt. Pulse to blend; pour the hot water through the feed tube with the machine running. Remove the cover and add the cracked wheat, honey, molasses, wheat germ, sunflower and sesame seeds. Pulse to blend. Drop in the shortening, and mix. The dough will be quite thick.

With the processor on, add flour, ¼ cup at a time, through the feed tube, to form a dense mass that will clean the sides of the work bowl and ride with the blade around the bowl.

KNEADING
1 min.

Once the dough ball forms, process for 1 minute to knead. If the dough is too dry, add water by the teaspoon. The dough should be soft, smooth, elastic, and slightly sticky when the kneading is completed.

FIRST RISING
1½ hours

Turn the dough out of the bowl, dust with flour, and knead for a few moments to be certain it is smooth and elastic. Drop into a greased bowl, cover tightly with plastic wrap, and put aside to double in volume, about 1½ hours.

SHAPING
8 mins.

Turn the dough out of the bowl, knead for a few moments to deflate, and put aside to rest for 3 or 4 minutes.

Divide the ball of dough into 2 pieces. Flatten each piece so that it is slightly longer than the baking pan. Fold lengthwise, pinch the seam together, and place in the pan, with the seam under. Push into the corners with your fingers.

SECOND RISING
1 hour

Cover the pans with wax or parchment paper and leave to rise until the dough is above the top of the pans, about 1 hour.

PREHEAT

Preheat the oven to 375° 20 minutes before baking.

BAKING
375°
40–45 mins.

Brush the loaves with the egg-milk wash and sprinkle liberally with sesame or sunflower seeds—or both. Place the loaves on the lower shelf of the oven; midway during baking turn the pans around and continue baking. When baked, the loaves will be crusty and a deep brown. Turn 1 loaf from its pan; rap the bottom with a forefinger. If the sound is hard and hollow, the bread is baked. If you wish a harder and darker crust, return the loaves to the oven without the pans for an additional 5 to 10 minutes.

(If using a convection oven, reduce heat 50°.)

FINAL STEP

Remove from the oven and allow to cool on a metal rack before slicing.

The loaf will keep fresh for several days at room temperature, or for 6 or 8 months when frozen.

Sesame-Nut Bread   [two loaves]

When we think of sesame in baking, the seeds sprinkled over the top of a bread or bun for good looks and good taste are what usually come to mind, rather than the rich and flavorful oil blended into the dough. This loaf has both, and the sesame connection is unmistakable and delicious.

The sesame oil in this recipe comes from Japan—a dark brown oil pressed from roasted sesame seeds. It can be found in stores specializing in Oriental foods or in large supermarkets. I used it first in soups—a marvelous flavor but a light hand is needed. The dark oil, unlike the light and nearly tasteless refined sesame oil, can be heavy and pervasive if poured too freely.

The sesame oil and the seeds (on the crusts) are combined with walnuts in a rich whole-wheat bread made with honey and eggs.

INGREDIENTS

1½ cups water
1 tablespoon sesame oil
2 tablespoons peanut or vegetable oil
¼ cup honey
3 cups whole-wheat flour
1 tablespoon salt
½ cup nonfat dry milk
2 packages dry yeast
2 eggs
1 cup bread flour, approximately
1 cup walnuts, chopped pea-size
1 egg, beaten, mixed with 1 tablespoon milk
2 tablespoons roasted sesame seeds

BAKING PANS

2 medium (8"-x-4") loaf pans, greased or Teflon

PREPARATION
10 mins.

Pour the water, oils, and honey into a saucepan. Heat over low flame to warm the mixture to 125°—just hot to the touch.

BY HAND
OR MIXER
15 mins.

Measure 2 cups whole-wheat flour into a mixing or mixer bowl and stir in the salt, dry milk, and yeast. Stir to blend.

Pour the heated liquid over the flour and beat 100 strong strokes with a wooden spoon, or for 2 minutes under the mixer flat beater. Break and drop in the eggs. Beat to blend.

Add the last cup whole-wheat flour and work it into the batterlike dough. Measure in the white flour, ¼ cup at a time, to form a shaggy mass that can be lifted from the bowl and placed on the work surface. Let the dough rest for 3 to 5 minutes to allow the whole-wheat flour to absorb its full complement of moisture, otherwise it may blot up all the moisture at the last moment—leaving a too-dry ball of dough.

KNEADING
10 mins.

With the dough hook in the mixer bowl, or by hand on a lightly floured surface, knead the dough, adding sprinkles of flour when moisture breaks through the dough. Knead the dough by hand with the help of a metal dough blade—lifting, turning, folding—until the dough is soft, elastic, and alive under your hands, about 10 minutes.

BY PROCESSOR
5 mins.

Insert the plastic dough blade.

Place 2 cups whole-wheat flour, the salt, dry milk, and yeast in the processor work bowl. Pulse to blend. Add the heated liquid to the dry ingredients. Pulse. Drop in the eggs.

With the machine running, add the last cup of whole-wheat flour and the bread flour, a small portion at a time.

KNEADING
50 secs.

When the dough has formed a ball that is carried around the bowl by the blade, knead for 50 seconds. If the dough seems too moist when taken from the work bowl, add sprinkles of flour to form a surface around the dough.

FIRST RISING
1 hour

Drop the dough into a greased bowl. Cover the bowl tightly with plastic wrap and put aside at room temperature to double in volume, about 1 hour.

SHAPING
10 mins.

Turn back the plastic wrap and punch down the dough.

Push and pull the dough into a 12" circle. Place half the walnut meats on the dough, fold in and knead for a few moments. Flatten the dough again and spread the balance of the nuts. Again fold in, and continue kneading until the nuts are disbursed evenly throughout the dough.

Divide the dough into 2 pieces, shape into balls, and let relax for 5 to 6 minutes.

Flatten each ball into an oval about the length of the pan. Fold lengthwise in half and pinch the seam tightly together. Drop into the prepared pans and push the dough into the corners with your fingers.

SECOND RISING
45 mins.

Cover the pans with wax paper or a Teflon sheet and leave at room temperature to rise to the level of the edge of the pan, about 45 minutes.

PREHEAT

Preheat the oven to 375° 20 minutes before baking.

BAKING
375°
40 mins.

Brush each loaf with the egg mixture and sprinkle liberally with sesame seeds. Place on the middle shelf of the oven, and bake until the loaves test done, about 40 minutes. The loaves will be a deep rich brown. Turn 1 loaf from its pan and tap the bottom crust to determine if it is hard and hollow. If not, return it in the pan to the oven for an additional 5 or 10 minutes.

(If using a convection oven, reduce heat 50°.)

FINAL STEP

Turn the loaves from the pans onto a metal cooling rack. Serve when cool.

Makes exceptionally good toast, and freezes well.

Sprouted Wheat Bread   [two loaves]

This loaf is all whole-wheat—from the whole-wheat sprouts cultivated for several days to a dough made only with whole-wheat flour. It is a delicious deep-crusted loaf with a rich wheaty flavor to be found only in an all-wheat loaf.

It takes about 3 to 4 days to grow a cup of whole-wheat sprouts in a glass jar. When a sprout has grown the length of the seeds, harvest the crop and proceed with bread baking. The liquid in the recipe is the water drained from the sprouting wheat.

A Dutch sprouted-wheat bread baked in the Jaarsma Bakery in Pella, Iowa (see the "Thrill of Discovery" chapter), reduces the time the wheat berries are prepared to 1½ days. The wheat is soaked in water for 12 hours, drained, and placed in a covered bowl for 24 hours. The tip of the sprout will have just started to peek through the berry when it is worked into the dough.

INGREDIENTS	¼ cup whole-wheat seeds or berries 2 cups warm water 2 packages dry yeast 2 cups warm liquid from soaking wheat (above) (105°–115°) ¼ cup brewer's yeast ¼ cup honey 3 tablespoons vegetable oil 4 to 5 cups whole-wheat flour, approximately 1 teaspoon salt
BAKING PANS	2 medium (8"-x-4") loaf pans, greased or Teflon
SPECIAL EQUIPMENT	1 quart jar with a piece of cheesecloth to fasten over the opening
PREPARATION 3–4 days	Place the whole-wheat seeds or berries in a quart jar 3 or 4 days before you plan to bake. Cover the mouth with cheesecloth and fasten tightly with a rubber band, which is not to be removed during the sprout growing period. Pour the warm water through the cloth into the jar. Turn the jar on its side and drain. Keep the berries moist, warm, and dark in a closet. Twice a day rinse the berries in a small amount of warm water poured through the cheesecloth; drain and reserve the water for a total of 2 cups needed to make the dough. When the sprouts are as long as the seed, continue with the bread-making.
BY HAND OR MIXER 15 mins.	On bake day, in a large mixing or mixer bowl sprinkle the dry yeast over the 2 cups water from the sprout jar. Stir with a fork to dissolve. Stir in the brewer's yeast, honey, and oil. Blend well with a wooden

spoon or under a mixer flat beater. Measure in 3 cups whole-wheat flour and the salt. Beat vigorously until the batter is smooth.

FIRST RISING
1 hour

Cover the batter with plastic wrap and leave at room temperature until doubled in size, about 1 hour.

\BY HAND
OR MIXER
8 mins.

Stir down. Add the sprouts and about 1 cup whole-wheat flour. Stir vigorously by hand or with the mixer flat beater for about 2 minutes. Add flour, if necessary, ¼ cup at a time, until the batter becomes a heavy mass. Dough made with whole-wheat is more sticky than white, so be patient. In time it will become elastic and smooth.

KNEADING
8 mins.

Lift the dough from the bowl and drop it onto the floured work surface. Or leave in the mixer bowl and work the dough under the dough hook. Knead by hand with a strong push-turn-fold motion, adding flour as needed to control the stickiness. Do not err on the side of too much flour—better soft and elastic than a hard ball. Knead for 8 minutes by hand or under the dough hook.

BY PROCESSOR
5 mins.

Prepare the sprouts, as above.

The sequence of ingredients varies from above. Use the plastic blade.

Measure 2 cups flour into the work bowl and add the dry yeast and brewer's yeast. Pulse to blend. Pour in the 2 cups wheat-soaking liquid. Pulse until it becomes a batter. Add the honey, oil, and salt.

With the processor running, add the balance of the whole-wheat flour, ¼ cup at a time, until the batter becomes a shaggy mass and whirls in a ball with the blade. The ball will clean the sides of the bowl as it spins.

KNEADING
50 secs.

Keep the machine running and knead for 50 seconds. The dough may be somewhat sticky when turned from the bowl but a few sprinkles of flour will form a surface over the dough. If moisture persists, however, add flour.

SECOND RISING
1 hour

Place the dough in a greased bowl, cover tightly with plastic wrap, and put aside at room temperature to double in volume, about 1 hour.

SHAPING
10 mins.

Punch down the dough and knead for a few seconds to press out the bubbles. Divide the dough into 2 pieces. Shape into balls and let rest on the counter for 3 or 4 minutes.

Form the loaf by pressing each ball of dough into a flat oval, roughly the length of the baking pan. Fold the oval in half, pinch the seam tightly to seal, tuck under the ends, and place in the pan, seam down.

THIRD RISING
45 mins.

Cover the pans with wax paper and leave until the center of the dough has risen slightly above the level of the edge of the pan, about 45 minutes.

PREHEAT

Preheat the oven to 375° about 20 minutes before baking.

BAKING
375°
25 mins.
300°
35 mins.

Bake in the moderately hot oven for 25 minutes, reduce heat to 300°, and continue baking for an additional 35 minutes. When the loaves are golden brown and tapping the bottom crust yields a hard, hollow sound, the bread is done. Midway during baking and again near the end of it, shift the pans so the loaves are exposed equally to temperature variations in the oven.

(If using a convection oven, reduce heat 50° and 25°.)

FINAL STEP

Turn the loaves from the pans onto a metal rack to cool before slicing.

This makes a delicious toast. The loaf freezes well, and will keep thus for several months.

Molasses Wheat Bread   [two loaves]

Molasses gives this loaf of bread its dark color and dark taste. Unsulphured molasses (blackstrap) has more bite to it than either light or dark Brer Rabbit, but the latter can be used with good results.

Twist the dough before dropping it into the loaf pan. Some believe that this makes the bread more tender. Regardless, it makes an attractive loaf.

INGREDIENTS

2 cups hot water (120°–130°)
$^1/_4$ cup molasses
$^1/_2$ cup nonfat dry milk
1 tablespoon salt
$2^1/_2$ cups whole-wheat flour
$2^1/_2$ cups bread or unbleached flour, approximately
2 packages dry yeast
3 tablespoons shortening, room temperature

BAKING PANS

2 medium (8"-x-4") loaf pans, greased or Teflon

BY HAND
OR MIXER
15 mins.

Into a mixing or mixer bowl pour the water, molasses, dry milk, salt, and 1 cup each whole-wheat and bread flours. Stir to form a thin batter. Sprinkle on the yeast and add the shortening. With a mixer flat beater beat for 1 minute at medium speed or use 75 strokes with a wooden spoon.

Add the balance of the whole-wheat flour (1½ cups). Beat at high speed for 3 minutes, or 150 strong strokes with the spoon. Stop the mixer. Gradually work in the white flour, first with the spoon and then by hand, or with a dough hook if using a mixer, until a rough and somewhat shaggy mass is formed.

KNEADING
8 mins.

Turn the dough onto a floured work surface and knead with a strong push-turn-fold motion. If the dough sticks to the work surface or your fingers, dust lightly with flour. Knead in this fashion for 8 minutes, or an equal length of time in the mixer bowl with the dough hook.

BY PROCESSOR
5 mins.

Attach the stubby plastic dough blade.

The sequence of adding ingredients is changed from above.

Measure 1 cup each of the whole-wheat and bread flours into the work bowl and follow with the hot water, molasses, dry milk, salt, yeast, and shortening. Pulse to blend into a smooth batter.

Add flour, ¼ cup at a time, to the batter until it forms a rough mass and is carried around the bowl by the thrust of the blade. If some flour remains dry in the bottom of the bowl, stop the machine and scrape it free with a spatula.

KNEADING
45 secs.

When the dough is riding on the blade and the sides are cleaned by the action of the dough, knead for 45 seconds.

FIRST RISING
1 hour

Shape the dough into a ball and place in a greased bowl. Cover the bowl tightly with plastic wrap and leave at room temperature until the dough has risen to about twice its original size, about 1 hour.

SHAPING
18 mins. ·

Punch down the dough and knead for 30 seconds to press out the bubbles that formed during rising. Divide into 2 pieces. Roll and press under the palms so that each piece is about half again as long as the pan and shaped somewhat like a fat French *baguette*. Let the dough rest for 5 minutes or it will resist twisting.

Twist each piece 2 or 3 times and place in the pan.

SECOND RISING
45 mins.

Cover the pans with wax paper and leave at room temperature until the center of the dough has risen ½" to 1" above the edge of the pan, about 45 minutes.

PREHEAT

Preheat the oven to 375° 20 minutes before baking.

BAKING 375° 35–45 mins.	Place the pans in the oven. When the loaves are dark brown and tapping the bottom yields a hard, hollow sound, they are done, about 35 to 45 minutes. If the crust is soft and gives off a dull thud, return to the oven, without the pans, for an additional 5 to 10 minutes. (If using a convection oven, reduce heat 40°.)
FINAL STEP	Remove the loaves from the oven and turn the hot bread onto a wire rack to cool before slicing.

Dark Sour Bread   [two long or round loaves]

There are 4 different wheat products plus cornmeal plus beer in this almost-black loaf of delicious bread. The beer is brought to steaming on the stove, and then the other ingredients are added.

   The bread, which has a moist, chewy texture, is ideal for a buffet or with just a piece of sharp cheese as a snack.

INGREDIENTS	2 cups flat beer $^1/_2$ cup water $^2/_3$ cup cornmeal 2 tablespoons butter 2 teaspoons salt $^1/_2$ cup molasses, unsulphured preferred 2 packages dry yeast $^1/_2$ cup *each* wheat germ and whole-wheat bran cereal 1 $^1/_2$ cups whole-wheat flour 1 cup bread or all-purpose flour, approximately
BAKING SHEET	1 baking sheet, greased or sprinkled with cornmeal
PREPARATION 15 mins.	In a saucepan bring the beer to a simmer. Add the water. Remove from the heat and stir in the cornmeal, butter, salt, and molasses. When it has cooled to lukewarm (105°–115°), add the yeast and stir to dissolve.
BY HAND	Stir in the wheat germ, bran cereal, and whole-wheat flour. Stir together with a wooden spoon. The dough will be heavy and unresponsive. Add the white flour, a small portion at a time, and work it in with your fingers and a dough blade. (The dough is too heavy for an electric mixer—the dough hook will just spin futilely in the air.)
KNEADING 8–10 mins.	Continue to knead and work the dough by hand, adding white flour if necessary to control the stickiness, for about 8 to 10 minutes.

BY PROCESSOR **6 mins.**	Attach the plastic dough blade. The sequence in which the ingredients are added varies from the above. Heat the beer, as above, and add all of the other ingredients, including the yeast, when 130° or below. Measure the whole-wheat flour, wheat germ, and bran cereal into the work bowl. Pulse. Pour the lukewarm beer mixture into the work bowl, and pulse to blend well.
KNEADING **45 secs.**	Adding the white flour may be too great a load for some processors; if so, the mixture should be taken from the machine and kneaded by hand. If not, add white flour to the work bowl. When the dough has become a mass that will travel on the blade, leave the machine on for 45 seconds to knead.
FIRST RISING **2 hours**	Drop the dough into a mixing bowl, cover with plastic wrap, and put aside at room temperature to double in volume, about 2 hours.
SHAPING **5 mins.**	The loaves may be shaped into long *baguettes,* ideal for small sandwiches, or into round loaves. Divide the dough and fashion the loaves of your choice.
SECOND RISING **1½ hours**	Cover the loaves with wax paper or a Teflon sheet and leave to rise until doubled in volume, about 1½ hours.
PREHEAT	Preheat the oven to 350° 20 minutes before baking.
BAKING **350°** **40 mins.**	Place the baking sheet on the middle shelf of the moderate oven. Bake for about 40 minutes, or until the loaves are crusty and almost black in color. Midway through baking, turn the sheet around so the loaves will bake evenly. (If using a convection oven, reduce heat 50°.)
FINAL STEP	Place the loves on a metal rack to cool. The loaves can be sliced thin, and make excellent toast. The bread will keep wrapped in foil for a fortnight or more.

Batter Whole-Wheat Bread   [two loaves]

An all-whole-wheat loaf, this is a batter bread, not to be kneaded. The slice is wheaty and chewy. Slice and serve with soft cheeses, topped with a wisp of ham.

INGREDIENTS	6 cups whole-wheat flour ¹/₄ cup sugar 1 tablespoon salt 2 packages dry yeast 3¹/₂ cups hot water (120°–130°)
BAKING PANS	2 medium (8"-x-4") loaf pans, greased or Teflon
BY HAND 13 mins.	In a large mixing bowl measure the flour and stir in the sugar, salt, and yeast. Pour in the hot water and stir 50 strokes to blend. This will be a soft batter, not to be kneaded. With a spoon, fill the pans two-thirds full. Wet your fingertips to push the batter into the corners, and to smooth.
RISING 30 mins.	Cover with wax paper and leave at room temperature to double in volume—but no more—about 30 minutes.
PREHEAT	Preheat the oven to 400° 20 minutes before baking.
BAKING 400° 15 mins. 350° 45 mins.	Bake in a hot oven for about 15 minutes, then reduce heat to 350° for an additional 45 minutes, or until the loaves test done. A metal skewer or cake testing pin inserted in the center of the loaf will come out clean and dry. (If using a convection oven, reduce heat 40° for each bake period.)
FINAL STEP	Remove the bread from the oven, turn from the pans, and place on a metal rack to cool before serving.

Royal Hibernian Brown Loaf   [one round loaf]

The Irish national loaf is brown soda bread, and this version from the Royal Hibernian Hotel in Dublin is one of the best—and richest. The hotel serves the bread warm and thinly sliced. Its richness comes from a generous portion of butter and eggs.

It is a striking loaf when it comes from the oven, unfolded like a giant blossom along cuts across the top.

For a more austere but equally delicious loaf of soda bread try the Scottish

Buttermilk Bread in the "White Breads" chapter, which has no eggs and a small portion of butter.

INGREDIENTS

2¹/₂ cups whole-wheat flour, stone-ground preferred
1 cup all-purpose flour, approximately
2 tablespoons sugar
1¹/₂ teaspoons baking soda
1 teaspoon salt
¹/₄ cup (¹/₂ stick) butter, room temperature
1 egg
1¹/₄ cups buttermilk (or 5 tablespoons buttermilk powder plus
    1¹/₄ cups water), room temperature

BAKING SHEET

1 baking sheet, greased or Teflon

PREHEAT

Preheat the oven to 400° 20 minutes before baking.

BY HAND
OR MIXER
18 mins.

In a bowl mix together all of the dry ingredients. With your fingers work in the butter until it is absorbed by the flour, and the mixture resembles tiny, soft bread crumbs.

Make a well in the center of the mixture. In a separate bowl lightly beat the egg and stir in the milk. Gradually pour the egg-milk mixture into the well, mixing first with a spoon and then by hand or mixer flat beater when it forms a stiff dough.

Lift the dough from the bowl and place on a lightly floured work surface. Work the dough with your hands and a dough knife to thoroughly blend all of the ingredients. Do not knead. The butter in the dough will make it easy to work without sticking to the work surface or the hands. Sprinkle with flour if it should stick.

BY PROCESSOR
5 mins.

Attach the steel blade.

Place the whole-wheat flour in the work bowl and add the sugar, soda, and salt. Pulse to blend. Drop in the butter and pulse 2 times to cut it into small pieces. In a bowl beat the egg and buttermilk together. Pour the mixture through the feed tube. Turn the machine on briefly to allow the flour to absorb the liquid. Let stand for 3 minutes to allow the flour to fully absorb the buttermilk.

Add ½ cup white flour through the feed tube, and turn on the processor only long enough to mix in the flour. The dough is *not* to be kneaded. Remove and feel the dough. If it is wet, add more flour, but frugally. Scrape from the bowl and pat into a ball with the hands. Sprinkle with flour if necessary to control the stickiness.

SHAPING 3 mins.	Shape into a plump round ball. Pat down the top slightly, and with a knife or razor blade cut a ½"-deep cross on the top.
BAKING 400° 45 mins.	Place the loaf on the baking sheet, and bake until it has browned and has opened dramatically along the cuts, about 45 minutes. (If using a convection oven, reduce heat 40°.)
FINAL STEP	Remove the bread from the oven and place on a wire rack to cool before cutting into thin slices. Although it can be frozen, it is better freshly baked.

Maple Syrup–Graham Bread   [two loaves]

In late winter and early spring when the warm days thaw and the cold nights freeze, the sap runs from metal spikes tapped into the maple trees and falls drop by drop into buckets—the first step leading to this delicious loaf of maple syrup bread.

Maple syrup gives this loaf a golden color, taste, and fragrance. This loaf deserves to be made with 100 percent maple syrup, not Log Cabin (less than 3 percent) nor Mrs. Butterworth's (less than 2 percent). The genuine article is expensive, upwards of $14 for a quart of this rich amber liquid.

More than a cup of maple syrup is blended with buttermilk and sour cream, and mixed with 2 flours, white and whole-wheat.

INGREDIENTS	2 cups all-purpose flour 2 teaspoons *each* baking powder and baking soda 1 teaspoon salt 2 cups whole-wheat flour 2 eggs, room temperature 1½ cups buttermilk, room temperature ½ cup sour cream, room temperature 1⅓ cups maple syrup
BAKING PANS	2 medium (8½"-x-4½") loaf pans, greased, lined with greased wax paper
PREHEAT	Preheat the oven to 325° (unless using a convection oven).

BY HAND
18 mins.
	In a large mixing bowl blend together the white flour, baking powder, baking soda, and salt. Measure and stir in the whole-wheat flour.
	    In a small bowl beat the eggs and blend in the buttermilk, sour cream, and maple syrup. Pour this mixture into the dry ingredients and stir well.
	    Pour or spoon the batter into the prepared loaf pans.

BAKING 325° I hour	Place the pans in the oven and bake until the loaves test (and look) done, about 1 hour. A metal skewer or cake testing pin inserted in the center of a loaf will come out dry if the loaf is done. (If using a convection oven, there is no need to preheat. Bake at 325° for 40 minutes, or until the loaves test done.)
FINAL STEP	Remove the bread from the oven. Turn the pans on their sides and gently tug on the paper to pull the loaves out. Allow the loaves to cool before slicing. There is a pleasant sweetness about this bread, especially when simply sliced and spread with sweet butter. Good, too, served with fruit.

Whole-Wheat Orange Bread

[one large or two small loaves]

This loaf is all whole-wheat, with ¹/₂ cup nuts to enhance the wheaty flavor. But what sets it off from the ordinary is a syrup made with the zest of 3 oranges and honey.

INGREDIENTS	*Syrup:* 3 medium oranges I ¹/₂ cups water I cup honey *Dough:* 2³/₄ cups whole-wheat flour 4 teaspoons baking powder I teaspoon salt I cup cold milk ¹/₂ cup roughly chopped pecans or walnuts
BAKING PANS	1 large (9"-x-5") loaf pan, or 2 small (7"-x-3") loaf pans, greased or Teflon, lined with buttered wax paper
PREPARATION 40 mins.	To make the syrup, strip the zest (the peel minus the inner white covering) with a French *zesteur* or an ordinary potato peeler. Cut the pieces into long strips and place them in a small saucepan with the water. Bring to a boil and cook slowly over low heat until the peel is tender, about 30 minutes. Pour off all but ¼ cup of the remaining liquid. Add honey to the orange liquid and peel, and boil over low heat until the syrup is thick. Set aside.
PREHEAT	Preheat the oven to 325° 15 minutes before baking.

BY HAND
5 mins.

To make the dough, in a mixing bowl blend together the whole-wheat flour, baking powder, and salt. Pour the milk into the saucepan with the orange syrup, and mix. Add the liquid gradually to the dry ingredients, and beat well. Add the nuts.

Pour the batter into the prepared pan(s), and spread with a wooden spoon or spatula.

BAKING
325°
1 hour

Bake on the middle shelf of the oven until the loaves are a light golden brown and test done when pierced in the center with a metal skewer or wooden toothpick, about 1 hour. If it comes out clean and dry, the loaf is done.

(If using a convection oven, reduce heat 25° and bake for 45 minutes or until it tests done, as above.)

FINAL STEP

Remove the bread from the oven and turn out onto a metal rack to cool before serving.

The bread gets better with age. Any time during the first week it is delicious unheated, served thinly sliced. Freezes well.

RYE BREADS

RYE IS THE GLAMOUR FLOUR of the dark grains. It can be used alone in a loaf (Dutch Roggebrood) or joined by cornmeal, potato, and whole wheat (Pumpernickel). It can be made sweet (Raisin Rye) or traditionally sour (Old Milwaukee).

One of the most important European cereal grains, rye is hardier than wheat, resistant to cold, and is the only grain other than wheat from which leavened bread can be made. The all-rye loaf, however, has little capacity for developing a gluten network to entrap the fermenting gases, hence it is quite dense and heavy. More times than not rye is mixed with white flour.

Many home bakers are discouraged by rye's characteristic stickiness and shy away from preparing one of the truly fine loaves. Use a dough scraper or blade, a putty knife with a wide blade, or the side of a metal spatula as an extension of your hand to work and knead the dough in early stages. Later, with your hands, keep a sprinkle of rye or white flour between the dough and the hands and work surface. Use sprinkles of flour with the dough hook to keep the dough from sticking to the sides of the bowl.

Rye Sour   [eight cups]

The foundation of some of the great rye breads, including Seeded Rye, is an acidic "sour," or starter, in which onions have been placed overnight. The sour may be kept alive and well in the refrigerator for several weeks (stirred and fed occasionally), but the onion chunks should be removed and discarded after the first day.

INGREDIENTS

2 medium onions, coarsely chopped
4 cups rye flour, stone-ground preferred
3¹/₂ cups hot water (120°–130°)
2 packages dry yeast
1 tablespoon caraway seeds

SPECIAL
EQUIPMENT

A length of cheesecloth in which to tie the onion pieces

PREPARATION
**Overnight–
24 hours**

Tie the onion pieces into a bag made with cheesecloth. Put aside for the moment.

In a large bowl measure the rye flour and water. Stir to mix. Sprinkle on the yeast and work it into the rye mixture. Add the caraway seeds.

When the mixture is thoroughly blended, push the onions down into the center of the sour. Cover tightly with plastic wrap and put aside overnight but no more than 24 hours.

Lift out the onions, scrape the sour off the cloth, and discard the onions.

The sour can now be used as part of the sponge in all sour rye breads. It can be refrigerated for later use.

Old Milwaukee Rye   [two to four loaves]

Old Milwaukee Rye bread has become a delicious classic in my kitchen. It was one of the first loaves of bread to come from my oven when I started baking, and it has been a favorite ever since. Over the years, it has become a classic (and a favorite) in other kitchens as well.

It begins with a sponge (or sour) rising and falling in a bowl under a taut plastic wrap that will bubble to its maximum goodness in about 3 days, give or take a few hours. After a day or so, a whiff of the fermented sponge will make manifest the historic relationship of the baker with the brewer.

I have baked hundreds of loaves of Old Milwaukee Rye, and each time I have done so I have had a warm thought for Bernadine Landsberg of Milwaukee, who sent me the recipe a long time ago.

The dough can be fashioned into 2 large round loaves—good for husky sandwiches—or 3 or 4 long, slender loaves, ideal for slicing thin to serve at a buffet or brunch.

Note: *This is a large amount of heavy dough for food processors. I suggest doing just half the recipe for that method.*

INGREDIENTS

Sponge:
2 cups medium rye flour
1 package dry yeast
1 tablespoon caraway seeds
2 cups warm water (105°–115°)

Dough:
1 cup hot water (120°–130°)
¼ cup molasses
2 tablespoons caraway seeds
1 egg, room temperature
1 tablespoon salt
2 cups rye flour
4 cups bread or all-purpose flour, approximately
3 tablespoons vegetable shortening
1 egg, beaten, mixed with 1 tablespoon milk

BAKING SHEET

1 baking sheet, greased, Teflon, or sprinkled with cornmeal, or 2 *baguette* pans, greased

PREPARATION
1–3 days

To make the sponge, in a large bowl measure the flour, yeast, seeds, and water. Blend well with 25 strokes of a wooden spoon. Cover the bowl snugly with plastic wrap so the sponge loses none of its moisture, which will condense on the plastic and fall back into the mixture. The dark brown pastelike batter will rise and fall as it develops flavor and a delicious aroma. Stir once each day.

The sponge, which will resemble a wet mash that's too thick to pour and too thin to knead, may be used anytime after 6 hours although the longer the better—up to 3 days, when it will have ceased fermentation. If it fails to bubble up after falling back anytime during the 3-day period, don't think it is dead. It's not. It's resting but gaining flavor all the time.

BY HAND
OR MIXER
20 mins.

To make the dough, on bake day, uncover the bowl and add the water, molasses, 1 tablespoon caraway seeds, egg, salt, rye flour, and about 2 cups white flour. Beat till smooth, about 100 strokes, or 3 minutes with the mixer flat beater. Add the shortening.

Stir in the balance of the white flour, ½ cup at a time, first with the spoon and then by hand or with the mixer dough hook. The dough should clean the sides of the bowl but it will be somewhat sticky, thanks to the perverse nature of rye flour.

KNEADING **8 mins.**	Turn the dough out onto a floured work surface and knead by hand (with the help of a dough blade) or under the mixer dough hook. If by hand, knead with a strong push-turn-fold rhythm until the dough is smooth. Add sprinkles of flour if necessary to control stickiness.
BY PROCESSOR **5 mins.**	Prepare the sponge, as above.

BY PROCESSOR
5 mins.

Prepare the sponge, as above.

Attach the plastic blade. Reduce the size of this recipe because the dough is so heavy.

Pour the sponge into the processor work bowl and add the hot water, molasses, 1 tablespoon caraway seeds, egg, and salt. Pulse to blend into a light batterlike dough. Add all of the rye flour. Pulse. Add the shortening.

With the machine on, measure in the bread flour, ¼ cup at a time. Add the last portion of the flour with care—no more than necessary to create a ball of dough that will ride the blade around the work bowl, cleaning it as it whirls.

KNEADING
45 secs.

Leave the machine running and knead for 45 seconds.

The dough will be somewhat sticky when it comes from the work bowl but a few sprinkles of white flour will make it easy to shape into a ball.

FIRST RISING
1 hour

Place the dough in a greased bowl and place plastic wrap over the top of the bowl. Leave at room temperature until the dough has doubled in bulk, about 1 hour.

PUNCH DOWN
10 mins.

Punch down and let rise for an additional 10 minutes.

SHAPING
6 mins.

Divide the dough. For 2 round loaves, mold each into a smooth ball and place on the baking sheet. Flatten the tops slightly. For a long slender loaf, roll the piece under the fingers and palms so that it stretches lengthwise to become a *bâton,* a French word that graphically describes the shape. Place the pieces side by side on the baking sheet or in the special twin pans made primarily for French *baguettes.*

SECOND RISING
40 mins.

Cover the loaves with wax paper. Leave until the loaves have doubled in bulk, about 40 minutes.

PREHEAT

Preheat the oven to 375° 20 minutes before baking.

BAKING
375°
40 mins.

Rye loaves should have the traditional design cut with a sharp knife or razor blade. Carefully slash 3 or 4 diagonal cuts across the top of each long loaf. For the round loaves, cut a tic-tac-toe design or 3 or 4 parallel cuts across the top of the loaves.

Brush the tops with the egg-milk wash for a shiny crust (or water for an unglazed one). Sprinkle the moist glaze with 1 tablespoon caraway seeds (which will stick better on the egg glaze).

Bake the loaves for about 40 minutes, or until they test done— tapping the bottom crust yields a hard hollow sound. The loaves will be dark brown, almost black. If the loaves appear to be browning too quickly, cover with a piece of foil or sack paper.

(If using a convection oven, reduce heat 40°.)

FINAL STEP

Remove from the oven and allow to cool on metal racks.

This bread keeps for at least a week or more in a plastic bag, and freezes for months at 0°.

Triple Rye Bread   [two large loaves]

Triple Rye is almost all rye—rye flakes, sprouted rye seeds, and rye flour— made with a sourdough starter (also of rye) that has been left to ferment for 2 days before baking begins. While the fermentation is taking place, rye berries are soaked in water and left to send out tiny sprouts. Rye berries and flakes (which look like suntanned oatmeal) can be found in specialty and health food stores.

There is no caraway, often added to impart its peculiar flavor to rye bread, because it might dominate the all-rye taste. If rye is not rye for you without the taste of caraway, add the seeds to the dough and sprinkle them over the tops.

This is wholly rye with the exception of bread flour added to allow the dough to rise.

INGREDIENTS

Sour:
2 cups rye flour
1 cup rye flakes
2 packages dry yeast
2 cups hot water (120°–130°)

Sprouts:
1/2 cup of rye berries (seeds)
3 cups water

Dough:
1 cup hot water (120°–130°)
1/4 cup molasses
1 tablespoon salt
1 cup rye flour

3¹/₂ cups bread or all-purpose flour, approximately
1 egg, beaten, mixed with 1 tablespoon milk

BAKING SHEET

1 baking sheet dusted with cornmeal if for hearth loaves, or greased pans if for conventional loaves or *baguettes*

PREPARATION
2 days

To make the sour, 2 days before mixing the dough pour the rye flour and flakes into a medium bowl. Add the yeast and hot water. Mix well and cover with plastic wrap. Set aside to ferment.

To grow the sprouts, measure the rye berries into a medium bowl and cover with the water. Put aside to soak for 8 to 12 hours. Drain. Cover the bowl with tight-fitting plastic wrap and leave to sprout for 24 hours. The sprouts will be small, just peeking out.

BY HAND
OR MIXER
10 mins.

To make the dough, pour all of the sour into a large mixing bowl and stir in the hot water and molasses. Add the sprouts, salt, and rye flour. Beat with a wooden spoon or a mixer flat beater to combine thoroughly.

Add the white flour, ½ cup at a time, to form a shaggy mass that can be lifted to the work surface, or until a mixer dough hook can move the dough in a piece. If the dough sticks to the sides of the bowl, add small sprinkles of flour.

KNEADING
10 mins.

If by hand, knead the dough with a strong push-turn-fold motion until it is smooth and elastic, about 10 minutes. If under a dough hook, knead at low to medium speed, adding sprinkles of flour if necessary, until the hook moves the dough cleanly around the bowl. If it does not, add a bit more flour. Knead for 10 minutes.

BY PROCESSOR
5 mins.

Prepare the sour and sprouts, as above.

The order of mixing changes from above. The sprouts are added last so they won't be chopped in the thin batter.

Attach the plastic blade.

Measure 1 cup white flour into the work bowl and add all of the sour, water, and molasses. Pulse to blend thoroughly. Add the salt and rye flour. Pulse. Add the sprouts.

The white flour can be added either through the feed tube or by taking off the cover each time. The latter gives the opportunity to see the dough more clearly than through the sides of the work bowl and also to feel and judge the dough as it develops.

Add more white flour, ¼ cup at a time, until the dough has formed into a ball that is carried by the blade, and the dough cleans (somewhat) the sides of the bowl.

KNEADING **45 secs.**	Leave the machine running and knead for 45 seconds. When turned from the bowl, the dough will be stickier than when done by hand or in the mixer. Sprinkle the dough with flour as you work it into a ball.
FIRST RISING **1 hour**	Place the dough in a greased bowl, cover with plastic wrap, and put aside to rise at room temperature until doubled in bulk, about 1 hour.
SHAPING **6 mins.**	To make the dough into round loaves, divide into 2 pieces and, with your hands, push and pat into smooth balls. Press on the top lightly to flatten the loaves somewhat. If the breads are to be made in a pan, press each piece into an oval the length of the bread pan, fold down the middle, pinch the seam to seal, and tuck in its ends. Drop into the pan and press into the corners.
SECOND RISING **40 mins.**	Cover the loaves lightly with wax paper and leave at room temperature to double in bulk, about 40 minutes.
PREHEAT	Preheat the oven to 400° about 20 minutes before baking.
BAKING **400°** **35–40 mins.**	With a razor, cut a design on the hearth loaves and slashes down the lengths of the other loaves. Brush with the egg-milk wash and place the loaves in the hot oven. Midway during baking, turn the loaves end for end to equalize the heat on each loaf. The loaves should be baked in 35 to 40 minutes. Turn one over and tap the bottom. If the loaf feels hard and crusty, the bread is done. (If using a convection oven, reduce heat 50°.)
FINAL STEP	Remove the bread from the oven and place on a metal rack to cool. Makes excellent toast.

Vortlimpa   [two long slender loaves]

Stout (or dark beer) tempered with molasses, orange zest, and fennel gives Vortlimpa a sweet, dark taste that will confound and delight the tongue. This was once voted the best loaf to ever come from my kitchen by a young woman who had studied for several years in Scandinavia and had fallen under the spell of its dark breads. However, others have found it too assertive.

Try it with goat cheese or feta.

INGREDIENTS	2 cups stout or dark beer 1 teaspoon salt 3 tablespoons butter

½ cup dark molasses
2 packages dry yeast
3 cups medium rye flour
2 cups bread or all-purpose flour, approximately
Zest of 1 orange, finely chopped
1 tablespoon ground or crushed fennel seed
1 tablespoon molasses mixed with 2 tablespoons water

BAKING SHEET

1 baking sheet, greased or Teflon, sprinkled with cornmeal

PREPARATION
10 mins.

In a medium saucepan heat the stout or beer, salt, and butter. When the butter has melted, remove from heat and add the molasses, stir, and let cool to lukewarm. Stir in the yeast.

BY HAND
OR MIXER
8 mins.

Measure 1½ cups rye and ½ cup bread flour into a large mixing bowl and pour in the stout mixture. Beat well by hand about 100 strokes, or with a mixer flat beater for about 2 minutes. Add the orange zest, fennel seed, and remaining 1½ cups rye. Stir and work the flour into the dough until it forms a rough, shaggy mass.

KNEADING
8 mins.

Attach a dough hook or turn the dough onto a floured work surface to work by hand. In the beginning it will be sticky. Rye dough always is. Handle the new dough gingerly, dusting well with flour, until you have struck a workable balance. This could mean the addition of a cup or more of white flour in the early part of the kneading—by hand or in the mixer. Gradually it will become even textured and no longer stick to your hands, the work surface, or the mixer bowl. Knead for at least 8 minutes after the dough has reached this point.

BY PROCESSOR
10 mins.

Prepare the beer mixture as above.
   Attach the plastic blade.
   Measure 1½ cups rye and 1 cup bread flour into the work bowl. When the beer mixture has cooled, pour into the flour, and add the orange zest and fennel. Pulse 2 or 3 times to blend. With the processor running, add the remaining flours, ¼ cup at a time, through the feed tube until the dough has formed a mass that is carried around the bowl by the thrust of the blade.

KNEADING
45 secs.

Keep the machine running and knead for 45 seconds.

FIRST RISING
1½ hours

Place the dough in a greased bowl, cover tightly with plastic wrap, and leave to rise at room temperature until double in bulk.

SHAPING 15 mins.	Turn the dough out onto the floured work surface and cut in half. Flatten each half with the palm of your hand into a long rectangle. Pushing the dough away from you with your palms, roll each into a long, slender cylinder. They should be about 12" to 14" long. Place the loaves on the prepared baking sheet. Be certain they are far enough apart that they don't touch when they rise. If they threaten to do so, fold a kitchen towel, dust well with flour, and lay between the loaves.
PREHEAT	Preheat the oven to 400° about 20 minutes before baking.
BAKING 400° 30 mins. 325° 45 mins.	Prick the top of each loaf with a toothpick, 1" or more deep in a dozen places, so steam can escape without lifting off the top. Bake in the hot oven for 30 minutes; turn heat down to 325°, and continue baking for 45 minutes more. Halfway through baking, turn the loaves and brush with the molasses-water glaze. About 4 minutes before the loaves are done, brush them again with the glaze and return to the oven until the glaze has set. They are done when the loaves are dark and shiny and the bottom crusts hard and sound hollow when tapped. (If using a convection oven, bake at 350° then 300°.)
FINAL STEP	Remove the bread from the oven and place on a wire rack to cool. To keep crisp, place in a paper sack. For a soft crust wrap in foil or plastic wrap.

Russian Black Bread   [two large loaves]

Onion powder, crushed fennel seeds, instant coffee granules, molasses, and vinegar are blended to make this loaf of chewy, dark, almost black bread. If available, use coarse pumpernickel rye flour rather than the usual medium rye, to give it a rough texture usually associated with European peasant breads.

It is fine for buffets, especially when it is shaped long and slender. A fat round loaf is good for sandwich slices.

INGREDIENTS	2 packages dry yeast 3$^1/_2$ cups bread or all-purpose flour, approximately 4 cups pumpernickel or medium rye flour 1 tablespoon salt 2 cups whole bran cereal 2 tablespoons crushed caraway seeds 1 tablespoon *each* instant coffee and onion powder

1 teaspoon crushed fennel seeds
2¹/₂ cups water
¹/₄ cup *each* cider vinegar and dark molasses
1 square (1 ounce) unsweetened chocolate
¹/₄ cup shortening
1 teaspoon cornstarch mixed into ¹/₂ cup cold water

**BAKING PANS
OR SHEET**

Two 8" cake pans, greased; or, if the dough is fairly stiff and will hold shape, use 1 baking sheet, greased or Teflon

**BY HAND
OR MIXER
20 mins.**

In a large mixing or mixer bowl mix the yeast, 1 cup white and 1 cup pumpernickel or rye flour, salt, bran cereal, caraway, instant coffee, onion powder, and fennel.

In a saucepan combine the water, vinegar, molasses, chocolate, and shortening. Place over low heat. When the liquid is warm (the chocolate and shortening need only be soft), add to the dry ingredients. Beat at medium speed with the flat beater for 2 minutes, scraping the bowl occasionally.

Add 1 cup white and 1 cup rye flour. Beat for 2 minutes, or about 100 strong strokes with a wooden spoon. Stir in 2 more cups rye and enough white flour to make a soft dough.

Work the flour into the dough first with a wooden spoon or dough hook, and then turn out to work with your fingers and hands.

**REST
15 mins.**

Before kneading, cover the dough with the bowl and let it rest for 15 minutes.

**KNEADING
8 mins.**

Knead by hand or with the mixer dough hook until the dough is smooth and elastic. If the dough is sticky, dust it and your hands with flour. Scrape away any sticky film that forms on the work surface, and dust it afresh. The dough should pull away and clean the sides of the bowl.

**BY PROCESSOR
6 mins.**

Use the short plastic dough blade.

Measure into the work bowl the yeast and 1 cup each white and rye flour, the salt, bran cereal, caraway, instant coffee, onion powder, and fennel. Pulse to blend.

In a saucepan combine the water, vinegar, molasses, chocolate, and shortening. Heat until the mixture is warm and the solids have softened.

With the processor running, pour the liquid into the work bowl and blend into a batterlike dough. Add 1 cup each white and rye flour, ¼ cup at a time, or all with the machine stopped and cover removed.

Process for 30 seconds. Add 2 cups rye flour and enough white flour to make a dough that will form a mass and ride the blade as well as clean the sides of the bowl.

KNEADING
45 secs.

With the processor on, knead for 45 seconds. Allow the dough to rest, as above, for 15 minutes.

FIRST RISING
1 hour

Place the dough in a bowl, cover tightly with plastic wrap, and leave at room temperature until puffy and doubled in bulk, 1 hour.

SHAPING
10 mins.

Punch down the dough with the fingers and turn out onto a lightly floured work surface. Cut the dough into 2 pieces and let the dough rest for 5 minutes. Shape each piece into a ball, flatten slightly, and place either in the cake pan or on a baking sheet.

SECOND RISING
45 mins.

Cover with wax paper and leave at room temperature until the loaves have doubled in bulk, 45 minutes.

PREHEAT

Preheat the oven to 350° about 20 minutes before baking.

BAKING
350°
1 hour

Bake for about 1 hour, or until a metal skewer inserted in the center of a loaf comes out dry and clean. When tapped on the bottom crust, it will sound hard and hollow.

Meanwhile, prepare the glaze. In a small saucepan heat the cornstarch and cold water. Cook over medium heat, stirring constantly, until the mixture boils. Hold the boil for 1 minute, stirring all the while.

When the bread is baked, remove from the oven and brush the loaves with the cornstarch mixture. Place back in the oven for about 3 minutes, or until the glaze has set.

(If using a convection oven, reduce heat 40°.)

FINAL STEP

Remove the bread from the oven, turn from the baking sheet or pan, and place on a metal rack to cool.

Raisin Rye Bread   [two round loaves]

Whenever I want to make brownie points in my house I add raisins to whatever I'm baking at the moment. Marje Clayton is a raisin freak. And nothing does it like this Raisin Rye Bread.

This loaf is a combination of light and dark raisins, plumped beforehand in water or brandy. It has a rich appearance and a fine taste (ask Mrs. Clayton). The loaf develops a rough, jagged crust in the rising that makes it unnecessary to slash with a sharp knife; the break expands naturally as the bread rises.

INGREDIENTS

Sponge:
2 cups rye flour
1 package dry yeast
1½ cups hot water (120°–130°)

Dough:
½ cup *each* light (Sultana) and dark raisins
⅓ cup water or brandy
1 tablespoon molasses
1 tablespoon vegetable oil
2 teaspoons salt
½ cup warm water (105°–115°)
1½ cups rye flour
1½ cups bread or all-purpose flour, approximately
1 egg and 1 teaspoon milk beaten together

BAKING SHEET

1 baking sheet, Teflon, or greased, or sprinkled with cornmeal

PREPARATION
2–3 hours

To make the sponge, in a bowl combine the rye flour and yeast. Pour in the hot water and blend into a light batter. Cover the bowl with plastic wrap and leave at room temperature until the sponge is bubbly, approximately 2 to 3 hours. It can be left longer (up to 2 or 3 days) to improve and strengthen the rye flavor.

In the meanwhile, plump the raisins in the water or brandy for 30 minutes or so. Drain, pat dry, and set aside. Keep the brandy; add it to the mixture.

In a small bowl combine the molasses, oil, salt, and warm water and pour into the sponge. Drop in the raisins.

BY HAND
OR MIXER
6 mins.

Alternately add about 1½ cups each rye and white flours to the sponge, first with a wooden spoon and then by hand, or with a flat beater in the mixer. If the dough is slack and sticky, add liberal sprinkles of white flour.

KNEADING
8 mins.

Sprinkle the work surface with flour and turn the dough onto it, or use the mixer dough hook, about 8 minutes. Knead until the dough is smooth and elastic. This will be a heavier than normal dough because of the high rye content.

BY PROCESSOR
8 mins.

Prepare the sponge as above.
Attach the plastic blade.
The raisins are to be added after kneading so they are not chopped by the blade.

Pour the sponge into the work bowl and add the molasses, vegetable oil, salt, and warm water (and, if desired, drained brandy). Pulse to blend.

Remove the cover and add the balance of 1½ cups rye flour. Pulse several times to mix thoroughly. With the processor running, add the white flour, ¼ cup at a time, until the dough forms a rough ball and is whirled around the work bowl by the force of the blade. At the same time the dough will clean the sides of the bowl.

KNEADING
2 mins.

Process to knead for 45 seconds.

Turn the dough out of the work bowl, press flat, and spread the raisins over the surface. Fold the dough into the middle and work in the raisins.

FIRST RISING
1 hour

Put the dough into a bowl, pat the surface with greased fingers, and stretch a piece of plastic wrap tightly across the bowl. Leave the dough at room temperature until doubled in bulk, 1 hour.

SHAPING
8 mins.

Punch down the dough, turn out onto the work surface, and divide into 2 pieces. Let rest for 5 minutes to relax. Shape into round loaves, slightly flattened, or into oblong loaves. Place them on a baking sheet.

SECOND RISING
45 mins.

Cover the loaves with wax paper and leave to double in size, 45 minutes.

PREHEAT

Preheat the oven to 350° 20 minutes before baking.

BAKING
350°
1 hour

Brush the loaves with the egg-milk mixture just before sliding them into the oven.

When the loaves are well browned and crusty and tapping the bottom crust yields a hard, hollow sound, they are done, about 1 hour.

(If using a convection oven, reduce heat 50°.)

FINAL STEP

Remove the loaves from the oven and place on a wire rack to cool before serving or freezing.

Sour Dill Rye Bread   [two loaves]

One cup of brine from a sour pickle jar (or barrel) joins with both dillweed and dillseed to produce a noteworthy rye loaf. Caraway seeds are included, too. Hearth loaves, I let them rise in cloth-lined baskets until they are high and round, and then turn them, upside down, directly onto the baking sheet.

This loaf is close kin to a dill rye in the original Complete Book of Breads *but the addition of the "pickle juice" gives it a personality of its own.*

INGREDIENTS

3 to 3¹/₂ cups bread or all-purpose flour, approximately
2 packages dry yeast
I cup sour dill pickle brine
³/₄ cup hot water (120°–130°)
2 tablespoons *each* vegetable shortening and sugar
I egg, room temperature
2 teaspoons salt
I tablespoon dried dillweed
I teaspoon caraway seeds
I teaspoon plus I tablespoon dillseed
I¹/₂ cups rye flour
I egg, beaten, mixed with I teaspoon milk

BAKING SHEET

1 baking sheet, greased or Teflon, sprinkled with cornmeal, and 2 round woven baskets, about 8" wide and 3" deep, loosely lined with cloths sprinkled with flour (optional)

BY HAND
OR MIXER
15 mins.

Measure 2 cups bread flour into a mixing or mixer bowl. Add the yeast, pickle brine, and hot water. Stir to form a thin batter. Add the shortening, sugar, egg, salt, dillweed, caraway seeds, and teaspoon dillseed. Beat by hand 100 strong strokes, or in the mixer with the flat beater for 3 minutes. Stop the mixer.

Add the rye flour and beat it into the batter with 25 vigorous strokes. Stir in the balance of the white flour, ½ cup at a time, first with the spoon and then by hand, or with the dough hook in the mixer. The dough will be a rough, shaggy mass, more sticky than an all-white dough. Sprinkle on additional white flour to control the stickiness.

KNEADING
8 mins.

Place the dough under a mixer dough hook, or turn onto a lightly floured work surface and knead with the rhythmic motion of push-turn-fold. If a film clings to the work surface, scrape it off with a dough blade or the edge of a metal spatula, and dust with flour. Occasionally crash the dough down on the work surface to break the kneading rhythm. Knead by hand or with the mixer for about 8 minutes. The dough should be smooth.

BY PROCESSOR
5 mins.

Use the plastic blade.

Measure 2 cups bread flour into the processor work bowl, and add the dry yeast. Pulse to mix. Pour in the pickle brine and hot water. Pulse. Add the shortening, sugar, egg, salt, dillweed, caraway seeds, and teaspoon dillseed. Turn on the machine and add all of the rye flour.

When the rye flour has been thoroughly absorbed into the mixture, add the white flour, ¼ cup at a time, until the dough forms a ball and is carried around the bowl by the thrust of the blade. The dough will clean the sides of the bowl.

KNEADING
45 secs.

Keep the machine running and knead for 45 seconds.

The dough will be sticky when first turned from the work bowl but a few sprinkles of flour will make it manageable.

REST
20 mins.

Round the dough into a ball, cover with a piece of foil or wax paper, and let rest for 20 minutes.

SHAPING
6 mins.

Knead the dough for 30 seconds to press out the bubbles, then divide it into 2 equal pieces and shape into balls. Place at opposite corners of the baking sheet, or in the cloth-lined baskets.

RISING
45 mins.

Cover the loaves with wax paper and leave at room temperature until they have risen to double their size, about 45 minutes.

PREHEAT

Preheat the oven to 375° 20 minutes before baking.

BAKING
375°
45 mins.

If the loaves have risen in the baskets, tip into your hand and quickly set each on the baking sheet or tip directly onto the sheet.

With a razor blade or sharp knife, slash the top of each into a design—parallel cuts, or a tic-tac-toe. Brush the loaves with the egg-milk wash and sprinkle with the tablespoon dillseed.

Bake in the oven until the loaves are crisp and hard, 45 minutes. Tap one loaf on its bottom. If it sounds hard and hollow, it is done. If not, return to the oven for an additional 5 to 10 minutes.

(If using a convection oven, reduce heat 50°.)

FINAL STEP

Remove the bread from the oven and place on a metal rack to cool. *Note:* For a chewy crust, brush with water while the bread is still hot.

Westphalian Pumpernickel
[one large or two small loaves]

The famous Westphalian ham must share honors with another of this German province's delicious foods—pumpernickel. It is a coarse, moist dark bread made with rye flour, and it must rest at room temperature for 12 to 18 hours, then bake slowly for at least 5 to 6 hours, so that the natural sugars in the rye flour will darken and sweeten the bread evenly.

Westphalian Pumpernickel is an unusual bread because there is no leaven, with the result that it is solid as a brick from inception to the last slice.

This version of the pumpernickel is easy to make, and begins with white sugar melted and burned in a skillet until it is almost black, the color the finished bread will be.

INGREDIENTS	¼ cup sugar 3 cups boiling water 4 cups stone-ground rye flour 1 cup bulgur or cracked wheat 2 teaspoons salt 2 tablespoons salad oil
BAKING PANS	1 large (9"-x-5") or 2 small (7"-x-3") bread pans, greased
PREPARATION 5 mins.	Pour the sugar into a heavy 10" frying pan, and place over medium-high heat. Stir constantly with a fork until the sugar is melted. Continue to cook until the sugar smokes and is black, about 3 minutes. Carefully add the boiling water and cook, stirring, until the sugar is dissolved. Set aside to cool somewhat.
BY HAND 8 mins.	In a large mixing bowl measure the rye flour, bulgur, salt, and oil. Pour in the cooled caramel liquid and stir until the dough is smooth and well blended. It will become quite dense as the flour and grain absorb the moisture.
REST 12–18 hours	Cover the bowl with plastic wrap and let stand at room temperature for 18 hours. (This step can be as few as 12 hours but for full flavor let the dough rest for a whole day.)
SHAPING 5 mins.	If making 2 loaves, divide the dough. Press the dough into the pan(s) with wet fingers, and smooth with a spatula dipped in water. The dough will be solid and unresponsive.
BAKING 200° 4 hours 300° 2 hours	Place a pan of boiling water in the oven beneath the middle shelf. Turn the oven to 200°. Cover the bread pan(s) tightly with aluminum foil and bake on the rack above the water for 4 hours. Reset the temperature to 300° and bake for another 2 hours, or until the loaf feels firm. (If using a convection oven, place a pan filled with boiling water on the bottom of the oven beneath the lower shelf. Bake for the full 5 hours at 200°. Remove when the loaf feels firm, as above.)
FINAL STEP	Remove the pan(s) from the oven and cool for 5 minutes before turning the loaves out onto a rack to cool completely. Wrap in clear plastic; refrigerate until chilled. Cut into very thin slices to serve.

Peasant Black Bread   [two hearth loaves]

Deeply toasted rye crumbs from old loaves give these long and almost black loaves the look and taste of a choice European peasant rye. When toasting the crumbs, let them get almost black but be careful not to burn them.

Postum is used, too, to color the loaves, the crusts of which are quite thick and hard when the bread comes from the oven. But the crusts will soften, stored in a plastic bag for a day or so.

INGREDIENTS

3 teaspoons Postum or instant coffee powder
2¹/₂ cups hot water (120°–130°)
¹/₄ cup dark molasses, unsulphured preferred
2 packages dry yeast
¹/₄ teaspoon ground ginger
2 cups dark-toasted fine rye bread crumbs (see Note)
3 cups stone-ground or pumpernickel rye flour
1 cup whole-wheat flour
4 tablespoons butter or margarine, melted
2 teaspoons salt
1 cup bread or all-purpose flour, approximately
1 teaspoon Postum mixed with 2 teaspoons water

BAKING SHEET

1 baking sheet, greased or Teflon

PREPARATION
20 mins.

In a large mixing or mixer bowl dissolve the Postum in the hot water. Stir in the molasses, yeast, ginger, and bread crumbs. Allow to stand until the crumbs are soaked and soft, and the mixture is warm to the touch, about 20 minutes.

BY HAND
OR MIXER
18 mins.

Add the rye and whole-wheat flours, butter or margarine, and salt; stir thoroughly by hand or with electric mixer. Measure the white flour, ¼ cup at a time, and stir vigorously with a wooden spoon or mixer flat beater until the dough is a rough, shaggy ball that can be lifted to the work surface, or left under the mixer dough hook.

REST
15 mins.

Cover the dough with a cloth or wax paper and let it rest for about 15 minutes.

KNEADING
10 mins.

Knead with a push-turn-fold motion—and the aid of a dough scraper—until the dough is smooth, about 10 minutes. Early in the process it will be sticky (add sprinkles of flour) but gradually it will become more elastic. Add sprinkles of flour to the dough in the mixer bowl if it sticks to the sides; knead for 10 minutes.

BY PROCESSOR **15 mins.**	Attach the plastic dough blade. Measure into the work bowl the Postum, hot water, molasses, yeast, and ginger. Pulse to blend. Add the rye and whole-wheat flours, butter or margarine, and salt. Pulse. The dough will be a thick batter. Allow it to stand for 10 minutes to allow the flours to be completely absorbed before adding the white flour. Add the white flour, a small portion at a time, to make a dough that will spin on the blade and clean the sides of the bowl.
KNEADING **45 secs.**	Leave the machine running for 45 seconds to knead. The dough may feel sticky when turned out on the work surface. If it does, sprinkle with white flour and work into a ball.
FIRST RISING **1½ hours**	Place the ball of dough in a bowl and pat with greased fingers to keep the surface from drying out. Cover the bowl tightly with plastic wrap and leave at room temperature until the dough is puffy to the touch and has risen to twice its original size, 1½ hours.
SHAPING **12 mins.**	Turn the dough onto the floured work surface, knead out the bubbles, and cut into 2 pieces. Form each into a round ball. Let rest for 3 minutes. Press each ball into a long, flat oval under your palms or with a rolling pin. Double over and pound several times down the middle of the long piece with the edge of your hand. Fold over, seal, and roll back and forth under your palms to fashion an 18"-long loaf. Repeat with the second piece.
SECOND RISING **45 mins.**	Cover lightly with wax paper and leave to rise until double in size, 45 minutes.
PREHEAT	Preheat the oven to 400° 20 minutes before baking.
BAKING **400°** **35 mins.**	Before baking, brush the loaves with the dissolved Postum. Bake in the hot oven for about 35 minutes, or until the bottom crust yields a hard, hollow sound when tapped. The loaves will be crusty and a deep brown, almost black. (If using a convection oven, reduce heat 50°.)
FINAL STEP	Remove the bread from the oven and cool on a metal rack. After the loaves have cooled, place them in plastic bags if you wish the crusts to be soft. For crispness, store in a paper bag. This loaf keeps for a fortnight or more in plastic. Will keep for months frozen at 0°.

Note: To make successive loaves even darker, save slices from new breads. Toast slices, crusts, and ends and store in the refrigerator or freezer for the next baking of black bread.

Sour Cream Rye Bread   [two loaves]

One of the fine cookbooks to come into the American kitchen in this baking renaissance is the Tassajara Bread Book, *and one of its fine recipes is for this Sour Cream Rye Bread.*

The crusty loaf is dark and heavy with full rye taste and texture. My loaves are dropped onto a baking stone placed in the oven earlier to preheat. The loaves are round and stabbed with a metal skewer, which lets the top crust expand but not lift too dramatically.

The original recipe called for nothing but rye flour, but the addition of a small portion of white makes it a better loaf.

INGREDIENTS	1 cup bread or all-purpose flour, approximately
	5 cups rye flour
	2 packages dry yeast
	1 cup sour cream, room temperature
	$^1/_4$ cup molasses
	1 teaspoon salt
	$^1/_4$ cup cooking oil
	$1^1/_2$ tablespoons caraway seeds
	1 cup hot water (120°–130°)

BAKING SHEET
OR BASKETS

1 baking sheet, greased or Teflon, sprinkled with cornmeal, and 2 cloth-lined baskets, 6" to 8" wide, sprinkled with flour (optional)

BY HAND
OR MIXER
10 mins.

Measure ½ cup bread flour, 2 cups rye flour, the yeast, sour cream, molasses, salt, oil, and 1 tablespoon caraway seeds into a large mixing or mixer bowl. Pour in the hot water and blend the ingredients thoroughly with a wooden spoon or with the mixer flat beater. Beat in the electric mixer at medium speed for 3 minutes, or for an equal length of time by hand.

Stop the mixer. Add the balance of the rye flour and, finally, the remaining ½ cup bread flour. Stir in these flours, ½ cup at a time, first with the spoon and then by hand. The dough will be a rough, shaggy mass that will clean the sides of the bowl. If the dough continues to be slack and sticky, sprinkle with small amounts of white flour.

KNEADING **7 mins.**	*Note:* The preponderance of rye flour makes this a heavy and sticky dough to work. A dough blade, a metal spatula, or a broad putty knife to turn the dough during kneading will help. Also 1 tablespoon shortening nearby in which fingertips can be touched will help control the stickiness.

Turn the dough out onto a floured work surface, or put under the mixer dough hook. The dough will be a sticky mass to start. If by hand, keep turning it with the dough blade and your fingers. Gradually it will become more workable, but will never become as elastic and alive as white dough. Knead for 7 minutes by hand or with the dough hook.

BY PROCESSOR **5 mins.**	Use the stubby plastic dough blade.

Measure into the work bowl ½ cup bread and 2 cups rye flours. Pulse. Sprinkle in the yeast and add the sour cream, molasses, salt, oil, and 1 tablespoon caraway seeds. Pour in the hot water, and pulse several times to blend thoroughly. With the machine running, add the balance of the rye flour, ¼ cup at a time, and the bread flour until the dough becomes a solid mass and rides around the bowl on the dough blade.

KNEADING **40 secs.**	Keep the machine running and knead for 40 seconds. If the machine stalls under this heavy load, stop it and knead the dough by hand, as above.

FIRST RISING **1 hour**	Place the dough in a bowl and pat with greased fingers. Cover the bowl tightly with plastic wrap and leave at room temperature until the dough has risen to twice its original size, about 1 hour.

SHAPING **5 mins.**	Punch down the dough and knead for 30 seconds to press out the bubbles. Use a sharp knife to cut the dough into 2 pieces. Form each piece of dough into a ball. Place on opposite corners of the baking sheet or in the cloth-lined baskets.

SECOND RISING **45 mins.**	Cover with wax paper and leave until the loaves have doubled in volume, 45 minutes. If the paper clings to the dough, elevate the dough on glass tumblers.

PREHEAT	Preheat the oven to 350° 20 minutes before baking.

BAKING **350°** **50–60 mins.**	If the loaves have raised in baskets, tip each raised loaf into your hand and quickly turn it right side up and onto the baking sheet. In either case, stab each loaf a dozen times across the top with a skewer.

Brush the loaves with water and sprinkle with the remaining

½ tablespoon caraway seeds. Bake. When the loaves are dark brown and crusty and tapping on the bottom crust yields a hard, hollow sound, they are done. If the loaves appear to be browning too quickly, cover with a piece of foil or brown paper sack. Midway during baking and again near the end of it, shift the loaves around so they are exposed equally to the oven's temperature variations.

(If using a convection oven, reduce heat 50°.)

FINAL STEP

Remove the loaves from the oven and lift them to a metal rack to cool before serving.

This rye keeps well for 2 or 3 weeks if it is wrapped tightly in foil or plastic. It freezes equally well.

Onion Rye Bread   [one large or two small loaves]

In the making and baking and eating this onion rye is a wholly satisfactory loaf of bread. It fills the kitchen with good smells while the onions are being chopped and the caraway seeds measured and set aside, and continues on through the kneading and the baking . . . and while eating!

It has a beautiful brown crust flecked with dark bits of onion.

INGREDIENTS

2½ cups bread or all-purpose flour, approximately
1½ cups rye flour, stone-ground preferred
2 tablespoons sugar
2 teaspoons salt
1 package dry yeast
1 cup milk, room temperature
½ cup hot water (120°–130°)
2 tablespoons vegetable oil
¾ cup finely chopped onion
2 tablespoons caraway seeds
1 egg, beaten, mixed with 1 tablespoon cream and 2 teaspoons water

BAKING PANS

1 large (9"-x-5") or 2 small (7"-x-3") baking pans, greased or Teflon

BY HAND
OR MIXER
8 mins.

Measure 1½ cups white flour into a mixing or mixer bowl, and add ½ cup rye flour, the sugar, salt, and yeast. Stir to blend well.

Make a well in the center of the flour and pour in the milk, hot water, and oil. With a spatula draw in the flour to make a thick batter and add the chopped onions and caraway seeds. If in the mixer, attach the flat beater and add the onions and caraway seeds and mix at medium speed.

Stir in the remaining 1 cup rye flour, and add the white flour, ¼ cup at a time, to make a mass that can be lifted from the bowl, if by hand. Or attach a dough hook and leave the dough in the mixer.

This is a heavy dough and not as responsive as dough made with white flour. Be patient. The longer it is worked in the hands or in the machine the easier to knead it becomes.

Caution: Occasionally when working with heavy dough it may be too stiff to be seized by the hook. Turn the dough out; knead it by hand for 2 or 3 minutes, and then put it back under the hook, if you wish, or continue by hand.

KNEADING
8 mins.

If by hand, turn the dough onto a floured work surface and knead aggressively with a push-turn-fold rhythm, about 8 minutes. Sprinkle lightly with flour if the dough is sticky. It will never become as elastic as white.

If using a mixer, continue with the dough hook, adding sprinkles of flour if the dough sticks to the sides, about 8 minutes.

BY PROCESSOR
6 mins.

Attach the short dough blade.

Measure 2 cups white and 1 cup rye flour into the work bowl and add the sugar, salt, and yeast. Pulse to blend. In a small bowl mix together the milk, hot water, and oil. With the processor running, pour the liquid through the feed tube to make a heavy batterlike dough, and add the chopped onions and caraway seeds.

With the processor running, add the remaining ½ cup rye flour, and follow this with the white flour, ¼ cup at a time, to form a heavy dough that will ride with the blade and clean the sides of the bowl. It will be sticky when turned from the bowl, so dust lightly with flour as you handle it.

KNEADING
45 secs.

With the machine on knead for 45 seconds.

FIRST RISING
1½ hours

Place the dough in a greased bowl, cover with plastic wrap, and put aside to double in volume, 1½ hours.

SHAPING
4 mins.

Turn back the plastic and punch down the dough. Lift it to the floured work surface. Shape into a ball and allow to relax for 3 or 4 minutes. Divide the dough in half if you wish to make 2 loaves. Press each piece into an oval the length of the bread pan, fold lengthwise, pinch the seam together, and tuck in the ends. Place the dough in the bread pan with the seam down.

SECOND RISING	Cover the dough with wax paper or foil and leave until double in volume, about 1 hour. It will be puffy when gently touched.
1 hour	

PREHEAT	Preheat the oven to 375° 20 minutes before baking.

BAKING	Brush the tops of the loaves with the egg-cream wash.
375°	Place the loaves on the middle shelf of the oven and bake until the crust is light golden brown, 30 to 40 minutes. Turn one loaf from the pan and test for doneness. If it sounds hard and hollow when rapped, it is done. If not, return to the oven without the pan(s) for an additional 10 minutes.
30–40 mins.	
	(If using a convection oven, reduce heat 40°.)

FINAL STEP	Turn the loaves onto a metal rack to cool. The kitchen will be beautifully perfumed.

Rye Bread with Sauerkraut   [two loaves]

Where but in Milwaukee (or a Bäckerei in Germany) would one expect to discover a rye bread made with sauerkraut and sauerkraut juice? And it is good company for a sauerkraut dish, such as Rippchen mit Kraut (smoked ribs).

This recipe came from Milwaukee but not from a bakery. Rather, it is from the imaginative test kitchen of Red Star Yeast.

INGREDIENTS	2½ to 3 cups bread flour, approximately (the amount of flour will depend on how much juice with the sauerkraut)
	2 cups rye flour
	2 packages dry yeast
	½ cup nonfat dry milk
	2 tablespoons sugar
	1 tablespoon caraway seeds
	2 teaspoons salt
	¼ teaspoon ground ginger
	1¼ cups hot water (120°–130°)
	2 tablespoons vegetable oil
	1 cup sauerkraut with its juice

BAKING PANS	2 medium (8"-x-4") loaf pans, greased or Teflon

BY HAND	In a large mixing or mixer bowl, combine 1 cup bread flour, ¼ cup rye flour, the yeast, dry milk, sugar, caraway, salt, and ginger. Stir to mix well.
OR MIXER	
12 mins.	

Add the hot water and oil to the mixture. Beat with a wooden spoon 100 strong strokes, or with a mixer flat beater for 3 minutes. By hand, gradually stir in the sauerkraut, remaining rye flour, and enough remaining bread flour to make a firm dough.

KNEADING
5 mins.

Knead the dough on a floured work surface for about 5 minutes. (The dough may be too dense to work well under the mixer dough hook.) Add sprinkles of flour if the dough is sticky.

BY PROCESSOR
5 mins.

Caution: The dough may be too dense for some processors. However, if there is no problem, attach the plastic dough blade and add the ingredients in the same order and quantities as listed above, except the remaining flours. Pulse to blend well.

With the machine on, add the balance of the rye flour, ¼ cup at a time, and then the white flour, until the dough has become a mass and spins around the work bowl with the dough blade.

KNEADING
30 secs.

Keep the machine running and knead for 30 seconds. If the blade should stop, remove the dough from the machine and finish by hand.

SHAPING
5 mins.

Note: The dough goes directly into the pans—there is no rising beforehand.

Divide the dough into 2 parts. On a lightly floured work surface, shape each piece into an oval, roughly the length of the bread pan. Fold the dough lengthwise, pinch the edges together, and drop into the pan, seam side down. Push the dough into the corners with your fingers.

RISING
40 mins.

Cover the loaves with wax paper and put them aside to double in volume, about 40 minutes.

PREHEAT

Preheat the oven to 375° about 20 minutes before baking.

BAKING
375°
35–40 mins.

Place the loaves in the oven and bake for 35 to 40 minutes, until the loaves are a light brown and sound hollow when tapped. If browning too quickly, cover loosely with foil the last 5 to 10 minutes of baking.

(If using a convection oven, reduce heat 50°.)

FINAL STEP

Remove from the pans and place on a metal rack to cool before slicing.

Buttermilk Rye–Whole Wheat Bread   [one loaf]

This bread has the flavor and texture of a rye loaf even though the rye is out-weighed by wheat (whole-wheat and bread flours). Further, it has the tangy bite of a sour-dough rye loaf when in fact it is buttermilk that gives it its good flavor. And since there is no time given to creating a sour and a sponge, this loaf can be made from scratch to the dining table or picnic or buffet in less than 4 hours.

INGREDIENTS

1 cup rye flour
1 cup whole-wheat flour
1 package dry yeast
1 tablespoon wheat germ
1 tablespoon caraway seeds
2 teaspoons salt
1 cup buttermilk, room temperature
3 tablespoons molasses
2 tablespoons vegetable oil or other shortening
1 cup bread or all-purpose flour, approximately

BAKING PAN
OR SHEET

1 large (9"-x-5") loaf pan or baking sheet, greased or Teflon

BY HAND
OR MIXER
10 MINS.

In a large mixing or mixer bowl combine the rye and whole-wheat flours, yeast, wheat germ, caraway, and salt. Mix well. In a saucepan heat the buttermilk, molasses, and oil or shortening until hot (120°–130°). Pour into the flour mixture. Blend by hand with 100 strong strokes of a wooden spoon, or 3 minutes at medium speed in the mixer with a flat beater.

By hand, gradually stir in the white flour to make a firm but not stiff dough.

KNEADING
8 mins.

Place the dough on a floured work surface, or keep in the mixer bowl under the dough hook, and knead for 8 minutes. If the dough contin-ues to be sticky, add sprinkles of white flour—but better too little flour than too much. Don't make a cannonball.

BY PROCESSOR
4 mins.

Attach the steel blade.

Measure all of the ingredients, except the white flour, into the work bowl. Pulse several times to thoroughly blend into a heavy batterlike dough. With the machine running, measure in the white flour, ¼ cup at a time, until the dough forms a rough mass and is carried around the bowl by the steel blade.

KNEADING **45 secs.**	Process to knead for 45 seconds.
FIRST RISING **1 hour**	Place the dough in a greased bowl, cover tightly with plastic wrap, and leave until doubled in bulk, about 1 hour.
SHAPING **4 mins.**	On a lightly floured work surface, roll or pat the dough into a 14"-x-7" rectangle. Starting with the short side, roll up tightly, pressing the dough into a roll with each turn. Pinch the edges and ends to seal. Place in the prepared pan. Or else shape the dough into a ball and press slightly to make a rounded loaf. Place on the baking sheet.
SECOND RISING **1–1½ hours**	Loosely cover the pan with a length of wax paper or plastic wrap and let rise until doubled, about 1 to 1½ hours.
PREHEAT	Preheat the oven to 375° about 20 minutes before baking.
BAKING **375°** **35–40 mins.**	Place the pan in the oven and bake for 35 to 40 minutes, until the loaf is a rich, dark brown and sounds hollow when tapped. (If using a convection oven, reduce heat 50°.)
FINAL STEP	Remove the bread from the pan or sheet and leave to cool on a metal rack before serving.

Pain Seigle   [three loaves]
(Rye Bread)

Fermentation and flavor for this typically French loaf of rye bread begin with a starter which begets a larger starter or sponge which, in turn, begets the dough. And ferment is what rye flour does best. One whiff of the batter bubbling under the plastic wrap pulled over the bowl will tell you just how potent is this brew.

While to many, caraway seeds are synonymous with rye bread, this is not so in France, where most rye loaves are baked without them. However, there is no reason caraway seeds in the dough or sprinkled across the crust could not be added if that is to your taste.

The onion-flavored Rye Sour in the beginning of this chapter can be substituted for the starter below.

INGREDIENTS   *Starter:*
1 cup rye flour
1 teaspoon dry yeast
1 cup warm water (105°–115°)

Sponge:
1¼ cups warm water (105°–115°)
1 cup bread or all-purpose flour
1½ cups rye flour

Dough:
½ cup hot water (120°–130°)
1 tablespoon salt
2½ cups rye flour, approximately
1 cup bread or all-purpose flour

Glaze:
1 egg yolk
1 tablespoon milk

BAKING SHEET   1 baking sheet, sprinkled with cornmeal or covered with parchment paper, or greased

PREPARATION   To make the starter, in a small bowl mix the flour, yeast, and warm
6–36 hours   water. Cover with plastic wrap and put aside at room temperature for at least 6 hours. More time, up to 36 hours, will give a deeper fermented taste to the dough.

8 hours   To make the sponge, remove the plastic wrap and stir down the starter. Add the warm water and the white and rye flours. Blend well and re-cover the bowl for a minimum of 8 hours at room temperature. As with the starter, a long rising period is desirable if you like your rye with a tangy bite.

BY HAND   To make the dough, on baking day, pour all of the sponge into a large
OR MIXER   mixing or mixer bowl. Add the hot water, salt, and 1 cup each rye and
15 mins.   white flour. Stir with a wooden spoon or with the mixer flat beater to develop a heavy mass that will cling tenaciously. Add the additional rye flour until it is a shaggy mass that can be turned out onto the work surface or left under the dough hook.

KNEADING   A basically rye dough does not need the longer kneading that an all-
5 mins.   white loaf demands. If you are kneading by hand, use a dough scraper or putty knife to turn and knead the dough in the beginning.

Throw down liberal sprinkles of white flour if moisture breaks through the surface or if the dough continues to cling to the mixer bowl. Continue kneading and working the dough. It will gradually lose its stickiness and become soft and elastic. However, in a rush to overcome the stickiness, don't overload the dough with so much flour that it becomes so heavy it defeats the leavening effect of the yeast. But don't skimp on flour or the dough will be slack and won't hold its shape on the baking sheet.

BY PROCESSOR
5 mins.

Make the starter and sponge as above.

Attach the plastic dough blade.

Pour the sponge into the processor work bowl. Add the hot water, salt, and 1 cup rye flour. Pulse to blend. With the machine running, add the white flour. Add the remaining rye flour, ¼ cup at a time, until the dough forms a mass and is spun around the bowl by the force of the blade. Add small portions of white flour if the dough does not form.

KNEADING
35 secs.

When the ball forms, knead with the machine on for 35 seconds.

FIRST RISING
40 mins.

Place the dough in a greased bowl, cover tightly with plastic wrap, and leave at room temperature for 40 minutes.

SHAPING
6 mins.

Uncover the bowl and punch down the dough. Turn onto a floured work surface and knead for a moment or two to press out the bubbles. Divide the dough, which will weigh about 3 pounds, into 3 pieces. Shape each into a round ball, pulling down with cupped hands to keep the surface of the dough taut.

SECOND RISING
30 mins.

Place the loaves on the baking sheet and cover with wax paper. Put in an undisturbed place at room temperature for 30 minutes.

PREHEAT

Preheat the oven to 400° 20 minutes before baking.

BAKING
400°
45 mins.

Rye breads take several forms in France. One style favors 8 cuts with a razor radiating from the top of a round loaf. In the oven the bread expands beautifully along these lines. Another favorite is to circle the top third of a raised round loaf with a razor cut that gives an attractive accent to its roundness.

For the star effect, make 8 radiating cuts about ¼" deep from the top of the raised loaf down the sides to within an inch of the baking sheet.

Create the other design by cutting a 6" circle around the top of the loaf with a razor blade. Cut about ¼" deep.

Mix together the egg and milk and brush the loaves with the glaze. Place in the oven. The bread is done when the bottom crust sounds hollow when tapped with the forefinger, about 45 minutes. The deep cuts to form the star will be a light brown while the outer crust will be a deep brown. Midway through baking, turn the baking sheet around so the loaves are exposed evenly to temperature variations in the oven.

(If using a convection oven, reduce heat 50°.)

FINAL STEP
Place the loaves on a metal rack to cool.

This bread freezes well. Sliced, it makes a fine sandwich companion with ham, beef, or cheese and goes well with soups, too.

Heavy Sour Rye Bread
[four small *baguettes* or two medium loaves]

This loaf is also known generically as "corn bread," but the only corn about it is the meal sprinkled on the baking sheet.

There is as much rye flour as bread flour in the recipe, hence it is heavier and more closely grained than other sour rye loaves. It is also left in the oven longer to bake. In commercial bakeries, the bread is sold by weight and not by the loaf.

There is no shortening or sugar in the recipe.

INGREDIENTS
4 cups Rye Sour (page 108)
¹/₂ cup water (if sour is stiff)
1 package dry yeast
1 tablespoon salt
4 to 4¹/₂ cups bread or unbleached flour, approximately
1 egg, beaten, mixed with 1 tablespoon water
1 tablespoon caraway seeds

BAKING PANS
2 small double *baguette* pans, greased lightly, or 1 baking sheet, sprinkled with cornmeal or covered with parchment paper

BY HAND
OR MIXER
15 mins.
The sour should be a heavy batter that can be poured. Pour into a large mixing or mixer bowl, and add the water, only if needed. Stir in the yeast and salt. Add 1 cup bread flour and stir into the sour with a wooden spoon or with the mixer flat beater. The mixture will be heavy and sticky. Be patient. It can soon be kneaded. Add more flour, ½ cup at a time, stirring it into the dough with a wooden spoon and then by

hand, or with the flat beater. Pick up the dough and place it on the floured work surface. Or leave in the mixer bowl to knead with the dough hook.

KNEADING
8 mins.

If the dough is sticky, sprinkle it liberally with flour and knead with a strong push-turn-fold motion. Use the dough blade or the edge of a metal spatula to scrape up the film of dough that may accumulate on the work surface. Knead by hand or under the dough hook for 8 minutes. The dough will clean the sides of the mixer bowl as the dough hook moves the dough around.

BY PROCESSOR
4 mins.

Fasten the short plastic dough blade.

Pour the sour, water (if needed), yeast, and salt into the work bowl. Pulse to mix. With the machine running, add the flour, ¼ cup at a time, until it becomes a ball of dough that is thrust around the bowl by the blade.

KNEADING
45 secs.

Keep the machine running and knead for 45 seconds.

FIRST RISING
30 mins.

Place the dough in a greased bowl, cover tightly with plastic wrap, and put aside to rise for 30 minutes.

SECOND RISING
30 mins.

Fold the plastic back and push the dough down with the fingers. Replace the cover and let the dough rise for a second time.

SHAPING
8 mins.

Turn the dough onto the floured work surface and divide it into the number of loaves desired. For slender *baguettes* roll each piece under your palms into the length desired. For other loaves, shape into round balls and flatten the tops slightly.

THIRD RISING
30 mins.

Cover the loaves with wax paper or aluminum foil and leave to rise until three-quarters proofed, about 30 minutes. Don't let them rise to full double volume as with many other breads.

PREHEAT	Preheat the oven to 425° about 20 minutes before baking.
BAKING 425° 40 mins.	With a razor blade or sharp knife, cut a design on the top of the loaves. Brush with the egg-water mixture and sprinkle liberally with caraway seeds.
	Three minutes before baking pour hot water in a pan and place on the bottom shelf of the oven to create steam. Place the pans or sheet on the middle shelf and bake until the loaves test done, about 40 minutes. Turn one loaf over, tap the bottom crust with a forefinger, and if the sound is hard and hollow, the bread is done. The loaves will be a light brown.
	(If using a convection oven, reduce heat 50°.)
FINAL STEP	Place the loaves on a metal rack to cool before serving.
	This bread freezes for up to 6 months at 0°. If a softer crust is desired, place the loaves in plastic bags.

Spicy Rye Bread   [two round or oblong loaves]

Cloves, allspice, and caraway mix with molasses and brown sugar to give this dark brown rye loaf a special spiciness. Like most recipes made with rye flour, this one will be sticky until suddenly there is the moment in kneading when stickiness ceases and all is smooth and well.

Four slashes are cut across the top of the loaf to prevent it from breaking on the sides. It also identifies the loaf as something special.

INGREDIENTS	2 teaspoons salt
	¹/₂ teaspoon *each* ground cloves and allspice
	I teaspoon caraway seeds
	2 tablespoons packed brown sugar
	3 tablespoons molasses, dark preferred
	1³/₄ cups hot water (120°–130°)
	2 packages dry yeast
	2 tablespoons shortening, room temperature
	2¹/₂ cups rye flour
	3 to 3¹/₂ cups bread or all-purpose flour, approximately
BAKING SHEET	1 baking sheet, greased or Teflon or dusted with cornmeal
BY HAND OR MIXER 15 mins.	In a large mixing or mixer bowl measure the salt, cloves, allspice, caraway seeds, sugar, molasses, and hot water. Add the yeast. Stir to blend. Add the shortening.

Measure the rye flour and 1 cup white flour into the bowl. Beat with a wooden spoon until smooth, about 100 strong strokes, or for 2 minutes at moderate speed with a mixer flat beater.

Put aside the electric mixer and add more flour, first with the spoon and then with your fingers. The dough, which will clean the sides of the bowl, will be a rough mass, a bit sticky but firm.

KNEADING
8 mins.

Put the dough under the mixer dough hook or turn out onto a lightly floured work surface and knead for 8 minutes. If the dough proves too heavy for the dough hook, knead by hand. Knead until the dough is smooth and elastic to the touch.

BY PROCESSOR
4 mins.

Attach the plastic blade.

The sequence of adding ingredients differs from above.

Measure 1 cup *each* rye and white flours into the work bowl. Pulse to blend. Add the salt, ground cloves, allspice, caraway seeds, hot water, sugar, and molasses. Pulse. Add the yeast and shortening. Pulse. Stop the machine to allow the yeast to dissolve before adding more flour, 1 minute.

Turn on the machine and add the balance of the flours, ¼ cup at a time, alternating between rye and white.

KNEADING
45 secs.

When the dough forms a ball and rides on the blade, knead for 45 seconds. If the dough is too heavy for the machine and slows or stops the blade, lift out the dough and knead by hand on the work surface.

FIRST RISING
1 hour

Place the dough in a greased bowl, turning once to film all sides. Cover with plastic wrap and leave to rise until double in volume, about 1 hour.

SHAPING
4 mins.

Divide the dough into 2 parts. Round each into a ball or oblong loaf (ideal for sandwiches) and place on opposite corners of the baking sheet.

SECOND RISING
45 mins.

Cover with a sheet of aluminum foil, shaping the foil so it does not touch the dough and stick. Leave until the loaves double in bulk, about 45 minutes.

PREHEAT

Preheat the oven to 375° 20 minutes before baking.

BAKING
375°
45 mins.

Uncover the loaves. With a sharp knife or razor slash the top of the loaves into a pattern. I make 4 slashes in a tic-tac-toe design to identify this type of loaf in my bread box or freezer. For many of their oblong rye loaves, the French make 4 short parallel cuts across the top of the loaves.

Bake the loaves until they are brown and test done when pierced with a toothpick, 45 minutes. If the pick comes out clean and dry, the loaf is done. Also, if when tapped the bottom crust yields a hard, hollow sound, they are done. Midway during baking, turn the loaves around on the baking sheet so they are exposed equally to temperature variations. Should the crust begin to darken early, cover with brown paper.

(If using a convection oven, reduce heat 50°.)

FINAL STEP
Remove the bread from the oven and place on a metal rack to cool.
Note: For a slightly glazed crust, brush with water or with an egg white mixed with water.

Pumpernickel Bread   [one large round loaf]

Caution: *If you are about to launch a career in baking, don't begin with this loaf, as delicious as it is. This has no white flour, only rye and whole wheat. It is a loaf for an advanced student, a baker who will tolerate the tedium of stickiness until, finally, the gluten forms and the dough kneads easily under the palms.*

The slices are moist and dark brown, almost black. Ideal for buffets, and sandwiches, or served with sliced cheese—and cold beer on the side.

INGREDIENTS
1³/₄ cups water
¹/₂ cup cornmeal
³/₄ cup molasses
1 tablespoon *each* butter and salt
2 teaspoons sugar
1¹/₂ teaspoons slightly broken caraway seeds
¹/₂ square (¹/₂ ounce) unsweetened chocolate
1 package dry yeast
1 cup mashed potatoes (may be prepared from instant)
3 cups rye flour
1 cup whole-wheat flour, approximately
1 egg white, beaten, mixed with 1 tablespoon cold water

BAKING SHEET
1 baking sheet, greased or Teflon, or dusted with cornmeal

PREPARATION
20 mins.
In a medium saucepan combine the water and cornmeal, and cook the mixture over low heat, stirring with a wooden spoon, until it becomes

thick and smooth, about 5 minutes. Remove from heat and add molasses, butter, salt, sugar, caraway seeds, and chocolate. Stir until well blended and pour into a mixing or mixer bowl. Set the mixture aside until it has cooled to warm (105°–115°), then stir in the yeast and mashed potato.

**BY HAND
OR MIXER
5 mins.**

When all the ingredients are blended, add the 3 cups rye and 1 cup whole-wheat flour. The dough will be stiff and sticky by hand or in the mixer.

**KNEADING
8 mins.**

Turn the dough onto a work surface liberally sprinkled with whole-wheat flour. Put a little vegetable oil on your fingers and hands before you start to knead. Keep the surface of the dough powdered with flour. Also have a scraper, such as a dough blade, to remove the gummy film of dough that accumulates on the work surface.

Some mixer dough hooks will knead the dense dough; others may not. If yours won't, knead by hand.

Be patient and presently the dough will respond and begin to clear the work surface, and your fingers. Knead until the dough is somewhat elastic, though it will still be stiff, about 8 minutes by hand or with the dough hook.

**BY PROCESSOR
5 mins.**

Prepare the liquid cornmeal mixture in a saucepan, as above. Don't add the yeast and potato yet.

Attach the plastic blade.

Measure 1 cup rye and 1 cup whole-wheat flour into the work bowl. Pulse to blend. Pour in the liquid cornmeal mixture plus the yeast and potato. Pulse.

If the blade has difficulty spinning in the dense mixture, stop the machine and move the dough to a work surface. Finish by hand.

**FIRST RISING
1 hour or more**

Place in a greased bowl, cover with plastic wrap, and leave at room temperature to rise. The dough will seem so heavy you might wonder how it could possibly rise. But it will, and it will double in bulk in about 1 hour.

**SHAPING
5 mins.**

Punch down the dough, knead out the air bubbles, and form into a round, smooth ball. It may be divided to form smaller loaves or rolls if you wish. Place on the baking sheet.

**SECOND RISING
1 hour**

Cover the loaf with wax paper and leave to rise until doubled in bulk, about 1 hour.

PREHEAT	Preheat the oven to 375° about 20 minutes before baking.

BAKING
375°
50 mins.
	Brush the loaf with the egg white–water mixture.
	    Place in the oven and bake for about 50 minutes, or until the bottom crust sounds hollow and hard when tapped with a finger. The loaf will be a rich dark brown. If the loaf appears to be browning too quickly, cover with a piece of foil or brown sack paper.
	    (If using a convection oven, reduce heat 40°.)

FINAL STEP	Remove the bread from the oven and place on a metal rack to cool. Pumpernickel is too heavy to toast, of course, but it keeps for a week or more wrapped in foil or plastic, and freezes for months at 0°.

Dutch Roggebrood   [two loaves]

Dutch Roggebrood is a solid loaf of unleavened rye to be sliced wafer thin and served buttered with thin slices of ham and cheese. It is one of three kinds of bread served at a Dutch breakfast. It will keep almost indefinitely wrapped in plastic.

The recipe was given to me by a Dutch woman in a small English inn in East Anglia, where we were cycling. I had just described for her a delicious bread I had eaten years before in Amsterdam. She knew immediately the bread I was talking about, and gave me this recipe.

The bread is steamed for 3 hours, and then baked for an additional hour. It is left in the turned-off oven to dry for yet another hour, for a total of 5 hours. There is little or no gluten in rye flour so the dough will not rise but remain a solid but delicious brick.

INGREDIENTS	3 or 4 potatoes, diced 2 cups potato water (see Preparation) $1/2$ cup molasses, unsulphured preferred 7 cups rye flour 1 tablespoon salt $1/2$ cup brewer's yeast 2 tablespoons ground caraway seeds
BAKING PANS	2 medium (8"-x-4") loaf pans, greased, plus a larger baking or roasting pan in which to place these 2 pans
PREPARATION 20 mins.	In a pot, boil the potatoes to get the 2 cups potato water. Save the potatoes for another use as only the water is used in this recipe.

BY HAND
15 mins.

Pour the boiling potato water into a large mixing bowl and add the remaining ingredients.

Be forewarned: all-rye is a sticky mess that won't get better no matter how long it is worked. When the dough has cooled, use a spoon (and your fingers, sparingly) to blend all of the ingredients together.

BY PROCESSOR
8 mins.

Make the potato water, as above. Set aside. This sequence differs from above.

Use a plastic blade.

Measure 4 cups rye flour into the work bowl and add the salt, brewer's yeast, and caraway seeds. Pulse to blend. Pour in the hot potato water and molasses. Pulse to mix thoroughly.

Add the rye flour, ¼ cup at a time. The addition of rye may create a dough that is too dense for the blade. If the blade slows or stops, scrape the dough onto a floured work surface or into a greased bowl and continue by hand.

SHAPING
8 mins.

Spoon the dough into the pans. Dampen your fingers and push the dough into the corners and smooth the surface.

Cover each pan tightly with foil. Place them in the larger pan and fill it with hot water an inch or so deep around the dough-filled tins. Cover the larger pan with a lid or improvise a cover with aluminum foil to keep the steam from escaping.

STEAM/BAKING
250°
3 hours
1 hour

Place the covered pan in the oven and set the temperature at 250°. Steam, covered, for 3 hours.

Lift out the larger pan, uncover, and then lift out the 2 bread pans. Remove the foil from each and return them by themselves to the oven for an additional hour, still at 250°.

No heat
1 hour

Turn off the heat. Turn the bread out from the pans and return them to the oven to dry, about 1 hour, for a total of 5 hours.

(Some home convection ovens will not hold both the bread tins and the large water-filled pan. I can just get a 13½"-x-8¾"-x-1¾" pan in my oven. It is a tight fit for 2 bread pans but it will work. The alternative is to reduce the recipe by half and steam/bake a single loaf in a smaller pan that will fit into the oven. Set the temperature at 225°, and follow the same times and procedures as above.)

FINAL STEP

Place on a metal rack to cool before slicing ⅛" thick to serve.

Seeded Rye   [two large loaves]
(also called New York Rye and Jewish Rye)

One of the most celebrated—and delicious—rye breads is one known by several names: Seeded, New York, and Jewish.

The secret ingredient long known only to bakers is a wet mash of crusts of old rye bread held over from an earlier baking. Many years ago in New York City when refrigeration facilities were not what they are today, the wet crusts were hidden from health inspectors, usually in a barrel. "Kid, what's in the barrel?" The reply from a child sitting on and protecting the barrel lid: "Pickles!"

The great flavor of this bread also depends on the leavening, a sour made with rye flour and onion slices (to give it acidity).

One of the finest bakers in the country is Michael London, who, with his wife, owns an outstanding bakery/deli in Saratoga Springs, New York. He has traveled widely searching for recipes and this one he found in a Jewish bakery in New York City. His recipe is for dozens of loaves so I have adapted it for the home baker.

A recipe for a Jewish or New York Rye was not in my first bread book, and I have heard about it ever since. So I am delighted to present it here.

INGREDIENTS	1½ cups rye bread pieces (see Preparation) 3 cups Rye Sour (page 108) 1 package dry yeast 1 tablespoon salt 2 tablespoons caraway seeds (more if you like the flavor) 4 cups bread or unbleached flour, approximately 1 egg, beaten, mixed with 1 tablespoon water
BAKING SHEET	1 baking sheet, greased or Teflon or dusted with cornmeal
PREPARATION 5 mins.	Soak in water a half dozen crusty slices of a previously baked loaf of rye (commercial rye is fine). Squeeze dry. Set aside 1½ cups for this recipe; the balance can be refrigerated or frozen for later use.
BY HAND OR MIXER 18 mins.	In a large mixing or mixer bowl drop in the squeezed-dry pieces of rye bread. Add the rye sour. With a wooden spoon or a mixer flat beater stir until the bread is thoroughly incorporated into the sour. Stir in the dry yeast, salt, and 1 tablespoon (or more) caraway. Add 2 cups white flour and mix vigorously into the sour. Add more flour, ¼ cup at a time, stirring first with a wooden spoon and then with the hands, or with the mixer flat beater. The dough may be sticky at

first but it will become elastic and smooth as it is worked. Lift the dough from the bowl and place it on the floured work surface. Or leave in the mixer bowl under a dough hook.

KNEADING
8 mins.

Knead the dough under a dough hook or with your hands for 8 minutes. If by hand, use a strong push-turn-fold motion, adding sprinkles of flour if the dough is sticky. But don't overload the dough with flour. It is better to keep it on the slack side.

BY PROCESSOR
5 mins.

Soak the bread, as above.

Use the plastic dough blade.

Place the bread pieces and the sour in the processor work bowl. Pulse several times to make certain the two are thoroughly blended. Add the yeast, salt, and 1 tablespoon caraway seeds. Pulse, and leave for a minute or two for the yeast particles to dissolve.

Add the white flour, ½ cup at a time, until the batter becomes solid and is carried around the bowl by the force of the blade.

KNEADING
45 secs.

Keep the machine running and knead for 45 seconds.

If the dough is too dense for your machine, turn the dough onto the work surface and proceed by hand.

FIRST RISING
30 mins.

Place the dough in a bowl, cover with plastic wrap, and leave at room temperature for 30 minutes.

SHAPING
5 mins.

Punch down the dough and turn out onto a floured work surface. Divide into 2 pieces. The dough may be fashioned into round loaves or long plump ones. Place the loaves on the baking sheet.

SECOND RISING
30 mins.

Cover the loaves with wax paper and put aside to rise for 30 minutes to proof only three-quarters, not the usual full proof of double in volume. This is not critical but it is nice to come close to this degree of proofing.

PREHEAT

Preheat the oven to 450° 20 minutes before baking, and prepare 1 cup hot water to pour into a pan on the bottom shelf 3 minutes before putting in the loaves. This will create the steam used in commercial ovens.

BAKING
450°
40 mins.

Cut the top of the loaves into a pattern with a razor blade or sharp knife. Try a tic-tac-toe design or diagonal cut across the top. Brush with the egg-water mixture. Sprinkle with 1 tablespoon caraway seeds.

Place in the hot oven. Midway through baking, turn the loaves around so they brown evenly. The loaves will bake a deep brown in about 40 minutes. Turn one loaf over and tap the bottom crust to determine if it is done. If it is not hard and crusty, return to the oven for 5 or 10 minutes.

(If using a convection oven, reduce heat 50°.)

FINAL STEP

Place the loaves on a metal rack to cool.

This is a delicious loaf that will be hard to keep in supply.

BARLEY BREADS

BARLEY FLOUR bakes into a dark loaf and is the principal ingredient of several of the European black breads.

Barley is one of the most ancient of the cultivated cereal grains. Grown by the Swiss lake dwellers in the Stone Age, barley mixed with water was one of the curatives prescribed by Hippocrates. The English and Dutch brought the grain to the early settlements in America and the Spanish introduced it into California.

Barley Banana Bread   [one large loaf]

Barley, a mild flour, is a near-perfect backdrop for this loaf because it allows the full flavor of bananas and nuts to come through. While there is no wheat in the bread, there is 1 cup rice flour, which is quite bland and combines well with the barley to make a good-tasting loaf.

If rice flour is in short supply in your kitchen, increase the amount of barley flour accordingly.

This recipe can be made with a mixer or food processor but I prefer to do it by hand in a mixing bowl because it is so easily done, and the cleaning up afterward is minimal.

INGREDIENTS

1 cup sugar
$^1/_2$ cup shortening, room temperature
2 eggs, room temperature
1$^1/_3$ cups mashed banana
1$^1/_2$ cups barley flour
1 cup rice flour
2 teaspoons baking powder
$^1/_2$ teaspoon salt
$^3/_4$ cup chopped walnuts

BAKING PAN	1 large (9"-x-5") baking pan, greased or Teflon, lined with buttered wax paper
PREHEAT	Preheat the oven to 350°.

BY HAND
18 mins.
	In a mixing bowl cream the sugar and shortening. Break in the eggs and stir in the mashed bananas.
	    In a second bowl, combine the barley flour, rice flour, baking powder, and salt. Stir the dry ingredients into the egg-banana mixture. When this is well blended, add the walnuts.
	    Pour the batter into the prepared baking pan. With a rubber spatula or spoon, push the batter slightly higher around the edges of the pan to compensate for the rising crown in the oven.

BAKING 350° 1 hour	Place the pan in the oven and bake until it tests done when a wooden toothpick, inserted in the center of the loaf, comes out clean and dry. (If using a convection oven, reduce heat 50°.)
FINAL STEP	Remove the bread from the oven. Allow it to cool for 10 minutes before turning the pan on its side and pulling the loaf out by tugging on the ends of the wax paper. Allow it to cool thoroughly. This bread is better the second day, after it has matured somewhat. It will keep well wrapped in foil in the refrigerator for up to two weeks.

Rieska   [one 14" loaf or two 8" loaves]
(Finnish Flat Barley Bread)

Finns use a variety of grains, and their breads have wonderful flavors and texture, especially this one—Rieska, a traditional loaf from Lapland and northern Finland. A velvety flat bread made with barley flour, it is cut in pie-shaped wedges, spread with plenty of butter, and served warm. It can be made with rye flour, but it won't be quite the same.

INGREDIENTS	2 cups barley flour (or rye) 3/4 teaspoon salt 2 teaspoons sugar 2 teaspoons baking powder 1 cup undiluted evaporated milk or half-and-half 2 tablespoons butter, melted
BAKING SHEET	1 baking sheet, greased or Teflon

PREHEAT	Preheat the oven to 425°.
BY HAND OR MIXER 15 mins.	In a medium-size mixing or mixer bowl combine the flour, salt, sugar, and baking powder. Stir in the milk or half-and-half and the butter by hand or with a mixer flat beater until a dough forms.
BY PROCESSOR 3 mins.	Attach the steel blade. Measure all of the dry ingredients into the processor work bowl, and pulse to blend. Pour the butter and the milk or half-and-half through the feed tube. Pulse until combined into a soft dough.
SHAPING 5 mins.	Spoon the dough onto the baking sheet, and pat the mass into a circle about 14" in diameter and about ½" thick. It will be soft and sticky, so work with hands dusted with flour. The dough may be divided in half to form two smaller 8" flat loaves. With the point of a knife lightly score the top to indicate 8 or 10 wedge-shaped servings, but do not cut through. Prick all over with the tines of a fork.
BAKING 425° 12–15 mins.	Place in the oven and bake until lightly browned, about 12 to 15 minutes. (If using a convection oven, reduce heat 50°.)
FINAL STEP	Remove the bread from the oven. Cut or break into wedge-shaped pieces after it has cooled. Serve immediately with butter.

Barley Orange Bread   [one large or two small loaves]

There is a velvety softness about breads made with barley flour, and in this loaf the light taste of orange complements the subtleness of the flour. The orange peel is simmered beforehand to subdue the otherwise strong orange taste, but if you wish an assertive orange, forgo the boiling process and let the orange come through.

The loaf is light brown in color, with a shiny golden crust.

INGREDIENTS

Rind of 2 oranges
1 cup sugar
½ cup water
2 cups barley flour
½ teaspoon salt
1 tablespoon baking powder
2 eggs, room temperature, lightly beaten
½ cup fresh or frozen orange juice
3 tablespoons butter or other shortening, melted

BAKING PANS	1 large (9"-x-5") or 2 small (7"-x-3") loaf pans, greased or Teflon, lined with greased wax paper
PREPARATION 50 mins.	In a saucepan barely cover the rinds from the oranges with water and boil gently for 10 minutes. Pour off the water; add more water and boil for another 10 minutes, or until tender. Pour off the water, and place the rinds under running tap water for a moment. Chop or grind the rinds in a food chopper or processor; return to the saucepan and add ½ cup each sugar and water; cook until thick and syrupy, about 25 minutes.
PREHEAT	Preheat the oven to 350° 20 minutes before baking.
BY HAND OR MIXER 15 mins.	When the orange mixture has cooled, sift the flour, ½ cup sugar, salt, and baking powder into a large bowl. Add the eggs, orange juice, shortening, and orange mixture. Combine—but don't overmix—and pour into either the large or 2 small loaf pans. The batter can be put together with a mixer using the flat beater but only until thoroughly mixed—not beyond.

BY PROCESSOR
3 mins.
	Prepare the orange mixture as above.
	    With the steel blade attached, measure all of the above ingredients into the mixer bowl, and pulse 2 or 3 times to blend—but no longer.
	    Pour the batter into the pan or pans.

BAKING 350° 1 hour	Place the pan(s) in the oven and bake for about 1 hour, or until the loaf is light brown and a metal skewer inserted in the center of it comes out clean and dry. If moist particles cling to the skewer, return the bread to the oven for an additional 10 minutes. Test again. (If using a convection oven, reduce heat 50°.)
FINAL STEP	Remove the bread from the oven and allow it to cool for 10 minutes before turning it out of the pan. Quick bread is more fragile when warm than a yeast loaf, so handle with care. Turn the pan on its side and pull the loaf out by tugging on the ends of the wax paper. Peel off the paper and let the bread cool on a metal rack before serving. It will develop a richer flavor if allowed to mature at least a day at room temperature wrapped in plastic or foil.

CORN BREADS

SOUTHERNERS LIKE their corn bread thin—about one inch deep in the pan, and they want it made with white cornmeal. White looks pure.

The North likes a thick corn bread—sometimes three inches deep in the pan—and made with yellow cornmeal. Yellow looks rich.

Few Europeans care for corn in any form. They consider it a "gross food" to be fed only to animals. Only Basque sailors who accompanied Columbus in 1492 liked it, and brought it back to become part of Basque cuisine (see *Taloa* in this chapter).

To new bread bakers without regional preferences, I confess that I find no difference in taste between white and yellow. I will choose one over the other on occasion because of the color.

Here are a dozen and a half of the best corn bread recipes.

Yankee Corn Bread   [nine servings]

Northerners like a golden corn bread made with yellow cornmeal. Unlike Southerners, who prefer a thin sheet of white corn bread that has little or no sugar in it, those in the North, with the exception of some in the New England states, like it sweeter.

This is a delicious Northern corn bread that will be acceptable in the South as well.

INGREDIENTS
I cup all-purpose flour
$^{1}/_{4}$ cup sugar
4 teaspoons baking powder
I teaspoon salt
I cup yellow cornmeal
2 eggs, room temperature
I cup milk
$^{1}/_{4}$ cup ($^{1}/_{2}$ stick) butter, melted
$^{1}/_{3}$ cup chopped crisp bacon

BAKING PAN	One 9"-x-9" baking pan, greased or Teflon
BY HAND 22 mins.	Sift together the flour, sugar, baking powder, and salt into a medium bowl. Stir in the cornmeal. In a small bowl beat the eggs with a fork, and add the milk and melted butter. Stir in the bacon bits. Add to the dry ingredients. Mix with a wooden spoon or spatula only to moisten the batter. Don't over-stir even if the batter is lumpy. Pour into the pan and level with the spoon.
PREHEAT	Preheat the oven to 425°.
REST 10 mins.	Let the batter rest for 10 minutes while the oven is heating.
BAKING 425° 25 mins.	Bake until the bread is raised and golden, about 25 minutes. Test with a wooden toothpick or metal skewer for doneness. Don't overbake or it will be dry. (If using a convection oven, reduce heat 50°.)
FINAL STEP	Remove the bread from the oven. Cut in squares and serve immediately from the pan—with lots of butter!

Sour Milk Corn Bread
[approximately eight bread servings,
or twelve–fourteen muffins or corn sticks]

Eggs, sour milk, and butter give this thin corn bread a fine open texture, not dense like many other corn breads. It has a pleasant eggy flavor.

Try breaking serving pieces off the yellow square rather than cutting it. It seems to taste better that way.

INGREDIENTS	1 cup *each* all-purpose flour and yellow cornmeal 1 teaspoon salt 1 teaspoon baking soda 1 cup buttermilk or sour milk, room temperature 2 eggs, room temperature, well beaten 2 tablespoons butter or other shortening, melted
BAKING TIN	One 9"-x-9" baking tin, Teflon or greased with bacon drippings or melted shortening, or 12 to 14 muffin tins or corn-stick molds, greased
PREHEAT	Preheat the oven to 450°.

BY HAND 18 mins.	In a large bowl blend together the flour, yellow cornmeal, and salt. In a smaller bowl or cup stir the baking soda into the buttermilk or sour milk. Pour this into the bowl of dry ingredients, and add the eggs. Stir in the melted butter or shortening. The mixing should be done quickly but don't beat beyond what is necessary to make a smooth batter. Pour the batter into the baking tin or muffin tins or corn stick molds.
BAKING 450° 30 mins.	Bake in the oven until the bread is well browned, and tests done when pierced with a wooden toothpick, about 30 minutes. If it comes out clean and dry, the loaf is done. If moist particles cling to the toothpick, return to the oven for 5 minutes. (If using a convection oven, reduce heat 50°.)
FINAL STEP	Remove the bread from the oven. This bread is best served hot and broken into pieces, rather than cut.

Southern Corn Bread   [nine servings]

Southerners like their corn bread white and thin. This corn bread will delight not only those in the South but in the rest of the country as well.

There is no wheat flour in the recipe, nor shortening. It is essentially corn, and that is what good corn bread is all about.

The batter is also excellent for corn sticks, enough for 12 to 14.

INGREDIENTS	2 eggs, room temperature 2 cups buttermilk, room temperature 1 teaspoon baking soda 2 cups white cornmeal 1½ teaspoons salt
BAKING PAN	One 9"-x-9" baking pan, greased or Teflon
PREHEAT	Preheat the oven to 450°. Heat the prepared baking pan in the oven while mixing the batter.
BY HAND OR MIXER 18 mins.	In a small bowl beat the eggs and add the buttermilk. In a mixing or mixer bowl stir together the baking soda, cornmeal, and salt. Pour in the egg-buttermilk mixture and beat with a flat beater or with a rotary beater until the batter is smooth. This can be done by hand, of course, but be certain the batter is smooth. Carefully pour the batter into the heated pan.

BAKING 450° 20–25 mins.	Return immediately to the oven and bake until set, 20 to 25 minutes. Insert a knife in the center of the bread, and when it comes out clean and dry, the corn bread is baked. (If using a convection oven, heat the pan, as above, before baking. Reduce heat 50°.)
FINAL STEP	Remove the bread from the oven. Serve hot, cut into squares, with lots of butter.

Broa   [one round loaf]
(Portuguese Corn Bread)

Broa is a finely textured Portuguese corn bread made with cornmeal spun in a blender, and leavened with yeast. It is not coarse and solid like so many other corn breads. In Portugal, the bread is served warm or cold with a famous dish of peas and eggs, and a potato-sausage soup.

INGREDIENTS	1½ cups yellow cornmeal 1½ teaspoons salt 1¼ cups boiling water 1 tablespoon olive oil 2 packages dry yeast 2 cups bread or all-purpose flour, approximately
BAKING SHEET	1 baking sheet, greased or Teflon
PREPARATION 5 mins.	Pulverize the cornmeal in a blender or food processor, ¼ cup at a time, until it is fine and powdery. The bread can be made without this step but the texture will not be as smooth.
BY HAND OR MIXER 20 mins.	In a large mixing or mixer bowl combine 1 cup of the powdered cornmeal, the salt, and boiling water. Stir until smooth. Stir in the olive oil, and cool the mixture until it is lukewarm. Then blend in the yeast. Gradually add the rest of the cornmeal and 1 cup flour, stirring constantly by hand, or with the mixer flat beater. Work the dough until it is a mass, adding ¼ cup or more flour if necessary to overcome the stickiness.
FIRST RISING 30 mins.	Place a length of plastic wrap tightly over the bowl, and leave at room temperature until the dough has doubled in volume, 30 minutes.

KNEADING 8 mins.	Turn the dough onto a floured work surface, and knead with a strong push-turn-fold motion. Meanwhile add flour, if necessary, to make a firm but not stiff dough. Knead by hand or with a dough hook in the mixer bowl for 8 minutes.

BY PROCESSOR
15–20 mins.
	Pulverize the cornmeal, as above, and attach the steel blade.
	    Pour the cornmeal into the work bowl and add the salt and boiling water. Pulse. Measure in the olive oil and cool until lukewarm. Add the yeast, and pulse to blend.
	    With the processor running, add the rest of the cornmeal and 1 cup white flour. Measure in additional flour, a small portion at a time, until the dough forms a mass and is thrust around the work bowl by the force of the blade. Allow the bread to rise, as above, before kneading.

KNEADING 50 secs.	With the machine running, knead the dough for 50 seconds.
SHAPING 3 mins.	Turn the dough from the work bowl. If the dough is sticky, dust it liberally with flour as you shape it into a round ball. Flatten it slightly and place on the baking sheet.
SECOND RISING 30 mins.	Cover the ball with wax paper and leave until it doubles in bulk again, 30 minutes.
PREHEAT	Preheat the oven to 350° about 20 minutes before baking.
BAKING 350° 40 mins.	Bake in the middle rack of the oven. When the loaf is golden and the bottom crust sounds hard and hollow when tapped, the loaf is done, about 40 minutes. If not, return to the oven for an additional 10 minutes. Test again. (If using a convection oven, reduce heat 50°.)
FINAL STEP	Remove the loaf from the oven and place on a rack to cool before serving.

Bacon Spoon Bread   [makes six servings]

Spoon bread, or batter bread, is a custardy corn bread served at the table as a soufflé from the dish in which it was baked. This version made with Cheddar cheese, a hint of garlic, and bits of bacon is unusually good. It rises impressively in the oven and is served puffed and creamy.

Spoon bread, according to legend, was created when a mixture used to make corn bread enriched by milk and eggs was left forgotten in a hot oven.

Virginians claim this happened in one of their kitchens, and as a consequence spoon bread has been one of their favored foods ever since.

INGREDIENTS

³/₄ cup cornmeal, yellow preferred
1¹/₂ cups cold water
2 cups shredded sharp Cheddar cheese
¹/₄ cup butter or shortening, room temperature
2 garlic cloves, crushed
¹/₂ teaspoon salt
1 cup milk
4 eggs, separated
¹/₂ pound fried bacon, in bits

BAKING DISH

One 2-quart casserole or soufflé dish, greased

PREHEAT

Preheat the oven to 325°.

BY HAND
18 mins.

In a saucepan stir the cornmeal into the cold water and place over medium heat. Bring to a bubbling boil, stirring constantly. When it is thick, perhaps 60 seconds, remove from heat. Stir in the cheese, butter, garlic, and salt. When the cheese is melted, pour in the milk. Stir in the egg yolks and add the bacon bits.

Beat the egg whites stiff, and fold them into the batter.

Pour the mixture into the casserole or soufflé dish. Level the batter with a rubber scraper or spatula.

BAKING
325°
1 hour

Bake until the bread is nicely browned, high, and puffy, about 1 hour. Slip a knife into the center of the casserole. If the blade comes out clean and dry, the spoon bread is done. If not, return to the oven for an additional 10 minutes.

(If using a convection oven, reduce heat 25°.)

FINAL STEP

Remove the bread from the oven and carry the dish to the table. Using 2 large spoons, cut into the bread and serve.

Corn Sticks   [fifteen to twenty sticks or muffins]

There is an appealing roughness about this corn bread whether it be made into corn sticks, muffins, or gems. Each grain is distinct and separate. Delicious.

INGREDIENTS

¹/₂ cup all-purpose flour
2 teaspoons baking powder
1 teaspoon sugar

¹/₂ teaspoon salt

1¹/₂ cups yellow or white cornmeal

1 egg, room temperature

³/₄ cup milk, room temperature

3 tablespoons butter, melted

BAKING MOLDS OR TINS	15 to 20 corn-stick molds or muffin tins, oiled
PREHEAT	Preheat the oven to 425°.
BY HAND 10 mins.	In a mixing bowl sift and stir together the flour, baking powder, sugar, and salt. Mix in the cornmeal and blend thoroughly. In another bowl beat the egg until it is light in color, and stir in the milk and melted butter. Using as few strokes as possible, stir the egg mixture into the cornmeal. The batter will be lumpy. Pour the batter into the greased corn-stick molds or muffin tins.
BAKING 425° 20–25 mins.	Bake in the oven until they are crisp and hard on the surface, about 20 to 25 minutes. (If using a convection oven, reduce heat 50°.)
FINAL STEP	Remove the bread from the oven. Serve hot with sweet butter.

Rich Corn Bread   [six servings]

This is an unusually rich corn bread—a dairyman's dream—made with cream, milk, butter, and eggs. Since some judge their corn bread as much by its thickness as by its flavor, the batter is only ½ inch deep in the pan and rises to 1¹/₂ inches. Absolutely delicious hot from the oven.

INGREDIENTS	1¹/₂ cups yellow cornmeal ¹/₂ cup bread or all-purpose flour 1 teaspoon *each* salt and sugar 1 tablespoon baking powder 1 cup milk 3 eggs, room temperature ¹/₄ cup heavy cream, room temperature ¹/₄ cup (¹/₂ stick) butter, melted
BAKING PAN	1 shallow 16"-x-12" baking pan, greased or Teflon, or a combination of smaller pans with the equivalent volume (two 9"-x-9" pans are about right)

PREHEAT	Preheat the oven to 400°.
BY HAND 12 mins.	In a mixing bowl measure the cornmeal, flour, salt, sugar, and baking powder. In a small bowl lightly beat the milk into the eggs and pour this into the bowl of dry ingredients. Beat until thoroughly blended. Pour in the cream and butter. Blend the mixture. Pour the batter into the baking pans to a depth of about ½".
BAKING 400° 20–25 mins.	Bake in the oven until the bread is nicely browned and tests done when a wood toothpick inserted in the center comes out clean and dry, 20 to 25 minutes. (If using a convection oven, reduce heat 50°.)
FINAL STEP	Remove the bread from the oven. Serve hot, cut into rectangles.

Toasted Cornmeal Bread   [two loaves]

More sophisticated than most corn breads, this loaf has a nice open texture, light brown color, and a nutlike taste. It is first leavened with a potato starter and then with yeast.

INGREDIENTS	*Sponge:* 1 cup Raw Potato Starter (page 242) ³/₄ cup *each* all-purpose flour and cold water *Dough:* 1 cup hot water (120°–130°) 1 package dry yeast ¹/₄ teaspoon ground ginger ¹/₂ cup nonfat dry milk 2 tablespoons maple or maple-flavored syrup 3 cups toasted cornmeal (see Notes) 3 cups all-purpose flour, approximately 2 teaspoons salt 2 tablespoons butter or margarine, room temperature
BAKING PANS	2 medium (8"-x-4") baking pans, greased or Teflon
PREPARATION Overnight	To make the sponge, the day before baking, empty the potato starter into a mixing bowl and stir in the flour and cold water. (See Notes.) Cover tightly with plastic wrap and set aside overnight. Scald the starter jar and set aside.

On baking day, stir the sponge and return 1 cup to the starter jar. Cover and place in the refrigerator for later use. Set aside the remaining 1 cup of starter.

**BY HAND
OR MIXER
20 mins.**

To make the dough, into a large mixing or mixer bowl pour the sponge, add the hot water, yeast, ginger, dry milk, syrup, toasted cornmeal, and 1½ cups all-purpose flour. Mix thoroughly. Add the salt, butter or margarine, and 1 cup additional flour. Stir 125 strokes with a wooden spoon, or with the mixer flat beater for 2 minutes. The dough will form a rough mass and clean the sides of the bowl.

**KNEADING
8 mins.**

If by hand, spread flour on the work surface and turn the dough onto it. Knead with a strong push-turn-fold motion, using only as much flour as necessary to make a smooth elastic dough that is not sticky. If using a mixer, knead with the dough hook. Knead by hand or mixer for 8 minutes.

**BY PROCESSOR
5 mins.**

Prepare the sponge, as above.

Use the short dough blade.

Pour the sponge into the work bowl and add the water, yeast, ginger, dry milk, syrup, toasted cornmeal, and 1 cup all-purpose flour. Pulse to mix thoroughly. Turn the machine on and add the salt and butter through the feed tube.

Add flour, ¼ cup at a time, until the dough forms a mass that is carried around the bowl by the thrust of the blade. If not all of the flour is pulled into the dough, stop the machine and scrape it free. The dough will clean the sides of the bowl.

**KNEADING
50 secs.**

Leave the machine running to knead for 50 seconds. The dough may still be sticky, so sprinkle liberally with flour when you take it from the work bowl.

**FIRST RISING
1 hour**

Place the dough in a bowl, cover tightly with plastic wrap, and put aside at room temperature until light and doubled in size, 1 hour.

**SHAPING
5 mins.**

Turn out the dough, divide into 2 equal pieces, and knead briefly to expel the bubbles. Push each piece into a flat oval, fold in half, press the seam together, and place in the pan with the seam under.

**SECOND RISING
50 mins.**

Cover the loaves with wax paper and leave to rise until light and doubled in volume, 50 minutes.

PREHEAT

Preheat the oven to 375° about 20 minutes before baking.

BAKING 375° 40 mins.	Place the pans in the oven. When golden brown and loose in the pans, the loaves are baked, about 40 minutes. They will sound hard and hollow when tapped on the bottom crust. (If using a convection oven, reduce heat 50°.)

FINAL STEP	Remove the bread from the oven and turn out from the pans onto a wire rack to cool.
	    The bread toasts beautifully, and freezes well for an indefinite period.
	    Notes: If you prefer, you can make the sponge with 1 package dry yeast and an additional ½ cup *each* flour and water. Leave overnight.
	    Toasted cornmeal, found in some specialty food stores, is called for, but I toast my cornmeal on a baking sheet or in an iron skillet in a 350° oven for about 30 minutes.

Plymouth Bread   [two loaves]

Cornmeal and molasses were in good supply in the early American settlements, and they came together in this fat brown loaf of good taste and unusual texture.

INGREDIENTS	2½ cups water ½ cup yellow cornmeal 2 tablespoons shortening ½ cup molasses 2 teaspoons salt 1 package dry yeast 4 to 5 cups bread or all-purpose flour, approximately 1 tablespoon milk (optional)
BAKING PANS	2 medium (8"-x-4") baking pans, greased or Teflon
PREPARATION 25–30 mins.	In a saucepan bring the water to a boil and very slowly pour the cornmeal into it, stirring all the while. This is important to keep the mixture smooth and free of troublesome and unattractive small balls of congealed meal. Boil over a medium heat for 5 minutes. Remove the pan from the burner, and add the shortening, molasses, and salt. Put aside to cool.
BY HAND OR MIXER 10 mins.	Pour the cooled cornmeal mixture into a mixing or mixer bowl. Add the yeast and blend for 1 minute in the mixer, or with a wooden spoon. Gradually add 2 cups flour and beat at medium speed for 3 minutes,

or 150 strokes with a wooden spoon. Stop the machine and stir in additional flour with the spoon, and then by hand, until a rough mass is formed. If slack or sticky, add up to ¼ cup more flour and work it into the dough.

KNEADING
8 mins.

Turn out onto a floured work surface and knead. Or leave the dough in the mixer for kneading with the dough hook. The dough will be smooth, elastic, and feel alive.

BY PROCESSOR
4 mins.

Heat the cornmeal-shortening mixture, as above, and put aside to cool.

Attach the plastic dough blade. Measure 2 cups white flour into the work bowl; pour in the cooled mixture and the yeast. Pulse 2 or 3 times to blend well.

With the machine running, add the remaining flour, ½ cup at a time, until the dough becomes a rough, shaggy mass, and is spun around the work bowl by the blade. The dough will clean the sides of the bowl.

KNEADING
45 secs.

Keep the machine running and knead for 45 seconds. Sprinkle flour over the dough and lift it out with the hands.

FIRST RISING
1 hour

Place the ball of dough in a lightly greased bowl, cover with plastic wrap, and leave at room temperature until it doubles in volume, about 1 hour.

SHAPING
10 mins.

Punch down the dough. Knead briefly to press out the air bubbles, and divide into 2 pieces. Press each piece into a flattened oval, fold in half, pinch the seam, plump into shape, and place in the pans.

SECOND RISING
45 mins.

Cover the loaves with wax paper and let rise until doubled in volume, 45 minutes.

PREHEAT

Preheat the oven to 350° 20 minutes before baking.

BAKING
350°
1 hour

Bake until the loaves are nicely browned, and tapping the bottom crust yields a hard, hollow sound, about 1 hour. If the bottom is soft, return the bread to the oven for an additional 5 to 10 minutes.

(If using a convection oven, reduce heat 50° and bake for 50 minutes.)

FINAL STEP

Remove the bread from the oven. A brush of milk across the crust will give the loaves a nice soft glaze.

This bread makes delicious toast. It freezes well at 0° for months.

Batter Corn Bread   [two loaves]

Batter Corn Bread, brown and golden when it comes from the oven, has the rough texture of quick corn breads, but is a batter bread that relies on yeast for leavening. Although the soft batter is not kneaded, it is allowed to rise before baking. It is hardly worth the bother of using a food processor and cleaning it.

This corn bread has a fine corn flavor and aroma, and can be frozen and reheated.

INGREDIENTS

2 packages dry yeast
3¹/₂ cups bread or all-purpose flour
1³/₄ cups yellow cornmeal
¹/₃ cup nonfat dry milk
1¹/₂ cups hot water (120°–130°)
¹/₂ cup (1 stick) butter, margarine, or other shortening
6 tablespoons sugar
2 teaspoons salt
2 eggs, room temperature, lightly beaten
1 tablespoon *each* milk and cornmeal

BAKING PANS

2 medium (8"-x-4") loaf pans, greased or Teflon

BY HAND
OR MIXER
25 mins.

In a large mixing or mixer bowl stir together the yeast, flour, cornmeal, and dry milk.

In another bowl pour hot water over the shortening, sugar, salt, and eggs. Combine. Add to dry mixture. Beat until well blended, about 50 strokes, or 1 minute with a mixer flat beater. The batter will be stiff.

Turn the batter into the loaf pans and push into the corners with a rubber scraper.

RISING
1 hour

Cover the tins with wax paper and put aside to rise at room temperature until the batter has doubled in bulk, about 1 hour.

PREHEAT

Preheat the oven to 375° 20 minutes before baking.

BAKING
375°
35 mins.

Before putting the loaves in the oven, carefully brush the tops with the milk and sprinkle lightly with the cornmeal.

Bake in the oven until golden and brown, about 35 minutes. When tapping the bottom crust yields a hard, hollow sound, and a wooden toothpick inserted in the middle comes out dry and clean, the loaves are done.

(If using a convection oven, reduce heat 50° and bake for 30 minutes.)

FINAL STEP

Remove the bread from the oven and turn the loaves out onto cooling racks. This bread is especially good served warm.

Freezes well.

Jalapeño Corn Bread [two pans, about eight servings]

This ranks as one of the best corn breads among my recipes. Chopped jalapeño peppers are in this delicious bread but lose their fierceness when baked. The peppers give the bread a provocative and spicy flavor that happily embraces the sharp Cheddar cheese, the creamed corn, and cornmeal. It is a handsome pan of bread—the yellow corn and the deeper yellow streaks of cheese, highlighted with bits of green pepper.

Served with or without butter, Jalapeño Corn Bread is almost a meal in itself. It is good with Mexican food, of course, also barbecued meats, grilled steaks, and hot dogs. It is an equally good companion to soup, a glass of red wine, or a bottle of cold beer.

INGREDIENTS

2^1/$_2$ cups yellow cornmeal
1 cup bread or all-purpose flour
2 tablespoons sugar
1 tablespoon salt
4 teaspoons baking powder
^{1}/$_2$ cup nonfat dry milk
3 eggs, room temperature
1^1/$_2$ cups warm water (105°–115°)
^{1}/$_2$ cup cooking oil
1 16-ounce can cream-style corn
6 to 8 jalapeño canned chili peppers, chopped (see Note)
2 cups grated sharp Cheddar cheese
1 large onion, grated

BAKING PANS

Two 9"-x-11" or 9"-x-9" baking pans, greased or Teflon.

PREHEAT

Preheat the oven to 425°.

BY HAND
18 mins.

In large bowl stir together the cornmeal, flour, sugar, salt, baking powder, and milk.

In a smaller bowl lightly beat the eggs and stir in the warm water and oil. Pour the liquid mixture into the cornmeal mix and stir in the corn, chopped peppers, cheese, and grated onion.

Pour the batter into the baking pans and spread evenly with a rubber scraper or a wooden spoon.

BAKING 425° 30 mins.	Bake until the bread tests done, about 30 minutes, and a wooden toothpick or metal skewer inserted in the center comes out clean. (If using a convection oven, reduce heat 50°.)
FINAL STEP	Remove the bread from the oven. Let the pans cool somewhat on metal racks before cutting the bread into serving pieces. This bread keeps well for several days, thanks to the oil and cheese, and may be frozen for months at 0°. *Note:* Jalapeño peppers are hot, hot and should be treated with respect. I use canned ones, and cut them up on a plate rather than the regular chopping board because they leave a hot afterglow that I might not want on the next food to be chopped. I am aware, too, that a bit of juice rubbed into the eye will bring a rush of tears and stop all preparations for a few moments. But nevertheless, even that is worth it for a bite of this bread.

Corn Bubble Bread   [one large round loaf]

Two layers of balls of dough expand in the oven to shape bubbles that are baked, pulled off, and served. Cornmeal gives this essentially white flour loaf a nice coarse texture. When the balls are stacked two deep in the large pan they will appear almost lost, but they soon expand in rising to make an intriguing solid loaf 3 to 4 inches deep.

The recipe calls for the dough to be refrigerated (as a convenience) but it can be baked straightaway with a 1-hour rising.

INGREDIENTS	5 cups bread or all-purpose flour, approximately 2 tablespoons sugar 1 tablespoon salt 1 cup yellow cornmeal 2 packages dry yeast 1 $^1/_2$ cups water $^1/_2$ cup milk 2 tablespoons shortening 4 teaspoons butter, melted
BAKING PAN	One 10" tube pan (as for an angel food cake), greased or Teflon
BY HAND OR MIXER 20 mins.	In a large mixing or mixer bowl blend 2 cups flour, sugar, salt, cornmeal, and yeast. In a saucepan, over low heat, combine the hot water, milk, and shortening. When the liquid is warm to the touch, pour it into the dry

ingredients, and beat for 2 minutes at medium speed of the mixer. Add about ½ cup flour to make the batter thick. Beat at high speed for 2 minutes. Scrape down the sides of the bowl twice during beating.

The beating can also be done by hand, of course. With a wooden spoon, beat for approximately the same length of time, or until the batter pulls away from the sides of the bowl in strands.

Turn off the mixer and stir in additional flour to make a rough mass that can be worked with the hands.

KNEADING
8 mins.

Turn the dough onto a lightly floured work surface and knead with a strong push-turn-fold action. The dough will be smooth and elastic, and feel alive under the hands. Knead for 8 minutes with the dough hook as well.

BY PROCESSOR
4 mins.

Attach the plastic dough blade.

There is no need to heat the milk, water, and shortening, as above.

Measure 2 cups white flour into the work bowl and add the sugar, salt, cornmeal, and yeast. Pulse to blend. With the machine running pour the liquids and shortening down the feed tube. When thoroughly blended, add additional white flour, ¼ cup at a time, to form a dough that will be whipped around the bowl by the blade and at the same time cleans the sides of the bowl.

KNEADING
45 secs.

Leave the machine on and knead for 45 seconds.

REST
20 mins.

Cover the ball of dough with a bowl and leave on the work surface to rest for 20 minutes.

SHAPING
15 mins.

Uncover the dough, punch it down, and knead briefly to collapse the air pockets. Divide it into 32 small pieces. The quickest and most accurate way is to divide the dough, with a knife, successively into 2-4-8-16 and finally 32 pieces.

Roll the pieces into balls between the palms. Arrange half of them in the first layer in the tube pan. They will not necessarily touch. Place the remaining 16 balls in a layer on top. Brush with 2 teaspoons melted butter.

REFRIGERATION
2–24 hours

Cover tightly with plastic wrap and place in the refrigerator from 2 to 24 hours.

PREHEAT

Take the pan from the refrigerator and, at the same time, preheat the oven to 375°.

REST 10 to 14 mins.	Uncover the pan and allow the dough to stand for 10 to 14 minutes. With a toothpick puncture any gas bubbles that may have formed on the surface of the dough balls.
BAKING 375° 55–60 mins.	Bake in the oven until the loaf is a deep brown, 55 to 60 minutes. Turn from the pan and tap the bottom crust to make certain it sounds hard and hollow. If not, return to the oven. (If using a convection oven, reduce heat 50° and bake for 45 minutes.)
FINAL STEP	Remove the bread from the oven, brush with the remaining melted butter, and place the loaf on a metal rack to cool. Serve the loaf at the table and let guests help themselves by picking off the "bubbles."

Johnnycake   [four to six servings]

In early America, this corn bread was called "journey cake"—fine to pack for a long horseback trip. Best served warm from the oven, even though it will be good later when eaten while traveling—or just staying in.

INGREDIENTS	**2 eggs, room temperature** **¹/₂ teaspoon salt** **2 tablespoons** *each* **sugar and melted butter** **I cup** *each* **cornmeal and all-purpose flour** **2 teaspoons baking powder** **I cup milk, room temperature**
BAKING PAN	One 8" square pan, greased or Teflon
PREHEAT	Preheat the oven to 425°.

BY HAND
OR MIXER
18 mins.
	Break the eggs into a large mixing or mixer bowl and add the salt. Whip until the eggs are light in color, then beat in the sugar and butter.
	    On a length of wax paper sift the cornmeal, flour, and baking powder. Alternately, add this and the cup of milk to the eggs. Blend well by hand or with a mixer flat beater.
	    Pour the batter into the prepared pan, and work it into the corners with a spatula or spoon.

BAKING 425° 20 mins.	Bake in the oven until raised and brown, about 20 minutes. Pierce the center of the loaf with a toothpick. If it comes out clean and dry, the bread is done. (If using a convection oven, reduce heat 50°.)

FINAL STEP	Remove the bread from the oven. Serve while warm . . . or on a journey.

Taloa   [eight large or sixteen small muffins]
(Corn Sandwich Muffins)

While a Taloa looks like an English muffin, it is basically corn, with a Basque background. The Taloa can be made with more cornmeal and less white flour but the more cornmeal used the less the muffin will rise, as the corn contributes nothing to the leavening effect of the yeast.

Slice open the chewy Taloa for a sandwich, or toast the halves for a different kind of breakfast bread. The Basques also scrape out most of the insides after it is baked, mix it with softened cream cheese, and return it to the Taloa, and it becomes a Marrakukua.

While the sprinkle of poppy seeds is not authentic, I thought the Taloa needed a contrasting touch.

INGREDIENTS	2 cups all-purpose flour, approximately 1 package dry yeast 2 teaspoons salt 1½ cups hot water (120°–130°) 2 cups yellow cornmeal 1 egg white, whipped with a few drops of water 2 tablespoons poppy or sesame seeds
BAKING SHEET	1 or 2 baking sheets, dusted with cornmeal
BY HAND OR MIXER 12 mins.	In a mixing or mixer bowl stir together 1 cup white flour, the yeast, salt, and hot water. Let stand for a minute or so to allow the yeast to dissolve. Pour in the cornmeal and blend with 25 strong strokes of a wooden spoon or rubber scraper, or for 2 minutes with a flat beater. Add the remaining flour, ¼ cup at a time, first with the spoon and then with the hands or under the dough hook to make an elastic ball of dough that cleans the sides of the bowl.
KNEADING 8 mins.	Leave in the mixer bowl if under the dough hook, or, if by hand, turn out on a floured work surface and knead with a push-turn-fold motion until the dough is smooth, soft, and does not stick, about 8 minutes. Avoid making the dough dense with too many sprinkles of flour.
BY PROCESSOR 4 mins.	Use the steel blade. Measure 1 cup white flour into the work bowl and add the yeast, salt, and hot water. Pulse to make a light batter. Remove the cover and

add the cornmeal. Replace the cover and pulse to blend. With the machine running, add flour through the feed tube to make a dough that will spin around the bowl with the blade.

KNEADING
45 secs.

Let the machine run for 45 seconds to knead.

FIRST RISING
1 hour

Place the dough in a greased bowl, cover with plastic wrap, and leave at room temperature until double in volume, about 1 hour.

SHAPING
10 mins.

Turn out the dough and knead for a moment to expel any bubbles. Divide the dough into pieces—8 for large muffins or 16 for the small.

Pat flat with the palm of your hand and roll into a circular disk with a pin. Larger muffins will be about 6" in diameter, and ½" thick; small ones will be about 4". When shaped, place on the prepared baking sheet(s).

SECOND RISING
50 mins.

Cover with wax paper and allow to rise for about 50 minutes.

PREHEAT

Preheat the oven to 450° about 20 minutes before baking.

BAKING
450°
20 mins.

Brush the muffins with the egg white and sprinkle liberally with the seeds of choice.

Place on the bottom shelf (if 1 baking sheet) or middle and bottom shelves (if 2 baking sheets, but switch pans after 12 minutes). If the oven will take only 1 sheet, let the reserved muffins rise for the additional time. On occasion Taloa may inflate to make it a convenient pocket for filling. Bake for 20 minutes, or until crusty when tapped with a finger.

(If using a convection oven, reduce heat 40°.)

Place on a metal rack to cool.

FINAL STEP

The muffins have no shortening and will not keep soft for more than a day or two. So use right away or freeze.

Biscuits au Maïs   [four dozen biscuits]
(Corn Biscuits)

Biscuits au Maïs gets its rich look from eggs, yellow cornmeal, and butter. It is true dessert bread—a light golden disk, a bit on the sweet side, perhaps, but a fine complement to a dish of strawberries or half of a grapefruit.

While these biscuits are unleavened, they achieve a pleasant plumpness in the oven.

INGREDIENTS	1/2 cup (1 stick) butter, room temperature
	1/2 cup sugar
	1 cup yellow cornmeal
	2 eggs, room temperature
	1 teaspoon salt
	1 1/2 cups all-purpose flour, approximately

BAKING SHEET	1 large baking sheet, greased or Teflon

PREHEAT	Preheat the oven to 375°.

BY HAND OR MIXER
15 mins.

In a large mixing or mixer bowl stir the butter into a soft mass with a wooden spoon or with the mixer's flat beater. Slowly add the sugar, and blend together, about 75 strokes, or for 2 minutes with the mixer. Add cornmeal, eggs, and salt. Beat until smooth. Add 1¼ cups flour. The mixture will be soft and moist but can be rolled flat with a rolling pin to a thickness of about ¼".

If too wet to work, add sprinkles of flour, blend in with your hands, and flatten with a rolling pin.

BY PROCESSOR
5 mins.

Use the steel blade for this small quantity.

Drop the butter and sugar into the work bowl. Turn on the processor and add the cornmeal, eggs, and salt through the feed tube. Add flour, ¼ cup at a time, to make a mixture that will form a soft ball and ride with the blade. If the dough is wet or slack, add sprinkles of flour. Turn from the bowl onto the work surface and roll flat.

The dough is not kneaded.

SHAPING
5 mins.

Use a 1½" round cookie cutter to cut about 48 pieces. Reassemble the scraps, roll again, and cut. Place on the baking sheet, but do not let the biscuits touch.

BAKING
375°
22 mins.

Place the baking sheet on the center rack, and bake until the biscuits are brown on the bottom, about 22 minutes. Near the end of baking, open the oven and turn the baking sheet around. If those biscuits on the outer edge are browning too fast, either remove them if they are done, or move to the center while pushing the lighter biscuits to the outside.

(If using a convection oven, reduce heat 50°.)

FINAL STEP

Remove the biscuits from the oven and cool slightly on a metal rack. Delicious served warm or equally good frozen and warmed for later service.

Steamed Corn Bread   [three small loaves]

While steamed corn bread has the color and texture of Boston Brown Bread (see "Blended Grains" chapter), it is less demanding in its ingredients; there is no blend of several flours—cornmeal and all-purpose only. These round loaves are great for sandwiches served with coffee, tea, or milk.

Steamed corn bread has another appeal—it can be prepared without an oven. Rafters down the Colorado River can steam it over a campfire, while young Scouts can do the same in the backyard.

In France this is called pain de maïs en sac *and is hung in a canvas bag or cloth over boiling water in a pot.*

INGREDIENTS

2 eggs
2¹/₂ cups buttermilk
¹/₂ cup molasses
I cup all-purpose flour
2 cups yellow or white cornmeal
2 teaspoons *each* salt and baking soda
¹/₂ cup raisins

KETTLE AND
BAKING CANS

Kettle with rack, large enough to hold three greased 1-pound coffee cans; aluminum foil held in place with string, rubber bands, or masking tape; rounds of buttered paper placed in bottoms of cans

PREPARATION
20 mins.

Fill the kettle with enough water to come halfway up the sides of the cans later and bring to a boil.

BY HAND
OR MIXER
17 mins.

In a large mixing or mixer bowl beat the eggs, buttermilk, and molasses with the mixer beater or a large wooden spoon until blended. Sift the flour, cornmeal, salt, and baking soda into the liquid mixture, and stir until smooth. Add the raisins and blend.

Pour the batter into the prepared cans, about two-thirds full. Cover tightly with a piece of aluminum foil to prevent steam from leaking into the containers—this can add unwanted moisture.

If using a cloth sack, fill only half full to allow the bread to expand.

STEAMING
3 hours

Place the cans on a rack in the large kettle of boiling water.

The filled sack may be placed in a steamer basket or suspended on a string above the boiling water.

Cover the kettle. Fashion a cover from heavy-weight aluminum foil and tie with a cord.

Steam in continuously boiling water over low heat. If necessary, replenish the water during the steaming.

DRYING
10 mins.

Remove the cans from the water and take off their lids (or peel back the cloth sack). Place them in a 400° oven for 10 minutes to partially dry the loaves.

FINAL STEP

Let the loaves rest in the cans on a metal rack for 15 minutes before turning them out. It may be necessary to loosen the loaves with a knife run around the inside edge of the can; do this carefully.

Slice into rounds and serve. Excellent, too, with Boston baked beans.

Corn Corn Bread   [eight servings]

This rich bread is double "corned" with cornmeal and corn fresh cut off the cob. It can be made with either white or yellow cornmeal, depending on regional preference (white for below the Ohio River, and yellow above). In this recipe I also use an all-purpose white flour milled in Knoxville, Tennessee, and famous throughout the South—White Lily. Other flours do as well but White Lily is more traditional.

INGREDIENTS

1 1/2 cups white or yellow cornmeal
1/2 cup all-purpose flour, White Lily preferred
1 teaspoon *each* salt and sugar
2 tablespoons baking powder
1 cup milk, room temperature
3 eggs, room temperature
1/4 cup heavy cream, room temperature (optional)
1/3 cup butter, melted
2 cups cooked fresh corn kernels (about 3 medium ears)

BAKING PAN

If a thick corn bread is desired, use one 9"-x-9" pan, greased. For thin corn bread, use one 16"-x-12" shallow baking dish or a combination of smaller pans with the equivalent volume, greased. It will be easier to remove servings of the corn bread from the pan if greased wax or parchment paper covers the bottom.

PREHEAT

Preheat oven to 400°.

BY HAND
12 mins.

In a mixing bowl measure the cornmeal, flour, salt, sugar, and baking powder.

Pour the milk into a small bowl and lightly beat in the eggs. Pour this into the bowl of dry ingredients. Beat thoroughly to blend. Pour in the cream, if desired, the butter, and corn kernels and stir into the mixture.

Pour the batter into the pans. The batter will be about ½" deep in the shallow pans, and about 1" in the deeper tin.

BAKING
400°
20–25 mins.

Bake in the oven until the bread is nicely browned and tests done when a wood toothpick or cake testing pin inserted in the bread comes out clean and dry, 20 to 25 minutes.

(If using a convection oven, reduce heat 50°.)

FINAL STEP

Remove the bread from the oven. It should be loose in the pan. Serve hot, cut into rectangles—and with butter on the side. Outstanding!

Gâteau au Maïs   [one small loaf]
(Corn Cake)

Beaten egg whites are the only leaven in this delightful small bread that I found while traveling through the Basque country, in the southwesternmost corner of France. This is the only region in Europe where bakers make as wide a variety of delicious breads prepared with corn as in the United States.

This is a dessert bread that is excellent served with fruit. I had it first with fresh pineapple slices. Superb.

It is sweet but not cloyingly so.

INGREDIENTS

½ cup sugar
¼ teaspoon salt
I cup yellow cornmeal
3 eggs, room temperature
½ cup (I stick) butter or margarine, melted

BAKING PAN

1 round (5½" diameter) charlotte pan or 1 small (7"-x-3") loaf pan, greased or Teflon, bottom lined with buttered wax paper

PREHEAT

Preheat the oven to 375°.

BY HAND
23 mins.

In a large bowl blend the sugar, salt, and ½ cup cornmeal.

Separate the eggs, and drop the yolks into the center of the dry mixture. Put the whites aside in a beater bowl.

Blend the butter or margarine slowly into the cornmeal mixture, drop by drop, as for mayonnaise. Add the balance of cornmeal.

Beat the egg whites until they are stiff; fold into the corn-butter mixture. It will be a thin batter.

Pour the batter into the prepared pan.

BAKING
375°
45 mins.

Place the pan in the center of the oven. Check the *gâteau* after 30 minutes—it should be raised and browning. Fifteen minutes later take from the oven and pierce with a metal skewer or wooden toothpick. If it comes out clean, the bread is baked.

(If using a convection oven, reduce heat 50°.)

FINAL STEP

Unmold onto a metal rack to cool. Slice thinly to serve.

This bread should freeze well but we have never had a slice left over with which to experiment.

BUCKWHEAT BREADS

IN MOST KITCHENS buckwheat is more legend than reality. For many years I thought it was grown only for my Grandmother Condon's buckwheat pancakes. It is sorely under-rated as a flour; it deserves better.

Buckwheat is not a true grain since it is an herb, not a grass. It was discovered by the Chinese in the cool mountain regions of that country about A.D. 1000 and brought to this country from Europe by the Dutch and grown along the Hudson River as early as 1625. The name derives from two words—*boc* (beech) and *whoet* (wheat).

Bauernbrot [two round loaves]

A Sauerteig (starter) begins this Austrian peasant loaf, which has the subtle, not-too-strong flavor of buckwheat. It is a moist bread that is excellent to serve at a buffet or tea. It is heavy, and tasty for a continental breakfast or to eat with cheese and slices of ham.

The loaf has a salty light-tan crust, but a slice reveals a dark brown interior.

INGREDIENTS

1 cup Rye Sour (page 108) (see Note)
4 cups buckwheat flour
2 cups all-purpose flour, approximately
1 package dry yeast
1½ cups hot water (120°–130°)
2 teaspoons salt
1 tablespoon caraway seeds
¼ cup molasses, dark preferred
1 tablespoon salt mixed with ¼ cup water

BAKING SHEET	1 large baking sheet, greased or Teflon
PREPARATION 1½ hours	In a large bowl blend together the buckwheat and white flours and set aside. In a large mixing or mixer bowl dissolve the yeast in the hot water, and add 2 cups of the combined flour mixture. Beat with a wooden spoon or mixer flat beater until smooth; the mixture will have the consistency of a batterlike porridge. If using a processor, attach short plastic blade. Blend the buckwheat and all-purpose flours in a bowl. Measure 2 cups of the flour mixture and the yeast into the processor work bowl. Pulse. Pour in the water and pulse until smooth. Cover the bowl with plastic wrap and let stand for 1½ hours.
BY HAND OR MIXER 10 mins.	Stir down the dough with a spoon, then add ½ cup starter, the salt, caraway seeds, and molasses. Add the remaining flour, 1 cup at a time, until the ball of dough is roughly formed and pulls away from the sides of the bowl. Don't force the dough to accept more of the flour than it needs to be firm—you don't want a cannonball.
KNEADING 8 mins.	Turn the dough onto a floured work surface and knead with a strong push-turn-fold action, or with the dough hook in the electric mixer, 8 minutes. The dough should be firm enough to hold its shape in a round ball. Add more of the flour mixture if needed.
BY PROCESSOR 5 mins.	Pulse and add ½ cup starter to the dough, the salt, caraway seeds, and molasses. While the machine is running, add more of the flour mixture until the dough is carried around the bowl by the thrust of the blade.
KNEADING 50 secs.	Leave the machine on for 50 seconds to knead. Turn off the machine, uncover, and dust the dough with flour before removing it from the bowl.
SHAPING 4 mins.	Divide the dough into equal parts and shape into round balls. Brush the loaves with water and place them on the baking sheet.
RISING 40 mins.	Cover the loaves with a length of wax paper and leave to rise for 40 minutes.
PREHEAT	Preheat the oven to 350° 15 minutes before baking.
BAKING 350° 40 mins.	Bake the loaves in the oven for 10 minutes. Open the oven door and quickly brush them with the salt water. Bake for 30 minutes longer, brushing them with salt water every 10 minutes. Test the loaves for

doneness by inserting a wooden toothpick in the center of the loaf. If it comes out dry and clean, the loaf is done.

(If using a convection oven, reduce heat 50°. Brush the loaves with the salt mixture every 10 minutes, as above.)

FINAL STEP   Remove the bread from the oven and place on a metal rack to cool.
Note: Sauerteig: A quick overnight starter or sponge can be made, if preferred, by combining ¼ cup *each* buckwheat and white flour, 1 package yeast, a pinch of sugar, and enough water to form a thick but wet batter. Cover with plastic wrap and let it work overnight. The starter will be light and frothy in the morning and ready to use in this recipe.

Buckwheat Bread   [4 small loaves]

Maybe it was because buckwheat was a special treat at my Grandmother Condon's house that it holds such a special place in my heart and on my palate. This recipe will bring back memories of buckwheat cakes on a cold winter's morning.

This bread seems to go best with bacon or sausage and eggs. The slices can also be fried in a batter and be as good as any griddle cakes ever served (see Pain Perdu in the "Special Breads" chapter).

The recipe calls for 2 cups from an established starter, but when I don't have one at the ready I make an overnight sponge.

INGREDIENTS   *Sponge:*
2 cups hot water (120°–130°)
2 cups all-purpose flour
1 tablespoon *each* salt and sugar
1 package dry yeast

Dough:
1½ cups hot water (120°–130°)
⅓ cup nonfat dry milk
4 tablespoons brown sugar or sorghum molasses
2 cups buckwheat flour
1 package dry yeast
4 tablespoons butter or margarine, room temperature
2 teaspoons salt
4 cups all-purpose flour, approximately
1 tablespoon butter, melted
2 tablespoons cream or canned milk

BAKING PANS AND TINS	The dough weighs about 4 pounds so I usually plan to make 4 loaves. It is nice to bake part of the dough in 1-pound coffee tins, which make attractive cylindrical loaves to be sliced for sandwiches or French toast. Oil the tins well. Place a round of buttered wax paper in the bottom of the coffee cans so the loaves will fall easily from the cans. For regular 1-pound loaves, use small (7"-x-3") loaf pans, greased or Teflon.
PREPARATION Overnight	To make the sponge, in a bowl mix together all the sponge ingredients. Cover with plastic wrap and leave at room temperature overnight. There will be enough sponge remaining to refrigerate and use for other recipes later.
BY HAND OR MIXER 10 mins.	In a large mixing or mixer bowl pour 2 cups sponge. Add the hot water, the milk, brown sugar or sorghum, and buckwheat flour. Add the yeast and beat 25 strokes, or for 1 minute with the mixer flat beater. Add butter or margarine and salt and stir about 150 strong strokes by hand, or with the mixer until the batter strings from the sides of the bowl. Add 3 cups white flour, 1 cup at a time, working first with the dough hook or hands. The dough will be moist and rough but will clean the sides of the bowl.
KNEADING 8 mins.	Turn the dough onto a working surface. Spread the remaining flour around the edge of the ball of dough and gradually work the flour into the dough as you knead—or as it works under the dough hook in the mixer bowl.

BY PROCESSOR
 4 mins.
	Prepare the overnight sponge, as above.
	     Attach the plastic blade.
	     Pour 2 cups sponge in the processor work bowl and add the water, milk, brown sugar or sorghum, and buckwheat flour. Pulse to blend into a batter. Add the yeast, shortening, and salt. Turn on the machine and, with it running, add about 3 cups white flour, 1 cup at a time, until the dough forms on the blade and is carried around the bowl by its thrust. Add more flour if necessary to form the mass of dough.

KNEADING 50 secs.	Leave the machine running and knead for 50 seconds. The dough may be sticky when turned from the work bowl but a few sprinkles of flour will help form it into a smooth, elastic ball.
FIRST RISING 1 hour	Grease a bowl and drop the dough into it. Cover with plastic wrap and leave at room temperature until the dough has doubled in bulk, about 1 hour.

SHAPING
5 mins.

Turn out the dough, knead briefly and lightly, and shape as desired. If placed in coffee cans, force the dough into the bottom with the fingers so that no pockets of air remain. The dough should reach two-thirds the way up the can. Else place in the loaf pans.

SECOND RISING
45 mins.

Brush the tops of the loaves with the melted butter, cover with wax paper, and leave to double in volume, about 45 minutes. The dough in the coffee tins should be at the top edge.

PREHEAT

Preheat the oven to 375° 20 minutes before baking.

BAKING
375°
45–55 mins.

Bake small loaves for 45 minutes; the larger loaves for about 10 minutes longer. Bake the loaves in the cans for 55 minutes.

Five minutes before the end of baking, brush the tops of the loaves with the cream or canned milk to give the crusts a rich, russet color.

Turn out one loaf from its pan or can and thump the bottom crust with the forefinger. A hard, hollow sound means the bread is baked. If it is not, return the loaf (removed from the pan, if you wish) to the oven for an additional 10 minutes. If the loaves appear to be browning too quickly, cover with a piece of foil or brown paper sack.

(If using a convection oven, reduce heat 50°.)

FINAL STEP

Remove the bread from the oven and turn onto a rack to cool before slicing.

Special Buckwheat Bread
[one medium or four small loaves]

It is the fruit—prunes or raisins—that gives an accent here to the special taste and aroma of buckwheat. For me, the smell of this bread baking in the kitchen is a reminder of a stack of my grandmother's buckwheat pancakes waiting on the breakfast table.

There is no flour other than buckwheat in it, so it is dark chocolate in color. Caution: you must like the uncompromised taste of buckwheat to enjoy this loaf.

INGREDIENTS

¹/₂ cup prunes or raisins
1³/₄ cups buttermilk
¹/₂ cup brown sugar
2¹/₃ cups buckwheat flour
1 teaspoon salt
1 teaspoon baking powder

BAKING PANS	1 medium (8"-x-4") loaf pan, or 1 small (7"-x-3") and 3 miniature (4"-x-2") loaf tins, greased or Teflon, lined with wax paper
BY HAND 15 mins.	Coarsely chop the prunes or raisins, place in a bowl, and soak (plump) the fruit in the buttermilk, about 10 minutes. Stir in the sugar, flour, salt, and baking powder. Pour the batter into the prepared pan or pans and work it into the corners with a spatula. Level off the tops.
PREHEAT	Preheat the oven to 325°, and let the pans rest for 10 minutes.
BAKING 325° 30–45 mins.	Place the pans in the oven and bake for 45 minutes (30 minutes for the miniature loaves), or until the loaves are a rich brown and test done when a wooden toothpick inserted in the center comes out clean and dry. (If using a convection oven, reduce heat 25°.)
FINAL STEP	Remove the bread from the oven. Turn the pans on their sides and gently pull the wax paper to slip the loaves onto the metal rack to cool. While the loaf is good warm from the oven, it is even more so the next day or the day following that.

OAT BREADS

ALL OF THE RECIPES here are made with rolled oats or oatmeal (one and the same) except one which calls for Scotch oatmeal, the cracked and unflattened whole grain. The oat groat is the edible part of the oat kernel, and whole groats become rolled oats.

Oat flour has no gluten strength and is seldom used in bread except in hypoallergenic diets.

English Oatmeal Bread   [two loaves or two dozen buns]

The English love their tea breads, and this is one of the very best. This nice dark loaf of oatmeal, whole-wheat, and white flours has a solid, pleasing bite. The oatmeal, which is not to be seen once it becomes part of the dark dough, is quite evident in the moist texture of the slice. The oatmeal is soaked in milk 2 hours beforehand.

George and Cecilia Scurfield, fine English home bakers and authors of a delightful Little Book of Bread Recipes—Home Baked, *also fashioned the oatmeal dough into "the most delicious buns."*

INGREDIENTS
2 cups oatmeal, plus 2 tablespoons for dusting
2 cups milk
1 package dry yeast
2 tablespoons butter, room temperature
2 teaspoons salt
1 cup whole-wheat flour
2 cups bread or unbleached flour, approximately
1 egg, beaten, mixed with 1 tablespoon water

BAKING PANS	2 small (7"-x-3") baking pans, greased or Teflon, or 1 baking sheet, sprinkled with cornmeal

PREPARATION
2 hours

In a large bowl soak the oatmeal in the milk for 2 hours.

If using a processor, attach the plastic dough blade before soaking the oatmeal in the work bowl.

BY HAND
OR MIXER
15 mins.

Stir the yeast into the oatmeal mixture; add the butter, salt, and whole-wheat flour. Beat in an electric mixer at medium speed for 1 minute, or by hand 100 strokes. Add ½ cup white flour and continue beating for 2 minutes more.

Stop mixer. Stir in the balance of the white flour, ½ cup at a time, first with the spoon and then by hand, or with the flat beater of the mixer. The dough will be a rough, shaggy mass that will clean the sides of the bowl. If, however, the dough continues to be slack and moist, and sticks to your fingers, the blade, or work surface, sprinkle with additional flour.

KNEADING
8 mins.

Put the dough under the dough hook, or turn onto a lightly floured work surface and knead with the rhythmic motion of push-turn-fold. The dough will become smooth and elastic. Occasionally change the kneading rhythm by raising the dough above the table and crashing it down hard against the surface. *Wham!* Knead by hand or under the dough hook for about 8 minutes.

BY PROCESSOR
5 mins.

Pulse to mix the oatmeal. Add the yeast, butter, salt, whole-wheat flour, and ½ cup white flour. Pulse 3 or 4 times to blend thoroughly. With the machine running, add the balance of the flour, ¼ cup at a time, through the feed tube. (It may take all of the flour to form a mass, or it may take less—add the last portion with care.)

KNEADING
50 secs.

When the dough becomes a rough ball and spins around the work bowl on the blade, leave the machine on for 50 seconds to knead. If the dough is sticky when taken from the work bowl, dust with sprinkles of flour to help form it into a smooth ball.

FIRST RISING
1½ hours

Place the dough in the mixing bowl and pat with buttered fingers to keep the surface from crusting. Cover the bowl tightly with plastic wrap and put aside at room temperature until it has risen to about twice its original size, as judged by how far it creeps up the sides of the bowl, 1½ hours. It can also be tested by poking a finger into it—the dent remains when the dough is risen.

SHAPING
5–10 mins.

Punch down the dough, turn it onto the work surface, and knead briefly to press out the bubbles.

For loaves: divide the dough into 2 pieces with a knife. Shape into balls, and let them rest under a towel for 3 to 4 minutes. Form each loaf by pressing a ball under your palms into a flat oval, roughly the length of the baking pan. Fold the oval in half, pinch the seam tightly to seal, tuck under the ends, and place in the pan, seam down.

For buns: roll the dough under the palms into a long sausagelike piece about 2" in diameter. With a sharp knife, cut it into equal lengths (perhaps 1½" long). Roll the small pieces into balls between your palms, or under your cupped palm press the dough hard against the work surface. The buns can be made any size you desire. Place them on the baking sheet spaced apart to give them room to rise.

SECOND RISING
45 mins.

Cover the pans or the buns with wax paper and leave at room temperature until they have risen to double in volume, and for the loaves, until the center of the dough has risen above the level of the edge of the pan, about 45 minutes.

Brush the raised breads with the egg wash and sprinkle with the 2 tablespoons oatmeal.

PREHEAT

Preheat the oven to 400° 20 minutes before baking.

BAKING
400°
30 mins.
350°
20–30 mins.

Bake in the hot oven for 30 minutes, reduce the heat to 350°, and continue baking for another 20 to 30 minutes, or until the loaves are a golden brown and test done. Turn one loaf out of its pan and tap the bottom crust with the forefinger. A hard, hollow sound means it is baked. If the loaves appear to be browning too quickly, cover with a piece of foil or brown sack paper. Midway during baking, and again near the end of it, shift the pans so the loaves are exposed equally to temperature variations in the oven.

(If using a convection oven, reduce heat 50° for each bake period.)

FINAL STEP

Remove the breads from the oven and place on a metal rack to cool.

Scotch Oatmeal Bread
[two medium loaves and one dozen rolls]

There is one kind of food, say the Scots, that is helpful to the brain and to the whole body throughout childhood and adolescence, and that is oatmeal. The Scots believe they have raised oats to the highest perfection and this loaf is a delicious affirmation.

There is no yeast in these loaves, yet they are as fat and pregnant as ones made with yeast. Cooked Potato Starter is the leavening force. However, if the starter is not at hand yeast can be used.

Scotch oatmeal, which is cracked whole-grain oats, is mixed with the starter the night before and, on baking day, blended with maple syrup, ginger, butter, and bread flour. Cinnamon and grated maple sugar (or sprinkles of brown sugar) are sprinkled on rectangles of dough, rolled tightly, and baked. The result is a colorful brown swirl through the loaves.

INGREDIENTS
1 cup boiling water
1 cup Scotch oatmeal (cracked whole-grain oats)
1 cup all-purpose flour
2 tablespoons brown sugar
3/4 cup Cooked Potato Starter (page 241), or 1 package dry yeast
    dissolved in 1/4 cup warm water
1 cup warm water (105°–115°)
1/2 cup nonfat dry milk
1/4 teaspoon ground ginger
1 teaspoon salt
3 tablespoons each soft butter and maple or maple-flavored syrup
4 to 5 cups all-purpose flour or unbleached flour, approximately
1 tablespoon ground cinnamon
1/4 cup grated block maple sugar or loose brown sugar
1/4 cup raisins (optional)
2 tablespoons butter, melted

BAKING PANS
2 medium (8"-x-4") baking pans, greased or Teflon, and 1 baking sheet, sprinkled with cornmeal

PREPARATION
Overnight
The night before, in a medium mixing bowl pour the boiling water over the Scotch oatmeal and stir well. Add ½ cup flour, the brown sugar, and starter (or dissolved yeast). Cover tightly with plastic wrap and leave until morning, about 10 hours.

If using a processor, insert the plastic blade, and measure the boiling water and oatmeal into the work bowl.

Pulse to mix. Add ½ cup flour, the brown sugar, and starter (or yeast). Pulse to blend, scrape down the sides of the bowl, cover, and leave overnight, 10 hours.

BY HAND
OR MIXER
20 mins.
On baking day, turn back the plastic covering, stir down, and add the warm water, dry milk, ginger, and salt. Blend in the butter, syrup, and 2 cups white flour. Stir 150 strong strokes with a wooden spoon or

with a mixer flat beater until the ingredients are well mixed and the batter strings from the sides of the bowl. Gradually add more flour, ½ cup at a time, first with the spoon and then by hand or under the mixer dough hook, until the dough forms a soft mass.

KNEADING
8 mins.

Knead with the dough hook or turn the dough out onto a work surface spread with flour. Keep flour dusted on the dough and hands until it is no longer sticky. It will be soft, elastic, and feel alive under your hands.

BY PROCESSOR
4 mins.

On baking day, add the warm water, dry milk, ginger, and salt to the work bowl. Pulse. Drop in the butter, syrup, and 2 cups flour. Pulse 5 or 6 times, or until the batter strings from the sides of the bowl. Add more flour, ½ cup at a time, until the dough forms a soft mass and is carried around the bowl by the force of the blade.

KNEADING
50 secs.

With the processor on, knead for 50 seconds.

FIRST RISING
1 hour

Place the dough in a greased bowl, cover with plastic wrap, and leave at room temperature until it is light and double in bulk, about 1 hour.

SHAPING
20 mins.

Punch down the dough, turn it out onto a floured work surface, and divide into 3 equal pieces—2 for loaves and 1 for rolls.

For loaves: roll each piece into a rectangle, sprinkle with cinnamon and grated maple sugar or brown sugar. (Raisins may also be sprinkled over the dough.) Roll the rectangle tightly, pinching the seam together and tucking under the ends. Drop into the pans, and brush the tops with the melted butter.

For rolls: divide the remaining portion of dough into the desired number of rolls, roll into balls under the palm of one hand, cupped, and pressing firmly down against the work surface. Brush with the melted butter and dip the tops into the maple or brown sugar. Sprinkle lightly with cinnamon.

SECOND RISING
50 mins.

Cover the loaves and rolls with wax paper and put them aside to rise to at least double in volume, about 50 minutes.

PREHEAT

Preheat the oven to 350° 20 minutes before baking.

BAKING
350°
30–60 mins.

Place the loaves and rolls in the oven. Bake the loaves for about 1 hour; the rolls will take no longer than 30 minutes. Test for doneness by turning over a loaf or roll and tapping the bottom crust. If it is hard and sounds hollow, it is baked. If the crust is soft and not browned, return to the oven for 5 or 10 minutes more.

(It is unlikely both loaf pans and baking sheet will fit into the convection oven at the same time, so cover and place the pan of rolls in the refrigerator while the loaves are baking. Reduce heat 50° and bake the loaves for 50 minutes, the rolls for about 25 minutes.)

FINAL STEP

Remove the breads from the oven. Turn out of the pans and place on a metal rack to cool.

Buttermilk Oaten Cakes [four "farls," or quarters]

I once drove a horse and an Irish gypsy wagon across County Cork. I loved the food but not the stubborn horse that sensed immediately that I knew nothing about his kind. Plodding along the back lanes, I discovered Buttermilk Oaten Bread or "cakes." They made up for the horse!

The traditional Irish oaten cakes were baked in front of the turf fire. The ones I sampled were not but delicious nevertheless. My Irish baker said to eat the cakes hot, with plenty of butter. He also said he urged parents to bake them for children: "They are excellent for young children, as they must be chewed well, so they strengthen the jaws and teeth."

This County Cork recipe was originally in pints and gills, but here it is in cups and fractions thereof.

INGREDIENTS

2 cups quick or old-fashioned oatmeal
1¼ cups buttermilk or sour milk
2½ cups bread or all-purpose flour
1 teaspoon salt
1 teaspoon baking soda

BAKING SHEET

1 baking sheet, greased, or Teflon, or sprinkled with cornmeal

PREPARATION
Overnight

In a bowl mix the oatmeal and buttermilk or sour milk, cover tightly with plastic wrap, and let stand overnight, until ready to proceed the next day.

PREHEAT

Preheat the oven to 350°.

BY HAND
10 mins.

In a separate bowl mix the flour, salt, and baking soda together, then work it gradually into the oatmeal mixture with a wooden spoon or your fingers. If the mixture is dry, add a little more milk. Keep the mixture soft.

SHAPING
5 mins.

When the dough is smooth, pat it into a round loaf about 1" thick. With a sharp knife, cut the dough into quarters, or farls, and place the sections side by side on the baking sheet.

BAKING	Bake in the oven until the quarters are a medium to deep brown, about
350°	40 minutes. To test for doneness, turn one farl over and tap. A hollow
40 mins.	sound means it is baked.

(If using a convection oven, reduce heat 50°.)

FINAL STEP	Remove the bread from the oven. Place the farls on a wire rack to cool.

When they have cooled, break them open with your fingers rather than cutting them. Slather with butter.

Raisin Oatmeal Bread   [one large or two small loaves]

The knife slicing the loaf will cut through the rolled oats to leave an intriguing pattern of light streaks against the almost-black bread. The bread has a molasses flavor that comes on stronger than do the 3 flours, the buttermilk, or the raisins and nuts. Nevertheless, combined in this moist, compact loaf, they make an unusual and delicious bread. The molasses can be reduced by as much as 1/4 cup to give a more balanced flavor.

INGREDIENTS	I cup *each* all-purpose flour, rye flour, and oatmeal
	I teaspoon *each* salt, baking soda, and baking powder
	1/4 cup sugar
	1/2 cup dark molasses
	1 1/4 cups buttermilk
	I cup raisins
	1/2 cup chopped walnuts

BAKING PANS	1 large (9"-x-5") or 2 small (7"-x-3") pans, buttered or Teflon, lined
	with buttered wax paper along sides and bottom

PREHEAT	Preheat the oven to 350°.

BY HAND	In a large bowl combine the flours, oatmeal, salt, baking soda, baking
20 mins.	powder, and sugar.

In a small bowl mix the molasses and buttermilk, and pour into the dry ingredients. Blend but don't beat. Add the raisins and walnuts. Stir together thoroughly.

Pour the batter into the pan, or pans, and level with a spoon or spatula.

BAKING	Place the pans in the moderate oven and bake for 1 hour. Smaller
350°	loaves will require only 45 minutes. Test for doneness with a wooden
45–60 mins.	toothpick.

(If using a convection oven, reduce heat 50°.)

FINAL STEP

Remove the bread from the oven. Allow the bread to cool for 15 minutes in the pan; then turn it on its side and tug free with the wax paper strips.

This bread is even more delicious the second or third day.

Orange Oatmeal Bread   [one large or two small loaves]

The orange zest, fruit, and juice give this loaf a delightful piquancy. The oatmeal gives it a rough chewy texture, though each slice is moist.

INGREDIENTS

1 orange
2 tablespoons plus $3/4$ cup sugar
$1^1/_2$ cups all-purpose flour
1 tablespoon baking powder
$^1/_2$ teaspoon salt
$^1/_4$ teaspoon baking soda
1 cup rolled oats
2 eggs
2 tablespoons butter, melted
$^2/_3$ cup warm water (105°–115°)

BAKING PANS

1 large (9"-x-5") or 2 small (7"-x-3") baking pans, buttered, then lined with buttered wax paper along sides and bottom

BY HAND
28 mins.

Grate the orange for its zest, then peel. Reserve zest. Cut off the outer white membrane and, with a sharp knife, cut the meat out of each section, leaving the tough sectional membranes intact. Discard the membranes and seeds. Cut the flesh into small pieces and add the orange zest. Sprinkle with the 2 tablespoons sugar and mix well. Set aside.

In a large bowl measure the flour, ¾ cup sugar, baking powder, salt, and baking soda. Stir in the rolled oats. In a separate bowl lightly beat the eggs and mix with the melted butter, reserved orange mixture, and water. Blend the liquid into the dry ingredients.

Pour the batter into the prepared loaf pan.

PREHEAT

Preheat the oven to 350° while letting the pan(s) rest for 10 minutes.

BAKING
350°
45–60 mins.

Bake the loaf or loaves in the oven until a wooden toothpick or cake testing pin inserted in the center of the loaf comes out clean and dry, 1 hour. The baking time will be about 15 minutes less for small loaves.

(If using a convection oven, reduce heat 50° and bake the large loaves for 50 minutes and the smaller ones for 35 minutes.)

FINAL STEP   Remove the bread from the oven. Carefully remove the bread from the pan(s), tugging gently on the wax paper to loosen it. Allow to cool slightly on a metal rack before serving.

Delicious served warm, spread with sweet butter.

Maple Oatmeal Bread   [two loaves]

Maple syrup—the truly natural product with nothing added—was discovered by the Indians who lived among the vast maple forests in North America, but it was the pioneer or Early American housewife who made the syrup's use into an art. Sugar was scarce, if available at all, but maple syrup was plentiful, and with it she made breads, biscuits, and pies and poured it over pancakes.

A fine example of this art is Maple Oatmeal Bread, which comes from an old New Hampshire farmhouse now turned inn—Staffords in the Field, which looks out over meadows and orchards and maple trees in the shadow of Mount Chocorua.

The loaf is a creation of the inn's baker, Ramona Stafford (her mother is the cook), who adapted it from a century-old recipe. The bread is baked for the evening meal at the inn, but Ramona says it is even better for lunch sandwiches—sweet and hearty with a chewy crust.

The loaf has an interesting texture, thanks to the oatmeal, and a light sweetness in taste, thanks to the syrup.

INGREDIENTS
2½ cups boiling water
1 cup quick or regular rolled oats
1 package dry yeast
¾ cup maple syrup (see Note)
2 teaspoons salt
1 tablespoon cooking oil
5 cups bread or all-purpose flour, approximately

BAKING PANS   2 medium (8"-x-4") loaf pans, greased or Teflon

PREPARATION
1¼ hours
In a large bowl pour the boiling water over the oatmeal and set aside to soak for 1 hour.

Sprinkle the yeast over the cooled oatmeal and stir to mix. Add the maple syrup, salt, cooking oil, and 3 cups flour. Blend all the ingredients. It will have the consistency of a heavy batter.

FIRST RISING
1 hour
Cover the bowl with plastic wrap and set aside to rise for about 1 hour.

BY HAND OR MIXER 10 mins.	Add additional flour, ½ cup at a time, to form a dough that can be lifted from the bowl and placed on the surface to knead until the dough is smooth and elastic, about 10 minutes. Add more flour if the ball of dough is sticky. The dough may also be placed under a dough hook in a mixer for an equal length of time. The dough should clean the bowl in the final stages of kneading.

BY PROCESSOR
5 mins.
	Prepare the oatmeal mixture, as above, and let rise.
	    Attach the short plastic dough blade.
	    After the soft batterlike dough has risen, transfer it to the processor work bowl. Add 2 cups flour and close the cover. Pulse to blend. Add flour through the feed tube, ¼ cup at a time, until the dough forms a ball and rides on the dough blade. Add no more flour than necessary to achieve this. It must be soft and elastic—not a hard ball.

KNEADING 50 secs.	Keep the machine running and knead for 50 seconds. The dough will be smooth and elastic.
SHAPING 5 mins.	Divide the dough into 2 pieces and shape into loaves. Drop each into a prepared pan. Push the dough into the corners.
SECOND RISING 45 mins.	Cover the pans with wax or parchment paper and leave at room temperature until the dough reaches the edge of the pan, about 45 minutes.
PREHEAT	Preheat the oven to 350° 15 minutes before baking.
BAKING 350° 40–50 mins.	This is a fairly slow oven, so allow 40 to 50 minutes for the bread to bake into a light brown loaf. Midway through baking, turn the pans end for end to balance the heat on the loaves. Turn one loaf out of its pan and tap the bottom crust with a forefinger. A hard, hollow sound means the bread is baked. If not, return to the oven for an additional 5 or 10 minutes. (If using a convection oven, reduce heat 50°.)
FINAL STEP	Remove the bread from the oven and turn the loaves from the pans. Place the loaves on a metal rack to cool before serving. The bread toasts beautifully. It can be kept frozen for an indefinite period at 0°. An admirable loaf. *Note:* While the bread can be made with the diluted "maple syrup" found on supermarket shelves, the delicate but definite flavor of real maple syrup will be lost.

Cinnamon Oatmeal Bread   [two loaves]

Miss Lucetta J. Teagarden, of Austin, Texas, has been my friend for years, though we have never met. She was one of my first readers and we have corresponded ever since. She is always on the hunt for recipes she likes, and which I, too, might like.

This Cinnamon Oatmeal Bread is one of them. She and a friend bake 15 loaves each year for Christmas giving, but I think it is too good to hold just for a special occasion. It is a special bread for anytime.

The large amount of oatmeal creates the effect of finely chopped nuts, and gives a slightly nutty flavor.

INGREDIENTS

1½ cups rolled oats
1½ cups boiling water
3 tablespoons butter or margarine
3 tablespoons honey
1 tablespoon brown sugar
2 teaspoons salt
½ cup raisins
1 package dry yeast
2 eggs, room temperature
4 to 5 cups bread or all-purpose flour, approximately
3 tablespoons butter, melted
1 cup granulated sugar
2 tablespoons ground cinnamon

BAKING PANS

2 medium (8"-x-4") loaf pans, greased or Teflon (this dough makes excellent rolls so half could be shaped into a loaf, while the balance could be made into small rolls)

PREPARATION
10 mins.

In a large bowl mix together the rolled oats and boiling water. Stir to blend, and add the butter or margarine, honey, brown sugar, salt, and raisins.

If using a processor, attach the plastic dough blade; pulse the rolled oats and boiling water together in the work bowl. Let stand for a few moments to be certain the oats have absorbed the water. Remove the cover and add the butter or margarine, honey, brown sugar, salt, and yeast. Pulse.

Let the mixture cool to no more than 130°.

BY HAND
OR MIXER
12 mins.

Add the yeast. Add the eggs and 2 cups flour. With a wooden spoon or with the mixer flat beater, stir vigorously for 2 to 3 minutes.

Work in additional flour, ½ cup at a time, with the spoon first and then with your hands—or dough hook, if you are using a mixer. The dough will become a soft mass that can be picked up and placed on the work surface, or left under the hook.

KNEADING
8 mins.

Knead with a strong push-turn-fold rhythm, adding flour if the dough is slack or wet and sticky. Knead for 8 minutes, or until the dough is soft and elastic. If under the dough hook in the mixer, add sprinkles of flour if the dough should cling to the sides of the bowl.

BY PROCESSOR
5 mins.

With the machine running, add the eggs and 2 cups flour. Add additional flour, ¼ cup at a time, until the dough becomes a soft mass that whirls with the blade and, at the same time, cleans the sides of the bowl. Work in the raisins by hand.

KNEADING
50 secs.

Process to knead for 50 seconds.

FIRST RISING
I hour

Place the dough in a buttered bowl, cover the bowl with plastic wrap, and put the dough aside to rise at room temperature until double in bulk, about 1 hour.

SHAPING
10 mins.

Turn the dough out of the bowl and divide into 2 pieces. With the hands and a rolling pin, shape each piece into a rectangle about 8" wide and 12" long. Butter the dough and sprinkle on the sugar and cinnamon.

Roll up the dough as for a jelly roll, and press the seams securely together. Drop each into a pan, seam down, and push into the corners and ends with your fingers.

SECOND RISING
45 mins.

Cover the pans with wax paper and put aside to rise until the center of the dough is slightly above the edge, about 45 minutes.

PREHEAT

Preheat the oven to 375° 20 minutes before baking.

BAKING
375°
40 mins.

Bake on the middle rack of the oven until the crusts are nicely browned, about 40 minutes. The bottom crust may be sticky with the melted sugar (which will harden as the loaf cools), but tap the crust to make certain it sounds hard and hollow.

(If using a convection oven, reduce heat 50°.)

FINAL STEP

When the loaves come from the oven, brush with more melted butter and turn out onto a metal rack to cool before serving.

BLENDED GRAIN BREADS

BLENDED GRAIN BREADS are coarser, denser, and darker than most other loaves. The taste is of no one grain but a blend of them all.

In these recipes there are a total of seven different flours and cereals; Sennebec Hill has six and War Bread four. Boston Brown Bread, while a steamed loaf, is in this chapter because it is made with cornmeal and rye and whole-wheat flours.

Dark Grains Bread   [two medium loaves]

With the consistency of a fine pumpernickel, Dark Grains Bread is much more than just another rye loaf. Here is a bread made of buckwheat, whole wheat, wheat germ, white, and only a modest portion of rye (the chief ingredient of many other dark and heavy loaves).

This dough is sticky and stiff to work but it rises surprisingly well, more than 1 inch above the edge of the pan in less than 1 hour. It must be kneaded by hand, being too heavy for a dough hook or food processor.

INGREDIENTS

2¹/₂ cups hot water (120°–130°)
¹/₃ cup nonfat dry milk
¹/₄ cup molasses, dark preferred
1 tablespoon salt
¹/₂ cup *each* wheat germ and buckwheat flour
2 packages dry yeast
2 tablespoons shortening, room temperature
1 cup rye flour
3 cups whole-wheat flour
1 to 1¹/₂ cups bread or all-purpose flour, approximately

BAKING PANS	2 medium (8"-x-4") metal or Pyrex baking pans, greased or Teflon

BY HAND
20 mins.

Into a large bowl pour the water, and measure and stir in the dry milk, molasses, salt, wheat germ, buckwheat flour, and yeast. Stir 50 strokes to blend well. Add the shortening. Add the rye and whole-wheat flours gradually, ½ cup at a time.

The batterlike dough will be thick—stir it 150 times until it pulls in strands from the sides of the bowl. Add the white flour, ½ cup at a time, first with the spoon and then by hand. It will create a rough mass that will not adhere to the sides of the bowl. If it is slack or wet, add sprinkles of white flour.

KNEADING
8 mins.

Spread white flour on the work surface and turn the dough onto it. To make the ball of dough easier to work, keep flour dusted on the dough, work surface, and hands while you knead. Shortly the dough will lose its stickiness. It will, however, remain firm and dense throughout the kneading. Knead for 8 minutes. At no point will it become either as elastic or as responsive as white dough. Because it is so sticky, use a dough scraper or metal spatula to keep the work surface scraped clean during kneading.

FIRST RISING
1 hour

Place the dough in the mixing bowl, pat it well with buttered fingers, cover the bowl tightly with plastic wrap, and leave at room temperature until the dough has doubled in bulk, about 1 hour.

SHAPING
6 mins.

Knock down the dough in the mixing bowl, divide into 2 equal pieces, flatten each into an oval, and fold in half. Pinch the seams together and plump each into a loaf, seam down. Place in the pans.

SECOND RISING
50 mins.

Cover the pans with wax paper and let double in volume.

PREHEAT

Preheat the oven to 375° 20 minutes before baking.

BAKING
375°
50 mins.

Place the loaves in the oven for 50 minutes. Test for doneness by turning one loaf out of its pan and thumping it on the bottom crust with a forefinger. A hard, hollow sound means the bread is baked.

(If using a convection oven, reduce heat 50°.)

FINAL STEP

Remove the bread from the oven and place on a metal rack to cool.

This is a delicious rough-textured bread that is excellent for sandwiches, especially served open-faced with sliced meats and cheeses at buffets.

Onion Triticale Bread   [one medium or two small loaves]

Triticale, a strange and relatively new word in the lexicon of the home baker, is a grain—a hybrid of wheat and rye, high in nutrients and fiber. Its name is a combination of the Latin words for the two grains. Triticale (rhymes with "daily") flour is superior for pastry doughs, with a higher protein content than either rye or wheat. However, its gluten content is low and requires gentler kneading. Triticale is most often found in health food stores and occasionally among the bulk grains in supermarkets.

In this recipe the triticale berries, not the flour, are used, and the leavening power comes from the wheat flour. This is an onion-flavored loaf that permeates the kitchen with good smells, delights with its good taste, and is especially good toasted.

A food processor does double duty in this recipe since it both chops the onions and "grinds" the triticale berries after they have been softened overnight in water.

INGREDIENTS	¹/₂ cup (3¹/₂ ounces) triticale berries ¹/₄ cup (¹/₂ stick) butter, room temperature 2 medium onions, finely chopped 2¹/₂ to 3 cups bread or all-purpose flour, approximately 1 package dry yeast 1¹/₂ teaspoons salt ²/₃ cup buttermilk, heated to tepid
BAKING PANS OR SHEET	1 medium (8"-x-4") or 2 small bread tins, greased or Teflon; or 1 baking sheet, greased
PREPARATION Overnight	Put the berries in a bowl, add hot tap water, and let stand overnight at room temperature. The berries will almost double in volume. (The soaked and drained berries may be stored and sealed in a plastic bag, for up to 5 days in the refrigerator.) Drain the berries the following day and set aside. In a medium skillet heat the butter over moderate heat. Add the chopped onions and cook, stirring, for about 5 minutes, or until very soft, but not browned. Set aside to cool to room temperature. Chop the soft berries by hand or put through a food grinder with a large grinder plate. Set aside.
BY HAND OR MIXER 8 mins.	Measure 1½ cups of flour into a mixing or mixer bowl and stir in the yeast and salt. By hand or with the mixer flat beater blend all but 2 tablespoons of the onions and all the chopped berries with this mixture.

Stir in the warmed buttermilk to make thick batter. If you are using the mixer, attach the dough hook. Add flour, ¼ cup at a time, until a rough, shaggy dough is formed.

KNEADING
8 mins.

Turn the dough onto a floured work surface, or leave in the mixer with the dough hook attached. Knead the dough for 8 minutes. If it is sticky, add sprinkles of flour. The dough will become a soft, elastic mass that will not stick to the hands nor to the sides of the mixing bowl. The dough will form a ball around the dough hook as it revolves.

BY PROCESSOR
5 mins.

Prepare the berries and the onions, as above.
Attach the steel blade.
Measure 1½ cups flour into the work bowl and add the yeast and salt. Pulse to blend. Scrape the triticale berries into this mixture and process for 30 seconds until the mixture is finely ground. Add all but 2 tablespoons of the sautéed onions. Pulse 4 or 5 times. Add the balance of the flour, ¼ cup at a time, until the dough forms a ball that rides with the blade, and at the same time cleans the sides of the bowl.

KNEADING
45 secs.

Process for 45 seconds to knead.

FIRST RISING
1 hour

Drop the ball of dough into a greased work bowl, cover with plastic wrap, and put aside to double in volume, about 1 hour.

SHAPING
4 mins.

The dough may be patted into a ball or rolled into a *baguette,* and placed directly on the baking sheet. Or it can be formed into 1 or 2 loaves and placed in the prepared pan(s).
Spread the balance of the cooked onions over the top of the loaves.

SECOND RISING
45 mins.

Cover the loaf or loaves with wax or parchment paper, and put aside to double in size, 45 minutes.

PREHEAT

Preheat the oven to 375° about 20 minutes before baking.

BAKING
375°
30–40 mins.

Place the loaves in the moderately hot oven until they are nicely browned and sound hollow when rapped on the bottom, 30 minutes. Turn the loaf from the pan. If you wish the sides to be browner, return it to the oven without the pan for 10 minutes.
(If using a convection oven, reduce heat 50°.)

FINAL STEP

Remove the bread from the oven and cool on a wire rack.
It is delicious as is or toasted. It may be frozen for several months at 0°.

Red River Pumpernickel Bread   [one large loaf]

Red River is a fertile valley in Canada that gives its name to an uncommonly good cereal which, in turn, makes an uncommonly good loaf of almost-black pumpernickel. Red River Cereal is a blend of cracked wheat, cracked rye, and whole flax. Fiber galore! Nothing added and nothing taken away.

Although I have suggested a large pan, the bread can be baked in medium or small tins.

INGREDIENTS	3 cups Red River Cereal
	1 teaspoon salt
	3 cups boiling water
	1/4 cup molasses
	2 teaspoons baking soda
	1 cup whole-wheat flour
BAKING PAN	1 large (9"-x-5") bread pan (or smaller tins of choice), greased
PREPARATION 2 hours–overnight	At least 2 hours before baking (or overnight) blend together in a mixing or mixer bowl the cereal, salt, hot water, and molasses. Cover with plastic wrap and put aside for the liquid to soften the grains.
PREHEAT	Preheat the oven to 275° about 20 minutes before baking.
BY HAND 12 mins.	With a wooden spoon stir the baking soda and whole-wheat flour into the cereal. It will be thick, but stir it sufficiently to blend all of the ingredients together. (It is not worth the cleaning to use either the electric mixer or food processor on this recipe.)
	Spoon or pour the mixture into the prepared pan. Push into the corners and smooth the top with a spatula. Settle the batter by tapping the pan gently against the table.
BAKING 275° 2½–3 hours	This will be in the oven for about 3 hours.
	Cover the pan with foil drawn tightly over the top. Place in the oven. After 2½ hours turn back the foil and check the loaf for doneness. It should be firm and a testing pin stuck into the center of the loaf will come out clean. If not, return it to the oven for up to an additional 30 minutes.
	Uncover the loaf for the last 15 minutes to remove the excess moisture gathered under the foil.
	(If using a convection oven, reduce heat 50°.)
FINAL STEP	The loaf will be fragile while still hot, so place the pan on a metal rack to cool before turning the bread out.

Wrapped in plastic the loaf will remain fresh in the refrigerator for a fortnight. While it can be frozen, fresh-baked and fresh-served is best.

The loaf is waxy when cut, so clean the knife under running water after cutting each slice.

Multi-Grain Bread   [three cylindrical loaves]

This golden and delicious loaf did not carry the Multi-Grain name when I first came upon it, but it seemed more descriptive than Trudi's Bread, which found its way to my kitchen in a manner that makes it impossible to trace the origin. I am sorry, for I would like to have personally thanked Trudi for this inspired loaf of many flours and cereals.

Thank you, Trudi.

Millet, not usually found in breads in the United States, is remarkable for its high protein content (16 to 22 percent). It thrives in tropical and arid countries and in this country is more often a feed crop.

INGREDIENTS

1 cup rolled oats
1 cup barley flour
1 cup millet
1 tablespoon brown sugar
2 teaspoons salt
2 cups hot water (120°–130°)
1/3 cup cooking oil, corn preferred
3 packages dry yeast
1 1/2 cups fresh or instant mashed potatoes
2 cups whole-wheat flour
3/4 cup rye flour
2 cups bread or all-purpose flour, approximately

BAKING CANS

Three 1-pound coffee cans, or cylindrical molds of equal volume, greased, lined with a buttered disc of wax paper cut to fit into the bottom of each (regular bread pans can be used, of course)

BY HAND
OR MIXER
12 mins.

Into a large mixing or mixer bowl measure the oats, barley, millet, brown sugar, and salt. Pour in the hot water and add the cooking oil. Stir to blend. Sprinkle in the yeast, and dissolve in the liquid. Add the mashed potatoes.

Measure in the whole-wheat and rye flours, and stir with a wooden spoon for 100 strong strokes, or 2 minutes with the flat beater of the mixer.

Add the white flour, ½ cup at a time, to form a shaggy mass that can be lifted from the bowl and placed on the work surface, or use the mixer dough hook. If the dough is sticky or slack, add sprinkles of flour.

KNEADING
8 mins.

On a floured work surface knead the dough with a strong push-turn-fold motion for about 8 minutes. It will not be as elastic as an all-white flour bread. Or knead with the dough hook for an equal length of time.

BY PROCESSOR
10 mins.

Attach the plastic dough blade.

Measure all of the ingredients into the work bowl with the exception of the rye, whole-wheat, and white flours, and pulse several times to thoroughly mix. With the processor on, pour all of the rye flour and 1 cup whole wheat through the feed tube. Add the white flour, a small portion at a time, until the dough forms into a mass that is swiftly carried around the bowl by the force of the blade. It will clean the sides of the bowl at the same time. If dry flour remains along the bottom edges of the bowl, stop the machine and pull it into the center with a rubber spatula.

KNEADING
45 secs.

Keep the machine running and knead for 45 seconds. Even though the dough has been kneaded for the proper length of time in the work bowl, it may be sticky when turned out on the work surface. A few sprinkles of flour will make it manageable.

FIRST RISING
1½ hours

Place the dough in a greased bowl, cover tightly with plastic wrap, and leave at room temperature until it has doubled in volume, about 1½ hours.

SHAPING
10 mins.

Turn the dough onto a floured work surface. Determine how much dough is needed to fill a can slightly more than half full. Cut 3 such portions from the dough. Place any remaining dough in an appropriate small loaf pan or brioche tin.

Pat each dough piece into a ball smaller than the diameter of the can. Drop it in, and force the dough into the bottom with fingers outstretched. Pat the dough to make it level.

SECOND RISING
1 hour

Cover the cans with wax paper and put aside to rise to the edge of the can (no further), about 1 hour.

PREHEAT

Preheat the oven to 375° 20 minutes before baking.

BAKING
375°
45 mins.

Since this bread will rise 1" or so higher than the tall coffee cans, be certain there is headroom for the loaves. It is better to bake them on a lower rack than have them try to push their way against the top of the oven.

Place the cans in the oven and bake until the bread is raised and nicely browned, about 45 minutes. Turn one of the loaves from its container and tap the bottom with a forefinger. If it is hard and crusty and sounds hollow, the loaves are done. If you wish a browner crust, return the loaves to the oven for an additional 10 minutes, without the cans.

(If using a convection oven, reduce heat 50°. Few convection ovens will accommodate the cylindrical cans on the lower shelf, so it is better to remove the shelf and place the can directly on the bottom pan.)

FINAL STEP

Gently turn the loaves from the coffee cans. Allow to cool before slicing.

Baked Brown Bread   [one large round loaf]

There is one major difference between Baked Brown Bread (also called "Dutch oven bread") and Boston brown bread—Baked is baked and Boston is steamed. This hearty, wholesome dark loaf is filled with raisins and nuts. It does not, however, have the softness nor fine texture of a steamed bread.

The baking begins in a cold oven; the heat is turned on at a moderate setting for only about an hour, half the time it takes to make the steamed version.

INGREDIENTS

¹/₂ cup yellow or white cornmeal
1¹/₂ cups all-purpose flour
1 cup *each* rye and whole-wheat flour
1 cup firmly packed brown sugar
1 cup molasses
2 teaspoons *each* baking soda and salt
2 cups buttermilk
1 cup broken walnuts

BAKING CONTAINER

1 Dutch oven (9" diameter) or equivalent covered casserole, greased

BY HAND
18 mins.

In a large bowl measure the cornmeal, all-purpose flour, rye and whole-wheat flours, brown sugar, molasses, baking soda, and salt. Pour in the buttermilk and mix well. Stir in the walnuts.

Pour the mixture into the Dutch oven or casserole. Cover. Do *not* preheat the oven.

BAKING 350° I hour	Place the bread in a cold oven. Turn the heat to 350° and bake the bread for about 1 hour. Test for doneness with a skewer or toothpick inserted in the loaf. If the probe comes out clean and dry, the bread is done. If moist particles cling to it, return the loaf to the oven for 5 or 10 minutes more. Test again. (If using a convection oven, reduce heat 50°.)
FINAL STEP	Remove the bread from the oven. This is a rather large loaf, so use care in removing from the Dutch oven to place it on the wire rack to cool.

Boston Brown Bread   [two cylindrical loaves]

Rye is the heart and soul of New England's legendary steamed bread, for it was the one grain that could be grown with relative ease in the cold climate. This bread began with the Puritans and has been handed down from one generation of cooks to the next. The version that is baked, not steamed, is above.

The rye is mixed with whole-wheat flour and cornmeal, and steamed on the top of the stove for about 2 hours to produce a moist brown cylinder that is spongy to the touch when done.

Two 1-pound coffee cans are my molds. Raisins are optional.

Serve this bread warm with a pot of molasses-flavored beans or a boiled dinner. It will more than justify its heritage.

INGREDIENTS	I cup cornmeal I cup rye flour I ½ teaspoons baking soda I teaspoon salt I cup whole-wheat or graham flour ³/₄ cup molasses, dark preferred 2 cups buttermilk or sour milk, room temperature I cup raisins, dusted with flour (optional)
BAKING CANS	Two 1-quart cylindrical molds, no. 2 cans, or 1-pound coffee cans, greased, each lined with a disk of buttered wax paper cut to fit the bottom of the container
BY HAND 15 mins.	In a large bowl sift together the cornmeal, rye flour, baking soda, and salt. Add the whole-wheat or graham flour.

In a small bowl stir the molasses into the buttermilk or sour milk. When thoroughly blended, pour it slowly, a little at a time, into the dry ingredients. Stir just enough to blend. Don't overstir. Add the raisins, if desired.

SHAPING
15 mins.

Divide the batter between the 2 cans or molds. The mix should come to slightly more than half the height of the coffee can. Double a piece of foil and press it tightly across the top of each can. Tie each foil top securely in place with a length of cord. Don't puncture the foil.

STEAMING
2 hours

In the bottom of a large kettle with cover place a rack on which the cans can rest. Pour in hot water up to half the height of the cans or molds, and bring the water to a slow boil. Cover. It may be necessary to add more hot water to the kettle during the 2-hour period. Steam until the bread is springy to the touch and no longer sticky. Probe one loaf with a wooden toothpick or metal skewer—if it comes out clean and dry, the loaves are done.

FINAL STEP

Remove the bread from the kettle and allow the tins to cool for a few minutes before turning them on their sides and slipping the breads out. Work with care because the loaves are fragile. Place them on a cooling rack and, ideally, serve warm slices.

Wheat and Oat Bread   [two medium loaves]

The raisins and the oatmeal are plumped by the boiling water in this recipe for a light brown loaf made with three wheat products—bran, whole-wheat flour, and white flour. When I first tasted this loaf years ago, it was called "health bread." I thought it deserved a better name.

This bread is a bit on the sweet side because of the $^3/_4$ cup molasses, a rather heavy portion that can be reduced to $^1/_2$ or $^1/_4$ cup.

INGREDIENTS

1 cup oatmeal
2 teaspoons salt
2 tablespoons shortening, room temperature
1 cup raisins
1 cup bran
3 cups boiling water
2 packages dry yeast
$^3/_4$ cup molasses
1 cup whole-wheat flour
5 to 6 cups bread or all-purpose flour, approximately

BAKING PANS	2 medium (8"-x-4") loaf tins, greased or Teflon
PREPARATION 30 mins.	In a large mixing or mixer bowl combine the oatmeal, salt, shortening, raisins, and bran; pour the boiling water over this mixture. Stir and set aside to cool to lukewarm. Test the mixture with a thermometer (or finger) to make certain it is not above 130°. Add the yeast and molasses.

If using a processor, plump the raisins alone in 2 cups boiling water for 30 minutes and drain.

This recipe may be too large for some food processors. If so, reduce the ingredients by half, with the exception of the yeast. The order of ingredients varies from above. The raisins are added to the dough *after* it has been kneaded.

Attach the short plastic dough blade. In the work bowl combine the oatmeal, salt, shortening, and bran. Pour the boiling water into the bowl—and allow to sit until lukewarm. This may take 30 minutes or so. (Meanwhile, plump the raisins.)

BY HAND OR MIXER 6 mins.	Stir in the whole-wheat flour and 2 cups white flour. Stir by hand or with the flat beater in an electric mixer. When it is a smooth batter, add additional flour ½ cup at a time, to make a rough mass that cleans the sides of the mixing bowl. If it is slack and inclined to be sticky, add liberal sprinkles of flour.
KNEADING 8 mins.	Lightly flour the work surface and turn the dough into the center of it, or leave it under the mixer's dough hook. Knead until smooth and elastic, about 8 minutes.
BY PROCESSOR 5 mins.	When the oatmeal mixture has cooled sufficiently, add the yeast and molasses. Pulse to blend. With the machine running, add the whole-wheat flour and 2 cups white flour. Gradually add more flour, as needed, to make a rough mass that will ride on the blade and clean the sides of the bowl.
KNEADING 2–3 mins.	Process to knead for 45 seconds. Turn the dough from the work bowl, sprinkle with flour, and press flat with the palms. Spread the raisins over the dough; turn in the sides to envelop the raisins. Knead the dough until the raisins are scattered evenly throughout.
FIRST RISING 1 hour	Place the dough in a greased bowl. Turn the dough once to film the entire ball. Cover the bowl tightly with plastic wrap, and leave at room temperature until the dough has doubled in bulk, about 1 hour.

SHAPING
20 mins.

Punch down the dough and divide it into 2 pieces; cover with a towel or wax paper. Let the dough rest on the counter for 10 minutes. Press each piece flat, fold in half, seal the seam by pinching tightly, and place each in the prepared pan.

SECOND RISING
45 mins.

Cover with wax paper, and let the dough rise until it has doubled in volume, about 45 minutes.

PREHEAT

Preheat the oven to 350° about 20 minutes before baking.

BAKING
350°
I hour

Place the pans in the oven and bake until the crusts are nicely browned. Turn one loaf out of its pan and tap the bottom crust with a forefinger. A hard, hollow sound means the bread is baked. If not, return to the oven for an additional 10 minutes.

(If using a convection oven, reduce heat 50° and bake for 50 minutes.)

FINAL STEP

Remove the bread from the oven and place the loaves on a wire rack until cooled.

Freezes well.

Sennebec Hill Bread   [two large or four small loaves]

Six cereals and flours—cornmeal, wheat germ, rolled oats, and rye, whole-wheat, and white flours—make this a fine and flavorsome loaf. It is a stiff dough to work, but it rises well, and results in a bread with a rough texture and a nutlike flavor.

The 4 egg yolks give this bread richness and enhance the color of the blend of dark grains.

INGREDIENTS

2 packages dry yeast
$^{1}/_{4}$ cup molasses
I tablespoon salt
$^{1}/_{3}$ cup cooking oil
I cup nonfat dry milk
4 egg yolks, room temperature
$^{1}/_{2}$ cup *each* rolled oats, yellow cornmeal, and wheat germ
2 cups hot water (120°–130°)
I cup rye flour
2 cups whole-wheat flour
3 cups bread or all-purpose flour, approximately

BAKING PANS

2 large (9"-x-5") or 4 small (7"-x-3") baking pans, greased or Teflon

BY HAND OR MIXER 18 mins.	In a large mixing or mixer bowl measure in the yeast, molasses, salt, oil, milk, egg yolks, oats, cornmeal, and wheat germ. Pour in the hot water. Beat on the low speed of the electric mixer or with a wooden spoon until well mixed. It will be a heavy batter; so with a spoon, or flat beater with the mixer, add the rye flour, whole-wheat, and 1 or 2 cups bread flour to make a firm dough.
KNEADING 8 mins.	If by hand, turn the dough out onto a floured work surface and knead. If the dough is sticky or slack, add small portions of white flour and work it into the dough. Knead for 8 minutes either by hand or under the dough hook in the mixer bowl.
BY PROCESSOR 5 mins.	Attach the plastic blade. Measure into the work bowl the yeast, molasses, salt, oil, dry milk, egg yolks, oats, cornmeal, and wheat germ. Pulse. Turn on the processor and pour the hot water into the bowl through the feed tube. Add the rye and whole-wheat flours and process for a few seconds. Add the white flour, ¼ cup at a time, until the dough forms a rough mass around the blade and cleans the sides of the bowl.
KNEADING 60 secs.	Process to knead for 60 seconds.
FIRST RISING 50 mins.	Grease a bowl lightly; drop the ball of dough into it, turning it so that all surfaces are filmed with oil. Cover the bowl tightly with plastic wrap, and leave at room temperature to rise until nearly double, about 50 minutes. For a somewhat finer texture, the dough may be punched down at the end of this time and allowed to rise again. However, this is not necessary. If you do decide on this extra rising, allow about 30 minutes more.
SHAPING 10 mins.	Turn the dough onto a floured surface; knead to press out the bubbles and divide the dough into 2 or 4 pieces, whichever number of loaves you choose to make. (See the Dough Volume chart on page 16.) Shape the pieces of dough into balls and let rest under a towel for 3 or 4 minutes. Form each loaf by pressing a ball of dough into a flat oval, roughly the length of the baking pan. Fold the oval in half, pinch the seam tightly to seal, tuck under the ends, and place in the pan, seam down.
SECOND RISING 45 mins.	Cover the pans with wax paper, and let the dough rise until it is doubled in volume, 45 minutes.

PREHEAT	Preheat the oven to 375° 20 minutes before baking.

BAKING	Bake in the moderately hot oven for 25 minutes; reduce heat to 350°
375°	and bake for an additional 20 minutes, until a deep golden brown.
25 mins.	Turn one loaf out of the pan and tap the bottom crust with a fore-
350°	finger. A hard, hollow sound means the bread is baked. If not, return
20 mins.	to the oven for an additional 5 to 10 minutes.

(If using a convection oven, reduce heat 50° for each bake period.)

FINAL STEP	Remove the bread from the oven. Turn the loaves out onto a metal rack
	to cool.

Makes a fine toast.

Three Flours Bread   [two large or four small loaves]

This crusty brown yeast loaf has an unusual flavor of a blend of 3 flours—whole wheat, soy, and white. The dough will weigh about 4 pounds, so I usually divide it and bake four 1-pound loaves in small tins.

These light and wheat-textured loaves are fine to send off with a departing houseguest or to take to a host or hostess.

INGREDIENTS	2¼ cups hot water (120°–130°)
	½ cup firmly packed brown sugar
	1 tablespoon salt
	½ cup shortening, room temperature
	4 cups whole-wheat flour
	1–2 cups bread or all-purpose flour, approximately
	2 packages dry yeast
	1½ cups soy flour

BAKING PANS	2 large (9"-x-5") or 4 small (7"-x-3") loaf pans, greased or Teflon

BY HAND	In a large mixing or mixer bowl pour the hot water over the brown
OR MIXER	sugar, salt, and shortening. Gradually beat in 3 cups whole-wheat and
8 mins.	1 cup white flour. Add the yeast, and beat with an electric mixer
	at medium speed for about 5 minutes, or 100 strong strokes with
	a large wooden spoon. The dough will pull away from the sides in
	ribbons.

Mix in the soy and the remaining cup whole-wheat flour. If the dough is too stiff to mix with a flat beater, attach the dough hook. If by hand, turn out onto a floured work surface and work in the flours.

KNEADING
8 mins.

If the dough is sticky in the hands as kneading begins, add a small amount of white flour. Depending on the flour, the dough may absorb up to a cup additional flour before it begins to feel light and springy. Knead with a strong push-turn-fold motion for about 8 minutes, or under the dough hook for the same length of time.

BY PROCESSOR
8 mins.

Attach the short plastic dough blade.

In the work bowl pour the hot water over the brown sugar, salt, and shortening. Pulse. Add 3 cups whole-wheat flour, 1 cup white flour, and the yeast. Process for 15 seconds to blend thoroughly. Stop the processor. If the flour in the bottom edge of the bowl has not blended with the dough, scrape it free with a spatula.

With the machine running, add the soy flour and the remaining whole wheat, ¼ cup at a time. The dough should form a rough mass and whirl around the bowl with the blade. If it does not, add small portions of white flour to give it body.

KNEADING
50 secs.

Knead with the processor running for 50 seconds.

The dough may be slightly sticky when taken from the bowl but a few sprinkles of flour will allow you to form it into a smooth ball.

FIRST RISING
1 hour

Place the dough in a bowl, cover tightly with plastic wrap, and leave at room temperature until doubled in bulk, about 1 hour.

SHAPING
5 mins.

Remove the plastic wrap and turn the dough out onto the floured work surface to knead lightly for about 45 seconds. Divide the dough into half or quarters and shape to fit the prepared tins.

SECOND RISING
50 mins.

Cover with wax paper and leave the dough to rise until the center of the dough has risen about 1" above the level of the edge of the pans, 50 minutes.

PREHEAT

Preheat the oven to 375° 20 minutes before baking.

BAKING
375°
35–45 mins.

Bake in the oven until well browned, about 35 minutes for small loaves and 45 minutes for larger ones. The loaves are done when a wood toothpick or testing skewer inserted in the center comes out clean. If the loaves have been baked in shiny tins, they may not be brown enough on the sides and bottom to please you. Turn them out of the tins and return them to the oven for an additional 5 minutes.

(If using a convection oven, reduce heat 50°.)

FINAL STEP

Remove the bread from the oven. Allow the loaves to cool completely on metal racks before slicing.

War Bread   [two large or three medium loaves]

War Bread has been a farmhouse loaf in New England kitchens for more than 150 years. When white flour was scarce, often in wartime, this blend of rolled oats, cornmeal, and whole wheat was added to the flour to make it go farther. It makes a delicious loaf that tastes equally good in less troubled times.

A young friend who likes it has suggested the name be changed to peace-meal bread.

INGREDIENTS	1 cup rolled oats
	1 cup cornmeal
	1 cup whole-wheat flour
	1 tablespoon lard or other shortening
	$^1/_3$ cup molasses
	1 tablespoon salt
	3 cups boiling water
	1 package dry yeast
	5 to 6 cups bread or all-purpose flour, approximately

BAKING PANS — 2 large (9"-x-5") or 3 medium (8"-x-4") baking pans, greased or Teflon

BY HAND
OR MIXER
25 mins.

In a large mixing or mixer bowl combine the rolled oats, cornmeal, whole wheat, shortening, molasses, and salt. Pour in the boiling water, stirring constantly, until the mixture is smooth. Set aside to cool to 120°–130°. Sprinkle the yeast on the batter, and blend.

Stir in the white flour, ½ cup at a time, first with the spoon and then by hand, or with the flat beater in the mixer. The dough will be somewhat heavy and dense and will not have the elasticity of white dough. Nevertheless, the dough will form a shaggy mass that cleans the sides of the bowl. Sprinkle on flour to control stickiness, if necessary.

KNEADING
8 mins.

Turn the dough onto a lightly floured work surface and knead with the rhythmic motion of push-turn-fold, or with the mixer dough hook, 8 minutes. The dough will become smooth. Sprinkle on more flour if the dough continues to stick to the work surface or your fingertips.

BY PROCESSOR
5 mins.

This recipe is too large for most food processors. Divide the ingredients in half (except the yeast) and attach the plastic blade.

In the work bowl measure the rolled oats, cornmeal, whole wheat, lard, molasses, and salt. Pulse to mix. With the machine running, pour in the boiling water. Allow the mixture to cool, and then add the yeast. Pulse.

Turn on the processor and add the white flour, ¼ cup at a time, until the dough forms a rough mass and rides on the blade. As it whirls around the bowl, it will clean away the film from the sides of the bowl. Add small portions of flour through the feed tube if the dough remains sticky.

KNEADING
50 secs.

When the dough forms a ball on the blade, knead for 50 seconds.

FIRST RISING
1 hour

Place the dough in a bowl and pat with butter or greased fingers to keep the surface from crusting. Cover the bowl tightly with plastic wrap and put aside for the dough to rise at room temperature until twice its original size—judged by how it creeps up the sides of the bowl—about 1 hour.

SHAPING
10 mins.

Punch down the dough and knead for 30 seconds to press out the bubbles. Divide the dough into 2 or 3 pieces. Shape into balls, and let them rest on the work surface for 3 to 4 minutes.

Form each loaf by pressing a piece of dough into a flat oval, roughly the length of the baking pan. Fold each oval in half, pinch the seam tightly to seal, tuck under the ends, and place in the pan, seam down.

SECOND RISING
50 mins.

Cover the loaves with wax paper and leave until the center of the dough has risen to an inch above the edge of the pan, 50 minutes.

PREHEAT

Preheat the oven to 350° 20 minutes before baking.

BAKING
350°
1 hour

Bake the loaves in the oven until they are nicely browned and test done, about 1 hour. Turn one loaf out of its pan and tap the bottom crust with a forefinger. A hard, hollow sound means the bread is baked. If not, return to the oven for an additional 10 minutes. If the loaves appear to brown too quickly, cover them with brown sack paper or foil. Midway during baking and again near the end, shift the pans so the loaves are exposed equally to the temperature variations in the oven.

(If using a convection oven, reduce heat 40°.)

FINAL STEP

Remove the bread from the oven and turn from the pans. Place on a metal rack to cool.

Pain Noir
(Black Bread)

[one loaf]

This delicious almost-black loaf of French Pain Noir is leavened with yeast, and made in a relatively short period of time. The flours are whole wheat, white, and rye.

The French do nothing to the top crust other than glaze it with egg, but I find a sprinkling of kosher or sea salt gives it a new dimension. The bread is a bit sweet, the crust a bit salty—a good marriage!

The bread is not solid and heavy as with most dark loaves but raised, with an open texture.

INGREDIENTS	$^1/_4$ cup cornmeal
	$^1/_2$ cup boiling water
	$^1/_3$ cup cold water
	1 package dry yeast
	1 square (1 ounce) unsweetened chocolate
	$^1/_2$ tablespoon butter
	$^1/_2$ cup molasses
	2 teaspoons salt
	2 teaspoons caraway seeds
	$^1/_2$ cup mashed potatoes (or $^1/_3$ cup instant flakes)
	$^2/_3$ cup whole-wheat flour
	$^1/_2$ cup rye flour
	$^1/_2$ cup all-purpose flour
	1 egg, beaten, mixed with 1 tablespoon water
	Coarse salt (optional)

BAKING SHEET

1 baking sheet, Teflon or sprinkled with cornmeal

PREPARATION
10 mins.

Stir the cornmeal into a pan containing the boiling water. Stir vigorously until the mixture is smooth. Add the cold water gradually, stirring constantly. When the mixture has cooled somewhat (110°), stir in the yeast.

In a small saucepan over very low heat melt together the chocolate and butter. Allow to cool to lukewarm.

BY HAND
OR MIXER
5 mins.

In a large mixing or mixer bowl combine the cornmeal and chocolate mixtures and add the molasses, salt, caraway, and mashed potatoes. Beat together with a heavy spoon or in an electric mixer for 2 or 3 minutes, until smooth. Add the whole-wheat flour and stir or beat for 2 minutes.

REST
1 hour

Cover the bowl with plastic wrap and set aside to rest for 1 hour while the dough ferments.

KNEADING
8 mins.

Add the rye flour. Stir to form a shaggy ball of dough that can be lifted to the work surface. Use a dough blade to turn, fold, and knead the dough, because it is very sticky to work, for 8 minutes. Add liberal sprinkles of white flour to keep the dough from sticking to the work surface and your hands. In most instances, the dough is too heavy for a dough hook (it pushes the dough against the sides of the bowl instead of kneading it). It will gradually become elastic even though sticky.

FIRST RISING 75 mins.	Place the dough in a greased bowl, turn to coat the ball, cover with plastic wrap, and put aside to double in volume, about 75 minutes.
REST 15 mins.	Turn back the plastic wrap, punch down the dough, re-cover, and let it rest for 15 minutes.
SHAPING 3 mins.	Turn the dough onto the work surface and shape into a round loaf.
SECOND RISING 45 mins.	Place the loaf on the prepared baking sheet. Cover and let rise until almost double in volume, about 45 minutes.
PREHEAT	Preheat the oven to 375° 20 minutes before baking.
BAKING 375° 10 mins. 350° 35 mins.	Brush the loaf with the egg wash. Sprinkle with coarse salt, if desired. Bake for 10 minutes, then reduce heat to 350° and bake for 35 minutes more, or until the loaf tests done. It will sound hollow when the bottom crust is tapped with a forefinger. (If using a convection oven, reduce heat 50° for each bake period.)
FINAL STEP	Place the loaf on a metal rack to cool before slicing. Excellent served with cheeses.

Red River White Bread   [two medium loaves]

Many years ago a miller in the rolling wheat country of the Red River Valley in Manitoba, Canada, urged his friends to try his new cereal, a blend of cracked wheat, cracked rye, and flax. They approved, and thus was born Red River Cereal.

The original recipe for this loaf, developed by the mill in St. Boniface, Manitoba, called for nearly 1 cup molasses. This was too strong for my taste and, besides, it masked the colorful grain particles scattered throughout the loaf.

INGREDIENTS
3 cups boiling water
2 cups Red River Cereal
2 tablespoons lard or other shortening
4 cups bread flour
2 packages dry yeast

1 tablespoon sugar
1 tablespoon salt
$^1/_3$ to $^2/_3$ cup molasses (optional)

BAKING PANS

2 medium (8"-x-4") loaf pans, greased or Teflon

PREPARATION
20 mins.

In a mixing or mixer bowl pour the boiling water over the cereal and shortening. Stir and put aside for 20 minutes.

BY HAND
OR MIXER
12 mins.

Measure 2 cups bread flour into the cereal mixture, stir, and add the yeast, sugar, and salt. (Up to $^2/_3$ cup molasses can be added here, but I prefer it without any.)

If by hand, stir more flour, ½ cup at a time, into the batter until it forms a soft mass that can be lifted from the bowl. If using a mixer, use the flat beater before changing to the dough hook.

KNEADING
10 mins.

Knead the dough with a rhythmic push-turn-fold motion, occasionally lifting the dough off the table and slamming it back down to hasten the formation of the gluten. Knead for 10 minutes. If under the dough hook, add sprinkles of flour if the dough sticks to the sides of the work bowl. Knead for 10 minutes.

The dough will be soft and elastic and peppered with bits of the cereal.

BY PROCESSOR
6 mins.

Prepare the cereal, as above.

Attach the plastic blade.

Place 2 cups flour in the work bowl and scrape in the cereal. Add the yeast, sugar, salt, and molasses, if desired. Pulse to make a smooth batter. With the processor on, pour additional flour down the feed tube or take off the cover and add ¼ cup at a time. Pulse several times after each addition. The dough is ready to knead when it forms a mass that is carried around the bowl by the force of the blade.

KNEADING
60 secs.

With the machine running, knead for 60 seconds. The dough will be smooth but slightly sticky when taken from the work bowl. Dust with flour to shape into a ball.

FIRST RISING
45 mins.

Place the dough in a greased bowl, cover with plastic wrap, and put aside to double in bulk at room temperature, about 45 minutes.

SHAPING
6 mins.

Divide the bread into 2 pieces and press each into an oval the length of the prepared bread pan. Fold down the length, pinch the seam together, tuck in the ends, and place in the pans. With your fingers push the dough into the corners and level it. The pans should be about two-thirds full. If there is an excess, place in a small pan.

SECOND RISING
35 mins.

Cover with wax paper and leave at room temperature until risen to the edge of the pans, about 35 minutes.

PREHEAT

Preheat the oven to 400° about 20 minutes before baking.

BAKING
400°
30–35 mins.

Before placing the pans in the oven, you may wish to cut a ½" slash down the center of each loaf, or another appropriate design.

Place in the oven for 30 to 35 minutes, or until golden brown and crusty. Midway during baking, turn the loaves around so the heat hits all sides equally.

(If using a convection oven, reduce heat 50° and the loaves need not be turned.)

FINAL STEP

Turn the loaves from the pans onto a metal rack to cool before slicing.

Makes superb toast.

Will keep fresh for several days and can be frozen at 0° for 3 to 4 months.

FRENCH AND ITALIAN BREADS

To PRODUCE A LOAF of fine French bread is not difficult. The glory of this loaf is its simplicity—flour, water, salt, and leavening are the basic ingredients of many of the doughs.

While the baking procedure is not elaborate, there are several steps to be done correctly and in sequence to produce the classic crusty loaf.

But first, the flour.

The French make their bread with flour milled from western European wheat. It is a soft wheat, with a medium gluten content.

The middle ground for the home baker in this country is to mix three parts all-purpose with one part bread flour. In several recipes in this book, this mixture is designated "all-purpose/bread flour" in the list of ingredients to indicate these proportions. Unbleached all-purpose flour can also be used alone with good results.

Equally important is the *boulanger*'s willingness to give the dough whatever time is necessary to allow it to develop taste and character. He will not rush it. He will not take shortcuts.

To give the dough time to develop its large open patternwork of cells, it must be allowed to rise in the bowl until it has at least fully doubled in volume. The shaped loaves, in turn, must be fully developed before they are placed in the oven. Less than full proofing means small loaves and a denser slice.

Several pans and techniques for making French loaves are described in the chapter on "Equipment." (For use of steam in the oven, see "Equipment," page 7.)

Judging by their popularity with home bakers throughout the United States and Canada—who have written and talked with me—I have chosen these ten breads.

A word about the delicious sourdough bread found in San Francisco, since this chapter contains several sourdough breads. Will it or will it not thrive away from the Bay Area? It has not for me. Several times I have started with a bona fide sample brought out of San Francisco by me or by friends, but after it has been in my kitchen for a while it has become Bloomington sourdough bread, thanks to the billions of yeast spores floating freely in my kitchen that simply overpower the special fungi and bacteria that makes S.F. sourdough so special. The same thing would happen in Ames, Iowa. After several months, San Francisco sourdough would become Ames sourdough. These changes are also enhanced by substantial changes of the sponge.

I corresponded for many months with University of California researchers at Berkeley and collected folders of information about the spore *Saccharomyces exiguus.* I came to appreciate that to bake S.F. sourdough bread consistently I would probably have to live there.

Pain de Campagne Honfleur
[four medium loaves or one large hearth loaf]
(Honfleur Country Bread)

The sense of disbelief when standing for the first time in front of the display windows of Monsieur André David's boulangerie in Honfleur, on the Normandy coast of France, is as powerful as that of a small boy standing for the first time before a candy-store window.

The most impressive sight is the window filled with big, husky 4-pound country loaves stacked like cordwood, each loaf decorated with stalks of wheat, fashioned from dough. In other windows are scores of other breads of all kinds, of all shapes and sizes, and in a full range of shades from golden to deep brown. For those puzzled as to the name of each, M. David has thoughtfully arranged in the largest window a display board on which each bread baked by him is displayed in miniature and identified with a legend underneath.

One of these, M. David's pain de campagne, is a husky, rough country loaf that begins with a starter enriched with honey. The yeast loves it.

M. David makes big loaves—18 inches to 2 feet across—most of which are cut into pieces and sold by the kilo. There are about 4½ pounds of dough in this recipe, enough for an impressive big country loaf, or 4 small-to-medium loaves. The large loaf has one marked advantage, however; it provides a wide canvas for the wheat stalks baked on the crust.

The decorating technique is described in this recipe.

INGREDIENTS

Starter:
1 tablespoon honey
1 cup hot water (120°–130°)
1 package dry yeast
1 cup bread or all-purpose flour, approximately
1 cup whole-wheat flour

Dough:
2 cups hot water (120°–130°)
1 tablespoon salt
2 cups whole-wheat flour
2 to 3 cups all-purpose/bread flour, approximately (see page 213)

BAKING SHEET

1 or 2 baking sheets, Teflon or greased and sprinkled with cornmeal. The number of sheets depends on the number of loaves to be made, and size of the oven, especially if it is convection.

PREPARATION
**4 hours–
overnight**

To make the starter, in a large mixing or mixer bowl dissolve the honey in the hot water and add the yeast. Add ½ cup each white and whole-wheat flour to make a thick batter. Add the balance of the flours to make a shaggy mass that can be worked with the hands. Knead for 3 minutes. Toss in liberal sprinkles of flour if the dough is slack or sticky.

Cover the bowl with plastic wrap and leave at room temperature for at least 4 hours. Left overnight it will gather even more flavor and strength.

BY HAND
OR MIXER
10 mins.

To make the dough, pour the hot water over the starter. Stir with a large wooden spoon or rubber scraper, or the flat beater of a mixer, to break up the dough. Add the salt.

Place 2 cups each of whole-wheat and white flour at the side of the mixing bowl, and add equal parts of each, ½ cup at a time, first stirring with a spoon and then working it with your hands, or with the dough hook. It may take more white flour to make a mass that is not sticky. Lift from the bowl if to be kneaded by hand, or leave in the mixer bowl if with the dough hook.

KNEADING
10 mins.

If by hand, place the dough on the floured work surface and begin to knead the dough aggressively with a strong motion of push-turn-fold. If the dough is slack and sticky, add sprinkles of flour. Once in a while lift the dough high above the work surface and bring it down with a crash to speed the process. Do this 3 or 4 times and then resume kneading. Knead by hand, or with the dough hook in the mixer bowl, for 10 minutes.

BY PROCESSOR
6 mins.

This is a big loaf and should be made only in a large-capacity home food processor. The dough will stall the blade of a lesser model.

Prepare the starter by hand, as above.

Attach the short plastic dough blade.

Pour the hot water over the starter, stir to mix, and scrape into the work bowl of the processor. Add salt. Pulse. Place 2 cups each whole-wheat and white flour at hand, and add equal parts of each, ¼ cup at a time, to the work bowl as the processor is running.

Add only enough flour to form a mass that will ride the blade and clean the sides of the bowl. Stop the machine and feel the dough. It should be moist and slightly sticky but not wet or slack. If it is so, add sprinkles of flour.

KNEADING
45 secs.

Knead the dough, with the processor running, for 45 seconds.

FIRST RISING
3–4 hours

Place the ball of dough in a greased bowl, cover tightly with plastic wrap, and leave at room temperature to double in volume, about 3 hours.

SHAPING
10 mins.

Push down the dough and turn out onto a well-floured work surface. Divide the dough into the desired number of pieces and shape with cupped hands into tight balls. Reserve 1 cup of dough to make the decorative wheat stalks later, if desired. They really only make sense if you are making one large round loaf that measures at least 12" across; anything smaller will not do the stalks justice.

Place the balls of dough on baking sheets and press down to flatten slightly.

SECOND RISING
2½ hours

Leave the loaves under wax paper to *triple* in size, about 2½ hours at room temperature.

DECORATING
15 mins.

Shortly before the loaf is completely raised, divide the reserved cup of dough into 3 pieces. Roll each into a long strand (under the palms) 12" to 14" long—no thicker than a lead pencil.

Place the strands parallel and, beginning 4" from one end, braid to the end. Turn the strand around and spread apart the strands to make it convenient to cut the wheat design on each.

With sharp-pointed scissors, make small cuts from the top down 5" of the strand—alternating right, center, and left—to create the illusion of grains of wheat protruding from the stalk before harvest. Leave the remainder of the stalk uncut and bare. Repeat the pattern for each strand.

Lightly brush the top of the loaf with water, and then position the wheat stalks. Fan the upper stalks apart.

PREHEAT

Preheat the oven to 425° 20 minutes before baking. Place a broiler pan on the bottom rack. Five minutes before the bread goes in the oven, pour 1 cup hot water in the pan to create a moist, steamy oven.

BAKING
425°
40–50 mins.

Place the loaves on the middle rack. Midway through baking shift the loaves to balance the effect of the oven's heat. The loaves are done when golden brown, in 40 to 50 minutes. The bottom crust will sound hard and hollow when tapped with a forefinger.

(If using a convection oven, measure beforehand and select the loaf size and pan size that will fit. Place a broiler pan on the floor of the oven and preheat at 375° 20 minutes before the bake period. Before putting the bread in the oven, pour 1 cup hot water into the pan. Bake for 45 minutes, or until the loaf sounds hollow when tapped, as above.)

FINAL STEP

Place on a metal rack to cool.

Freezes well.

If for a party or simply out of pride, present the loaf complete with wheat stalks at the table before slicing.

Pain de Campagne Madame Doz
[two 2-pound hearth loaves]
(Madame Doz's Peasant Loaf)

I towered over Madame Doz in height only. At ninety-nine years of age, she stood head and shoulders above me in knowledge of baking. For most of those years Madame Doz had lived with her family on a 60-acre farm high on the mountain above the French presidential Château de Vizalle, south of Grenoble.

Her wood-fired oven, no longer used, was in a shed behind the house, and a brown hen, nesting in one of the old cloth-lined wicker baskets once used to form the loaves, clucked her disapproval when Madame Doz and I came to the door. The oven's interior chamber, which held the fire and where the bread was baked, was about 8 feet long and 4 feet wide, ample space, said Madame Doz, to bake all at one time a 2-week supply of bread for the family.

The peasant bread baked by Madame Doz was made with levain, *a portion of dough left from the previous bake. She kept the* levain *for 1 and sometimes 2 weeks in a corner of the dough tray under the top of a big walnut table in the kitchen.*

The boulangers in the valley below Madame Doz use ascorbic acid in their dough because they believe it helps the cellular formation of the loaves. It is the only additive allowed the French boulanger. I have made it optional in this recipe.

A levain *can be kept by the home baker in the refrigerator for a period of days, as Madame Doz did in her cool mountain kitchen, but it must be dough made without sugar or shortening or it may spoil. Keep the* levain *in a container that will allow the dough to expand during its first hours in the refrigerator. To make the* levain *there must first be a starter.*

In the following recipe you may wish to take off 1 cup of levain *for future bakings.*

INGREDIENTS

Starter:
1½ cups bread or all-purpose flour
1 package dry yeast
⅔ cup hot water (120°–130°)
⅓ cup buttermilk, room temperature
1 teaspoon vinegar

Levain:
1 cup water, room temperature
2 cups stone-ground or plain whole-wheat flour
½ cup wheat germ
1 cup bread or all-purpose flour

Dough:
2 cups water, room temperature
Pinch of ascorbic acid (optional)
4½ cups all-purpose/bread flour, approximately (see page 213)
4 teaspoons salt dissolved in 4 teaspoons water

BAKING SHEET
OR PANS

1 baking sheet, greased or Teflon, for round *boules;* long pans for *baguettes* or *ficelles,* greased

PREPARATION
12–36 hours

To make the starter, measure the flour into a medium mixing or mixer bowl, and stir in the dry yeast. Pour in the hot water, buttermilk, and vinegar. Stir to make a heavy batter. Cover tightly with plastic wrap and let the batter stand at room temperature for a minimum of 12 hours, or until it rises and falls, or as long as 24 to 36 hours if more convenient.

6–12 hours

To make the *levain,* uncover the bowl containing the starter. Stir in the water, whole-wheat flour, and wheat germ. The *levain* is to be a soft ball of dough, not a batter, so add sufficient white flour, about 1 cup, to make a solid mass. Work in the flour by hand or with the dough hook. Re-cover and leave at room temperature for a minimum of 6 hours. It can be left longer if convenient. The ball of dough will rise and spread under the plastic wrap and then take on the appearance of a heavy batter.

BY HAND OR MIXER 2¼ hours

The white flour is made into a soft dough and then blended with the ball of *levain.* The salt is not added until later in the kneading. But don't forget it—set it aside now as a reminder.

To make the dough, uncover the *levain,* stir it down with a rubber scraper or by hand, and lift onto the work surface. Shape into a round ball and set aside.

Pour the water into the bowl, and add the optional ascorbic acid and 1½ cups flour. Stir to blend into a thick batter. Add flour, about ¼ cup at a time, to make a soft dough that can be lifted from the bowl. Place it on the work surface and knead until it is smooth, adding sprinkles of flour if it is sticky.

KNEADING 20 mins.

Press the *levain* into a flat oval and cover with the ball of white dough. Fold the two together and continue folding and kneading by hand or with a dough hook in the mixer until the two are completely blended.

The combined doughs should be elastic yet firm, so add additional flour as the kneading begins. A test is to shape the dough into a ball and see how well it retains its shape when you remove your hands. If the dough slouches badly, it needs more flour. If it holds its shape yet is elastic and responds to a finger pushing back—there may be enough flour. On the other hand, it should not be a stiff ball.

The combined doughs will blend into a light brown ball, sprinkled with tiny darker brown flakes. Use a forceful push-turn-fold motion for about 8 minutes, aggressively throwing the ball of dough down against the work surface from time to time. If the dough remains sticky, cover it with sprinkles of flour or knead under the mixer dough hook for the same length of time.

Stop the kneading for a moment and press the dough flat with a depression in the center. Into this, put the salt-water solution. Fold the dough over the liquid and return to kneading.

The dough may be slick and squishy until the liquid is absorbed; if so, sprinkle with a bit of flour. Knead for an additional 8 minutes, or a total of 16.

BY PROCESSOR
8 mins.

Both the *levain* and the ball of white dough can be made by hand in a bowl, as above.

Attach the short plastic dough blade.

Drop the *levain* into the processor's work bowl. Pulse for a moment and then drop in the ball of white dough. Pulse until the 2 doughs are well blended. Pour the salt mixture into the bowl, and pulse to blend. Add ¼ cup of flour to absorb the liquid. If the dough is sticky and does not clean the bowl, add sprinkles of flour.

KNEADING
45 secs.

When the dough forms a shaggy mass and rides on the dough blade as it whirls around the bowl, knead for 45 seconds.

FIRST RISING
2 hours

Place the dough in the washed and greased bowl, cover tightly with plastic wrap, and leave at room temperature until it has more than doubled in volume, 2 hours.

SHAPING
10 mins.

Remove the plastic wrap and punch down dough with extended fingers. Turn onto the work surface and divide into as many pieces as you wish loaves. The dough will weigh about 4 pounds.

Whether the dough is shaped as a *boule* (round loaf) or as *baguettes* or *ficelles,* it may be placed to rise directly on the baking sheets or in pans in *bannetons,* or *sur couche.*

SECOND RISING
1½ hours

Cover with a cloth or wax paper and leave at room temperature to rise to *triple* its original bulk, about 1½ hours.

PREHEAT

Place a broiler or other shallow pan in the oven; preheat to 450° about 20 minutes before baking. Five minutes before baking, pour 1 cup hot water in the pan to create steam. Use a long-handled container to pour the water so you don't burn yourself.

BAKING
450°
35–40 mins.

Uncover the loaves. Those in *bannetons* are turned over onto the baking sheet. Those in the cloth folds *(couches)* are rolled onto a length of cardboard, then lifted and rolled off onto the baking sheet. Leave those already in pans or on a baking sheet.

With a razor blade cut the tops with diagonal slashes.

Place the loaves on the middle rack of the oven, or, if the top shelf is also used, be aware that bread bakes faster there and must be interchanged with breads on the lower shelf midway through baking.

The loaves are done when a golden brown and crusty, in 35–40 minutes. Turn over one loaf and tap the bottom crust with a forefinger. If it sounds hard and hollow, the bread is baked.

(If using a convection oven, place 1 cupful water in a shallow pan on the floor 5 minutes before putting in the bread. Reduce heat 75°.)

FINAL STEP

Place the loaves on a metal rack to cool, or stack on end so the air can move around them freely. The loaves will crackle loudly as the crusts cool and crack.

Try to wait until almost cool before breaking into chunks or slicing.

Pain Ordinaire Carême
[four *baguettes, boules,* or *couronnes*]
(A Daily Loaf)

The great eighteenth-century French cook and founder of la grande cuisine, *Antonin Carême, wrote of grand dishes for princes and kings, yet he created an ordinary loaf of bread that has been passed down from one generation of bakers to the next for more than 175 years.*

Carême, who has been called the cook of kings and the king of cooks, wrote: "Cooks who travel with their gastronomically minded masters can, from now on, by following this method, procure fresh bread each day."

This excellent bread is made with hard-wheat bread flour to give the dough the ability to withstand the expansion it undergoes when it rises more than three times its original volume. Baking at high heat provides the oven-spring that makes possible the formation of a large cellular structure, the distinguishing characteristic of pain ordinaire.

INGREDIENTS

6 cups bread or unbleached flour, approximately
2 packages dry yeast
2¹/₂ cups hot water (120°–130°)
2 teaspoons each salt and water

BAKING SHEET
OR PANS

1 baking sheet, Teflon or greased and sprinkled with cornmeal, or 4 *baguette* pans, greased.

BY HAND
OR MIXER
10 mins.

The early part of this preparation, beating a batter, can be done by an electric mixer. However, don't overload a light mixer with this thick batter. If by hand, stir vigorously for an equal length of time.

Measure 3 or 4 cups of flour into the mixing bowl and add the yeast and hot water. The mixer flat beater or whisk should run without undue strain. The batter will be smooth and pull away from the sides as the gluten develops. It may also try to climb up the beaters and into the motor. If it does, push it down with a rubber scraper. Mix for 10 minutes. When about finished, dissolve the salt in the water and add to the batter. Blend for 30 seconds or more.

KNEADING
10 mins.

If the machine has a dough hook, continue with it and add additional flour, ¼ cup at a time, until the dough has formed under the hook and cleans the sides of the bowl. If it is sticky and clings, add sprinkles of flour. Knead for 10 minutes.

If by hand, add additional flour to the beaten batter, ½ cup at a time, stirring first with a utensil and then working by hand. When the dough is shaggy but a solid mass, turn onto a work surface and begin kneading with an aggressive push-turn-fold motion. If the dough is sticky, toss down sprinkles of flour. Break the kneading rhythm occasionally by throwing the dough down hard against the countertop—an excellent way to encourage the development of the dough.

BY PROCESSOR
5 mins.

Attach the short plastic dough blade.

Measure 4 cups flour into the work bowl, and add the yeast. Pour the hot water slowly through the feed tube to make a thick batter. (A too-thin batter may try to climb up the inside of the stem that holds the blade.) Process the batter for 60 seconds. Stop the machine; add the salt, 2 cups flour, and the 2 teaspoons water. Pulse several times to blend thoroughly. If the dough continues to be wet, add more flour.

KNEADING
45 secs.

When the dough forms a mass and is whirled around the bowl by the blade, let the machine continue to run and knead for 45 seconds.

It will be a soft dough when taken from the bowl but a few sprinkles of flour will allow you to pat and shape it into a ball.

FIRST RISING
2 hours

Place the dough in a large greased bowl, cover with plastic wrap, and leave at room temperature for 2 hours. The dough will more than treble in volume—and may even be pushing against the plastic covering.

SECOND RISING
1½ hours

Turn back the plastic wrap and turn the dough onto the work surface to knead briefly, about 3 minutes. Return the dough to the bowl and re-cover with wax paper. Allow to rise to more than triple its volume, about 1½ hours.

SHAPING
10 mins.

The dough will be light and puffy. Turn it onto the floured work surface and punch it down. Don't be surprised if it pushes back, for it is quite resilient. Divide into as many pieces as you wish loaves. One-quarter (10 ounces) of this recipe will make a *baguette* 22" long and 3" to 4" in diameter. Allow pieces of dough to rest for 5 minutes before shaping.

For *boules* or round loaves, shape the pieces into balls. Place in cloth-lined baskets *(bannetons)* or position directly on the baking sheet. For *baguettes,* roll and lengthen each dough piece under your palms to 16" to 20", and 3" to 4" in diameter. Place in a pan or on a baking sheet or in the folds of a long cloth *(couche)*.

This loaf's characteristic *couronne* or "crown" can be made in several ways. One is to flatten the piece of dough, press a hole through the center with your thumb, and enlarge the hole with your fingers. Another is to roll a long strand 18" to 24" and curl into a circle, overlapping and pushing together the ends. Yet a third way is to take 2 or 3 shorter lengths of dough and join them together in a circle, not overlapping top and bottom but pressing the ends together side by side into a uniform pattern—this one will be irregular but attractive.

THIRD RISING
1 hour

Cover the loaves with a cloth, preferably of wool, to allow air to reach the loaves and to form a light crust. Leave at room temperature until the dough has risen to more than double its size, about 1 hour.

PREHEAT

Before preheating the oven to 450° (very hot) 20 minutes before baking, place a broiler pan on the floor of the oven or bottom rack so it will be there later. Five minutes before baking, pour 1 cup hot water into the hot pan. Be careful of the burst of steam—it can burn. I use a long-handled cup to reach into the oven when I pour.

BAKING
450°
25–30 mins.

Carefully move the loaves in baskets and in *couches* to the baking sheet. Make diagonal cuts down the lengths of the long loaves and tic-tac-toe designs on the *boules*.

Place on the middle shelf of the oven.

The loaves are done when a golden brown, 25 to 30 minutes. Turn one loaf over and if the bottom crust sounds hard and hollow when tapped, the loaf is done.

(If using a convection oven, reduce heat 50°.)

FINAL STEP

Place on a rack to cool. One of the exciting sounds in the kitchen is the crackle of French bread as it cools. Crackle away!

Spread with butter and enjoy with any dish.

French Bread with Egg Whites   [two long *baguettes*]

Folding stiffly beaten egg whites into the dough before it is kneaded produces this crusty, light loaf of French bread. The air beaten into the egg whites has little effect on the texture of the bread, but a measure of its lightness is evident from the combined weight of two 18-inch loaves—less than 1 1/2 pounds.

INGREDIENTS	2 egg whites
	3 to 3 1/2 cups bread flour, approximately
	1 package dry yeast
	1 tablespoon sugar
	1 teaspoon salt
	1 cup hot water (120° to 130°)
	2 tablespoons butter, room temperature
	1 teaspoon cornstarch and 1/2 teaspoon salt mixed with 1/3 cup water
	3 tablespoons sesame or poppy seeds

BAKING PANS OR SHEET

2 *baguette* pans or 1 baking sheet, greased and lightly sprinkled with cornmeal

BY HAND OR MIXER
10 mins.

Just before preparation, beat the egg whites until they are stiff, and set aside.

Measure 2½ cups bread flour into a mixing or mixer bowl, and add the yeast, sugar, and salt. Pour in the hot water and the butter; beat 50 strong strokes with a wooden spoon, or for 2 minutes with the mixer flat beater. Fold in the egg whites by hand or with the flat beater. It will take a few moments for the soft dough to accept the egg whites. It is easier and faster to do this with the electric mixer than by hand.

Add flour, ¼ cup at a time, until the mixture is no longer moist but soft and elastic. If it continues to be sticky, add sprinkles of flour.

Lift the dough from the bowl and place on the lightly floured work surface, or, if in the electric mixer, attach the dough hook.

KNEADING
10 mins.

This is a soft dough that will be slightly tacky but not sticky. Knead the dough by hand with a push-turn-fold rhythm, adding sprinkles of flour if the moisture breaks through the dough and is sticky. Occasionally lift the dough above the work surface and bring it crashing down to speed the development of the gluten network. If in the mixer, add sprinkles of flour if the dough persists in sticking to the sides of the bowl. Knead for 10 minutes.

BY PROCESSOR
6 mins.

Prepare the egg whites, as above.

Attach the steel blade.

Measure 2 cups bread flour into the processor work bowl, and add the yeast, sugar, and salt. Pulse to blend. Pour in the hot water and add the butter. Pulse 2 or 3 times. Drop the beaten egg whites into the batterlike dough, and pulse several times to blend and make smooth.

Remove the cover and add flour, ¼ cup at a time, until the dough forms a soft mass and is whipped around the bowl on the steel blade. At the same time it will partially clean the bowl. Each time the cover is removed to add flour, feel the dough to determine when enough flour is enough—not solid, not wet.

KNEADING
45 secs.

With the machine running, knead for 45 seconds.

The dough will be quite soft when it is taken from the work bowl, but sprinkles of flour will make it easier to shape and drop into a greased bowl to rise.

FIRST RISING
1 hour

Place the dough in a greased bowl, cover tightly with plastic wrap, and put aside to rise at room temperature to double in bulk, about 1 hour.

SHAPING
10 mins.

Divide the dough into equal parts and roll each under the palms of your hands into a 15"-long *baguette.* Lay the dough either in the French bread pans or directly onto the prepared baking sheet, keeping the loaves apart so they won't touch during rising and baking.

SECOND RISING
1 hour

Brush the loaves with the cornstarch-salt mixture and sprinkle with sesame or poppy seeds—or both. Let rise, uncovered, until doubled in bulk, about 1 hour.

PREHEAT

Preheat the oven to 350° 20 minutes before baking, and place the broiler pan on the floor of the oven, beneath the bottom rack. Five minutes before baking pour 1 cup hot water into the pan to create steam for a crispy crust. Be careful not to burn yourself. (I use a long-handled cup for this.)

BAKING
350°
30–40 mins.

Bake in the moderate oven for 30 to 40 minutes, or until the crust is risen and a golden brown. Turn one loaf over and thump with the fore-finger to make certain it sounds hard and hollow. If not, return to the oven for a few minutes.

(If using a convection oven, reduce heat 40°.)

FINAL STEP

Remove the loaves from the oven, lift from the pans, and place on a metal rack to cool.

Pain de Campagne Poilâne

[one large or four medium loaves]

Pierre and Lionel Poilâne (père et fils) *are the most celebrated of Parisian bakers, and their most celebrated bread is the round 2-kilogram (4.4-pound) peasant loaf baked in a wood-fired oven in the basement of the* boulangerie *built over the ruins of a fourteenth-century Gothic abbey on the rue du Cherche-Midi.*

Each of the big Poilâne loaves measures about a foot in diameter and is slashed across its domed top with the traditional and functional jets that allow the crust to spread and the dough to expand. Poilâne's most famous design is a cluster of grapes made of dough, complete with twisted tendrils, on a large leaf resting on the loaf. The wheat stalk design described in the Pain de Campagne Honfleur earlier is also appropriate here.

The Poilânes have their flour grown and milled in the south of France, and while it is difficult to duplicate precisely in the United States, the whole-wheat starter in this recipe imparts a fermentation, flavor, and color that is close to the original and which drew praise from Pierre.

Allow 3 days to prepare this recipe.

INGREDIENTS

Starter:
1 cup fine or stone-ground whole-wheat flour
1 cup nonfat dry milk
2 packages dry yeast
1 cup hot water (120°–130°)

Sponge:
2 cups hot water (120°–130°)
3 cups bread or all-purpose flour

Dough:
1 tablespoon salt
3 cups all-purpose/bread flour (see page 213)

BAKING SHEET
OR PANS

1 baking sheet or 2 twin open-ended *baguette* pans, greased or Teflon

PREPARATION
24 hours

To make the starter, in a medium bowl, measure the flour, nonfat dry milk, and yeast. Stir in the hot water to make a batter. Cover tightly with a length of plastic wrap and set aside at room temperature. The batter will rise and fall and continue to ferment and bubble during a 24-hour period.

24 hours

The next day, make the sponge: turn back the plastic wrap and pour the hot water into the starter. Stir in the white flour. The batter will be thick. Re-cover and leave at room temperature, another 24 hours or at least overnight.

**BY HAND
OR MIXER
20 mins.**

To make the dough, remove the plastic wrap from the bowl. Stir briefly and add the salt. With a large wooden spoon or rubber scraper, stir in the white flour, ½ cup at a time, by hand or in an electric mixer. When the dough becomes dense and difficult to stir, work in the flour with your hands or with a dough hook.

While this is an elastic, soft dough, sufficient flour must be worked into the mass to enable the shaped loaves to rest on the baking sheets without slumping, as hearth loaves are prone to do.

**KNEADING
10 mins.**

Knead the dough with a dough hook, or turn the dough out of the bowl onto a floured work surface and let rest for 3 to 4 minutes before kneading. If the dough seems slack, without body, or is sticky, throw down liberal sprinkles of flour to work into it during the early kneading.

A dough scraper in hand is convenient for keeping the work surface free of the film that often collects while the dough is moist and sticky. Lift the dough above the work surface occasionally and bang it down hard to break the kneading motion, and, at the same time, hasten the development of the dough, 10 minutes.

**BY PROCESSOR
6 mins.**

Prepare the starter and sponge by hand in a medium bowl, as above.

To make and knead the dough on the third day, attach the short plastic dough blade and scrape the sponge into the work bowl. Add the salt. Pulse.

With the processor running, add flour, ¼ cup at a time, until the dough becomes a mass that will ride on the blade around the bowl.

**KNEADING
45 secs.**

Let the machine run for an additional 45 seconds to knead the dough. It may be sticky when it is taken from the bowl, but sprinkles of flour will allow it to be formed into a ball and dropped into the bowl to rise.

**FIRST RISING
1½ hours**

Wash and grease the bowl. Drop the dough into the bowl and cover tightly with plastic wrap. Leave at room temperature until the dough more than doubles, about 1½ hours.

**SHAPING
15 mins.**

Punch down the dough and turn it onto the work surface.

For a large loaf use all of the dough, about 4 pounds. If making a grape leaf and cluster, reserve 1 cup of dough.

The dough may be divided into small loaves. While the loaves may be put directly on the baking sheet to rise, they will have better shape if first placed in cloth-lined baskets *(bannetons)* or wedged between folds of cloth *(couches)*. After the second rising they are transferred to the baking sheet.

If long French bread pans are available, the dough may be placed in these to rise and to bake, without being transferred to a baking sheet.

In forming a ball of dough for the basket, pull the surface taut under cupped hands. Place the ball of dough in the basket with the smooth surface down and wrinkled side up. When the dough is turned on the baking sheet, the smooth surface will be on top and the seam under.

In rolling a length of dough for a *baguette* or *bâtard,* keep it taut by striking the length of dough with the side of your palm 2 or 3 times as it gets longer. After making a crease down its length, fold in two (lengthwise) and continue rolling. This forces out air that is trapped in the dough that might cause unsightly bubbles in the bread, in addition to stretching the surface of the dough.

SECOND RISING
2 hours

Carefully cover the loaves with wax paper or woolen cloth. Leave at room temperature until the dough triples in volume, about 2 hours. The large cell structure so characteristic of French bread depends on this extra period of rising.

DECORATING
15 mins.

Shortly before the dough is completely raised, make top decorations, if desired.

Grape: If possible, use a grape leaf, cluster, and tendrils or a picture to model the decoration. Roll the dough ⅛" thick for the leaf, trace the design, and cut with a dough wheel, razor, or sharp knife. Work carefully to trace the veins of the leaf. Pinch off 2 dozen small pieces of dough, and roll into balls between your palms or on the work surface. Carefully roll out a long string of dough to resemble a tendril. Reserve. They will be assembled on top of the risen loaf.

To make wheat stalk decorations, see page 216.

PREHEAT

Place a broiler pan on the bottom shelf of the oven 20 minutes before baking. Preheat oven to 425°. Five minutes before the bread is to go into the oven, pour 1 cup hot water into the pan. Be careful of the sudden burst of steam. It can burn.

BAKING
425°
35–40 mins.

Uncover the loaf or loaves, lightly brush the tops with water, and position the decoration. If you are not making any decoration, slice the top with 5 or 6 parallel *jets* or cuts in one direction, turn the loaf, and slice 5 or 6 parallel cuts in the other to end up with a checkerboard pattern.

Place the loaves or loaf on the middle and top rack if both are needed, and change their positions 20 minutes into baking.

The water should boil away about the time the loaves begin to take on color so that the bread will finish in a hot, dry oven for a brown, crispy crust, 35 to 40 minutes. If the water has not evaporated, use less next time.

The loaves are baked when a light golden brown and are hard and crusty when tapped with a forefinger. If the bottom crust is not crisp, turn the loaves over in the pans and return to the oven for 10 minutes.

(If using a convection oven, place a shallow pan on the bottom. Three minutes before baking pour 1 cup hot water into the pan to create steam. Reduce heat 50°.)

FINAL STEP

Remove the bread from the oven and turn out, if necessary. Place on metal racks to cool. The bread is best when cooled, which allows the baking process to be completed. Warming bread after it has cooled is another matter. But fresh out of the oven it should be cooled or nearly so before it is introduced to the knife.

Pain Italien   [two husky 2-pound loaves]
(Italian Bread)

There is a small but telling difference between French and Italian breads. In this loaf from Monaco, near where France and Italy meet on the Mediterranean, there are two ingredients that surprised me—oil and dry milk. Normally, Italian loaves are made with just flour, yeast, salt, and water. No sugar, of course.

This loaf is the pride of Monsieur Albert Phillips, at 6 rue Grimaldi, down the hill from Prince Rainier's palace. He has been influenced over the years by a knowledgeable clientele on what is and what is not Pain Italien.

The best results with this recipe can be obtained with bread flour. Its high gluten content allows the maximum expansion of the dough in rising and in the oven.

INGREDIENTS

1 tablespoon salt
1 tablespoon malt syrup
$\frac{1}{2}$ cup nonfat dry milk
2 packages dry yeast
3 cups warm water (105°–115°)
6 cups bread or unbleached flour, approximately
1 tablespoon vegetable oil

BAKING SHEETS	1 large or 2 small baking sheets, greased or Teflon
BY HAND OR MIXER **15 mins.**	This is a good recipe in which to let the electric mixer work for about 10 minutes in the early stages of developing the dough as a soft batter.

In a medium bowl combine the salt, malt syrup, dry milk, yeast, and warm water. Stir to dissolve the malt, which is heavy and thick.

In a mixing or mixer bowl place 4 cups flour and form a well in the center. Pour in the malt-milk-yeast mixture; stir to form a batter. Add the oil. Beat with the flat beater at medium speed for 10 minutes. Scrape down the sides of the bowl, if necessary. If by hand, beat with a large wooden spoon for an equal length of time.

Stop the mixer. Add additional flour, ½ cup at a time, stirring first with a spoon and then working the flour into the dough by hand. When the dough is firm, take it from the bowl.

KNEADING
10 mins.

The dough will be soft, elastic, and warm to the touch.

Occasionally break the kneading pattern of push-turn-fold by throwing the dough down hard against the work surface. Do this a half dozen times and then return to push-turn-fold.

The dough hook of the electric mixer is fine for working this dough, but be mindful that this large amount of dough may force some of it up and over the protecting collar and into the spring mechanism. Push the dough back by holding a rubber spatula between it and the collar while the dough hook revolves.

BY PROCESSOR
5 mins.

Attach the short plastic dough blade.

The order of ingredients differs from above.

Measure 3 cups flour then the other ingredients into the work bowl. Pulse several times to blend thoroughly. Add flour, ¼ cup at a time. Rather than pour the flour through the feed tube, it is just as quick, and less messy, to stop the machine, remove the cover, and measure in the flour.

KNEADING
45 secs.

When the dough becomes a mass that is carried around the bowl by the blade, let the machine run to knead for 45 seconds.

FIRST RISING
2 hours

Return the dough to a large washed and greased bowl, cover with plastic wrap, and leave at room temperature until the dough has *tripled* in volume, 2 hours. This may mean that the dough will press up against the plastic wrap.

SECOND RISING
30 mins.

Turn back the plastic wrap, punch, and deflate the dough with extended fingers. Turn the dough over, re-cover the bowl, and allow the dough to rise for 30 minutes more.

SHAPING **5 mins.**	The dough can be shaped into a *boule* or made into *bâtards* and the longer *baguettes.* Turn the dough onto a floured work surface and knead briefly to press out the bubbles. Divide the dough, which will weigh about 4 pounds, into 2 pieces or as many as you wish. Form each into a ball and cover with a towel. The dough or a portion of it may also be rolled under the palms into a stubby *bâtard* 12" to 14" long or the classic long *baguette.*
REST **20 mins.**	Let the dough rest for 20 minutes.
SHAPING **15 mins.**	For a *boule,* shape the dough into a ball, gently pulling the surface of the dough taut with your cupped hands. Place on the baking sheet and press the dough into a flat loaf—about 8" in diameter by 1½" thick. Repeat for each loaf.
THIRD RISING **1 hour**	Loosely cover the loaves with a towel or piece of wool (I use a piece of army blanket) so that some air reaches the surface of the dough to form a light crust. Leave at room temperature for about 1 hour.
PREHEAT	Preheat the oven to 425° about 20 minutes before baking.
BAKING **425°** **40–50 mins.**	Cut a tic-tac-toe design on the loaves if they are flat. Brush the loaves with water and place in the oven. This bread is baked in a dry oven, so no pan of water is needed. If 2 shelves are used, rotate the baking sheets 2 or 3 times after the loaves begin to brown, about 20 minutes. The loaves are done when they are a golden brown, 40 to 50 minutes, and the bottom crust sounds hard and hollow when tapped with a forefinger. If the oven is too small to accept all of the loaves at one time, cover and reserve those to be held in the refrigerator. (If using a convection oven, reduce heat 40°.)
FINAL STEP	Place the loaves on a metal rack to cool.

Italian Batter Bread   [one large peasant loaf]

There is no kneading necessary to make this Italian peasant bread—only 20 to 25 minutes of beating the batter with a wooden spoon, by hand, or with a mixer dough hook. It has been called the "mother" loaf by Italian bakers because it is so basic—just yeast, flour, salt, and water. It has a crackly crust that, when torn apart, reveals a not-quite-white crumb of coarse and open texture.

The dough is soft and wet, and never solid enough to knead by hand. After it has been beaten to develop the gluten, the dough is left to rise and then poured into a pan to rise until doubled in bulk and very puffy.

This is an adaptation of a recipe brought back from Italy by one of the editors of Sunset *magazine, the fine regional publication for the Far West states and Hawaii.*

While this bread can be made by hand, beating the batterlike dough is a tiresome process. Perhaps not so for an Italian farm woman who has the time and the wrist strength, but the machine is a nice option with no compromise on quality. The recipe is written for a mixer or perhaps a food processor. But if you are in a cabin high in the mountains and only a wooden spoon is at hand, then by hand, of course.

INGREDIENTS

1³⁄₄ cups hot water (120°–130°)
4 cups bread flour, approximately
2 packages dry yeast
2 teaspoons salt

BAKING PAN

One 14" pizza pan with lip, or, if using a convection oven, one 10"-x-15" baking sheet, with an edge, greased and sprinkled liberally with cornmeal

BY MIXER
35 mins.

Start with the mixer flat beater or wire whip and as the batter gets heavier change to the dough hook.

Pour the hot water and 2 cups flour into the mixer bowl. With the mixer running, add the yeast and salt. Beat at medium speed for 3 minutes. Measure in additional flour, ¼ cup at a time, until the batter is thick and heavy. When a spoonful of dough is lifted from the bowl it will be quite elastic and stretchy.

When the dough is so thick and rubbery that it jams the flat beater or wire whip, change to the dough hook (or pick up a wooden spoon). Beat at high speed for 25 minutes. If the mixer becomes hot or the dough climbs up the hook, let the dough rest as long as 15 minutes, then continue.

BY PROCESSOR
7 mins.

Be forewarned: the soft dough may climb up the protruding stem and lock the blade to the bowl. If it does you have an unholy mess!

If you must, pour the hot water into the work bowl; add 2 cups flour, the yeast, and salt. Pulse to make a thin batter. Add another cup flour (and perhaps ¼ cup more) to make a wet, soft dough that will hold its shape when the machine is stopped. But no stiffer.

Process for 2 minutes. As the gluten is formed by the whirling blade, the dough will become quite smooth and elastic (as you will discover when you lift the blade from the shaft). Be careful: the blade is extremely sharp. Don't let the dough rise in the work bowl but transfer it to another bowl; wash the processor bowl and shaft before the film hardens.

FIRST RISING **2–3 hours**	Scrape down the sides of the bowl, cover tightly with plastic wrap, and put aside at room temperature to triple in volume, 2 to 3 hours.
SHAPING **10 mins.**	Uncover the bowl but do not stir or punch down the dough. Gently scrape it onto the prepared pan. With liberal sprinkles of flour, carefully tuck the dough edges under to shape a rounded loaf about 12" in diameter.
SECOND RISING **1 hour**	Sprinkle the dough with flour, and cover with a flour-dusted cloth. Let rise at room temperature until doubled and very puffy, about 1 hour.
PREHEAT	Preheat the oven to 400° 20 minutes before baking.
BAKING **400°** **50 mins.**	Bake on the center shelf of the hot oven until golden brown and crusty, about 50 minutes. Turn the loaf over to be certain it is well browned on the bottom and sounds hollow and hard when thumped. (If using a convection oven, reduce heat 50°.)
FINAL STEP	Transfer to a metal rack to cool before tearing the bread into chunks or slicing.

Schiacciata   [one large round loaf]

I adapted the recipe for a traditional Italian sweet bread, Schiacciata, by making it with less sugar, no raisins or herbs, and yet retaining the fine taste and open texture of the original. It is crusty, eggy, a bit on the dry side, but a delight toasted or not.

I am certain that somewhere in Italy there is a twin of this loaf in an oven. It is simply too good not to have been already developed by some Italian baker.

INGREDIENTS	3½ to 5 cups bread or all-purpose flour, approximately 2 packages dry yeast 1 cup hot water (120°–130°) ¼ cup olive oil 1 tablespoon lard, room temperature 1 tablespoon sugar 2 teaspoons salt 1 egg

BAKING SHEET	1 baking sheet, Teflon or sprinkled liberally with cornmeal
BY HAND OR MIXER 8 mins.	In a mixing or mixer bowl measure 1½ cups flour, and sprinkle in the yeast. Mix thoroughly. Pour in the hot water. Beat the batter by hand or under the flat beater of the mixer for 2 minutes. Add the oil, lard, sugar, salt, and egg. Stir in the balance of the flour, ¼ cup at a time, to form a mass that can be taken from the bowl and dropped on the floured work surface. Add more flour, if necessary, to control stickiness.
KNEADING 15 mins.	It will be helpful to turn and work the dough with a metal dough blade or spatula while kneading. Occasionally lift the dough off the work surface and send it crashing back. The gluten in the dough loves it! Of leave the dough in the mixer bowl and knead under the dough hook for an equal length of time, 15 minutes. Sprinkles of dough will control the stickiness, and the dough will clean the sides of the electric mixer bowl when sufficient flour has been added.
BY PROCESSOR 5 mins.	Insert the plastic blade. Measure 2 cups flour into the work bowl; add the yeast. Pulse to blend. Pour in the hot water. Pulse. Add the oil, lard, sugar, salt, and egg. Turn on the processor and add flour, ¼ cup at a time, through the feed tube, until the dough becomes a mass that will clean the sides of the bowl and ride on the blade.
KNEADING 50 secs.	Leave the machine on to knead for an additional 50 seconds. The dough may be sticky when it is turned from the work bowl. A few sprinkles of flour will make it easy to move it to the baking sheet.
RISING 1 hour	Place the ball of dough on the prepared sheet, flatten somewhat with your hand, and cover with a towel or a length of wax paper. Leave the baking sheet at room temperature for 1 hour, or until the dough has doubled in bulk.
PREHEAT	Place a broiler pan on the floor of the oven. Preheat the oven to 450° 20 minutes before baking. Five minutes before baking, pour 2 cups hot water into the pan to create steam. Do this with care so as not to burn yourself.
BAKING 450° 35–40 mins.	Bake in the hot oven until the bread is raised and a golden brown, about 35 to 40 minutes. Turn the loaf over and tap the bottom crust for doneness; there should be a hard and hollow sound. If the crust

does not feel hard and crispy, return to the oven for 10 minutes. Cover with foil or brown paper if the top crust appears to be browning too quickly.

(If using a convection oven, reduce heat 40°.)

FINAL STEP

Remove the loaf from the oven, move from the sheet, and allow to cool on a metal rack before slicing.

It is a large loaf and sometimes I cut it into 2 pieces—one for family use and the other as a gift.

Braided Peasant Loaf [two loaves]

This is a basic peasant-type bread with open texture and good crust, thanks to the unusual treatment of the dough as it rises. After kneading, it is put into a bowl and every 10 minutes for 1 hour it is pushed back down into the bowl. Finally, after 5 deflations, it is allowed to rise to double in volume. Each time it is punched down, the elastic network formed by the gluten expands and gives it more lift.

This unique way of preparing dough was given to me by Ethel Scheer, the outstanding baker at the Vintage 1847, the equally outstanding restaurant in Hermann, Missouri. (Her Kaffee Kuchen is in the "Thrill of Discovery" chapter.)

INGREDIENTS

3¹/₂ cups bread or all-purpose flour
1 teaspoon salt
2 packages dry yeast
1 tablespoon sugar
1¹/₂ cups hot water (120°–130°)
2 tablespoons vegetable shortening
1 egg white, beaten, mixed with 1 teaspoon water

BAKING SHEET

1 baking sheet, Teflon, greased, or sprinkled with cornmeal

BY HAND
OR MIXER
8 mins.

In a mixing or mixer bowl measure 2 cups flour and sprinkle in the salt, dry yeast, and sugar. Pour in the hot water and add the shortening. Beat the mixture with a wooden spoon, or with a mixer flat beater for 2 minutes to make a smooth batter. Measure in additional flour, ½ cup at a time, stirring it into the wet batter. When the dough has formed a mass, work it with the hands, with sprinkles of flour to control the stickiness, until it can be lifted from the bowl and placed on a floured work surface.

If in the mixer, the last portion of flour may have to be worked into the dough by hand because it may be too thick for the flat beater and yet not thick enough for the dough hook.

KNEADING
10 mins.

Knead the dough for 10 minutes, either by hand or with the dough hook (or a combination of both). By hand, use a strong push-turn-fold motion, occasionally lifting up the dough and crashing it down, until the dough is smooth, elastic, and feels alive under your hands.

BY PROCESSOR
5 mins.

Attach the steel blade.

Measure 2 cups flour into the work bowl and add the salt, yeast, and sugar. Pulse to blend. Pour in the hot water and turn the machine on for 30 seconds to form a batter. Drop in the shortening. Pulse again to blend.

Add flour, ¼ cup at a time, through the feed tube or remove the cover to add it, until the dough forms a mass and spins around the bowl on the blade. Don't overload with flour, however. It is better to have the dough slack than hard as a rock. If the dough is too hard it may stop the machine.

KNEADING
45 secs.

Leave the machine on and knead for 45 seconds.

When the dough is turned from the work bowl it may seem sticky. A few sprinkles of flour as you mold the dough into a ball is usually sufficient.

FIRST RISING
1½ hours:
Six 10-minute
periods
30 mins.

Note: This unusual treatment of the dough calls for it to be pushed down into the bowl every 10 minutes for 1 hour.

Place the dough in a greased bowl, cover tightly with plastic wrap, and put aside at room temperature.

Set a timer for 10 minutes. When the bell rings, turn back the plastic wrap and punch down the dough with your fingertips; turn it over. Cover.

Again set the timer for 10 minutes, and proceed as above. Do this 4 more times.

After the last push-down, cover the bowl tightly with the plastic wrap and leave to rise until double in bulk, about 30 minutes.

SHAPING
12 mins.

Punch down the dough and turn onto the floured work surface. Divide the dough in half. With a knife or dough blade cut one half into 3 equal parts, by measurement or weight.

To braid, roll each of the 3 small pieces into a strand about 16" long. Lay them side by side and braid loosely, beginning in the middle; turn the dough around and finish the braid. Repeat for the second dough half.

SECOND RISING 30 mins.	Place the braided dough on the baking sheet, cover with a piece of foil, plastic wrap, or parchment paper, and allow to double in bulk, about 30 minutes.
PREHEAT	Preheat the oven to 400° about 20 minutes before baking.
BAKING 400° 35–40 mins.	Brush the braids with the egg white mixture.

BAKING
400°
35–40 mins.

Brush the braids with the egg white mixture.

Place in the oven to bake until a light golden brown and crisp, about 35 to 40 minutes. Turn one of the loaves over and tap the bottom with a forefinger. It is done if it sounds hard and hollow and is well browned. If not, return to the oven for 5 or 10 minutes to complete baking.

(If using a convection oven, reduce heat 50°.)

FINAL STEP

Remove from the oven and allow to cool for a few minutes before placing on a baking rack to cool. The braided loaf is more fragile than a solid loaf so it must be handled with care. Lift the loaves off the baking sheet with the help of a spatula.

Blue Ribbon French Bread   [two loaves]

The blue ribbon won by this loaf at the Indiana State Fair almost 20 years ago has hung over my desk since I started to write cookbooks—to buoy me when it seemed there were more good recipes to be baked than there were words to describe them. Somehow I have always managed to find both.

A personal note: my mother and my sister were consistent award winners for their baked goods at the fair. It was a time of year when it seemed both were baking night and day. And then came the euphoric moment when the morning newspaper carried the names of the winners. There they were— the names of my mother, Lenora, and Martha as blue ribbon winners. Both the challenge of entering my breads in the state fair, and the happy moment of winning many years later, were heightened by my memories of those moments a long time ago.

INGREDIENTS

1 package dry yeast
2 tablespoons nonfat dry milk
1 tablespoon sugar
1 tablespoon salt
4 to 5 cups all-purpose flour, approximately
2 cups hot water (120°–130°)
1 tablespoon butter, room temperature
1 tablespoon *each* cold water and coarse salt

BAKING SHEET	1 baking sheet, greased or Teflon
BY HAND OR MIXER 15 mins.	In a large mixing or mixer bowl stir together the yeast, dry milk, sugar, salt, and 2 cups flour. Pour in the hot water and add the butter. Blend with 100 strong strokes with a wooden spoon, or for 2 minutes with the flat beater of the mixer. Stir in the balance of the flour, ½ cup at a time, first with the spoon and then by hand, or in the mixer. The dough will be a shaggy mass, elastic but not sticky; it will clean the sides of the bowl. If, however, it continues to be moist, sprinkle on additional flour.
REST 10 mins.	Turn the dough onto a lightly floured work surface and let it rest for 10 minutes.
KNEADING 10 mins.	Knead with the rhythmic 1-2-3 motion of push-turn-fold. The dough will become smooth and elastic, and bubbles may rise under the surface of the dough. Break the kneading rhythm by throwing the dough down hard against the work surface. Knead by hand or with the mixer for 10 minutes.
BY PROCESSOR 5 mins.	Use the steel blade. Measure the dry ingredients and 2 cups flour into the work bowl. Pulse to blend. Pour in the hot water and add the butter. Pulse 4 or 5 times to mix thoroughly. With the processor on, add additional flour through the feed tube, ¼ cup at a time, until the dough forms a mass and rides atop the steel blade as it whirls around the bowl. When this happens turn off the machine and allow the dough to rest for 10 minutes.
KNEADING 50 secs.	Turn on processor and knead for 50 seconds.
FIRST RISING 1¼ hours	Place the dough in a greased bowl, cover tightly with plastic wrap to retain moisture, and leave at room temperature until the dough doubles in volume, about 1¼ hours.
SHAPING 15 mins.	Punch down the dough and turn it onto the lightly floured work surface again. Knead for 30 seconds to press out the bubbles, cut into 2 pieces, and form each into a ball. For a round loaf, place the dough on a corner of a baking sheet or in a small basket, lined loosely with a cloth and sprinkled with flour. For a long loaf, roll the ball into a rectangle, about 10"x16". Roll the dough under your palms into a long loaf which can be placed directly

on the baking sheet or in a long cloth-lined basket. Later, after it has risen, it will be turned from the basket directly onto the baking sheet.

SECOND RISING
45–50 mins.

Place the baking sheet and/or the baskets in a warm place and cover the loaves carefully with a length of wax paper. Leave until the loaves have doubled in volume, about 45 to 50 minutes.

PREHEAT

Prepare the oven by placing a large, shallow roasting pan under the bottom shelf of the oven. Preheat the oven to 400° 20 minutes before baking. Three minutes before placing the loaves in the oven, pour 1 pint hot water in the pan. Be careful of the steam that will suddenly erupt.

BAKING
400°
45 mins.

If the loaves have raised in baskets, simply tip the raised loaf into your hand and quickly turn the loaf right side up and onto the baking sheet. Brush with cold water and sprinkle with the coarse salt.

With a razor blade or a sharp knife, slash the round loaves with a tic-tac-toe design, the long loaves with diagonal cuts.

Bake the loaves until they are golden brown, 45 minutes. Turn over one loaf and tap the bottom crust; a hard hollow sound means the bread is baked. If not, return to the oven for an additional 10 minutes. Midway during baking and again near the end of it, shift the loaves on the baking sheets so they are exposed equally to the temperature variations of the oven.

(If using a convection oven, reduce heat 25°.)

FINAL STEP

Remove the loaves from the oven and place them on wire racks to cool.

This bread is delicious reheated. Place uncovered in a 350° oven for 20 minutes. It also keeps well frozen at 0°.

STARTERS

THERE ARE TWO basic starters used in this book—wild and yeast-fortified.

A true starter, be forewarned, can be whimsical and maddening in its formative days. Once established, it is a joy to have in the refrigerator. Some starters are boosted with yeast, but the amount is small and its presence will be lost in the long fermentation period that follows. The yeast, of course, makes it a sure thing and takes away some of the gamble—and some of the magic.

The French cut off, and set aside for use the next day, a small portion of each day's batch of dough. This portion is called the "chef" or *levain* and allows a desired strain of yeast (with its special taste and texture) to be carried forward indefinitely. It is described in the preceding chapter on French (and Italian) breads.

All starters and sponges (especially those for salt-rising bread) demand warmth in their formative stages. With the door slightly ajar, the pilot light in one of my gas ovens maintains a perfect 90°. With the door closed it jumps to 100°, which is also acceptable. I sometimes borrow my wife's yogurt maker, a series of small glass jars nestled in a heated plastic box that holds a constant 90°. I divide the mixture among the jars and I am certain to get one or more viable starters or sponges.

Other warm places likely to be good nurturing havens for sponges include the top of the water heater or refrigerator or any enclosed area where heat collects. The light in an electric oven can provide heat, too. Turn the oven on for a moment—just until the air inside feels a little warmer than room temperature. Place the starter inside, close the door, and turn on the light—or prop open the door just enough to keep the light on.

There are two easy ways to replenish starters.

One is to replace the cupful taken out of the jar to make a loaf of bread with ¾ cup flour and ¾ cup liquid (water, potato water, or milk). Stir, then allow the mixture to ferment at room temperature for a day or so before returning, covered, to the refrigerator.

The other way is to pour all of the starter into a bowl and add an equal amount of flour and liquid, as above. Stir the mixture well and take out however much starter is required by the recipe. This offers an opportunity to wash and scald the jar in which the starter has been stored. Return the starter to the bottle and allow it to ferment at room temperature for a day before returning it to the refrigerator.

A starter should be used at least once a week. If not, stir it down after 3 or 4 weeks, spoon out, and discard half of it and replenish the balance according to one of the methods described above.

Some starters can be frozen successfully, but if yours doesn't bounce back to life after thawing, it may need help with a sprinkling of dry yeast. Bring the starter to room temperature, stir in the yeast, and allow it to bubble before using.

Cooked Potato Starter   [six cups]
This is made in 2 steps, several days apart.

4 tablespoons cornmeal
2 tablespoons sugar
1½ teaspoons salt
1 cup milk
3 medium potatoes, peeled
1 quart water
3 tablespoons sugar
2 teaspoons salt

In a saucepan stir the cornmeal, 2 tablespoons sugar, 1½ teaspoons salt, and milk together; bring to the scalding point. Stir constantly. Pour this into a small bowl or glass container, cover tightly with plastic wrap, and leave in a warm place (90°) for 2 to 4 days, or until it ferments and becomes light and frothy. Stir each day.

When the mixture is spongy, cook the potatoes in a pot with the water until tender. Reserve the water, and add more if necessary, to make 3 cups of liquid. Mash the potatoes and put through a sieve or food mill. Stir in the reserved liquid, sugar, and salt. When cool, stir in the fermented cornmeal. Cover and let stand in a warm place. Stir down each time it becomes bubbly. Next day, put the mixture into a 2-

quart jar, cover, and place in the refrigerator to age for about 3 days before using.

Stir the potato starter down each time before using, and replenish when the starter has been reduced to 1 or 1½ cups. Prepare a new mixture of potato, potato water, sugar, and salt, and proceed as before.

Raw Potato Starter   [two cups]

I cup warm water (105°–115°)
1¼ cups bread or all-purpose flour
I teaspoon *each* salt and sugar
I medium potato, peeled and grated

In a 2-cup measure mix together the water, flour, salt and sugar. Add the grated potato sufficient to make a full 2 cups.

Pour the mixture into a widemouthed glass jar or bowl that will hold about 1 quart (to allow for expansion during fermentation).

Place a cheesecloth over the container and allow to rest in a warm place (90°) for 24 hours. Stir and cover tightly with plastic wrap, which will retain the moisture. The mixture will become light and foamy in 2 or 3 days. Stir down each day.

Pour the fermented starter into a glass jar fitted with a tight lid, and place in the refrigerator. In 3 or 4 days, when a clear liquid collects on top of the mixture, it will have ripened sufficiently for use.

Honey Starter   [three cups]
This is a yeast-boosted starter.

I package dry yeast
2½ cups warm water (105°–115°)
2 tablespoons honey
2½ cups bread or all-purpose flour

Combine the ingredients in a quart jar with a tight-fitting cover. Seal the jar and let the mixture ferment in a warm place for 5 days, stirring daily. Store in the refrigerator.

Replenish the starter with water and flour in equal portions.

Hops Starter   [six cups]

3 cups water
1 quart fresh hops, or ¼ cup packaged dry hops
½ cup white or yellow cornmeal
2 cups mashed potatoes
3 tablespoons sugar
2 teaspoons salt

In a saucepan bring the water to a boil and steep the hops for 20 minutes. Drain and reserve the liquid; discard the hops. If necessary, add water to make 3 full cups of liquid.

Pour 1 cup hops liquid into a saucepan and stir in the cornmeal. Bring to a boil over medium heat, stirring constantly. When it thickens slightly, remove from heat.

In a large mixing bowl combine the cornmeal mixture, mashed potatoes, sugar, salt, and remaining 2 cups hops liquid. Cover the bowl with a length of cheesecloth and set in a warm place (85°–90°) for 24 to 48 hours, or until well fermented and bubbly. Stir every 8 hours or so during this period.

When the starter is frothy and smells pleasantly fermented, pour it into a 2-quart jar with a tight-fitting lid. Store in the refrigerator until clear liquid has risen to the top, about 2 days. Stir down—and your hops starter is ready to use.

Yogurt Sourdough Starter   [two cups]

Excellent to give taste and texture to sourdough French breads, this starter is made with yogurt, milk, and flour—and, later, fortified with yeast when making the dough. Use in making Homecoming Sourdough French Bread in the "Sourdough Breads" chapter.

1 cup skim or low-fat milk
3 tablespoons plain yogurt
1 cup bread or all-purpose flour

Sterilize a 1½-quart glass, ceramic, rigid plastic, or stainless-steel container with boiling water. Wipe dry with a clean cloth.

In a saucepan heat the skim or low-fat milk to 90°–100°. Remove from heat and stir in the yogurt. Pour into the warm container, cover tightly, and let stand in a warm place for 8 to 24 hours. The starter should have the consistency of yogurt. If some liquid rises to the top, stir it back in. However, if the liquid has turned a light pink, it indicates the milk has started to break down; discard and start again.

After the mixture has formed a curd which will flow only slowly when the container is tilted, gradually stir the flour into the starter until it is smooth. Cover tightly and let stand in a warm place until the mixture is full of bubbles and has a good sour smell, 2 to 5 days. When half of the starter has been used it can be replenished by stirring in ½ cup milk and ½ cup flour.

To store, refrigerate. Bring to room temperature before using.

Fermented Grape Starter   [four cups]

This recipe for a grape-fermented starter was not in the bread book, but collected much later and published in Cooking Across America. *Nevertheless, it deserves to have a place here.*

This unusual starter is the creation of Karen Mitchell, whose Model Bakery is in St. Helena, deep in California's Napa Valley. It makes some of the best sourdough bread in the San Francisco Bay Area, and does it with a highly successful leavening of fermented grapes and flour.

Not all her breads are made with natural grape yeast, but they are the ones that are the most sought after.

Whenever she needs a new starter Karen goes to an old vineyard nearby that has not been "nuked," that is, sprayed with sulfur, and picks a bucket of the valley's Gamay grapes.

Here, in her words, is the recipe for the grape starter.

"I crush the grapes in the pail, cover it with a cloth to keep out the fruit flies, and put it aside for a week near the ovens where it is about 100°. By then, it will be a bubbly sort of wine, with a sugar content of between 1 and 2 percent. I strain off the juice, and discard the skins and stems.

"Each day I lightly feed the juice with small portions of whole wheat flour. By the end of two weeks, I have a starter the consistency of a thick batter."

SOURDOUGH BREADS

FERMENTATION IN THE EARLY stages of making the dough—lasting for hours and even days—is responsible for the delicious tanginess of sourdough breads. Very often it begins with the development of a starter (see "Starters" chapter), or it may be a heavy sponge made specially for a particular loaf.

There are a number of sourdough breads in the book, not all of them in this chapter. Old Milwaukee Rye is found in the chapter on rye breads and several sourdough French breads are in the "French Breads" chapter.

Homecoming Sourdough French Bread
[two round or long loaves]

Not quite a French peasant loaf but nevertheless delicious, this bread came out of my oven the first time to feed guests visiting from afar for a homecoming football game. Our team lost but the bread, said one guest, made it all worthwhile.

The sponge, which begins with a sourdough starter, is left to ferment for 1 or 2 days—depending on the degree of sourness desired. The egg-white wash applied just before the loaf goes into the oven and again at the end gives a glossy shine over a fine crackly crust.

This is a delicious bread not only for homecomings but for anytime, best when served warm or rewarmed. Although it can be frozen it always tastes better freshly baked.

INGREDIENTS

Sponge:

1 cup starter of choice (pages 241–44)
1½ cups warm water (105°–115°)
2½ cups bread or all-purpose flour
2 teaspoons sugar

Dough:

1 package dry yeast
2 teaspoons salt
½ teaspoon baking soda
3 to 4 cups bread or all-purpose flour, approximately

Glaze:

1 egg white, beaten, mixed with 1 tablespoon water

BAKING SHEET

1 baking sheet, Teflon, greased, or sprinkled with cornmeal

PREPARATION
1 or 2 days

To make the sponge, in a large mixing or mixer bowl combine the starter, water, flour, and sugar. Stir well and cover the bowl with plastic wrap. Put in a warm place (80°–90°) for 24 to 48 hours. Stir down each day.

BY HAND
OR MIXER
8 mins.

To make the dough, on bake day stir down the sponge and add the yeast, salt, and baking soda. Blend thoroughly. If by hand, stir in 3 to 4 cups flour with a wooden spoon and then use your hands to make a rough, shaggy mass that cleans the sides of the bowl. If using a mixer, begin with the flat beater and change to a dough hook when the dough gets heavy. Use 3 to 4 cups flour.

KNEADING
10 mins.

If by hand, turn the dough onto a lightly floured work surface and knead with the rhythmic motion of push-turn-fold. The dough will become smooth and elastic under the hands.

By mixer, add flour if necessary to form a soft ball that revolves around the dough hook, and cleans the sides of the bowl. Knead by hand or mixer for 10 minutes.

BY PROCESSOR
5 mins.

Prepare the sponge as above.

Attach the plastic dough blade.

Pour the sponge into the work bowl and add the yeast, salt, and baking soda. Pulse to blend. With the processor on, add flour, ¼ cup at a time, until the batter becomes a rough mass spinning with the blade, and cleaning the sides of the bowl.

KNEADING **60 secs.**	Keep the machine running and knead for 60 seconds.

When the dough is turned from the bowl it will be slightly sticky but sprinkles of flour will make it manageable. If it is too slack or wet, return to the bowl, add flour, and pulse several times. If the dough is dry, add 1 or 2 teaspoons of water, and process.

REST **10 mins.**	This dough does *not* rise before shaping, as do most yeast breads. When the kneading is completed put the dough under a towel to rest for 10 minutes.

SHAPING **20 mins.**	Punch down the dough and with a sharp knife cut in half. Form each half into a ball.

For round loaves, place each dough ball on a corner of the baking sheet and press into ovals or place in a small basket, lined loosely with a cloth sprinkled with flour.

For long loaves, press each dough ball down with your palms; roll the dough back and forth across the work surface until it is about 16" long. If the dough pulls back, allow it to rest for a few minutes or strike it hard with a fist down the length of the loaf. This will take much of the resistance out of the dough.

The long loaf, like the round one, can either be placed on the baking sheet or in a long cloth-lined basket sprinkled with flour from which it will be turned onto the baking sheet after rising.

RISING **1½ hours**	Place the baking sheets or basket in a warm place and cover carefully with a length of parchment or buttered wax paper. Leave until the loaves have doubled in volume.

PREHEAT	Place a large, shallow roasting pan on the bottom shelf of the oven. Preheat to 400° 20 minutes before baking. Fill the pan with about ½" of boiling water 5 minutes before baking. The water should boil away by the time the loaves begin to brown. If it does not, use less water next time.

BAKING **400°** **45 mins.**	If the loaf has risen in a basket, tip the dough into your hand and quickly turn it, right side up, onto the baking sheet. Brush the loaves with the egg-white wash.

With a razor blade, cut diagonal slashes in each long loaf, or a tic-tac-toe design on each round one.

Place the loaves in the oven. Midway during baking and again near the end of it, shift the loaves on the baking sheet so they are exposed equally to the temperature variations of the oven. Ten minutes before the bread is done, brush again with the egg-water mixture.

Bake until the loaves are a glossy brown, 45 minutes. Turn over one loaf and tap the bottom crust with a forefinger. A hard, hollow sound means the bread is baked. If not, return to the oven for an additional 5 to 10 minutes.

(If using a convection oven, reduce heat 50°.)

FINAL STEP

Remove the bread from the oven. It will make a cheery crackling sound on the rack as it cools. Serve warm or rewarmed.

Sourdough Oatmeal Bread   [two medium loaves]

Flecked with oats, this creamy, thick, and crusty loaf is only mildly sour or tart.

This is one of the first sourdough recipes I collected and it came via another cookbook author, Jack Mabee, of San Francisco. His small sourdough cookbook, no longer in print, introduced thousands of home bakers to the tangy delights of a sourdough loaf.

INGREDIENTS

Sponge:
1 cup starter of choice (pages 241–44)
1 cup warm water (105°–115°)
1 1/2 cups bread or all-purpose flour

Dough:
1 cup hot water (120°–130°)
1/2 cup nonfat dry milk
2 tablespoons honey
1 package dry yeast
1 cup quick oatmeal
1 tablespoon sugar
1 teaspoon *each* salt and baking soda
2 to 4 cups bread or all-purpose flour, approximately

BAKING PANS

2 medium (8"-x-4") baking pans, greased or Teflon. (For other combinations of pan sizes, see Dough Volume chart, page 16.)

PREPARATION
8–10 hours
or overnight

To make the sponge, begin the night before by mixing the starter, warm water, and flour into a large mixing or mixer bowl. Cover with plastic wrap and put in a warm place (85°–90°) for 8 to 10 hours or overnight. The starter will bubble and foam to about double its original size.

BY HAND
OR MIXER
15 mins.

To make the dough, on bake day turn back the plastic wrap, stir down the sponge, and measure in the water, dry milk, and honey. Sprinkle on the yeast. Stir in the oatmeal, sugar, salt, and baking soda. This can be done by hand with a wooden spoon or in the mixer with a flat beater.

Measure in the flour, ¼ cup at a time. If by hand, use a wooden spoon and then your hands. If using a mixer, attach the dough hook. The dough will be a rough shaggy mass that will clean the sides of the bowl. If the dough continues to be moist, add liberal sprinkles of flour.

KNEADING
10 mins.

If by hand, turn the dough onto a lightly floured work surface and knead for 10 minutes with the rhythmic motion of push-turn-fold.

If using a dough hook, knead at low speed in the mixer bowl and add flour, if necessary, until the dough forms a soft ball around the revolving arm, about 10 minutes. It will clean the sides of the bowl. The dough will feel smooth and satiny under your hands.

BY PROCESSOR
10 mins.

Prepare the sponge, as above.

Attach the plastic blade.

Pour the sponge into the work bowl, and add the water, dry milk, honey, and yeast. Pulse to blend. Add the oatmeal, sugar, salt, and baking soda. Pulse.

With the processor on, add the flour, ¼ cup at a time, until the heavy batter becomes a rough dough that spins with the blade and cleans the sides of the bowl. If flour clings to the bottom of the work bowl, scrape free with a spatula.

KNEADING
60 secs.

Process to knead for 60 seconds. The dough will be slightly sticky when turned from the bowl. Add sprinkles of flour, if needed, and knead briefly by hand.

REST
10 mins.

Shape the dough into a ball and leave on the work surface to rest under a towel for 10 minutes.

SHAPING
10 mins.

Knead the dough for 30 seconds to press out the bubbles. With a sharp knife divide the dough into 2 pieces. Shape into balls, and let rest for 3 to 4 minutes.

Form each loaf by pressing a ball of dough into a flat oval, roughly the length of the baking pan. Fold in half, pinch the seam tightly to seal, tuck under the ends, and place in the pan, seam down.

RISING
1¼ hours

Place the pans in a warm place, cover with wax paper, and leave until the center of the dough has risen above the edge of the pan, 1¼ hours.

PREHEAT	Preheat the oven to 400° 20 minutes before baking.
BAKING 400° 20 mins. 350° 25 mins.	I identify sourdough loaves with a slash lengthwise down the center of the crust. You may wish to do the same. This also allows the breads to expand along the slash and not pull the top crust away from the sides. Bake the loaves in the hot oven for 20 minutes, reduce the heat to 350°, and continue baking for an additional 25 minutes, or until the loaves test done. Midway during baking and again near the end of it, shift the pans so the loaves are exposed equally to the oven's temperature variations. When the loaves are a golden brown and tapping the bottom crust yields a hard and hollow sound, they are done. (If using a convection oven, reduce heat 50° for each bake period.)
FINAL STEP	Remove the bread from the oven and place on a metal rack to cool. This makes delicious toast, and freezes well for 4 to 6 months at 0°. *Note:* For a soft crust, brush the loaves with melted butter while the bread is hot.

Sourdough Whole-Wheat Bread   [two loaves]

A sponge composed of whole-wheat flour, water, and a cup of sourdough starter bubbles and foams for 24 hours before it takes command of this delicious loaf of almost all whole wheat. This is a satisfying dough to work, soft and pliable.

INGREDIENTS	*Sponge:* 1 cup starter of choice (pages 241–44) 1 1/2 cups warm water (105°–115°) 2 cups whole-wheat flour *Dough:* 1 package dry yeast 2 teaspoons salt 3 to 4 cups whole-wheat flour 1 cup bread or all-purpose flour, approximately
BAKING PANS	2 medium (8"-x-4") loaf pans, greased or Teflon
PREPARATION 8–10 hours or overnight	To make the sponge, the night before mix the starter, water, and flour in a mixer or mixing bowl. Cover with a length of plastic wrap and put in a warm place (80°–85°) for 8 to 10 hours, or overnight. The sponge will bubble and foam and rise to double its original volume.

**BY HAND
OR MIXER
20 mins.**

To make the dough, turn back the plastic wrap, stir down the sponge, and sprinkle yeast over the surface of the mixture. Add the salt. If you are using a mixer, attach the flat beater, and measure in the whole-wheat flour, ¼ cup at a time. Mix for 2 minutes at medium speed. If by hand, measure in the whole-wheat flour, mixing first with a spoon and then by hand.

When all of the whole-wheat flour has been mixed in, let the dough rest for 8 to 10 minutes while the flour completely absorbs the moisture. At this point attach the mixer dough hook.

Stir in the white flour, ¼ cup at a time, to make a soft dough that will form a rough mass that can be lifted from the bowl, or left in the mixer under the dough hook. The ball will be somewhat sticky because of the large volume of whole-wheat flour.

**KNEADING
10 mins.**

If by hand, use a spatula, putty knife, or dough scraper to help turn the dough. At the same time press with the palm of your other hand. Slowly the dough will become responsive and less sticky. If under the dough hook, add sprinkles of white flour so that a soft ball forms around the revolving arm. Knead by hand or with the dough hook until the dough is soft and elastic, 10 minutes. If it persists in sticking, sprinkle on additional small portions of white flour.

**BY PROCESSOR
15 mins.**

Prepare the sponge, as above.

Attach the plastic blade.

Pour the sponge into the processor work bowl and add the yeast and salt. Pulse to blend. With the processor running, add all of the whole-wheat flour, ¼ cup at a time. When the flour has been mixed in, turn off the machine and let the heavy batter rest for 8 to 10 minutes.

Add the white flour, ¼ cup at a time, with the processor running, to form a rough mass that will ride with the blade and clean the sides of the bowl.

**KNEADING
60 secs.**

Process to knead for 60 seconds. The dough will be slightly sticky when turned from the bowl but sprinkles of flour will make it manageable.

**RESTING
15 mins.**

Cover the dough with plastic wrap or a towel and let rest on the work surface for 15 minutes.

**SHAPING
10 mins.**

Push the dough down and knead for 30 seconds to press out the bubbles. With a sharp knife, divide the dough into two pieces. Shape into balls, and let rest for 3 to 4 minutes.

Form each loaf by pressing a ball of dough into a flat oval, roughly the length of the baking pan. Fold the oval in half, pinch the seam tightly to seal, tuck under the ends, and place in the pan, seam down.

RISING

2 hours

Place the pans in a warm place, cover with wax paper, and leave until the center of the dough has risen to the level or slightly above the edge of the pan, 2 hours.

PREHEAT

Preheat the oven to 425° 20 minutes before baking.

BAKING

425°

20 mins.

350°

35 mins.

Slit the top of each loaf lengthwise with a stroke of a razor blade or sharp knife.

Brush with water, and bake in the hot oven for 20 minutes. Brush the loaves again with water, reduce heat to 350°, and continue baking for an additional 35 minutes, or until the loaves are browned and test done when tapped on the bottom with the forefinger. Midway during the baking period and again near the end of it, shift the pans in the oven so they are exposed equally to its temperature variations.

(If using a convection oven, reduce heat 50° for each bake period.)

FINAL STEP

Place the bread on a metal rack to cool.

Sourdough Loaf   [two large loaves]

A fine bread with a tingling sharp taste—creamy on the inside, golden brown on the outside. The sponge, which is yeast boosted, can be heard bubbling across a quiet kitchen during the first 2 days of fermentation, and then it becomes passive and silent. Only 1½ cups of sponge is used in this recipe. You can refrigerate the rest for later use.

INGREDIENTS

Sponge:

1 package dry yeast

1¾ cups bread or all-purpose flour

1 tablespoon salt

1 tablespoon sugar

2½ cups hot water (120°–130°)

Dough:

5 to 6 cups bread or all-purpose flour, approximately

3 tablespoons sugar

1 teaspoon salt

1 package dry yeast

⅓ cup nonfat dry milk

1 cup hot water (120°–130°)
2 tablespoons shortening

BAKING PANS

2 large (9"-x-5") baking pans, greased or Teflon

PREPARATION
4 or 5 days

To make the sponge, in a medium bowl blend the yeast, flour, salt, and sugar and add the hot water. Stir for 30 seconds. Cover with plastic wrap to retain moisture, and place in a warm spot (80°–85°). Stir the sponge down each day.

BY HAND
OR MIXER
15 mins.

On baking day, make the dough in a large mixing or mixer bowl. Measure 1 cup flour and stir in the sugar, salt, yeast, dry milk, and hot water. Add the shortening and 1½ cups of sponge. Beat for 3 minutes with the mixer flat beater at medium-high speed, or for an equal length of time with a wooden spoon.

Stop the mixer, and attach the dough hook. Stir in the balance of the flour, ½ cup at a time, until the dough is a rough, shaggy mass that will clean the sides of the bowl. Or mix in by hand. If the dough continues to be moist and sticky, sprinkle with flour. The dough will form a soft ball around the hook, and clean the sides of the bowl.

KNEADING
8 mins.

If by hand, turn the dough onto a lightly floured work surface and knead with the rhythmic motion of push-turn-fold. If using a mixer, knead under the dough hook. Either way, knead for 8 minutes.

If the dough should be sticky, sprinkle with small additions of flour. If by hand, occasionally break the kneading rhythm by raising the dough above the work surface and throwing it down hard against the table.

PROCESSING
5 mins.

Prepare the sponge, as above.

Attach the plastic dough blade.

Measure 3 cups flour into the work bowl and add the sugar, salt, yeast, and dry milk. Pour in the hot water. Pulse to blend. Add the shortening and 1½ cups of sponge.

With the processor running, add flour, ¼ cup at a time, to form a rough mass that swirls with the blade and cleans the sides of the bowl.

KNEADING
60 secs.

Knead with the processor on for 60 seconds.

The dough will be slightly sticky when turned from the bowl but a few light sprinkles of flour will make it manageable.

FIRST RISING
1 hour

Place the dough in a greased or buttered bowl, cover tightly with plastic wrap, and leave at room temperature until the dough has risen to about twice its original volume, about 1 hour.

SHAPING	Punch down the dough with the fingertips and knead for 30 seconds to
10 mins.	press out the bubbles. Put the dough on the lightly floured work sur-

SHAPING
10 mins.

Punch down the dough with the fingertips and knead for 30 seconds to press out the bubbles. Put the dough on the lightly floured work surface and cut in half with a sharp knife. Shape each half into a ball, and let rest under a towel for 5 minutes.

Form each loaf by pressing a ball of dough into a flat oval, roughly the length of the baking pan. Fold the oval in half, pinch the seam tightly to seal, tuck under the ends, and place in the pan, seam down.

SECOND RISING
50 mins.

Cover the pans with a length of wax paper and leave until the loaves have doubled in size, 50 minutes. Ideally, the top of the dough should have risen to about 1" above the level of the pans.

PREHEAT

Preheat the oven to 400° 20 minutes before baking.

BAKING
400°
30–40 mins.

Bake the loaves until they are a golden brown and test done, about 30 minutes. Turn one loaf out of its pan and tap the bottom crust with a forefinger. A hard, hollow sound means the bread is baked. If not, return to the oven for an additional 5 to 10 minutes. Midway during baking and again near the end of it, shift the loaves so they are exposed equally to the temperature variations of the oven. If you wish a darker crust, remove the loaves from the pans during the final 10 minutes of baking.

(If using a convection oven, reduce heat 50°.)

FINAL STEP

Remove the bread from the oven. Turn from the pans and cool on a wire rack.

Note: For a softer crust, brush the bread with melted butter while the bread is still hot.

Sourdough Potato Bread   [two medium loaves]

Potato starter—no yeast—lifts this loaf grandly above the pan and gives it the wonderful taste and texture that potato alone can produce. Later on, packaged potato flakes are used in the sponge so there is no fuss about peeling and boiling potatoes.

INGREDIENTS

Sponge:
1 cup Raw or Cooked Potato Starter (pages 241–44)
1 cup bread or all-purpose flour
$1/4$ cup sugar
$1/4$ teaspoon ground ginger
1 cup water
$1/2$ cup instant potato flakes

Dough:

$\frac{1}{2}$ cup hot water (120°–130°)

$\frac{1}{3}$ cup nonfat dry milk

3 to 4 cups bread or all-purpose flour, approximately

$\frac{1}{4}$ teaspoon *each* baking soda and cream of tartar

$\frac{1}{4}$ cup vegetable shortening, room temperature

1 teaspoon salt

2 tablespoons cream (optional)

2 tablespoons butter, melted (optional)

BAKING PANS	2 medium (8"-x-4") loaf pans, greased or Teflon, or a selection of pans and baking sheets, according to the Dough Volume chart (page 16)
PREPARATION 2 hours Overnight	To make the sponge, in a stoneware, ceramic, or glass bowl (not metal or plastic) stir together 1 cup starter and the flour. A soft ball will form. Let it rest, uncovered, for 2 hours. In a separate bowl stir together the sugar, ginger, and water. Pour over the starter mixture. Sprinkle the potato flakes over the surface. Cover tightly with a length of plastic wrap and set aside in a warm place (80°–85°) for 8 to 10 hours, or overnight.
BY HAND OR MIXER 15 mins.	The sponge will be foamy and expanding up the sides of the bowl. Stir it down. Add the hot water, dry milk, 2 cups flour, baking soda, and cream of tartar. Beat 100 strokes with a wooden spoon, or if using a mixer, stir with the flat beater at medium speed for 2 minutes. Measure in the shortening and salt. Attach the dough hook for the mixer. Work in the balance of the flour, ¼ cup at a time. The dough will be a rough, shaggy mass that will clean the sides of the bowl. In the mixer the dough will form a soft ball around the revolving dough hook. If the dough continues to be sticky, add sprinkles of flour.
KNEADING 10 mins.	Turn the dough onto a lightly floured work surface and knead with the rhythmic motion of push-turn-fold. If using the mixer, leave under the dough hook. Knead for 10 minutes. The dough will become smooth and elastic. Sprinkle more flour if the dough is slack or moist and continues to stick to your hands or the sides of the mixer bowl.

BY PROCESSOR
4 mins.
	Prepare the sponge, as above.
	    Attach the plastic dough blade.
	    On baking day, scrape the sponge into the processor work bowl and add the hot water, dry milk, 2 cups flour, baking soda, and cream of tartar. Pulse to blend thoroughly. Measure in the shortening and salt. Pulse several times to blend.

With the processor on, add flour, ¼ cup at a time, until a mass has formed on the blade. The dough will clean the sides of the bowl.

KNEADING
60 secs.

Knead for 60 seconds with the processor running.

The dough will be slightly sticky when turned from the bowl. If it is wet, return it to the bowl and add sprinkles of flour. Knead in with a pulse or two.

REST
20 mins.

Form the dough into a ball, and let it rest under a cloth on the work surface for 20 minutes.

SHAPING
15 mins.

Punch down the dough and knead for 1 minute to press out the bubbles. Divide the dough into as many pieces as you want loaves. Shape the pieces into balls, and let them rest for 3 or 4 minutes.

Form each loaf by pressing the ball under your palms into a flat oval, roughly the length of the pan. Fold the oval in half, pinch the seam tightly to seal, tuck under the ends, and place in the pan, seam down.

RISING
45 mins.

Brush the tops of the loaves with melted butter, cover loosely with wax or parchment paper, and leave to rise until the dough has doubled in bulk, 45 minutes. The center of the top will rise above the sides of the pan.

PREHEAT

Preheat the oven to 375° 20 minutes before baking.

BAKING
375°
45 mins.

Bake the loaves in the oven until they are a lovely golden brown and test done, 45 minutes. Midway during baking, shift the pans so the loaves are exposed equally to temperature variations. If you wish a deep brown crust, remove the loaves from the pans during the last 10 minutes of baking.

Five minutes before the end of baking brush the loaves with a swish of cream or melted butter for a rich-looking crust.

(If using a convection oven, reduce heat 50°.)

FINAL STEP

Remove the breads from the oven and turn from the loaf pans. Allow the loaves to cool before slicing.

This bread toasts beautifully, keeps well wrapped for a week or more, and will freeze for an indefinite period at 0°.

Starter White Bread   [two medium loaves]

The life and movement of dough is a constant wonder. This loaf, leavened only with a starter, begins as a heavy blob of dough about the size of an orange on the bottom of the bowl. Warm water is poured over it, and 8 hours later the sponge is foamy and light on the surface of the water.

Lard makes a softer, richer texture, which is why I use it in this loaf.

INGREDIENTS

Sponge:
$\frac{1}{2}$ cup starter of choice (pages 241–44)
$\frac{3}{4}$ cup bread or all-purpose flour
2 tablespoons sugar
$\frac{1}{4}$ teaspoon ground ginger
1 cup water

Dough:
$\frac{1}{2}$ cup nonfat dry milk
3 to 4 cups bread or all-purpose flour
$\frac{1}{4}$ teaspoon *each* baking soda and cream of tartar
2 teaspoons salt
$\frac{1}{4}$ cup lard or other shortening, room temperature, plus
    2 tablespoons, melted, to brush

BAKING PANS

2 medium (8½"-x-4½") loaf pans, greased or Teflon

PREPARATION
2 hours

To make the sponge, the night before, stir the starter and flour together in a bowl to form a soft ball. Use a wooden spoon rather than your fingers because the mixture will be moist and sticky. Let stand for 2 hours uncovered.

Overnight

Meanwhile, in a small bowl or measuring cup combine the sugar, ginger, and water. Pour the liquid over the dough, cover the bowl tightly with plastic wrap, and leave at room temperature overnight.

BY HAND
OR MIXER
20 mins.

To make the dough, next day turn back the plastic wrap and thoroughly blend the floating sponge into the water. Add the dry milk, ½ cup flour, baking soda, cream of tartar, and salt. Beat 50 strokes by hand or with a mixer flat beater.

Add the ¼ cup lard or other shortening and 1 cup flour, then beat into a smooth batter. Work in the balance of the flour, a portion at a time, first with the spoon and then by hand or under a dough hook. The dough will be a rough, shaggy mass that will clean the bowl. If the dough is slack and moisture breaks through, add small amounts of flour as you work the dough.

KNEADING 8 mins.	Turn the dough onto a lightly floured work surface and knead with the rhythmic motion of push-turn-fold, or put under the dough hook. The dough will become smooth and elastic and bubbles will rise under the surface of the dough. Break the kneading rhythm by occasionally throwing the dough down hard against the countertop. Knead for about 8 minutes by hand or with the dough hook.
BY PROCESSOR 5 mins.	Make the sponge, as above. Attach the plastic blade. Pour all of the sponge into the work bowl and add the dry milk and 1 cup flour, baking soda, cream of tartar, salt, and ¼ cup shortening. Pulse to blend thoroughly. With the machine on, add the balance of the flour through the feed tube, a portion at a time. After the mixture absorbs the flour, the ball of dough will clean the sides of the bowl as it whirls with the blade.
KNEADING 45 secs.	Keep the machine running and knead for 45 seconds.
REST 20 mins.	Let the dough rest on the countertop, covered with a tea towel or wax paper for 20 minutes.
SHAPING 10 mins.	Try a twin loaf. Divide the dough into 2 portions, then each loaf portion into halves. Make each twin into a roll the length of the pan. Place side by side in the pan. Brush the tops with the melted shortening.
RISING 2 hours	Cover the pans and leave until the dough has risen to double in bulk, 2 hours. Starter is not a fast leavening agent so it will take longer to rise than yeast breads.
PREHEAT	Preheat the oven to 375° 20 minutes before baking.
BAKING 375° 45 mins.	Bake the loaves at 375° until they are golden brown, about 45 minutes. When tapping the bottom crust yields a hard, hollow sound, the loaves are done. If not, return to the oven—without the pans if you wish a deep brown crust—for an additional 5 to 10 minutes. Midway during baking and again near the end of it, shift the pans so the loaves are exposed equally to temperature variations in the oven. (If using a convection oven, reduce heat 50°.)
FINAL STEP	Remove the bread from the oven and turn the loaves onto a metal rack to cool before serving or freezing. This loaf will keep for several months in the deep freeze. Excellent toasted, too.

California Sourdough Whole-Wheat Bread
[two medium loaves]

When questioned about my very favorite bread from among the several thousand that I have baked, I hedge. It's like being asked which child you favor. However, if pressed to give two favorites, this bread is one of them.

And for good reason. This loaf led me into writing about home baking. Many years ago while rafting down the Colorado River, through the Grand Canyon, I told the passengers in my boat about a wonderful bread I had developed. One of the passengers was an editor for Sunset, *a magazine at home in the Bay Area, where devotees of sourdough French bread are legion (and vocal). The editor bought the recipe and I became a professional.*

The loaf has withstood the test of time and I talk about it in glowing terms today just as I did two decades ago while floating downstream on a raft.

The chief reason, of course, is that it is delicious.

During the 3 days when the sponge is fermenting in the bowl, a whiff under the plastic wrap will be strongly alcoholic. I add 1 cup whole or cracked wheat grains to the sponge to give the bread the texture of a provincial loaf.

Toasted, and under a piece of fine cheese, makes a marvelous combination.

This is a large recipe of heavy dough for the food processor. I suggest dividing the recipe in half.

INGREDIENTS

Sponge:
2 cups hot water (120°–130°)
2 packages dry yeast
$^1/_3$ cup nonfat dry milk
3 cups whole-wheat flour, stone-ground preferred
1 cup whole or cracked wheat grains

Dough:
$^1/_4$ cup dark molasses
1 tablespoon salt
3 tablespoons vegetable shortening
2$^1/_2$ to 3 cups bread or all-purpose flour, approximately

BAKING PANS

2 medium (8"-x-4") loaf pans, greased or Teflon

PREPARATION
3 days

To make the sponge, 3 days before baking begin it in a large bowl by blending together the hot water, yeast, dry milk, and whole-wheat flour.

Cover the bowl tightly with plastic wrap so the moisture will not evaporate. Leave at room temperature for 3 days. Once each day stir the mixture briefly. The sponge will rise and then fall during this period. Even when fallen and it looks to be inactive, the sponge will continue to ferment.

1 hour

One hour before making the dough, in a bowl soak the cracked grains in hot water to cover. Drain, press dry through a sieve, and stir into the sponge. They will have a nice crunchiness about them.

**BY HAND
OR MIXER
15 mins.**

To make the dough, stir into the sponge the molasses, salt, and shortening. If by hand, stir in the white flour with a wooden spoon and then when it becomes too heavy, with your hands. If using a mixer, begin with the flat beater and attach the dough hook when the spongy dough gets heavy.

There are times when the dough hook will not accept the dough and will revolve ineffectively in a pattern around but not in the dough. If this happens, turn out the dough onto the floured work surface and continue by hand. When the dough becomes soft and elastic it may be returned to the mixer to be kneaded.

**KNEADING
10 mins.**

If by hand, turn the dough onto a floured work surface and knead with a rhythmic motion of push-turn-fold. It is a heavier dough than all white, but presently the gluten will begin to form and the dough will become soft and pliable. Add small sprinkles of flour to control the stickiness, if necessary. Under the hook, the dough will form a soft ball and clean the sides of the bowl as the arm revolves. Knead for 10 minutes.

**BY PROCESSOR
5 mins.**

A reminder that this may be too much dough for the food processor. To be on the safe side, reduce the quantities of the ingredients by half for both sponge and dough.

Prepare the sponge as above.

Attach the short plastic dough blade.

Pour or scrape the sponge into the work bowl and add the molasses, salt, and shortening. Pulse several times to blend. With the processor running, add flour, ¼ cup at a time, through the feed tube until the batter becomes a heavy mass that rides with the blade and cleans the sides of the bowl. Stop the machine, uncover, and feel the dough. It should be soft and slightly sticky. If wet, add flour and pulse to achieve a soft, elastic texture.

**KNEADING
60 secs.**

Process to knead the dough for 60 seconds.

FIRST RISING **2 hours**	Place the dough in a mixing bowl and pat with buttered or greased fingers to keep the surface from crusting. Cover the bowl with plastic wrap and leave at room temperature until the dough has risen to about double its original volume, 2 hours. Because this is leavened with only the 3-day-old sponge, it will not rise as fast as if it had been made with a fresh charge of yeast.
SHAPING **15 mins.**	Punch down the dough. Knead for 30 seconds to press out the bubbles. Divide the dough in half with a sharp knife. Shape into balls, and let rest under a towel for 5 minutes. Shape by pressing each ball under your palms into a flat oval, roughly the length of the baking pan. Fold the oval in half, pinch the seam tightly to seal, tuck under the ends, and place in the pan, seam down.
SECOND RISING **1¼ hours**	Cover the pans with wax or parchment paper and leave until the center of the dough has risen even with the edge of the pan, about 1¼ hours.
PREHEAT	Preheat the oven to 375° about 20 minutes before baking.
BAKING **375°** **40–50 mins.**	With a sharp razor, slash each loaf down the center; then make several small diagonal cuts, as branches from a limb. Bake in the oven until the loaves are deep brown and crusty, 40 to 50 minutes. Turn one loaf out of its pan and tap the bottom with a forefinger. A hard, hollow sound means the bread is baked. If not, return to the oven, without the pan, for an additional 10 minutes. Midway during baking, shift the pans to different parts of the oven or simply exchange positions. (If using a convection oven, reduce heat 50°.)
FINAL STEP	Remove the bread from the oven. Turn the loaves onto a metal rack to cool before serving. This bread will keep, wrapped, for at least a month, and can be frozen for 6 months or more at 0°. Toasting brings out the special flavor and aroma of this delicious loaf.

Pumpernickel au Ferment Aigre
[two large round loaves]
(Sourdough Pumpernickel)

This loaf of dark, coarse bread begins with a sourdough starter, and any one of many in this book will do. But this bread doesn't depend solely on a starter to leaven the dough. Yeast is added to allow an otherwise dense loaf to develop an open grain. For flavor and texture, both the potato and the water in which it is cooked are used in the recipe.

INGREDIENTS

Sponge:
1 cup starter of choice (pages 241–44)
$^1/_4$ cup molasses
$^3/_4$ cup potato water (can be reserved from cooking the potato, below)
2 cups stone-ground whole-wheat flour

Dough:
1 cup boiling water
$^1/_4$ cup cornmeal
1 cup mashed potatoes
1 package dry yeast
1 tablespoon salt
2 tablespoons cooking oil
2 tablespoons caraway seeds
1 cup whole-wheat flour
3 cups rye flour
$^1/_2$ cup bread flour, approximately
1 egg, beaten, mixed with 1 tablespoon water
Coarse salt (optional)

BAKING SHEET

1 baking sheet, Teflon or sprinkled with cornmeal

PREPARATION
8–10 hours

To make the sponge, in a large bowl combine the starter, molasses, potato water, and whole-wheat flour. Mix thoroughly, cover the bowl with plastic wrap, and leave at room temperature until the sponge has doubled in volume, about 8 to 10 hours.

BY HAND
OR MIXER
20 mins.

In a small bowl pour the boiling water over the cornmeal, stirring vigorously with a fork or wire whip. Add the mashed potatoes and mix well. Allow to cool, then add the sponge and yeast, salt, cooking oil, and 1 tablespoon caraway seeds. Beat well by hand with a heavy spoon, or if using an electric mixer, with a flat beater.

Add the whole-wheat and rye flours, ¼ cup at a time, stirring all the while. Stir in ½ cup white flour to make a mass that will pull away from the bowl. The dough will be stiff (probably too stiff for a dough hook), but if it should remain slack and sticky, add sprinkles of white flour.

KNEADING
8 mins.

Turn the dough onto a lightly floured work surface—countertop or breadboard—and knead with a rhythmic motion of push-turn-fold. A dough blade to turn and fold the dough will make the job easier. The dough will become elastic, in about 6 or 8 minutes, but will remain somewhat sticky. Control stickiness with sprinkles of flour.

BY PROCESSOR
7 mins.

Prepare the starter and sponge, as above.

Attach the plastic blade.

In a small bowl pour the hot water over the cornmeal and add the mashed potatoes. When the mixture has cooled, scrape it into the work bowl and add the sponge, yeast, salt, cooking oil, and 1 tablespoon caraway seeds. Pulse to blend.

With the machine running, add the whole-wheat and rye flours, ¼ cup at a time. Add white flour to make a mass that will ride the blade and clean the sides of the bowl.

KNEADING
45 secs.

Keep the machine running and knead for 45 seconds.

FIRST RISING
3 hours

Place the dough in a greased bowl, cover with plastic wrap, and let rise until double in volume, about 3 hours.

SHAPING
5 mins.

Punch down and remove the dough from the bowl. Divide into 2 pieces. Shape each into a ball and press down on top with the palm of your hand to flatten it somewhat.

Slash a tic-tac-toe design in the tops and place on the baking sheet.

SECOND RISING 1 hour	Cover the loaves with plastic wrap or a cloth and set aside to rise at room temperature until almost doubled in size, about 1 hour.
PREHEAT	Preheat the oven to 375° 20 minutes before baking.
BAKING **375°** 1 hour	Brush the loaves with the egg-water glaze, sprinkle with 1 tablespoon caraway seeds (coarse salt is another option), and place on the lower shelf of the oven.

Bake for 1 hour, or until the loaves test done—the bottom crusts will sound hard and hollow when tapped with a forefinger.

(If using a convection oven, reduce heat 50°.)

FINAL STEP Remove the loaves from the oven and place them on a metal rack to cool before cutting.

This bread will keep for several days at room temperature. It freezes admirably.

Marvelous for sandwiches, buffets, and picnic lunches.

SALT-RISING BREADS

THIS IS A NATURAL WAY to make bread, but also one of the most difficult and temperamental. No yeast is used. If the sponge doesn't bubble up during the night to produce its oddly sweet odor, have *no* patience. Throw it out. It is only a sacrifice of cornmeal and milk. Begin again, but try another way—different milk, another brand of cornmeal. There is no easy explanation of why one combination will work and another will not.

The phrase "salt-rising" refers to the old kitchen practice of keeping the bowl of starter nested overnight in a bed of salt, which is easy to heat and will retain the heat nicely. It does not refer to the bread's peculiar taste.

Salt-rising bread loves warmth. Warm everything it touches—the bowl, the cups, and the spoons. Don't let it chill. Search out a place in the kitchen where the temperature is consistent over a twenty-four-hour period. The ideal place for the starter is between 90° and 100°. I sometimes place it on a shelf near the hot water heater. The pilot light in my gas stove keeps the temperature at a constant 90°, with the door slightly ajar. My wife's yogurt machine of jars nested in a heating unit is fine, too. The sponge and dough demand less heat and attention as the bacteria strain grows and strengthens.

Always use whole milk. I have used nonfat dry milk but not always with success.

The smell of salt-rising bread hot out of the oven or toasted is one of baking's most distinctive aromas. The taste and texture are equally so.

Sister Abigail's Salt-Rising Bread   [two medium loaves]

"Take scalded milk and pour over cornmeal . . ." So began the recipe for the salt-rising bread baked by Sister Abigail, a member of one of Ohio's several Shaker communities at the turn of the century.

However, Sister Abigail's recipe became more complicated as she heated more milk, added this ingredient and that, and then put everything in a saucepan set in a bowl filled with hot water. This is to caution the home baker that this Shaker recipe, while it produces a good loaf of salt-rising bread, is a painstaking one, calling for a warm kitchen, and a work schedule that will accommodate the rather unpredictable risings of the starter and dough.

However, the feeling of accomplishment when taking a well-raised loaf from the oven, can be considerable reward for the effort involved.

INGREDIENTS

Starter:
1 cup fresh milk
$^1/_2$ cup cornmeal

Sponge:
2 cups fresh milk
$^3/_4$ teaspoon salt
1 tablespoon sugar
5 tablespoons lard or other shortening
1 teaspoon baking soda

Dough:
$2^1/_2$ cups bread or all-purpose flour, approximately

BAKING PANS

2 medium (8"-x-4") baking pans, greased or Teflon

PREPARATION
2–6 hours

To make the starter, in a saucepan, scald the milk, then pour it over the cornmeal in a small bowl. Stir to mix. Do not cover. Leave open to the air, and move to a warm place (90°–100°). Leave until the mixture bubbles, from 2 to 6 hours. This must be an active fermentation—not just 1 or 2 solitary bubbles making their way through the cornmeal. The action must expand the mixture and make it light and fluffy. If it doesn't, get a new starter going. You are at the mercy of bacteria!

1–2 hours

To make the sponge, in a large saucepan heat the 2 cups milk to luke-warm and stir in the salt, sugar, shortening, and baking soda. Add the starter.

Fill a large bowl with hot water and carefully set the saucepan of sponge in the bowl to provide a constant flow of warmth while this larger batch ferments and begins to bubble, 1 to 2 hours. Replenish the hot water 2 or 3 times during the period. (See Note.)

BY HAND
OR MIXER
6 mins.

Empty the warm bowl, wipe it dry, and use it to combine the milk mixture and the flour. Stir in the flour, ¼ cup at a time, first with the spoon and then by hand. The dough will be a rough, shaggy mass that will clean the sides of the bowl. If the dough continues to be sticky, add sprinkles of flour. If using a mixer, stir in the flour with the flat beater until it becomes too heavy to work. Substitute the dough hook and continue adding flour until a soft ball forms around the revolving arm.

KNEADING
10 mins.

Knead by hand or in the mixer for 10 minutes. Expect the dough to have a slightly different consistency than the usual yeast-raised bread. It will not feel as alive, nor will it be as elastic.

BY PROCESSOR
5 mins.

Prepare the starter and sponge, as above.

Attach the plastic dough blade.

Pour the fermented sponge into the processor work bowl and add the salt, sugar, shortening, and baking soda. Add 2 cups flour. Pulse to blend. With the processor running, add the balance of the flour, ¼ cup at a time, until a mass forms and is carried with the blade. The mass will clean the sides of the bowl as it whirls.

Stop the machine and pinch the dough. If the dough is dry, add water by teaspoons, with the machine running. If wet, add flour by tablespoons.

KNEADING
60 secs.

With the processor running, knead for 60 seconds.

The dough should be slightly sticky and elastic. Pull and stretch the dough between your hands to test its consistency; if necessary, return to the work bowl to process a few seconds more.

SHAPING
4 mins.

The dough goes directly into the pan.

Divide the dough into 2 pieces. Shape each into an oval, roughly the length of the baking pan. Fold the oval in half, pinch the seam tightly to seal, tuck under the ends, and place in the pan, seam down.

RISING
2–3 hours

Place the pans in a warm place (90°), cover with wax paper, and leave until the dough has doubled in volume—2 or 3 hours depending on how warm the loaves are kept during this period. A temperature of 90° is ideal.

PREHEAT

Preheat the oven to 350° about 20 minutes before baking.

BAKING
350°
15 mins.
425°
45 mins.

Bake in a moderate oven for 15 minutes, advance heat to 425°, and bake for an additional 45 minutes, a total of 1 hour, or until raised and a light brown. When tapping the bottom crust yields a hard, hollow sound, the bread is done. If not, return to the oven for an additional 5 to 10 minutes. Midway during the baking and again near the end of

it, shift the pans so the loaves are exposed equally to temperature variations in the oven.

(If using a convection oven, reduce heat 50° for each bake period.)

FINAL STEP

Turn the loaves from the pans and place on a metal rack to cool.

Expect salt-rising bread to be a rather heavy, solid loaf. It will not
have the lightness or the buoyancy that a yeast-leavened loaf will have.
Note: If you wish to ferment the sponge the old-fashioned way, heat 2
or 3 pounds of coarse rock salt (the kind used in a home ice cream
freezer) in the oven until the salt is quite warm to the touch (about
110°). Pack this around the container of sponge and leave for 1 to 2
hours, as above.

Salt-Rising Bread   [two small loaves or one medium]

*An uncomplicated way to make a loaf of good salt-rising bread is with this
recipe published in 1912 by the Ladies Aid Society of the First Presbyterian
Church in Polson, Montana. Living in the heart of Flathead Indian country, the
church women of the valley were fine cooks and bakers, and salt-rising bread
was a specialty.*

*Preparation begins the day before, with cornmeal in a small bowl over which
scalding hot milk is poured. The mixture will ferment and be light and foamy by
morning. The active mixture is added to the batter in a large bowl to begin the
fermentation process over again but on a larger scale.*

*The batter will develop a strong smell not unlike that of a soft ripe cheese, and
it is here the lovers of salt-rising bread are usually sorted out from the nonlovers.
To the former, it is a glorious aroma, to the latter, an unpleasant smell.*

INGREDIENTS

$1/4$ cup fresh milk
2 tablespoons cornmeal, stone-ground preferred
$1 1/2$ teaspoons sugar
1 cup hot water (120°–130°)
$1/2$ teaspoon *each* salt and baking soda
$3 1/2$ to 4 cups bread or all-purpose flour, approximately
$1/4$ cup shortening, lard preferred, room temperature
Oil or melted lard, to brush

BAKING PANS

2 small (7"-x-3") or 1 medium (8"-x-4") loaf pan, greased or Teflon

PREPARATION
8–10 hours
or overnight

The evening before, in a saucepan scald the milk. In a small bowl pour
the scalding hot (but not boiling) milk over the cornmeal and 1 teaspoon sugar. Stir together and cover tightly with plastic wrap. Place in

a warm spot (90°–100°) where it will remain for 8 to 10 hours. A bubbly foam will develop over the surface of the cornmeal and it will smell sweet and fermented.

BY HAND
20 mins.

In a large mixing or mixer bowl (warmed under hot water tap), pour the hot water over the ½ teaspoon sugar, salt, and baking soda. Stir this briefly with a large spoon. Gradually add 1½ cups flour to make a thick batter. Stir until smooth—about 50 strokes. The batter should be lukewarm to the touch. Not hot. Stir in the fermented cornmeal mixture.

FIRST RISING
2 hours

Cover the bowl tightly with plastic wrap; return to the warm place until the batter has bubbled and foamed to more than double its volume, about 2 hours.

When you turn back the plastic wrap the aroma will be quite strong.

BY HAND
OR MIXER
10 mins.

With the wooden spoon or flat beater mix in the shortening. Gradually add flour, ¼ cup at a time, first with the spoon and then by hand. Work it well between the fingers, adding more flour, if necessary, until the dough has lost its wetness and a rough mass has formed. If using a mixer, when the dough becomes heavy remove the flat beater and replace it with the dough hook. Continue adding flour until a rough mass forms under the hook.

KNEADING
10 mins.

Turn the dough onto a floured work surface and begin the kneading process. This dough will feel alive under your palms, elastic and soft. The dough under the dough hook will form a soft ball around the revolving arm. Add sprinkles of flour if the dough sticks to the sides of the bowl. Knead for 10 minutes.

BY PROCESSOR
5 mins.

The first 2 steps in the preparation of the dough will be done in 2 bowls, as above. Processing will come later.

Attach the steel blade.

After the batter has risen for the second time and the shortening has been added, pour the mixture into the processor work bowl. With the machine running, add flour, ¼ cup at a time, to form a rough mass that whirls with the blade and cleans the sides of the bowl. If flour remains along the bottom edge of the bowl, scrape it free with a spatula.

KNEADING
60 secs.

With the processor running, knead for 60 seconds.

SHAPING
10 mins.

Divide the dough in half. Roll each piece into a rectangle, fold in half, pinch the seam closed, and shape the dough into a loaf. Place in the pan, seam to the bottom. The dough usually fills only half the pan. Brush the tops lightly with oil or melted lard.

SECOND RISING
50 mins.

Cover with wax paper and allow to rise until the dough has doubled, about 50 minutes.

PREHEAT

Preheat the oven to 375° about 20 minutes before baking.

BAKING
375°
45 mins.

Place the pans in the oven. When the loaves are nicely browned and tapping the bottom crust yields a hard and hollow sound, about 45 minutes, they are done.

(If using a convection oven, reduce heat 50°.)

FINAL STEP

Remove the bread from the oven and turn out immediately onto a metal cooling rack.

Toasting enhances the flavor of salt-rising bread. It may be kept frozen for several months at 0°.

FESTIVE BREADS

In AUTUMN, the appearance on the grocer's shelves of stacks of candied fruit and mountains of nuts in all of their wonderful variety—priceless ingredients for the festive breads—is a sure sign of the approaching holidays. In summer, the candied fruit would have melted in the heat and its sweetness would have drawn the ants. But as the days grow short and the nights cool, it is safe to bring it home and begin preparation for a joyous time of baking from early November through Thanksgiving, Christmas, New Year's, and on into the Easter celebrations.

Of course, not all festive breads are baked for the holidays, or made with candied fruit and nuts. A child's birthday, any time of the year, deserves a festive bread. Challah, the delicious Jewish loaf, is a Sabbath bread. Panettone is for weddings and christenings as well as the holidays.

A suggestion: shortly after the holidays, candied fruit is reduced in price to clear the grocer's shelves; so if you have space in the freezer, buy a supply. It will assure that you have candied fruit to bake with in the months when it can't be found in the market.

Mother's Christmas Bread
[two large or four small loaves]

For many years our family's favorite loaf has been Mother's Christmas Bread. It was not my mother's bread, although she was a fine home baker, but one brought to this country from Norway more than a century ago by the great-great-grandmother of a friend. Dates, nuts, candied fruit, and butter make this one of the best tasting and most colorful of the festive loaves.

I consider it an all-around festive loaf that can be used for any holiday occasion—Christmas, New Year's, Easter, birthdays, anniversaries—shaped into any number of special forms that give it a life out of the ordinary, such as a stollen, a wreath, or a tier of braids.

It also makes a fine piece of toast on either a festive or nonfestive occasion. The small loaves are ideal for gift giving.

INGREDIENTS

7 cups bread or unbleached flour, approximately
2 cups hot milk (120°–130°)
2 packages dry yeast
1 egg, room temperature
$\frac{1}{2}$ cup sugar
1 teaspoon salt
1 cup (2 sticks) butter, room temperature
$\frac{1}{2}$ cup halved glacéed cherries, plus 6 more halves for decorating
1 cup finely diced mixed candied fruit
1 cup date bits or crystals
1 cup coarsely broken walnuts or pecans, plus 12 whole nuts for decorating
1 egg, beaten, mixed with 1 tablespoon cream or milk

BAKING PANS

2 large (9"-x-5") or 4 small (7"-x-3") loaf pans, greased or Teflon

PREPARATION
2 hours

In a large mixing or mixer bowl combine 2 cups flour, the hot milk, and yeast. When the flour and milk are well blended, cover the bowl with plastic wrap and leave it at room temperature to ferment and bubble for 2 hours.

BY HAND
OR MIXER
12 mins.

Lightly beat the egg and add to the mixture. Add the sugar, salt, and butter. Beat well by hand, about 50 strokes, or for 2 minutes with the mixer flat beater. Continue beating and adding flour, ½ cup at a time, until the dough is soft and no longer sticky.

KNEADING
10 mins.

Turn the dough out onto a floured work surface, and knead with a rhythmic and strong push-turn-fold motion, or in the mixer bowl with the dough hook, until the dough is smooth and elastic, about 10 minutes. If moisture persists in breaking through, add sprinkles of flour.

BY PROCESSOR
5 mins.

Mix the flour, milk, and yeast as above.

Attach the short plastic blade.

Scrape the flour-milk mixture into the processor work bowl and add the egg, sugar, salt, and butter. Pulse to blend into a thick batter.

Add ½ cup flour to the work bowl, either through the feed tube or by removing the cover, and pulse several times to blend before adding more flour. When the dough has formed a rough ball and is carried around the bowl by the force of the blade, the kneading has begun.

KNEADING **50 secs.**	Let the machine run for 50 seconds. When the dough is turned out of the bowl it may be more sticky than when done by hand. Dust liberally with flour as you form it into a ball.
REST **15 mins.**	Let the dough rest under a cloth or a length of wax paper. Meanwhile, mix the cherries, candied fruit, dates, and nuts together in a bowl and sprinkle with flour to keep the pieces separate.
KNEADING **5 mins.**	Press the dough flat with the hands, and sprinkle about half of the fruit-nut mixture over it. Turn the edges of the dough over the fruit and nuts and fold the mixture into the body of the dough. Again press flat; sprinkle on the balance of the mixture. Knead until the mixture is well distributed throughout the dough.
FIRST RISING **1 hour**	Return the dough to the large bowl, cover with plastic wrap, and leave at room temperature until doubled in volume, about 1 hour.
SHAPING **10 mins.**	Turn the dough onto a floured work surface and knead briefly to press out the bubbles. With a knife or dough blade divide the dough. Shape into balls and let rest for 5 minutes. Form each loaf by pressing the dough into a flat oval, roughly the length of the baking pan. Fold each oval in half, pinch the seam tightly to seal, tuck under the ends, and place in the pan, seam down.
SECOND RISING **45 mins.**	Cover the pans with wax or parchment paper and leave at room temperature until doubled in bulk, about 45 minutes.
PREHEAT	Preheat the oven to 350° about 20 minutes before baking.

BAKING
350°
50 mins.
	Brush the loaves with the egg-milk wash, and place the 12 glacéed cherry halves and whole nut meats in a random pattern over the top of the loaves.
	    Bake in a moderate oven until the loaves are a deep brown, 50 minutes. Turn one loaf out of its pan and tap the bottom with a forefinger. If it sounds hard and hollow, it is done. If the tops of the loaves appear to be browning too quickly, cover with a piece of foil or brown sack paper. Midway during baking and again at the end, shift the pans so they are exposed equally to temperature variations in the oven.
	    (If using a convection oven, reduce heat 50°.)

FINAL STEP	Remove the bread from the oven. Slip the hot loaves carefully from the pans and leave on wire racks until they are cool.

Julekage   [one large or two small loaves]
(Danish Christmas Fruit Loaf)

This festive loaf is filled with many good things—butter and eggs, candied fruit, golden raisins, almonds—and with the delicate and gingery taste of cardamom. Celebrated throughout Scandinavia, Julekage may be baked in a loaf pan or as a ball on a baking sheet.

Pearl sugar or crushed sugar cubes are sprinkled over the top before the bread goes into the oven. The Julekage is then drizzled with a snowy-white almond icing when it comes from the oven and has cooled.

A handsome festive offering.

INGREDIENTS

Dough:

3 to 4 cups bread or all-purpose flour, approximately

I package dry yeast

I¹/₂ teaspoons salt

¹/₄ cup sugar

¹/₄ cup nonfat dry milk

¹/₂ cup hot water (120°–130°)

¹/₂ teaspoon *each* vanilla extract, grated lemon peel, and ground cardamom

¹/₂ cup (1 stick) butter, room temperature

2 eggs, room temperature, lightly beaten

¹/₃ cup mixed candied fruit, chopped medium fine

¹/₃ cup golden raisins

¹/₃ cup slivered almonds

Glaze:

I egg, beaten, mixed with ¹/₄ teaspoon salt and 2 tablespoons milk

¹/₃ cup pearl sugar or crushed sugar cubes

Icing:

I cup confectioners' sugar

I tablespoon water

I teaspoon vegetable oil

¹/₂ teaspoon almond extract

BAKING PANS
OR SHEET

1 large (9"-x-5") or 2 small (7"-x-3") baking pans, greased or Teflon; for a hearth loaf: 1 baking sheet, greased or Teflon or covered with parchment paper

BY HAND
OR MIXER
8 mins.

Measure 1 cup flour into a large mixing or mixer bowl, and add the yeast, salt, sugar, and dry milk. Stir to blend. Pour in the hot water and mix to a thick batter. Add the vanilla, lemon peel, and cardamom. Stir to blend. Add the butter and beat with 75 strong strokes using a wooden spoon, or for 3 minutes with the mixer flat beater, until the butter is worked into the dough. Pour in the eggs, and beat into the dough.

Add flour, a small portion at a time, until the dough becomes a shaggy mass that can be lifted from the bowl and placed on the floured work surface, or left in the mixer under the dough hook.

KNEADING
10 mins.

Knead the dough under the hands with a strong push-turn-fold movement or with the mixer dough hook, 10 minutes. The dough will become shiny and elastic, a pleasure to work.

BY PROCESSOR
8 mins.

Attach the steel blade.

Measure 1 cup flour into the processor work bowl and add the dry ingredients. Pulse to blend. With the processor on, pour the hot water through the feed tube. Stop. Remove the lid and add the vanilla, lemon peel, and cardamom. Also cut the butter into several pieces and drop it into the work bowl. Turn on the machine and while the butter is being worked into the dough, add the eggs, one at a time.

Add flour, ¼ cup at a time, either through the feed tube or by removing the cover each time, until the dough is a mass that will begin to clean the sides of the work bowl as it is whirled around by the blade.

KNEADING
45 secs.

Let the processor run for 45 seconds to knead.

Remove the cover from the work bowl and pinch the dough. It may be slightly sticky, but a few sprinkles of flour will form a coating over the dough so it can easily be worked into a ball.

FIRST RISING
1³/₄ hours

Place the dough in a greased bowl, cover tightly with plastic wrap, and leave at room temperature until the dough has risen to about twice its original size, about 1¾ hours.

KNEADING
5 mins.

Punch down the dough and press it flat on the work surface. Mix the candied fruit, raisins, and almonds together, and spread half the mixture across the dough. Fold over the dough; knead until the fruit and nuts disappear. Press the dough flat and sprinkle the balance of the mixture across the top. Knead until the fruit and nuts are mixed evenly throughout the dough.

SHAPING
10 mins.

For 2 loaves, divide the dough with a sharp knife. Shape into balls and let rest under a towel for 3 to 4 minutes.

If the loaf or loaves are to be baked in pans, press each dough ball into a flat oval, roughly the length of the pan. Fold the oval in half, pinch the seam tightly to seal, tuck under the ends, and place in the pan, seam down.

For a hearth loaf, press the ball of dough to flatten somewhat and place on the baking sheet.

For both, brush with some of the egg-milk glaze.

SECOND RISING
1½ hours

Cover the dough with wax paper and leave at room temperature until doubled in bulk, about 1½ hours.

PREHEAT

Preheat the oven to 375° about 20 minutes before baking.

BAKING
375°
30–40 mins.

Uncover the loaves and again brush with the egg-milk glaze. Liberally sprinkle the sugar over the tops.

Bake the loaves in the center of the oven until the crust is golden, 30 to 40 minutes. To test, tap the bottom of one loaf with a forefinger. A hard, hollow sound means the bread is baked. If the tops appear to be browning too quickly, cover with a piece of foil or brown sack paper. Midway during baking and again near the end of it, shift the pans so the loaves are exposed equally to temperature variations in the oven.

(If using a convection oven, reduce heat 75°.)

ICING
5 mins.

While the loaves are in the oven prepare the icing. Measure the confectioners' sugar into a small bowl and add the water, vegetable oil, and almond extract. Stir together with a fork until smooth. If the icing is too thick to spread and drizzle down the sides, add a few drops of water. If the icing is thin and watery, add sugar.

FINAL STEP

Remove the bread from the oven, and cool on wire racks.

Spread the icing over the cooled loaves, and drizzle down the sides. *Don't ice if it is first to be frozen.*

Julekage will keep exceptionally well for up to 3 weeks if it is wrapped tightly in foil or plastic.

Bohemian Christmas Bread
[two medium braided loaves]

At least one braided bread decorated by the home baker is a must for the holidays and this Bohemian Christmas Bread is a good one for the table and to make for friends. Frosted and dotted with pecans and cherries, it is a holiday spectacle.

INGREDIENTS	¹/₂ cup raisins
	¹/₂ cup water or brandy
	5 to 6 cups bread or all-purpose flour, approximately
	2 packages dry yeast
	1¹/₂ teaspoons salt
	¹/₂ cup sugar
	¹/₄ teaspoon dried mace
	Rind of 1 lemon, grated
	1¹/₄ cups hot milk (120°–130°)
	2 eggs or 4 egg yolks, room temperature
	¹/₄ cup (¹/₂ stick) butter, room temperature
	¹/₂ cup chopped almonds

Topping:
1 cup confectioners' sugar mixed with 1 tablespoon warm water
    or milk and ¼ teaspoon almond extract
¹/₂ cup whole pecans
8 red and green candied cherries, halved

BAKING SHEET	One 11"-x-17" baking sheet (or smaller for convection ovens), greased or Teflon
PREPARATION 30 mins.	Place the raisins in a small bowl and cover with the water or brandy. Soak for 30 minutes. Then drain and pat dry.
BY HAND OR MIXER . 18 mins.	Place 2½ cups flour in a large mixing or mixer bowl and add the yeast, salt, sugar, mace, and lemon rind. Stir to blend. Pour in the heated milk, and stir with a wooden spoon 50 strong strokes, or for 2 minutes with the mixer flat beater, to make a heavy batter.
	Drop in the eggs or egg yolks and beat to blend with the dough. When the eggs have been absorbed, stir in the butter. Beat until smooth. Blend in the raisins and almonds. Gradually stir in more flour (about 3 cups) to form a soft, elastic dough.
KNEADING 10 mins.	Turn the dough onto a lightly floured work surface, if kneading by hand. Or leave in the bowl with the mixer dough hook. Knead until the dough is smooth and elastic, 10 minutes. If the dough should continue to be sticky, dust lightly with sprinkles of flour. The dough in the mixer should clean the sides of the bowl, and draw into a ball around the hook.
BY PROCESSOR 6 mins.	Plump the raisins, as above.
	Attach the short plastic blade.

Measure 2½ cups flour into the processor work bowl and add the yeast, salt, sugar, mace, and lemon rind. Pulse 2 or 3 times to blend. With the processor running, pour the heated milk through the feed tube to make a sticky, heavy batter.

Turn on the machine and add the eggs or egg yolks. Remove the cover and add 1 cup flour. Pulse to blend. Add the butter. Pulse. Add the raisins and almonds. Turn the processor on and add flour, ¼ cup at a time, to form a mass that will spin with the blade and at the same time partially clean the sides of the bowl.

KNEADING
45 secs.

Knead the dough under the blade for 45 seconds.

FIRST RISING
1½ hours

Place in a greased bowl and turn to coat all of the dough. Cover with plastic wrap and leave until the dough has doubled in bulk, about 1½ hours.

SHAPING
25 mins.

Punch down the dough and turn onto a floured work surface. Divide the dough in half, and place one half in the bowl to reserve.

Divide one piece of dough into 4 equal parts. Let it rest for 8 to 10 minutes. Shape 3 of the 4 pieces into smooth, ropelike strips, about 14" long. Place them side by side on the baking sheet. Beginning in the middle, braid toward each end. Pinch the ends together and tuck under.

Divide the fourth piece into 3 equal parts and shape into strands about 10" long, as above. Braid the strands. With the side of the hand strike a channel down the center of the larger braid, or with a knife make a ¾" cut along the top. Lay the smaller braid in the depression and push it into the other braid.

Repeat with the second dough half.

SECOND RISING
1 hour

Cover with wax paper. Let rise until double in bulk, about 1 hour.

PREHEAT

Preheat the oven to 400° about 20 minutes before baking.

BAKING
400°
10 mins.
350°
40 mins.

Note: The pecans and cherries can be tucked into the braids now and baked into the loaf—very attractive.

Place the pan in the hot oven for 10 minutes. Turn the temperature down to 350° for an additional 40 minutes, or until the bread tests done when tapped on the bottom crust.

(If using a convection oven, reduce heat by 50° for each bake period.)

FINAL STEP

Carefully lift the somewhat fragile loaves off the baking sheet with a metal spatula and place on a rack to cool. Allow the braids to cool for 20 or 30 minutes.

Drizzle on the confectioners' icing. Decorate with cherries and pecans placed at random over the braids.

Makes superb toast.

Challah

[two braided loaves]

Challah is a lovely yellow egg-rich and light-textured white bread steeped in Jewish history.

While the word challah *(pronounced hal-la) has come to mean this loaf of braided bread, the preparation of the dough for baking in the Jewish kitchen is "the act of challah" in which the woman takes a small part of the dough to burn as an offering. She thereby reenacts her origin at the Creation, according to the Old Testament, when she sprang from man's rib. The remaining dough may be baked as she chooses, usually in the braided form.*

During Rosh Hashanah and Yom Kippur, Challah is baked in the form of a ladder, symbolizing the hope that prayers of thanksgiving will mount to heaven. On Rosh Hashanah, it is customary to dip a slice of challah in honey to symbolize the sweetness of the New Year.

INGREDIENTS

2 packages dry yeast
5 cups bread or all-purpose flour, approximately
2 tablespoons sugar
2 teaspoons salt
$^1/_3$ cup butter or margarine, room temperature
1 cup hot water (120°–130°)
1 pinch of saffron
3 eggs
1 egg white
1 egg yolk (from egg above), beaten, mixed with 2 tablespoons sugar
    and 1 teaspoon cold water
1 teaspoon poppy seeds

BAKING SHEET

1 large baking sheet, greased or Teflon

BY HAND
OR MIXER
15 mins.

In a large mixing or mixer bowl combine the yeast, 2 cups flour, sugar, salt, and butter or margarine. Gradually add the hot water and beat forcefully by hand, or at medium speed using the mixer flat beater, for 2 minutes. Scrape the bowl occasionally.

Add the saffron, eggs, and egg white (reserving the yolk). The batter will be thick. Beat at high speed for 2 minutes. Continue to add flour with a wooden spoon or change to a dough hook in the mixer. Add about 3 additional cups of flour, one at a time, until the rough mass is no longer sticky. If it continues to be moist, add small amounts of flour until the dough cleans the sides of the bowl.

KNEADING **10 mins.**	Turn the dough onto a floured surface and knead until it is smooth and elastic. This is a lovely dough to work under the hands. Or knead in the mixer bowl under the dough hook. Knead for 10 minutes.
BY PROCESSOR **8 mins.**	Attach the plastic dough blade. Pour the yeast, 3 cups flour, sugar, salt, and butter or margarine into the work bowl. Gradually add the hot water through the feed tube. Pulse several times to blend. Scrape down the bowl. With the processor running, add the saffron, eggs, and egg white. The batter will be quite thick. Add flour, ¼ cup at a time, through the feed tube or by taking the cover off, until the dough forms a rough mass that is whirled around the bowl by the blade. The dough will partially clean the sides of the bowl at the same time.
KNEADING **45 secs.**	With the machine running knead the dough for 45 seconds.
FIRST RISING **I hour**	Place the dough in a greased bowl, cover tightly with plastic wrap, and set aside until it has doubled in bulk, about 1 hour.
SHAPING **25 mins.**	Punch down the dough and knead out the bubbles. Divide the dough in half. To braid, divide each half into 3 equal pieces. Under your palms roll each into a 12" length. Lay the rolls parallel to each other. Start the braid in the middle and work to one end. Pinch the ends securely together. Turn around and complete the other end. Repeat with the other dough half. Carefully brush the braids with the egg glaze. Sprinkle liberally with poppy seeds.
SECOND RISING **I hour**	Don't cover the braids for the second rise. They will double in bulk, about 1 hour.
PREHEAT	Preheat the oven to 400° about 20 minutes before baking.

BAKING **400°** **30–40 mins.**	Bake until the braids are a shiny brown, 30 to 40 minutes, and test done when a wooden toothpick inserted in the center comes out dry and clean. (If using a convection oven, reduce heat 50°.)
FINAL STEP	Carefully remove the bread from the baking sheet and cool on wire racks. A long braided loaf fresh from the oven is fragile and should be moved with care (and a spatula under its bottom). Do not cut until it has cooled and firmed a bit.

Hoska   [two braided loaves]

One of my favorite breads, this Czechoslovakian loaf has 3 successively smaller tiers of braids. It is a spectacular holiday bread that is glazed and decorated with whole almonds and bakes to a beautiful deep brown. It is light, tender, and a bit sweet.

I often make Hoska for my classes because the rich dough is a pleasure to work, and the braids are fun to make. Also, I have learned the trick of keeping the braids from toppling over as they rise in the oven, which can be discouraging to any home baker when it happens. (In the beginning, I held them in place with toothpicks and metal skewers, but the loaves resembled porcupines more than they did breads.) For my secret, read on.

INGREDIENTS	5^1/$_2$ cups bread or all-purpose flour, approximately 2 packages dry yeast ^{1}/$_4$ cup nonfat dry milk 2 teaspoons salt ^{3}/$_4$ cup sugar 1^1/$_4$ cups hot water (120°–130°) 2 eggs, room temperature ^{1}/$_2$ cup (1 stick) butter, room temperature ^{1}/$_4$ cup chopped citron ^{1}/$_4$ cup white or dark raisins ^{1}/$_4$ cup chopped almonds 1 tablespoon butter, melted 1 egg, beaten, mixed with 1 tablespoon water ^{1}/$_2$ cup whole blanched almonds
BAKING SHEET	1 baking sheet, greased or Teflon
BY HAND OR MIXER 12 mins.	Measure 3 cups flour into a mixing or mixer bowl and add the yeast, dry milk, salt, and sugar. Stir to blend. Pour in the hot water and beat 60 strong strokes with a wooden spoon or for 2 minutes with the mixer

flat beater. Drop in the eggs, one at a time, blending each into the soft batter. Add 1 cup flour, and after it has been absorbed, stir in the butter. Beat 100 strokes, or for 3 minutes with the flat beater, until the mixture is smooth. Stir in additional flour, first with the spoon and then by hand. If with the mixer, attach the dough hook. The dough will be soft but not sticky.

KNEADING
10 mins.

By hand, turn out onto a lightly floured work surface and knead for 10 minutes, until it is smooth and elastic. Or knead for 10 minutes in the mixer, adding sprinkles of flour so the dough will clean the sides and form a ball around the dough hook. The dough is so rich with butter that it will quickly lose its stickiness. If the dough seems moist (or "slack," as bakers call it) work in more flour.

BY PROCESSOR
5 mins.

Attach the short plastic dough blade.

Measure 2½ cups flour into the work bowl and add the yeast, dry milk, salt, and sugar. Pulse to blend. With the processor running, pour the hot water through the feed tube. Stop the machine. Open the cover to see if all of the flour has been pulled into the blade. If it has not and dry flour remains, scrape it into the center with a spatula. Pulse to blend.

Add the eggs, pulse, and measure in 1 cup flour. Pulse to mix together. Add the butter, and pulse. With the machine running, add flour, ¼ cup at a time, until the dough forms a mass that cleans the sides of the work bowl (partially), and rides on the blade.

KNEADING
45 secs.

Keep the machine running and knead for 45 seconds.

FIRST RISING
1 hour

Place the ball of dough in a greased bowl, and cover tightly with plastic wrap. Allow to double in bulk, about 1 hour.

KNEADING
10 mins.

Punch down the dough and turn out onto a floured work surface.

In a small bowl mix together the citron, raisins, and chopped almonds. Sprinkle about half the mixture over the top of the dough. Begin to knead it into the dough. Flatten the dough again, and spread the remainder of the mixture on top. Continue working the dough with the fingers until the fruit and nuts are distributed throughout the dough.

Working the fruit in now, rather than earlier, makes it unlikely the fruit will discolor the dough during a lengthy kneading.

SHAPING
25 mins.

Divide the dough in half. Put one half back in the bowl to shape later.

Braiding the dough is fascinating once you get the hang of it. If the braid doesn't look right the first time, unbraid and do it again.

Rather than balance the braids one on top of the other and pray they stay in place, form a deep channel in each braid as it is laid down by hitting the dough sharply down the center with the side of your hand. Do it several times if necessary. Lay the second braid in the channel, and then strike a channel down it in turn. Finally lay in the top braid.

Divide the first half into 2 equal parts. Divide one of these into 3 equal pieces. Roll each under your palms, pulling and patting, until they are about 14" long. (Children's putty requires the same technique.) Place the 3 strands, which now look like small ropes, on the baking sheet and braid. Knock a channel down the center of the braid, as described above. Brush with some of the melted butter. Divide *two-thirds* of the second piece into 3 equal pieces. Form a second and smaller braid about 12" long. Place this in the channel made in the first braid. Knock a channel in this braid. Brush with butter. With the remaining small piece of dough, make a third braid about 10" long. This is placed triumphantly on the second braid. Butter as above.

Form the second loaf in the same manner with the dough half reserved in the bowl.

SECOND RISING
45 mins.

Cover the loaves carefully with wax paper and leave at room temperature until doubled, about 45 minutes.

PREHEAT

Preheat the oven to 375° about 20 minutes before baking.

BAKING
375°
45 mins.

Brush the braided loaves with the egg glaze and randomly decorate each loaf with about 18 or 20 whole almonds.

Place the loaves in the oven and bake for about 45 minutes. When testing the dark brown loaves, be aware that they are fragile while warm. Lift with a metal spatula. If the bottom crust is a deep brown and sounds hard and hollow when tapped with a forefinger, it is done. On the other hand, it may be easier to insert a toothpick or metal skewer into the center of the loaf. If the pick comes out clean, it is done.

(If using a convection oven, reduce heat 50°.)

FINAL STEP

Remove the bread from the oven and cool on wire racks.

Kulich   [two loaves]
(Russian Easter Bread)

Kulich was the traditional Easter bread of Russia and so delicate a creation that bakers put pillows around the pan of dough so that it would not fall. It was forbidden to walk through the kitchen with heavy boots until the loaves were safely out of the oven.

These precautions are unnecessary today.

The initials XV—meaning "Christ is risen"—are shaped on the top of the loaf with tiny strips of dough, or sprinkled on the frosting with colored sprinkles. It was also traditional for a small rose to be placed across the frosting. With this recipe, it is possible to make one of each design.

The decorated top is cut off and replaced each time the loaf is sliced. To some, the frosted top resembles the snow-covered domes of Russian churches.

INGREDIENTS	2$\frac{1}{2}$ to 3$\frac{1}{2}$ cups bread or all-purpose flour, approximately
	$\frac{1}{4}$ cup sugar
	1 teaspoon salt
	1 teaspoon grated lemon peel
	2 packages dry yeast
	$\frac{1}{4}$ cup nonfat dry milk
	$\frac{3}{4}$ cup hot water (120°–130°)
	2 tablespoons butter, room temperature
	1 egg, room temperature
	$\frac{1}{4}$ cup *each* chopped almonds and raisins
	1 cup confectioners' sugar mixed with 1 tablespoon milk and $\frac{1}{2}$ teaspoon vanilla extract (optional)
	Colored sprinkles
	1 rose, fresh, paper, or plastic (optional)

BAKING TINS

Two 1-pound coffee cans, or other containers of equal volume, greased

BY HAND
OR MIXER
20 mins.

In a large mixing or mixer bowl combine 1 cup flour, the sugar, salt, lemon peel, yeast, and dry milk.

Pour the water in a saucepan and place over low heat. Add the butter only to soften. Pour the liquid into the dry ingredients and beat 100 strokes with a large wooden spoon, or for 2 minutes at medium speed with the mixer flat beater. Scrape the bowl. Add the egg and ½ cup or more flour to make a thick batter. Beat at high speed for 2 minutes, or 150 strokes with the spoon.

By hand, with the spoon and fingers work in additional flour to make a soft dough that cleans the sides of the bowl. By mixer, attach the dough hook and add sprinkles of flour until the dough cleans the sides of the bowl and surrounds the dough hook in one ball.

KNEADING
10 mins.

Turn onto a lightly floured work surface and knead with a strong push-turn-fold action until the dough is smooth, elastic, and feels alive under your hands, about 10 minutes. In the mixer, give the dough hook an equal length of time.

BY PROCESSOR
8 mins.

Attach the steel blade.

Measure 1½ cups flour into the work bowl and add the sugar, salt, lemon peel, yeast, and dry milk. Pulse to blend. With the machine running, pour the hot water through the feed tube. The mass will be thick but sufficiently moist to dissolve the yeast. Follow this with the butter and egg. Stop the machine when blended.

Add flour, ¼ cup at a time, with the machine running. When the dough has become a mass that cleans the sides of the bowl and whirls with the blade, stop the machine. Remove the cover and pinch the dough to determine if it is firm enough to hold its shape. If it is soft and wet, it needs more flour. Add small amounts at a time.

KNEADING
45 secs.

Knead the dough with the machine running for 45 seconds.

FIRST RISING
1 hour

Place the dough in a greased bowl, turning to coat the entire ball. Cover the bowl with plastic wrap and leave at room temperature to double its size, about 1 hour.

KNEADING
5 mins.

Punch down the dough and turn it onto the floured work surface. Press the dough flat, sprinkle with the almonds and raisins, and work them into the dough.

SHAPING
15 mins.

Divide the dough into 2 large pieces, with a small piece the size of a golf ball set aside to make the initials.

With the hands, shape each large piece into a ball and, with smooth side up, press into the greased coffee cans. (It is easier to first shape the dough roughly in a teardrop shape so no air is forced under the dough to the bottom of the can where it will be difficult to press out.) Be certain the dough fills only *half* the tin. If necessary, reduce the amount of dough and bake the excess in another container.

To create the letters "XV" in dough, roll out the small reserved piece into a pencil-thin strand about 24" long and no more than ¼" in diameter. Cut into 4 pieces. Cross two strands to form the "X"—and place the other two to make the "V."

SECOND RISING 45 mins.	Cover the cans with wax paper and let the dough rise until it has almost reached the top of the tins, about 45 *watchful* minutes. Don't let the dough rise above the tops.
PREHEAT	Preheat the oven to 350° about 20 minutes before baking. Be certain the shelf is placed to allow the dough sufficient headroom to rise in the oven.
BAKING 350° 35 mins.	Place the cans in the moderate oven until the bread turns a light golden brown, about 35 minutes. Insert a wooden toothpick or metal skewer in the center of the loaf. If it comes out clean and dry, the bread is baked. (If using a convection oven, reduce heat 50°.)

FINAL STEP	Let the bread cool in the tins for about 10 minutes before turning onto a metal cooling rack. (The bread will have shrunk away from the sides of the cans.)
	    To decorate the loaf without the dough initials frost with confectioners' icing and allow it to drip down the sides as icicles might. Form the "XV" with colored sprinkles or simply place a rose across the top.
	    The decorated top is sliced off and is either used to cover the loaf while it is being eaten or is presented to an honored guest at the Easter feast.

Sugarplum Bread   [one large and six baby loaves]

For a greater part of the year a loaf of bread is just a loaf of bread, but during the holiday season it becomes a gift of love from the home baker to the family and to friends. And a slice for Santa Claus, of course.

In England it is Sugarplum Bread—of which visions "dance in their heads." It is made with a rich dough flavored with nutmeg, candied mixed fruit and peel, and raisins.

In this recipe the dough is made into 1 large round loaf and 6 small ones. The latter are fine for holiday callers, especially young carolers.

INGREDIENTS	5 to 6 cups bread or all-purpose flour, approximately 1/2 cup sugar 2 teaspoons salt 2 packages dry yeast 1/3 cup nonfat dry milk 1 1/3 cups hot water (120°–130°) 1/4 cup vegetable shortening

2 eggs, slightly beaten
$1/2$ teaspoon vanilla extract
$1/4$ teaspoon ground nutmeg
$1/2$ cup candied mixed fruit and peel
1 cup raisins

Topping:
1 cup confectioners' sugar mixed with 1 to $1 1/2$ tablespoons fresh
    lemon juice
12 red candied cherries and slivers of green candied cherries
6 walnut halves

BAKING SHEET
AND
MUFFIN TIN

1 baking sheet, greased or Teflon, and 1 large muffin pan with 6 cups, greased or Teflon

BY HAND
OR MIXER
15 mins.

Measure 2 cups flour into a large mixing or mixer bowl and stir in the sugar, salt, yeast, dry milk, and hot water. Blend thoroughly and add the shortening, eggs, vanilla, nutmeg, chopped mixed fruit and peel, and raisins. Stir for 2 minutes with a wooden spoon, or with a mixer flat beater at medium speed for an equal length of time.

Stir in the balance of the flour, ½ cup at a time, first with the spoon and then by hand. The dough will be a rough, shaggy mass that will clean the sides of the bowl. If the dough continues to be moist and sticky, add several sprinkles of flour.

KNEADING
10 mins.

If by hand, turn the dough onto a lightly floured work surface and knead with a rhythmic motion of push-turn-fold. If using a mixer, knead under the dough hook. Add sprinkles of flour until the dough cleans the sides of the bowl and forms a mass around the hook. The dough will become smooth and elastic. Occasionally break the kneading rhythm by throwing the dough hard against the work surface. Knead for 10 minutes.

BY PROCESSOR
8 mins.

Attach the plastic dough blade.

Measure 2¾ cups flour into the processor work bowl and add the sugar, salt, yeast, and dry milk. Pulse to blend. With the machine on, pour the hot water through the feed tube. When the water has been absorbed by the flour—and with the machine running—add the shortening, eggs, vanilla, nutmeg, chopped mixed fruit and peel, and raisins. Add flour, a small portion at a time, through the feed tube, to form a shaggy mass that cleans the sides of the work bowl and spins with the blade.

KNEADING **45 secs.**	With the processor running, knead the dough for 45 seconds. The dough may be slightly sticky when turned from the bowl. If so, dust lightly with flour while forming it into a ball.
FIRST RISING 1½ **hours**	Place the dough in a greased bowl, cover tightly with plastic wrap, and leave at room temperature until it has risen to about twice its original size, about 1½ hours.
SHAPING 15 **mins.**	Divide the dough in half. Knead each piece for 30 seconds to press out the bubbles. Shape one piece into a ball, flatten slightly on top, and place on the baking sheet. Divide the remaining half into 6 pieces. Shape each into a ball. Place in muffin cups, and press down. The dough will be almost level with the tops of the cups.
SECOND RISING 1 **hour**	Cover the dough with wax paper and let rise until it has nearly doubled in volume, about 1 hour.
PREHEAT	Preheat the oven to 350° 20 minutes before baking.
BAKING **350°** 20–35 **mins.**	Bake the large loaf in the moderate oven for 35 minutes, until golden brown. The small loaves will be done in about 20 minutes. The bread is done when tapping the bottom yields a hard and hollow sound. (If using a convection oven, reduce heat 50°.)
FINAL STEP	Remove the bread from the oven and place on a metal rack to cool. Frost the large loaf with a drizzle of the confectioners' icing. Circle with red candied cherries and slivers of green candied cherries. For the small loaves, drizzle the tops and cap each with a perfect walnut half.

Barm Brack   [two medium loaves]

It is part of the Irish tradition on All Hallows' Eve to bake a wedding ring into this festive tea bread. The finder can be confident that he or she is to become engaged before the year is out.

Barm Brack (literally "yeast bread") is one of the few examples of yeast in Irish cooking.

INGREDIENTS	4 to 5 cups bread or all-purpose flour, approximately ½ cup sugar 2 teaspoons salt 1 teaspoon grated lemon peel 2 packages dry yeast ½ cup (1 stick) butter, room temperature

³/₄ cup water
¹/₂ cup milk
2 eggs, room temperature
1¹/₂ cups golden raisins
¹/₂ cup chopped mixed candied fruit
1 teaspoon sugar dissolved in 1 tablespoon water

BAKING PANS	2 medium (8"-x-4") loaf pans, greased or Teflon
BY HAND OR MIXER 15 mins.	In a large mixing or mixer bowl measure 1½ cups flour, sugar, salt, lemon peel, and yeast. In a saucepan combine the butter, water, and milk and heat over a low flame until the liquid is hot (120°–130°). Add to the dry ingredients and beat by hand with a wooden spoon, or with the mixer flat beater at medium speed for 2 minutes, scraping the bowl occasionally. Add the eggs and ¾ cup flour, or enough to make a thick batter. Beat vigorously by hand or at high speed in the mixer for 2 minutes. Add flour, ¼ cup at a time, beating with the spoon and working with your hands, or in the mixer using a dough hook, to form a shaggy mass that can be lifted from the bowl and placed on the work surface.
KNEADING 10 mins.	Knead the dough, by hand on a floured work surface or in the mixer, until it is smooth and elastic, about 10 minutes. If the dough is sticky, add liberal sprinkles of flour. The dough will leave the sides of the bowl in the mixer and gather around the dough hook.
BY PROCESSOR 10 mins.	Attach the plastic dough blade. Measure 2½ cups flour into the work bowl and add the sugar, salt, lemon peel, and yeast. Pulse to mix well. In a saucepan combine the butter, water, and milk and heat over a low flame until the liquid is hot. With the processor running, add the warm liquid; add the eggs. With the machine running add flour, a portion at a time, to form a rough mass that cleans the sides of the bowl and is whirled by the force of the blade.
KNEADING 45 secs.	Allow the machine to run for 45 seconds to knead the dough.
FIRST RISING 45 mins.	Place the dough in a greased bowl, cover tightly with plastic wrap, and leave at room temperature until the dough has risen to about twice its original size (judged as it expands up the sides of the bowl), about 45 minutes.

SHAPING 20 mins.	Punch down the dough and turn onto the floured work surface. Work in the raisins and candied fruit. Divide the dough in half, shape each half into a ball, and let rest under a towel for 5 minutes. Form each loaf by pressing a ball, under your palms or with a rolling pin, into a flat oval, roughly the length of the baking pan. Fold the oval in half, pinch the seam tightly to seal, tuck under the ends, and place in the loaf pan, seam down.
SECOND RISING 1 hour	Cover the dough loosely with wax paper and let rise until it has doubled in bulk, about 1 hour. The dough should be just above the edge of the loaf pan.
PREHEAT	Preheat the oven to 375° about 20 minutes before baking.
BAKING 375° 35–40 mins.	Bake in the moderately hot oven until the loaves test done, 35 to 40 minutes. Turn out one loaf and tap the bottom with a forefinger. A hard, hollow sound means the light golden brown loaf is done. If not done, return to the oven—without the pan, if you wish a deep brown crust—for an additional 10 minutes. Finally, brush the crusts with the sugar glaze. Return to the oven for 2 or 3 minutes, or until shiny. (If using a convection oven, reduce heat 50°.)
FINAL STEP	Remove the bread from the oven. While the bread is warm, cut thick slices and serve with ample butter. This bread will keep for several days wrapped in plastic or foil. It also freezes nicely.

Gugelhupf   [one large loaf]

There are conflicting stories about who elevated gugelhupf to its present gastronomic height. Was it Marie Antoinette in the late 1700s (she loved the creation), or Carême, the great chef, who popularized the bread in Paris in the early 1800s? Or was it the skill and devotion of a man named George who set up a pâtisserie-boulangerie in the rue de Coq in Paris in 1840?

No matter. Gugelhupf is a triumph large enough to be shared by all three.

And there are as many ways to spell gugelhupf as there are days in the week—suglhupf, kugelhupf, and kougloff, to name but three. And as you might expect, there are even more recipes than names for this fine yeast-raised bread.

This is one of the best, from the bakery of Jean Pierre Scholler in Strasbourg.

M. Scholler has an equally delicious loaf—Gugelhupf Complet Bio-logique—made with whole wheat (plus only 1 cup bread flour). This is a break with tradition, for festive breads are usually made only with white flour. The recipe below can be used for making the whole wheat loaf by using white flour in the starter but substituting whole wheat flour in the dough.

Gugelhupf even has a pan of its own in which the dough rises to resemble an almond-studded crown. If no gugelhupf pan is at hand, a bundt or angel food pan will impart almost the same élégance, especially when sprinkled with a delicate snow of confectioners' sugar.

INGREDIENTS

Sponge:
1¼ cups bread or all-purpose flour, approximately
1 package dry yeast
½ cup warm water (105°–115°)

Dough:
½ cup currants or raisins
¼ cup dry white wine
3½ cups bread or all-purpose flour, approximately
4 eggs, beaten, room temperature
2 tablespoons warm water (105°–115°)
⅓ cup sugar
2 teaspoons salt
½ cup (1 stick) butter, room temperature
⅓ cup sliced almonds, plus 24 whole almonds
1 tablespoon confectioners' sugar

BAKING PAN

One large 2-quart *gugelhupf* pan preferred, or 1 bundt or angel food pan; if too much dough for the pan, have a small standby such as a large *brioche* or *charlotte* pan

PREPARATION
6 hours–
overnight

To make the sponge, in a medium bowl measure 1 cup flour and add the yeast and warm water. Beat by hand to fashion a rough ball of dough. Add flour if the ball of dough is too sticky to shape. Cover the bowl tightly with plastic wrap and leave at room temperature for a minimum of 6 hours, or overnight. The sponge will spread across the bowl as it ferments and rises.

1 hour

An hour or so before preparing the dough, soften and plump the currants or raisins in the white wine for about 1 hour. (The original recipe called for rum or kirsch, but I found either too dominant.) Drain off the wine.

BY HAND
OR MIXER
15 mins.

To make the dough, in a large mixing bowl or mixer pour 2 cups flour and fashion a well at the bottom. Pour in the beaten eggs, warm water, sugar, and salt. Slowly pull in flour from the sides while stirring with a large wooden spoon, or with the mixer flat beater. Cut the butter into several pieces and drop into the egg-flour mixture. Beat with 75 strong strokes, or for 2 minutes in the mixer. Add additional flour to form a soft mass that can be worked with the hands or under the dough hook without sticking.

KNEADING
15 mins.

Uncover the sponge, stir or punch down, and turn onto a floured work surface.

Turn out the dough and pat and punch into a large flat oval. If by hand, place the sponge in the center of the oval, fold the dough over the sponge, and knead together. If using a mixer, drop the sponge into the bowl with the dough and knead together for about 10 minutes.

The white sponge will gradually blend with the yellow eggy dough as the two become a fine, elastic mass in about 10 minutes. Add sprinkles of flour if needed.

Let the dough rest on the floured work surface. Drain the currants and pat them dry on paper toweling. Flatten the dough and drop the currants into the center. Fold the dough over the currants and knead until the fruit is distributed evenly throughout, about 5 minutes.

BY PROCESSOR
10 mins.

Prepare the sponge, as above. Plump the raisins or currants.

Attach the plastic dough blade.

Measure 2 cups flour into the work bowl, and with the machine running pour in the beaten eggs. Add the water, sugar, and salt. Pulse to blend. Drop in the butter. Pulse several times.

With the machine on, add flour, ¼ cup at a time, until the mixture forms a shaggy mass that cleans the sides of the bowl and is carried around by the force of the blade.

KNEADING
1¼ mins.

Keep the machine running and knead for 45 seconds.

Uncover the work bowl and add the risen sponge. Process until the two are thoroughly blended, about 30 seconds.

Incorporate the raisins as above.

FIRST RISING
2–3 hours

Place the dough in a large bowl, cover with plastic wrap, and leave at room temperature until doubled in bulk, from 2 to 3 hours. The dough takes a while to begin rising but then performs admirably in the latter stages.

SHAPING
15 mins.

Turn back the plastic covering and punch down the dough with your outstretched fingers. Before preparing the pan, experiment with the amount of dough needed to fill the mold to the halfway point. At this point, you also will know if an additional pan is necessary for the balance of the dough. Put the dough aside for a moment.

With your fingers, smear the mold with a liberal film of cold butter to which the almonds will cling. Push the almond slices against the walls of the pan. Place the whole almonds uniformly along the bottom. Reserve some almonds if an additional pan is necessary.

Flatten the ball of dough into an oval roughly the diameter of the pan. With your fingers, tear and fashion a hole in the center through which the pan tube will slip. Drop the dough into place in the pan and push down with your fingers.

Butter an overflow pan, if you are using one, and place the almonds against the sides of the pan. Put the dough in the pans, as above.

SECOND RISING
1 hour

Tear a hole in a length of wax paper and fit over the pan's tube. Put aside for the dough to rise to the edge of the pan at room temperature, about 1 hour.

PREHEAT

Preheat the oven to 400° about 20 minutes before baking.

BAKING
400°
40–60 mins.

Place the pans on the middle shelf. Midway during baking, change the positions of the pans so they heat evenly.

A small loaf may be baked in 40 minutes. Check with a metal skewer or wooden pick to determine if done. Test a larger loaf in about 1 hour. Loaves should have a deep brown crust.

Many gugelhupf pans are made with shiny metal, which makes it difficult to achieve a deep brown crust. If necessary, remove the loaf from the pan and return to the oven for 5 to 8 minutes for a deeper tan.

(If using a convection oven, reduce heat 50°.)

FINAL STEP

Remove the bread from the oven (and from its pan) and place on a metal rack to cool. While it may be served as soon as it is cool, *boulangers* suggest allowing the bread to mature for 1 or 2 days before cutting.

Sprinkle the loaf with the confectioners' sugar. It makes a handsome piece for a special breakfast, brunch, or buffet.

Italian Panettone   [four medium hearth loaves]

Unlike the many panettone baked in tall cylindrical pans, this loaf is baked on a baking sheet or directly on the hearth without benefit of a mold. A rich and classy touch is dropping a tablespoon of butter on the center of the developing crust 5 minutes after it has been in the oven. Voilà! Eccolo!

I found the loaf in Monsieur Albert Phillips's boulangerie in Monaco, just down the hill from the royal palace, and only a few miles away from Italy, the home of the panettone. Italy makes a substantial contribution to the variety of breads available in the tiny principality, as well as to that part of France that fronts it.

The original of this recipe was a classic example of starting with a cup of flour, some yeast, and a little water and carrying it through several sponges to make more than 5 pounds of dough. This adaptation eliminates two of the sponges with no loss of flavor or texture.

Of course, the dough can be baked in an ordinary loaf pan or a cylindrical one if preferred over this hearth loaf.

This is a large recipe that can easily be halved.

INGREDIENTS

Starter:
³/₄ cup bread or all-purpose flour, approximately
1 package dry yeast
¹/₄ cup hot water (120°–130°)
1 teaspoon malt syrup (optional) (see Note)

Dough:
1¹/₄ cups hot milk (120°–130°)
7 cups bread or all-purpose flour, approximately
2 teaspoons salt
¹/₂ cup (1 stick) butter, room temperature
4 egg yolks, room temperature
2 eggs, room temperature
1 cup sugar
¹/₂ cup chopped candied mixed fruit or citron
2 tablespoons chopped pine nuts
1 tablespoon ground or crushed aniseed
²/₃ cup raisins
4 tablespoons butter

BAKING SHEET

1 or 2 baking sheets, greased or Teflon

PREPARATION
6 hours–
overnight

To make the starter, measure ¹/₂ cup flour into a small bowl, stir in the yeast, and add the hot water and malt syrup, if desired. Add more flour to make a soft ball, and knead briefly for 2 or 3 minutes. Cover the bowl with plastic wrap and leave at room temperature for a minimum of 6 hours, or overnight.

BY HAND OR MIXER
15 mins.

To make the dough, scrape the starter into a large mixing or mixer bowl and pour the hot milk over it. Stir in 2 cups flour, the salt, and butter.

In a separate bowl, beat together the egg yolks, eggs, and sugar until light and frothy, about 3 minutes. Slowly pour this into the flour mixture, blending well.

With a wooden spoon or the mixer flat beater stir in additional flour, ½ cup at a time, until the dough becomes thick and can be lifted out of the bowl, or left in the mixer bowl to knead with the dough hook.

KNEADING
15 mins.

Dust the work surface with liberal sprinkles of flour, and begin to knead the dough with the help of a dough scraper, or in the mixer. Use a rhythmic push-turn-fold motion, occasionally varying this by banging the dough down hard on the work surface. The dough will become soft, elastic, and a pleasure to work after kneading for 10 minutes.

Cover the dough with a cloth and let rest while preparing the fruits and nuts.

Mix the candied fruit or citron and pine nuts with the ground aniseed and raisins.

Flatten the dough into an oval and spread half of the fruit-nut mixture over the top. Fold into the dough and knead until it disappears, then repeat with the balance of the mixture. Knead the dough thoroughly so the fruits and nuts are well distributed, about 5 minutes.

BY PROCESSOR
8 mins.

Prepare the starter, as above.

Attach the plastic dough blade.

Scrape the starter into the processor work bowl, and add 2½ cups flour. Pulse briefly. Pour in the hot milk; pulse to combine. Add the salt and butter. Pulse 3 or 4 times. Add 2 more cups flour.

In a separate bowl beat together the egg yolks, eggs, and sugar until light yellow and frothy, about 3 minutes. With the machine running, slowly pour the mixture through the feed tube.

Add flour, ¼ cup at a time, through the feed tube or by removing the cover. Pulse each time until well blended. Add flour until the heavy batter is a shaggy mass riding on the blade. It will also clean the sides of the bowl.

KNEADING
6 mins.

Knead the dough for 45 seconds with the machine on.

When the dough is turned out of the work bowl it may be somewhat sticky. Sprinkle lightly with flour and knead the dough by hand for a moment or so. The stickiness will disappear.

Incorporate the fruit and nuts as above.

FIRST RISING
2 hours

Place the dough in a greased bowl, cover tightly with plastic wrap, and set aside undisturbed for about 2 hours at room temperature to more than double in volume.

SHAPING
5 mins.

Remove the plastic wrap and punch down the dough with your fingers. Lift the dough to a flour-dusted work surface and divide into 4 pieces (for medium-size loaves). Shape each into a ball with cupped hands. Place on 1 or 2 baking sheets, as needed. Flatten the tops of the loaves slightly.

SECOND RISING
1½ hours

Arrange lengths of wax paper over the loaves so the surfaces will not dry out. Leave at room temperature until the loaves have doubled in bulk, 1½ hours.

PREHEAT

Preheat the oven to 375° about 20 minutes before baking.

BAKING
375°
40 mins.

Before placing in the oven, cut an **X** with a razor blade on top of each of the balls. The cut should be about ½" deep and extend to a point halfway down the sides. (The butter comes later.)

Place the baking sheets on the top and middle shelves if baking with both trays, otherwise use the middle shelf. Five minutes after the bread has been placed in the oven, open the door, pull the shelf forward, and drop 1 tablespoon butter in the center of the loaf where **X** crosses. Close the oven door. Midway during baking, shift the baking sheets from top to bottom and bottom to top. The loaves are done when deep brown and sound hollow when the bottom crust is tapped with a forefinger, 40 minutes.

(If using a convection oven, reduce heat 50°.)

FINAL STEP

Place the loaves on a metal rack to cool.

This is a lovely, light bread that is excellent for any festive occasion. Serve it for brunch, a breakfast, or a tea.

Freezes well but should be used within 8 weeks for the full measure of flavor.

Note: Malt syrup or extract can be found in most large supermarkets, sometimes in the section devoted to home-brewed beverages. Blue Ribbon Malt Extract is one of the foremost products.

Stolle de Noël   [three loaves]
(Christmas Stollen)

The holiday season begins for Jean Pierre Scholler, one of the fine bakers in Strasbourg on the banks of the Rhine, when he commences the annual bake of Stolle de Noël, the Christmas stollen.

Almonds, orange and lemon peel, raisins, currants, and schnapps or brandy are the good things that are part of his special Christmas bread. His loaves range from ¹/₂ pound to those weighing more than 3 pounds and are brushed with melted butter the moment they come from the oven. Not only does it enhance the flavor, says M. Scholler, but the stolle will keep for up to 3 or 4 weeks. When the bread has cooled, M. Scholler sprinkles it lightly with confectioners' sugar.

A rare Christmas treat—as a gift or to serve to friends.

INGREDIENTS

Starter:
1 cup bread or all-purpose flour, approximately
1 package dry yeast
¹/₂ cup hot milk (120°–130°)

Dough:
1¹/₂ cups hot milk (120°–130°)
¹/₃ cup sugar
2 teaspoons salt
5¹/₂ cups bread or all-purpose flour, approximately
¹/₂ cup (1 stick) butter
1 tablespoon schnapps or brandy (optional)
1 cup coarsely chopped almonds
¹/₂ cup *each* candied orange peel and candied lemon peel
   (or ¹/₃ cup mixed candied fruit)
¹/₃ cup raisins
¹/₄ cup currants
1–2 tablespoons butter, melted
Confectioners' sugar

BAKING SHEET

1 large (14"-x-17") baking sheet, greased or Teflon

A smaller baking sheet is necessary in most convection ovens so you may be able to bake only 1 or 2 loaves at a time. Refrigerate the reserve stollen during the first baking.

PREPARATION
3 hours–
overnight

To make the starter, measure the flour into a small bowl and stir in the yeast and then the hot milk. Add flour sufficient to make a soft dough that can be kneaded without sticking. Knead on the work surface for 3 minutes. Return to the bowl and cover with plastic wrap. Leave at room temperature for at least 3 hours, or overnight if more convenient.

BY HAND
OR MIXER
12 mins.

To make the dough, scrape the starter into a large mixing or mixer bowl and cover with the hot milk. By hand or the mixer flat beater stir in the sugar, salt, and 2 cups flour. Divide the butter into small pieces and drop into the bowl. Add schnapps or brandy, if desired.

With a large wooden spoon beat with vigor about 60 to 70 strokes to cream the butter into the thick batter, or for 2 minutes with the mixer. The dough will begin to pull away from the bowl in heavy strands. This is good. Work in additional flour to make a shaggy mass that can be lifted from the bowl—or leave in the mixer bowl under the dough hook.

KNEADING
20 mins.

Dust the work surface lightly with flour and turn out the dough, if by hand. Knead with a strong motion. Don't baby the dough. Bang it down hard against the work surface to hasten development of the gluten network. It is a soft and elastic dough to work. It will be responsive under the hands—and feel alive! In the mixer the dough will pull away from the sides and mass around the dough hook. It will have the same alive feeling when handled.

When finished kneading, allow the dough to rest for 5 minutes.

Mix the peels and nuts together in a bowl or on the work surface.

With your fingers, punch down the dough into an oval and spread half of the peel-nut mixture and raisins and currants over the top. Fold it in, and when it has disappeared, fold in the balance of the mix. Knead until the mixture is evenly distributed, about 5 minutes.

(The mixture may be worked into the dough with the mixer dough hook or fed through the processor feed tube into the dough while pulsing.)

BY PROCESSOR

Prepare the starter, as above.

Attach the short plastic dough blade.

Scrape the starter into the processor work bowl, and add 3 cups flour. Turn on the machine and pour in the 1½ cups hot milk, the sugar, and salt. The dough will be a thick batter at this point. Divide the butter, as above, and drop into the work bowl. Add schnapps or brandy, if desired. Pulse several times until the dough pulls away from the bowl in heavy strands.

Measure in additional flour, ½ cup at a time, to make a shaggy mass that cleans the sides of the bowl and rides around the bowl atop the blade.

KNEADING 10 mins.	With the machine running knead for 45 seconds. Let the dough rest for 5 minutes, then incorporate the peels and raisins and currants as above.
FIRST RISING 1¼ hours	Place the dough in a greased bowl, cover with plastic wrap, and set aside to rise at room temperature until doubled in volume, about 1¼ hours.
SHAPING 10 mins.	Turn the dough onto the work surface and cut into 3 pieces. Cover with a cloth and let the dough rest for 5 minutes. With a rolling pin, roll out a piece of dough into an oval about 10" long by 8" wide by ½" thick. Brush the surface with melted butter. Fold lengthwise in half, allowing 1" of the lower edge to project. Place on the baking sheet. Repeat with the other pieces.
SECOND RISING 1 hour	Cover the dough with wax paper and leave at room temperature for 1 hour.
PREHEAT	Preheat the oven to 350° about 15 minutes before baking.
BAKING 350° 45 mins.	Remove the wax paper and set the sheet on the middle shelf of the oven. Turn the sheet around 30 minutes into baking. The stollen is done when deep brown on the top crust and when the bottom crust tapped with a forefinger sounds hard and hollow, about 45 minutes. (If using a convection oven, reduce heat 50°.)
FINAL STEP	Immediately brush with more melted butter when removed from the oven and placed on a metal rack. When the loaves are completely cooled, sprinkle with confectioners' sugar. If the loaves are to be frozen, sprinkle with sugar after they come out of the freezer and are thawed.

Choreki   [two large or four small braided loaves]
(Grecian Sweet Braid)

Choreki will lend a festive air to any occasion with shiny braids sprinkled with sesame seeds and chopped almonds. Three eggs give this loaf tenderness. There is a faint suggestion of anise, but it does not overwhelm the other delicate flavors of this special bread.

The recipe makes 2 large loaves for the family or 4 smaller ones, the latter ideal for gift giving. The recipe can, of course, be halved.

INGREDIENTS

5 to 5$^1/_2$ cups bread flour, approximately
2 packages dry yeast
I cup hot water (120°–130°)
$^1/_3$ cup nonfat dry milk
I teaspoon ground aniseed
$^1/_2$ cup (I stick) butter, room temperature
$^1/_4$ cup sugar, plus 2 tablespoons to sprinkle
I teaspoon salt
3 eggs, room temperature
I egg, beaten, mixed with I tablespoon milk
2 tablespoons *each* chopped almonds and sesame seeds
sugar to sprinkle

BAKING SHEET

1 large baking sheet, greased or Teflon

BY HAND
OR MIXER
15 mins.

In a mixing or mixer bowl measure 3 cups flour and add the yeast. Stir to blend.

In a saucepan over low heat measure the hot water, dry milk, aniseed, butter, ¼ cup sugar, and salt. Mix and heat until the butter is soft, about 110° or warm to the touch. Stir well and pour slowly into the dry ingredients. Beat 25 strokes by hand, or for 2 minutes with the mixer flat blade, and add the eggs.

Add flour, ½ cup at a time, until the dough is roughly shaped and cleans the bowl. Add sprinkles of flour if the dough is sticky.

KNEADING
10 mins.

Turn the dough onto a floured work surface, or leave in the mixer bowl under the dough hook. Knead until smooth and elastic, 10 minutes by hand or hook.

BY PROCESSOR
5 mins.

Insert the plastic blade.

The order of adding the ingredients differs from above.

Measure 4 cups flour into the work bowl and add the yeast, dry milk, aniseed, sugar, and salt. Pulse to blend. With the processor running pour the hot water through the feed tube. Turn off the machine when a heavy but moist batter has formed to allow the yeast cells a moment or so to be absorbed. Drop in the butter. Pulse to blend. Add the eggs.

Turn on the processor and add flour through the feed tube, ¼ cup at a time, until a rough mass begins to form. Add the balance of the flour until the dough cleans the sides of the bowl and rides with the blade as it spins.

KNEADING
45 secs.

With the processor running knead for 45 seconds. The dough should be slightly sticky and very elastic when kneading is completed. Pull and stretch the dough between your hands to test its elasticity; if necessary, return the dough to the work bowl to process for a few more seconds.

FIRST RISING
I hour

Place the dough in a greased bowl, cover with plastic wrap, and set aside to double in volume, about 1 hour.

REST
10 mins.

Turn the dough onto a floured work surface and knead briefly. Divide the dough into as many pieces as you wish loaves; cover with a cloth and allow to rest for 10 minutes.

SHAPING
15 mins.

To shape, divide one of the dough portions into 3 smaller but equal pieces. Roll each under your palms into long ropes (about 16" long for the large loaf). Place the ropes side by side on the work surface. Start in the middle and loosely braid toward the end. Turn the strands around and complete the braid. Pinch the ends so the braids will not break loose when they rise.

Repeat for the other 2 dough portions.

SECOND RISING
I hour

Place the loaves on the baking sheet, cover with a length of wax paper, and put aside to rise until puffy and doubled in volume, about 1 hour.

PREHEAT

Preheat the oven to 350° about 20 minutes before baking.

BAKING
350°
45 mins.

Before the loaves go into the oven, brush the egg glaze over the braids. Sprinkle with the almonds and sesame seeds, then the 2 tablespoons sugar.

Bake in the oven until well browned and a wooden toothpick or metal skewer inserted in the center comes out clean and dry, 45 minutes.

(If using a convection oven, reduce heat 50°.)

FINAL STEP   Remove the bread from the oven and place on a wire rack to cool.

It is delicious warm from the oven—but don't cut into the loaves until they have cooled considerably. When butter is spread on a slice it should not melt into the bread.

Anise Kuchen   [two to four loaves]

Bright colored ribbons appear to have been baked as part of this festive bread from Germany. Paper strips, which the real ribbons later replace, are fastened around the loaf before it goes into the oven and the dough pushes into a large four-leaf clover. The golden brown loaf, speckled with bits of orange and lemon peel, has a spicy anise flavor.

This bread makes a thoughtful gift for the holidays. It can be made into 2, 3, or 4 loaves, according to the size desired. Of course, for the smaller loaves reduce the width of the ribbons accordingly.

INGREDIENTS

1 cup (2 sticks) butter, room temperature
$1/2$ cup sugar
Peel of 1 lemon, grated
Peel of 1 orange, grated
$1/2$ teaspoon *each* dried mace and grated nutmeg
3 tablespoons crushed or ground aniseed
3 eggs, room temperature
7 cups bread or all-purpose flour, approximately
2 packages dry yeast
1 teaspoon salt
$1/2$ cup nonfat dry milk
$1 1/2$ cups hot water ($120°$–$130°$)
1 teaspoon salad oil

BAKING SHEET   1 large baking sheet, greased or Teflon

SPECIAL
EQUIPMENT

Four strips of 30"-x-1½" (or other width of choice) heavy brown sack paper, lightly greased; plus colored ribbon the same size as the paper strips; adjust number and size for more loaves

BY HAND
OR MIXER
20 mins.

In a large mixing or mixer bowl cream the butter by hand with a wooden spoon or with the mixer flat beater and gradually add the sugar, blending until the butter is soft and fluffy. Mix in the lemon and orange peels, mace, nutmeg, and ground aniseed. Add the eggs, beating well after each addition.

Measure 2 cups flour, the dry yeast, salt, and dry milk into the bowl, stir to blend and pour in the hot water. With strong strokes of the wooden spoon or with the flat beater, measure additional flour, ½ cup at a time, until the dough is soft and not sticky. Work it with your hands when it becomes dense and difficult to beat with a wooden spoon, or use the dough hook.

KNEADING
10 mins.

Turn the dough onto the work surface sprinkled lightly with flour, or leave in the mixer work bowl. Allow the dough to rest for a minute or two before kneading. Knead until the dough is smooth and elastic, 10 minutes. Add small portions of flour if the dough continues to be slack (moist).

BY PROCESSOR
10 mins.

Insert the steel blade and later, when the flour is added, change to the short plastic blade.

Place both the butter and sugar in the work bowl and pulse until blended. Add the peel of lemon and orange, mace, nutmeg, and aniseed; pulse. Drop the eggs into the work bowl. Pulse several times until the mixture is thoroughly blended.

Change to the short blade.

Measure in 2 cups flour, the yeast, salt, and dry milk. Pulse to blend. With the machine running, pour in the hot water. The dough will be a heavy batter. Add flour, ¼ cup at a time, either through the feed tube or by removing the cover each time, until the dough forms a shaggy mass that cleans the bowl and spins with the blade as it whirls.

KNEADING
45 secs.

Keep the machine running and knead for 45 seconds.

FIRST RISING
50 mins.

Place the dough in a large greased bowl, cover with plastic wrap, and leave at room temperature until doubled in bulk, about 50 minutes.

SHAPING
15 mins.

Turn the dough onto the work surface, punch down to press out the gassy bubbles, and cut into as many pieces as you wish loaves.

Shape each piece into a rectangular loaf—about 8" x 5" for the large loaves. Place on the baking sheet. Grease the tops lightly with salad oil using your fingers or a brush. Tie each loaf with 2 of the paper strips— one lengthwise and one crosswise.

Pin, clip, or staple the paper ribbons together quite loosely—enough so that a finger can slip easily under the paper after it is fastened in place, but not so loosely that depressions will not be left in the finished loaves—so the dough can expand evenly. The paper will leave depressions for the colored ribbons to be tied there later. Repeat with the other pieces.

SECOND RISING 40 mins.	Cover the dough with wax paper and leave at room temperature until almost doubled in bulk, 40 minutes.
PREHEAT	Preheat the oven to 350° 15 minutes before baking.
BAKING 350° 45 mins.	Bake in the oven until golden brown and tapping the bottom crust yields a hard hollow sound, about 45 minutes. Turn the sheet or the loaves midway during baking so they will have even exposure. (If using a convection oven, reduce heat 50°.)
FINAL STEP	Remove the bread from the oven. When the breads have cooled on a wire rack, remove the paper strips and replace with bright ribbons. A fine and tasty gift, and particularly good when toasted. The loaf can be frozen at 0° for 5 to 6 months.

Christopsomo   [two round loaves]
(Greek Christmas Bread)

An early Christian cross—an X with ends split and curled into circles—decorates this Greek Christmas bread. A round loaf with the cross on the top, it is rich with eggs and scented with anise.

Initials, birth dates, and ages can also be fashioned to celebrate other occasions.

INGREDIENTS	6 to 7 cups bread or all-purpose flour, approximately 2 packages dry yeast 1/4 cup nonfat dry milk 1 teaspoon salt 2 teaspoons crushed aniseed 1 cup hot water (120°–130°) 3/4 cup sugar 4 eggs, room temperature, slightly beaten 1 cup (2 sticks) butter, room temperature 10 candied cherries or walnut halves 1 egg white, slightly beaten
BAKING SHEET	1 baking sheet, greased or Teflon
BY HAND OR MIXER 12 mins.	Measure 2 cups flour into a large mixing or mixer bowl and add the yeast, dry milk, salt, and aniseed. Pour in the hot water and blend with 50 strong strokes of a wooden spoon, or for 30 seconds with the mixer flat beater.

In a small bowl beat the sugar and eggs together and add to the thin batter. Add 1 cup flour and stir well. Add the butter and blend until it is completely absorbed.

Add the balance of the flour, ¼ cup at a time, until the dough is a shaggy mass that can be lifted from the bowl and placed on the floured work surface, or left in the mixer bowl under the dough hook.

KNEADING
10 mins.

Knead the dough, by hand or dough hook, until it is smooth and elastic, soft but not sticky. However, if the dough is slack (moist), add additional sprinkles of flour. Knead for about 10 minutes.

BY PROCESSOR
10 mins.

Attach the plastic dough blade.

Measure 2 cups flour into the work bowl; add the yeast, dry milk, salt, and aniseed. Pulse to blend. With the machine running, pour hot water through the feed tube. Stop the machine. The dough will be heavy and wet.

In a small bowl stir together the sugar and eggs and pour this mixture into the work bowl. Pulse 1 time, and immediately add 2 cups flour. Pulse several times to mix thoroughly. Add the butter. Pulse again and blend.

Add flour, ¼ cup at a time, either through the feed tube or by removing the cover, until the dough becomes a mass and cleans the sides of the bowl as it whirls.

KNEADING
50 secs.

With the machine running knead for 50 seconds.

FIRST RISING
1½ hours

Place the dough in a large greased bowl, cover tightly with plastic wrap, and set aside at room temperature until almost doubled in size, about 1½ hours.

SHAPING
20 mins.

Knead the dough briefly to work out the bubbles, and turn onto a floured work surface. Cut the dough in half. Return one half to the bowl while making the first loaf.

Pinch off 2 small pieces from the larger piece, each about 2" in diameter, and set aside. Work the large piece into a smooth ball, and place on one corner of the baking sheet. Flatten it into an 8" round loaf, about 2" to 3" thick.

Shape each of the small balls into 12"-long strands by rolling and stretching each under your palms. Cut a 4"-long slash into each end of the 2 strands. Cross the strands at the center of the round loaf. Do not press down. Curl each slashed end to form a circle to embrace either a nut or cherry—about 1½" in diameter. Place the nuts or cherries in each circle as well as in the center of the cross. Carefully brush the loaf with the egg white, taking special care to brush where the strands join the loaf. Repeat with the other dough half.

SECOND RISING I hour	Cover the loaves with wax paper resting above the surface on water tumblers so the paper does not touch and stick to the dough. Let rise until almost doubled in size, about 1 hour.
PREHEAT	Preheat the oven to 350° about 20 minutes before baking.
BAKING 350° 45 mins.	Bake the loaves on the center shelf of the moderate oven until a golden brown and a wooden toothpick inserted in the center of the loaf comes out clean, about 45 minutes. (If using a convection oven, reduce heat 50°.)
FINAL STEP	Remove the bread from the oven. Let cool on a wire rack. Cut into wedges or slices. Serve it warm, spread with butter or, later, toast and serve with honey. Wrap in foil to reheat in a 350° oven for about 20 minutes. Freezes well.

Portuguese Honey Bread   [three small loaves]

Portuguese Honey Bread is a brick—a delicious brick that gains flavor and a degree of tenderness as it ages for 5 or more days. It is spicy rich, flavored with sugar, honey, and molasses, as well as with butter, sweet sherry, and 4 spices.

Each loaf comes out of the oven a solid brown brick that is allowed to age before it is thinly sliced to be served with tea or eggnog or holiday punch. Unlike traditional holiday fruit cake, Portuguese Honey Bread contains only a small quantity of fruit and nuts.

Because they travel well, I have shipped these dense little loaves at Christmas time by air to friends on both coasts and in Europe. Transit time allows their goodness to grow.

INGREDIENTS	I cup (2 sticks) butter, room temperature ³/₄ cup molasses I¹/₂ cups sugar ¹/₃ cup honey ¹/₄ cup instant potato flakes ¹/₄ cup sweet sherry

¹/₃ cup chopped candied fruit

1 tablespoon finely diced candied citron

¹/₂ cup broken walnuts

³/₄ teaspoon ground cloves

2 teaspoons ground aniseed

2 tablespoons ground cinnamon

¹/₄ teaspoon freshly ground black pepper

¹/₂ teaspoon baking soda

6 cups all-purpose flour

BAKING TINS

3 small (7"-x-3") baking tins, Teflon or buttered, lined with buttered wax paper

**BY HAND
OR MIXER
20 mins.**

Note: The mixer flat beater can be used in the early stages of preparing the dough; later on, it will become so thick and dense that a wooden spoon and your hands will be a necessity.

In a large mixing or mixer bowl cream the butter, molasses, sugar, and honey until fluffy. Blend in the potato flakes, sherry, candied fruit, citron, walnuts, cloves, aniseed, cinnamon, pepper, and baking soda.

Stir in 3 cups flour, best done with a heavy spoon. Add the remaining 3 cups flour. You will now have a heavy, crumbly mixture with neither the elasticity of yeast dough nor the creaminess of the usual batter.

**BY PROCESSOR
10 mins.**

Attach the steel blade.

Use the processor to blend together all of the above ingredients, except the flour. Turn the batter from the work bowl into a mixing bowl and beat in the flour by hand with a wooden spoon. Otherwise the heavy mixture may stall the processor.

PREHEAT

Preheat the oven to 250°.

**SHAPING
10 mins.**

Divide the mixture among the 3 tins. Press the dough into the corners and pat the tops smooth—the fingerprints will come out as the loaves rise in the oven. The dough will come to about ½" below the top of the pan.

**BAKING
250°
3 hours**

Bake in the moderately low oven for 3 hours. The loaves will rise an inch or so, and longitudinal cracks will appear in the brown tops.

(If using a convection oven, bake at 250° but check after 2 hours to determine with a cake testing pin or metal skewer if the loaves are done.)

FINAL STEP   Cool in the tins on a wire rack for 10 minutes. With care, turn the loaves from the pan. Gently peel off the wax paper and discard. The loaves are fragile when warm and could be broken.

The bread may be sliced when warm, but after the loaves have cooled they are to be aged, wrapped tightly in foil for at least 5 days at room temperature. The loaves may be kept sealed in foil for months, and can be frozen indefinitely. Slice thinly to serve.

Mâkos és Diós Kalács   [two long loaves]
(Hungarian Christmas Bread)

Black poppy seeds and raisins swirling through golden brown dough create an impressive and delicious loaf that celebrates Christmas for the Hungarians.

INGREDIENTS   *Dough:*
3 1/2 cups bread or all-purpose flour, approximately
2 packages dry yeast
1/2 teaspoon salt
1/4 cup nonfat dry milk
2/3 cup hot water (120°–130°)
1/4 cup sugar
1 cup (2 sticks) butter, room temperature
1 tablespoon grated lemon peel

Filling:
1 cup ground poppy seeds
1 cup sugar
1/2 cup raisins
1/2 cup milk
1 tablespoon grated lemon peel
1 egg, beaten, mixed with 1 teaspoon water

BAKING SHEET   One 11"-x-17" baking sheet, greased or Teflon. A smaller sheet will be necessary for most convection ovens. Be certain there is a 1" clearance around the pan.

BY HAND
OR MIXER
12 mins.   In a mixing or mixer bowl measure 2 cups flour and add the yeast, salt, and dry milk. Pour in the hot water. Blend with a large wooden spoon for 100 strong strokes, or for 2 minutes with the mixer flat beater. In a smaller bowl cream together the sugar, butter, and grated lemon peel. Spoon this mixture into the batter, mixing thoroughly.

Add additional flour, ¼ cup at a time, until the dough has formed a soft ball.

KNEADING
10 mins.

If by hand, turn onto a floured work surface to knead. If using the mixer, attach a dough hook. Knead with a strong push-turn-fold rhythmic motion, adding sprinkles of flour if the dough sticks to the hands or the work surface. In the mixer, add sprinkles, as needed, until the ball of dough cleans the sides of the bowl and rotates with the dough hook. Knead by hand or with the mixer for 10 minutes, until the dough is soft and elastic.

BY PROCESSOR
8 mins.

Attach the steel blade.

The sequence of adding ingredients differs from above.

In a small bowl cream together the sugar, butter, and lemon peel. Set aside.

Measure 1⅓ cups flour in the work bowl and add the yeast, salt, and dry milk. Pulse to blend. With the processor running, pour the hot water through the feed tube. It will be a very thick, moist batter that will allow the yeast particles to be absorbed. Stop the machine and add the sugar-butter mixture by the spoonful. Pulse several times to blend.

With the machine running, add additional flour, ¼ cup at a time, until the batter becomes a rough ball riding on the blade as it whirls.

KNEADING
45 secs.

With the machine running, knead the dough for 45 seconds.

FIRST RISING
1 hour

Turn the dough into a bowl, cover tightly with plastic wrap, and put aside at room temperature to double in volume, about 1 hour.

FILLING
20 mins.

While the dough is rising, prepare the poppy seed filling. Combine the ground poppy seeds, sugar, raisins, milk, and lemon peel and cook in a double boiler over water until the mixture is of spreading consistency. Stir constantly. It will thicken in about 10 minutes. Remove from the heat and cool to room temperature.

SHAPING
10 mins.

Punch down the dough, divide into 2 pieces, and roll each into a long rectangle about ¼" thick. Spread the pieces with the cooled filling. Roll like a jelly roll. Pinch the seams tightly together so the filling does not bubble out when it heats and the dough begins to expand.

SECOND RISING
30 mins.

Place the rolls on the baking sheet. Brush with some of the egg glaze.

Cover the rolls with wax paper laid across water glasses above the surface so the paper does not touch the moist dough. Let rise, 30 minutes. Brush again with the glaze.

PREHEAT	Preheat the oven to 325° about 20 minutes before baking.
BAKING **325°** **50 mins.**	Place the loaves on the middle shelf of the moderate oven. If the tops seem to brown too rapidly in the latter part of the baking, cover with a piece of brown paper or foil. Bake for about 50 minutes, or until a deep brown. (If using a convection oven, reduce heat to 300°.)
FINAL STEP	Remove the bread from the oven and with a spatula under the loaf lift and place on a metal rack to cool. The breads are fragile when warm, so handle them with care.

Finnish Easter Bread   [one or two large loaves]

The Finnish call this festive loaf that celebrates Easter and the arrival of spring, Pääsiäisleipä, a cylindrical bread that is traditionally baked in milking pails to celebrate the arrival of new calves.

*   The loaf, pleasantly pungent with lemon, orange, and cardamom, is cut into quarter wedges, and each wedge into triangular slices. It is delicious served with all sorts of cheese.*

INGREDIENTS	*Sponge:* 2 cups bread flour 2 packages dry yeast 1½ cups light cream or undiluted evaporated milk, room temperature ½ cup hot water (120°–130°) *Dough:* 5 egg yolks 1 cup sugar 1 cup (2 sticks) butter, room temperature 1½ teaspoons salt 2 teaspoons *each* ground cardamom and grated lemon peel 2 tablespoons grated orange peel 1 cup golden raisins 1 cup chopped or slivered almonds 1 cup milk, room temperature 2 cups rye flour 4 to 5 cups bread flour, approximately Butter, melted

BAKING PAILS

One 4-quart or two 2-quart ungalvanized sand pails, or two 2-pound coffee cans or the equivalent in volume in other combinations of pails or cans, greased

PREPARATION
1 hour

To make the sponge, in a mixing bowl combine the bread flour and the yeast. Stir in the light cream and hot water. With a large wooden spoon or mixer flat beater mix until the batter/sponge is smooth and without lumps. Cover with plastic wrap and let the sponge rise at room temperature until it has doubled in volume, about 1 hour.

If using a processor, make half a batch of sponge. Measure 1¼ cups bread flour into the work bowl; add the yeast, pulse and pour in ¾ cup cream and the water through the feed tube. Run the machine for 30 seconds, until the sponge is a thick batter. Keep the work bowl covered and allow the sponge to rise to the top in about 1 hour.

BY HAND
OR MIXER
15 mins.

To make the dough, remove the plastic wrap, stir down, and add the egg yolks, sugar, butter, salt, cardamom, lemon peel, orange peel, raisins, and almonds. Beat well until thoroughly combined. Stir in the milk and rye flour until blended. Stir in the white flour, ½ cup at a time, to make a firm dough. Work the flour into the dough with the fingers or attach the mixer dough hook.

KNEADING
10 mins.

Sprinkle a small amount of flour on the work surface and turn the dough onto it; or leave in the mixer bowl under the dough hook. Knead with a strong push-turn-fold motion by hand until the dough is smooth and elastic, about 10 minutes, or with the dough hook for an equal length of time. The dough will clean the sides of the bowl. If it does not, sprinkle lightly with flour.

BY PROCESSOR
5 mins.

Note: This recipe is too large for most food processors in one batch. Mix and knead the dough in 2 different batches or make only half the recipe.

Attach the plastic dough blade.

To make the dough: pulse to deflate the sponge. Add ingredients in the order above, pulsing several times after each addition to blend thoroughly.

With the machine running, add the balance of the white flour, ½ cup at a time. The batter will become a rough mass. Stop the machine, lift off the cover, and pinch to test the dough for moisture. If it is quite moist and sticky, add sprinkles of white flour. It has enough flour when it begins to clean the sides of the bowl and ride with the blade as it spins.

KNEADING **50 secs.**	With the machine running, knead for 50 seconds.
FIRST RISING **I hour**	Drop the dough into a greased bowl, cover with plastic wrap, and put aside to rise to double in volume, about 1 hour.
SHAPING **I5 mins.**	Punch down and work the dough into a smooth ball. To make 1 large loaf, place the dough in the 4-quart pail. It should only come halfway up the pail. If there is an excess, bake a smaller loaf as well. If making 2 loaves, divide the dough equally. Again, the dough should only come halfway up the sides of the container.
SECOND RISING **45 mins.**	Cover the pail or can loosely with wax paper and leave to rise until the dough *almost* reaches the top, about 45 minutes. If it rises too high in the oven, it may lean and break or push into the top of the oven.
PREHEAT	Preheat the oven to 350° 20 minutes before baking. Arrange the shelves so that the tall pail or cans will go on the lowest shelf to provide sufficient headroom.
BAKING **350°** **I to I¹/₄ hours**	Place the loaf or loaves in the moderate oven. The large gallon-size loaf will take about 1¼ hours, while the 2-pound loaves will bake in about 1 hour. Test for doneness with a long straw or a wooden or metal skewer. If the bread is baked, the straw will come out clean and dry from the center of the loaf. (It is unlikely that any home-size convection oven will accommodate these tall baking cans or pails. Determine if the cans or pails will fit into the oven before baking. There should be at least a 2" or 3" clearance. Reduce heat 50°.)
FINAL STEP	Remove the bread from the oven and immediately brush the top with melted butter. Allow the loaf to rest for about 15 minutes before turning it onto a metal cooling rack.

Golden Beehive Bread   [one large woven basket]

Golden beehive bread is an eye-catching creation of dough that can be presented at almost any festive occasion of the year. It is literally good enough to eat.

The beehive is shaped from dough twisted around an inverted bowl and baked. When it comes from the oven it resembles a beehive. Turn it over and it is a beautiful (and edible) basket that can be a centerpiece filled with dips and spreads or Easter eggs or Christmas ornaments, depending on the season.

You can have both the bread to eat and the bowl if you bake two identical loaves. In that case, double the recipe below.

This can be done in one baking with two identical bowls or one at a time with the same bowl. This finished "hive" crowns the other as a sphere about the size of a soccer ball. The top lifts off to be eaten. The bottom is the basket (the bowl may be left in place) to fill with whatever good things you wish.

This recipe is for a butter- and egg-rich dough that is suitable for the most festive occasion. However, it can be made with any of the yeast-raised doughs. Made with simple French or Italian bread dough, it is ideal to carry to a tailgate party to serve with a stew or chili. Or perhaps baked to resemble a football.

There is one caution: the long coil is made with about 10 short strands pinched together as the coil is built. Because this takes time, the beehive is slipped back into the refrigerator to retard the rising while each new length is twisted so that the finished beehive will rise uniformly as one piece.

Forming dough into shapes began centuries ago, but this new method is from the innovative kitchen of Sunset, the fine West Coast regional magazine. I carried it one step farther by joining the halves.

INGREDIENTS	5$\frac{1}{2}$ to 6 cups bread flour
	1 package dry yeast
	$\frac{1}{2}$ teaspoon salt
	$\frac{1}{2}$ cup sugar
	$\frac{3}{4}$ cup milk (or $\frac{3}{4}$ cup water with $\frac{1}{3}$ cup nonfat dry milk) (120°–130°)
	1 tablespoon grated lemon peel
	5 eggs, room temperature
	$\frac{1}{2}$ cup (1 stick) butter, room temperature
	1 egg, beaten, mixed with 1 teaspoon milk
BAKING SHEET	1 baking sheet
SPECIAL EQUIPMENT	One 2- or 2½-quart ovenproof glass or metal mixing bowl (9" wide x 4" deep)
BY HAND OR MIXER 12 mins.	In a mixing bowl measure 2 cups flour, the yeast, salt, and sugar (also dry milk powder if used). Stir in the milk (or water) and lemon peel. By hand, with a wooden spoon, or with a mixer flat beater, beat until it is a smooth batter. Add the eggs, one at a time, blending after each is dropped into the bowl. Stir in the butter.

Add flour, ½ cup at a time, until the dough is a rough mass that can be lifted from the bowl to knead by hand or left in the bowl under the dough hook. If the dough is sticky, add liberal sprinkles of flour.

KNEADING
10 mins.

Knead the dough by hand with a strong push-turn-fold motion, or with a dough hook in the mixer, adding flour if needed, until it becomes smooth and elastic, about 10 minutes.

BY PROCESSOR
9 mins.

Attach the plastic blade.

Measure 3 cups flour into the work bowl; add the yeast, salt, and sugar. Pulse to blend. Pour the milk (or water and dry milk) through the feed tube while the machine is running, and add the lemon peel. Also while the machine is running, add the eggs, one at a time, and the butter.

The dough will be a wet mass and will need more flour. Add flour, ½ cup at a time, either through the feed tube or by removing the cover. Stop adding flour when the dough has become a rough ball and is riding around the work bowl on the blade.

KNEADING
50 secs.

Knead the dough in the machine for 50 seconds.

Turn the dough from the bowl. It may be quite moist to the touch, but this is no problem. Dust with flour as you form it into a ball to rise.

FIRST RISING
1 hour

Place the dough in a greased bowl, cover tightly with plastic wrap, and let rise at room temperature until doubled in bulk, about 1 hour.

CHILLED RISING
2 hours or
overnight

Turn the dough onto the work surface and knead for 2 or 3 minutes. Return the dough to the bowl, cover, and place in the refrigerator for 2 hours or overnight.

SHAPING
20 mins.

Wrap the outside of the bowl with foil, folding the excess inside. Press the foil against the surfaces of the bowl. Generously grease and place the bowl upside down on the baking sheet.

Remove the dough from the refrigerator. It will be chilled and hard; work it under the hands for a few moments to make it supple. Divide the dough into 20 equal pieces. This is easy to do by first rolling the dough into a 20" length and, with a yardstick, marking into 1" pieces. *Note:* Keep the pieces of dough in the refrigerator until needed to allow all parts of the beehive to rise together when completed.

Work 2 pieces of dough under your palms into ropes 18" to 20" long, and about 3/8" thick. Pinch the ends of the 2 ropes together and twist. If the dough resists twisting, allow it to relax before proceeding.

Starting low on the rim, wrap the twist around the bowl. While making a new twist, place the bowl in the refrigerator to keep chilled. When adding a new twist, pinch the ends together to join. Don't *stretch* the twist as it mounts up the bowl, but do pat it frequently into its new shape.

Depending on the size of the bowl over which the beehive is shaped, the twists of dough may not completely reach around the bowl. A small opening may be left at the top of the beehive, which is perfectly acceptable.

REST
20–30 mins.

Cover the shaped bowl lightly with plastic wrap and leave at room temperature for 20 to 30 minutes to become slightly raised and puffy.

PREHEAT

Preheat the oven to 350° about 20 minutes before baking.

BAKING
25–30 mins.

Brush the hive carefully with the egg glaze. Place the baking pan on the middle or lower shelf of the oven and bake until well browned, about 25 to 30 minutes.

(If using a convection oven, reduce heat 50°.)

FINAL STEP

Place the bowl on a cooling rack and allow the hive to cool for 15 minutes.

Crumple a large piece of foil into a loose ball with the same diameter as the depth of the bowl. This will support the beehive when it is lifted from the bowl. Carefully slip the bread from the bowl and place it on the crumpled foil.

Serve upside down for a beehive or open side up for a basket. To eat, tear off serving-size pieces.

If made ahead, cool, wrap well, and freeze. Thaw uncovered, then place on a baking sheet and warm in a 350° oven for 7 to 10 minutes.

Election Day Bread   [one large tube loaf]

Legend would have you believe that once upon a time a loaf of this delicious bread would have bought a vote or two on Election Day in some places in the New England states. While this is nearly impossible to authenticate, the bread itself is very real and very good. The proof is in the eating.

I have served this to poll watchers in my garage during the day, and then again that evening to neighbors gathered in front of the television set watching election results.

The loaf is studded with nuts and bits of fruit. It has a lovely smell of cinnamon and nutmeg. It may be frosted with confectioners' icing or served plain as it comes from the oven.

This is a batter bread to be prepared in two easy stages, so don't be carried away by election results and add so much flour that it must be kneaded.

INGREDIENTS

Dough:

4^1/$_2$ cups bread or all-purpose flour, approximately

2 packages dry yeast

2 teaspoons plus 1 cup granulated sugar

1^1/$_2$ cups hot water (120°–130°)

2 teaspoons salt

1^1/$_4$ teaspoons ground cinnamon

^{1}/$_4$ teaspoon *each* ground cloves and dried mace

^{1}/$_2$ teaspoon grated nutmeg

^{3}/$_4$ cup (1^1/$_2$ sticks) butter or other shortening, room temperature

2 eggs, room temperature

1^1/$_2$ cups raisins

^{3}/$_4$ cup chopped nuts

^{1}/$_2$ cup chopped citron

Icing:

1 cup confectioners' sugar

1^1/$_2$ tablespoons orange juice

^{1}/$_2$ teaspoon vanilla extract

Pinch of salt

BAKING PAN

One 10" tube pan, greased or Teflon

BY HAND
OR MIXER
10 mins.

Measure 1½ cups flour into a mixing or mixer bowl and add the yeast and 2 teaspoons sugar. Stir in the hot water and beat 150 strong strokes with a wooden spoon, or for 2 minutes with a mixer flat beater.

FIRST RISING
30 mins.

Cover the bowl with plastic wrap and set in a warm place. Let the batter rise high in the bowl, about 30 minutes, and stir down.

While the batter is rising, on a length of paper sift together the remaining 3 cups flour with the salt and spices.

In a small bowl cream together the butter or shortening and the 1 cup sugar, and add the eggs.

Remove the plastic wrap; stir down the batter. Spoon in the creamed mixture and blend thoroughly. Add the spice mixture a spoonful at a time, beating after each addition. The mixture must be smooth.

Dredge the raisins, nuts, and citron in 1 tablespoon flour, and stir them into the mixture.

BY PROCESSOR
30 mins.

Attach the plastic blade.

Measure 1½ cups flour into the work bowl and add the yeast and 2 teaspoons sugar. Pour in the warm water and pulse to make a smooth batter. Let the batter rise in the covered work bowl for about 30 minutes.

While the batter is rising, sift together the remaining flour, salt, and spices. In a small bowl cream the butter, sugar, and eggs. Add this to the batter and pulse. Add the flour-spice mixture, ½ cup at a time, through the feed tube or by removing the cover each time. Pulse after each addition. The mixture must be smooth.

Add the dredged raisins, nuts, and citron. Pulse only briefly.

SECOND RISING
1½ hours

Pour the batter into the pan. Level off with a spoon, which will slip more easily over the sticky batter if first dipped in water.

Cover the pan with wax paper and leave at room temperature until the batter has risen to twice its original height, 1½ hours.

PREHEAT

Preheat the oven to 375° 20 minutes before baking.

BAKING
375°
1¼–1½ hours

This is a thick batter and will take considerable time in the moderate oven to bake. With a metal skewer test for doneness when the loaf appears light golden brown, 1¼ to 1½ hours.

(If using a convection oven, reduce heat 50°.)

FINAL STEP

Remove the loaf from the oven. Let it rest in the pan for 10 minutes before turning onto a metal rack to cool.

Mix together the icing ingredients and spread over the top while the bread is still warm, or leave plain.

Don't forget to vote!

Swiss Christmas Bread   [two medium loaves]

During the Christmas season the baking begins the night before with a mixture of fruit and nuts steeping in brandy. It fills the kitchen with the delightful aroma of a very special kind of loaf in the making.

A slice will show a swirl of brandied fruit in a dough that has taken on some of the russet tint of the liquor.

INGREDIENTS

$^1/_2$ cup *each* sliced dried pears, raisins, chopped blanched almonds, and mixed chopped red and green candied cherries
$^1/_4$ cup finely chopped citron
I teaspoon grated lemon peel
$^1/_2$ teaspoon *each* ground cloves, cinnamon, and nutmeg
$^1/_2$ cup brandy
I cup milk
$^1/_4$ cup ($^1/_2$ stick) butter, room temperature, plus 3 tablespoons melted for brushing
$^1/_4$ cup sugar
2 teaspoons salt
4 cups bread or all-purpose flour, approximately
I package dry yeast
I egg, room temperature
I cup confectioners' sugar mixed with 2 tablespoons milk and $^1/_8$ teaspoon almond extract
8 whole almonds, plus $^1/_4$ cup slivered almonds
4 red candied cherries, halved

BAKING PANS

2 medium (8"-x-4") loaf pans, greased or Teflon

PREPARATION
Overnight

In a bowl combine the pears, raisins, almonds and red and green cherries. Add the citron, lemon peel, and spices. Cover with the brandy. Stir the mixture several times during the evening so that it has the opportunity to absorb as much brandy as possible. Cover tightly with plastic wrap and let marinate overnight.

BY HAND
OR MIXER
25 mins.

On baking day, in a saucepan heat the milk (120°–130°), and add the butter, sugar, and salt. The butter need not melt. Measure 2 cups flour into a mixing or mixer bowl. Pour in the milk mixture and any brandy that has not been soaked up by the fruit. With a wooden spoon or with a mixer flat beater pull the flour into the milk. Add the yeast; stir. Beat the egg lightly and add to the dough batter.

Add flour, ¼ cup at a time, until the dough is a soft but cohesive mass. Dust with flour if it is sticky.

KNEADING
10 mins.

If by hand, turn out onto a floured work surface and knead with a strong push-turn-fold motion until the dough is smooth and elastic, about 10 minutes. Or knead with a dough hook in the mixer bowl for an equal length of time.

BY PROCESSOR
8 mins.

Marinate the dried fruit, as above.

Use the stubby plastic blade.

Heat the milk, butter, sugar, and salt, as above. Measure 2 cups flour into the work bowl and pour in the milk. Pulse to blend into a smooth batter. Sprinkle in the yeast and add the egg. Turn on the machine for 15 seconds.

Gradually add flour, either through the feed tube or directly into the bowl, until the dough becomes a mass that is spun around the bowl by the force of the blade. If the blade has not picked up all the flour along the sides, stop the machine and scrape the flour toward the blade. Resume.

KNEADING
50 secs.

Turn on the machine and knead for 50 seconds.

When the dough is first turned from the work bowl it may be somewhat sticky. If so, sprinkle with flour as it is worked into a ball.

FIRST RISING
1 hour

Drop the dough into a greased bowl, cover tightly with plastic wrap, and put aside at room temperature until doubled, about 1 hour.

SHAPING
15 mins.

Spread the brandied fruit on a paper towel and pat dry. Dust the crust lightly with flour. Press the dough flat and spread about half of the fruit on top of it. Fold in the fruit, kneading gently, and then add the rest of the fruit in a similar manner. The moist fruit may leave brown streaks through the dough, but this is attractive when the bread is sliced.

Divide the dough in half. Pat and roll each half into an oblong about the length of the prepared pans. Tuck the ends under and drop the shaped loaves into the pans.

SECOND RISING
1½ hours

Cover loosely with wax paper or a tea towel and leave until double in bulk and slightly above the edge of the pan, about 1½ hours.

PREHEAT

Preheat the oven to 400° 20 minutes before baking.

BAKING
400°
10 mins.
350°
40 mins.

Brush the loaves with melted butter and place in the hot oven. After 10 minutes reduce heat to 350° and bake for 40 minutes longer, until golden brown. Turn one loaf out of the pan and test for doneness by rapping the bottom crust. If it sounds hard and hollow it is done. Midway during baking, shift the loaves so they are exposed evenly to the oven's heat.

(If using a convection oven, reduce heat 50°.)

FINAL STEP

Remove the bread from the oven. Turn out onto a wire rack to cool.

Frost the cooled loaves with the confectioners' icing. Almonds and red cherries placed on the icing add a festive note.

Kolach   [two fat 2-pound loaves]

The Circle of Serbian Sisters in Milwaukee reached back to a homeland in the Balkans for this egg- and butter-rich bread that is braided and then coiled on the baking sheet to rise impressively into a loaf of twined golden brown ropes.

The loaf is baked and served most often on one's patron saint day, but it is equally good anytime.

"God, I could live on this bread," wrote James Orgill, who is always searching out little-known but delicious recipes and passing them along to me. Like Mr. Orgill, I could live on this bread. Almost.

Kolach is an unusually fine loaf to be made with so few ingredients. True, some are especially rich.

INGREDIENTS

1½ cups (3 sticks) unsalted butter, room temperature
4 egg yolks
4 tablespoons sugar
1 teaspoon salt
2 teaspoons minced lemon zest
1 teaspoon lemon juice
2½ cups hot milk (120°–130°)
6½ cups bread or all-purpose flour, approximately
2 packages dry yeast
1 egg yolk, beaten, mixed with 1 tablespoon milk
¼ cup whole nuts (your choice)

BAKING SHEET

1 large baking sheet, Teflon or sprinkled with cornmeal

BY HAND
OR MIXER
10 mins.

In a mixing or mixer bowl cream by hand or with a mixer flat beater the butter, egg yolks, sugar, salt, lemon zest, and juice. Mix the milk with the butter and egg yolk mixture. Measure in 2 cups flour. Add the yeast. Stir to blend well.

When the batter is smooth, add flour, ½ cup at a time, and each time stir vigorously. When the dough has formed a mass that can be lifted out of the bowl and placed on the floured work surface, the dough is ready to knead. Or, if with a mixer, attach the dough hook. Add sprinkles of flour if the dough continues to be sticky during the kneading period.

KNEADING
10 mins.

Knead the dough with an aggressive push-turn-fold motion or under the dough hook for 10 minutes, or until the dough is smooth and elastic. At this point it should not stick to the work surface or to the sides of the mixer bowl.

BY PROCESSOR
6 mins.

Attach the short plastic dough blade.

The sequence for adding ingredients varies from above.

Place the butter, egg yolks, sugar, salt, lemon zest, and juice in the work bowl and pulse several times to cream. Measure 3 cups flour into the bowl. Add the yeast. With the machine running, pour the milk through the feed tube.

When the dough is a smooth batter, stop the machine and add flour, ¼ cup at a time, either through the feed tube or by removing the cover. If flour around the edges of the bowl is not pulled in by the blade, remove the cover and scrape the flour into the center and under the blade.

KNEADING
60 secs.

When the dough becomes a mass and rides around the work bowl on the blade, knead for 60 seconds. As it spins the dough will clean (somewhat) the sides of the bowl.

When the dough is first turned from the bowl it may seem quite moist—sprinkle with flour and knead for a few moments.

FIRST RISING
1 hour

Place the dough in a greased bowl, cover tightly with a length of plastic wrap, and put aside at room temperature to double in bulk, about 1 hour.

SHAPING
15 mins.

When the dough has risen, turn onto a floured work surface and divide in half. Divide each half into 3 equal parts. With the palms of your hands, roll each part into a rope about 24" long. Braid.

Place the braid on the baking sheet and coil it. Tuck the end of the

braid into the coil so that it doesn't break loose as the dough rises. With your hands, gently push the coils into a symmetrical shape.

SECOND RISING
50 mins.

Cover the 2 coils with parchment paper or a cloth and put aside at room temperature until the dough doubles in bulk, about 50 minutes.

PREHEAT

Preheat the oven to 350° about 20 minutes before baking.

BAKING
350°
I hour

Brush the loaves with the egg-milk glaze, and carefully push the nuts into a pattern over the top of the loaves.

Place the baking sheet in the moderate oven and bake until golden, about 1 hour. Turn one of the loaves over. If it is brown, and sounds hard and hollow when tapped with a forefinger, the loaves are done.

(If using a convection oven, reduce heat 50°. Some convection ovens will not accommodate a baking sheet suitably large to take both loaves at once. It may be necessary to bake separately—placing the reserved loaf in the refrigerator or cool place while the first loaf bakes.)

FINAL STEP

The first thing to do is admire the twined braids. Beautiful! Call in the family to look at them.

Allow the loaves to cool for 10 minutes before lifting them with a metal spatula and placing them on a metal rack to cool.

Delicious toasted.

Luffen   [five loaves]

Luffen came to my kitchen from the Carmelite Monastery of Mary Immaculate in New Jersey. Mother Mary Joseph, O.C.D., included it in a letter she wrote to me that said my bread books were much used by the sisters—but one thing concerned them. In many recipes, the Mother Superior wrote, I call for nonfat dry milk. The convent, on the other hand, had its own dairy herd of Guernsey milk cows—would it be all right to substitute fresh milk for dry?

I assured her it was and explained that I use the powder simply because it is more convenient to have in households no longer dedicated to gallons of fresh milk for thirsty youngsters.

This is her delicious Luffen—and made with fresh milk, of course. I changed her recipe in only one small way—I plumped the raisins in brandy.

This is a large recipe—5 pounds of dough—ample to make several Luffen for family and gifts to friends. I make five 1-pound loaves, about 12 inches long.

The recipe can easily be cut in half for fewer loaves or for ease in working the dough.

INGREDIENTS	¹/₂ cup raisins
	¹/₃ cup brandy
	1¹/₂ cups milk
	1 cup (2 sticks) butter
	6 cups bread flour, approximately
	2 packages dry yeast
	2 cups sugar
	1 tablespoon salt
	2 teaspoons *each* ground cinnamon, allspice, and nutmeg
	2 eggs, room temperature
	1 tablespoon finely chopped lemon zest or peel
	1 tablespoon lemon juice
	¹/₂ cup *each* chopped citron and pecans or walnuts
	1 egg, beaten, mixed with 1 tablespoon milk
	¹/₄ cup slivered almonds or pecans

BAKING SHEET   1 large baking sheet, Teflon or greased or sprinkled with cornmeal

PREPARATION
1 hour

In a bowl soak the raisins in the brandy for 1 hour. Drain and pat dry with a paper towel.

BY HAND
OR MIXER
10 mins.

In a saucepan heat the milk and butter. It need only be about 125° to soften or melt the butter.

In a large mixing or mixer bowl measure 3 cups flour, the yeast, sugar, salt, and spices. Stir to blend. Pour in the milk, add the eggs, and mix into a thick batter. Add the lemon zest or peel and juice; blend.

Stir in flour, ½ cup at a time, and work briskly with a wooden spoon or a mixer flat beater. The dough should be soft to knead so don't over-load with flour. When it is a shaggy mass, lift it from the bowl and place on a floured work surface. If using a mixer, replace the flat beater with a dough hook.

KNEADING
10 mins.

Knead the dough with a rhythmic press-turn-fold motion, adding heavy sprinkles of flour if the dough is sticky. If using a dough hook the dough should come together in a smooth ball that rotates around the bowl with the hook. Add sprinkles of flour if the dough sticks to the sides. Knead for 10 minutes by hand or hook. Finish kneading by working in the plumped raisins and nuts.

BY PROCESSOR
6 mins.

This is a large recipe and some food processors may overheat and stall. Halve the recipe, if needed.

Plump the raisins, as above. Heat the milk and butter, as above.
Insert the short dough blade.

Measure 3 cups flour into the work bowl, and add the yeast, sugar, salt, and spices. Pulse to blend. Uncover and pour in the heated milk-butter mixture and add the eggs, lemon zest and juice. Pulse several times to make a smooth batter. Add the citron and nuts.

Add ¼ cup flour at a time, either into the feed tube or directly into the bowl, pulsing each time to blend the ingredients with the flour. The dough is ready to knead when a mass has formed and is spun around the work bowl by the dough blade.

KNEADING
50 secs.

Turn the machine on and knead for 50 seconds.

Remove the cover and pinch the dough to test its consistency. Even when fully kneaded it will at first be more sticky than dough worked by hand. Sprinkle lightly with flour and form into a ball. By hand knead in the plumped raisins which otherwise would be chopped into bits by the blade.

FIRST RISING
2–3 hours

Place the dough in a greased bowl, cover with plastic wrap, and put aside to rise at room temperature to double in bulk, 2 to 3 hours. (The dough is quite heavy and takes a long time to rise.)

SHAPING
18 mins.

Punch down the dough and divide into 5 pieces. Divide each piece into 3 parts; roll under your palms into a strand about 14" long. Start from the center and braid loosely. Turn the dough around and finish the braid. Repeat for each loaf.

Place the braided bread on the baking sheet. If the oven will not accommodate all the breads at one time, cover and refrigerate several loaves until the first loaves go into the oven.

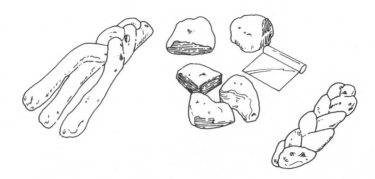

SECOND RISING
I hour

Brush the braids with some of the egg-milk glaze. Cover lightly with wax paper and leave at room temperature to rise, about 1 hour.

PREHEAT

Preheat the oven to 400° 20 minutes before baking.

BAKING
400°
40 mins.

Brush the loaves again with the glaze and sprinkle lightly with the almond slivers or chopped pecans.

Place in the hot oven and bake until the loaves are a golden brown and are hard and crusty when tapped on top with a finger, about 40 minutes—don't attempt to turn the hot braids over to test as for other loaves because they are fragile until cooled.

(If using a convection oven, reduce heat 50°.)

FINAL STEP

Carefully lift the braids off the baking sheet with a large metal spatula and slide onto a rack to cool.

These butter-rich loaves will keep fresh for a fortnight, and can be frozen at 0° for 3 or 4 months.

Note: Try decorating one or more of the loaves by dusting with confectioners' sugar. Handsome!

Bara Brith
(Speckled Bread)

[one medium loaf]

The Welsh have been famed for many years for their sweet breads and Bara Brith or "speckled bread" is one of the best. A solid loaf and solidly good, Bara Brith was originally made for special occasions such as Easter, Christmas, and the harvest festival. A north Wales specialty, it has a rich, fruity mixture under a firm, nutty crust.

The recipe is an adaptation of the Bara Brith recipe in the unusual British cookbook, Farmhouse Cookery—Recipes from the Country Kitchen, *published by the Reader's Digest Association Limited, London.*

INGREDIENTS	2¹/₂ cups bread or all-purpose flour, approximately 1 package dry yeast 1 teaspoon salt ¹/₄ cup sugar 1 teaspoon ground cinnamon ¹/₂ cup milk 1¹/₂ tablespoons lard, room temperature 2 eggs, room temperature 1 cup currants ¹/₂ cup golden raisins ¹/₂ cup water, brandy, or wine ¹/₂ cup chopped mixed candied fruit
BAKING PAN OR SHEET	1 baking sheet, or medium (8"-x-4") loaf pan, greased
BY HAND OR MIXER 8 mins.	Into a mixing or mixer bowl pour 1 cup flour and add the dry ingredients. In a saucepan, heat the milk and lard over a gentle flame until warm. The lard need not be wholly dissolved. Break and stir in the eggs. Stir the milk mixture into the flour by hand or with the mixer flat beater until the batter is smooth and creamy. Add flour, a small portion at a time, to form a dough that can be lifted from the bowl and placed on the floured work surface to knead. Or it can be left in the mixer under the dough hook.
KNEADING 10 mins.	Knead the dough by hand with a strong push-turn-fold motion, adding sprinkles of flour if the dough is sticky. If using a mixer, add flour if the dough sticks to the sides of the bowl. The dough will leave the sides of the bowl and form a ball around the dough hook. Knead for 10 minutes.

BY PROCESSOR
8 mins.
	Prepare the milk-lard-eggs mixture, as above.
	    Attach the steel blade.
	    The sequence for adding ingredients differs from above.
	    Measure 1½ cups flour into the work bowl and add the dry ingredients. Pulse to blend. With the processor running, slowly pour the milk-lard-egg mixture through the feed tube. Stop the machine and add ½ cup flour. Pulse several times. Add small portions of flour, if necessary, to make a mass that rides with the steel blade and cleans the sides of the bowl.

KNEADING 50 secs.	With the machine running, knead for 50 seconds. The dough should be slightly sticky and very elastic when the

kneading is complete. Pull and stretch the dough between your hands to test the consistency; if necessary, return the dough to the work bowl to process a few seconds more.

FIRST RISING
1 hour

Place the dough in a greased bowl, cover tightly with plastic wrap, and put aside at room temperature to rise for 1 hour.

While the dough is rising, plump the currants and raisins in the water, brandy, or wine for 45 minutes. Drain the liquid from the currants and raisins, and pat dry with a paper towel. Mix with the chopped fruit.

SHAPING
6 mins.

Turn the dough onto a floured work surface. Knead for a moment or so to press out the bubbles. Allow the dough to relax for 3 or 4 minutes.

Press the dough into a flat oval and spread with half of the fruit mixture. Knead into the dough, and then add the balance of the fruit. This is a considerable amount and pieces may persist in dropping out. Push them back into the dough.

If baking on the sheet, round up the dough into a ball or roll into a tubular shape and place on the sheet. If using a loaf pan, press the dough into an oval roughly the length of the pan, fold lengthwise, pinch the seam tightly together, tuck in the ends, and put it in the pan.

SECOND RISING
1½ hours

Cover with wax or parchment paper and put aside to nearly double in bulk, about 1½ hours.

PREHEAT

Turn the oven to 350° 20 minutes before baking.

BAKING
350°
35 mins.

Cut a slash ½" deep down the center of the loaf, whether on the sheet or in the pan. It will allow for expansion in the oven without breaking apart the crust.

Place the loaf on the middle shelf of the moderate oven. Bake for 35 minutes.

Test for doneness by turning the loaf out of the pan and rapping the bottom crust with a forefinger. If the crust sounds hard and hollow, the bread is baked. If not, return to the oven for 10 minutes in the pan.

(If using a convection oven, reduce heat 50°.)

FINAL STEP

Remove from the oven and allow to cool before slicing. Delicious for a special brunch or tea—or anytime.

Portuguese Nut and Fruit Bread   [two round loaves]

The good taste of this delicate bread rests heavily on almonds as well as butter, raisins, fruit peel, and a garniture of candied fruit.

This loaf is striking in appearance—rising up and around a small ovenproof cup that forms a center hole during the baking. Observe the season with appropriate ornaments nestled in the center—colored glass balls at Christmas, eggs at Easter, and on and on.

Finely textured, moist, and delicious, this bread can be a treat—for breakfast, brunch, or at a buffet supper.

INGREDIENTS

Dough:

5 to 6 cups bread or all-purpose flour, approximately

1 cup sugar

3 teaspoons salt

2 packages dry yeast

1/2 cup nonfat dry milk

1 1/2 cups hot water (120°–130°)

1/2 cup (1 stick) butter, room temperature

3 eggs, room temperature

3 tablespoons *each* raisins, diced mixed candied peel,
  and chopped almonds

Toppings:

1 egg, room temperature, lightly beaten

Whole almonds

Red and green candied fruit

Whole pine nuts

Coarse decorating sugar

BAKING SHEETS
AND CUPS

2 baking sheets, greased or Teflon; 2 2½" ovenproof baking cups, buttered on the outside

BY HAND
OR MIXER
20 mins.

In a large mixing or mixer bowl measure 2 cups flour and the dry ingredients. Stir together. In a small bowl pour the hot water over the butter, stir; pour over the dry ingredients. Beat 100 strokes with a wooden spoon, or for 3 minutes at medium speed with the flat beater in the mixer. Add the 3 eggs, one at a time, and continue beating until blended. Stop the mixer and attach the dough hook. Gradually work in the remaining flour, ½ cup at a time, sufficient to make a soft mass that cleans the sides of the bowl. In the mixer, the dough will form a soft ball around the hook and clean the bowl except for a small spot on the bottom (which indicates the dough is not too dry).

KNEADING
13–15 mins.

If by hand, turn the dough onto a floured work surface and knead with a strong push-turn-fold motion for 10 minutes, until the dough is smooth and elastic. Add sprinkles of flour if the dough is wet and sticky. Knead with the dough hook for 8 minutes.

Flatten the dough into a large oval; scatter the raisins, peel, and almonds over it. Fold the edges in and begin to work the mixture into the dough. (A dough hook may be used but a processor blade may tear or cut the fruit.)

BY PROCESSOR
4 mins.

Attach the plastic dough blade.

Measure 3½ cups flour into the work bowl and add the dry ingredients. Pulse to blend. In a small bowl stir together the hot water and butter and, with the processor on, pour the liquid through the feed tube. Add the eggs, one at a time. Stop the machine to allow the ingredients to rest.

Turn on the processor and add flour, ¼ cup at a time, through the feed tube. Sufficient flour will have been added when the batter becomes a mass that cleans the sides of the bowl and revolves with the blade.

KNEADING
1 min.

When the dough forms a ball, process for 1 minute to knead.

Stop the machine and feel the dough. If it is dry, add water by the teaspoon, with the machine running. If too wet, add flour. Pull and stretch the dough between your hands to test consistency; if it is not elastic, return the dough to the work bowl and process for a few seconds more.

Knead in the raisins, fruit peel, and nuts, as above.

FIRST RISING
1 hour

Return the dough to the bowl, pat with buttered fingers, cover tightly with plastic wrap, and set aside at room temperature to double in volume, 1 hour.

SHAPING
20 mins.

Punch down the dough, turn it onto the work surface, and knead briefly to press out the bubbles. Divide the dough in half. Poke or tear a hole in the center of each half. Gently enlarge the hole with your fingers until it will slip over the small cup. Pat in shape and place the dough and its center cup on a baking sheet.

SECOND RISING
50 mins.

Cover with wax or parchment paper and leave until double in volume, 50 minutes. You can test if it has risen by poking a finger in it; the dent will remain if the dough is ready.

PREHEAT

Preheat the oven to 350° about 20 minutes before baking.

BAKING
350°
I hour

Brush the loaves with beaten egg and decorate with the almonds, candied fruit, and pine nuts. Press these gently into the dough. Sprinkle with decorating sugar.

Bake in the oven until golden brown and crusty, 1 hour. If the loaves are placed in the oven on 2 shelves, alternate the pans midway during baking. Turn the loaves on the baking sheets so they are exposed evenly to the oven heat.

(If using a convection oven, reduce heat 50°. It is unnecessary to shift loaves or baking sheets, as above.)

FINAL STEP

Remove the bread from the oven and carefully place the loaves on a metal rack to cool. Don't tear the inner ring of dough when removing the cup from the warm dough. Cut around it on the underside with a sharp knife if it is reluctant to drop out.

The bread will keep for days wrapped in foil or plastic. It also freezes well for several months.

CHEESE BREADS

TO ALL SORTS OF BREADS cheese gives its taste.

It may be added in the mixture as just another ingredient so that it becomes indistinguishable except for the subtle richness and aroma it gives the loaf. It may be encased in a blanket of dough so that it retains its form or it may be sprinkled on the top to melt into the crust and add color and appeal.

Many of the recipes here call for sharp Cheddar cheese of good quality. All the cheeses called for are natural, with one exception—a process cheese is called for in the Twisted Cheese Loaf. Cheese shaved or grated for bread sticks or the tops of loaves should be one of the Cheddars, fresh Parmesan, Swiss, or a similar dry cheese.

There are two things that should be remembered about cheese in bread. It will soften the loaf and give it a closer grain. Therefore, the loaf should be baked longer to avoid a slight sogginess caused by the melted cheese.

Cheese is a great food, and it is a high compliment to bread to use cheese in its preparation.

Roquefort Cheese Bread   [two medium loaves]

The cheesemakers of the small French town of Roquefort-sur-Soulzon have for centuries stood militant over the good name and incomparable flavor of their much-prized cheese. If it is not made with sheep's milk or aged in the region's extraordinary limestone caverns, it is not Roquefort. And these cheesemakers will pursue to the ends of the world anyone who dares call his blue-veined cheese, no matter the quality, a Roquefort!

A slice of deep brown Roquefort bread is as delicious as Roquefort crumbled in a salad or spread on toast. Because the veins running through the cheese are a deep blue, the bread, understandably, is colored a rich off-white.

This recipe is from those vigilant Roquefort cheesemakers, and while I have made respectable loaves with a domestic blue-veined cheese, it is just not the same as the genuine article.

There is a glorious smell in the house when this bread is baking.

INGREDIENTS	1½ cups milk
	4 ounces (1 cup) Roquefort cheese, room temperature, crumbled
	2 tablespoons butter, room temperature
	1 egg, beaten
	¼ cup sugar
	1 teaspoon salt
	4½ to 5 cups bread or all-purpose flour, approximately
	2 packages dry yeast

BAKING PANS   2 medium (8"-x-4") loaf pans, greased or Teflon

BY HAND
OR MIXER
15 mins.

In a medium saucepan heat the milk and add the crumbled cheese, butter, egg, sugar, and salt. Stir until the cheese has melted into the liquid. Set aside.

In a mixing or mixer bowl measure in 3½ cups flour and the yeast. Stir to blend. By hand or with the mixer flat beater, stir the milk-cheese mixture into the flour to become a thick batter. Beat with 50 strong strokes, or for 2 minutes in the mixer. Add flour, ¼ cup at a time, until the dough forms a shaggy ball and can be lifted from the bowl to a floured work surface. In the mixer, the dough will clean the sides of the bowl and at the same time form a ball around the dough hook.

KNEADING
10 mins.

Knead by hand with the strong motion of push-turn-fold, adding sprinkles of flour if the dough is sticky. The dough is rich in butterfat and will be soft and elastic under the hands. Knead by hand or with the dough hook for 10 minutes.

BY PROCESSOR
8 mins.

Heat the milk and other ingredients, as above, and set aside.

Attach the short dough blade.

Measure 3½ cups flour into the work bowl and sprinkle on the yeast. Pulse to blend. With the motor on, slowly pour the milk-cheese mixture through the feed tube. Stop the machine. The dough will be a thick batter and quite sticky. With the processor running, add flour, ¼ cup at a time, through the feed tube. The dough will form a ball that cleans the sides and bottom of the work bowl.

KNEADING
1 min.

Process for 1 minute to knead.

Stop the machine, uncover, and pinch off a small piece of dough the size of a golf ball. If it can be pulled and stretched with the fingers, it is sufficiently kneaded. If necessary, to achieve an elastic ball, return the dough to the work bowl with a small bit of flour to process for a few more seconds.

FIRST RISING
1 hour

Place the dough in a greased bowl, cover with plastic wrap, and put aside to double in volume, about 1 hour.

SHAPING
4 mins.

Place the dough on a floured work surface, then divide the dough in half. Work and roll each half into a tubular shape the length of the loaf pan. Press the dough down into the corners of the pan with your fingers.

SECOND RISING
40 mins.

Cover the loaves and allow to rise to ½" above the edge of the pan, about 40 minutes.

PREHEAT

Preheat the oven to 375° 15 minutes before baking.

BAKING
375°
30–40 mins.

With a razor blade or sharp knife, cut a ½"-deep slit down the length of each loaf.

Place the loaves on the middle shelf of the moderately hot oven. The cheese-rich dough will brown quickly, so after 20 minutes cover the loaves with a length of foil. Turn the loaf pan around midway during baking so the loaves are exposed to an equal range of temperatures. (If using a convection oven, reduce heat 50°.)

FINAL STEP

Remove the bread from the oven. Allow to cool completely on a wire rack before slicing.

The Roquefort cheesemakers suggest storing the loaf in a covered container that has a few tiny openings for ventilation. I don't want to cross them, but I find it more convenient to keep my cheese bread in an ordinary paper sack (to retain a crisp crust) or a plastic bag. This bread freezes beautifully. In reheating or toasting, the loaf casts a wonderful fragrance throughout the house—an ideal loaf to have to bake before a prospective buyer comes to visit.

Twisted Cheese Loaf   [two medium loaves]

Cheese and beer have always been the best of companions but never more so than in this bread—a lovely braided yellow loaf—mellow with cheese and piquant with beer. Two cheeses are used—process and Swiss. In my original recipe I used only the process variety, but a friend, Dr. Maurice Barry, Jr., of Rochester, Minnesota, gave it an inspired touch by swirling Swiss cheese dice throughout the dough.

INGREDIENTS	1 12-ounce can or bottle beer, or 1½ cups milk
	½ cup hot water (120°–130°)
	2 tablespoons sugar
	1 tablespoon salt
	2 tablespoons butter or margarine
	1 8-ounce package process Swiss or American cheese
	5 cups bread or all-purpose flour, approximately
	2 packages dry yeast
	8 ounces natural Swiss cheese, cut into ¼" cubes

BAKING PANS	2 medium (8"-x-4") loaf pans, greased or Teflon

PREPARATION	In a large saucepan combine the beer or milk, hot water, sugar, salt,
15 mins.	butter, and process cheese and heat until hot. The cheese need not melt completely. Lift off the heat and cool to warm.

BY HAND	In a large mixing or mixer bowl put 2 cups flour and the yeast. Pour in
OR MIXER	the warm cheese mixture and beat by hand with a wooden spoon 100
8 mins.	strong strokes, or for 3 minutes at medium speed with the mixer flat beater. Stir in the balance of the flour, ½ cup at a time, first with the spoon and then by hand. If using the mixer, change to a dough hook when the dough becomes too heavy to stir with the flat beater.
	The dough will be a rough, shaggy mass that will clean the sides of the bowl. If the dough continues to be slack and moisture breaks through, add small amounts of flour.

KNEADING	If by hand, turn the dough onto a lightly floured work surface and
10 mins.	spread the Swiss cheese bits over it. Fold the dough over on the cheese and knead with the rhythmic motion of push-turn-fold. The dough will become smooth and elastic, and bubbles will form under the surface of the dough. Break the kneading rhythm occasionally by throwing the dough down hard against the work surface.
	If using a mixer, drop the cheese bits into the bowl while the mixer is running. The dough will clean the sides of the bowl and form a ball around the revolving hook. If it does not, add sprinkles of flour. Knead by hand or mixer for 10 minutes.

BY PROCESSOR	Combine all of the ingredients except the flour, yeast, and Swiss cheese
5 mins.	dice in a large saucepan, as above.
	Attach the plastic dough blade.
	Measure 3½ cups flour and the yeast into the processor work bowl. Pulse to blend. With the motor running, slowly pour a portion of the

cooled cheese mixture through the feed tube to form a wet mass in the bowl. Do not make it a thin batter. Keep it on the heavy side. Take off the cover and add ¾ cup flour. Pulse several times until the flour is completely absorbed. With the processor running, add the balance of the mixture and flour, ¼ cup at a time, until the dough forms a ball and is carried around the bowl by the force of the blade.

KNEADING
50 secs.

With the machine running, knead for 50 seconds.

When first turned out of the work bowl, the dough will be slightly sticky but a dusting of flour will take the stickiness away.

Work the cheese bits into the dough by hand.

FIRST RISING
1 hour

Place the dough in a buttered bowl and turn over to coat the ball completely to prevent crusting. Cover the bowl tightly with plastic wrap and leave at room temperature until the dough has risen to about twice its original size (as judged by how high it creeps up the bowl), about 1 hour.

SHAPING
15 mins.

Punch down and knead the dough for 30 seconds to deflate. Divide the dough in half. (Each half will weigh about 1½ pounds.) Roll each half into a 12"-x-6" rectangle. Cut each rectangle lengthwise into three 2" strips leaving them joined at one end by a ½" piece. Braid the strips. Tuck under the ends to make the dough about the same length as the bake pan. Place in the pan.

SECOND RISING
45 mins.

Place the pans in a warm place, cover with wax or parchment paper, and leave until the center of the dough has risen ½" above the level of the edge of the pan, 45 minutes.

PREHEAT

Preheat the oven to 350° 20 minutes before baking.

BAKING
350°
45 mins.

Bake until the loaves are a golden brown, about 45 minutes. They are done when tapping the bottom crust yields a hard, hollow sound. If not, return the loaves to the oven for an additional 5 to 10 minutes. Midway during baking, and again near the end, shift the loaves so they are exposed equally to the temperature variations in the oven. If the loaves appear to be browning too quickly, cover with a length of foil.

(If using a convection oven, reduce heat 50°.)

FINAL STEP

Remove the bread from the oven. Turn from the pans and place on a metal rack to cool before slicing.

Toasted, this bread is superb.

Pepper Cheese Loaf   [two small loaves]

Pepper Cheese is a fickle loaf. Eaten cold, the pepper dominates. Warm from the oven or toasted, the cheese flavor comes to the fore. Whichever, it is unusual and delicious.

The cheese creates swirls and small fissures of yellow, while the pepper makes a pattern of black specks throughout the white dough.

Baked in coffee cans, the cylindrical loaf is cut into round slices for the table.

INGREDIENTS	3 to 4 cups bread or all-purpose flour, approximately
	1 package dry yeast
	2 tablespoons sugar
	1 teaspoon salt
	2 teaspoons freshly ground black pepper
	1 cup hot water (120°–130°)
	1 tablespoon shortening
	8 ounces (2 cups) sharp Cheddar cheese, coarsely grated

BAKING PANS
OR CANS

Two 1-pound coffee cans or, if desired, 2 small (7"-x-3") loaf pans, greased

BY HAND
OR MIXER
15 mins.

In a mixing or mixer bowl blend 1 cup flour, the yeast, sugar, salt, and ground pepper. (The cheese comes later, after the first rising.) Add the hot water and shortening. Beat with a spoon 100 strong strokes, or for 30 seconds with the mixer. Then, at mixer high speed, beat for 3 minutes more. Scrape the bowl once or twice.

Stir in additional flour, ½ cup at a time, to form a soft but elastic dough.

KNEADING
10 mins.

If by hand, turn out on a floured work surface and knead with a strong push-turn-pull motion. With the mixer, attach the dough hook. Knead for 10 minutes. Add more flour to control stickiness, if necessary.

BY PROCESSOR
5 mins.

Attach the steel blade.

Measure 2 cups flour into the processor work bowl and add the yeast, sugar, salt, and pepper. Pulse to blend. With the machine on, pour the hot water through the feed tube. Stop the processor, remove the cover, and drop in the shortening. Replace the cover, turn the machine on, and add the balance of the flour, ¼ cup at a time, through the feed tube. The dough will form a rough mass that cleans the sides of the bowl and spins with the blade. Remove the cover and feel the dough with your fingers. It should be slightly sticky, but if it is wet, add small portions of flour.

KNEADING
50 secs.

With the processor running, knead the dough for 50 seconds.

FIRST RISING
45 mins.

Place the ball of dough in a lightly greased bowl, cover tightly with plastic wrap, and leave at room temperature until the dough has doubled in bulk, about 45 minutes. You can test if it has risen sufficiently by poking a finger in it; the dent will remain.

SHAPING
10 mins.

Punch down the dough and work it briefly under your hands to press out the bubbles.

Spread half of the cheese over the dough and fold in. Knead for 1 minute and sprinkle on the balance of the cheese. This is not an easy job because the dough doesn't want to accept the cheese. After a few minutes of tucking in loose pieces, however, it will, and all will be well.

Divide the dough in half. Shape each half into a ball and let them rest for 3 minutes. One ball should fill the prepared coffee can about halfway, no more. Press each dough ball into a container, and push down with your fingers all around the sides to force the dough to the bottom—and to press out any air.

For loaf pans, form by pressing each ball of dough into a flat oval, roughly the length of the baking pan. Fold the oval in half, pinch the seam tightly to seal, and tuck under the ends.

SECOND RISING
1 hour

Cover the containers with wax paper and leave until the center of the dough has risen to the edge of the can or above the loaf pan, about 1 hour.

PREHEAT

Preheat the oven to 400° 15 minutes before baking.

BAKING
400°
35 mins.

Bake until the crust is a deep brown, 35 minutes, and the loaves test done. Turn out one loaf from its can or pan and tap the bottom crust with a forefinger. A hard, hollow sound means the bread is baked. If not, return to the oven (without the pan, if you wish a browner crust) for an additional 5 or 10 minutes. If the loaves appear to be browning too quickly, cover with a piece of foil or brown sack paper.

(If using a convection oven, reduce heat 50°.)

FINAL STEP

Remove the bread from the oven. Turn from the containers and place on wire racks to cool. Serve either warm (not hot) from the oven or reheated later.

This bread freezes especially well, and will keep frozen 6 months or longer at 0°. A fine bread with a soup dinner, great for unusual sandwich slices on a buffet, and superb toasted, always.

Cheese Caraway Batter Bread
[one large or two small loaves]

This loaf has a positive cheese and spicy flavor that makes a slice (especially toasted) great for a barbecue, a soup dinner, or to serve with a salad. Like other batter breads, it is best served fresh (but cool) from the oven. It has a dark crust and a light interior speckled with caraway seed.

INGREDIENTS

2½ cups bread or all-purpose flour
1 package dry yeast
1 teaspoon crushed or ground caraway seeds
2 tablespoons sugar
2 teaspoons salt
1 cup hot water (120°–130°)
4 ounces (1 cup) Cheddar cheese, grated
2 tablespoons butter or vegetable shortening

BAKING PANS

1 large (9"-x-5") or 2 small (7"-x-3") loaf pans, greased or Teflon

BY HAND
OR MIXER
6 mins.

In a large mixing or mixer bowl measure 1½ cups flour, followed with the yeast, caraway seeds, sugar, and salt. Stir to blend, and pour in the hot water. Add the cheese and butter or shortening. Beat with a heavy wooden spoon 100 vigorous strokes, or for 2 minutes with the mixer flat beater. (The beating is a substitute for kneading to form the necessary gluten in a yeast bread.)

Add the balance of the flour (1 cup); beat to blend into a smooth batter.

BY PROCESSOR
5 mins.

Attach the steel blade.

Measure all of the flour into the work bowl and add the dry ingredients. Pulse to mix well. Pour the hot water through the feed tube with the machine running. Stop the processor, uncover, and drop in the cheese and shortening. Process for 25 seconds to form a thick batter.

FIRST RISING
45 mins.

Pour the batter into a greased bowl, cover tightly with plastic wrap, and put aside in a warm place until it has doubled in bulk, 45 minutes.

SHAPING
6 mins.

Stir down the batter with 25 strokes and pour into the prepared loaf pan(s). Spread evenly with a spatula, and pat the top of the loaf with a floured hand to smooth the surface. Pan(s) will be about half filled.

SECOND RISING
45 mins.

Cover with wax or parchment paper and leave at room temperature until it has doubled in bulk, 45 minutes. It will rise to the lip of the pan.

PREHEAT	Preheat the oven to 375° 20 minutes before baking.
BAKING 375° 45 mins.	Bake on the center shelf of the moderate oven. The crust will be dark, and sound hard and hollow when rapped with the forefinger, about 45 minutes. (If using a convection oven, reduce heat 50°.)
FINAL STEP	Remove the bread from the oven and turn from the pan(s) to a wire rack. Let it cool before slicing.

Buttermilk Cheese Bread
[one large or two smaller loaves]

Sharp Cheddar cheese and buttermilk give their good flavors to this quick-rising loaf leavened with both yeast and baking powder, a practice of kitchens in the Old West to make certain that if one didn't make the dough rise the other one would. If both did, so much the better.

It is a very alive dough, though not as finely textured as other white breads, and it will rise handsomely above the edge of the tins. Preparation time of the bread is cut considerably because there is only one rising, and that in the pan.

INGREDIENTS	4½ to 5 cups bread or all-purpose flour, approximately 2 packages dry yeast 2 teaspoons *each* baking powder and salt 2 tablespoons sugar ¾ cup hot water (120°–130°) 1¼ cups buttermilk, room temperature 4 ounces (1 cup) sharp Cheddar cheese, shredded 1–2 tablespoons butter, melted
BAKING PANS	1 large (9"-x-5") or 1 medium and 1 small loaf pan, greased or Teflon
BY HAND OR MIXER 15 mins.	In a mixing or mixer bowl, combine 2½ cups flour, the yeast, baking powder, salt, and sugar. Stir to blend. Pour the hot water and buttermilk into the flour, and beat with a wooden spoon 75 strong strokes, or for 3 minutes with the mixer flat beater to make a smooth batter. Scrape down the sides of the bowl with a rubber spatula, and stir in the cheese. Add the remaining flour, ¼ cup at a time, until the dough forms a rough mass and cleans the sides of the bowl. Insert the mixer dough hook if the mass is too heavy and solid for the flat beater.

KNEADING **8 mins.**	Knead by hand on a floured surface or by dough hook in the mixer to make a soft elastic ball, 8 minutes. Add sprinkles of flour if the dough is slack or wet and sticky.
BY PROCESSOR **5 mins.**	Attach the short plastic blade. Measure 3 cups flour into the processor work bowl and add the yeast, baking powder, salt, and sugar. Pulse to blend. With the processor running, pour in the hot water and only enough buttermilk to make a heavy batter, about ¾ cup. Remove the cover and stir in the cheese. Add 1 cup flour and the balance of the buttermilk. Pulse several times to blend all of the ingredients to make a batter. Turn on the machine and add flour, ¼ cup at a time, to make a dough that will form a ball and ride on the blade. It will clean the bowl as it rotates.
KNEADING **50 secs.**	Knead the dough for 50 seconds. Remove the cover; check the consistency of the dough by pinching it between the fingers. It will be slightly sticky but soft and elastic. A few sprinkles of flour will make it easy to lift the dough from the bowl.
SHAPING **10 mins.**	Press and push the dough into an oval (or ovals) slightly longer than the pans. Fold lengthwise, and pinch the edges tightly together. With the seam down, push in the ends. Fit the dough into the pan, pressing it snugly into the corners.
RISING **1 hour**	Cover the pan(s) with wax or parchment paper and leave at room temperature until doubled in bulk, 1 hour. The top of the dough will have risen about 1" above the pan. You can test by poking a finger in it; the dent will remain if the dough is fully risen.
PREHEAT	Preheat the oven to 425° about 20 minutes before baking.
BAKING **425°** **35–40 mins.**	Place the pan(s) on a low shelf so the bread will not brown too quickly. The loaves will be done when they are deep brown and pull away from the sides of the pan, 35 to 40 minutes. When tapping the bottom yields a hard, hollow sound, the bread is done. If not, return to the oven—without the pan if you want a deep brown crust—for an additional 5 to 10 minutes. However, if the tops of the loaves appear to be browning too quickly, cover with a piece of foil or brown sack paper. (If using a convection oven, reduce heat 50°.)

FINAL STEP

Remove the bread from the oven. Turn from the pan(s) and place on a wire rack to cool.

While the bread is still hot, brush with melted butter for a lovely rich glow.

Swiss Cheese–Potato Bread   [one large ring loaf]

Swiss cheese melts and spreads through this handsome and delicious loaf to create a soft and tender slice. Basically a potato bread, the loaf bakes to a light brown with dark pieces of crusted cheese melted into the surface.

While it can be baked in a number of different shapes, it seems more at home in a tube pan, either an angel food tin or a bundt pan—I like the hills and valleys of the latter.

INGREDIENTS

3 cups bread or all-purpose flour, approximately
1 package dry yeast
1 teaspoon *each* sugar and salt
1/4 cup instant potato flakes
1 1/2 cups hot water (120°–130°)
1/4 cup (1/2 stick) butter or margarine, melted
2 eggs, room temperature
4 ounces (1 cup) Swiss cheese, finely diced or coarsely grated

BAKING PAN
AND SHEET

One 8" tube pan (angel food, bundt, or gugelhupf), greased or Teflon; 1 baking sheet

BY HAND
OR MIXER
12 mins.

Measure 1½ cups flour into a large mixing or mixer bowl and stir in the yeast, sugar, salt, potato flakes, and hot water. Beat by hand 30 strong strokes, or for 1 minute in the mixer. Add the melted butter or margarine, eggs, and Swiss cheese. Beat by hand 100 strokes, or for 2 minutes with the mixer turned to high. Stop the mixer.

Stir in the balance of the flour, ½ cup at a time, first with the spoon and then by hand, or with the mixer flat beater and then the dough hook. The dough will be a rough, shaggy mass that will clean the sides of the bowl. However, if it continues to be slack (wet), add small portions of flour.

KNEADING
8 mins.

Turn the dough onto a lightly floured work surface and knead with the rhythmic motion of push-turn-fold. Add light sprinkles of flour if necessary. In the mixer, with the dough hook, the dough will completely clean the sides of the bowl and form a ball around the revolving hook. The dough will be smooth and elastic. Knead by hand or mixer for 8 minutes.

BY PROCESSOR
5 mins.

Attach the steel blade.

Measure 2 cups flour into the work bowl and add the yeast, sugar, salt, and potato flakes. With the machine running, pour 1 cup hot water through the feed tube to form a thick batterlike mass. Drop in the butter or margarine and add 1 cup flour. Pulse several times until the butter and flour are completely absorbed into the dough. Drop in the eggs and pulse to blend. With the machine on, pour in the remaining ½ cup hot water. Stop the machine and pinch the dough. If it is wet, add 1 or 2 tablespoons flour, pulsing to blend each.

KNEADING
1 min.

Once the dough forms a ball, process for 1 minute to knead.

The dough should clean the sides of the work bowl. If the dough is wet and sticks to the sides of the machine, add a bit more flour. If it appears dry, add water by the teaspoon. The dough should be soft, smooth, and *slightly* sticky when kneading is complete.

FIRST RISING
1 hour

Place the dough in a greased mixing bowl and pat with buttered or greased fingers. Cover the bowl tightly with plastic wrap and leave at room temperature until the dough has doubled in volume, about 1 hour.

SHAPING
6 mins.

Punch down the dough, turn it onto the floured work surface, and let it rest for 2 minutes. It can be shaped in one of two ways. One is to roll it under your palms to about 20" in length. Lay the length of dough in the prepared pan. Overlap the ends slightly and pinch together.

Or, flatten the ball of dough and, with your fingers, punch a hole in the center and widen this to slip over the tube. Either way, push the dough firmly into the bottom of the pan.

SECOND RISING
45 mins.

Cover the pan with a length of foil or wax paper and let rise until the dough has doubled in volume, 45 minutes.

PREHEAT

Preheat the oven to 375° 20 minutes before baking.

BAKING
375°
45 mins.

Place the pan in the moderate oven. Bake until a metal skewer inserted in the center of the loaf comes out clean and dry, about 45 minutes. Ten minutes before the baking is done, carefully turn the loaf out of the pan onto a baking sheet. Return to the oven. This will give the loaf a lovely overall brown that it would not otherwise have. But handle carefully. It is fragile when hot.

(If using a convection oven, reduce heat 50°.)

FINAL STEP   Take the bread from the oven. Slide the loaf off the baking sheet onto a metal rack to cool before slicing.

Tabasco Cheese Bread
[one large round or four miniature loaves]

A dash or two of hot pepper sauce (Tabasco, in my kitchen) stirred into the grated Cheddar gives this loaf a nippy cheese flavor. The loaf has a highly glazed crust and slices streaked with yellow cheese.

Make this recipe in small or miniature pans for children, who will love it toasted. Baked in a larger pan, it is excellent for sandwiches.

INGREDIENTS   3 to 4 cups bread or all-purpose flour, approximately
1 package dry yeast
2 teaspoons salt
1¼ cups hot milk (120°–130°)
3 tablespoons butter or margarine
4 ounces (1 cup) sharp Cheddar cheese, room temperature, grated
¼ to ½ teaspoon Tabasco or other hot pepper sauce, as desired
1 egg yolk, beaten, mixed with 1 tablespoon milk or cream

BAKING PANS   1 round 8" cake pan or 4 miniature bread pans, greased or Teflon

BY HAND
OR MIXER
15 mins.

In a mixing or mixer bowl measure 2 cups flour and add the yeast and salt. Pour in the hot milk. Blend well with 50 strokes of a wooden spoon or for 2 minutes with a mixer flat beater. Add the butter or margarine and cheese; blend into the batter.

Mix in the hot sauce.

Measure in additional flour, ¼ cup at a time, and stir by hand or with the flat beater until the dough is a rough mass and has lost its wetness. It will clean the sides of the bowl. If using a mixer, attach the dough hook.

KNEADING
10 mins.

If by hand, turn the dough onto a lightly floured work surface. Knead with a strong push-turn-fold motion. Add sprinkles of flour if the dough should be sticky in the early stages of kneading. In the mixer, add light sprinkles of flour until the dough cleans the bowl and gathers as a ball around the hook. Knead for 10 minutes.

BY PROCESSOR
5 mins.

Attach the steel blade.

Place 2 cups flour in the work bowl, and add the yeast and salt. Pulse to blend. With the processor running, pour the hot milk through the feed tube. Remove the cover and add the butter or margarine, cheese, and hot sauce. Close the cover and pulse 6 or 7 times to blend.

Start the processor and add flour, ¼ cup at a time, through the feed tube or with the cover off, until the dough forms a ball and is spun around the bowl by the force of the blade.

KNEADING 1 min.	Process for 1 minute to knead. Remove the cover and pinch off a small piece of the dough. It will be slightly sticky. Stretch it between the fingers. It should be elastic.
FIRST RISING 1 hour	Place the dough in a large greased bowl, cover tightly with plastic wrap, and leave at room temperature until it has doubled in volume, about 1 hour.
SHAPING 15 mins.	Punch the dough down into the bowl, knead briefly, and turn out onto the floured work surface. Cut the dough into as many pieces as you have decided to make loaves. For the round loaf, shape the dough into 1 ball. Press into the cake pan, filling out to the edges. For miniature loaves, press each dough piece into a flat oval, roughly the length of the pan. Fold the oval in half, pinch the seam tightly to seal, tuck under the ends, and place in the pan, seam down.
SECOND RISING 50 mins.	Cover the pans loosely with wax or parchment paper and leave until the loaves have doubled in bulk, or just begin to peek over the edge of the pans, 50 minutes.
PREHEAT	Preheat the oven to 400° 20 minutes before baking.
BAKING 400° 10 mins. 350° 20–30 mins.	Brush the bread with the egg glaze. Place in the hot oven for 10 minutes, and then reduce heat to 350°. Bake the small loaves for an additional 20 minutes. Bake the large loaf for 25 to 30 minutes, until golden brown. When tapping the bottom of the crust yields a hard, hollow sound, the bread is done. (If using a convection oven, reduce heat 50° for each bake period.)
FINAL STEP	Remove the bread from the oven. Turn from the pans and leave on a wire rack to cool.

Cheese Bread Ring   [one loaf]

Its crust richly embedded with sesame seeds, this Cheese Bread Ring is a bat-ter bread baked in a tube or gugelhupf pan. Sandwiched between two layers of rich dough is a filling of Cheddar cheese—creamed and spiced with several dashes of Tabasco and a liberal spoonful of garlic powder.

This is an adaptation of the winning Pillsbury Bake-Off® Contest creation of Kayleen Sloboden, of Puyallup, Washington.

INGREDIENTS

2 tablespoons butter, room temperature
3 tablespoons sesame seeds

Filling:
6 ounces (1½ cups) Cheddar or mozzarella cheese, shredded
2 dashes of Tabasco or other hot sauce
¼ teaspoon garlic powder
¼ cup (½ stick) butter, softened

Batter:
1½ cups milk
½ cup (1 stick) butter, room temperature
4 to 5 cups bread or all-purpose flour, approximately
2 packages dry yeast
¼ cup sugar
1½ teaspoons salt
2 eggs, room temperature

TUBE PAN

One 12-cup or 10" tube pan (I use a gugelhupf pan with impressive results.)

PREPARATION
10 mins.

Liberally butter the bottom and sides of the tube pan, and coat with the sesame seeds. Wrap a small piece of foil tightly around the tube, and butter. The foil will slip out *with* the loaf when it is unmolded; the bread in the center will not stick as it otherwise might.

BY HAND
OR MIXER
13 mins.

To make the filling, in a medium mixing or mixer bowl place the shredded cheese and, by hand or in the mixer, stir in the hot sauce, garlic powder, and softened butter.

Taste for seasoning, and add more hot sauce if you wish. Set aside.

To make the batter, in a small saucepan, heat the milk and butter until warm. Set aside.

Measure into a mixing or mixer bowl 2½ cups flour and add the yeast, sugar, and salt; blend well. Add the milk and butter and the eggs to the flour mixture—and beat by hand 50 strong strokes, or for 2 minutes with the mixer flat beater. Add the balance of the flour, ¼ cup at a time, and mix until it forms a smooth, stiff yet elastic batter.

Spoon half of the batter into the tube pan, taking care to disturb the sesame coating as little as possible. Spoon the filling evenly over the batter to within ½" of the sides of the pan. Spoon the remaining batter over the filling.

BY PROCESSOR
14 mins.

Prepare the tube pan, as above.

Note: The food processor is ideal for creaming together the ingredients for the filling.

For the batter, heat the milk and butter, as above.

Attach the plastic blade.

Measure 2½ cups flour into the work bowl and add the yeast, sugar, and salt. Pulse to blend. With the machine running, pour in half of the milk-butter mixture, and add the eggs. Stop the machine, and add 2½ cups flour. Turn on the machine, and add the balance of the warm liquid. Process the batter, which should be thick yet elastic, for 30 seconds.

Spoon the batter and filling into the pan, as above.

RISING
45 mins.

Cover the pan with plastic wrap and put aside at room temperature to double in volume, to the edge of the pan, about 45 minutes.

PREHEAT

Preheat the oven to 350° 20 minutes before baking.

BAKING
350°
40–50 mins.

Place the pan in the oven and bake until the bread is golden brown and feels firm and solid when tapped with a forefinger, 40 to 50 minutes.

(If using a convection oven, reduce heat 50°.)

FINAL STEP

Remove the bread from the oven and place on a metal rack to cool for 5 minutes. If the dough has overflowed the sides, the bread may stick, so carefully pry loose with the point of a knife.

Turn the loaf over. The foil collar around the tube will allow the bread to come free.

It is a handsome loaf and should be displayed to family and friends (and photographed) before slicing.

Galette de Gannat   [two round loaves]
(Gannat Cheese Bread)

This beautiful brown speckled bread is made from a 200-year-old recipe given to me by Monsieur Louis Malleret, the secretary of the Société Culturelle de Gannatois (a region in central France), a respected amateur chef and the proprietor of the town of Gannat's only bookstore.

While the old recipe called for no leavening, this yeast-raised adaptation produces a more open-textured and lighter bread. The original recipe also calls for Gruyère cheese, which is expensive, so I often substitute Swiss cheese, with fine results.

INGREDIENTS	4½ cups bread or all-purpose flour, approximately
	2 packages dry yeast (see Note)
	2 teaspoons salt
	6 eggs, room temperature
	1 cup (2 sticks) butter, room temperature, cut into small chunks
	8 ounces (2 cups) Gruyère or Swiss cheese, grated

BAKING SHEET

1 baking sheet, greased or Teflon

BY HAND OR MIXER 12 mins.

In a large mixing or mixer bowl stir together 1 cup flour, the yeast, and salt. With a wooden spoon or rubber scraper, form a well in the flour. Break the eggs, one at a time, and drop them into the bowl. Each time pull flour in from the sides to mix with the eggs. By mixer, beat at medium speed with the flat beater, adding the eggs one at a time until the last is blended in. When all of the eggs have been added and blended well, the dough will be a heavy batter. Drop the butter pieces into the bowl. Stir to blend the butter into the mixture.

When the butter has been worked into the batter, add flour, ½ cup at a time, stirring first with the spoon and then by hand, or with the mixer dough hook. The dough is rich in butterfat and will not be sticky. Add flour sufficient to make a ball of dough that is elastic yet does not slump when left to rest for a moment or two. If using a dough hook, the dough will clean the sides of the bowl and gather as a ball around the revolving hook.

KNEADING 9 mins.

If by hand, knead with a strong push-turn-fold motion, or with the dough hook, for about 6 minutes.

Press the dough into a flat circle. Spread the grated cheese over the dough; fold the dough over the cheese. Or drop the cheese into the mixer bowl with the dough hook turning. Knead for an additional 2 or 3 minutes to distribute the cheese evenly throughout the dough.

BY PROCESSOR 6 mins.

Attach the plastic dough blade.

Measure 2 cups flour into the processor work bowl and sprinkle in the yeast and salt. Pulse to blend. To make it convenient to add the eggs, first break them into a small bowl, stir lightly, and then—with the machine running—pour slowly through the feed tube. Stop the machine. Add 1 cup flour and the butter pieces. Pulse several times to make a heavy batter. With the machine running, add small portions of flour to make an elastic dough that will clean the sides of the bowl and spin with the blade.

KNEADING **45 secs.**	Keep the machine running and knead for 40 seconds. Remove the cover and sprinkle the cheese over the dough. Pulse several times to mix the cheese thoroughly into the dough.
FIRST RISING **1½ hours**	Place the dough in a bowl, cover tightly with plastic wrap, and leave to double in volume, about 1½ hours.
SHAPING **5 mins.**	Turn the dough from the bowl and divide in half. Each piece will weigh about 1¼ pounds. With your hands, shape each into a round loaf or *galette*—10" in diameter and about ¾" thick. Place on the baking sheet.
SECOND RISING **40 mins.**	Cover the loaves with wax paper. Leave at room temperature for about 40 minutes.
PREHEAT	Preheat the oven to 375° about 20 minutes before baking.
BAKING **375°** **40 mins.**	Place the loaves on the middle shelf of the oven. Midway through baking, turn the baking sheet around. The *galettes* are done when they are light brown and heavily freckled (thanks to the cheese bits), 40 minutes. Carefully turn over one loaf with a spatula to be certain the bottom crust is dark brown and feels solid to the tap of the forefinger. (If using a convection oven, reduce heat 50°.)
FINAL STEP	Place the loaves on a metal rack to cool. Cut the warm *galette* in wedges to serve with butter. They can be frozen and reheated with excellent results. *Note:* If you wish to make this bread the old way, leave out the yeast. Put the dough aside to rest for 1 or 2 hours before shaping. It will not rise, of course, but the dough will have matured nevertheless.

Gâteau de Gannat   [three 2-pound loaves]
(Gannat Clabber Bread)

Since the sixteenth century this loaf has been a favorite of the Gannatois region of France, where it is known as Gâteau de Gannat or Pompe au Fromage. *It was introduced to me several years ago by Monsieur Louis Malleret of Gannat.*

It is a lovely brown loaf, light in weight and texture, that rises high to be served on all occasions, especially festive ones. This authentic Gâteau de Gannat differs from those found in the boulangeries *because it forgoes the commercial cheeses and is made without brandy. Also, there is no sugar.*

Its most curious ingredient is fromage blanc, *clabber made in the kitchen from whole milk treated with rennet. Whipped cottage cheese may be substituted, but the clabber is easy to make and the whey, the clear liquid that drains from the clabber, is vitamin-packed. The whey can be saved and used in place of milk or water in other recipes.*

This is a large recipe. The 3 loaves make it worthwhile to spend time making the clabber or whipping the cottage cheese. The rennet (Junket) tablets may be found where the ice cream mixes and custard mixes are shelved in most supermarkets.

When Craig Claiborne spent several days in my kitchen while I did recipes for a New York Times *food article, the Gannat Clabber Bread turned out to be one of his favorites.*

INGREDIENTS

Clabber:
2 quarts whole milk, room temperature
¼ rennet tablet
   or
1 pound large-curd cottage cheese

Dough:
8 cups bread or all-purpose flour, approximately
1 package dry yeast
1 tablespoon salt
10 eggs, room temperature
½ cup (1 stick) butter or margarine, room temperature, cut into chunks

Glaze:
1 egg, beaten, with 1 tablespoon milk

BAKING PANS OR SHEET

3 round cake pans with 1" sides or 1 baking sheet, greased or Teflon

SPECIAL EQUIPMENT

A 3-foot length of cheesecloth to drain clabber

PREPARATION
12 hours

To make the clabber, the day before, warm the milk to 70° and pour into a medium-size crock. Crush ¼ rennet tablet, dissolve in a spoonful of milk, and stir into the bowl of milk. Cover with plastic wrap and leave at least 12 hours at room temperature. When the milk has curdled, pour the curds into the cheesecloth and suspend over a bowl to drain.

6 hours

I use a large square of cheesecloth, double thickness, placed over a large bowl as I fill it with curds. Then I tie the corners together, lift the bag from the bowl, and fasten to a shelf brace and allow it to drain over the bowl for 6 hours.

Empty the clabber into a bowl and keep refrigerated until ready to proceed. Bottle and refrigerate the whey for use in other breads.

10 mins.

Or as a substitute for clabber, cream 1 pound large-curd cottage cheese in a blender or food processor or mash and whip with a fork in a bowl, about 10 minutes.

BY HAND
OR MIXER
15 mins.

To make the dough, in a large mixing or mixer bowl stir together 2 cups flour, the yeast, and salt. Form a well in the bottom of the bowl and break in the eggs, one at a time. Stir with a wooden spoon or with a mixer flat beater until the eggs are worked into the flour. Pour in 2 cups clabber and stir well into the egg-flour mixture. Drop the butter or margarine pieces into the bowl.

Add flour, 1 cup at a time, blending in the pieces of butter or margarine first with the spoon and then with your hands. In the mixer, blend first with the flat beater and then attach a dough hook.

Dough will be smooth and easy to work because of the clabber and butter.

KNEADING
10 mins.

Turn the dough onto a floured work surface and knead with a forceful motion of push-turn-fold. Occasionally crash the dough down against the work surface to vary the kneading. In the mixer, the dough will pull away from the sides of the bowl and form a ball around the dough hook. Knead for 10 minutes.

BY PROCESSOR
7 mins.

This recipe may be too large for most food processors; if so, reduce all ingredients by half except the yeast.

Make the clabber, as above.

Attach the plastic dough blade.

Measure 2 cups flour into the work bowl and add the yeast and salt. Pulse to blend. To make it easier to add the eggs, break them into a small bowl, stir lightly and, with the machine running, pour slowly through the feed tube. Follow the eggs with 2 cups clabber and chunks of butter. When the ingredients have been absorbed into a thick batter, stop the machine. Remove the cover and add 1 cup flour. Replace the cover and pulse to blend.

Add the balance of the flour, ¼ cup at a time, with the machine running. Don't overpower the dough with too much flour. Remove the cover and feel the dough. It should be soft, elastic, but only slightly sticky.

KNEADING
45 secs.

With the machine on, knead for 45 seconds.

FIRST RISING
1½ hours
or longer

"Don't rush the dough," said my mentor, M. Malleret. Let it mature and develop good flavor, he urged.

Place the dough in a greased bowl and cover tightly with plastic. Leave for at least 1½ hours, preferably longer, until double in bulk.

SHAPING
15 mins.

Punch down the dough and divide into 3 pieces (if you have made a full recipe). Press into balls and allow to relax for 5 minutes.

If you're using pans, place the dough in the center of each pan and with the palms of your hands and fingers press the dough flat and into the sides. It may pull back; if it does, let it rest a few minutes and repeat.

If you're using a baking sheet, round the pieces of dough between cupped hands, place on the sheet, and flatten the dough to half its rounded height.

SECOND RISING
1½ hours

Cover the pans or sheet with wax paper and leave at room temperature until the dough has doubled in volume, 1½ hours.

PREHEAT

Preheat the oven to 400° 20 minutes before baking.

BAKING
400°
35 mins.

Brush the loaves with the egg glaze and place in the oven. (If your oven can take only 2 loaves, punch down one-third of the dough and set aside.) Watch the loaves. If they brown too fast, cover with foil or brown sack paper the last 15 minutes of baking. Turn one loaf over; if the bottom crust sounds hard and hollow when tapped with the forefinger, the bread is done.

(If using a convection oven, it is unlikely 3 loaves can be baked at the same time. Shape only as much dough as can be accommodated. Punch down the balance and set aside at room temperature. Bake at 350°.)

FINAL STEP

Place the bread on a metal rack to cool.

M. Malleret called this loaf "a noble old dish," and it is an especially appropriate gift for the holidays. Excellent toasted.

Cheddar Cheese Bread   [two medium loaves]

There are 2 cupfuls of sharp Cheddar cheese in this recipe—more than ¹/₄ pound for each of 2 delicious loaves.

Because of its high butterfat content the dough is soft, pliable, and easy to work. Not at all sticky.

A toasted slice is a good base for a creamed dish—creamed mushrooms, chicken à la king and, the author's favorite, chipped beef.

INGREDIENTS	**2 cups water**
	¹/₄ cup sugar
	2 teaspoons salt
	2 tablespoons butter, room temperature
	¹/₂ cup nonfat dry milk
	8 ounces (2 cups) sharp Cheddar cheese, grated
	6 cups bread or all-purpose flour, approximately
	I package dry yeast

BAKING PANS

2 medium (8½"-x-4½") baking pans, greased or Teflon

PREPARATION
15 mins.

In a saucepan heat the water to scalding (but barely) over low heat and stir in the sugar, salt, butter, dry milk, and 2 cups (8 ounces) cheese. Remove from heat and stir until the butter and cheese are melted. Set aside to cool sufficiently so that you can test the water comfortably with a finger (120°).

BY HAND
OR MIXER
10 mins.

In a mixing or mixer bowl combine 2½ cups flour, the cheese mixture, and yeast. With an electric mixer, beat for 2 minutes at medium speed, or 150 strong strokes with a wooden spoon.

Add the additional flour, 1 cup at a time, stirring with a wooden spoon and then by hand until the dough is roughly formed and leaves the sides of the bowl. If it is wet or slack, add additional small portions of flour. Use the dough hook in the mixer.

KNEADING
6–10 mins.

If by hand turn the dough out onto a floured work surface and knead with a strong push-turn-fold motion until it is smooth and elastic, about 10 minutes. If under a dough hook, knead for 6 or 8 minutes in the mixer bowl.

BY PROCESSOR
6 mins.

Heat the butter-cheese mixture, as above.

Attach the plastic blade.

Pour the mixture into the work bowl and add 2½ cups flour and the yeast. Mix by turning the machine on and off several times. Add the flour, ½ cup at a time, processing after each addition, until the dough is no longer wet but soft and slightly sticky. Process until the dough forms a ball (add a tablespoon flour if necessary).

KNEADING
50 secs.

Let the ball spin on blade for 50 seconds to knead.

FIRST RISING
1 hour

Place the dough in a bowl (it need not be greased because of the butterfat in the dough) and cover with plastic wrap drawn tightly over the bowl. Let sit in a warm place (80°–100°) until the dough has doubled in bulk, about 1 hour.

SHAPING
3 mins.

Remove the plastic wrap and turn out the dough onto a floured work surface. Punch down the dough and divide in half. Flatten the dough pieces with your palms, fold in half, pinch the seams together, turn the seams under, and plump the loaves to fit into the baking pans.

SECOND RISING
45 mins.

Cover the pans with wax paper or cloth and return to the warm place until the dough has doubled in volume, 45 minutes. It will rise about 1" above the edge of the pans.

PREHEAT

Preheat the oven to 375° 20 minutes before baking.

BAKING
375°
45 mins.

Place the bread in the oven and bake until a cake testing pin inserted in the middle of the loaf comes out clean and dry, 45 minutes. The bottom, when the loaf is turned out of the pan, is brown and hard to the touch. This loaf browns easily, so watch it closely after 30 minutes. If necessary, cover with foil or brown paper to keep it from scorching.

(If using a convection oven, no preheating is necessary. Reduce heat 50° and bake for 40 minutes. Don't let the loaves become too brown.)

FINAL STEP

Remove the bread from the oven. Turn the loaves out of their pans and leave on a metal rack to cool before slicing.

It is outstanding toasted. Cut the slices thin—no more than ½" thick.

Pain Battu au Fromage   [two medium loaves]
(Cheese Batter Bread)

Along the French and Italian border this fine bread carries a French name, but its chief ingredient is a famous Italian cheese—Parmigiano, subtly flavored and one of the cornerstones of Italian cuisine. While the French think of sprinkling it over onion soup or a dish to gratinée, the Italians embrace it lovingly for a major role in Italian cookery, including this delicately flavored loaf.

Use only quality Parmigiano cheese—Parmigiano-Reggiano if possible—bought in one piece and grated in your kitchen. The Parmigiano cheese sold in shaker-top cans is a poor substitute.

This is a yeast-raised batter bread, which means there is no kneading. However, there is some stir-beating by hand or in the mixer. If by hand, turn some of the chore over to a helpmate.

INGREDIENTS	3¹/₂ cups bread or all-purpose flour
	1 package dry yeast
	2 teaspoons salt
	¹/₃ cup nonfat dry milk
	1¹/₂ cups hot water (120°–130°)
	2 tablespoons butter, melted and cooled (below 130°)
	1 tablespoon honey
	2 eggs, room temperature
	4 ounces (1 cup) fresh Parmigiano cheese, grated, 2 tablespoons reserved for garnish

BAKING PANS

2 medium (8"-x-4") baking pans, greased or Teflon

PREPARATION
25 mins.

To make a sponge, pour 2 cups flour into a mixing bowl and add the yeast, salt, and dry milk. Stir to blend. Add the hot water. Stir.

Add the cooled melted butter to the mixture.

Add the honey, eggs, and cheese.

Beat the sponge for 10 minutes with a wooden spoon to blend. If in a mixer, use the flat beater for 8 minutes.

If using a processor, attach the plastic blade. Pour 2 cups flour into the work bowl and add the other ingredients, including the hot water. Pulse to blend.

REST
1 hour

Cover the bowl with plastic wrap and set aside to ferment for about 1 hour. It will bubble and become puffy.

BY HAND
OR MIXER
10 mins.

To make the batter, remove the plastic wrap and stir down the sponge. Add additional flour, ½ cup at a time, to thicken the sponge. Beat thoroughly each time. The sponge will become a thick batter that will pull away from the bowl in sheets. When the batter has absorbed the flour, continue to beat for another 3 or 4 minutes.

BY PROCESSOR
30 secs.

Pulse to deflate the sponge.

Add 1 cup flour, ½ cup at a time, through the feed tube. Turn the machine on for 30 seconds. Remove the lid and test the elasticity of the batter. It should be sticky and thick, yet soft enough to spoon into pans later.

FIRST RISING **1 hour**	Cover the work bowl and leave at room temperature to double in volume, about 1 hour.
SHAPING **5 mins.**	Stir down the batter with a wooden spoon. Spoon the dough in equal amounts into the 2 baking pans. Moisten your fingers and push the dough into the corners.
SECOND RISING **45 mins.**	Cover the bowls with wax or parchment paper. Because the batter may stick to the paper, rest the paper on drinking glasses above the pans. The dough will rise to the edge of the pans in about 45 minutes.
PREHEAT	Preheat the oven to 375° 20 minutes before baking.

BAKING
375°
45 mins.
	Sprinkle the 2 tablespoons grated cheese over the tops of the loaves.
	    Place the pans in the oven. Midway through baking, turn the pans around to equalize heat. The loaves will brown and test done in about 45 minutes.
	    (If using a convection oven, reduce heat 50°.)

FINAL STEP	Remove the bread from the oven. Turn from the pans and place on a metal rack to cool before slicing.

Cheese Shortbread   [one dozen pie-shaped servings]

It may look like ordinary piecrust, but it isn't. It is a rich, short, and delicate wedge of goodness, fragile in the making and fragile in the cutting—but a joy to eat with coffee and tea even in crumbs and pieces.

INGREDIENTS	4 ounces (1 cup) Swiss cheese, grated, room temperature 7 tablespoons butter, softened ¼ teaspoon salt 1½ cups bread or all-purpose flour
BAKING PAN **AND SHEET**	One 9" layer cake pan or flan ring on baking sheet, lightly buttered

PREHEAT	Preheat the oven to 400°.
BY HAND OR MIXER 10 mins.	In a medium mixing or mixer bowl combine the cheese with the butter, salt, and flour. Work the mixture with your hands until it is a soft ball. If too sticky, add a bit more flour; if too stiff, add a teaspoon cold water. This may be done with a mixer flat beater but the dough may be too heavy to thoroughly blend the ingredients.
BY PROCESSOR 4 mins.	Attach the steel blade. Place all of the above ingredients in the work bowl, and process 3 or 4 times until a soft ball has formed.
SHAPING 15 mins.	With a rolling pin, roll out the dough between 2 lengths of wax or parchment paper until it is slightly larger than the bottom of the pan or ring. Peel back the paper with care, quickly invert the dough over the pan, and let it drop in. Press the dough snugly to the bottom. Neatly trim around the circle of dough because shortly you will be giving it a new edge. Fashion the scraps into a long, thin roll—long enough to go around the inside of the pan. Press the new edge into the pastry, and flute it as you would a piecrust. With a knife or pastry wheel, cut the shortbread 6 times across to make a dozen servings. If a flan ring was used, remove it and spread the wedges ½" apart on the baking sheet underneath. Whether the wedges are separated or not, the demarcations will remain and make it easier to cut after it comes from the oven.
BAKING 400° 14 mins.	Bake on a middle shelf of the oven until the shortbread is only faintly browned, about 14 minutes. Don't overbake; it can burn quite easily. (If using a convection oven, reduce heat 50°.)
FINAL STEP	Remove the bread from the oven. When the shortbread has cooled, cut down the lines again and remove from the baking pan. Serve warm or at room temperature. Delicious.

Rye Bread with Brie   [one large wreath]

A ripe Brie cheese sits in the center of this wreath of braided almost-black pumpernickel-rye bread, which has been given an extra fillip with beer. The bread is shaped and baked around a pan that's the same diameter as the cheese. When time to serve, place the cheese inside the bread wreath, slice the braid thinly, and spread the Brie lavishly.

Because a good Brie is sometimes hard to find, the wreath can be baked and frozen in advance against the day a truly ripe cheese and an occasion for a party coincide.

This recipe is an adaptation of one in Sunset *magazine, the fine Pacific Coast regional publication.*

INGREDIENTS

1¼ cups beer, flat and room temperature
¼ cup molasses
1 teaspoon salt
2 tablespoons butter, softened
1 egg yolk
¼ cup cocoa powder
1 tablespoon caraway seeds
2 cups stone-ground or pumpernickel rye flour
2 cups bread or all-purpose flour, approximately
2 packages dry yeast
1 egg white, beaten, mixed with 1 tablespoon water
1 5" or 8" round of Brie cheese

BAKING SHEET
AND PAN

1 large (14"-x-17") or 2 medium (10"-x-15") baking sheets; 1 5" or 8" round cake pan, outer sides buttered. Determine beforehand the size Brie you intend to serve. The large party-size Brie is 8" in diameter while smaller cheeses are 4" or 5". Select a cake tin of the same diameter.

BY HAND
OR MIXER
12 mins.

In a bowl combine the beer, molasses, salt, softened butter, egg yolk, cocoa, and caraway.

In a mixing or mixer bowl measure 1 cup rye and 1 cup white flour and the yeast. Blend the beer mixture and the flour, stir with 75 strong strokes, or for 3 minutes with a flat beater until there's a smooth batter. Add the remaining 1 cup each rye and white flour, ¼ cup at a time, to make a heavy mass.

If, in the beginning, the dough hook does not stir the dough but presses it aside, remove the dough and knead by hand for 3 or 4 minutes. Return the dough to the mixer. Sufficient gluten will have formed by then to make the dough pliable under the hook.

KNEADING
8 mins.

If by hand, knead the dough with a strong push-turn-fold motion. Because of the greater rye flour content, the dough will be stickier and less pliable than one made with white. Use liberal sprinkles of white flour to control the stickiness while kneading.

In the mixer, the dough will begin to pull away from the sides of the bowl and cling to the hook. If it does not, add small sprinkles of white flour. This will never become as soft and responsive as a white dough.

BY PROCESSOR
5 mins.

Attach the plastic blade.

The sequence for adding ingredients is different from above.

Measure 2 cups rye and 1 cup white flour and the yeast into the work bowl.

In a separate bowl mix together all of the remaining ingredients, as above.

With the processor running, slowly pour the beer mixture through the feed tube. The batter will be heavy. Add flour, ¼ cup at a time, through the feed tube or by removing the cover each time, until the dough has become a ball and is riding on the blade. The dough will clean the sides but not as cleanly as with an all-white dough.

KNEADING
45 secs.

With the processor running, knead the dough for 45 seconds.

FIRST RISING
1½ hours

Place the dough in a greased bowl, cover with plastic wrap, and let rise at room temperature until doubled in bulk, about 1½ hours.

SHAPING
15 mins.

Turn the dough out of the bowl, and knead on a lightly floured board to press out the bubbles.

Divide the dough into 3 pieces. Roll each piece into a smooth 36"-long strand. Place the strands side by side. Starting in the center, loosely braid the strands out to each end. Wrap the braid around the buttered cake pan placed on the baking sheet. (If using 2 medium sheets have them overlap.) Stretch the braid slightly, if needed, to join the ends together. Pinch to seal.

SECOND RISING
45–60 mins.

Cover the wreath with plastic wrap and let rise until almost double in bulk, 45 minutes to 1 hour.

PREHEAT

Preheat the oven to 375° about 20 minutes before baking.

Brush the braid with the egg glaze, taking care not to allow the liquid to accumulate around the pan, else the bread might stick.

Place the baking sheet(s) in the moderate oven and bake the braid for 25 or 30 minutes, until the loaf tests done. The dough itself is almost black, so it's not possible to gauge doneness by a brown crust.

(It is unlikely a home convection oven is wide and long enough to accept the large pan and braid. But if it can be done, reduce heat 50°.)

Remove the bread from the oven. Carefully slide the wreath onto a rack to cool. Loosen the braid around the pan and lift it off.

To serve, place the wreath on a large tray. Cut a 3" section into ¼"-thick slices (to give the wreath some give), then fit the Brie into the center—spreading the braid if necessary to make it fit. Set the bread slices back in place. Garnish with a cluster of grapes, if desired.

Let the guests have the fun of making their own servings.

Wrap airtight to store at room temperature for a day; or freeze, wrapped, for longer storage.

POTATO BREADS

Long a favorite of the American home baker, potato in bread produces a crisp crust and a moist slice, with a delightful home-baked flavor. Instant potato flakes can be substituted for the boiled potato, but then you forgo the dividend of the potato water that adds so much flavor to the bread.

Experiment, too, with potato flour and potato starch. In a recipe that calls for 4 cups white flour, substitute ½ cup potato flour or starch for 1 cup white flour. Increase the proportion over a number of bakings until you have found the most desirable crispness and crunchiness.

Sister Jennie's Potato Bread   [two medium loaves]

There is a delicious potato flavor in this loaf of Shaker bread that rises high and grandly above the edge of a loaf pan. The moisture in the potato supplies most of the liquid.

Sister Jennie was a member of a Shaker community in Ohio years before yeast was reliable, and she allowed 8 hours for this loaf to rise. With today's yeasts it can be done in considerably less time.

She also advised: "Bread rises more quickly in the daytime when the kitchen fires are kept going than at night when only the embers smolder on the hearth; therefore 4 hours is equal to 12 hours of rising at night."

Finally: "Bread is the one food one can eat thrice daily and not tire of."

INGREDIENTS

1 cup plain mashed potatoes (instant flakes and water are fine)
2 eggs, beaten
½ cup sugar
1 teaspoon salt

1 package dry yeast
$\frac{1}{2}$ cup hot water (120°–130°)
4 to 5 cups bread or all-purpose flour, approximately
$\frac{1}{2}$ cup (1 stick) butter, room temperature

BAKING PANS

2 medium (8"-x-4") baking pans, greased or Teflon

**BY HAND
OR MIXER
10 mins.**

In a large mixing or mixer bowl combine the potatoes, eggs, ¼ cup sugar, salt, yeast, warm water, and 2 cups flour. Stir into a rough batter. Kneading will come later.

**FIRST RISING
1½ hours**

Cover the bowl tightly with plastic wrap and set aside until the batter doubles in volume, 1½ hours.

Meanwhile, cream the butter with the remaining ¼ cup sugar. Set aside.

**DOUGH
10 mins.**

Remove the plastic wrap and beat down the batter. Stir in the creamed butter and sugar. Add the balance of the flour, ½ cup at a time, using a wooden spoon or a mixer flat beater. When the batter gets heavy, replace the beater with a dough hook. The dough will be a rough, shaggy mass that will clean the sides of the bowl. If the dough continues to be moist and sticky, sprinkle with small amounts of flour.

**KNEADING
10 mins.**

If by hand, turn the dough onto a lightly floured work surface and knead with a rhythmic motion of push-turn-fold. If using a mixer, knead with the dough hook (and add flour if necessary) until the dough cleans the sides of the bowl. The dough will form a soft ball around the hook as it turns. Knead for 10 minutes. The dough will be smooth and elastic when stretched between the hands.

**BY PROCESSOR
5 mins.**

Attach the plastic dough blade.

In the work bowl combine the potatoes, eggs, ¼ cup sugar, salt, yeast, and water. Pulse to blend. Scrape down the bowl with a spatula if some of the ingredients are thrown out of reach of the short blade. Add 1½ cups flour and pulse to blend.

**FIRST RISING
1½ hours**

Cover the work bowl with a length of plastic wrap and leave until the batter has doubled in bulk, about 1½ hours.

Cream the butter and sugar, as above.

**DOUGH
5 mins.**

Pulse 4 or 5 times to beat down and deflate the batter. Drop in the creamed butter and sugar; pulse to blend thoroughly. Turn on the processor and add the balance of the flour, ¼ cup at a time, until the batter becomes a mass that cleans the sides of the bowl. Stop the machine, feel the dough, and determine if it needs more flour to make a moist mass.

KNEADING
50 secs.

Knead with the processor running for 50 seconds.

The dough should be elastic and slightly moist when turned from the bowl. Light sprinkles of flour will make it manageable under the hands.

SECOND RISING
1½ hours

Place the dough in a mixing bowl and pat with buttered or greased fingers. Cover the bowl with plastic wrap and leave until the dough has risen to about twice its original volume, about 1½ hours. You can test if it has risen by poking a finger into it; the dent will remain if it is ready.

SHAPING
10 mins.

Punch down the dough, turn it out onto the work surface again, and knead for 30 seconds to press out the bubbles. With a sharp knife, divide the dough in half. Shape into balls. Let rest under a towel for 3 to 4 minutes.

Form the loaves by pressing each ball into a flat oval, roughly the length of the bread pan. Fold the oval in half, pinch the seam tightly to seal, tuck under the ends, and place in the pan, seam down.

THIRD RISING
40 mins.

Place the loaves in a warm place, cover with wax or parchment paper, and let rise to double in volume, above the edge of the pans, 40 minutes.

PREHEAT

Preheat the oven to 375° 20 minutes before baking.

BAKING
375°
40 mins.

Bake the loaves until they are a golden brown, about 40 minutes. Turn one loaf out of its pan and tap the bottom crust with a forefinger. A hard, hollow sound means the bread is baked. If not, return to the oven for an additional 10 minutes. If the tops of the loaves appear to be browning too quickly, cover with a piece of foil or brown sack paper. Midway during baking and again near the end of it, shift the pans so the loaves are exposed equally to temperature variations in the oven.

(If using a convection oven, reduce heat 50°.)

FINAL STEP

Remove the bread from the oven. Turn from the pans and place on a metal rack to cool before slicing.

This loaf will keep well for several days at room temperature. It will keep for 4 to 5 months at 0° in the freezer.

It makes fine toast.

Potato Bread   [one braid and one pan loaf]

There is a wonderful fragrance about this bread that reaches into every nook of the house. In this recipe there can be no substitute for potato water—the liquid in which the potatoes are boiled. Instant potato flakes could be used as the chief ingredient but alone do not produce an important by-product, the starch-rich water.

This recipe makes a lovely white loaf that is delicious warm from the oven, or toasted.

INGREDIENTS

2 small- to medium-size potatoes
2 cups water
5 cups bread or all-purpose flour, approximately
2 packages dry yeast
1 tablespoon salt
2 tablespoons sugar
¼ cup (½ stick) butter

BAKING PAN
AND SHEET

1 medium (8"-x-4") loaf pan, greased or Teflon, and 1 baking sheet

PREPARATION
30 mins.

In a pot boil the peeled potatoes in the water. (Add nothing to the potatoes during cooking.) Pour off the liquid and reserve, adding more water if necessary to get 1¾ cups potato water. Rice or mash the potatoes and set them aside.

BY HAND
OR MIXER
8 mins.

Measure 3 cups flour into a mixing or mixer bowl, and add the yeast, salt, and sugar. Blend. Into a saucepan pour the potato water, the butter, and potatoes. Place over medium heat until the liquid is hot (120°) to the touch, and the butter has softened or melted. Add to the flour mixture.

Add flour, ¼ cup at a time, to form a rough mass. If by hand, beat with 100 vigorous strokes with a wooden spoon or spatula and then work with your hands until the dough is smooth. If using a mixer, attach the dough hook and allow it to work for 3 minutes. The dough may be slightly sticky. The stickiness will disappear with sprinkles of flour.

KNEADING
10 mins.

Turn the dough onto a floured work surface and knead with the firm rhythm of push-turn-fold until it becomes smooth and elastic. Add small sprinkles of flour if the dough sticks to the surface or hands. If by mixer, continue kneading under the dough hook, adding flour if needed. The dough will clean the sides of the bowl and form an elastic ball that will rotate with the hook. Knead for 10 minutes.

BY PROCESSOR
6 mins.

Prepare the potatoes, as above.

Attach the short plastic dough blade.

Measure 4 cups flour into the work bowl and add the yeast, salt, and sugar. Pulse to blend. Prepare the potato water, butter, and mashed potatoes as above. Turn on the processor and pour the liquid through the feed tube. A heavy batter will form. Add flour, ¼ cup at a time, through the feed tube and process until the dough cleans the sides of the bowl, and forms a ball which will spin with the blade.

KNEADING
50 secs.

Knead with the processor running for 50 seconds.

The dough may be slightly sticky when taken from the bowl. If so, add light sprinkles of flour and work it under the hands for a moment or so.

FIRST RISING
1½ hours

Place the dough in a greased bowl, cover tightly with plastic wrap, and put aside to rise to double in volume, about 1½ hours.

SHAPING
8 mins.

Punch down the dough and move to a floured work surface. Divide into 2 equal pieces.

For the braid, divide one piece into 3 equal parts. Let rest for a few minutes and then roll each part under your palms into 14" lengths. If they resist and pull back, hit the dough hard with your fist all along the length. Finish rolling. Braid the 3 parts loosely into a loaf.

For the pan loaf, press the second dough piece into a flat oval roughly the length of the prepared baking pan. Fold down the length, pinch the seam together, tuck under the ends, and drop into the pan. Push the dough into the corners with the fingers.

SECOND RISING
40 mins.

Cover the dough with wax or parchment paper and leave at room temperature to rise, 40 minutes.

PREHEAT

Preheat the oven to 400° 20 minutes before baking.

BAKING
400°
15 mins.
350°
25 mins.

Bake in the hot oven for 15 minutes; reduce heat to 350°. Continue baking until the loaves are golden crusty brown, an additional 25 minutes. If the loaves appear to be browning too quickly, cover with foil. The loaves are baked when tapping the bottom crust yields a hard, hollow sound.

(If using a convection oven, reduce heat 50° for each bake period.)

FINAL STEP

Remove the bread from the oven. Place the loaves on a metal rack to cool before serving. It is best to lift and move the braid with a metal spatula, since it is fragile while hot.

Potato Starter White Bread   [two medium loaves]

This loaf is a country kind of bread made with country kinds of ingredients, including a raw potato starter and, for shortening, lard.

A starter must be made and allowed to double in volume so there is enough for this recipe as well as to replenish the starter jar.

This Potato Starter Bread has a delicious flavor, especially when toasted. The dough also makes delicious dinner rolls.

INGREDIENTS

1 cup Raw Potato Starter (page 242)
³/₄ cup *each* hot water (120°–130°) and flour
1¹/₄ cups hot water (120°–130°)
¹/₂ cup nonfat dry milk
2 tablespoons sugar
¹/₂ teaspoon ground ginger
1 package dry yeast
4 to 4¹/₂ cups bread or all-purpose flour, approximately
2 tablespoons lard or other shortening, room temperature
2 teaspoons salt

BAKING PANS

2 medium (8"-x-4") baking pans, greased or Teflon

PREPARATION
Overnight

The night before preparing the dough, pour the starter into a bowl and add the ¾ cup hot water and flour. Mix well. Cover tightly with plastic wrap and place in a warm spot overnight.

BY HAND
OR MIXER
20 mins.

On bake day, turn back the plastic covering, stir down, and pour 1 cup of the starter into a large mixing or mixer bowl. Set aside. Return the remaining starter to the jar and place in the refrigerator for future starter breads.

To the starter in the bowl add the 1¼ cups hot water, milk, sugar, ginger, yeast, and 1½ cups flour. Stir thoroughly and let stand for 3 minutes. Add the shortening, salt, and 1½ cups additional flour.

If by hand, stir more flour into the batter, ¼ cup at a time, with a wooden spoon to form a rough, shaggy mass that can be lifted from the bowl and placed on the work surface. If using a mixer, begin stirring with the flat beater and replace with a dough hook when the dough becomes heavy.

KNEADING
10 mins.

Spread flour on the work surface and turn out the dough. Knead with a strong push-turn-fold motion until it is smooth and elastic. If moisture should break through, sprinkle flour on the dough and hands. Soon the dough will lose its stickiness and feel alive and somewhat rubbery. In the mixer, the dough will form a soft ball around the hook as it revolves and, at the same time, clean the sides of the bowl. If it remains sticky, add liberal sprinkles of flour. Knead for 10 minutes.

BY PROCESSOR
5 mins.

Prepare the overnight starter, as above.

Attach the short plastic dough blade.

The following day scrape 1 cup of the starter into the work bowl. (Return the balance of the starter to the refrigerator.) Add the 1¼ cups hot water, milk, sugar, ginger, yeast, shortening, salt, and 1½ cups flour. Process to blend.

With the processor running, add flour, ¼ cup at a time, through the feed tube, until the batter becomes a mass that cleans the sides of the bowl and rides with the blade.

KNEADING
50 secs.

With the machine running process for 50 seconds.

FIRST RISING
1 hour

Place the dough in a bowl, cover tightly with plastic wrap, and set aside to double in bulk, about 1 hour.

SHAPING
12 mins.

Punch down the dough and turn it onto the work surface. Knead for 30 seconds to press out the bubbles. Divide the dough in half. Shape each half into a loaf by flattening into an oval as wide as the length of the pan. Fold in half, seal the seam tightly, and pat into shape. Place in the pan with seams and ends tucked under.

SECOND RISING
45 mins.

Cover the pans with wax or parchment paper and leave until the dough has doubled in bulk to reach the edge of the pans, about 45 minutes.

PREHEAT

Preheat the oven to 375° 20 minutes before baking.

BAKING
375°
45 mins.

Bake the loaves until a deep brown and loose in their pans, 45 minutes.
    (If using a convection oven, reduce heat 50°.)

FINAL STEP

Remove the bread from the oven. Turn the loaves onto a wire rack to cool before serving.

Irish Freckle Bread   [two medium loaves]

It doesn't take much imagination to see freckles all over these delicious loaves when really they are raisins or currants. But no one need know. When I was in Ireland my hostess called them "freckles" and I dared not challenge her. Like so much of the Irish cuisine, this has potato as well as the water in which the potato was boiled.

The mashed potato can be prepared with potato flakes but then there will be no potato water.

INGREDIENTS	I potato, peeled and quartered I¹/₂ cups water 5 cups bread or all-purpose flour, approximately 2 packages dry yeast ¹/₃ cup sugar I teaspoon salt 2 eggs, room temperature ¹/₂ cup (I stick) butter, melted and cooled I cup dark raisins or currants
BAKING PANS	2 medium (8½"-x-4½") loaf pans, greased or Teflon
PREPARATION 30–40 mins.	In a pot boil the potato in the water for 20 to 30 minutes. Reserve 1 cup of the water (120°–130°) and put the potato aside to cool before mashing it.
BY HAND OR MIXER 5 mins.	Pour 1½ cups flour in the mixing bowl and add the potato, yeast, sugar, and salt. Pour in the cup of potato water and beat until a smooth batter.
FIRST RISING 1–1¹/₂ hours	Cover the bowl with plastic wrap and set the dough aside to rise and become puffy, about 1 to 1½ hours.
KNEADING 10 mins.	Stir down the batter and add the eggs, butter, and raisins. Stir to mix thoroughly. Add more flour, ½ cup at a time, to make a soft, elastic ball of dough. Don't add too much flour—the dough should be quite soft. If it is sticky, add sprinkles of flour. Knead with a strong push-turn-fold motion until the dough becomes smooth, about 10 minutes. Knead for an equal length of time if using a mixer dough hook.
BY PROCESSOR 5 mins.	Prepare the mashed potato, as above. Attach the short plastic dough blade. For the dough, place 2 cups flour in the work bowl and add the yeast, sugar, and salt. Pulse to blend. In a small bowl mix the mashed potato and 1 cup potato water. Turn on the processor and pour the potato mix through the feed tube.
I to 1¹/₂ hours	Turn off the machine, sprinkle flour over the top of the batterlike dough, replace the cover and leave at room temperature to ferment until risen and puffy, about 1 to 1½ hours.

KNEADING
45 secs.

Pulse the processor to stir down the batter. Add the eggs, butter, and raisins or currants. Pulse to blend. Through the feed tube, with the machine running, add flour, ½ cup at a time, until the dough becomes a ball and rides on top of the blade. It will clean the sides of the bowl. Knead for 45 seconds.

SHAPING
15 mins.

There are two different ways to form Freckle Bread.

For both the dough is divided into 4 pieces and allowed to rest for 5 minutes before shaping.

For one, roll each piece lengthwise into a cylinder as long as the bread pan. It will be about 2" in diameter. Repeat with a second, and place the 2 pieces side by side in the pan. They will rise together and present a divided crust down the length of the loaf.

The second loaf can be formed in the same fashion, or the pieces can be shaped into balls and placed side by side. They will rise together to look like two half loaves.

SECOND RISING
45 mins.

Cover with wax paper and leave in a warm place to rise to the edge of the pans, about 45 minutes at room temperature.

PREHEAT

Preheat the oven to 375° 20 minutes before baking.

BAKING
375°
35 mins.

Place the pans in the oven and bake until the crusts are nicely browned, 35 minutes. Turn one loaf out of its pan and tap the bottom crust with a forefinger. A hard, hollow sound means the bread is baked. If not, return to the oven for an additional 10 minutes.

(If using a convection oven, reduce heat 50°.)

FINAL STEP

Remove the bread from the oven and place the loaves on a wire rack until cooled.

Toasts beautifully. Freezes well.

VEGETABLE BREADS

A VEGETABLE IS A VEGETABLE in most kitchens and seldom is it considered an ingredient for bread, which is a shame. Some lend a most interesting texture and taste to a loaf.

There are six vegetables in these ten recipes, hardly a major challenge to a green thumb, but they make delicious breads. Carrots, onion, pumpkin, tomato, zucchini, and rhubarb are the six, although smaller portions of these and other vegetables are among the ingredients elsewhere in the book.

Onion Lover's Bread [one large or two small loaves]

Each braid of this loaf is filled with a mixture of onions, butter, garlic salt, Parmesan cheese, poppy seeds, and paprika. Its antecedents can be traced to pizza, but it took imagination and daring to wrap 6 such ingredients in a lovely bread dough, braid into a twist, and bake.

The result—but you must love onions and/or pizza—is uncommonly good.

INGREDIENTS

Dough:
1 package dry yeast
4 cups bread or all-purpose flour, approximately
1¼ cups water
¼ cup sugar
1½ teaspoons salt
⅓ cup nonfat dry milk
½ cup (1 stick) butter, softened
1 egg, room temperature, lightly beaten

Filling:
¼ cup (½ stick) butter, melted
1 cup finely chopped onions, or ¼ cup onion flakes
1 tablespoon *each* grated Parmesan cheese and poppy seeds
1 teaspoon *each* garlic salt and paprika

BAKING SHEET   1 baking sheet, greased or Teflon (or 1 loaf pan)

BY HAND
OR MIXER
20 mins.

Note: The filling is prepared after the dough has been made and set aside to rise.

To make the dough, in a large mixing or mixer bowl stir the yeast and 2 cups flour together. In a saucepan heat the water, sugar, salt, dry milk, and butter (about 125°). When the butter is quite soft, but not necessarily melted, add the egg and pour all the liquid into the flour. Blend with a wooden spoon or mixer at low speed until moistened. Increase the speed to medium and beat for 2 minutes with the mixer flat beater, or wooden spoon, if preferred.

Stop the mixer, attach the dough hook, and add flour, ¼ cup at a time, to make a soft dough that forms a ball around the hook as it revolves and cleans the sides of the bowl.

This dough must rise first before kneading.

FIRST RISING
1 hour

Cover the bowl tightly with plastic wrap and let the dough rise at room temperature until light and doubled in volume, 1 hour.

FILLING

Meanwhile, make the filling. Melt the butter in a medium saucepan. Remove from heat and stir in the remaining ingredients. Mix thoroughly and set aside until ready to form the braids.

KNEADING
10 mins.

If by hand, knock down the dough and turn out on a floured work surface. The dough may be sticky because it is so soft. However, toss or throw the dough down hard against the work surface until it becomes elastic and is no longer sticky. Small sprinkles of flour will also help. If using a mixer, add flour, if necessary, to form a soft, elastic ball around the dough hook as it revolves. It will clean the sides of the bowl. Knead for 10 minutes.

BY PROCESSOR
8 mins.

Note: Unlike the dough above, this one will be kneaded immediately following its preparation.

Attach the plastic dough blade.

The sequence for adding ingredients varies from above.

In a saucepan heat the water, sugar, salt, dry milk, butter, and egg until the mixture is about 125° and the butter is quite soft. It need not melt.

Measure the yeast and 2½ cups flour into the work bowl. Turn on the processor and pour the liquid through the feed tube. Add flour, ¼ cup at a time, to form a heavy mass that rides on the blade and cleans the sides of the bowl. The dough should be soft and elastic. Add liberal sprinkles of flour if it is wet, and teaspoons of water if dry.

KNEADING
1 min.
	Knead with the machine running for 1 minute.
	    The dough will be slightly sticky when turned from the bowl but small sprinkles of flour will make it manageable.
	    Let the dough rise, as above.

SHAPING
18 mins.
	Allow the dough to relax for 5 minutes and then roll the piece into a 12"-x-18" rectangle. For one loaf, cut into three 4"-wide strips, or, for two loaves, six 9"-x-4" strips. If the strips pull back and shrink when they are cut, let them rest for 3 or 4 minutes—and roll to size.
	    Carefully spread the filling on the pieces, leaving a ½" margin around the edge. This permits a good bond that will hold and not open when the braids rise.
	    Roll each piece from the long side. Stop the roll 1" from the edge. *Lift the edge up to the roll and pinch together.* Don't roll to the edge, for this will push the filling onto the clear margin and make it difficult to get a firm seal.
	    Lift the rolls onto the baking sheet and braid 3 rolls together, pinching the ends together tightly.

SECOND RISING 45 mins.	Cover with a length of wax paper and leave at room temperature until the braids have doubled in bulk, 45 minutes.
PREHEAT	Preheat the oven to 350° 20 minutes before baking.
BAKING 350° 40 mins.	Bake on the middle shelf of the moderate oven. When the loaves are a golden brown and tapping the bottom crust yields a hard, hollow sound, they are done, about 40 minutes. (If using a convection oven, reduce heat 25° and bake for 35 minutes.)
FINAL STEP	Remove the bread from the oven. As with all braided loaves, handle the hot bread with care. Move with the help of a spatula to cool.

Pumpkin-Walnut Bread [two medium loaves]

Pumpkin in bread adds a new taste dimension to pumpkin's popularity, which began at least 9,000 years ago in the Mexican highlands. There are 2 cups chopped walnuts divided between the 2 loaves, and these add color and roughness to the texture that is pleasing.

Either fresh-cooked or canned pumpkin can be used. Substituting dark brown sugar for light will give the bread a richer look.

INGREDIENTS

1³/₄ cups fresh or canned cooked pumpkin
1¹/₂ cups firmly packed brown sugar
¹/₂ cup (1 stick) butter, room temperature
3 eggs, room temperature, lightly beaten
4 cups sifted all-purpose flour, approximately
2 tablespoons baking powder
1 teaspoon ground cinnamon
¹/₂ teaspoon *each* salt and grated nutmeg
2 cups chopped walnuts

BAKING PANS

2 medium (8"-x-4") loaf pans, lined with buttered wax paper

PREHEAT

Preheat the oven to 350°.

BY HAND
OR MIXER
15 mins.

In a large mixing or mixer bowl blend together the pumpkin, brown sugar, butter, and eggs. On a length of wax paper sift together the flour, baking powder, cinnamon, salt, and nutmeg.

Spoon 3 cups of the dry ingredients into the pumpkin mixture. Mix thoroughly. Stir in the walnuts by hand or with the flat beater. Add more flour if necessary to make a firm batter.

BY PROCESSOR
5 mins.

I have not made this bread with a processor because the steel blade would cut the nuts too finely. But the processor could be used following the sequence as above, with the nuts stirred by hand into the batter.

SHAPING
5 mins.

Spoon or pour the batter into the prepared pans. Push the mixture into the corners.

BAKING
350°
1 hour

Bake in the moderate oven until the loaf is a deep brown and tests done when a metal skewer inserted in the center comes out clean and dry, 1 hour. If moist particles cling to the probe, return the loaf to the oven for an additional 5 to 10 minutes. Test again.

(If using a convection oven, reduce heat 50°.)

FINAL STEP

Remove the bread from the oven, and allow to cool for 10 minutes before turning the loaves out of the pans. Warm quick bread is more fragile than a yeast loaf and should be handled with care.

This loaf will develop a richer flavor if allowed to age several days before slicing. It will keep for at least 2 weeks wrapped in plastic or foil.

Carrot Bread   [two medium loaves]

A wonderfully moist and delicate loaf, there are 2 cups finely shredded carrots in a dough already quite yellow with 4 eggs.

I usually bake carrot bread in two 1-pound coffee cans and serve it either sliced in wedges or in rounds.

INGREDIENTS	4 eggs, room temperature 2 cups sugar 1¼ cups salad oil 3 cups bread or all-purpose flour 2 teaspoons baking powder 1½ teaspoons baking soda ¼ teaspoon salt 2 teaspoons ground cinnamon 2 cups finely shredded raw carrots
BAKING PANS OR CANS	2 medium (8"-x-4") loaf pans, greased and lined with wax paper; or two 1-pound coffee cans, buttered, and a circle of buttered wax paper placed on the bottom of the cans
PREHEAT	Preheat oven to 350°.
BY HAND OR MIXER 10 mins.	In a large mixing or mixer bowl beat the eggs, and add the sugar gradually, beating until thick. Add the oil gradually, and continue beating until thoroughly combined. Stir in the flour, baking powder, baking soda, salt, and cinnamon. Blend until the mixture is smooth. Stir in the carrots.
BY PROCESSOR 5 mins.	Attach the steel blade. Drop the eggs into the work bowl, cover, turn the processor on, and add the sugar gradually through the feed tube. Pour in the oil gradually. Remove the cover and measure in the flour, baking powder, baking soda, salt, and cinnamon. Replace the cover and pulse to blend until the mixture is smooth. Add the shredded carrots. Pulse to blend.
SHAPING 2 mins.	Pour or spoon the batter into the pans.
REST 10 mins.	Allow the batter to stand in the pans about 10 minutes.
BAKING 350° 1 hour	Place tall cans on the lower oven shelf or the crowns may push against the top of the oven. Bake until the loaves are a light golden brown and test done when a metal skewer inserted in the center of a loaf comes

out clean and dry, 1 hour. If the batter clings to the probe, return the bread to the oven for an additional 5 to 10 minutes. Test again.

(If using a convection oven, reduce heat 50°.)

FINAL STEP

Remove the bread from the oven. Let the loaves stand in the pans for 10 minutes before turning the bread onto a metal rack to cool. Patiently allow the loaves in the coffee cans to work free by gently forcing them downward.

This loaf will keep for several weeks and freezes particularly well.

Tomato-Caraway Bread   [two slender loaves]

A single cup of tomato juice is sufficient to color 2 slender loaves a salmon pink and to give a definite but not overpowering taste of tomato. The caraway seeds sprinkled on beaten egg brushed on the crust may be substituted with either poppy or sesame seeds giving equally good results. The dark seeds (caraway or poppy) contrast nicely with the pinkish brown crust.

INGREDIENTS

3 to 3¹/₂ cups bread or all-purpose flour, approximately
I package dry yeast
I cup plus I tablespoon tomato juice
I tablespoon butter or margarine, room temperature
I teaspoon salt
I tablespoon sugar
I egg, slightly beaten
I tablespoon caraway or other seeds

BAKING SHEET

1 baking sheet, Teflon or dusted with cornmeal

BY HAND
OR MIXER
20 mins.

In a large mixing or mixer bowl measure 1 cup flour and the yeast; stir. Pour the tomato juice into a saucepan, add the butter or margarine, salt, and sugar, and warm over a low heat (120°–130°) to melt or soften the butter. Pour the tomato blend into the flour and beat with 50 strokes with a wooden spoon, or for 30 seconds at low speed with a mixer flat beater. Add ½ cup flour and beat 150 strong strokes with the spoon, or for 3 minutes at moderate speed with the mixer.

Continue to add flour and beat by hand with a spoon or with the mixer dough hook. The dough will be a soft mass that cleans the sides of the bowl.

KNEADING
10 mins.

If by hand, turn the dough onto a work surface lightly dusted with flour, and begin the kneading process—push-turn-fold. If using a dough hook in a mixer, knead until the dough is a soft ball gathered around the revolving hook. Knead by hand or mixer for about 10 minutes. Add sprinkles of flour if moisture should break through. The dough should clean the sides of the mixer bowl.

BY PROCESSOR
5 mins.

Attach the steel blade.

The sequence of ingredients differs from above.

Heat the tomato juice in a saucepan, add the butter or margarine, salt, and sugar and warm to melt or soften the butter. In the work bowl measure 1 cup flour and the yeast. Pulse to blend. With the machine running, pour the tomato blend through the feed tube. Add flour, ¼ cup at a time, until the batter becomes a solid mass that rides with the blade and cleans the sides of the bowl.

KNEADING
I min.

Knead with the machine running for 1 minute.

If the dough is dry, add water by the teaspoon, with the machine running. If the dough is wet, add flour by the tablespoon. The dough will be slightly sticky and very elastic when the kneading is completed. Pull and stretch the dough between your hands to test consistency.

FIRST RISING
I hour

Place the dough in a buttered or greased bowl, cover tightly with plastic wrap, and set aside until the dough has doubled in bulk, 1 hour.

SHAPING
10 mins.

Turn the dough onto the floured work surface and divide into 2 pieces. Pressing down with your palms, roll each piece back and forth so that it becomes a long, slender cylinder about 18" long and 2½" wide. Place on the baking sheet.

SECOND RISING
45 mins.

Cover with wax or parchment paper and leave until the loaves have doubled in size, about 45 minutes.

PREHEAT

Preheat the oven to 375° 20 minutes before baking.

BAKING
375°
30 mins.

Brush the loaves with the beaten egg and sprinkle with the caraway or other seeds.

Place on the middle shelf of the moderate oven. When lightly browned and tapping the bottom crust yields a hard, hollow sound, they are done, 30 minutes.

(If using a convection oven, reduce heat 50°.)

FINAL STEP

Remove the bread from the oven. Place on a metal rack to cool before slicing or freezing.

Onion Twist Bread   [two medium loaves]

A package of onion soup mix is the heart of this loaf, which has the strength of aroma and taste to please the most discriminating onion fancier. While that savory flavor is less strong after the loaf has cooled, it renews itself with vigor in the toaster.

Don't look for salt among the ingredients below. It is in the soup mix.

The bread looks good as a twist—2 long pieces wrapped together and dropped in a baking pan. The twist can also be laid directly on a baking sheet. However, be certain the ends are pinched together tightly.

INGREDIENTS

4 to 4½ cups bread or all-purpose flour, approximately
2 packages dry yeast
½ cup nonfat dry milk
1½ cups hot water (120°–125°)
2 tablespoons vegetable shortening, room temperature
2 tablespoons sugar
1 1⅜-ounce package onion soup mix
2 tablespoons grated Parmesan cheese
1 egg, room temperature
Butter, melted

BAKING PANS
OR SHEET

2 medium (8"-x-4") baking pans, greased or Teflon; or 1 baking sheet, Teflon or sprinkled with cornmeal

BY HAND
OR MIXER
20 mins.

In a large mixer or mixing bowl combine 2 cups flour and the yeast.

In a saucepan measure the dry milk, water, shortening, sugar, soup mix, and cheese. Stir over low heat until hot (125°). Pour this into the flour, add the egg, and beat with a wooden spoon 100 strokes, or with a mixer flat beater for 1 minute. Scrape down the bowl.

Beat with a spoon or turn the mixer to medium for 2 minutes. Stir in more flour to form a soft dough that will clean the sides of the bowl. Remove the flat beater and attach the dough hook.

KNEADING
10 mins.

Sprinkle the work surface with flour and turn the dough onto it; knead until smooth and elastic. Add sprinkles of flour if moisture breaks through. Knead by hand or under the dough hook for 10 minutes. The dough in the mixer will form a soft ball around the revolving blade, and clean the sides of the bowl.

BY PROCESSOR
8 mins.

Attach the short plastic dough blade.

The sequence for adding ingredients varies slightly from above.

Heat the milk, water, shortening, sugar, soup mix, and cheese over low heat until about 125°. Stir in the egg.

Combine 2½ cups flour and the yeast in the work bowl. With the processor running, pour the liquid through the feed tube. Stop the machine once or twice and scrape down the sides of the bowl. Turn on the machine and add flour, ¼ cup at a time, until the batter becomes a solid mass that will clean the sides of the bowl as it rides on the blade.

KNEADING
1 min.

Knead with the machine running for 1 minute.

The dough will be slightly sticky when turned from the bowl but sprinkles of flour will make it manageable. If not, return the dough to the bowl and add flour.

REST
20 mins.

Turn the dough onto the floured work surface, cover with an inverted bowl or a cloth, and let rest for 20 minutes.

SHAPING
20 mins.

To make the twisted loaves, divide the dough into 4 parts. Roll each under the palms into a 12"-long cylinder. Allow the dough to rest for 5 minutes.

Twist 2 cylinders together and press the ends to seal. Tuck under the ends and place the loaf in a pan. Repeat with second loaf. The loaves can also be baked right on a baking sheet, placing them 2" apart.

RISING
45 mins.

Cover with wax paper or foil until doubled in size, 45 minutes. The dough will rise about ½" above the edge of the pan.

PREHEAT

Preheat the oven to 375° 20 minutes before baking.

BAKING
375°
40 mins.

Bake in the oven until the crusts are nicely browned, about 40 minutes. The loaves will draw away from the sides of the pan. When tapping the bottom crust yields a hard, hollow sound, the bread is done.

(If using a convection oven, reduce heat 50°.)

FINAL STEP

Remove the bread from the oven. Turn out onto cooling racks.

While the loaves are still hot, brush with the melted butter for a nice soft finish.

Zucchini-Basil Muffins   [two dozen medium muffins]

These delicious muffins, flavored with basil and Parmesan cheese, underline the goodness and variety zucchini offers even at summer's end when the vegetable is almost too plentiful in the garden and on the market. Everybody seems to have zucchini! It seems hardly a treasure, yet come a cold winter's day these muffins will gladden the hearts of family and guests.

Don't peel the zucchini. Shred the entire vegetable; the green slivers will contrast nicely with the creamy batter.

INGREDIENTS	2 eggs, room temperature
	$3/4$ cup milk
	$2/3$ cup cooking oil
	$2^1/2$ cups all-purpose flour
	$1/4$ cup sugar
	1 tablespoon baking powder
	2 teaspoons salt
	2 cups shredded zucchini
	2 tablespoons minced fresh basil
	$1/2$ cup grated Parmesan cheese

MUFFIN TINS   Muffin tins with total of 22 to 24 cups, buttered or Teflon

PREHEAT   Preheat the oven to 425°.

BY HAND
12 mins.

In a large bowl break and beat the eggs. Add the milk and oil.

In another bowl measure the flour, sugar, baking powder, and salt. Stir thoroughly. Add the dry ingredients to the egg mixture, 1 cup at a time, and stir until it becomes a thick, moist batter. It need not be beaten until perfectly smooth—a few lumps are no problem.

Gently stir in the zucchini and basil, but only enough to mix it well.

Spoon the batter into the prepared muffin tins, filling each cup halfway.

Sprinkle Parmesan cheese over the top of each muffin.

BAKING
425°
15–22 mins.

Place the muffin tins in the oven and bake for 20 to 22 minutes, or until the muffins are a golden brown and the cheese is melted across the tops. Turn a muffin out of the tin and tap the crust to be certain it is hard, not soft. If the muffin mix is poured into very small muffin cups the baking time will be less, about 15 minutes.

(If using a convection oven, reduce heat 50° and bake for about 18 minutes, or until the muffins test done, as above.)

FINAL STEP   Allow the muffins to cool about 10 minutes in the tins before turning them onto a metal rack to cool.

These freeze well to serve that winter's day when the thoughts of summer's bountiful zucchini harvest are but warm memories.

Tomato-Cheese Bread [one medium loaf]

This is a handsome brown loaf studded with red tomato bits that can be assembled, baked, and served in less than 2 hours—including the time spent picking the tomatoes in the garden. While it is baking, the odor is reminiscent of pizza. Delightful. This is an adaptation of a recipe from a fine bread book by Mel London, Bread Winners.

INGREDIENTS

2 cups whole-wheat flour
2 teaspoons baking powder
Pinch of baking soda
1 teaspoon salt (optional)
$1/2$ teaspoon garlic powder
1 teaspoon crushed oregano
1 teaspoon (4 leaves) finely chopped fresh basil
$1/2$ cup shredded mozzarella cheese
$1/2$ cup grated Parmesan cheese
$1 1/2$ cups tomatoes, peeled, seeded, and chopped, juice reserved
$1/2$ to $3/4$ cup milk
2 eggs
$1/4$ cup cooking oil
1 tablespoon honey

BAKING PAN

1 medium ($8 1/2$"-x-$4 1/2$") loaf pan, greased or Teflon, long sides and bottom lined with greased wax paper

PREHEAT

Preheat the oven to 350°.

BY HAND
15 mins.

In a large bowl mix the flour, baking powder, baking soda, spices, and cheeses.

In another bowl, drain the chopped tomatoes, saving the juice. Add the milk to the juice to make 1 cup of liquid; stir in the eggs, oil, and honey. Pour this and the tomatoes into the flour mixture and stir until it becomes a moist, thick batter.

Pour or spoon the batter into the prepared loaf pan. Push the batter into the corners and smooth the top with a spatula.

BAKING
350°
60–70 mins.

Bake for 60 to 70 minutes. If the bread has browned before the baking time is complete, cover the top with a foil tent and continue baking until it tests done and the bottom sounds hollow when tapped with a finger.

(If using a convection oven, bake on the lower shelf and reduce heat 50°. Bake for 50 minutes. If a cake testing pin comes out moist, return to the oven for an additional 5 to 10 minutes.)

FINAL STEP   Turn out onto a cooling rack. Don't slice until the loaf has thoroughly cooled.

This is a moist loaf and will keep at room temperature for several days. Freezes well.

Marbled Bread   [three loaves]

Three doughs—white, green (spinach), and pink (tomato)—are rolled or twisted together to make this spectacular loaf. Or each can be baked as a separate loaf.

This adaptation is from the famous kitchen of LeNotre in Paris by the way of The Pleasures of Cooking, the fine Cuisinart publication.

There is no better demonstration of the speed of the food processor than this recipe, which calls for 3 different doughs to be made within a very short period of time. The food processor does these in less than 30 minutes.

Note: *The 3 loaves share most of the same ingredients. The shared ingredients are followed by those ingredients needed to make each special loaf.*

INGREDIENTS   *For Each Loaf:*
3 1/2 cups bread or all-purpose flour, approximately
I package dry yeast
I teaspoon salt
I teaspoon sugar
2 tablespoons butter
I egg, room temperature

For Spinach:
18 ounces fresh spinach, stemmed and washed (to make I cup puree)
1/4 cup milk

For White:
2 tablespoons milk
2/3 cup hot water (120°–130°)

For Tomato:
2 tablespoons milk
I cup tomato sauce

BAKING SHEETS   1 to 3 baking sheets, greased or Teflon

PREPARATION
5 mins.   In a medium saucepan cook the washed spinach, covered, with the water still clinging to the leaves, until the leaves are just wilted, about 2 minutes. Drain and squeeze out as much moisture as possible. Puree

the spinach in a blender or processor until finely chopped. Scrape down the work bowl. With the motor running, gradually add the milk until the spinach is pureed, about 45 seconds. Set aside.

Note: Only instructions for the white loaf follow since the 3 loaves are so similar. For the tomato and spinach loaves simply add the ingredients above.

**BY HAND
OR MIXER
8 mins.**

Measure 2 cups flour into a mixing or mixer bowl and add the yeast, salt, and sugar. Form a well in the flour and drop in the butter, egg, milk, and hot water. Stir vigorously with a wooden spoon for 100 strokes, or with a flat beater for 2 minutes.

Add flour, ¼ cup at a time, to form a shaggy mass that can be lifted to the floured work surface to be kneaded.

**KNEADING
10 mins.**

If by hand, turn and fold the dough with a rhythmic motion of push-turn-fold. Occasionally lift the dough above the table and bring it crashing down against the work surface. Add sprinkles of flour if the dough is sticky. If using a mixer, knead with the dough hook at low speed and add flour, if necessary, until the dough forms a soft ball around the revolving hook and cleans the sides of the bowl. Knead for 10 minutes. The dough will be smooth and elastic when stretched between your hands.

**BY PROCESSOR
5 mins.**

Attach the steel blade.

The order of ingredients varies slightly from above.

Measure 2½ cups flour into the work bowl and add the yeast, salt, sugar, and butter. Pulse to blend. In a separate bowl stir together the egg, milk, and hot water. With the processor running, pour the liquid through the feed tube to form a heavy batter. Add flour, ¼ cup at a time, until the dough rides with the blade and cleans the inside of the bowl.

**KNEADING
1 min.**

Knead the dough with the processor running for an additional 1 minute. If the dough is wet, add flour through the feed tube by the tablespoon; if dry, add water by the teaspoon.

When turned from the bowl the dough will be slightly sticky. Dust lightly with flour to control the stickiness.

**FIRST RISING
40 mins.**

Place the dough in a greased bowl (or plastic bag) and set aside to rise, about 40 minutes. Proceed with the other 2 loaves.

**SHAPING
20 mins.**

Turn each of the 3 loaves onto the floured work surface, and divide each into 3 pieces of equal size (a total of 9). Allow them to relax for about 5 minutes.

For rolled loaves: with your hands and a rolling pin shape the white dough into a rectangle about 15"-x-7"-x-¼". If the dough pulls back, put it aside for a moment and proceed with the others. The tomato and spinach rectangles are made slightly smaller, 14" x 6" x ¼", to fit on top of the white.

To assemble, start with 1 white layer and stack 1 each pink and green dough on top of the other. Roll from the long side into a cylinder and pinch the seam and ends together tightly. Place the loaf seam side down on a prepared baking sheet. Repeat the stacking and rolling with the remaining doughs.

With a razor, cut 3 diagonal slashes, ¼" deep, across the top of each loaf.

For twisted or braided loaves: roll each of the 9 pieces into an 18"-long rope under your palms.

Lay 3 ropes of different colors side by side, and either twist together or braid. Place on the prepared baking sheet(s).

SECOND RISING
30–40 mins.

If there is room in the oven for only 1 bake sheet and 1 loaf, cover and place the other loaves in reserve in the refrigerator and bring one at a time out to rise while the first loaf bakes.

Cover the loaves with parchment paper or greased plastic wrap and set aside to double in bulk, 30 to 40 minutes.

PREHEAT

Preheat the oven to 375° about 20 minutes before baking.

BAKING
375°
40 mins.

Be certain the seams of the loaves are closed before putting them in the oven. Bake until a light golden brown, 40 minutes. Turn a loaf over and tap bottom with a forefinger. If it sounds hard and hollow it is baked. If not, return to the oven for 5 to 10 minutes more.

(If using a convection oven, reduce heat 50°.)

FINAL STEP

Remove from the oven and allow to cool on a metal rack before slicing.
Colorful when cut!

Pain au Rhubarbe   [two small loaves]
(Rhubarb Bread)

Rhubarb is a big, showy plant that is one of the first in the garden to peep through the earth to announce that winter is over, and that it won't be long before its juicy and slightly acid stalks will be ready to be pulled and taken to the kitchen.

To many in this country, the first thought might well be for pie (indeed, rhubarb's common name is "pieplant"); to the French, however, it could be for a loaf of rhubarb bread. Compact and moist, a slice is filled with delicious surprises each time the tongue touches a nugget of rhubarb.

Both the flavor and color are in the rhubarb skin, so don't peel it off. Later in the summer it may get tough and stringy. Then be more selective and choose the new, slender stalks. If freshly picked rhubarb isn't available, frozen rhubarb is now in almost all supermarkets.

This is an appealing loaf—speckled and brown with bits of nuts and rhubarb.

(It can be made into 1 large loaf but it is a rich, specialty bread that seems to dictate smaller loaves. The smaller loaves are also nice to use as gifts.)

INGREDIENTS	1 egg $1/2$ cup honey $1/2$ cup (1 stick) butter, melted 1 cup orange or pineapple juice $1 1/2$ cups rhubarb, chopped into $1/4$" bits (see Note) $3/4$ cup walnuts, chopped into $1/4$" bits 2 cups all-purpose flour 2 teaspoons baking powder $1/2$ teaspoon baking soda $1/2$ teaspoon salt $1/4$ teaspoon ground ginger
BAKING PANS	2 small (7" x 3") loaf pans, greased or Teflon, long sides and bottom of pans lined with buttered wax paper
PREHEAT	Preheat the oven to 350°.
BY HAND 20 mins.	In a medium bowl beat the egg with the honey, butter, fruit juice, rhubarb, and walnuts. In a separate bowl mix the flour, baking powder, baking soda, salt, and ground ginger. Mix the flour with the wet ingredients in stages, starting with 1 cup flour stirred in. Thereafter, add flour 1 tablespoon at a time to form a batter that can be poured or spooned into the pans. Dumping all of the flour into the bowl at one time might result in a too-hard and too-stiff mixture. If this happens, however, push it into the corner of the pans with moistened fingers. Spread the batter into the corners with a spatula or your fingers. Leave the sides slightly higher than the center to allow for the loaf to expand and level off in the oven.

BAKING
350°
45 mins.

Bake in the moderate oven for about 45 minutes. The crust will be browned when done, and a metal skewer or cake testing pin will come out clean and dry when inserted in the middle of the loaf.

(If using a convection oven, reduce heat 50° and bake for 40 minutes, testing for doneness, as above.)

FINAL STEP

The loaf will be fragile when it first comes from the oven. Allow it to cool for 10 minutes before turning the pan on its side and gently tugging the paper to loosen.

Let the loaf mature, or age, overnight before serving. Then it is delicious!

Note: The only use for a food processor in this recipe is to chop the rhubarb, but do so with care—it may make rhubarb puree! Using a knife is more satisfactory, and less trouble to clean up.

Pain d'Ail   [two medium loaves]
(Garlic Bread)

More often than not garlic butter is spread on slices of French bread, but in this unusual recipe, creamy garlic butter becomes part of the dough. The loaf carries within it the appealing fragrance of the garlic clove.

I found this recipe one August day at the Great Garlic Recipe Contest and Cook-Off in Gilroy, California, which its residents modestly claim is the "garlic capital of the world." The figures to substantiate this are impressive: 16,000 acres of garlic under cultivation in the fields around the town, producing nearly 200 million pounds of the bulbs each year.

Only 4 to 6 cloves of that tremendous harvest are needed in this recipe, yet the taste comes forward, not like a sledgehammer, but as delicately as a feather. Even one who doesn't care for garlic might be coaxed to try a slice of this.

There are legends and folk tales galore about the miraculous curative powers of this vegetable. In the sixteenth century, for instance, the Parisians ate garlic with fresh butter during the month of May, quite convinced that this "rustic diet" strengthened their health for the whole year.

While this recipe is made with the same combination—garlic and fresh butter—the author promises not a cure but a slice of delicious bread.

INGREDIENTS	4 to 6 garlic cloves, peeled (depending on strength desired)
	1/4 cup (1/2 stick) butter, room temperature
	5 to 5 1/2 cups bread or all-purpose flour, approximately
	1 package dry yeast
	2 teaspoons salt
	1 tablespoon sugar
	1/3 cup nonfat dry milk
	2 1/4 cups hot water (120°–130°)

BAKING PANS   2 medium (8"-x-4") baking pans, greased or Teflon

PREPARATION
8 mins.

In a saucepan blanch the garlic cloves in boiling water for 1 minute; remove and place under cold running water for a few moments. Pound into a smooth paste in a mortar or put through a garlic press. Soften the butter and mix with the garlic. Set aside.

BY HAND
OR MIXER
5 mins.

Measure 3 cups flour into a mixer or mixing bowl and add the yeast, salt, sugar, and dry milk. Stir to blend.

If by hand, pour the water into the flour and stir vigorously with a wooden spoon to blend thoroughly. Drop in the garlic butter and mix it into the batter. Add flour, 1/4 cup at a time, to develop a shaggy, rough dough mass that can be lifted to the work surface to knead.

If using a mixer, attach the flat beater. With the mixer running, pour in the water to form a thick batter. Drop in the garlic butter and mix for 2 minutes at medium speed. Add flour, 1/4 cup at a time. When the dough clings to the flat beater without mixing, attach the dough hook. Add more flour if necessary to form a soft ball around the revolving hook.

KNEADING
10 mins.

If by hand, place the dough on the floured work surface and knead with a push-turn-fold motion to create a dough that is soft and elastic. Add sprinkles of flour if sticky.

If under the mixer dough hook, continue with the machine running. If the dough should cling to the sides of the bowl add light sprinkles of flour. The dough will form a soft ball around the revolving arm. Knead for 10 minutes by hand or in the mixer.

BY PROCESSOR
5 mins.

Prepare the garlic butter, as above, and set aside.

Attach the short plastic dough blade.

Measure 4 cups flour into the work bowl and add the yeast, salt, sugar and dry milk. Pulse to blend. With the machine running, pour the water through the feed tube to form a heavy batter. Drop in the garlic butter and process for a few seconds to blend.

Uncover the work bowl and add ½ cup flour. And at the same time with a rubber spatula loosen and push to the center any dry ingredients stuck along the outer edges of the bowl. With the machine running add flour through the feed tube, ¼ cup at a time, to form a mass that will spin with the blade and clean the sides of the bowl.

KNEADING
1½ mins.

Knead with the processor running for 1½ minutes.

The dough should be slightly sticky and very elastic when kneading is complete. Pull and stretch the dough between your hands to test its consistency; if necessary, return the dough to the work bowl to process a few seconds more.

FIRST RISING
1 hour

Place the dough in a greased bowl, cover tightly with plastic wrap, and put aside to double in volume, about 1 hour.

SHAPING
5 mins.

Turn the dough onto the work surface, knead briefly to push out the air bubbles, and divide in half. Press each half into a flat oval, about the length of the pan. Fold in half lengthwise, pinch the seam together, tuck in the ends, and drop seam down into the baking pan.

SECOND RISING
45 mins.

Cover the pans with parchment or wax paper and let rise until the dough has doubled in volume, about 1" above the pan rim, 45 minutes.

PREHEAT

Preheat the oven to 375° 20 minutes before baking.

BAKING
375°
40 mins.

Place the baking pans on the middle shelf of the oven. The loaves will be a light brown when baked, about 40 minutes. To test for doneness, turn one loaf out of its pan and thump the bottom crust. If it sounds hard and hollow, the bread is done. If not, return to the oven for an additional 10 minutes, without the tin.

(If using a convection oven, reduce heat 50°.)

FINAL STEP

Turn the loaves from the pans onto a rack to cool.

HERB AND
SPICE BREADS

BREADS MADE WITH HERBS and spices fill the house with provocative aromas and gladden the tongue with piquant tastes.

An herb is the leaf of a plant grown in the temperate zone, such as basil. A spice is part of a plant grown in the tropics—root, seed, leaf, or bark—such as pepper.

While herbs and spices are used frequently in recipes throughout the book, they do not dominate or take charge of the flavor as they do in this chapter. There are three exceptions, strongly spiced, found elsewhere: Jalapeño Corn Bread, Pepper Cheese Loaf, and Tabasco Cheese Bread.

Herbs and spices are perishable. So use them shortly after purchase while the flavors are at their best. Keep spices tightly closed and store in a cool place away from the light. Refrigerate or freeze herbs.

Schiacciata con Zibibbo   [one large loaf]
(Flatbread with Raisins)

This is a traditional Italian sweet bread, seasoned with rosemary leaves dropped into hot olive oil, and speckled with raisins. During the Italian grape harvest, some bakers use freshly picked grapes but others hold that raisins are equally good and not so seasonal.

This feathery light bread, with an open texture, is baked in a jelly roll pan from which it is usually served cut into 16 or 18 pieces. It is ideal for breakfast, brunch or lunch for 6, 8, or 10 guests.

INGREDIENTS	1 cup raisins
	1/2 cup olive oil
	2 tablespoons lard
	2 tablespoons fresh or dried rosemary leaves
	4 1/2 cups bread flour, approximately
	2 packages dry yeast
	1 cup hot water (120°–130°)
	2/3 cup sugar
	1 teaspoon salt
	2 eggs, room temperature

BAKING PAN

1 baking pan (16" x 11") greased with a bit of olive oil

PREPARATION
20 mins.

In a small bowl plump the raisins in warm water to cover for 20 minutes. Drain, pat dry with paper towels, and set aside. In a small saucepan heat the olive oil and lard and bring to a low boil. Drop in the rosemary leaves; simmer for 5 minutes. Remove from the heat and let stand to cool.

1 hour

Measure 1½ cups flour into a mixing bowl and blend in the yeast. Form a well in the center of the flour; pour in the hot water. With a spatula pull in flour from the edges to make a thick batter/sponge. Cover with plastic wrap and let stand until the sponge has risen over the remaining flour, about 1 hour.

If using a processor, attach the plastic dough blade. Measure 1½ cups flour into the work bowl and add the yeast. Pulse. Push the flour to the sides of the bowl. Pour the water into the center and, with a spatula, pull in the flour from the sides to form the sponge. Let rise, as above.

BY HAND
OR MIXER
8 mins.

When the sponge has risen and is bubbly, add ¼ cup of the oil-rosemary mixture, ⅓ cup sugar, salt, and the eggs.

Stir briskly with a wooden spoon or mixer flat beater until all of the ingredients are smoothly blended together.

Add flour to the batter, ½ cup at a time, stirring vigorously after each addition, until the dough is a rough, shaggy mass that can be lifted from the bowl and placed on the work surface. Or with a mixer, change to the dough hook.

KNEADING
15 mins.

Knead the dough for 15 minutes by hand or under the dough hook. Add sprinkles of flour if the dough sticks to your hands or does not clean the sides of the mixer bowl.

Three minutes before the dough is finished add the raisins which, if added earlier, would have been torn apart and would have discolored the dough. If the dough in the mixer does not accept the raisins, put the dough on the counter and work them into the dough by hand. Knead for 2 minutes.

BY PROCESSOR
5 mins.

Plump the raisins, then heat the oil, lard, and rosemary, as above.

When the sponge has doubled, add ¼ cup of the oil-rosemary mixture, ⅓ cup sugar, salt, and the eggs. Pulse several times to blend.

Add flour, ¼ cup at a time, through the feed tube, until the dough forms and rides with the plastic blade to clean the bowl.

KNEADING
5–6 mins.

With the machine running, knead for 50 seconds.

Remove the dough from the work bowl, sprinkle lightly with flour, and knead for a moment or so and then flatten into an oval. Spread half of the raisins over the dough, fold the sides over to cover them, and then begin kneading to get them into the dough. This will take about 4 or 5 minutes.

SHAPING
8 mins.

Prepare the pan by oiling it with 1 teaspoon of the oil mixture. Place the dough on the pan and spread it out with your fingers to cover the surface completely. Don't rush the dough or it may get stubborn and pull back. Walk away from it for a minute or two if the dough gets tense. Pour the remaining oil mixture over the dough and spread it with your fingers. Sprinkle the remaining ⅓ cup sugar over the top.

RISING
1 hour

It is not necessary to cover the pan because of the olive oil spread over the dough. Allow the dough to rise to double in volume, about 1 hour. The dough will have risen above the edge of the pan and be quite puffy. The surface will be irregular, with small pools of oil in the valleys.

PREHEAT

Preheat the oven to 375° 20 minutes before baking. Be certain the large pan will fit comfortably into the oven with space left around the edges or the heat trapped underneath may scorch the bread.

BAKING
375°
30–35 mins.

Bake for 30 to 35 minutes, or until the top is a golden brown. The thin bread will bake rapidly.

(If using a convection oven, reduce heat 50°. The large pan may create a problem. If so, divide and fit the dough into 2 smaller pans. Leave one aside while the first is baking, about 30 minutes. Then do the second one.)

FINAL STEP

Remove from the oven. Cut into serving-size rectangles, and serve hot or cold.

This is a delicious bread warmed over and pieces split horizontally toast beautifully.

Pfeffernuss Brot   [two medium loaves]
(Pepper Spice Bread)

Aniseed, ground allspice, cinnamon, and freshly ground black pepper are the pepper and spice in this delicious German loaf—a derivative of the much-loved Pfeffernuss spice cookie.

This recipe and several for delicious soups came to my kitchen from a friend in Kansas whose German forebears came to the Plains State from Russia, where they had colonized choice land along the Volga and Black Sea at the invitation of German-born Catherine the Great. They fled to this country, where their heritage of fine cooking is preserved in recipes of a cookbook, Küche Kuchen, collected by the American Historical Association of Germans from Russia.

Preparation begins by first making a sponge which has the strength to lift the rather heavy dough, rich with butter and eggs, into a lovely dark-brown loaf with an open texture.

INGREDIENTS

Sponge:
4$\frac{1}{2}$ to 5$\frac{1}{2}$ cups bread flour, approximately
2 packages dry yeast
I teaspoon salt
$\frac{1}{2}$ cup sugar
$\frac{1}{2}$ cup nonfat dry milk
I$\frac{1}{2}$ cups hot water (120°–130°)

Dough:
$\frac{1}{2}$ cup (I stick) butter, room temperature
2 eggs
$\frac{1}{2}$ cup molasses (or $\frac{1}{4}$ cup *each* honey and dark corn syrup)
I teaspoon freshly ground black pepper
2 teaspoons ground aniseed
$\frac{1}{2}$ teaspoon *each* ground allspice and cinnamon
$\frac{3}{4}$ cup roughly broken walnuts

BAKING PANS
OR SHEET

2 medium (8"-x-4") loaf pans or 1 baking sheet, greased or Teflon

PREPARATION
2 hours

To make the sponge, in a mixing or mixer bowl measure 2 cups flour and add the yeast, salt, sugar, and dry milk. Stir in the water to make a batter. Cover with plastic wrap and put aside at room temperature to bubble and rise to more than twice its original volume, about 2 hours.

If using a processor, attach the plastic dough blade. Measure 2 cups flour into the work bowl and add the yeast, salt, sugar, and dry milk. Pulse to blend. Pour in the water. Pulse several times to make a thick batter. Leave the bowl on the machine, covered, and allow the sponge to rise to the top of the bowl, about 2 hours.

BY HAND
OR MIXER
10 mins.

To make the dough, uncover the sponge and stir in the butter. Add the eggs one at a time. Use a wooden spoon, if by hand, or the flat beater in the electric mixer. Pour in the molasses, blend, and add the pepper and spices. Add the broken walnuts.

When all of the ingredients have been added, stir in additional flour, ½ cup at a time, until the dough is a rough mass that can be lifted to the work surface—or left in the mixer bowl and kneaded under the dough hook.

KNEADING
10 mins.

If the dough is somewhat sticky, sprinkle lightly with flour and begin kneading with a strong push-turn-fold motion. Or knead under the mixer dough hook, adding sprinkles of flour if the dough sticks to the sides of the bowl. Knead by hand or in the machine for 10 minutes until the dough is smooth and elastic.

BY PROCESSOR
4 mins.

To make the dough, pulse to deflate the sponge. With the machine running, add the butter, eggs, and molasses through the feed tube. Stop the machine. Add the pepper and spices. Pulse to blend.

Turn on the machine and add the flour, ¼ cup at a time, until the dough forms a rough mass that is swirled around the bowl by the force of the blade. Stop, remove the cover, and pinch the dough to test for texture. If it is sticky, add light sprinkles of flour, pulsing between each addition.

KNEADING
45 secs.

When you have judged the dough to have sufficient flour, turn on the machine and knead for 45 seconds.

Lift the dough out of the bowl. It may be somewhat sticky; if so, dust it with flour as you work it into a ball.

FIRST RISING
1½ hours

Place the ball of dough in a greased bowl, cover with plastic wrap, and leave at room temperature to double in bulk, about 1½ hours.

SHAPING	Divide the dough in half. Set one half aside while making the first loaf.
12 mins.	For a braided loaf, divide the dough half into 3 parts, and roll each under your palms into a rope about 12" to 14" long. Braid from the middle to one end, pinch to close, and then turn the braid around and braid to the other end. Place on the baking sheet. Repeat for the second piece.
	For pan loaves, flatten each dough half into an oblong the length of the baking pan. Fold down the center. Pinch the seam to seal, tuck in the ends, and drop into the baking pan, seam down.
SECOND RISING	Cover the loaves with a cloth or wax paper and leave at room temperature until they are puffy and have doubled in volume, about 45 minutes.
45 mins.	
PREHEAT	Preheat the oven to 350° 20 minutes before baking.
BAKING	Bake in the moderate oven for about 50 minutes for the large braided loaves, or 35 minutes for the medium pan loaves. The loaves should turn dark brown.
350°	
35–50 mins.	(If using a convection oven, reduce heat 50°.)
FINAL STEP	Remove the breads from the oven and place on a metal rack to cool.
	Because this is a rich and filling bread, I often cut the large braids into pieces to give to friends.

Savory Bread   [two medium loaves]

Tabasco, a clove of garlic, and minced onion—plus spices—blend together to give a delightful fragrance and flavor to this loaf, which bakes to a fat plumpness. The seasonings are found in a buttered layer in the loaf.

Excellent with soups, barbecue meats, and pasta.

Use all fresh garlic and onion—no powdered or dried products!

INGREDIENTS

1½ cups water
6 tablespoons plus ½ cup (1 stick) butter, room temperature
5 cups bread or all-purpose flour, approximately
1 tablespoon sugar
2 teaspoons salt
2 packages dry yeast
½ cup nonfat dry milk
2 eggs, room temperature, lightly beaten
2 garlic cloves, crushed and finely chopped (see Note)
2 teaspoons minced or grated onion

1 teaspoon dried thyme

1/2 teaspoon *each* caraway seeds and freshly ground black pepper

1/4 to 1/2 teaspoon Tabasco, according to taste

1 egg yolk, beaten, mixed with 1 tablespoon cream or milk

BAKING PANS	2 medium (8½"-x-4½") loaf pans, greased or Teflon
PREPARATION 10 mins.	In a saucepan heat the water and 6 tablespoons butter until the water is hot (120°–130°). The butter need not melt.
BY HAND OR MIXER 6 mins.	In a large mixing or mixer bowl combine 2 cups flour and the sugar, salt, yeast, and dry milk. Pour the water/butter into the flour and mix. Add the eggs to the batter. Beat with a mixer flat beater at low speed until the flour is moist; increase speed to medium and beat for 3 minutes. If by hand, beat 100 strong strokes with a wooden spoon, or until the batter begins to string away from the sides of the bowl. Blend in the additional 3 cups flour with your fingers. Work the dough into a shaggy mass that is no longer sticky.
KNEADING 8 mins.	Turn the dough onto a floured work surface and knead for about 8 minutes. It will become alive, warm, and elastic under your hands. If under a dough hook, knead for the same length of time. The dough will clean the sides and bottom of the bowl. If not, add sprinkles of flour.
BY PROCESSOR 5 mins.	Prepare the butter and water, as above. Attach the short plastic dough blade. Measure 2 cups flour into the work bowl and add the sugar, salt, yeast, and dry milk. Pulse to blend. With the machine running, pour in the water/butter mixture. Stop the machine; scrape the bottom edge of the bowl with a spatula to pull in dry flour. Add the eggs and pulse 2 or 3 times to make a smooth batter. Add flour, ¼ cup at a time, until the batter becomes a soft, elastic ball that will whirl around the bowl with the blade.
KNEADING 45 secs.	With the machine running, knead for 45 seconds. The dough may seem sticky when taken from the bowl; if so add sprinkles of flour as you shape it into a ball. It will develop a smooth covering that will make it easier to place in a greased bowl to rise.
FIRST RISING 1 hour	Return the dough to the bowl and pat with buttered fingers. Cover the bowl with plastic wrap and leave at room temperature to rise until the dough has doubled in bulk, about 1 hour. While the dough is rising, in a small bowl cream the ½ cup butter and garlic. Add the onion and seasonings.

SHAPING
15 mins.

Punch down the dough and remove from the bowl. Divide in half and roll each half into an 8"-x-14" rectangle.

With a spatula spread half the seasoned butter over the dough, leaving 1". Roll up each rectangle and pinch the seam tightly closed. Tuck in the ends and drop into the pans.

SECOND RISING
1 hour

Cover the loaves with wax paper and leave until the dough reaches the top of the pan, about 1 hour.

PREHEAT

Preheat the oven to 350° about 20 minutes before baking.

BAKING
350°
45 mins.

Brush the loaves with the egg yolk glaze.

Place the pans in the oven. Bake until the crusts are bright brown, 45 minutes. Test by tapping the underside of one loaf with the forefinger. If it sounds hard and hollow, it is done.

(If using a convection oven, reduce heat 40°.)

FINAL STEP

Remove the bread from the oven. When you turn the loaves out of their pans, do so over paper towels because some of the butter may have run out of the seams and collected in the bottom of the tins. Place the loaves on a metal rack to cool before serving.

This loaf toasts and freezes well. It should not, however, be served with delicately flavored dishes. It is a rugged bread that demands and gets attention.

Note: The garlic cloves are best crushed under the flat surface of a kitchen knife with a blow of the fist before chopping finely.

Six Herbs Bread   [one medium or three mini-loaves]

To the delight of the baker and the herbalist, this light and airy loaf presents a choice of one or more of six herbs—dill, savory, basil, oregano, thyme, or marjoram. Select your favorite herbs for one medium loaf or divide the dough, and work some herbs into one piece of dough and perhaps a different selection into the others.

INGREDIENTS

1 package dry yeast
3$\frac{1}{2}$ cups bread or all-purpose flour, approximately
1 tablespoon sugar
1 teaspoon salt
$\frac{1}{2}$ cup nonfat dry milk
1$\frac{1}{4}$ cups hot water (120°–130°)
1 tablespoon shortening, room temperature

Choice of these dried herbs, alone or in combination:
2 teaspoons dillweed
2 teaspoons savory
1 tablespoon basil
1 teaspoon oregano
1 teaspoon thyme
1½ teaspoons marjoram
(Double measurements if using fresh herbs, finely chopped)

BAKING PANS

1 medium (8½"-x-4½") or 3 miniature (5½"-x-3 ¼") loaf pans, greased or Teflon

BY HAND
OR MIXER
6 mins.

In a large mixing or mixer bowl blend the yeast and 1½ cups flour. Add the sugar, salt, milk, and hot water. Beat with a wooden spoon 25 strong strokes, or for 3 minutes at medium speed with a mixer flat beater. Add the shortening. Continue beating until the soft batter pulls away in strings from the sides of the bowl, about 2 minutes. Gradually add the additional flour, ¼ cup at a time, first with the spoon and then by hand, until the dough has formed a rough mass and can be kneaded.

KNEADING
8 mins.

If the dough feels slack or moist or wet beneath the skin when it is turned out onto the work surface, add sprinkles of flour. Knead with a strong rhythmic motion of push-turn-fold until the dough is smooth and satiny, and feels alive under your fingers, about 8 minutes. Knead for the same length of time under the dough hook in the mixer.

BY PROCESSOR
5 mins.

Attach the steel blade.
    The order of ingredients varies slightly from above.
    Measure 1½ cups flour into the work bowl and add the yeast, sugar, salt, and dry milk. Pulse to blend. Pour in the hot water and add the shortening. Turn on the machine and add flour, ¼ cup at a time, through the feed tube until a rough ball of dough forms around the blade and the sides of the bowl are wiped clean by the dough.

KNEADING
50 secs.

With the machine running, knead for 50 seconds.
    When taken from the bowl, the dough may be of the ideal consistency yet sticky. Sprinkle with flour and shape with your hands into a smooth ball.

FIRST RISING
1 hour

Place the dough in a greased bowl, turning to film all sides. Cover the bowl with plastic wrap and leave at room temperature until the dough has doubled in bulk, about 1 hour.

SHAPING 15 mins.	Turn the dough out onto the floured work surface. Knead the dough briefly to work out the bubbles. If for 3 loaves, divide the dough. Flatten the dough under your palms and sprinkle on one or more of the herbs of choice. Fold in the herbs; knead for 2 minutes, or until the herbs are mixed throughout the piece.
	Shape each dough piece into an oval the length of a bread pan, fold lengthwise, pinch the seam securely, and place in the pan, seam down. Repeat using different herbs, if desired.
SECOND RISING 45 mins.	Cover the pan(s) with wax paper and leave until the dough has doubled in size or has expanded above the edge of the pan, about 45 minutes.
PREHEAT	Preheat the oven to 375° 20 minutes before baking.
BAKING 375° 45 mins.	Bake on the middle shelf of the oven until the loaf is a golden brown, and tests done when a wooden toothpick inserted in the center of the loaf comes out dry and clean, about 45 minutes.
	(If using a convection oven, reduce heat 50°.)
FINAL STEP	Remove the bread from the oven and immediately turn the loaves onto a metal rack to cool.
	The fragrance in the kitchen while this loaf bakes and cools is alone worth whatever time it takes to make.

Whole-Wheat Herb Bread   [two medium loaves]

Sage and nutmeg blend their flavors and aroma in this lightly textured loaf made with whole-wheat and white flours. While it can be made with margarine, I use butter to enhance the good flavor.

INGREDIENTS	2 cups whole-wheat flour
	2 packages dry yeast
	$^1/_3$ cup nonfat dry milk
	3 tablespoons sugar
	2 teaspoons salt
	2 teaspoons crushed caraway seeds
	$^1/_2$ teaspoon *each* grated nutmeg and dried sage
	1$^1/_2$ cups hot water (120°–130°)
	2 tablespoons butter or other shortening, room temperature
	1 egg, room temperature
	2 to 2$^1/_2$ cups bread or all-purpose flour, approximately
BAKING PANS	2 medium (8½"-x-4½") loaf pans, greased or Teflon

**BY HAND
OR MIXER
20 mins.**

In a large mixing or mixer bowl blend the whole-wheat flour, yeast, dry milk, sugar, salt, caraway, nutmeg, and sage. Pour in the hot water and beat with the mixer flat beater at medium speed for 1 minute, or 50 strong strokes with a large wooden spoon. Add the shortening and egg. Beat for 1 minute.

Stir in the white flour, ½ cup at a time, first with the spoon and then by hand, or with the flat beater. The dough will be a rough, shaggy mass that will clean the sides of the bowl. If the dough is slack and moisture breaks through, add sprinkles of flour.

**KNEADING
8 mins.**

Turn out the ball of dough onto a floured work surface, and knead, adding a little more flour to control stickiness, if needed, until the dough is smooth and elastic, about 8 minutes. Knead an equal length of time under a dough hook in the mixer bowl.

**BY PROCESSOR
5 mins.**

Insert the steel blade.

Measure the whole-wheat flour into the work bowl and add the yeast, dry milk, sugar, salt, caraway, nutmeg, and sage. Pulse to blend. In a small bowl mix together the hot water, shortening, and egg. With the machine running, pour the liquid through the feed tube. Add the white flour, ¼ cup at a time, until the heavy batter becomes dough and forms a ball on and around the blade. The film on the sides of the bowl will be swept clean by the dough.

**KNEADING
50 secs.**

Knead with the machine turned on for 50 seconds.

When the dough is turned out of the work bowl it may be somewhat sticky. Sprinkle with flour and work into a ball.

**FIRST RISING
1 hour**

Place the dough in a greased bowl, cover tightly with plastic wrap, and leave at room temperature until the dough has risen to twice its original size and is puffy, about 1 hour.

**SHAPING
10 mins.**

Turn the dough onto the floured work surface and cut in half. Each half can be formed into a loaf either by simply pressing and rolling by hand into a shape to fit the loaf pan, or rolling with a pin into a rectangle which is folded, the seam pinched shut, the ends tucked in and placed in the pan. Either will produce a handsome loaf.

**SECOND RISING
40 mins.**

Cover the pans loosely with wax paper and leave until the dough has doubled in bulk and risen to the height of the pans, about 40 minutes.

PREHEAT

Preheat the oven to 375° 20 minutes before baking.

BAKING
375°
45 mins.

Bake the loaves until they are a golden brown, 45 minutes. Turn one loaf out of a pan and tap on the bottom crust with your forefinger. A hard, hollow sound means the bread is done. If not, return to the oven for an additional 5 to 10 minutes, out of the pans if you want a deep brown crust. Midway during baking, shift the pans so the loaves are exposed equally to temperature variations in the oven.

(If using a convection oven, reduce heat 50°.)

FINAL STEP

Remove the bread from the oven and immediately turn out the loaves onto wire racks to cool completely before slicing.

This is an excellent sandwich bread and toasts beautifully. These loaves freeze well.

Pesto Bread   [two medium loaves]

Pesto—the thick Italian sauce made with basil, garlic, cheese, and olive oil—comes to mind most often with thoughts of soups and pastas. It is so rich and good and flavorful that I often transgress and spread it on a slice of country bread.

In the search for a better pesto and a better bread, I married the two in the heat of the oven. The pesto ingredients came together on the dough, which made it easy to prepare. But if you have some pesto already prepared on hand, by all means use it. A half cup can substitute for the basil, cheese, and garlic in the recipe.

INGREDIENTS

5 to 6 cups bread or all-purpose flour, approximately
1 package dry yeast
2 tablespoons sugar
2 teaspoons salt
2 cups hot water (120°–130°)
3 tablespoons olive oil
$1/2$ cup prepared pesto, room temperature
or
$1/4$ cup finely chopped fresh basil leaves; $1/3$ cup grated Parmesan
    cheese; $1/2$ clove garlic, crushed and finely minced

BAKING PANS

2 medium (8"-x-4") baking pans, greased or Teflon

BY HAND
OR MIXER
6 mins.

Measure 2 cups flour into a mixing or mixer bowl and add the dry ingredients. Stir to blend. Pour in the hot water and 2 tablespoons olive oil. Beat with 30 strong strokes of a wooden spoon, or with the mixer flat beater.

(The pesto mixture will be added after the first rising.)

Add flour, ¼ cup at a time, to form a ball of shaggy dough that can be lifted from the bowl and placed on the work surface. Leave it in the bowl if the dough hook is to be used.

KNEADING
8 mins.

With a dough blade to help turn and fold, knead the dough with a rhythmic motion—adding sprinkles of flour when it becomes sticky—until the ball is smooth and elastic, about 8 minutes. Knead under the dough hook in the mixer bowl for the same length of time.

BY PROCESSOR
5 mins.

Insert the plastic dough blade.

Add 2 cups flour and the dry ingredients, hot water, and 2 tablespoons olive oil to the work bowl. Pulse several times to blend. Sometimes with the shorter dough blade the flour along the outer edge of the bottom does not get pulled in by the blade. If this happens, stop the machine and loosen the flour with a rubber spatula; resume pulsing.

Add flour through the feed tube, ¼ cup at a time, until a ball of dough begins to form and is whirled around the bowl by the force of the blade.

KNEADING
50 secs.

With the machine running, knead for 50 seconds.

The dough may be slightly sticky when it is taken from the bowl. Dust your hands with flour and sprinkle flour lightly over the dough. Knead by hand for several moments to form a dry surface around the ball.

FIRST RISING
40 mins.

Put the dough in a greased bowl, cover tightly with plastic wrap, and put aside to double in bulk, about 40 minutes.

SHAPING
15 mins.

Divide the dough in half. Press and roll each half into a rectangle the width of the baking pan and about 10" to 12" long. The dough will be thin.

Spread olive oil over the center half of the rectangle, leaving a wide oil-free margin at each end so the seam will stick together and not be pulled apart. Spread the prepared pesto or basil leaves and cheese over the oil, and press in lightly. Sprinkle the garlic bits over the top.

(If using already prepared pesto, spread it over the same center section only, avoiding the ends.)

Roll the dough, jelly-roll fashion, to form a loaf. Pinch the dough together and tuck in the ends. Place in the prepared pan with the seam under. Push the dough into the corners with your fingers.

SECOND RISING **40 mins.**	Cover the pans with wax paper or plastic wrap and leave to rise to the height of the pan, about 40 minutes.
PREHEAT	Preheat the oven to 375° 20 minutes before baking.
BAKING **375°** **40 mins.**	Bake the loaves until a dark golden brown, about 40 minutes. Turn a loaf from the pan to test for doneness. Use care because the hot bread is fragile along the seams until cool and firm. (If using a convection oven, reduce heat 50°.)
FINAL STEP	Allow the loaves to cool in the pans for 10 minutes. Turn the bread out on its side so there is little stress to the bottom seam, which may be fragile when hot. Fine to serve with a pasta or a steaming bowl of minestrone. Delicious toasted.

Dilly Casserole Bread   [one loaf]

Once upon a time, Dilly Casserole Bread was on every home baker's list of favorite loaves. It deserves to be again.

The major ingredient is cottage cheese. Some recipes call for dillweed instead of dillseeds while others recommend butter instead of margarine. Whatever the refinements, it is a fine bread and is easy to make—and sends forth a delightful aroma while being baked, toasted, and eaten.

When fresh dill is in the market or in the garden, by all means use it. It gives the loaf a special lift that's not possible with dried herbs, good as they may be.

INGREDIENTS	1 cup cottage cheese, room temperature 2 tablespoons sugar 1 tablespoon instant onion 1 tablespoon fresh or dried dillweed or dillseeds 1 teaspoon salt $^1/_4$ teaspoon baking soda 2 eggs, room temperature 1 package dry yeast $2^1/_2$ cups bread or all-purpose flour, approximately $^1/_2$ teaspoon butter, melted Dash of salt
CASSEROLE	One 1½-quart casserole (approximately 7" wide by 4" deep), greased
PREPARATION **10 mins.**	In a saucepan heat the cottage cheese until warm to the touch (110°–120°).

BY HAND **OR MIXER** 12 mins.	Turn the cottage cheese into a mixing or mixer bowl and add the sugar, onion, dill, salt, baking soda, eggs, and yeast. Add flour, ½ cup at a time, to make a stiff batter, beating well after each addition with a wooden spoon, if by hand, or with the mixer flat beater. This is a heavy batter, not a dough, and will not be kneaded.
BY PROCESSOR 5 mins.	Heat the cottage cheese, as above. Attach the steel blade. Measure 1 cup flour into the work bowl and add the other ingredients as in method above. Pulse to blend well. Add flour, ¼ cup at a time, until the batter is quite thick. This is not a dough and so will not be kneaded.
FIRST RISING 1 hour	Cover the dough with plastic wrap and let rise in a warm place for about 1 hour.
SHAPING 5 mins.	Remove the plastic wrap and stir down the batter with 20 strong strokes. Pour or spoon the batter into the casserole.
SECOND RISING 45 mins.	Cover with wax paper and leave until the batter doubles in volume, about 45 minutes. Keep the wax paper from touching the expanding batter or it may collapse when the paper is pulled away.
PREHEAT	Preheat the oven to 350° 20 minutes before baking.
BAKING 350° 40–45 mins.	Bake the loaf until it is deep brown and crusty, 40 to 45 minutes. A wooden toothpick or metal skewer inserted in the center will come out clean and dry when the bread is done. If moist particles cling to the probe, return the loaf to the oven for an additional 5 to 10 minutes. Cover with foil or brown paper for the last 15 minutes to prevent excessive browning. (If using a convection oven, reduce heat 50°.)
FINAL STEP	Remove the bread from the oven and immediately brush with butter. Sprinkle salt lightly over the crust. Allow the bread to cool for 10 minutes before removing it from the casserole and placing it on the metal rack to cool.

Briarpatch Herb Bread   [two medium loaves]

It is always a special delight to find something special in one's own backyard. The Briarpatch is a few miles away in Terre Haute, but I claim it, especially after finding Briarpatch Herb Bread, the creation of one of the country's outstanding herbalists, Pearl (Toadi) Lloyd.

With more than 150 herbs to choose from in her private herb garden, Mrs. Lloyd chose these 4—oregano, chives, basil, and parsley—to make this loaf which is served at every meal. She has tried over the years to introduce other breads, but the clientele wants only this herb loaf.

Ideally, the herbs should be fresh, but dried can be substituted.

INGREDIENTS

2 cups bread or all-purpose flour, approximately
1 package dry yeast
2 tablespoons sugar
⅓ cup nonfat dry milk
1¾ cups hot water (120°–130°)
1 egg
3 tablespoons finely chopped fresh parsley,
    or 1 tablespoon dried
1 teaspoon chopped fresh oregano, or ⅓ teaspoon dried
½ teaspoon grated nutmeg
1½ tablespoons finely chopped fresh chives,
    or ½ tablespoon dried
1 tablespoon finely chopped fresh basil
2 tablespoons cooking oil
2 teaspoons salt
3 cups whole-wheat flour
1 tablespoon butter, melted

BAKING PANS

2 medium (8½"-x-4½") loaf pans, greased or Teflon

PREPARATION
20 mins.

Measure 1½ cups flour into a mixing or mixer bowl and stir in the yeast, sugar, and dry milk. Pour in the hot water. Blend into a thin batter. Break in the egg and add the parsley, oregano, nutmeg, chives, and basil. Beat this mixture by hand briskly or in a mixer for 2 minutes.

If using a processor, attach the plastic dough blade. Add 1½ cups white flour, the yeast, sugar, dry milk, and hot water. Close the lid and pulse to blend into a smooth batter. Add the egg and the herbs and nutmeg. Pulse to blend.

Allow the mixture to ferment and become bubbly, about 15 minutes. There is no need to cover it for this short period.

BY HAND	Add cooking oil, salt, and 2 cups whole-wheat flour to the mixture and
OR MIXER	beat with a wooden spoon or with the mixer flat beater until the flour
10 mins.	has been worked into the batter. Let stand for 3 minutes to allow the

BY HAND OR MIXER
10 mins.

Add cooking oil, salt, and 2 cups whole-wheat flour to the mixture and beat with a wooden spoon or with the mixer flat beater until the flour has been worked into the batter. Let stand for 3 minutes to allow the whole-wheat particles to fully absorb the moisture (and not suddenly become a dry cannonball) before adding more flour.

Alternate between the white and whole-wheat when adding small portions of flour to form a rough shaggy ball of dough.

KNEADING
8 mins.

Lift the dough to a floured work surface, or leave under the dough hook of the mixer. Knead by hand with a rhythmic push-turn-fold motion until the dough is smooth and elastic, about 8 minutes. Add sprinkles of flour to control the stickiness. Knead with the dough hook for 8 minutes as well.

BY PROCESSOR
5 mins.

Pulse to beat the bubbles out of the fermented batter. Add the oil, salt, and 2 cups whole-wheat flour. Pulse once or twice. With the machine running, add ¼ cup flour, alternating between the white and whole wheat, until a rough ball forms around the blade and the dough cleans the sides of the bowl.

KNEADING
50 secs.

Run the machine for 50 seconds to knead.

FIRST RISING
40 mins.

Grease the mixing bowl, drop in the dough, cover tightly with plastic wrap, and leave at room temperature to rise until double in bulk, about 40 minutes.

SHAPING
5 mins.

Divide the dough into 2 pieces and shape each into a ball. Press each ball into an oval roughly the length of a bread pan and fold in half lengthwise. Pinch the seam to seal, and place in the baking pan with the seam under.

SECOND RISING
35 mins.

Cover the pans with wax paper and leave to rise until the dough reaches the height of the pan, about 35 minutes.

PREHEAT

Preheat the oven to 400° 20 minutes before baking.

BAKING
400°
35 mins.

Place the pans in the oven and bake until golden brown with flecks of herbs over the crust, about 35 minutes. Turn one loaf from its pan and test for doneness by tapping the bottom with a forefinger. If it is hard and sounds hollow, the loaves are done. If not, return them to the oven for an additional 8 to 10 minutes.

(If using a convection oven, reduce heat 50°.)

FINAL STEP

Turn the loaves out onto a metal rack to cool before slicing. While still hot, brush the bread with the melted butter.

Mrs. Lloyd reheats the bread to serve warm. I like my slice cooled and spread with butter, but toasted for breakfast. A wonderful way to start a healthful day. Freezes well.

Sage and Celery Bread   [one large or two small loaves]

This loaf, a particular delight when the slice is toasted, is flavored with sage, nutmeg, and celery seeds and is easy to make.

INGREDIENTS

3 to 3½ cups bread or all-purpose flour, approximately
1 package dry yeast
1½ teaspoons salt
¼ cup nonfat dry milk
2 tablespoons sugar
½ teaspoon grated nutmeg
1 tablespoon chopped fresh sage, or 1 teaspoon dried
2 teaspoons celery seeds
1 cup hot water (120°–130°)
2 tablespoons shortening, room temperature
1 egg, room temperature
Butter, melted, or milk

BAKING SHEET,
PANS, TINS, OR
CASSEROLE

1 baking sheet, 9" pie pan, or 2-quart casserole, greased or Teflon; or two 6" brioche tins, greased

BY HAND
OR MIXER
15 mins.

In a mixing or mixer bowl measure 1½ cups flour and add the dry ingredients. Pour in the hot water and add the shortening and egg. Mix thoroughly, 150 strong strokes with a wooden spoon, or for 2 minutes with a mixer flat beater.

Gradually add additional flour, ¼ cup at a time, until the dough is formed into a rough, shaggy mass. If moisture persists in breaking through, add sprinkles of flour and work it into the dough.

KNEADING
8 mins.

Knead on a lightly floured work surface or under the dough hook until the dough is a smooth, elastic ball, about 8 minutes. In the early stages keep flour dusted on your fingers and on the work surface. The dough will grow responsive and alive under your hands, and will clean the sides of the bowl.

BY PROCESSOR 4 mins.	Attach the steel blade.
	Measure 1½ cups flour and all of the other ingredients, except the melted butter, into the work bowl. Pulse several times to blend. With the processor on, add the balance of the flour through the feed tube, ¼ cup at a time. After the flour absorbs the liquid, the ball of dough will clean the sides of the bowl as it whirls with the blade.
KNEADING 45 secs.	With the machine running, knead for 45 seconds.
FIRST RISING 1 hour	Return the dough to the bowl, pat with buttered fingers, cover the bowl tightly with plastic wrap, and leave at room temperature (72°) until the dough has doubled in volume, about 1 hour.
SHAPING 8 mins.	Punch down the dough and turn onto the floured work surface again. Knead for 30 seconds to press out the bubbles that have formed throughout the dough.
	For a large loaf, shape into a ball; place on the baking sheet, pie plate, or casserole. Push down to flatten somewhat. For 2 loaves, divide the dough and fashion each into a ball. Put each into a 6" brioche tin, and press the dough down into the corners.
SECOND RISING 50 mins.	Cover the loaf (loaves) with a length of wax paper. Let rise until double in bulk, about 50 minutes.
PREHEAT	Preheat the oven to 400° 20 minutes before baking.
BAKING 400° 30–35 mins.	Place in the oven, and bake for 30 to 35 minutes, or until a loaf tests done when tapped on the bottom with a forefinger. The sound will be hard and hollow.
	(If using a convection oven, reduce heat 50°.)
FINAL STEP	Place the bread on a wire rack to cool.
	While still hot, brush the loaf (loaves) with melted butter or milk to give the crust a velvet softness.

Pain de Provence

[one medium loaf or two slender *baguettes*]

The mixture of herbs—herbes de Provence—is the heart and soul of this delicately flavored loaf from southern France.

INGREDIENTS	*Herbes de Provence (fresh or dried):* ¹/₄ cup *each* savory, thyme, and fennel 2 teaspoons lavender flowers ¹/₂ cup basil *Dough:* 3 cups bread or all-purpose flour, approximately 1 package dry yeast 1 teaspoon salt ³/₄ cup hot water (120°–130°) ¹/₄ cup liqueur, Beauchant preferred, or substitute Grand Marnier or orange Curaçao
BAKING PAN OR SHEET	1 medium (8½"-x-4½") loaf pan or twin *baguette* pan, greased or Teflon, or 1 baking sheet, sprinkled with cornmeal
PREPARATION 5 mins.	In a jar combine the herbes de Provence ingredients. Since this is twice as much as is needed for this recipe, set aside ½ cup, if fresh, or 2 table- spoons, if dried, and freeze or store the balance. The mixture may also be found in many supermarkets or fine food shops.
BY HAND OR MIXER 5 mins.	Measure 1½ cups flour into a mixing or mixer bowl and stir in the yeast and salt. Pour in the hot water and the liqueur; beat into a smooth batter with a wooden spoon or a mixer flat beater. Stir in the herbes de Provence. Add flour, a small portion at a time, until the batter becomes a shaggy mass that can be lifted from the bowl to the work surface or placed under the dough hook.
KNEADING 8 mins.	This is a small amount of dough and easy to knead. Knead with a rhythmic push-turn-fold, using a dough blade or scraper to help in the work. Occasionally throw the dough down hard against the work sur- face to speed the kneading process. Knead by hand or with the dough hook for about 8 minutes, until the ball of dough is smooth and elas- tic. Add sprinkles of flour to control stickiness.

BY PROCESSOR
4 mins.
	Prepare the herbes, as above.
	    Attach the steel blade.
	    Place 1 cup flour, the yeast, salt, hot water, and liqueur in the work
	bowl. Pulse to mix. Add the herbes. Pulse. With the machine running,
	add flour, ¼ cup at a time, until the dough forms a ball and is carried
	around the bowl by the force of the blade. The dough will partially
	clean the sides when enough flour has been added.

KNEADING **50 secs.**	With the machine running, knead for 50 seconds.
FIRST RISING **45 mins.**	Place the dough in a greased bowl, cover with plastic wrap, and leave at room temperature until it has doubled in bulk, about 45 minutes.
SHAPING **5 mins.**	Punch down the dough and form a ball. Press the ball into an oval roughly the length of the bread pan. Fold in half lengthwise, pinch shut the seam, and place in the pan, seam down. If making *baguettes,* divide the dough into 2 pieces and roll into slender ropes about 12" long and 1½" thick. Place in a regular twin *baguette* pan or on a baking sheet.
SECOND RISING **35–40 mins.**	Cover the loaf (loaves) loosely with wax paper or plastic wrap and leave to double in volume, 35 to 40 minutes.
PREHEAT	Preheat the oven to 375° 20 minutes before baking.
BAKING **375°** **30 mins.**	Bake until the loaf is a light golden color, about 30 minutes. When the loaf seems done, turn the bread over and tap the bottom with a forefinger. It should be hard and sound hollow. (If using a convection oven, reduce heat 50°.)
FINAL STEP	Turn onto a metal rack and allow to cool before slicing. Serve with almost any spread. Delicious toasted.

Butter-Beer Batter Bread   [one medium loaf]

For this rich loaf a melted stick of butter is poured over the batter, which is baked with the butter slowly moving to the bottom—and then, out of the oven, turned upside down so the butter goes back through the loaf. From top to bottom and then bottom to top, the loaf becomes permeated with butter all along the way.

The recipe is from Georgia where self-rising flour is widely used, as it is in most of the South. The loaf carries with it the fine fragrance of fresh oregano leaves.

Barbara St. Amand grew the oregano in her Kennesaw, Georgia, garden and flew north with the recipe and the herb to bake test loaves in my kitchen.

INGREDIENTS	3 cups self-rising flour (see Note) ¹/₄ cup sugar ¹/₂ teaspoon salt 1 12-ounce can beer ¹/₂ cup finely chopped fresh oregano leaves ¹/₂ cup (1 stick) butter, melted

BAKING PAN	1 medium (8½"-x-4½") loaf pan, greased or Teflon
PREHEAT	Preheat the oven to 350°.
BY HAND OR MIXER 5 mins.	Measure the flour, sugar, and salt into a mixing or mixer bowl. Stir to blend. Pour in the beer and add the oregano leaves. With a wooden spoon or a mixer flat beater, work the batter for a few moments to be certain all of the ingredients are thoroughly blended.
BY PROCESSOR 3 mins.	Attach the steel blade.
	Place the flour, sugar, and salt in the work bowl. Pulse 2 times to mix the dry ingredients. With the machine running, pour in the beer and add the chopped oregano. Stop the machine when the ingredients are blended.
SHAPING 3 mins.	Pour or spoon the batter into the prepared loaf pan. Pour the warm butter carefully over the top of the batter. It will not be absorbed into the batter until baking begins.
BAKING 350° 45–50 mins.	Bake the loaf for 45 to 50 minutes, or until golden brown. Test with a toothpick or a metal skewer to determine if it is done. Inserted into the heart of the loaf, it will come out dry and clean.
	(If using a convection oven, reduce heat 50°.)
FINAL STEP	Remove the pan from the oven but don't turn out the loaf for 15 minutes and until somewhat cooled.

Hold a baking rack against the top of the loaf and quickly but carefully turn upside down so the top of the loaf is on the bottom. Put it aside to cool—and to allow the butter to drift back into the loaf.

Fingers may get buttery when a slice is eaten out of hand, but it's a small price to pay for something so rich, so good.

Note: If self-rising flour is not at hand, substitute an equal amount of all-purpose flour plus 1 tablespoon baking powder and an additional ½ teaspoon salt.

Minted Yogurt Bread   [one medium loaf]

Minted Yogurt Bread could claim a distant kinship with an American favorite, Dilly Casserole Bread, but as a new bread it can stand on its own good taste and texture. Rather than cottage cheese and dill, this loaf is made with yogurt and coarsely chopped fresh mint. The first bite is delicious, but the second and third are even more so as the palate senses that this is a brand-new taste.

It is unusual, too, because it is made without salt (the mint and lemon add enough piquant flavor), and sugar has been replaced with honey.

The recipe was created in a baking session in my kitchen by one of Atlanta's most imaginative cooks, Barbara St. Amand, who also writes about food and teaches cooking as well.

INGREDIENTS	2½ cups bread or all-purpose flour, approximately 1 package dry yeast 1 cup plain yogurt, room temperature 3 tablespoons coarsely chopped fresh mint Zest of 1 lemon 2 teaspoons honey 1 teaspoon butter, melted
BAKING PAN	1 medium (8½"-x-4½") loaf pan, greased or Teflon
BY HAND OR MIXER 15 mins.	In a mixing or mixer bowl measure 1 cup flour and the yeast. Stir to blend. Pour in the yogurt, mint, lemon zest, and honey. Beat together with a wooden spoon or mixer flat beater until thoroughly mixed into a batterlike dough. Add additional flour, ¼ cup at a time, first stirring with the spoon and then working with your hands, until a rough ball of dough has formed. This will be too thick for the beater blade, so attach the dough hook and stir with it.
KNEADING 8 mins.	If by hand, lift the ball of dough from the bowl and place on the work surface. Knead with your hands or the help of a dough blade until the dough is soft and elastic. If it is sticky, add sprinkles of flour. Knead by hand or with the dough hook in the mixer for 8 minutes.
BY PROCESSOR 5 mins.	Attach the steel blade. The order of adding the ingredients differs from above. Measure 2½ cups flour, the yeast, mint, and lemon zest into the processor work bowl. Turn off and on 3 times to mix. Add the honey and yogurt. Pulse several times to form a rough ball of dough that rides on the blade and cleans the sides of the bowl. Add small amounts of flour through the feed tube, if necessary, to develop the dough ball.
KNEADING 1 min.	Turn the machine on and knead for 1 minute. The dough may be somewhat sticky when turned out of the bowl, but a few sprinkles of flour as you shape the dough under your hands will make it less so.

FIRST RISING 1 hour	Place the dough in an oiled bowl, cover with plastic wrap, and let rise to double in bulk, about 1 hour.
SHAPING 3 mins.	Punch down the dough. Shape into a ball; flatten the dough into an oval roughly the length of the pan. Fold in half lengthwise, pinch the edges into a seam, and place seam down in the pan.
SECOND RISING 40 mins.	Cover the loaf pan with a length of wax paper and leave until it has doubled in volume, about 40 minutes. The center should rise slightly above the edge of the pan.
PREHEAT	Preheat the oven to 350° 20 minutes before baking.
BAKING 350° 35 mins.	Bake the loaf until it is light golden in color, and tests done when tapped on the bottom crust with a forefinger, about 35 minutes. It should sound hard and hollow. (If using a convection oven, reduce heat 50°.)
FINAL STEP	Remove from the pan immediately and brush with the melted butter. Cool on a rack before slicing. Particularly delicious toasted. Minty!

Pain Nord Africain au Coriandre
[three medium or two large loaves]
(North African Coriander Bread)

The French colonial influence on North Africa has been considerable, but Algiers and Morocco, in turn, have left their imprint on the French way of life, including its cuisine. A delicious example is this loaf flavored with coriander, treasured in the North African kitchen for its taste described by a famous French boulanger, *Cécile Chemin, as "slightly bitter and spicy yet sweet."*

Coriander is prized in many countries, including Mexico, China, Italy, and the United States. A plant known to man for many centuries, the Chinese thought it had the power to confer immortality. If that is so, then it comes as yet another dividend with this delicious bread.

INGREDIENTS	2 cups milk 6 tablespoons butter $1/2$ cup honey 7 cups bread or all-purpose flour, approximately 2 packages dry yeast 2 teaspoons salt 4 teaspoons ground coriander $1/4$ teaspoon *each* ground ginger and cloves

½ teaspoon ground cinnamon
2 eggs
1 tablespoon grated orange or lemon peel

BAKING PANS

3 medium (8½"-x-4½") or 2 large (9"-x-5") loaf pans, greased or Teflon

PREPARATION
6 mins.

In a saucepan pour the milk and add the butter and honey. Place over low heat for 5 or 6 minutes to take the chill off the milk and soften the butter (about 125°).

Measure 3 cups flour in a mixing or mixer bowl and add the dry ingredients. Stir them together well.

BY HAND
OR MIXER
10 mins.

Pour the milk mixture into the flour, add the eggs and citrus peel, and beat by hand 200 strokes, or for 3 minutes with the flat beater in a mixer.

Add flour, ½ cup at a time, until the dough is a shaggy mass.

KNEADING
8–10 mins.

While it may still be sticky, turn the dough onto a floured work surface and begin kneading. If sticky, add sprinkles of flour. Knead with a strong push-turn-fold motion until the dough is elastic and smooth, about 8 to 10 minutes. If under a dough hook, knead for 10 minutes. The dough should clean the sides of the bowl. If the dough sticks to the bowl, add sprinkles of flour. Soon it will become a compact ball.

BY PROCESSOR
3 mins.

Heat the butter mixture, as above.

Attach the plastic dough blade.

Pour 3 cups flour into the work bowl and add all of the dry ingredients. Pulse to mix. Add the eggs and citrus peel. Pour the butter-milk-honey mixture into the bowl. Turn on for 30 seconds before adding flour, ¼ cup at a time, through the feed tube. The dough mass will begin to clean the sides of the bowl and ride on top of the blade.

KNEADING
45 secs.

With the machine running, knead for 45 seconds.

FIRST RISING
50 mins.

Turn the dough out of the mixer or processor bowl to check consistency by hand. The dough should be smooth and elastic. Grease the bowl. Place the dough back in the bowl and cover tightly with plastic wrap. Leave at room temperature to double in volume, about 50 minutes.

SHAPING
20 mins.

Punch down the dough and divide into 2 or 3 pieces, according to the pans being used. Make into balls and leave under a cloth to rest for 10 minutes before shaping into loaves.

Press each ball into a flat oval, fold lengthwise, and pinch the seam together. Tuck in the ends to fit the pan and drop the dough into place. Press down with your fingers to flatten the dough and push it into the corners.

SECOND RISING
40 mins.

Cover the pans and leave at room temperature for the dough to rise about 1" above the sides of the pans, about 40 minutes.

PREHEAT

Preheat the oven to 375° 20 minutes before baking.

BAKING
375°
35 mins.

If desired, cut a tic-tac-toe or a diagonal pattern on the top of the loaves to give them your personal touch.

Place on the lower shelf of the oven and bake until a golden brown, about 35 minutes. Turn out a loaf and tap on the bottom with a forefinger. If there's a hard, hollow sound, the bread is done.

(If using a convection oven, reduce heat 50°. Place the loaves on the lower shelf. If the oven is too small for all the loaves at once, place the second or third loaf, covered, in the refrigerator until it can be baked. The bread will be done when it is a golden brown, about 25 minutes.)

FINAL STEP

Turn the loaves onto a metal rack to cool—and enjoy the wonderful aroma before slicing.

Pain au Cumin   [two medium loaves]
(Cumin Bread)

There is a special delight in making, baking, and eating this loaf spiced with cumin—the slightly pungent smell of the seed as it is being roasted and ground, and again when the loaf is baked. And then the warm, sharp taste of the first bite. Cumin is found most often in Mexican, Oriental, and Indian dishes, especially in curries and chili, so its appearance in bread is a surprise.

There is a surprising combination of ingredients to support the cumin—milk, honey, butter, orange juice, and two kinds of flour, white and whole wheat.

This recipe is translated from a fine French cookbook, Tous Les Pains, *by Cécile Chemin.*

INGREDIENTS	4 teaspoons cuminseed
	I cup milk
	½ cup honey
	6 tablespoons butter
	2 teaspoons salt
	I cup orange juice
	2½ cups whole-wheat flour
	2½ cups bread or all-purpose flour, approximately
	2 packages dry yeast

BAKING PANS 2 medium (6"-x-4") loaf pans, greased or Teflon

**PREPARATION
13 mins.**

In a small skillet or pan roast the cuminseed (to enhance their flavor) over medium heat until the seeds darken, about 6 minutes. Allow the seeds to cool and then grind in a mortar and pestle, a blender, or coffee grinder. Set aside. (The seeds can be used whole rather than ground, but much of their pungency will be lost and packaged ground cumin is a poor second choice.)

In a medium pan pour the milk and add the honey, butter, salt, orange juice, and ground cumin. Heat over low flame to warm the milk (about 125°), and soften the butter.

**BY HAND
OR MIXER
3 mins.**

In a large mixing or mixer bowl pour 1 cup each white and whole-wheat flours, and sprinkle on the yeast. Pour in the milk mixture and beat with a wooden spoon until the batter is smooth. If using a mixer, use the flat beater for about 3 minutes.

Add ½ cup each of the 2 flours, blend, and continue adding small portions of each until the dough is a shaggy mass that can be lifted out of the bowl and onto a floured work surface.

**KNEADING
10 mins.**

Knead the dough with a strong motion of the arms and hands, pushing down on the dough mass, and then folding and turning. Continue kneading until the dough is smooth and elastic, about 10 minutes. If under a dough hook, add no more flour once the dough cleans the sides of the bowl. Knead in the mixer for 10 minutes.

BY PROCESSOR
4 mins.

Roast and grind the cuminseed, as above.

The order of ingredients differs from above.

Attach the plastic dough blade.

Pour 1 cup each whole-wheat and white flours into the work bowl. Add the milk, honey, butter, salt, orange juice, yeast, and cumin. Pulse to blend all of the ingredients, wet and dry, into the flour.

Add additional flour, equal amounts each of white and whole wheat, pulsing after each addition to blend.

KNEADING
45 secs.

When the dough mass becomes a ball and rises to the top of the blade, knead for 45 seconds.

The dough will clear the sides of the bowl. If it doesn't, the dough is still too wet and needs more flour.

FIRST RISING
1 hour

Place the ball of dough in a greased bowl, cover with plastic wrap, and put aside at room temperature to double in volume, about 1 hour.

SECOND RISING
45 mins.

Turn back the plastic wrap, punch down the dough with your fingers, and turn over the ball in the bowl. Replace the plastic wrap and allow the dough to rise for a second time, about 45 minutes.

SHAPING
10 mins.

Turn the dough onto a floured work surface, cut in half, and shape into balls. Let them rest for 5 minutes.

To shape a loaf, press each ball into a flat oval, roughly the length of the baking pan. Fold the oval in half, pinch the seam tightly to seal, tuck under the ends, and place in the pan, seam down.

THIRD RISING
30 mins.

Cover the pans with wax or parchment paper, and leave at room temperature until the dough rises above the edges of the pans about ½", about 30 minutes.

PREHEAT

Preheat the oven to 375° 20 minutes before baking.

BAKING
375°
35 mins.

Place the pans on the middle shelf of the oven and bake until nicely browned, about 35 minutes. Turn one loaf from its pan and tap the bottom. It is done if the crust has a hollow sound. Midway during baking, turn the loaves end for end to bake uniformly.

(If using a convection oven, reduce heat 50°.)

FINAL STEP

All through the preparation and baking there has been a delicate odor of cumin in the kitchen. Place the loaves on a metal rack to cool. When the loaves have cooled, it is time to taste-test a slice.

Excellent toasted. Freezes well.

Pain d'Epices   [two small loaves]

Pain d'Epices is a traditional French spice bread made with honey and a mixture of rye and white flours. There are 4 spices, a touch of rum, and almonds, currants, and orange rind.

A fine bread to serve thinly sliced with coffee or tea or a glass of wine, Pain d'Epices improves with age, so don't plan to slice it for at least 2 or 3 days—despite the temptation to do so.

INGREDIENTS

1 cup honey
1 cup hot water (120–130°)
¼ cup sugar
Pinch of salt
2 teaspoons baking soda
1 teaspoon baking powder
¼ cup rum or water
1½ teaspoons ground aniseed
1 teaspoon ground cinnamon
¾ teaspoon ground ginger
¼ teaspoon ground cloves
2 cups rye flour
1½ cups unbleached or all-purpose flour
1 teaspoon grated orange rind
⅔ cup chopped almonds
½ cup currants or raisins (if the latter, chop fine)

BAKING PANS

2 small (7"-x-3") loaf pans, greased or Teflon, bottom and sides lined with buttered wax paper

PREHEAT

Preheat the oven to 400°.

**BY HAND
23 mins.**

In a large bowl pour the hot water over the honey. Add the sugar, salt, baking soda, and baking powder. Stir to dissolve and blend.

Pour in the rum or water, and add the spices. Measure in 1 cup each rye and white flours. Stir together. When the ingredients are blended, add 1 additional cup rye and ½ cup white flour. The batter will be thick but smooth.

Add the orange rind, almonds, and currants. Stir 25 strokes to blend thoroughly.

With a large spoon and rubber scraper, fill the pans three-quarters full. If the dough sticks to the scraper, dip in water. Wet fingers are also good to push the dough into the corners of the pans.

BAKING	Place the loaves on the middle shelf. After 10 minutes reduce heat to
400°	350°, and bake for an additional 50 minutes. The loaves will rise about
10 mins.	1" above the sides of the pans. They will be a deep brown when baked,
350°	with a large crevice running the length of each loaf, which is desirable.
50 mins.	Test for doneness with a cake pin or metal skewer thrust into the center of a loaf. If it comes out clean and dry, the bread is done.

(If using a convection oven, reduce heat 50° for each bake period.)

FINAL STEP	Place the pans on a metal rack. Turn each loaf on its side and gently tug free with a wax paper tab. When the loaves have completely cooled, wrap in aluminum foil or place in a plastic bag to age for several days.

This bread keeps exceptionally well and is an ideal gift for sending to friends overseas, on the other coast, or around the corner.

Swedish Cardamom Braid   [one plump loaf]

Three strands of dough—rich with butter, eggs, raisins, and cardamom—are woven and baked into a handsome plump loaf. Braided bread has a crafted look that delights the eye, and this loaf in particular has the taste to delight the palate as well.

INGREDIENTS	3 cups bread or all-purpose flour, approximately
	1 package dry yeast
	$1/4$ cup sugar
	$1/2$ teaspoon salt
	$1/4$ cup nonfat dry milk
	$1/2$ cup hot water (120°–130°)
	$3/4$ cup (1 $1/2$ sticks) butter, softened at room temperature
	1 egg, room temperature
	1 teaspoon ground cardamom
	$1/3$ cup light or dark raisins
	1 egg white, slightly beaten with 2 tablespoons sugar

BAKING SHEET	1 large baking sheet, greased or Teflon (or 2 smaller sheets for convection ovens)

BY HAND OR MIXER 15 mins.	In a mixing or mixer bowl measure 1 cup flour and add the dry ingredients. Blend with a wooden spoon. Pour in the hot water and stir with 25 strong strokes, or for 2 minutes with the mixer flat beater.

Cut the soft butter into several pieces and drop into the batterlike dough. Add the egg, cardamom, and raisins.

Stir in additional flour, ¼ cup at a time, first with the spoon and then by hand, or with the beater and then the dough hook. The dough will form a rough mass and clean the sides of the bowl. Because of the large amount of shortening, the dough will not be sticky. It will be firm but not stiff.

KNEADING
8 mins.

Turn the dough out onto a lightly floured work surface. With a strong push-turn-fold action, knead until the dough is smooth and elastic, for about 8 minutes. Or knead in the mixer under the dough hook for the same length of time.

BY PROCESSOR
5 mins.

Attach the steel blade.

Measure 1 cup flour into the work bowl and add the dry ingredients. Pulse to blend. Pour in the hot water. Pulse several times until the batter is smooth. Drop in the butter, egg, and cardamom and with the machine running add flour, ¼ cup at a time, until the batter becomes a shaggy, rough ball of dough carried around the bowl by the force of the blade.

KNEADING
50 secs.

Knead for 50 seconds with the machine running.

If the dough clings to the sides of the bowl, add a few sprinkles of flour. The raisins may be added to the dough the last few seconds of the kneading process but they will be cut into small bits by the blade. Or the raisins can be worked into the dough after the first rising.

FIRST RISING
1 hour

Return the dough to the bowl (it need not be greased again because of the high butter content of the dough). Cover the bowl with plastic wrap and put aside at room temperature until the dough has doubled in volume, about 1 hour.

SHAPING
20 mins.

Punch down the dough and turn it onto a floured work surface. Knead briefly to work out the bubbles.

Divide the dough into 3 equal parts. Roll each part under your palms into a strand about 14" long. Beginning in the middle of the strands, braid loosely to one end, reverse the loaf, and again braid from the middle to the end. Pinch the ends closed. Place on the baking sheet.

SECOND RISING
1 hour

Cover the dough with wax paper and leave until doubled in bulk and puffy to the touch, about 1 hour.

PREHEAT

Preheat the oven to 350° 20 minutes before baking.

BAKING
350°
45 mins.

Before baking, brush the braid with the egg white glaze.

Bake until the crust is a rich brown, about 45 minutes. A wooden toothpick or metal skewer inserted in the center of the loaf should come out clean and dry.

(If using a convection oven, reduce heat 40°.)

FINAL STEP

Remove the braid from the oven. Use a metal spatula to lift the braid off the baking sheet, because the hot loaf is somewhat fragile and might break. Cool on a wire rack.

This bread keeps well, toasts beautifully (but must be watched), freezes well, and overall, is a wholly satisfying baking experience.

Orange-Cinnamon Swirl Bread   [two medium loaves]

Sugar and spice and everything that's nice is what this loaf is made of—cinnamon, egg, butter, orange juice, and grated orange peel.

INGREDIENTS

6 cups bread or all-purpose flour, approximately
2 packages dry yeast
$1/3$ cup nonfat dry milk
$1/2$ cup granulated sugar
$1 1/2$ teaspoons salt
$1 1/4$ cups hot water (120°–130°)
$1/4$ cup ($1/2$ stick) butter, room temperature
1 tablespoon grated orange peel
$3/4$ cup orange juice
1 egg, room temperature
1 tablespoon ground cinnamon mixed with $1/2$ cup sugar
2 teaspoons water

Frosting:
1 cup confectioners' sugar
1 teaspoon grated orange peel
4 teaspoons orange juice

BAKING PANS

2 medium (8"-x-4") loaf pans, greased or Teflon

BY HAND
OR MIXER
15 mins.

Measure 2 cups flour into a large mixing or mixer bowl and add the dry ingredients. Pour in the hot water and stir vigorously to blend into a thin batter. Add the butter, orange peel, orange juice, and egg.

Add flour, ¼ cup at a time, stirring with strong strokes after each addition until the dough becomes a rough shaggy mass that can be turned out onto a floured work surface. Or use the mixer flat beater until the dough gets too thick to beat, and then attach the dough hook.

KNEADING
8 mins.

Knead for 8 minutes by hand or with the dough hook. Add a bit more flour if the moisture works through the surface and sticks to the work counter or the sides of the mixer bowl.

BY PROCESSOR
6 mins.

Attach the plastic dough blade.

Measure 2 cups flour into the work bowl and add the dry ingredients. Pulse to blend. Pour in the hot water and turn on the machine to form a thin batter. Turn off and add the butter, orange peel, juice, and egg.

With the machine running, add flour, ¼ cup at a time, until a ball of dough forms and is carried around the bowl by the blade. The moving dough will clean the sides of the bowl.

KNEADING
45 secs.

With the machine running, knead for 45 seconds.

If the dough is somewhat sticky when turned from the work bowl, sprinkle with flour and knead for a moment or two.

FIRST RISING
1 hour

Place the dough in a greased bowl, turning the dough to be certain it is filmed on all sides. Cover the bowl tightly with plastic wrap and put aside until the dough has doubled in bulk, 1 hour.

SHAPING
25 mins.

Fold back the plastic wrap and punch down the dough. Turn it onto the floured work surface and divide into 2 pieces. Cover with wax paper and let rest for 10 minutes.

Roll each piece into a 15"-x-7" rectangle. Each will be about ½" thick. Spread each piece with the cinnamon-sugar mixture. Sprinkle each with 1 teaspoon water and smooth with a spoon or spatula. Roll from the narrow side. Seal the edges securely by pinching tightly along the seams. Tuck in the ends and place seam down in the pans.

SECOND RISING
45 mins.

Cover the pans with wax paper and let stand until the dough has doubled in bulk, about 45 minutes.

PREHEAT

Preheat the oven to 375° 20 minutes before baking.

BAKING
375°
10 mins.
325°
30 mins.

Bake for 10 minutes then reduce heat to 325°, and bake for 30 minutes more, or until the loaves are nicely browned and test done when tapped on the bottom with a forefinger. The sound will be hard and hollow.

(If using a convection oven, reduce heat 50° for first bake period.)

FINAL STEP

Remove the bread from the oven. Turn out onto a metal rack to cool.

Blend together the frosting ingredients and when the loaves have cooled, spread over the top of the bread.

Good warm, and fine toasted.

Rosemary-Garlic Bread   [two medium loaves]

It was a day for marvelous aromas and refreshingly new tastes, when 8 members of the Evansville Herb Society came to my kitchen to teach and be taught—they, herbs; I, breads. One of many outstanding recipes developed by us that day was this loaf of Rosemary-Garlic Bread. Not mentioned in the name is another herb—parsley.

Mary M. Lovett, who crosses the Ohio River from Owensboro, Kentucky, to Evansville, Indiana, to meet with the society, brought this recipe.

INGREDIENTS

3 cups whole-wheat flour

2¹/₂ cups bread or unbleached flour, approximately

2 packages dry yeast

2 teaspoons salt

2 teaspoons freshly ground black pepper

2 cups hot water (120°–130°)

¹/₄ cup olive oil

3 garlic cloves, finely minced

¹/₄ cup finely chopped fresh parsley

3 tablespoons minced fresh rosemary (or 1 tablespoon dried)

BAKING PANS

2 medium (8"-x-4") bread pans, greased or Teflon

BY HAND
OR MIXER
12 mins.

In a mixing or mixer bowl measure 1 cup each whole-wheat and white flours. Stir in the yeast, salt, and black pepper and blend. Add the hot water and olive oil, and beat 50 strong strokes with a wooden spoon, or for 2 minutes with the mixer flat beater, until the batter is smooth.

Stir in the herbs. Mix well. Measure in 2 cups whole-wheat flour, and add the balance of the white flour, ¼ cup at a time, until the batter becomes dough and forms a rough, shaggy mass.

KNEADING
8 mins.

Knead the dough by hand or with a mixer dough hook. If by hand, use a rhythmic push-turn-fold motion, and occasionally lift the dough from the table and crash it down onto the work surface. A metal dough blade, as an extension of the hand, is useful in lifting and turning the dough. Knead for about 8 minutes by hand or with the dough hook.

BY PROCESSOR
5 mins.

Attach the plastic dough blade.

Add to the work bowl 1 cup each whole-wheat and white flours, the yeast, salt, and pepper. Add the liquids and herbs. Pulse to blend and to form a light batter. With the machine running, add flour, first whole-wheat and then white, about ¼ cup at a time. Stop the machine once or twice to scrape flour from the bottom edge of the bowl.

KNEADING
45 secs.

When the dough forms a rough mass and rides with the blade, cleaning the sides of the bowl, leave the machine on to knead for 45 seconds.

FIRST RISING
30–60 mins.

Drop the dough into a greased bowl and cover tightly with plastic wrap. Put either in a warm place (90°) for 30 minutes, until doubled in bulk, or leave at room temperature for about 1 hour.

SHAPING
10 mins.

Punch down the dough. Divide in half. Roll each half into a ball and put aside to rest for 5 minutes.

Press each ball into an oval, roughly the length of the pan. Fold lengthwise, press the seam together, and place in the prepared pan, seam down.

SECOND RISING
1 hour

Cover the pans with wax paper and leave to rise until double in bulk, about 1 hour. The dough will reach the height of the pan.

PREHEAT

Preheat the oven to 400° 20 minutes before baking.

BAKING
400°
35–40 mins.

Uncover and place on the middle shelf of the oven. Bake until the loaf is a deep brown and crusty, 35 to 40 minutes. Turn one loaf from its pan and tap the bottom crust with your forefinger. The bread is done if it sounds hollow and hard.

(If using a convection oven, reduce heat 50°.)

FINAL STEP

Turn the loaves onto a metal rack to cool before slicing.

The bread is delicious toasted, keeps well at room temperature for several days, and can be held frozen for a year at 0°.

FRUIT AND NUT BREADS

FRUIT AND NUTS are made for each other. They are admirable companions, especially in the kitchen. Here, they are teamed in half of the thirty recipes in this chapter, and stand alone in the others. For instance, Pain Allemand aux Fruits (German Fruit Bread) is made with prunes, apricots, figs, raisins, and orange and lemon juices but no nuts, while German Raisin Bread combines the fruit with almonds.

There are thirteen kinds of fruit and four kinds of nuts among the ingredients in this chapter.

Hana Banana–Nut Loaf   [one medium loaf]

Hana, on the island of Maui in the Hawaiian Islands, is at the other end of an incredibly tortuous 52.5-mile road—crossing 57 narrow bridges—built in 1910 for horse-drawn wagons. (A T-shirt—"I Survived the Road to Hana"—celebrates the drive.) Much of it is less than 2 lanes wide. It is the last remote place in Hawaii where one can go to get away from hordes of tourists and yet arrive at an outstanding hotel, the Hana-Maui, hedged on one side by the Pacific and the other by a 15,000-acre cattle ranch.

The road is through rain forests, across volcanic slopes, over open range, and along beaches of black and gold sand and lava cliffs glistening with ocean spray.

Four hours later, at the end of the road, I found April Sue Noelani Tanaka Burns, whose marvelous smile was an Aloha warmer than the word. Noelani, which means "heavenly mist," was twenty-five when she took over from her mother as head baker at the Hana-Maui in 1984. Her banana-nut bread has become famous with hotel guests, who carry home as gifts as many loaves as they eat while in residence. Noelani's recipe calls for the expensive Hawaiian nut, the macadamia, but I have used almonds with equal success. Also, I have added (as an option) shredded coconut because I like the flavor it gives and it reminds me of the stately coconut palms along the Hana coast.

INGREDIENTS

6 tablespoons (³/₄ stick) butter, room temperature
¹/₃ cup sugar
2 eggs, room temperature
1¹/₂ cups mashed bananas
1¹/₂ cups all-purpose flour
1 teaspoon baking soda
¹/₂ teaspoon baking powder
¹/₄ teaspoon *each* salt and vanilla extract
1 cup coarsely broken macadamia nuts
¹/₂ cup shredded coconut (optional)

BAKING PAN

1 medium (8"-x-4") baking pan, greased or Teflon, sides and bottom lined with buttered wax paper

PREHEAT

Preheat the oven to 350°.

BY HAND
OR MIXER
12 mins.

In a mixing or mixer bowl cream the butter and sugar together and add the eggs, one at a time. Mix in the banana puree. This can be done by hand or with a mixer flat beater. Stir in 1 cup flour and add the baking soda, baking powder, salt, and vanilla extract. Stir to blend and add the remaining ½ cup flour. Add the broken nuts and coconut, if desired.

Stir only to blend the ingredients thoroughly and moisten the flour. Don't overstir or the loaf will be tough.

BY PROCESSOR
8 mins.

Attach the steel blade.

The sequence for preparing the ingredients differs from above.

Put the nuts in the work bowl; pulse only twice. Add the flour, baking soda, baking powder, and salt. Pulse to blend. Remove and reserve the mixture.

Put the eggs and sugar in the work bowl and process to mix, about 30 seconds. Add the butter and pulse several times to mix thoroughly with the eggs and sugar. Add the bananas and vanilla extract. Pulse to mix. Add the flour-nut mixture, drop in the coconut, and pulse only until the dry ingredients disappear. Don't overmix.

SHAPING
3 mins.

Pour and spoon the mixture into the prepared pan. Level with the spatula.

BAKING 350° I hour	Place the pan on the middle shelf of the moderate oven and bake for about 1 hour, or until dark brown and a cake tester inserted in the center comes out clean. (If using a convection oven, reduce heat 50°.)
FINAL STEP	Gently lay the loaf on its side on a metal cooling rack and tug at the ends of the wax paper to slip the loaf from the pan. Allow the bread to cool before cutting.

Blueberry-Pecan Bread   [one large or two small loaves]

A family blueberry picker visits a pick-it-yourself farm in northern Indiana to bring me fresh berries for this loaf, which also includes pecans, orange juice, orange rind, and butter. Huckleberries may be substituted. Also, I have used frozen blueberries with excellent results.

*   I do not use the food processor in this recipe because the blade cuts the berries into bits.*

INGREDIENTS	2 cups bread or all-purpose flour ²/₃ cup sugar I ¹/₂ teaspoons baking powder ¹/₂ teaspoon *each* baking soda and salt Juice and grated rind of I orange 2 tablespoons butter, room temperature ¹/₂ cup boiling water, approximately I cup fresh blueberries or huckleberries, washed and dried (or frozen berries, thawed) I cup chopped pecans
BAKING PAN(S)	1 large (9"-x-5") or 2 small (7"-x-3") loaf pans, greased or Teflon, lined with buttered wax paper
PREHEAT	Preheat the oven to 350°.
BY HAND OR MIXER 23 mins.	In a large mixing or mixer bowl sift together 1¾ cups flour, and the dry ingredients. In a measuring cup pour the juice and orange rind and add the butter. Add boiling water sufficient to make ¾ cup. By hand or with the mixer flat beater stir the liquid into the dry ingredients, blending well.

In a separate bowl combine the berries, pecans, and ¼ cup flour. Add this to the batter, taking care not to mash the berries.

Pour or spoon the batter into the prepared pan or pans.

BAKING
350°
1 hour

Place the pans in the oven and bake until the bread is a light brown and tests done when a wooden toothpick inserted in the loaf comes out clean and dry.

(If using a convection oven, reduce heat 50°.)

FINAL STEP

Remove the bread from the oven. Turn the pan on its side; carefully pull the loaf out by gently tugging on the wax paper lining. Cool on a metal rack.

Chopped Apple Bread   [two medium loaves]

Chopped Apple Bread is a hodgepodge of dough, apples, and nuts—a wonderful mix that produces a handsome and delicious loaf that makes marvelous toast. When everything is chopped in pieces spread before you on the table you might wonder how it can produce something as orderly as a loaf of bread. But it does.

I found the recipe first at Mrs. London's Bakeshop in Saratoga Springs, New York, and then had its goodness confirmed in the Jaarsma Bakery in Pella, Iowa. The only difference is that one version is made with pecans and the other, walnuts. In Pella this is called "Dutch Apple-Pecan."

The apple mixture will become part of the dough after the first rise.

INGREDIENTS

Dough:
6½ to 7 cups bread or all-purpose flour, approximately
2 packages dry yeast
1 tablespoon salt
½ cup dry milk
2½ cups hot water (120°–130°)
3 tablespoons shortening

Apple Mix:
2 cups apples, chopped into ¾-inch cubes
2 eggs, lightly beaten
½ cup walnuts or pecans, chopped into ½" (pea-size) pieces
⅓ cup brown sugar
1 tablespoon ground cinnamon

BAKING PANS	2 medium (8"-x-4") loaf pans, greased or Teflon, lined with buttered wax or parchment paper
BY HAND OR MIXER 10 mins.	In a mixing or mixer bowl combine 3 cups flour with the dry ingredients. Pour in the hot water and stir in the shortening. With strong strokes, beat the batter 100 times by hand, or for 2 minutes with the dough hook in the mixer. Add flour, ½ cup at a time, to make a dough that can be lifted from the bowl and placed on the work surface, or lift in the mixer bowl under the dough hook.
KNEADING 10 mins.	If by hand, turn the dough onto the work surface and knead with a push-turn-fold rhythm. The dough will become elastic and smooth. If it is sticky, add sprinkles of flour. If under the hook, the dough will form a ball around the dough hook as it revolves. Knead for 10 minutes. If soft dough clings to the bottom third of the bowl, add flour. Ideally, there should be a spot of dough, about the size of a 50-cent piece, adhered to the bottom, which indicates that the dough is neither too wet nor too dry.
BY PROCESSOR 5 mins.	Attach the plastic dough blade. Measure 4 cups flour into the work bowl and add the dry ingredients. Pulse to blend. With the machine running, pour in hot water sufficient to make a heavy, moist batter. Drop in the shortening. Add the balance of the water. Add flour, ¼ cup at a time, to create a mass that cleans the sides of the bowl and spins with the blade. Add more flour if necessary.
KNEADING 50 secs.	Knead with the processor running for 50 seconds. The dough may be slightly sticky when turned from the bowl, but a few sprinkles of flour will bring it under control.
FIRST RISING 1 hour	Place the dough in a greased bowl, cover tightly with plastic wrap, and set aside to double in volume, about 1 hour.
SHAPING 12 mins.	Punch down the dough and place it on the floured work surface. Roll and press the dough into an 18" square, about ½" thick. Let the dough rest for a few moments. *Note:* The following should be done on a chopping board to protect the work surface. Spread the chopped apples uniformly over the surface of the dough. Pour the beaten eggs over the apples. Add the nuts. Sprinkle on the sugar and cinnamon.

Fold the dough into a package. This will be the last time there will be a semblance of order in preparing the bread.

Using a dough scraper or large knife, chop the dough with random blows into pieces about 1" in size. Uniformity is of no great consequence.

When the apple dough has been well chopped, toss or scoop the pieces into the prepared loaf pans, two-thirds full.

SECOND RISING 40 mins.	Cover the pans with wax or parchment paper and put aside to rise slightly above the edge, about 40 minutes.
PREHEAT	Preheat the oven to 375° 20 minutes before baking.
BAKING 375° 45 mins.	Place in the oven and bake until rich golden brown, about 45 minutes. Test for doneness with a cake testing pin. If it comes out clean and dry, the bread is done. (If using a convection oven, reduce heat 50°.)
FINAL STEP	Turn out the hot bread with care onto a metal rack to cool. It will be somewhat fragile while hot.

Lemon-Nut Bread   [one medium loaf]

Flavored with lemon and nuts, this loaf is rich and moist. A thick mixture of lemon juice and sugar is laid on the crust with a spoon when the loaf comes from the oven. The crust is pricked with a metal skewer or wooden toothpick and the syrup spooned on.

INGREDIENTS	1/2 cup shortening 1 3/4 cups sugar 2 eggs, room temperature, lightly beaten 1 1/4 cups bread or all-purpose flour 2 teaspoons baking powder 1/4 teaspoon salt 1/2 cup milk, room temperature 1/2 cup finely chopped walnuts Juice and grated rind of 1 lemon
BAKING PAN	1 medium (8"-x-4") loaf pan, greased or Teflon, lined with greased wax paper
PREHEAT	Preheat the oven to 350°.

BY HAND
OR MIXER
12 mins.

In a large mixing or mixer bowl cream together the shortening and 1 cup sugar. Add the eggs. On a length of wax paper sift together the flour, baking powder, and salt, and spoon this into the egg mixture, alternately with the milk. Add the walnuts and grated rind. Blend thoroughly—but only enough to mix well. Overworking the batter will toughen it.

BY PROCESSOR
5 mins.

Attach the steel blade.

Cream the shortening and 1 cup sugar in the work bowl with 4 or 5 pulses. Add the eggs and pulse. On a length of wax paper, sift together the flour, baking powder, and salt. Turn on the processor and spoon the flour through the feed tube, alternately with the milk. Stop the machine, uncover, and add the walnuts and lemon rind. Replace the cover and pulse 5 or 6 times to blend—but only to mix. No kneading.

SHAPING
3 mins.

Pour or spoon the heavy batter (or dough) into the prepared pan. Push the batter into the corners with a spatula or spoon.

BAKING
350°
1 hour

Bake on the middle shelf of the oven for an hour, until light golden in color. Pierce the loaf with a metal skewer. If it comes out clean and dry, the loaf is done. (Keep skewer handy for the crust-piercing procedure to follow.)

(If using a convection oven, reduce heat 50°.)

FINAL STEP

Remove the bread from the oven but leave in the pan. Prick the top with 20 or 30 holes, using a wooden pick or a metal skewer.

Mix together ¾ cup sugar and the lemon juice. Spoon it on the bread. If there is a long break in the crust (and there should be) be sure to coat this well. Slowly the crust will absorb all of the lemon mixture.

Allow the loaf to stand for 15 minutes, and then carefully turn it on its side and remove from the pan. Handle gingerly since quick breads can be fragile while warm.

Cool completely before serving at a gala breakfast, brunch, teatime, or as a late afternoon special snack.

Coconut-Banana Bread   [one large loaf]

This loaf has the smell of toasted coconut and the taste of banana. The coconut flakes are toasted in the oven before they are mixed with the banana. Later, in the oven, as part of the dough, the flakes will bake a deep brown against the lighter brown crust. It is a moist loaf that is fine for tea sandwiches—or to serve on any special occasion.

INGREDIENTS	1 cup flaked coconut
	1/4 cup (1/2 stick) butter or margarine, room temperature
	2/3 cup sugar
	2 eggs, room temperature
	3 tablespoons milk
	1 teaspoon lemon juice
	1/2 teaspoon almond extract
	2 cups sifted all-purpose flour
	1 teaspoon baking powder
	1/2 teaspoon *each* baking soda and salt
	1 cup mashed ripe bananas (about 2 medium bananas)

BAKING PAN

1 large (9"-x-5") loaf pan, greased or Teflon, lined with greased wax paper cut to size

PREPARATION
25 mins.

Toast the coconut on a baking sheet in a moderate oven (350°) until lightly browned, 15 minutes. Stir the flakes occasionally and keep a watchful eye on them so they don't burn. Remove from the oven and set aside to cool. Leave the oven on.

BY HAND
OR MIXER
5 mins.

In a large mixing or mixer bowl fitted with the flat beater cream together the butter and sugar. Beat in the eggs, one at a time. Stir in the milk, lemon juice, and almond extract. Sift the flour again into the mixing bowl with the baking powder, baking soda, and salt. Blend thoroughly. Work the bananas into the mixture and gently fold in the toasted coconut. (Reserve a large pinch of coconut to sprinkle on the top of the loaf.)

BY PROCESSOR
5 mins.

Toast the coconut, as above.
    Attach the steel blade.
    The sequence of adding ingredients varies from above.
    Process the bananas into a liquid in the work bowl. Stop the machine, remove the cover, and add the butter, sugar, eggs, milk, lemon juice, and almond extract. Pulse to blend together. Add the sifted flour, baking powder, baking soda, and salt. Add the coconut. Again pulse only to mix the ingredients.

SHAPING
5 mins.

Pour the mixture into a loaf pan, pushing the dough into the corners and leveling the top with a rubber scraper.

BAKING
350°
1 hour

Bake until light brown, 1 hour. A metal skewer or wooden toothpick inserted in the center of the loaf should come out clean.
    (If using a convection oven, reduce heat 40°.)

FINAL STEP

Remove the bread from the oven. Let the loaf cool in the pan for about 10 minutes before carefully turning it out onto a wire rack. Allow it to cool completely before serving.

Nubby Peanut Loaf   [one medium loaf]

For kids and folks who love peanuts in a whole-wheat loaf, this is for them— chopped peanuts scattered liberally throughout the dough. Serve it fresh from the oven, or for sandwiches—or toasted for breakfast.

INGREDIENTS

1 1/2 cups whole-wheat flour
1 package dry yeast
1/3 cup nonfat dry milk
3 tablespoons sugar
1 teaspoon salt
1 cup hot water (120°–130°)
2 tablespoons shortening
1 egg, room temperature
3/4 cup finely chopped salted peanuts
1 1/2 to 2 cups all-purpose flour, approximately

BAKING PAN

1 medium (8"-x-4") baking pan, greased or Teflon

BY HAND
OR MIXER
8 mins.

Measure the whole-wheat flour into a mixing or mixer bowl and add the dry ingredients. Stir together with either a spoon or flat beater at low speed. Add the water and shortening. Beat for 30 seconds at low speed, and add the egg and chopped peanuts.

Stir in sufficient white flour to make a thick batter and beat at medium speed, or by hand, for 3 minutes. Replace the flat beater with the dough hook. Gradually add additional flour, first by spoon and then by hand, until a rough mass has formed.

KNEADING
10 mins.

If by hand, turn the dough out onto a lightly floured work surface and with a push-turn-fold motion knead the dough until smooth and elastic. If using a mixer, knead until the dough gathers around the dough hook and cleans the sides of the bowl. Add liberal sprinkles of flour if the dough is wet and won't form a ball. Knead for 10 minutes.

BY PROCESSOR
5 mins.

Attach the plastic dough blade.

The sequence of adding ingredients differs slightly from above.

Measure the whole-wheat and 1 cup white flour into the work bowl and add the dry ingredients. With the processor on, pour the hot water through the feed tube, and add the shortening, egg, and peanuts. The batter will be quite thick.

Continue processing and add flour to make a rough mass—moist but not wet—that rides on the blade and cleans the bowl.

KNEADING 1 min.	With the machine running, knead the dough for 1 minute.
FIRST RISING 1 hour	Place the dough in a greased bowl, cover tightly with plastic wrap, and leave at room temperature until it has doubled in volume, about 1 hour.
SHAPING 5 mins.	Punch down the dough and turn out onto a floured work surface. Shape into a loaf by pressing it into a flat oval, folding in half, pinching the seam together tightly, and placing in the bread pan, seam down.
SECOND RISING 45 mins.	Cover the pan with wax paper and leave until the center of the dough is slightly above the top of the pan, 45 minutes.
PREHEAT	Preheat the oven to 400° 20 minutes before baking.
BAKING 400° 40 mins.	Place the loaf in the oven and bake for 40 minutes, until a rich brown. When a wooden pick inserted in the loaf comes out clean and dry, the bread is done. If the crust browns too quickly in the last half of the bake period, cover the loaf with foil or brown paper. (If using a convection oven, reduce heat 50°.)
FINAL STEP	Remove the bread from the oven. Turn the loaf out of the pan onto a metal rack to cool before slicing.

Lemon Rich Tea Loaf   [one large or two small loaves]

This bread is surprisingly robust in its outward appearance despite its genteel name. It is a fat loaf with a deep brown crust. Inside, the egg-rich bread is finely textured and delicately flavored with lemon.

INGREDIENTS
3/4 cup milk, scalded
1/4 cup sugar
1/4 cup (1/2 stick) butter, room temperature
1 egg, room temperature
2 egg yolks, room temperature
1 package dry yeast
1/2 teaspoon salt
1 1/2 teaspoons grated lemon peel
1/4 teaspoon lemon extract
3 cups bread or all-purpose flour, approximately

BAKING PAN	1 large (9"-x-5") or 2 small (7"-x-3") loaf pans, greased or Teflon
BY HAND OR MIXER 20 mins.	Pour the hot milk into a large mixing or mixer bowl and add the sugar and butter. Stir to melt and allow to cool to lukewarm.

BAKING PAN

1 large (9"-x-5") or 2 small (7"-x-3") loaf pans, greased or Teflon

BY HAND
OR MIXER
20 mins.

Pour the hot milk into a large mixing or mixer bowl and add the sugar and butter. Stir to melt and allow to cool to lukewarm.

Beat the egg and yolks together in a small bowl. Stir the egg mixture and yeast into the milk in the mixing bowl. Add the salt, lemon peel, and extract.

Gradually stir in the flour by hand or with the flat beater in the mixer to make a soft dough. Work the dough with your hands or under the dough hook until it is smooth.

There is no other kneading. Because of the butter, this dough will not be sticky even though it is quite soft and somewhat moist.

BY PROCESSOR
5 mins.

Attach the steel blade.

The sequence of adding ingredients differs from above.

Measure 1½ cups flour into the work bowl and add the yeast, sugar, and salt. Pulse to blend. In a separate bowl pour the hot milk and add the butter. Stir to melt and allow to cool. When lukewarm, pour the mixture into the flour, and pulse 3 or 4 times.

In a separate bowl beat together the egg and yolks and stir in the grated lemon peel and extract. With the machine running, pour the egg mixture through the feed tube into the work bowl.

Add flour, ¼ cup at a time, through the feed tube until a soft mass forms on the whirling blade. At the same time it will clean the sides of the bowl. Stop the machine so the dough is not unnecessarily worked as one would do if kneading. Turn the dough from the bowl. Sprinkles of flour will make it easy to shape into a ball.

FIRST RISING
1¼ hours

Place the ball of dough in a greased bowl, cover tightly with plastic wrap, and let rise until doubled in bulk, about 1¼ hours.

SHAPING
5 mins.

Turn the dough out onto a floured work surface and press out the bubbles by kneading briefly. Flatten the dough into an oval or divide into 2 pieces and make 2 small ovals. Fold in half, pinch the seam together tightly, tuck under the ends, and place in the pan(s).

SECOND RISING
1 hour

Cover the pan(s) with wax paper and set aside. Let the dough rise until it has doubled in volume, perhaps 1" above the side of the pan, 1 hour.

PREHEAT

Preheat the oven to 375° 20 minutes before baking.

BAKING 375° 10 mins. 350° 30 mins.	Bake for 10 minutes in the moderate oven; reduce heat to 350° for an additional 30 minutes, or until the loaf is deep brown. The loaf is done when a tap on the bottom crust sounds hard and hollow; crusty, not soft. (If using a convection oven, bake at 325° and 300°.)
FINAL STEP	Remove the bread from the oven. Turn out onto a metal rack and allow the loaf or loaves to cool before slicing, or freezing. This bread toasts beautifully.

Cranberry-Nut Bread   [one large or two small loaves]

This bread is a treat whenever the bright red cranberry is on the market, especially during the weeks of Thanksgiving and Christmas. Cranberries give the loaf a slight tartness and spot it with bits of bright color. Orange peel and orange juice heighten the flavor.

*   I usually make 2 small loaves—one for home and the other to give as a gift.*

INGREDIENTS	2 cups bread or all-purpose flour I cup sugar 1½ teaspoons baking powder ½ teaspoon baking soda I teaspoon salt ¼ cup shortening ¾ cup orange juice I tablespoon grated orange rind I egg, room temperature, slightly beaten ½ cup chopped walnuts or pecans I cup coarsely chopped cranberries
BAKING PANS	1 large (9"-x-5") or 2 small (7"-x-3") loaf pans, greased or Teflon, long sides and bottom lined with buttered wax paper

BY HAND
OR MIXER
6 mins.
	In a large mixing or mixer bowl sift together the flour and dry ingredients. If by hand, use a pastry blender or 2 knives to cut in the shortening until the mixture resembles coarse cornmeal. In the mixer, use the flat beater.
	    In a small bowl combine the orange juice, grated rind, and the beaten egg. Pour the liquid into the dry ingredients and mix just enough to dampen. Don't beat. Carefully fold in the nuts and cranberries.
	    The mixture will be stiff and must be pushed into the corners of the

pan with a spoon or spatula. Form it slightly higher on the sides to compensate for the rising crown.

PREHEAT

Preheat the oven to 350°, allowing the filled pans to rest for 20 minutes.

BAKING
350°
1 hour

Bake in the oven until the loaves are a rich brown and test done when pierced in the center with a metal skewer or wooden toothpick, 1 hour. If it comes out clean and dry, the loaf is baked. If moist particles cling to the pin, return the loaf to the oven for an additional 5 to 10 minutes.
(If using a convection oven, reduce heat 50°.)

FINAL STEP

Remove the bread from the oven. Carefully turn from the pan, peel the wax paper away, and cool on a metal rack. An easy way to remove the loaf is to turn the pan on its side, then tug gently at the leading edges of the wax paper to work the loaf loose.

Allow the loaf to age overnight before slicing.

Glazed Raisin Bread   [one large or two smaller loaves]

A slice of this loaf is moist, finely textured, and studded with dark raisins. Lemon or orange juice is mixed into the confectioners' icing to give a pleasant taste contrast to the buttermilk-and-egg dough. This is an all-around satisfactory loaf, especially for the new baker.

INGREDIENTS

1 cup seedless raisins
¼ cup (½ stick) butter or other shortening
¼ cup sugar
1½ teaspoons salt
1 package dry yeast
¾ cup buttermilk, room temperature
4 cups all-purpose flour, approximately
2 eggs, room temperature, slightly beaten
1 cup sifted confectioners' sugar mixed with 1½ tablespoons orange
   or lemon juice

BAKING PANS

1 large (9"-x-5") or 1 medium (8"-x-4") and 1 small (7"-x-3") loaf pan, greased or Teflon

BY HAND
OR MIXER
15 mins.

In a large mixing or mixer bowl combine the raisins, butter, sugar, salt, yeast, and buttermilk. Measure in 1½ cups flour and beat well—75 strokes by hand or for 1 minute with the mixer flat beater. Pour in the eggs. Blend thoroughly.

If in the mixer, change to the dough hook.

Gradually add the remaining flour, ½ cup at a time, until the mass of dough is soft and has dropped away from the sides of the bowl. If the dough continues to be moist and sticky, add sprinkles of flour.

KNEADING
8 mins.

Turn out onto a lightly floured work surface and knead vigorously by hand, or under the dough hook in the mixer bowl. The dough will become smooth and elastic in about 8 minutes.

BY PROCESSOR
4 mins.

Attach the plastic dough blade.

The sequence of adding ingredients differs from above.

Measure 2 cups flour into the processor work bowl and add the sugar, salt, yeast, and shortening. Pulse several times to mix thoroughly. Pour in the buttermilk, and with the processor running, add 1 cup flour. Drop in the eggs and raisins. Continue adding flour, ¼ cup at a time, until a mass forms on the blade.

KNEADING
50 secs.

When the dough cleans the sides of the bowl, process for 50 seconds to knead.

The dough, when turned out of the bowl, should be slightly sticky—not at all dry. If it is so, add 1 or 2 teaspoons water and continue processing.

FIRST RISING
1½ hours

Place the dough in a bowl, pat it with buttered fingers, cover the bowl with plastic wrap, and leave to rise until doubled in size, 1½ hours.

SHAPING
20 mins.

Turn back the plastic wrap, punch down the dough, turn it onto the work surface, and let it rest for 10 minutes.

Divide the dough into as many pieces as you wish loaves and form each by rolling into a flat rectangle—as wide as the length of the pan. Roll up the dough, sealing well at each turn. Press down on the ends of the loaf to seal, and tuck under as you place in the pan.

SECOND RISING
50 mins.

Cover with wax paper and allow the dough to double in bulk, 50 minutes. You can test if it has risen by poking a finger in it; the dent will remain.

PREHEAT

Preheat the oven to 375° 20 minutes before baking.

BAKING
375°
40 mins.

Bake until the loaves are well browned and loose in their pans, 40 minutes. Turn one loaf out of its pan and tap the bottom crust with a forefinger. A hard, hollow sound means the bread is done. If it is soft, return to the oven for 5 to 10 minutes.

(If using a convection oven, reduce heat 50°.)

FINAL STEP

Remove the bread from the oven and place on a wire rack.

When cooled, drizzle the sugar-juice over the loaves.

Selkirk Bannock   [three loaves]

In 1859 a baker named Robbie Douglas opened a shop in the Scottish town of Selkirk, near Edinburgh. He made and sold a bannock that was to bring fame to Robbie and to the community. He bought butter made from milk produced on selected pastures and imported his raisins from Turkey.

His fame and recipe still live on. This is an adaptation of his original recipe that I found in Edinburgh. It is a weighty, rounded loaf, flat on the bottom and curved gently on the top, with about half its weight in fruit.

The Selkirk bakery where I found the recipe says that the bread "is cut into thin slices and eaten with or without butter. It is rich but not over-rich, and the butter that it contains is very noticeable. It is very economical since little is required and it keeps well. Wrapped in a cloth and placed in a tin, it will keep moist and palatable for a month or longer."

INGREDIENTS	4 to 5 cups bread or all-purpose flour, approximately 1 package dry yeast 2 teaspoons salt 1½ cups hot water (120° to 130°) 1 cup (2 sticks) butter, room temperature ½ cup lard, room temperature 1 cup sugar 2 pounds sultana or dark raisins
BAKING PANS	3 round 8" or 9" cake pans, with 1½" sides, greased or Teflon

BY HAND
OR MIXER
15 mins.

Measure 1 cup flour into a large mixing or mixer bowl and stir in the yeast, salt, and hot water, and put aside for a moment. Cream together the butter, lard, and sugar in a separate bowl. Thoroughly combine with the flour mixture.

Stir in flour, ½ cup at a time, first with a spoon and then by hand as the dough becomes more firm. If using a mixer, begin with the flat beater and replace with the dough hook when the dough gets heavy.

The dough will be buttery and oily, hence won't cling. Add flour sufficient to make a dough that is firm but elastic.

KNEADING
10 mins.

Place the dough on a lightly floured work surface and knead by hand for 2 minutes with a strong push-turn-fold motion, or knead for an equal length of time with the mixer dough hook.

Add the raisins. This is a large measure and it will take a few minutes for the dough to accept them all, but in the meantime you will be kneading the dough as you work them in. Knead by hand or with the dough hook for 8 minutes, or until all of the raisins are in, and the dough is an elastic but firm ball that will hold its shape in the pan.

BY PROCESSOR
5 mins.

Attach the plastic blade (the steel blade will cut up the raisins).

Measure 2½ cups flour into the processor work bowl and add the yeast, salt, and hot water. Pulse to mix, and then let stand while creaming together the butter, lard, and sugar in a separate bowl.

Drop the butter mixture into the work bowl and pulse 6 or 7 times to blend thoroughly. Add the raisins. Turn the processor on and add flour through the feed tube, ¼ cup at a time, to form a soft mass that will clean the sides of the work bowl as the dough is whirled around by the blade.

KNEADING
1 min.

With the machine running knead for 1 minute.

The dough should be moist but not wet. It may be slightly sticky when turned from the work bowl, but sprinkles of flour will make it easy to work into a ball.

SHAPING
6 mins.

Divide the dough into 3 parts. Mold each piece into a large round bun, and place in a pan. It should not touch the sides of the pan but rise up in a gentle curve away from the sides.

RISING
30 mins.

Cover the pans with wax paper and leave the dough at room temperature until risen, about 30 minutes.

PREHEAT

Preheat the oven to 350° 20 minutes before baking.

BAKING
350°
1–1¼ hours

Bake on the middle shelf of the oven. When tapping the bottom crust yields a hard, hollow sound, the loaves are done, about 1 to 1¼ hours. If the crust should brown too quickly, cover with a piece of foil or brown sack paper.

(If using a convection oven, reduce heat 50°.)

FINAL STEP

Remove the bread from the oven. Carefully place the loaves on metal racks to cool.

Honey-Pineapple Bread   [one large or two small loaves]

While this honey-colored loaf has a full cup of honey among its ingredients, it is the unmistakably tropical aroma of pineapple—in its preparation as well as in the loaf—that sets it apart. Whole bran and walnuts are added to give it a pleasant and slightly rough texture.

A good slice to go with coffee, or a glass of port.

INGREDIENTS	2 tablespoons salad oil
	I cup honey
	I egg, room temperature, slightly beaten
	2 cups bread or all-purpose flour
	2 teaspoons baking powder
	I teaspoon salt
	I cup whole bran
	I cup pineapple juice
	¾ cup chopped walnuts
BAKING PAN	1 large (9"-x-5") or 2 small (7"-x-3") loaf pans, greased or Teflon, bottom lined with greased wax paper
PREHEAT	Preheat the oven to 350°.
BY HAND OR MIXER 10 mins.	In a mixing or mixer bowl measure in the oil, honey, and egg. This sticky mess does blend together, so stir it well for about a minute by hand or with a mixer flat beater. Add the flour, baking powder, salt, whole bran, and pineapple juice. Stir just enough to absorb the dry ingredients. Fold in the nuts.
BY PROCESSOR 5 mins.	Attach the steel blade. Measure the oil, honey, and egg into the work bowl, and pulse 3 or 4 times to blend. With the machine stopped, add the flour, baking powder, salt, whole bran, and pineapple juice. Pulse only long enough to absorb the dry ingredients. Drop in the nuts and pulse to fold them in. Do so briefly so the blade does not chop the nuts more finely.
SHAPING 5 mins.	Spoon or pour the batter into the pan or pans, filling only halfway. Push into the corners and level the top with a spoon or spatula.
BAKING 350° I–1¼ hours	Bake until the loaf or loaves are honey colored, 1 to 1¼ hours. The loaves will test done when a wooden toothpick or metal skewer inserted in the center comes out clean and dry. No batter will be sticking to it. (If using a convection oven, reduce heat 25°.)
FINAL STEP	Remove the bread from the oven and allow to cool in the pan for 10 minutes before removing to a wire rack. Peel the paper off the bottom of each loaf. Allow the loaf to age at least a day for a richer and more flavorful bread.

German Raisin Bread   [two medium or three small loaves]

A big swirl of raisins, nuts, candied fruit, and cinnamon gives this nut-encrusted loaf its character and exceptionally good taste. Whole almonds or pecans are baked into the bottom and top crusts, while the crumb is finely textured and moist with potato.

Preparation begins with making a sponge.

INGREDIENTS

Sponge:
2 cups bread or all-purpose flour
2 packages dry yeast
2 teaspoons salt
1 tablespoon butter, softened at room temperature
1/2 cup finely sieved cooked potato, or 2 tablespoons instant potato
    flakes mixed with 1/2 cup water
1 1/4 cups warm milk (105°–115°)

Dough:
2 eggs, room temperature, lightly beaten
1/2 cup sugar
2 tablespoons butter, melted
1/2 teaspoon ground cinnamon
2 to 3 cups bread or all-purpose flour, approximately

Filling:
3/4 cup *each* raisins and coarsely chopped candied cherries
1/2 cup finely chopped almonds or pecans
1/4 cup chopped citron
1/4 cup sugar
1 teaspoon ground cinnamon
2 tablespoons butter

Topping:
12 whole almonds or pecans
1 egg, beaten
2 to 3 tablespoons butter

BAKING PANS

2 medium (8"-x-4") or 3 small (7"-x-3") loaf pans, greased or Teflon

PREPARATION
2 hours

To make the sponge, in a large mixing or mixer bowl stir 2 cups flour, the dry yeast, and salt. Add the butter and potato. Stir in the warm milk. Mix thoroughly—100 strokes. Cover the bowl tightly with plastic wrap and set aside for 2 hours, or until the sponge has doubled in volume.

BY HAND
OR MIXER
10 mins.

Turn back the plastic wrap and stir the sponge briefly. Add the eggs, sugar, melted butter, and cinnamon. Gradually add more flour, sufficient to form a soft mass that cleans the sides of the bowl. If using a mixer, begin with the flat beater and then, when the mass begins to form, change to a dough hook.

KNEADING
10 mins.

If by hand, turn the dough onto a floured work surface and knead with a strong push-turn-fold motion until the dough is smooth and elastic. If using a mixer, add flour, if needed, to form a soft ball around the dough hook that cleans the sides of the bowl. Knead until the dough has lost all of its stickiness and is soft and elastic when pulled between the hands, 10 minutes.

BY PROCESSOR
4 mins.

Prepare the sponge in a separate bowl, as above.

Attach the plastic dough blade.

Scrape the sponge into the work bowl with a spatula. Add 1 cup flour, and pulse to blend. With the processor running, add the eggs, sugar, melted butter, and cinnamon.

Add flour, ¼ cup at a time, until the mass gathers on the blade and cleans the sides of the bowl. Stop the machine and feel the dough. It should be slightly sticky. If wet to the touch, add more flour.

KNEADING
50 secs.

With the processor running knead for 50 seconds.

When taken from the bowl the dough will be sticky, but a few sprinkles of flour will make it possible to knead a few times by hand before putting aside to rise.

FIRST RISING
1 hour

Place the dough in a greased bowl, cover, and let rise until double in bulk, about 1 hour.

Meanwhile, prepare the filling. In a bowl combine the raisins, candied cherries, nuts, and citron. In a cup combine and have ready the sugar and cinnamon. Melt the butter in a small saucepan.

SHAPING
30 mins.

Turn the dough onto the lightly floured work surface and knead briefly to press out the bubbles. Divide the dough into however many loaves you have decided to bake.

Roll each piece into a rectangle (9" x 12" for a medium loaf). Brush with the butter and spread on the sugar and cinnamon mix. Leave a dry margin around the edges so that a strong seam can be made. Divide the fruit-nut mixture among the pieces of dough. Smooth in place but keep it away from the margins.

Roll as you would a jelly roll, starting from a short side. Make the roll tight to avoid air spaces in the finished loaf. When the roll is almost to the end of the rectangle, lift up the edge of dough and pinch it to the roll. Don't take the roll all the way to the edge because this would push the filling into the cleared margin. Fold the ends to seal.

Scatter a few nuts on the bottom of the pans before fitting in the loaves.

SECOND RISING I hour	Cover the loaves with wax paper and leave them to double in volume, 1 hour.
PREHEAT	Preheat the oven to 350° 20 minutes before baking.
BAKING 350° 45 mins.	Beat the egg in a cup; dip the nuts in the egg and then lightly press in a pattern on top of each loaf. Bake in the oven until the loaves are nicely browned and loose in their pans, 45 minutes. Turn one loaf out of its pan and tap the bottom crust with a finger. A hard, hollow sound means the bread is done. If not, return the loaf to the oven for 10 minutes, and without the pan if you wish a deeper brown crust. (If using a convection oven, reduce heat 50°.)
FINAL STEP	Remove the bread from the oven. Turn the loaves onto wire racks to cool. Brush each loaf generously with melted butter.

Vel's Date Bread   [two small loaves]

The Hindostan Women's Booster Club (20 members) in a small farming community near my home in southern Indiana put together a book of favorite recipes to help underwrite the club's "service and work."

This is a rich brown waxy loaf packed with date and walnut bits.

INGREDIENTS	I ½ cups chopped dates or crystals I ½ cups boiling water I ¼ cups sugar I egg, room temperature 2 teaspoons baking soda ½ teaspoon salt I teaspoon vanilla extract I tablespoon butter, melted 2 ½ cups all-purpose flour I cup chopped walnuts

BAKING PANS	2 small (7"-x-3") loaf pans, greased or Teflon, sides and bottoms lined with buttered wax paper
PREPARATION 20 mins.	Put the dates into a large mixing bowl, then pour the boiling water over them. Soak for 20 minutes.
PREHEAT	Preheat the oven to 325°.
BY HAND 15 mins.	Stir the sugar, egg, baking soda, salt, vanilla, and melted butter into the soaking dates.

In a separate bowl measure the flour and add the chopped walnuts. Add the flour-nut mixture to the wet ingredients and mix thoroughly.

Pour the mixture into the pans. Push into the corners with a spatula and smooth the tops. |
| BAKING 325° 50 mins. | Bake until the loaves are a rich brown, 50 minutes, and test done when a metal skewer inserted in the center comes out dry and clean. If moist particles cling to the probe, return the pans to the oven for an additional 10 minutes.

(If using a convection oven, reduce heat 25°.) |
| FINAL STEP | Remove the bread from the oven. Allow to cool in the pans for 10 minutes before turning the pans on their sides to pull out the loaves with a gentle tug on the paper lining. Cool on a wire rack.

This loaf will keep nicely for a fortnight or more at room temperature. Keeps frozen for several months. |

Apricot-Nut Bread   [two large loaves]

Rolled oats gives this no-knead bread its handsome rough texture. Dried apricots and pecans are expensive, but they are worth having in this dark, molasses-flavored bread.

INGREDIENTS	1 cup rolled oats
$^1/_4$ cup dark molasses
$^1/_4$ cup sugar
$^1/_2$ teaspoon *each* grated nutmeg and ground ginger
3 teaspoons salt
2 cups boiling water
2 packages dry yeast
$4^1/_2$ cups all-purpose flour
$^3/_4$ cup finely cut dried apricots
$^3/_4$ cup chopped pecans
2 tablespoons butter or margarine

BAKING PANS	2 large (9"-x-5") loaf pans, greased or Teflon
BY HAND OR MIXER 20 mins.	In a large mixing or mixer bowl combine the rolled oats, molasses, sugar, nutmeg, ginger, and salt. Pour the boiling water over. Blend, and let cool until the mixture is lukewarm to the touch. Add the yeast.
	Add 2½ cups flour. Blend with about 20 strokes or for 30 seconds with the mixer flat beater. Add remaining flour, ½ cup at a time, with the apricots, pecans, and shortening. Mix well. It will be a soft batter. There is no kneading.
BY PROCESSOR 20 mins.	Attach the plastic blade.
	Measure the rolled oats, molasses, sugar, nutmeg, ginger, and salt into the work bowl and pour in the boiling water. Pulse. Allow the mixture to cool to lukewarm. Sprinkle the yeast over the mixture. Pulse several times to mix well.
	With the processor on, add the flour, ½ cup at a time, with the apricots, pecans, and shortening. Pulse several times to blend thoroughly.
FIRST RISING 1 hour	Cover the bowl with plastic wrap and leave at room temperature until doubled in bulk, about 1 hour.
SHAPING 4 mins.	Remove the plastic wrap; beat down the dough (or pulse if in the processor). Pour into the pans.
SECOND RISING 45 mins.	Cover the pans lightly with wax paper and let the dough reach the top of the pans, 45 minutes. However, elevate the wax paper on tumblers so it won't touch the batter.
PREHEAT	Preheat the oven to 375° about 20 minutes before baking.
BAKING 375° 50 mins.	Bake until the loaves test done when pricked with a metal skewer, 50 minutes. They are done if the pin comes out clean. If not, leave them in the oven for 5 minutes longer.
	(If using a convection oven, reduce heat 50°.)
FINAL STEP	Take the bread from the oven. Carefully remove from the loaf pans to wire cooling racks.
	Allow the bread to develop its full flavor for a day or so before slicing.

Raisin-Nut Bread   [one long loaf]

When the long strands of this rich dough, thick with chopped walnuts and raisins, are braided, some of the nuts and raisins will fall out. Push them back in anywhere. Others will have the appearance of wanting to come out but won't. They will be surrounded and held firmly in an elastic grip when the dough expands.

There is a rugged handsomeness about this loaf that could come only from the hands of a home bread-maker.

INGREDIENTS

3 to 3¹/₂ cups bread or all-purpose flour, approximately
1 package dry yeast
¹/₄ cup sugar
1 teaspoon salt
¹/₂ cup nonfat dry milk
1¹/₄ cups hot water (120°–130°)
¹/₄ cup shortening, room temperature
¹/₂ cup *each* seedless raisins and chopped walnuts

Topping:
½ cup confectioners' sugar
2 tablespoons milk
¹/₄ teaspoon vanilla extract
Several candied cherries, halved

BAKING SHEET

1 baking sheet, greased, Teflon, or covered with parchment paper

BY HAND
OR MIXER
15 mins.

In a large mixing or mixer bowl measure 1½ cups flour and the dry ingredients. Pour in the hot water and add the shortening. Beat well with 150 strong strokes, or with the mixer flat beater for 2 minutes. Stir in the raisins and nuts. Gradually add flour, ¼ cup at a time, first with a wooden spoon and then by hand until a rough, soft mass has formed. If using the mixer, remove the flat beater and attach the dough hook. Add flour until the dough forms a soft ball around the dough hook and moves with it.

KNEADING
10 mins.

If by hand, spread flour on the work surface and turn the dough onto it. If the dough is moist (slack) and sticky, work in a little more flour. Presently it will become elastic and no longer sticky. When kneading in the mixer, the dough should pull away from the bowl. If not, add sprinkles of flour. Knead for 10 minutes.

BY PROCESSOR
5 mins.

Attach the steel blade. The raisins and nuts are worked into the dough after taking it from the work bowl, otherwise the blade could chop them into small bits.

Measure 2 cups flour and dry ingredients into the work bowl. Process to blend. With the machine running, pour in the hot water and drop in the shortening.

Add flour, ¼ cup at a time, through the feed tube to form a soft mass that will clean the sides of the work bowl and move with the blade. Add more flour, if necessary.

KNEADING
1 min.

Process to knead for 1 minute.

The dough will be slightly moist when turned out of the bowl. Flatten the dough into an oval and spread with the raisins and nuts. Turn in the edges and work the raisins and nuts into the dough. Add light sprinkles of flour as you work.

FIRST RISING
1½ hours

Place the ball of dough in a bowl, pat with butter or shortening on your fingertips, and cover tightly with plastic wrap. Put aside until the dough has doubled in bulk, 1½ hours. You can test if it has risen sufficiently by poking a finger into it; the dent will remain.

SHAPING
25 mins.

Remove the plastic wrap, punch down the dough, and turn it onto the floured work surface again. Divide the dough into 3 equal pieces. Cover and rest for 10 minutes. The rest period is important. The gluten must relax, otherwise you are constantly trying to stretch it when it wants to pull back.

Roll each piece into a strand about 20" long. Give the dough time to relax as it is being worked by rolling the first strand to only 10", and then do the second and third strands to get them started. Return to the first, which has now relaxed, and complete the strand to its full 20". Then go back to the other two. If some of the nuts and raisins spill out, tuck them back into a fold.

Lay the 3 strands side by side and braid loosely, starting in the center, working to either end. Pinch the ends together tightly. Avoid stretching the strands and braiding them too tightly. They need room to expand. Place the braid on the baking sheet.

SECOND RISING
1 hour

Cover the braid with wax or parchment paper and put aside to double in volume, 1 hour.

PREHEAT

Preheat the oven to 375° 20 minutes before baking.

BAKING
375°
25–30 mins.

Be certain the ends of the braid are tightly pinched together at the ends before placing it in the oven. Bake until the loaf is a light brown, 25 to 30 minutes. Test by piercing between the strands with a toothpick or cake testing pin. If it comes out dry, and not damp with uncooked dough, the braid is done.

(If using a convection oven, reduce heat 50°.)

FINAL STEP

Remove the bread from the oven. Handle the hot braids carefully, as they may pull apart. Lift from the sheet with a spatula and place on a metal rack to cool.

In a bowl mix together the sugar, milk, and vanilla. While slightly warm, spread the crust with the confectioners' icing. Decorate with the candied cherries.

If the braid is to be given as a gift or to be carried away, place a piece of cardboard under it, trimmed to size.

Raisin-Orange Bread   [2 medium loaves]

Raisin-Orange Bread is a fat, moist loaf replete with raisins. It is iced with a frosting of chopped walnuts beaten into a blend of confectioners' sugar, butter, and orange juice.

There are bits of orange peel in the yellow eggy dough, which contrasts nicely with the dark raisins. The dough rises in the oven 2 or 3 inches above the pan to give the bread an open and airy texture.

INGREDIENTS

Dough:
5 to 5¹/₂ cups bread or all-purpose flour, approximately
2 packages dry yeast
1¹/₄ cups water
¹/₂ cup nonfat dry milk
Rind of 1 orange, grated
¹/₂ teaspoon ground ginger
¹/₂ cup *each* butter and sugar
2 teaspoons salt
2 eggs, room temperature
1¹/₂ cups raisins

Glaze:
1 cup confectioners' sugar
2 teaspoons butter, room temperature
¹/₂ cup finely chopped walnuts
2 to 4 tablespoons orange juice

BAKING PANS

2 medium (8"-x-4") baking pans, greased, Teflon, or filmed with vegetable spray

BY HAND
OR MIXER
20 mins.

In a large mixing or mixer bowl measure 3 cups flour and sprinkle the yeast over it. Blend with a spoon or mixer flat beater. In a saucepan measure the water, dry milk, orange rind, ginger, butter, sugar, and salt.

Heat over a low flame until it is hot (120°), stirring constantly. Pour this mixture into the flour and yeast, add the eggs, and beat by hand or with the mixer until the flour becomes a smooth batter. Beat for 3 minutes at high speed, or for the same length of time with a wooden spoon.

Stop the mixer, scrape down the bowl, and stir in the raisins. Gradually add more flour to form a soft mass that cleans the sides of the bowl. Work the flour in by hand when the dough gets too stiff for the spoon, or attach the dough hook, if using the mixer.

KNEADING
10 mins.

Turn the soft dough out onto a lightly floured work surface, and knead with a strong push-turn-fold motion until smooth and elastic. If the dough is sticky or too moist (slack), add ½ cup flour and work into the dough. If using the mixer, the dough should form a soft, elastic ball around the revolving dough hook. Add sprinkles of flour if the dough clings to the sides. Knead for 10 minutes.

BY PROCESSOR
5 mins.

Attach the plastic dough blade.

Measure 3 cups flour and the yeast into the work bowl. Pulse to blend. In a saucepan heat the water, dry milk, orange rind, ginger, butter, sugar, and salt until just hot to the touch (120°).

With the processor on, pour the liquid through the feed tube. Stop the machine and drop in the eggs and raisins. Pulse to blend. With the machine on, add flour through the feed tube to form a soft mass that will clean the sides of the bowl.

KNEADING
50 secs.

Knead with the processor running for 50 seconds.

FIRST RISING
1¼ hours

Place the dough in a greased bowl, cover tightly with plastic wrap, and put aside at room temperature until doubled in size, 1¼ hours. The dough can be tested by poking a finger in it; the dent will remain.

REST
15 mins.

Punch down the dough in the bowl, turn it out onto the floured work surface, and knead briefly. Let rest under a towel or piece of wax paper for about 15 minutes.

SHAPING
5 mins.

Divide the dough into 2 parts. Press each part into a flat oval, fold in half, pinch the seam tightly closed, and pat into the shape of a loaf. Drop into the pans and with a sharp knife or razor blade, make 3 diagonal slashes ¼" deep across the top of each loaf.

SECOND RISING
1 hour

Cover the pans with wax paper and leave until the dough has doubled in volume, about 1 hour.

Meanwhile, prepare the topping. In a bowl blend the confectioners' sugar with the soft butter, walnuts, and orange juice to spreading consistency.

PREHEAT

Preheat the oven to 375° about 20 minutes before baking.

BAKING
375°
50 mins.

Place the loaves in the hot oven until well browned, about 50 minutes. When tapping the bottom crust yields a hard, hollow sound, they are done.

(If using a convection oven, reduce heat 50°.)

FINAL STEP

Remove the bread from the oven. While the loaves are warm, spread the topping over the crusts. However, allow the loaves to cool before slicing.

Orange-Nut Bread   [one large or two small loaves]

There is a jagged tear down the center of the light brown crust of this loaf in which an orange and sugar mix is spooned while the loaf is still in the oven. Fresh or frozen orange juice and grated orange rind gives a fine flavor to this waxy bread of orange and nuts.

INGREDIENTS

2¹/₂ cups all-purpose flour
3 teaspoons baking powder
I teaspoon salt
I cup sugar
¹/₃ cup nonfat dry milk
¹/₄ cup shortening, room temperature
¹/₄ cup fresh or frozen orange juice
³/₄ cup water
I egg, room temperature
3 tablespoons grated orange rind
I cup chopped walnuts
¹/₂ cup sugar mixed with 3 tablespoons orange juice

BAKING PANS

1 large (9"-x-5") or 2 small (7"-x-3") loaf pans, greased or Teflon, sides and bottom lined with buttered wax paper

PREHEAT

Preheat the oven to 350°.

BY HAND
15 mins.

Into a large bowl sift the dry ingredients. With a pastry blender or your fingers cut in the shortening. Pour in the orange juice, water, and the egg. With a large wooden spoon mix only enough to dampen the dry ingredients. Add the grated rind and chopped walnuts and mix them well—but don't overbeat.

Pour or spoon the batter into pans. Spread with a rubber scraper. Leave the sides slightly higher than the center, to allow the batter to expand and level off in the oven.

BAKING
350°
1 hour

Bake in the moderate oven for about 50 minutes, until light brown. Remove the loaf from the oven and carefully spoon the sugar-juice mixture over the crust. Return to the oven for 10 minutes, or until the loaf tests done. A wooden toothpick or metal skewer will come out clean and dry when inserted in the middle of the loaf. If moist particles cling to the probe, return the loaf to the oven for an additional 10 minutes.

(If using a convection oven, reduce heat 50°.)

FINAL STEP

Remove the bread from the oven. Let cool for 10 minutes. With the loaf pan turned on its side, carefully coax out the bread by tugging gently on the wax paper ends. Continue cooling on a wire rack.

Allow the loaf to age overnight before serving.

Orange Bread   [two medium loaves]

Unlike other orange breads that fall into the quick-bread category, this handsome loaf, flavored with orange juice and orange peel, is yeast-raised. The crust is deep brown and the slice a light orange.

INGREDIENTS

2 cups hot water (120°–130°)
1/4 cup fresh or frozen orange juice
1/4 cup grated orange rind
1/2 cup sugar
2 teaspoons salt
3 tablespoons shortening, room temperature
7 cups bread or all-purpose flour, approximately
1 package dry yeast
1 egg, room temperature
2 tablespoons milk or cream

BAKING PANS

2 medium (8"-x-4") baking pans, greased, Teflon, or coated with vegetable spray

BY HAND
OR MIXER
15 mins.

In a large mixing or mixer bowl combine the hot water, orange juice, rind, sugar, salt, and shortening. Stir in 3 cups flour and the yeast. Add the egg. Beat 150 strong strokes with a wooden spoon, or for 3 minutes with the mixer flat beater, until the batter is smooth and begins to pull away from the sides of the bowl in strands. Gradually add more flour, ½ cup at a time, until a soft mass of dough is formed. Attach the dough hook, if using the mixer.

KNEADING
10 mins.

If by hand, turn the dough onto a lightly floured work surface and knead with a strong push-turn-fold motion until it is smooth and elastic. If the dough seems slack or unduly moist, add ¼ cup or so additional flour. In the mixer the dough should form a soft ball around the hook and clean the sides. If it clings to the sides, add liberal sprinkles of flour. Knead by hand or in the mixer for 10 minutes.

BY PROCESSOR
8 mins.

Attach the plastic blade.

The sequence for adding ingredients differs from above.

Measure 4 cups flour into the work bowl and add the yeast. Pulse to blend. In a separate bowl combine the hot water, orange juice, rind, sugar, salt, and shortening. Lightly beat in the egg. With the machine running, pour the liquid through the feed tube to form a heavy batter.

Add flour, ¼ cup at a time, to form a mass that cleans the sides of the bowl and travels with the blade around the bowl. Stop the machine. Feel the dough. It should be only slightly sticky. If wet, add flour; if dry, add water. Replace the cover.

KNEADING
1 min.

Turn the machine on and knead the dough for 1 minute. Dust the dough with flour when removing from the bowl to make it easier to handle.

FIRST RISING
1½ hours

Place the dough in a greased bowl, turning once to coat all surfaces, and cover tightly with a length of plastic wrap. Put the bowl aside at room temperature to allow the dough to double in volume, about 1½ hours.

SHAPING
10 mins.

Turn back the plastic wrap, punch down the dough with a blow of the fist, and let rest for 5 minutes.

Divide the dough into 2 pieces. Form a ball with each piece, flatten it into an oval, fold in half, pinch the seam closed, and pat into a loaf that will fit into the pan.

SECOND RISING
1 hour

Cover the pans with wax paper and leave until the dough rises about 1" above the pan, 1 hour.

PREHEAT

Preheat the oven to 375° 20 minutes before baking.

BAKING **375°** **45 mins.**	Place the loaves on the middle shelf of the moderate oven and bake until the crusts are a golden brown and the loaves are loose in their pans, 45 minutes. When a tap on the bottom crust yields a hard, hollow sound, the bread is done. (If using a convection oven, reduce heat 50°.)
FINAL STEP	Remove the bread from the oven. Turn from the pans, and place on a wire rack. While still hot, brush the loaves with milk or cream for a lovely soft look. I sometimes rub the crusts with the wrapping paper from a stick of butter.

Cherry-Pecan Bread   [one medium loaf]

The slice is pink studded with red cherry pieces and pecan chunks. With its light brown and shiny crust, it is an especially handsome loaf.

*   The maraschino flavor, however, is not pronounced, despite a dozen cherries and the cherry juice. There is also orange juice.*

INGREDIENTS	1 4-ounce bottle maraschino cherries (juice reserved) 1 egg, room temperature 1 cup sugar 2 tablespoons butter, melted 1/4 cup *each* orange juice and water 2 cups all-purpose flour 3 teaspoons baking powder 1/4 teaspoon baking soda 1 teaspoon salt 1 cup chopped pecans
BAKING PAN	1 medium (8"-x-4") loaf pan, greased or Teflon
PREHEAT	Preheat the oven to 350°.
PREPARATION **5 mins.**	Pour off the cherry juice and reserve. There should be ¼ cup. With a sharp knife, quarter the cherries.
BY HAND **OR MIXER** **18 mins.**	In a mixing or mixer bowl beat the egg, add the cherries, and stir in the sugar and melted butter with a large wooden spoon or spatula, or with a mixer flat beater. Pour in the cherry and orange juices and water. On a length of wax paper, sift or stir together the flour, baking powder, baking soda, and salt. Add these to the liquid, a spoonful at a time, and blend together thoroughly. Add the chopped nuts, and stir in.

Pour the batter into the prepared pan. Push into the corners and level with a spoon or spatula.

BAKING
350°
1¼ hours

Bake until the crust is well browned (and perhaps cracked open). When a wooden toothpick inserted in the loaf comes out clean and dry, the loaf is done.

(If using a convection oven, reduce heat 50°.)

FINAL STEP

Remove the bread from the oven. Let rest in the pan for 10 minutes before removing to a wire rack to cool.

This loaf is better seasoned for a day or so before slicing. Wrap with foil or plastic wrap.

Loyalist Bread   [two medium loaves]

During the American Revolution families loyal to George III fled to Nova Scotia. More than 30,000 were exiled to Canada and lost everything except their loyalty to the crown and whatever they could carry with them. Women escaped with their recipes.

Loyalist Bread is one of the recipes they saved, and decades later it and others were collected in a fine volume, The Blueberry Connection, *written by Beatrice Ross Buszek, who lives in Granville Centre, Nova Scotia, which is noted for its blueberries.*

It is a handsome loaf with a craggy crust and, when cut, pools of blueberries. Because this bread is so simple to make by hand I have not included instructions for mixer or food processor. Also the blades would chop the blueberries into bits—and the berry left whole is dramatic when the loaf is sliced.

INGREDIENTS

2 tablespoons shortening, melted
2 cups sugar
2 cups buttermilk
2 eggs, lightly beaten
4½ cups all-purpose flour
5 teaspoons baking powder
1 teaspoon baking soda
1 teaspoon salt
2 cups cleaned blueberries
1 cup chopped walnuts

BAKING PANS

2 medium (8"-x-4") loaf pans, greased or Teflon, lined with buttered wax paper

BY HAND **11 mins.**	In a bowl mix the melted shortening together with the sugar, buttermilk, and beaten eggs. Into a large bowl measure the dry ingredients. Form a well in the bottom and pour in the buttermilk mixture. Stir together with 15 or 20 strokes. Drop in the blueberries and walnuts and blend into the batter. Pour or spoon the batter into the prepared pans, and push into the corners.
PREHEAT	Allow the pans to stand for 20 minutes while preheating the oven to 350°.
BAKING **350°** **1–1½ hours**	Place in the oven and bake for 1 to 1½ hours. The crust will be a lovely light brown. Test with a toothpick inserted into the center of a loaf. If it comes out clean and dry, the bread is done. (If using a convection oven, reduce heat 50°.)
FINAL STEP	Remove from the oven and allow the breads to cool for 10 minutes before turning the pans on their sides. Tug the bread loose with the ends of the wax paper. Allow to cool further on a wire rack.

Pain aux Noix   [three round loaves]
(Nut Bread)

This dark, dense, and delicious Pain aux Noix was created for Fauchon of Paris in the celebrated boulangerie *of Monsieur Pierre Poilâne (see the "Thrill of Discovery" chapter). More than ½ pound walnuts are worked into this all-whole-wheat loaf.*

A slice is a deserving companion at any meal. Toasted and served with cheese, it is even better.

The Fauchon bread is fashioned into a small boule, *a round loaf, but it can easily be made into other shapes and sizes to accommodate almost any need.*

INGREDIENTS	4 cups whole-wheat flour, approximately (see Notes) 2 packages dry yeast ½ cup nonfat dry milk 2 teaspoons salt 2½ cups hot water (120°–130°) 1 tablespoon plain malt syrup (not hop-flavored) (see Notes) 2 tablespoons butter, softened 1 cup bran flakes (see Notes) 2½ cups broken English walnuts 1 egg, beaten, mixed with 1 tablespoon milk

BAKING SHEET

BY HAND
OR MIXER
15 mins.

KNEADING
10 mins.

BY PROCESSOR
5 mins.

KNEADING
30 secs.

1 baking sheet, greased or Teflon

In a mixing or mixer bowl measure 1 cup whole-wheat flour and the dry ingredients. Stir to blend well. In a small bowl mix together the hot water, malt syrup, and butter. Pour the liquid into the flour and stir to a thick batter. Mix the bran flakes into the wet ingredients. Let rest for 3 or 4 minutes while large particles absorb their fill of moisture. Stir vigorously by hand with a wooden spoon or, if in the mixer, with the dough hook. Cautiously add flour to make a mass that can be lifted from the bowl.

While whole-wheat dough is not as elastic as white dough, it nevertheless must not be made into a solid ball that cannot be kneaded. The tendency in working with 100 percent whole wheat is to add too much flour too soon to overcome stickiness and then discover that the flour has absorbed all of the moisture—and the dough is hard. Sprinkles of *white* flour will help control the stickiness and yet not overflour the dough.

The nuts are to be added after the first rising.

Turn the ball of dough onto the floured work surface, or leave in the mixer under the dough hook. Occasionally the dough may be too dense for the hook and lie there impassively. In this event, turn out the dough on the work surface and finish the kneading by hand. Knead for 10 minutes. Use a dough scraper or putty knife to help turn the dough and clean the work surface in the early moments of kneading. Keep light sprinkles of flour between the dough, hands, and work surface. Bang the dough down hard against the work surface to relieve the tedium of kneading.

Use the short plastic blade.

The order of adding ingredients differs slightly from above.

Measure 2 cups whole-wheat flour, bran flakes, yeast, dry milk, and salt into the processor work bowl. In a small bowl stir together the hot water, malt syrup, and butter. With the processor running, pour the liquid through the feed tube. Stop the machine and let the heavy batter rest for 2 or 3 minutes while the bran absorbs its fill of moisture.

Turn on the processor and add whole-wheat flour, ¼ cup at a time, until the batter forms a mass that will clean the sides of the bowl.

Process to knead for 30 seconds.

FIRST RISING
1–1¼ hours

Place the dough in a greased bowl, cover with plastic wrap, and leave at room temperature until the dough has doubled in bulk, 1 to 1¼ hours.

SHAPING
10 mins.

Place the dough on the work surface and push into a large flat oval. Pour half the nuts on the dough and fold in. When they have disappeared, repeat with the balance of the nuts. Some of the nuts may have a tendency to fall out of the dough as it is worked. Keep pushing them back into the dough as it is kneaded and soon they will stay in place.

Divide the dough into 3 equal parts (or the number of loaves desired). Let the dough rest for 5 minutes to relax it before shaping.

With cupped hands, turn each piece of dough into a smooth ball, the cut surfaces pulled together under the ball. Flatten each ball slightly with a gentle pat of your palm. Place on the baking sheet.

SECOND RISING
50 mins.

Cover the *boules* with wax or parchment paper and leave at room temperature, 50 minutes.

PREHEAT

Preheat the oven to 375° 20 minutes before baking.

BAKING
375°
35 mins.

Brush the loaves with the egg-milk glaze and cut the top of each with 4 shallow cuts with a razor blade. These can be made in a tic-tac-toe pattern or as parallel cuts across the loaf.

Place the sheet on the middle shelf of the oven, and bake for 35 minutes, until dark brown. Turn one loaf over and tap the bottom crust with the forefinger. If it has a hollow sound and hard feel, it is baked. Halfway during baking, turn the baking sheet around to equalize the oven temperature on the loaves.

(If using a convection oven, reduce heat 50°.)

FINAL STEP

Place the loaves on a metal rack to cool.

Good to eat cool, toasted, or reheated. Freezes well and will keep at 0° for 4 or 5 months.

Notes: Bran flakes will add a healthy roughness to the bread's texture, particularly if the whole-wheat flour is finely ground. If your whole-wheat flour is stone-ground or pumpernickel, forget the bran flakes and add 1 additional cup whole-wheat flour.

Malt syrup is an ideal nutrient for yeast and will quickly boost it on its way.

Pain Allemand aux Fruits
[two large or three medium loaves]
(German Fruit Bread)

Strasbourg, a lovely French city on the Rhine, reflects in many ways the German influence from across the river. One is in its cuisine, and this unusual fruit bread—not fruit cake—is a delicious example of what each has done for the other.

There are no less than 17 ingredients in this loaf, but after all have been gathered the actual preparation of the bread is not difficult. All of the fruits are dried. The taste of each is subtle but definite.

This is a rich and moist festive bread, and the ample recipe will reward you with one for good eating at home and others as gifts (or to be frozen for another day).

INGREDIENTS	I cup pitted prunes
	I cup dried apricots
	$^1/_2$ cup dried figs
	$^1/_2$ cup light or dark raisins
	5 cups bread or all-purpose flour, approximately
	2 packages dry yeast
	I cup hot water (120°–130°)
	I cup fruit juice (orange, pineapple, or apricot), warmed
	I teaspoon *each* aniseed and ground cinnamon
	$^1/_2$ teaspoon ground cloves
	I teaspoon grated lemon zest
	$^1/_4$ cup honey
	2 teaspoons salt
	$^1/_2$ cup (I stick) butter, melted
	$^1/_2$ cup *each* finely chopped hazelnuts and almonds
BAKING PANS	2 large (9"-x-5") or 3 medium (8"-x-4") loaf pans, greased or Teflon
PREPARATION 10–40 mins.	*Note:* If the dried fruit is hard, soak for 30 minutes in a bowl of hot water. If the fruit has been in a vacuum pack and soft, do not soak.

Chop the dried fruit finely. It can be chopped in a food processor, but pulse quickly. Don't turn it into a puree. Each piece should be distinct, larger than a grain of rice but smaller than a pea. However, use the raisins whole, not chopped.

The fruit will be kneaded into the dough after the first rising.

BY HAND
OR MIXER
10 mins.

Pour 2 cups flour into the work bowl, stir in the yeast and add the water and fruit juice. Stir in the spices, zests, honey, salt, butter, and nuts. Beat by hand or in a mixer until the ingredients are thoroughly mixed and smooth, about 3 minutes.

Add flour, ½ cup at a time, and stir into the mixture until it forms a rough mass.

KNEADING
8 mins.

Lift the dough from the bowl and place on a floured work surface. Knead the dough until it is pliable, soft, and no longer sticky, about 8 minutes. If under a dough hook, knead the dough for an equal length of time.

BY PROCESSOR
5 mins.

Attach the plastic dough blade.

Add 2 cups flour, yeast, liquids, spices, zest, honey, salt, butter, and nuts to the work bowl. Pulse to mix thoroughly. Let stand for 1 minute until the yeast is dissolved.

Add flour, ¼ cup at a time, through the feed tube. When the dough forms a ball, it will clean the sides of the bowl and ride on the top of the blade.

KNEADING
45 secs.

With the machine running, knead for 45 seconds.

FIRST RISING
50 mins.

Place the dough in a greased bowl, cover with plastic wrap, and set aside to double in volume, about 50 minutes.

SHAPING
18 mins.

Mix all of the dried fruit together, and dust with flour so the pieces will not stick together. This will not always be possible because of moisture in the fruit. No matter; it may take a little longer to spread it through the dough.

Punch down the dough, turn out onto a floured work surface, and knead to shape a ball. Press the ball flat, spread a third of the fruit on the dough, fold it in, and knead for a moment. Continue adding fruit until all of it has been incorporated.

Divide the dough. Round into balls and let rest for 10 minutes.

Flatten the balls with your fingers, fold each oval in half, pinch the seams tightly together, turn the seams under, and plump the loaves to fit into the pans.

SECOND RISING
45 mins.

Cover the pans with wax paper or a cloth and let set at room temperature until the dough has doubled in volume, 45 minutes. It will rise about 1" above the edge of the pans.

PREHEAT	Preheat the oven to 350° 20 minutes before baking.
BAKING **350°** **45 mins.**	A design cut into the surface of the loaf with a razor or sharp knife will give it personality. Make a slash the length of the loaf, about ½" deep. Or make diagonal slashes across the width of the loaf or those that radiate from the lengthwise cut. Bake until a cake testing pin inserted comes out clean and dry, about 45 minutes. The loaf browns easily, so watch it closely after the first 30 minutes. If necessary, cover with foil or brown paper to keep it from getting too brown and perhaps burning. Turn one loaf out of the pan and test for doneness. (If using a convection oven, reduce heat 50°.)
FINAL STEP	Remove the bread from the oven and turn from the pans to a wire rack. Let it cool before slicing. Although this toasts nicely, it seems to be even more delicious untoasted.

Bran-Date Bread Deluxe   [one medium loaf]

The bran dominates this handsome loaf, but gradually the palate is aware of wheat and the richness of the walnuts and dates. It is a heavy, moist block that makes wonderful sandwiches with butter or cream cheese.

This recipe is one adapted from an early edition (1943) of The Joy of Cooking *in which the authors said, in the best Michelin tradition, "this recipe is worthy of three stars." It remains so after more than four decades.*

INGREDIENTS	2 cups finely chopped dates or date crystals 2 cups boiling water 2 eggs, room temperature ³/₄ cup brown sugar 2 cups whole-wheat flour 2 teaspoons baking powder 1 teaspoon baking soda 2 cups bran flakes ¹/₂ teaspoon vanilla extract 1 cup chopped walnuts
BAKING PAN	1 medium (8"-x-4") loaf pan, greased or Teflon, long sides and bottom lined with buttered wax paper
BY HAND OR MIXER 18 mins.	Place the dates in a bowl and pour the boiling water over them. Set aside. In a mixing or mixer bowl beat the eggs until light and slowly add

the brown sugar, beating constantly. When this is creamy, gradually add 1 cup whole-wheat flour, the baking powder, and baking soda. Add half the date mixture and the other cup whole-wheat flour, the bran, and vanilla. When this is blended, add the second portion of the date mixture and the chopped nuts.

BY PROCESSOR
5 mins.

Soak the date bits in boiling water, as above.

Attach the steel blade.

The order of adding the ingredients differs from above.

Measure 1 cup wheat flour, the bran, baking powder, baking soda, and sugar into the work bowl. Pulse several times to mix well. With the processor running, pour the date-water mixture through the feed tube. Stop the processor, add the other cup flour, the eggs, and vanilla. Replace the cover and process for 5 to 6 seconds—not to knead but to blend thoroughly. Blend in the chopped nuts.

SHAPING
3 mins.

Pour or spoon the mixture into the pan.

PREHEAT

Preheat the oven to 350°, allowing the batter to stand for 20 minutes while the oven heats.

BAKING
350°
1 hour

Place the pan on the middle shelf of the oven and bake until the loaf is a deep crusty brown and tests done when a wooden pick inserted in the center of the loaf comes out clean and dry.

(If using a convection oven, reduce heat 50°.)

FINAL STEP

Remove the bread from the oven. Turn the pan on its side and pull the loaf out by tugging gently on the wax paper edges. Peel the paper from the loaf and leave it to cool on a metal rack.

This loaf will be better after it has been allowed to age overnight. It keeps well for several days wrapped in plastic, or frozen at 0° for several months.

Familia-Raisin Bread   [three small loaves]

Swiss Familia, a cereal rich with fruit and nuts, is one of the chief ingredients in this loaf adapted from a recipe created by a 1984 Pillsbury Bake-Off® Contest winner, Bonnie Komlos, of Ambridge, Pennsylvania. I have substituted Familia for the granola in Bonnie's version because the Swiss product is 25 percent bran and includes whole-wheat and rye flakes, hazelnuts, dried apple flakes, crushed almonds, and wheat germ flakes. An impressive array of good things.

Familia, imported from Switzerland, can be found among the cereals in most supermarkets. If you cannot find Familia, substitute granola.

INGREDIENTS

3 to 3½ cups bread or all-purpose flour, approximately
1 package dry yeast
½ cup nonfat dry milk
1 teaspoon salt
1½ cups hot water (120°–130°)
⅓ cup honey
¼ cup vegetable oil
½ cup Familia (or granola)
¼ cup sunflower seeds
½ cup raisins
1 tablespoon orange zest or finely chopped rind
1 egg, beaten, mixed with 1 tablespoon milk

BAKING PAN

3 small (7"-x-3") loaf pans, greased or Teflon

BY HAND
OR MIXER
8 mins.

Into a large mixing or mixer bowl measure 2½ cups flour and the dry ingredients. Stir to blend. Mix in the hot water, honey, and oil. When the ingredients have been blended, add the Familia, sunflower seeds, raisins, and orange zest or rind. Blend. Stir by hand for 2 minutes, or with the mixer flat beater at medium speed for 2 minutes.

Add flour, ¼ cup at a time, to form a mass that can be lifted from the bowl, or left under the mixer dough hook. Add liberal sprinkles of flour if the dough is sticky.

KNEADING
10 mins.

Knead by hand with a strong push-turn-fold rhythm until the dough becomes soft and elastic and has lost its stickiness. Add sprinkles of flour if needed. If using the mixer, continue under the dough hook until the dough cleans the bowl and forms a ball around the rotating hook.

Add sprinkles of flour if the dough sticks to the sides. Knead for 10 minutes.

BY PROCESSOR
5 mins.

Attach the plastic dough blade.

Measure 2½ cups flour into the work bowl and add the dry ingredients. Pulse to blend. In a small bowl mix the hot water, honey, and oil; with the machine running, pour the liquid through the feed tube. Stop the machine and add the Familia, sunflower seeds, raisins, and orange zest or rind. Pulse 6 or 7 times to blend the fruit and nuts into the heavy batter. Add sufficient flour to form a dough that will clean the sides of the bowl and ride with the blade.

KNEADING **45 secs.**	Process to knead for 45 seconds.
FIRST RISING **1 hour**	Place the dough in a greased bowl, cover tightly with plastic wrap, and put aside to rise until double in volume, about 1 hour.
SHAPING **8 mins.**	Punch down the dough and place on the floured work surface. Divide into 3 pieces. Shape each into a ball, and then press the dough into an oval the length of the prepared loaf pan. Fold the oval, pinch the seam together, tuck in the ends, and drop into the pan. Push the dough with your fingers into the corners.
SECOND RISING **45 mins.**	Cover the pans with wax or parchment paper and put aside to let rise to the edge of the pans, about 45 minutes.
PREHEAT	Preheat the oven to 375° 20 minutes before baking.

BAKING
375°
35 mins.
	Brush the loaves with the egg-milk wash.
	    Place the pans on the middle shelf of the moderate oven. Bake until a golden brown, about 35 minutes.
	    (If using a convection oven, reduce heat 50°.)

FINAL STEP	Remove from the oven and turn the loaves out of the pans. Let cool on a metal rack. This loaf freezes nicely and will keep for several months at 0°.

Peanut Batter Bread   [one large or two small loaves]

While it may sound like a loaf dreamed up just for kids, its appeal is universal. It has a crunchy bite provided by the chunky peanut butter and finely chopped peanuts. The peanuts give the loaf only a light brown color but a solid flavor of nuts.

I had expected this loaf to appeal principally to children, so I was delighted to find adults joining me in enjoying it, too.

INGREDIENTS	1¼ cups hot water (120°–130°) ¼ cup finely chopped salted peanuts ¼ cup chunk-style peanut butter ¼ cup firmly packed brown sugar 2 teaspoons salt 3 cups bread or all-purpose flour 1 package dry yeast
BAKING PANS	1 large (9"-x-5") or 2 small (7"-x-3") loaf pans, greased or Teflon

BY HAND OR MIXER 15 mins.	In a mixing or mixer bowl measure the water, peanuts, peanut butter, sugar, salt, 1½ cups flour, and yeast. Beat at medium speed with the mixer flat beater for 2 minutes, scraping the sides and bottom of the bowl occasionally. Or use a wooden spoon—200 strong, vigorous strokes by hand. Add the rest of the flour, ½ cup at a time, to make a smooth batter. Beat until the flour has been completely absorbed.
BY PROCESSOR 4 mins.	Attach the steel blade. The order of adding ingredients differs from above. Measure 2½ cups flour into the work bowl and add the yeast, brown sugar, salt, and chopped peanuts; pulse to blend. With the machine running, pour the water through the feed tube and add the peanut butter. Stop the machine. Uncover and add the balance of the flour. Cover and pulse 6 or 8 times to thoroughly blend the flour in with the other ingredients. Transfer the batter to a bowl to let rise.
FIRST RISING 45 mins.	Cover the bowl tightly with plastic wrap and put aside at room temperature until the batter has doubled in bulk, 45 minutes.
SHAPING 5 mins.	Stir down the batter with a dozen strong strokes. Spread evenly in the pan or pans. Dampen your fingers and pat the top of the loaves to smooth the surface.
SECOND RISING 40 mins.	Cover the pans with wax or parchment paper and leave until the batter has doubled and is about level with the top of the pan, 40 minutes.
PREHEAT	Preheat the oven to 375° 20 minutes before baking.
BAKING 375° 45 mins.	Place the pan(s) in the oven until the bread is lightly browned and loose in its pan(s), about 45 minutes. Cover with foil if the bread starts to brown too fast. When tapping the bottom crust yields a hard, hollow sound, it is baked. If not, return to the oven, without the pan if you wish a deep brown, for an additional 5 to 10 minutes. Midway during baking, shift the pans so the loaves are exposed equally to temperature variations. (If using a convection oven, reduce heat 50°.)
FINAL STEP	Remove the bread from the oven. Cool on a wire rack before serving. Freezes well.

Raisin Coffee Cake   [two 8" round cakes]

While it is called a cake (kaffe kuchen in German), it is really a delicious yeast-raised bread that was regularly on my mother's breakfast table. This version is filled to bursting with raisins—1 cup for each cake.

INGREDIENTS

Dough:
3^1/$_2$ cups bread flour, approximately
2 packages dry yeast
1 teaspoon salt
2 tablespoons sugar
^{3}/$_4$ cup milk, room temperature
^{1}/$_4$ cup (^{1}/$_2$ stick) butter, room temperature
2 eggs, room temperature
2 cups raisins

Topping:
^{1}/$_2$ cup bread or all-purpose flour
^{1}/$_4$ cup (^{1}/$_2$ stick) butter, room temperature
^{1}/$_4$ cup sugar
^{1}/$_2$ teaspoon ground cinnamon
2 tablespoons butter, melted

BAKING PANS

Two 8" round cake pans, greased or Teflon

BY HAND
OR MIXER
15 mins.

Into a large mixing or mixer bowl pour 2 cups flour and add the dry ingredients. Stir to blend well. Pour in the milk, stir, and drop in the butter. With a wooden spoon or with the mixer flat beater stir until the mixture has absorbed the butter, and then drop in the eggs, one at a time. It will be a heavy batter.

Add the balance of the flour, ½ cup at a time, until the dough becomes a shaggy mass that can be placed on the work surface, or left in the mixer under the dough hook. If the dough is sticky, add scant sprinkles of flour.

The raisins will be added after the first rising.

KNEADING
10 mins.

Turn the dough out onto a lightly floured work surface and knead for 10 minutes with a strong push-turn-fold motion. The dough will become smooth and elastic. Add light sprinkles of flour if the dough sticks to the hands or the work surface. If using a dough hook in a mixer bowl, the sides of the bowl should be wiped clean by the force of the revolving ball of dough, 10 minutes.

BY PROCESSOR
7 mins.

Attach the steel blade.

Measure 2 cups flour and the dry ingredients into the work bowl. Pulse to blend. Pour in the milk, and process briefly to blend the ingredients. Drop the eggs through the feed tube while the machine is running, and add the butter. The batter will be thick.

Add the balance of the flour, ¼ cup at a time, until the dough forms a mass that cleans the sides of the bowl and is pushed around the bowl by the blade.

KNEADING
45 secs.

Let the machine run for 45 seconds to knead.

The dough may be sticky when lifted from the bowl but it will become smooth with a few sprinkles of flour.

FIRST RISING
I hour

Place the dough in a greased bowl, cover tightly with plastic wrap, and put aside at room temperature to double in volume, about 1 hour.

SHAPING
10 mins.

Remove the dough from the bowl and knead for a moment or so to deflate. Press the dough into an oval and spread the raisins over the top. Work these into the dough with a kneading motion.

When the raisins are evenly mixed throughout the dough, divide the dough into 2 pieces. Place each piece in a prepared cake pan; spread and pat the dough with the hands to cover the bottom of the pans. If the dough should draw back as it is worked, allow it to relax for a few minutes and then return to the task.

SECOND RISING
1½ hours

Cover the pans with a cloth or sheet of wax paper and leave at room temperature to double in volume, about 1½ hours.

While the dough is rising, prepare the streusel topping. Measure the flour into a bowl and drop in the butter. The flour must be worked into the butter until it resembles coarse crumbs. This can be done between the fingers or, better, with a wire pastry blender. Work in the sugar and cinnamon. Set the mixture aside.

If using a food processor, with the steel blade in place, combine the flour, butter, sugar, and cinnamon in the work bowl. Process until the ingredients resemble coarse meal.

PREHEAT

Preheat the oven to 350° 20 minutes before baking.

BAKING
350°
30 mins.

Uncover the cakes and brush with melted butter. Sprinkle the streusel topping generously over the tops.

Bake on the middle rack of the oven for about 30 minutes, or until a pick inserted in the center of the cake comes out clean.

(If using a convection oven, reduce heat 50°.)

FINAL STEP

Cool the cakes on a wire rack.

These freeze well.

Italian Olive Bread   [one loaf]

Olives pop up in the most unexpected places, and none more surprising than a loaf of Italian bread, rich in eggs and butter. It is almost as rewarding to look at a slice of olive bread, of black and green olives sheared off by the bread knife in a mosaic pattern, as it is to have it for brunch and snacking.

This Italian-born bread is made throughout that country with one or two of many kinds of olives—Spanish-style green ones stuffed with pimiento, ripe black ones, salt cured as well as the black niçoise-style berries (which is what they really are). Authentic olive breads often are made with unpitted olives, but then expect some hard bites.

This recipe is adapted from one in Sunset magazine, published in California, where olives of a quality equal to the Italian are harvested. While I lived for many years in San Francisco and environs, and traveled Italy extensively, I had never tasted bread made with olives until I baked this loaf in my Indiana kitchen.

For a large gathering this recipe can easily be doubled and baked in one long loaf. Great for an autumn tailgate party and served with thin slices of cured ham, hard-boiled eggs, or a ripened goat cheese.

INGREDIENTS

2½ to 3 cups bread or all-purpose flour

1 package dry yeast

2 tablespoons sugar

1 teaspoon salt

⅓ cup hot water (120°–130°)

2 eggs

¼ cup (½ stick) butter, room temperature

½ cup green pimiento-stuffed olives

½ cup pitted ripe black olives (or other olives of choice)

1 egg yolk, beaten

BAKING SHEET

1 baking sheet (14"-x-16"), greased, Teflon, or sprinkled with cornmeal

BY HAND
OR MIXER
15 mins.

In a mixing or mixer bowl pour 2 cups flour and add the dry ingredients. Stir to blend. Form a well in the flour and pour in the hot water. With a wooden spoon pull flour into the water to form a batter. Break the eggs and drop into the batter. Vigorously stir the eggs and batter together until the eggs have been absorbed. Cut the butter into 2 or 3 pieces and drop into the mixture. With a wooden spoon or mixer flat beater, mix until the batterlike dough is smooth and silky, about 2 minutes.

Stir in flour, ½ cup at a time, until the dough is a ball and can be turned out of the bowl onto a floured work surface. The dough should not be sticky because of the high fat content of the butter and eggs. But if it is, add sprinkles of flour.

KNEADING
8 mins.

Knead by hand or under a dough hook until the dough is smooth and elastic, about 8 minutes. Knead with a strong push-turn-fold motion, and occasionally lift the dough and throw it back onto the work surface. Be aggressive.

BY PROCESSOR
2 mins.

Attach the steel blade.

Place 2 cups flour in the work bowl and add the dry ingredients. Pulse to blend. Remove the cover and add the hot water, eggs, and butter. Turn on the machine for 30 seconds.

Add flour, ¼ cup at a time, through the feed tube, pulsing after each addition.

KNEADING
45 secs.

When the batter becomes dough and begins to clean the sides of the bowl, knead for 45 seconds. During kneading, the dough will ride with or on the blade.

FIRST RISING
1½ hours

Place the dough in a greased bowl and set aside at room temperature to rise. Because of its richness, the dough is slow to begin rising, but it will double in bulk in about 1½ hours.

SHAPING
15 mins.

Drain the olives and mix the green and black ones together so they can be uniformly scattered over the dough. Set aside.

Punch down the dough and turn onto the floured work surface. Pat and push the dough into a 14" square. Allow it to relax for 3 or 4 minutes before scattering the olives. Press the olives lightly into the dough.

Roll up the dough as for a jelly roll to enclose the olives and place seam side down on a baking sheet. Tuck the open ends of the dough under to make a smooth surface. Pat the loaf to flatten and shape into an oval about 2" thick.

SECOND RISING
30 mins.

Cover the loaf with wax paper or plastic wrap and leave at room temperature until puffy, about 30 minutes.

PREHEAT

Preheat the oven to 350° 20 minutes before baking.

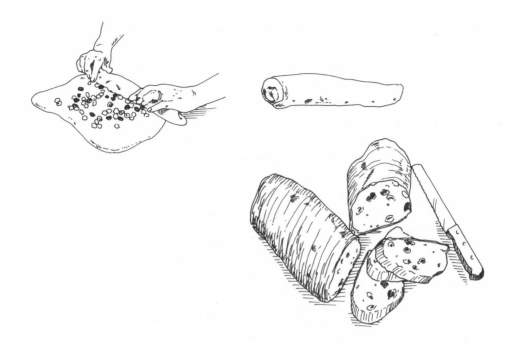

BAKING	Uncover the loaf and brush with the beaten egg yolk.
350°	Bake in the oven until richly browned, about 45 minutes.
45 mins.	(If using a convection oven, reduce heat 50°.)

FINAL STEP

Place on a rack to cool for at least 10 minutes. Serve warm or at room temperature.

If made ahead, let cool, package airtight, and let stand overnight at room temperature. Freeze to store longer; let thaw, wrapped, for at least 6 hours. To reheat, place the unwrapped loaf in a 325° oven for 20 to 30 minutes.

The bread is delicious sliced and toasted. Spread slices with anchovy or unsalted butter.

Fresh Strawberry Bread   [one medium loaf]

Strawberries are usually served as jam on top of a slice of bread, not in the bread itself. This loaf combines the best of two worlds—a slice of strawberry bread, spread with cream cheese, topped with thin slices of the fresh berries.

The women of Holland, Michigan, most of them of Dutch descent, have gone into family recipe files to put together a fine Junior Welfare League cookbook, Eet Smakelijk (Eat Well and with Taste). This is from the kitchen of Mrs. William G. Beebe.

INGREDIENTS

1 pint fresh strawberries, washed and hulled
1³/₄ cups bread or all-purpose flour
1 teaspoon baking soda
1 teaspoon salt
¹/₄ teaspoon baking powder
³/₄ cup sugar
¹/₃ cup butter or other shortening
2 eggs
¹/₃ cup water
¹/₂ cup chopped walnuts
Cream cheese, softened (optional)

BAKING PAN

1 medium (8½"-x-4½") loaf pan, greased or Teflon, long sides and bottom lined with buttered wax paper

PREHEAT

Preheat the oven to 350°.

PREPARATION
5 mins.

Crush enough of the strawberries to fill 1 cup. Pour into a small saucepan and heat over a medium flame. Cook for 1 minute, stirring constantly. Cool. Slice the remaining strawberries and chill.

BY HAND
8 mins.

In a medium bowl combine the dry ingredients, except the sugar.
    In a large mixing bowl cream the sugar and shortening; then add the eggs and water, mixing until light and fluffy.
    Add the flour mixture to the creamed mixture, mixing well to blend. Stir in the crushed strawberries and walnuts.
    Pour or spoon the mixture into the prepared pan.

BAKING
350°
1 hour

Bake for 1 hour, or until a pick inserted in the center comes out clean.
    (If using a convection oven, reduce heat 50°.)

FINAL STEP

Remove the bread from the oven. When the loaf has cooled in the pan for 10 minutes, turn onto a rack to cool.
    Present to your guests thin slices spread with softened cream cheese and topped with the reserved chilled strawberries. Families will like it, too.

LITTLE BREADS

R ANGING FROM POPOVERS and Buttery Rowies to Kaiser Rolls and Sumsums, these wonderful small breads have been assembled in this chapter devoted to one-bite or two-bite recipes. There is no other reason for presenting Swiss Croissants in a chapter with English Muffins except neither are very big and both are very good.

German Sour Cream Twists
[three dozen large or four dozen small twists]

This is a crispy, flaky, sugar-crusted delicacy rich with sour cream, butter, and eggs. These can be made any size but I like twists 4 by 1 inch for several bites at breakfast, or petite ones 2 by ¹/₂ inch for one-bite pieces at a buffet or tea service.

Note: *This is a dough rich in fat and easy to work but it will not be as elastic as other yeast doughs. It will rise and become puffy nevertheless.*

INGREDIENTS

3¹/₂ to 4 cups all-purpose flour, approximately
1 teaspoon salt
1 package dry yeast
1 cup sour cream, room temperature
1 egg, room temperature
2 egg yolks, room temperature
¹/₂ cup (1 stick) butter, room temperature
¹/₂ cup margarine or other solid shortening
1 teaspoon vanilla extract
1 cup sugar

BAKING SHEET   1 large or 2 small baking sheets, lightly greased or covered with parchment paper, or Teflon

BY HAND
OR MIXER
10 mins.

Measure 2 cups flour into a mixing or mixer bowl and add the salt and yeast. Stir to blend. In a saucepan heat to lukewarm and stir together the sour cream, egg, egg yolks, butter, and shortening. Add the vanilla. If by hand, form a well in the flour and pour in the liquid to make a thick batter. Beat vigorously with a wooden spoon. Add flour, ¼ cup at a time, to form a rough, shaggy mass that can be lifted to the work surface to knead.

If using a mixer, attach the flat beater, turn to medium speed, and pour in the liquid. Beat for 2 minutes. Attach the dough hook. Add flour, ¼ cup at a time, to create a dough that is soft and forms around the dough hook as it revolves.

The dough will be quite buttery and be filmed with considerable oil. Light sprinkles of flour will keep it manageable.

KNEADING
5 mins.

If by hand, begin to work with a dough blade, spatula, or putty knife, turning and folding the dough. Then use your hands. Knead for 5 minutes. If using the dough hook in the mixer bowl knead for 5 minutes. Add sprinkles of flour if the dough is wet with oil.

BY PROCESSOR
5 mins.

Attach the plastic dough blade.

Measure 2½ cups flour into the work bowl and add the salt and yeast. Pulse.

Prepare the sour cream, egg, egg yolks, butter, shortening, and vanilla, as above. With the machine running, pour the lukewarm liquid through the feed tube to form a thick batter.

Add flour, ¼ cup at a time, until a rough ball of dough forms and rides with the blade. The dough will clean the bowl as it spins.

KNEADING
30 secs.

Process the dough to knead for 30 seconds.

FIRST RISING
1½ hours

The dough is so buttery that there is no need to grease the bowl beforehand. Place the dough in the bowl, cover with plastic wrap, and set aside to double in bulk, 1½ hours.

SHAPING
10 mins.

Remove the dough from the bowl and form into a ball. Liberally sprinkle sugar on the work surface and on the ball of dough. Roll out the dough to an 18" length, occasionally sprinkling on sugar. Fold the dough in half lengthwise and then into quarters. Roll out the dough again into a rectangle 18" x ½". Sprinkle with sugar.

Rather than use the rolling pin, I often press and shape the dough under the palms of my hands. The twists may be made large or small. With a pizza cutter or knife held against a yardstick, cut the rectangle into lengths—1" wide by 4" long for the larger twist, and ½" wide by 2" for the smaller ones. Twist each piece and place 1" apart on the prepared baking sheet(s).

SECOND RISING
1 hour

Cover the twists with parchment or wax paper and set aside to become puffy and raised, about 1 hour.

PREHEAT

Preheat the oven to 375° about 20 minutes before baking.

BAKING
375°
25 mins.

Uncover the twists and sprinkle liberally with sugar.
Place in the oven and bake until lightly browned, about 25 minutes. (If using a convection oven, reduce heat 40°.)

FINAL STEP

Immediately lift the twists from the baking sheet with a spatula, otherwise the sugared bottoms will stick and never part from the pan in whole pieces. Place on a metal rack to cool.

Chinese Steamed Buns   [one dozen buns]

A steamed bun, one of the delights of the Chinese cuisine, is soft, puffy, and delicious. Originally from northern China where rice is not grown, the steamed bun has long since moved from a regional bread to a favorite item on most Chinese menus. It is especially good served with duck and pork.

Don't discard the buns when they have lost their freshness. Slice ¼" thick, dip in an egg-milk mixture, and fry or deep-fry. Sprinkle with confectioners' sugar and serve as a sweet treat.

The bun can easily be transformed into bao—"bread with a heart." It can be given that heart from any of a number of different fillings. One of my favorites is char siu bao, a bun stuffed with a mixture of barbecued pork, green onions, sesame oil, soy sauce, and sugar (see below). There are also lop chong bao (sausage), siu mai bao (shrimp), and gai bao (chicken).

This recipe for the steamed bun and the char siu filling came from China by way of Hawaii, where for years street vendors sold them from baskets hanging at the ends of long, sturdy poles balanced on shoulders. Today these buns have become a standard dim sum item and are found almost everywhere in the islands served as snacks with tea, as hors d'oeuvres and appetizers at parties, and sent to work in a brown bag lunch.

Char siu, *the principal ingredient in the filling, is barbecued pork, brushed while cooking with a sweet reddish sauce. It can be bought in Chinese markets in large American cities, and in most Chinese restaurants. However, an excellent substitute, with little change in flavor, is roast pork or ham.*

The recipe for making the char siu *filling follows the one for the steamed buns.*

INGREDIENTS

3 cups bread or all-purpose flour, approximately
I package dry yeast
¹/₄ cup sugar
¹/₄ cup nonfat dry milk
I cup hot water (120°–130°)
I tablespoon shortening
¹/₂ teaspoon baking powder

SPECIAL
EQUIPMENT

A bamboo steamer, set in a wok containing water, is ideal. Western-style steamers can be substituted.

Cut 3" circles of parchment or wax paper to place under the buns so they do not stick to the steamer bottom.

BY HAND
OR MIXER
12 mins.

Into a mixing or mixer bowl measure 2 cups flour and add the dry ingredients, except the baking powder. Stir to blend, and fashion a well in the flour. Pour the hot water into the well and drop in the shortening. Let stand for a moment to soften the shortening. With a wooden spoon or mixer flat beater, stir vigorously for 2 minutes. Sprinkle in the baking powder. Add flour, ¼ cup at a time, mixed into the body of the dough until it forms a rough but elastic mass that can be lifted from the bowl. If using a mixer, attach the dough hook.
Note: Don't overload this dough with flour. It must be soft and elastic so that later the small pieces can be stretched over the filling with ease.

KNEADING
10 mins.

If by hand, lift the dough to a floured work surface and knead with a strong rhythm of push-turn-fold. Add sprinkles of flour if the dough is sticky, but keep it on the moist side rather than making a hard ball. If under the dough hook, the dough will clean the sides of the bowl and form a ball around the hook. If it sticks to the sides, add small portions of flour, but be niggardly. Knead for 10 minutes.

BY PROCESSOR
4 mins.

Attach the steel blade.

Measure 2¼ cups of flour into the work bowl and add the dry ingredients, except the baking powder. Blend. With the processor running, pour the water through the tube; add shortening. Stop machine and sprinkle in the baking powder.

Add flour, ¼ cup at a time, with the processor on. The amount of flour is sufficient when the dough cleans the sides of the bowl and rides on the blade.

KNEADING
50 secs.

Process with the machine running for 50 seconds.

The dough will be somewhat sticky when taken from the machine, but a dusting of flour will make it possible to work.

RISING
45 mins.

Place the dough in a greased bowl, cover tightly with plastic wrap, and put aside at room temperature to double in volume, 45 minutes.

SHAPING
12 mins.

Plain: Punch down the dough, and divide into 12 equal pieces. Form each into a ball by rolling under a cupped palm. Press down with force.

Filled: Form the dough into balls, as above. Let them rest a moment and then flatten each into a 4" circle. Place a spoonful of filling in the center of each circle; gather the dough over the filling, make small pleats, and pinch the seam tightly closed.

REST
10 mins.

Place each ball with the seam down on a circle of wax or parchment paper on the steamer rack. Let the balls rest for 10 minutes but no longer. Be precise about the timing.

While the buns are resting, bring the water in the wok or conventional steamer to a boil.

STEAMING
15–20 mins.

Lower the rack into the steamer. If the steamer cover is metal (rather than bamboo) fold a small towel and place under the cover (and above the buns) so the cloth will absorb the steam and not let drops of moisture rain on the buns as they are being cooked. Cover and steam for 15 to 20 minutes. Be certain the water does not boil away during the process.

FINAL STEP

Lift the rack out of the steamer. Let cook for a moment or two and take out the rolls. Serve warm.

To reheat the buns, cover with foil and place in a 350° oven for 15 minutes.

Char Siu

Almost any cooked meat or seafood mixture can be used to fill a steamed bun.
This one happens to be my favorite.

INGREDIENTS

1 teaspoon sesame oil
$^1/_2$ pound *char siu* or roast pork or ham, finely diced
3 tablespoons chopped green onions
$2^1/_2$ tablespoons sugar
4 teaspoons soy sauce
$^1/_4$ teaspoon salt
1 teaspoon grated ginger
2 teaspoons all-purpose flour
2 teaspoons cornstarch
$^1/_4$ cup water

PREPARATION
10 mins.

In a saucepan, heat the oil and stir-fry the diced meat for 30 seconds. Add the onions, sugar, soy sauce, salt, and grated ginger.

Mix the flour and cornstarch with the water. Stir into the *char siu* mixture. Cook over medium heat for about 3 minutes, until the mixture thickens. Put aside to cool.

I like the filling to have a smooth texture, so when it cools I process it for 3 seconds.

Lenora's Yeast Rolls   [two to three dozen pieces]

In this book a person's name is seldom bestowed on a recipe unless in good conscience it could not be otherwise. Even a mother's.

So it is for an elegant and delicious dinner roll made by my mother that this recipe is named. It is a lovely, light, golden roll that won for her several blue ribbons at the Indiana State Fair. She was an outstanding cook, but no matter what special dish she placed before her guests, it was her rolls that drew the most flattering remarks from men—and requests for the recipe from the wives.

Lenora called them, simply, her "yeast rolls." Here is her recipe to be made into most of the dinner roll shapes—Parker House, bowknots, rosettes, butterhorns, crescents, cloverleafs, fan-tans, and pan rolls.

INGREDIENTS

1 egg, room temperature
$^1/_4$ cup sugar
$^1/_2$ cup mashed potato or prepared instant
$^3/_4$ cup milk, room temperature
$^1/_3$ cup ($^5/_8$ stick) butter, softened

$^1/_2$ teaspoon salt
3 to 3$^1/_2$ cups all-purpose flour, approximately
I package dry yeast
$^1/_4$ cup ($^1/_2$ stick) butter, melted

**BAKING SHEET,
MUFFIN PANS,
AND/OR CAKE
PAN**

Baking sheet or sheets for Parker House, bowknots, rosettes, butterhorns, and crescent rolls. Cloverleafs and fan-tans are placed in muffin tins, while pan rolls are set in 8" or 9" cake pans. Select the proper ones and grease.

**BY HAND
OR MIXER
15 mins.**

In a large mixing or mixer bowl blend the egg and sugar. Add the potato, milk, softened butter, and salt. Mix together either with a wooden spoon or mixer flat beater. Add 2 cups flour and the yeast. Beat 100 strokes, or for 1 minute in the mixer. Gradually add flour, ½ cup at a time, first with the wooden spoon and then by hand as the dough becomes firm. If using a mixer, attach the dough hook.

Work the flour into a moist ball until it cleans the sides of the bowl and has lost much of its stickiness. Under the dough hook, the dough will clean the sides of the bowl and form a ball about the revolving hook.

It is an easy dough to work because of its high butterfat content.

**KNEADING
8 mins.**

If by hand, turn the soft dough onto a floured work surface and knead with a strong push-turn-fold motion until it becomes smooth and velvety under your hands. Or knead under the dough hook in the mixer. If the ball of dough sticks to the sides of the bowl during kneading, add sprinkles of flour. Knead for 8 minutes.

**BY PROCESSOR
3 mins.**

Attach the steel blade.

The sequence of adding ingredients varies from above.

Measure 1½ cups flour into the work bowl and add the yeast, sugar, and salt. Pulse to blend. With the processor running, pour the milk through the feed tube, and add the egg, softened butter, and the potato.

Add flour, ¼ cup at a time, either by taking off the cover or using the feed tube, until the batter becomes a rough mass of dough. If the ball of dough does not clean the sides of the bowl, add small portions of flour.

**KNEADING
I min.**

When the dough has formed a ball, process for 1 minute to knead.

Stop the machine and test the dough with your fingers. If it is too dry, add water by the teaspoon with the machine running; if it is too wet, add flour by the tablespoon. The dough should be very elastic when stretched between the hands. If not, return to the work bowl and process for a few more seconds.

FIRST RISING
1¼ hours

Return the dough to the bowl, stretch a length of plastic wrap across the top, and leave at room temperature until the dough has risen to double in volume, 1¼ hours.

SHAPING
20 mins.

The dough (4 cups of which will weigh about 2 pounds) can be made into one shape of dinner roll or divided among the various shapes, as desired, in about 20 minutes.

Dust the work surface with flour. Divide the dough in half.

PARKER HOUSE

(28 to 32 pieces):

Roll the first half into a circle, ⅜" thick. Cut with a 2½" or 3" biscuit cutter. Place a light rolling pin in the center of the small rounds of dough. Carefully roll toward each end to create a valley through the center of the round. The center will be about ⅛" thick while the ends will be thicker. Or you may press the rounded handle of a knife into the dough to achieve the same results. Keep the rolling pin or knife handle dusted with flour as you work. Carefully brush each round to within ¼" of the edges with the melted butter. This will allow the baked roll to open as a pocket.

Fold over the round of dough so the cut edges just meet. Pinch with the fingers to seal, and press the folded edge (the hinge) securely. Place each roll about ½" apart on a baking sheet as it's completed. Repeat with the remainder of the dough, as desired.

BOWKNOTS AND
ROSETTES

(24 pieces):

With your palms, roll each dough half into a 12" rope. Divide the rope into 12 pieces. Roll each into a slender 8" rope. For a bowknot, tie each into a simple knot. For a rosette, tie a simple knot and bring one end up and through the center of the knot, bringing the other end over the side and under. Place on a baking sheet 1" apart; press the ends to the sheet to keep them from untying.

BUTTERHORNS
AND CRESCENTS

(16 pieces):

Roll each dough half into an 8" circle. Let the dough relax for 3 or 4 minutes before cutting into 8 wedges with a pastry wheel or knife. Roll up the wedge, toward the point, pulling and stretching the dough slightly as you roll. For butterhorns, place each on the baking sheet, with the points under. For crescents, roll the wedge in the same manner but curve each into a crescent as it is placed on the baking sheet.

CLOVERLEAF	(12 pieces):

With your palms, roll each dough half into a 16" rope. If the rope draws back, allow it to relax for 3 or 4 minutes before proceeding. Cut each rope into 18 pieces. Shape each into a small ball; place 3, in triangle formation, in each muffin cup.

FAN-TANS (24 pieces):

Roll each dough half into an 8"-x-16" rectangle—twice as long as it is wide. If the dough pulls back, let it relax for a few minutes. Brush with melted butter. With a pastry wheel or knife, cut the dough across the narrow width into five 1½" strips. Stack the 5 strips and cut the stack into 12 pieces. Place each into a 2½" muffin cup with the cut side of the dough up.

PAN ROLLS (24 pieces):

With your hands roll each dough half into a 12" rope. Cut into 12 pieces. Shape each into a tight ball under a cupped palm. Arrange in the pan.

SECOND RISING
30 mins.

Brush the roll tops with melted butter, cover with wax paper, and leave at room temperature until the rolls have doubled in size, 30 minutes.

PREHEAT

Preheat the oven to 400° 20 minutes before baking.

BAKING
400°
12–15 mins.

Place the rolls in the oven and bake until a golden brown, about 12 to 15 minutes.

(If using a convection oven, reduce heat 40°.)

FINAL STEP

Remove from the oven and immediately brush with melted butter. Place on a metal rack to cool.

Delicious served warm from the oven.

Gipfelteig
(Swiss Croissants)

[about four dozen rolls]

The Gipfelteig is small (about 1 ounce), rich, and certainly one of the most praiseworthy morsels to be found in Switzerland—specifically in a 100-year-old Bäckerei in Wichtrach, 40 kilometers south of Bern, on the way south and east to the resort areas of Thun and Interlaken and the great glacier at Grindelwald.

We have gone back to this Swiss village a number of times because of the delicious breads and pastries baked by Rolf and Verena Thomas and because they have become good friends, beginning from the day we stopped at the

*Hotel Kreuz (10 rooms) down the road and discovered that the lovely crois-
sants came from just two doors away.*

*Four of Herr Thomas's delicate Gipfelteigs will fit comfortably on the flat of
the hand as compared to one French croissant to which it is closely related.*

*If there is one different ingredient in this small bread that contributes so
much to its extraordinary flavor it's the Schweinefett, country lard, used in
making the dough. It imparts a flavor that is difficult to duplicate with any
other shortening. Herr Thomas prefers margarine over butter for the rest of the
shortening because he feels it lets the lard flavor come through more clearly.
And for him it is less expensive.*

*The dough is rolled unusually thin—$1/8$ inch or less—before the triangles are
cut. There are 55 layers of dough and margarine when all of the turns have
been made. Herr Thomas agrees that not all of the layers are retained in
rolling, but enough remain, he believes, to impart a special texture not found in
other croissants.*

Note: *The preparation of the dough before it is cut into triangles is best done
the night before baking, since the layered dough must be thoroughly chilled
before the final step.*

INGREDIENTS

6 cups bread or all-purpose flour, approximately
2 packages dry yeast
4 teaspoons salt
$1/4$ cup sugar
2 cups hot water (120°–130°)
6 tablespoons lard, room temperature
I cup (2 sticks) margarine
I egg, beaten, mixed with I tablespoon milk

BAKING SHEETS

1 or 2 baking sheets, greased or Teflon (1 baking sheet means 2 baking
periods)

BY HAND
OR MIXER
25 mins.

In a large mixing or mixer bowl combine 3 cups flour and the dry
ingredients. Pour the hot water into the bowl. Stir to make a smooth
batter. Allow this to stand for 15 minutes.

The lard, at room temperature, is added to the batter and blended
with 25 strong strokes of a large wooden spoon or the flat beater in the
mixer bowl. Pour in additional flour, ½ cup at a time, and stir first with
a utensil and then with your hands to make a shaggy mass that cleans
the sides of the bowl. If using the mixer, remove the flat beater and
replace it with the dough hook.

KNEADING
10 mins.

Lift the dough to the floured work surface and knead with a strong push-turn-fold rhythm to develop the dough into a soft, elastic mass. If using a mixer, the dough will clean the sides of the bowl and form a ball around the dough hook. Toss down light sprinkles of flour to control stickiness if it develops. Knead for 10 minutes.

BY PROCESSOR
20 mins.

This is a large recipe for most food processors so I suggest doing it in 2 batches.

Attach the plastic dough blade.

In the work bowl measure together 2 cups flour and the dry ingredients. Pulse. With the processor on, pour 1 cup hot water through the feed tube. Pour 1 cup hot water into the work bowl. Add the lard. Pulse to make a smooth batter. Allow this to stand for 15 minutes.

Turn on the processor and add flour, a small portion at a time, through the feed tube to make a rough ball that will ride on the blade and clean the sides of the bowl.

KNEADING
50 secs.

Process to knead for 50 seconds.

LAYERING
20 mins.

Unlike the French *boulanger* preparing layered croissants with cold margarine or butter, Herr Thomas does not chill the margarine before spreading it with his fingers across the rectangle of dough.

Knead the margarine with a pastry scraper to soften and cream. Set aside.

With a rolling pin and your fingers, roll and stretch the dough into a 14"-x-18" rectangle. Let it rest for 3 or 4 minutes to retain its shape. With your fingers or a rubber scraper, spread the margarine over the dough, leaving a 1" border of dough around the edges. This will allow the dough to seal together and hold in the fat when rolled.

Turn 1: Fold and overlap the dough lengthwise in 3 sections— as one would fold a business letter. The rectangle now measures about 6" x 14" and is 3 layers deep.

Turn 2: Lightly flour the dough and work surface. Turn the dough so the short sides of the rectangle are at 6 o'clock and 12 o'clock and roll out into a new rectangle—12" x 18". Fold again into thirds.

REFRIGERATION
3 hours or
overnight

Wrap the dough in a double thickness of damp towel so the surface of the dough will not dry out. Slip the dough packet into a plastic bag, lay on a baking sheet, and place in the refrigerator.

LAYERING
4 mins.

Turn 3: Unwrap the dough and place on the floured work surface. Carefully roll out the dough into a 12"-x-18" rectangle. Fold into thirds. This is the final turn before rolling dough into a thin sheet.

SHAPING
20 mins.

Have the work surface sprinkled with flour so the dough will move easily under the rolling pin. (This may also be done on a pastry cloth and with a cloth stocking on the pin.)

Roll the dough into a rectangle—about 18" x 36"—and very thin, about ⅛". Let the dough rest before cutting with a pastry wheel or the dough will draw back when cut.

With a yardstick as a guide, trim the dough and cut into 3 lengthwise sections 6" wide. The Gipfelteig triangles are 4" x 6". Mark each section at 4" intervals, alternating on the right and left sides of the section, to produce a series of long triangles.

Lay the triangles to one side. If there are too many to bake at one time, reserve the surplus in the refrigerator, separated by small pieces of wax paper.

With the rolling pin, roll each triangle back and forth one time to press it out and make thinner. Hold the point under a finger. With the other hand, roll up the dough toward the point. Place on the baking sheet about 1½" apart, with the tip under the body of the Gipfelteig to keep it from unrolling in the oven. Shape into a crescent.

RISING
1 hour

Brush each piece with the egg-milk glaze and leave uncovered at room temperature for about 1 hour.

PREHEAT

Preheat the oven to 375° 20 minutes before baking.

BAKING
375°
25 mins.

Brush the pieces again with the glaze.

Place the sheet or sheets on the middle shelf of the oven. Fifteen minutes later, shift the baking sheet(s) and quickly inspect the crescents. They are small and brown rapidly the final few minutes of baking. If your oven is hotter than it should be, be prepared to take out the breads a few minutes early. Bake for 10 minutes after inspecting.

(If using a convection oven, reduce heat 50° and use the same caution as above.)

FINAL STEP

Remove the Gipfelteig from the oven and cool on a metal rack. Serve while warm if possible.

To freeze, cool first on a rack and package airtight. Thaw before returning to a 350° oven for 12 minutes.

Petites Galettes Salées   [about forty-five pieces]
(Little Salted Biscuits)

On a discovery trip to Grenoble, on the Isère River in southeastern France, I found not only several outstanding recipes for big, husky loaves of peasant bread, but this recipe for bite-size little biscuits—ideal for entertaining, served alone or with spreads. The salt is in them—not sprinkled on.

INGREDIENTS

½ cup (1 stick) butter, room temperature, cut into pieces
½ cup hot water (120°–130°)
2¼ cups all-purpose flour, approximately
¼ cup nonfat dry milk
4 teaspoons sugar
2 teaspoons salt

BAKING SHEET

1 baking sheet

BY HAND
OR MIXER
15 mins.

Drop the butter into a mixing or mixer bowl. Pour in the hot water, which will further soften the butter. Let stand for 5 minutes.

By hand or with the mixer flat beater, stir in ¾ cup flour and the dry ingredients. This will be a soft batter. Add the rest of the flour, ¼ cup at a time, to form a ball of dough.

KNEADING
3 mins.

There is no leavening in this dough so it is not necessary to develop gluten as for a yeast-raised product. The kneading or working the dough is simply to blend ingredients and make a smooth dough.

If by hand, turn the dough onto a dusted work surface and work until the dough is smooth. If using a mixer, attach the dough hook. Add sprinkles of flour to give body to the dough, if needed. Work (or knead) the dough for about 3 minutes.

BY PROCESSOR
4 mins.

Attach the steel blade.

Prepare the butter and hot water, as above.

Place 1½ cups flour and the other dry ingredients in the work bowl; pulse to blend. With the processor running, pour the liquid through the feed tube into the bowl. Stop the machine.

Add flour, ¼ cup at a time, through the feed tube or by taking off the cover.

KNEADING
5 secs.

Stop the processor, and feel the dough. If it is soft and smooth, process for 5 seconds.

It may be slightly sticky but it will become manageable with a dusting of flour.

REST 1 hour	Place the dough in a bowl, cover with plastic wrap, and put aside at room temperature for 1 hour.
PREHEAT	Preheat the oven to 400° 20 minutes before baking.
SHAPING 10 mins.	Turn the dough onto a floured work surface and roll into a rectangle about 10" x 18"—and no more than ⅛" thick. Don't rush. Pull gently with your hands to form the rectangle. When the rectangle has been formed, lay a yardstick across the dough and mark off the rectangle in 2" squares. Cut with a pastry wheel or knife. (A pastry wheel or jagger, especially the latter, which is a wheel with a scalloped edge like pinking shears, creates a handsome *galette* and does not tear or pull the dough as a knife would do.) Prick each dough piece with the sharp tines of a fork 3 or 4 times. Lift each biscuit carefully and place on the baking sheet. If the sheet won't hold them all, cover the balance with paper and leave on the work surface.
BAKING 400° 15–20 mins.	Place in the oven, but stand by because these bake rapidly, in 15 to 20 minutes. Look at the biscuits after 8 minutes. They should be light brown with somewhat darker edges and brown on the bottom. Don't be afraid to shuffle them around to achieve uniform baking. If some are fatter than others and feel soft when pressed on top, return to the oven. But watch them! (If using a convection oven, reduce heat 50°.)
FINAL STEP	As they are removed from the oven, place on a metal rack to cool. Delicious warm. They will stay fresh for days in a closed container, and freeze well.

Ka'achei Sumsum   [about two dozen small bagels]
(Salted Sesame Bagels)

Sumsum is a small salted sesame bread traditional with Syrian Jews on a Sabbath morning over coffee. I had my first sumsum at a Paris sidewalk cafe with tea, not coffee, and it was equally good.

Rich with butter, the sumsum is not sweet. Roll out a piece of dough 6 inches long, curl it around the index finger, and let the tip of one end rest on the tip of the other. That's a sumsum.

INGREDIENTS	¹/₂ cup sesame seeds 3 cups bread or all-purpose flour, approximately

1 package dry yeast
1 teaspoon salt
1 cup hot water (120°–130°)
1 cup (2 sticks) butter or margarine, melted
1 egg, beaten

BAKING SHEET

1 baking sheet, greased, Teflon, or covered with parchment paper

PREPARATION
10 mins.

Spread the sesame seeds on a baking sheet and place in a 350° oven for 10 minutes, or until they are a dark golden brown. Stir once or twice.

BY HAND
OR MIXER

Into a mixing or mixer bowl measure 2 cups flour and sprinkle in the yeast and salt. Stir to blend well. Pour in the hot water and the melted butter (warm but not hot). Beat 100 strokes with a wooden spoon or for 2 minutes with the mixer flat beater. Add the balance of the flour, ¼ cup at a time, stirring first with a utensil and then working in the flour with your hands. If using a mixer, change to the dough hook when the dough gets too dense for the flat beater.

KNEADING
10 mins.

Turn the dough onto the floured work surface and knead aggressively with a rhythmic motion of push-turn-fold. If using a mixer, the dough should clean the sides of the bowl and form a ball around the dough hook. It is a rich dough and will soon lose its stickiness. Knead for 10 minutes.

BY PROCESSOR
4 mins.

Toast the seeds, as above.
    Attach the steel blade.
    Add 2 cups flour and the dry ingredients to the work bowl. Pulse to blend. With the machine running, pour the hot water through the feed tube, and follow with the melted butter. It will be a thick, wet batter. Stop the machine and prepare to add the flour, ¼ cup at a time, through the feed tube, or by removing the cover for each addition.
    Turn on the processor and add the flour. When the dough forms a rough ball and cleans the sides of the bowl, stop the machine, remove the cover, and check the consistency of the dough with your fingers. It should be slightly sticky, but if too wet, add 1 or 2 tablespoons flour and process again. If too dry, add teaspoons of water and process.

KNEADING
1 min.

Process for 1 minute to knead.
    The dough should be slightly sticky and very elastic when the kneading is complete. Dust the dough with flour before stretching it between your hands to test. If it stretches poorly—breaks apart— return the dough to the processor for a few seconds more.

RISING 2 hours	Cover with plastic wrap and leave at room temperature. Because of its richness, it takes about 2 hours for the dough to double in bulk in the bowl.
SHAPING 12 mins.	Divide the dough into 24 equal pieces and roll each into a tight ball. Set aside. Roll the first ball under your palm into a 6" length. Press the ends into points. Form the piece into an overlapping circle on the baking sheet. Place your index finger down against the sheet and wrap the length of dough around it, letting the end overlap on the top of the piece underneath. Press the ends gently to join. Repeat for the other pieces, and place 1½" apart on the baking sheet.
PREHEAT	Preheat the oven to 375° 20 minutes before baking. Meanwhile, brush the *sumsums* with the beaten egg and sprinkle liberally with sesame seeds. (Try poppy seeds on some for an attractive variation.) Let them rest, uncovered, during preheating.
BAKING 375° 35 mins.	Unlike the conventional bagel that is first cooked in boiling water, these go directly into the oven. They are done when a bright golden yellow and firm when pressed, 35 minutes. (If using a convection oven, reduce heat 50°.)

FINAL STEP	Allow the bagels to cook on a metal rack.
	    Delightful served with coffee or tea—or anytime.
	    They keep well in a bread box. Also freeze well.

Benne Seed Biscuits   [about two dozen biscuits]

The wild sesame seed is known to Southern cooks as the benne seed, its use especially favored in this thin biscuit. The seed has an uncommon flavor that will intrigue guests. The dough is rolled wafer thin and baked no longer than 8 to 10 minutes.

INGREDIENTS	¹/₂ cup benne or sesame seeds 2 cups all-purpose flour, approximately ¹/₂ cup (1 stick) butter or margarine, room temperature 1 teaspoon baking powder ¹/₂ teaspoon salt, plus more for sprinkling ¹/₂ cup milk
BAKING SHEET	1 baking sheet, greased or Teflon

PREPARATION 10 mins.	Spread the seeds on a cookie sheet and toast in a 350° oven for 10 minutes. Toasting (or roasting) greatly enhances the seeds' flavor.
PREHEAT	If the oven has cooled after toasting the benne seeds, heat again to 350° before starting the dough.
BY HAND **OR MIXER** 10 mins.	Measure the flour into a mixing or mixer bowl. If by hand, rub in the butter or margarine with your fingers, or cut in with a pastry cutter. If using a mixer, drop small pieces into the mixer bowl under the flat beater. Stir in the baking powder, ½ teaspoon salt, and milk. Blend thoroughly with 30 or 40 strokes, or for 1 minute in the mixer. If the dough is sticky and moist, add small portions of flour. Add the benne or sesame seeds and work them into the dough.

BY PROCESSOR
3 mins.
	Toast the seeds, as above.
	    Attach the steel blade. This is a quick operation so pulse the processor only enough to mix the ingredients.
	    Place all the ingredients, in the order above, and include the benne seeds in the work bowl. Pulse 5 or 6 times—just enough to mix thoroughly. Feel the dough. If it is too sticky to be rolled, add flour.

SHAPING 5 mins.	Lightly flour the work surface and turn out the dough. Roll wafer thin (⅛" or thickness of 2 seeds placed side by side), and cut circles with a 2" cookie or biscuit cutter. Arrange the circles on the baking sheet.
BAKING 350° 8–10 mins.	Place the baking sheet in the oven and bake for 8 to 10 minutes. (If using a convection oven, reduce heat 50°.)
FINAL STEP	Remove the biscuits from the oven. Place them on a metal rack and sprinkle lightly with salt. Serve while still warm; they are equally good at room temperature.

Bialys [two dozen bialys]

Bialys and bagels go together, at least in the marketplace. Where one is sold the other is certain to be found nearby. The bagel probably holds a slight edge in popularity, but the bialy, a dimpled bun with an onion filling, is closing fast.

Both are solid, chewy, and delicious. Both come from the same Eastern European Jewish culture. The bialy was brought to this country by immigrants from Bialystok, a city in Poland, near the Russian border.

Growing up in a small town in Indiana, far from bialys and bagels, I did not appreciate their enthusiastic following until I wrote my first book—and did not include the bialy (or the bagel)! Letters have continued to challenge me over the years—"How can the Complete Book of Breads *be complete if it does not have the bialy (and the bagel)?" This recipe makes it complete.*

INGREDIENTS

Filling:
2 tablespoons onion flakes
2 teaspoons poppy seeds
1 tablespoon vegetable oil
1 teaspoon salt

Dough:
4½ cups bread or all-purpose flour, approximately
5 teaspoons sugar
2 teaspoons salt
1 package dry yeast
1¾ cups hot water (120°–130°)

BAKING SHEET

1 baking sheet, sprinkled with cornmeal or covered with parchment paper

PREPARATION
2 hours

To make the filling, soak the onion flakes in water for about 2 hours. Drain and press out the water with a paper towel. If the onion flakes are coarse, mince fine in a food processor or blender. Combine in a bowl with the poppy seeds, oil, and salt, and set aside.

BY HAND
OR MIXER
10 mins.

To make the dough, measure 3 cups flour into the mixing or mixer bowl and add the dry ingredients. Stir to blend. Form a well in the flour and pour in the hot water. With a wooden spoon pull the flour from the sides into the middle and beat until a medium batter. If using a mixer, attach the flat beater and, with the machine running, pour in the hot water. Add flour, ¼ cup at a time, until the batter becomes a rough but elastic dough. Attach the dough hook, if using the mixer.

KNEADING
10 mins.

Turn the dough from the mixing bowl and knead with strong push-turn-fold strokes; crash the dough down against the work surface occasionally to help develop the gluten. If the dough is sticky, dust with sprinkles of flour. If under the dough hook, the dough will clean the sides of the mixer bowl and form a ball around the hook. If it persists in sticking to the sides, add small portions of flour while the mixer is running. Knead for 10 minutes, until the dough is smooth and elastic when stretched.

BY PROCESSOR 5 mins.	Attach the plastic dough blade. Measure 3½ cups flour into the work bowl and sprinkle in the dry ingredients. Pulse several times to mix well. With the processor running, pour the hot water through the feed tube. Stop the machine, remove the cover, and with a rubber spatula pull all of the dry flour into the center. Pulse. Add 1 cup flour. Pulse for 3 seconds to blend. With the machine running, add flour, ¼ cup at a time, until the batter becomes a mass that is carried around the bowl by the force of the blade and cleans the sides.
KNEADING 50 secs.	When the dough has formed a ball, knead for 50 seconds. If the dough is slightly sticky when taken from the bowl, dust lightly with flour.
FIRST RISING 1 hour	Place the dough in a greased bowl, cover with plastic wrap, and set aside to double in volume at room temperature, about 1 hour.
SECOND RISING 45 mins.	With your fingers or fist punch down the dough, re-cover, and let double in volume again, about 45 minutes.
SHAPING 12 mins.	Take the dough from the bowl and divide into 4 equal parts. Divide each part into 6 pieces. Roll each piece into a tight ball under a cupped palm. Let the balls rest for 10 minutes under a length of wax paper or a cloth. With hard blows of your palm or under a rolling pin, shape each ball into a 4" circle, about ½" thick. Place on the prepared pan.
THIRD RISING 30 mins.	Cover the circles with wax or parchment paper and put aside to rise to slightly *less* than double, 30 minutes. A baker would say "three-quarter proof."
FILLING 8 mins.	With care not to deflate the outer part of the bialy, push a deep depression in the center with the thumbs. Stretch the dough uniformly outward until the well is at least 1½" across, and thin on the bottom. Place about ½ teaspoon of the onion filling in the well.
FOURTH RISING 25 mins.	Cover the bialys with wax paper and allow them to rise until almost doubled, 25 minutes.
PREHEAT	Preheat the oven to 450° 20 minutes before baking.
BAKING 450° 25 mins.	Place the bialys on the middle shelf of the hot oven and bake until a light brown, about 25 minutes. (If using a convection oven, reduce heat 50°.)

FINAL STEP	Place the baked bialys on a metal rack to cool.
	A bialy is delicious sliced in half horizontally and buttered, or spread with cream cheese. Delicious, too, toasted. Or filled as for a sandwich.

Gâteaux au Poivre　　[four dozen little cakes]
(Pepper Cakes)

The pepper cake of Limoux, a small town in southern France, is not a cake but a tiny, twisted, golden wreath of yeast-raised dough, speckled with pepper and formed around the finger. It is most often served as an hors d'oeuvre or snack with drinks or coffee or tea.

It is a spécialité of the boulangerie of Roger Rebolledo, a smiling man with the arms and shoulders of a gymnast.

"Be careful with the yeast—not too much or the gâteaux will be too fat," he explained. "They must be petite and delicate. Allow them no time to rise before you put them in the oven. Allow them to bake just long enough to be a shade beyond golden. . . . And always use fresh ground pepper," he added.

Since pepper is the most important single ingredient in these small gâteaux, grind it fresh if you can. If a grinder is not part of your batterie de cuisine, buy a fresh container of ground pepper at a large market where there is a fast turnover on the spice shelves.

Don't expect perfection the first time. Not until the third batch did I succeed in making a truly delicate, pencil-thin strand. And it was not before the fourth batch that I succeeded in making a perfect round-the-finger wreath. M. Rebolledo said he had been doing it for more than two decades.

INGREDIENTS	2^1/$_2$ cups all-purpose flour, approximately
	1 level *teaspoon* dry yeast (see Note)
	2 teaspoons freshly ground black pepper
	1 teaspoon salt
	^{2}/$_3$ cup hot water (120°–130°)
	^{3}/$_4$ cup (1^1/$_2$ sticks) butter, room temperature, cut into pieces
	1 egg or egg yolk, beaten, mixed with 1 teaspoon water
BAKING SHEET	1 baking sheet, greased, Teflon, or covered with parchment paper
BY HAND OR MIXER 10 mins.	In a large mixing or mixer bowl measure 1½ cups flour and the dry ingredients. Pour in the water and mix by hand for 50 strokes or with the mixer flat beater for 1 minute to thoroughly blend the ingredients. Crop in the butter pieces and work them into the flour until they are completely absorbed. Add flour (about 1 cup) until the dough forms a smooth, buttery mass.

KNEADING **5 mins.**	If by hand, turn the dough onto a floured work surface and knead. It will be an easy task because of its high butter content, but if it seems too moist or too sticky, toss down several liberal sprinkles of flour and work them in. If using the mixer, attach the dough hook, and add small portions of flour if the dough sticks to the bowl. Knead for 5 minutes.
BY PROCESSOR **4 mins.**	Attach the steel blade. Measure 1½ cups flour into the work bowl and add the dry ingredients. Turn on the machine and slowly pour the warm water through the feed tube. Stop the machine and add the pieces of butter. With the machine running, add flour, ¼ cup at a time, through the feed tube until the heavy batter becomes a dough. The dough will become a ball that cleans the bowl as it rides on the blade.
KNEADING **45 secs.**	Process the dough for 45 seconds to knead. The dough will be slightly sticky when it is turned out of the work bowl, but light sprinkles of flour will make it manageable.
PREHEAT	Preheat the oven to 425°. (This dough goes directly into the oven after shaping so whatever leavening effect there is takes place in the oven. A vigorous rising might tear the delicate wreaths apart.)
SHAPING **20 mins.**	The dough will weigh about 1½ pounds. Divide it into 6 or 8 pieces. Roll each piece into a rough cylinder. Lay both hands on the center of the roll and move the dough back and forth across the work surface—slowly spreading your hands apart to make the roll longer and thinner. But don't force the dough to spread because it may tear. Be firm when you push *down* on the roll with the hands. You can't collapse it. When one strand seems to be resisting, move on to another. Return to the first and continue the motion. When the strand gets so long that the ends get tangled (more than 18") cut in half. Presumably the strand will be as thin as, if not thinner than, a pencil. If not, continue rolling under your palms. Twist 2 slender strands together. The double strand will try to unwind when you lay it down, so press the ends to the work surface until they relax in the twisted position. Go on to the next pair. When all the strands have been paired, hold the tip of your index finger against the work surface. Wrap the dough around your finger to form a small wreath. Allow enough additional length so that the ends can be pinched together (about 5" overall) and cut with a knife or scis-

sors. Make certain the strands don't untwist before overlapping and pinching together.

Place on the baking sheet ½" apart. Repeat for all the double strands. When all *gâteaux* have been made, brush with the egg-water glaze. For an extra peppery taste, sprinkle a bit of ground pepper over the glaze.

BAKING

425°

22 mins.

Move the sheet directly to the hot oven—no rest period or rising. Look at the cakes after 15 minutes. If those along the outside edges of the sheet are browning too quickly, push them to the center and move the center cakes to the outside. The cakes will bake dry with little moisture left in them.

(If using a convection oven, reduce heat 50°.)

FINAL STEP

Remove from the oven and let cool on a metal rack.

They will remain fresh for several weeks in an airtight container. Or they will freeze nicely for several months.

Honey-Bran Muffins   [two or three dozen muffins]

Honey-Bran Muffins are the creation of the two fine cook/owners of The Ark, a restaurant in the village of Oysterville on the shore of Willapa Bay in Washington. Oyster boats and crab boats come and go outside the ordinary-looking one-story blue building surrounded by piles of oyster shells. It belongs to Jimella Lucas and Nanci Main, for whom James Beard "blew the trumpet and waved the banners."

But it is inside, at lunch, when baskets of these delicious muffins (and dishes of cranberry butter) come to the table that one realizes it has indeed been worthwhile to make the journey to this remote spot on the Pacific Coast, a few miles from where the Lewis and Clark expedition ended.

The Ark muffins taste rich because they are rich—buttermilk, honey, butter, eggs, brown sugar, bran, nutmeg, the option of chopped dates or raisins, and, the final touch, chopped walnuts.

INGREDIENTS

2 cups buttermilk

¹/₂ cup honey

³/₄ cup (1 ¹/₂ sticks) butter, melted

3 eggs, room temperature

2 cups packed brown sugar

3 cups sifted cake flour

2 tablespoons baking soda

2 teaspoons salt

1/2 teaspoon freshly grated nutmeg, or 1 tablespoon grated
   orange rind

3 cups bran flakes

1/2 cup *each* chopped dates or raisins and chopped walnuts

MUFFIN TINS   Several muffin tins, greased or lined

PREHEAT   Preheat the oven to 400°. Be certain the oven is right on 400° (or a bit
                   more) or the muffins will sink. Use a reliable thermometer.

BY HAND   In a large bowl combine the buttermilk, honey, butter, eggs, and brown
15 mins.   sugar. Stir well to blend.

                   In a second bowl sift the cake flour, baking soda, salt, and nutmeg or
                   orange rind. Stir in the bran flakes.

                   Pour the liquid mixture into the flour, and blend well with a wooden
                   spoon or spatula. Briefly stir in the dates or raisins and walnuts. Over-
                   stirring can make the muffins tough. The batter will be thick but easily
                   spooned into the tins.

                   Spoon the batter into the lined muffin tins to three-quarters full. If
                   only one or two muffin tins are available, it may be necessary to bake a
                   second or third time. Place the remaining batter in the refrigerator to
                   reserve.

BAKING   Bake in the hot oven for 20 to 25 minutes, until golden brown.
400°   (If using a convection oven, reduce heat 50°.)
20–25 mins.

FINAL STEP   Remove the muffins from the oven and cool on a wire rack.
                   Serve, enjoy, and imagine you are lunching at The Ark at the edge of
                   the quiet waters of Willapa Bay.

Mother's Biscuits   [two dozen biscuits]

*My mother baked such beautiful baking powder biscuits that for a long time I
felt intimidated by the thought of doing them myself. Finally, I dared.*

*The recipe that started me along this delicious byway was from a delightful
book,* Cross Creek Cookery, *by Marjorie Kinnan Rawlings, author of* The
Yearling. *The mother is hers. My mother's recipe was never committed to
paper. But after a consultation with my sister, I am satisfied this biscuit is
as good as my mother's. I have no qualms about putting it here as a loving
tribute to all mothers and to the millions of biscuits they have baked for happy
children.*

INGREDIENTS	2 cups all-purpose flour, approximately 4 teaspoons baking powder $\frac{1}{2}$ teaspoon salt 2 tablespoons butter I scant cup milk, room temperature
BAKING SHEET	1 baking sheet, greased and cornmeal-dusted, Teflon, or covered with parchment paper
PREHEAT	Preheat the oven to 450°.
BY HAND OR MIXER 10 mins.	In a mixing or mixer bowl combine the dry ingredients and sift twice. Work in the butter with your fingertips, a wire pastry blender, or with a mixer flat beater, until the batter resembles coarse grain. Add only enough milk to hold the dough together. The exact amount varies with the flour.

BY PROCESSOR
4 mins.
	Insert the steel blade.
	   This will be a quick mixing operation. On-off pulses only. Don't let the machine run.
	   Measure the dry ingredients into the work bowl. Pulse to blend. Drop the butter into the work bowl; pulse 3 or 4 times, until it resembles coarse grain.
	   Pour in half the milk through the feed tube. Pulse 3 or 4 times. Add more milk but only enough to hold the dough together. Pulse 2 or 3 times. Remove the cover and feel the dough. It should be slightly sticky. Dust with flour to make it easy to handle.

SHAPING 6 mins.	While it is considered heresy to handle biscuit dough needlessly, Mrs. Rawlings's mother believed that to make a flaky, layered biscuit one should roll out the dough, fold it over itself in 4 layers, roll out again to a thickness of $\frac{1}{2}$", and cut with a 2" cookie cutter. Place the biscuits on the baking sheet.
BAKING 450° 12–14 mins.	Bake in the oven until a golden brown and raised to about $1\frac{1}{2}$" to 2", 12 to 14 minutes. (If using a convection oven, reduce heat 50°.)
FINAL STEP	Remove the biscuits from the oven. Serve hot.

Kaiser Rolls [eighteen rolls]

One of the most popular hard and crusty rolls is the Kaiser, known in some parts of the country as the Vienna. There are two secrets in making the Kaiser. One is egg and egg white among the ingredients. The other is a moist oven—steam from a pan under the rolls and water brushed on the dough beforehand, or a light spray into the oven before and during baking.

Perhaps the most difficult thing about a Kaiser is to shape it into a roll that looks somewhat like its traditional shape of a 5-petal blossom. First attempts will probably be irregular, but properly formed or not, the rolls are large, tender-crusty, delicious.

Dusting the pieces of dough with rye flour before shaping them prevents the sections of the rolls running together, and leaves the "petals" intact.

INGREDIENTS

4½ cups bread or unbleached flour, approximately
1 package dry yeast
1 tablespoon sugar
1 teaspoon salt
1½ cups hot water (120°–130°)
1 teaspoon malt extract, if available
1 egg
1 egg white
1 tablespoon shortening
Rye flour, for dusting
Poppy seeds

BAKING SHEET

1 baking sheet, greased or covered with parchment paper

BY HAND
OR MIXER
8 mins.

Into a mixing or mixer bowl measure 3½ cups flour and add the dry ingredients. Stir to blend well. Pour in the hot water and malt extract. Mix for 1 minute with a wooden spoon or the mixer flat beater until a smooth but heavy batter forms. Add the egg, egg white, and shortening. Beat together until the mixture is smooth. If using the mixer, remove the flat beater and continue with the dough hook. Add flour, ¼ cup at a time, until the dough is a solid but soft mass that can be lifted from the bowl, or left under the dough hook.

KNEADING
10 mins.

Turn the dough out onto a lightly floured work surface. Knead the dough with a strong push-turn-fold motion, adding liberal sprinkles of flour if the dough is wet. In the mixer, the dough will clean the sides of the bowl and form a ball around the dough hook. If, however, the dough continues to cling to the sides, add sprinkles of flour. Knead for 10 minutes.

BY PROCESSOR
4 mins.

Attach the plastic dough blade.

Measure 3½ cups flour into the work bowl and add the dry ingredients. Pulse to blend. With the machine running, pour the hot water through the feed tube. The dough will be a thick batter. Drop in the egg, egg white, and shortening. Pulse 7 or 8 times to blend completely.

Add flour, ¼ cup at a time, until the dough forms a ball and rides the blade. If the dough is wet and sticks to the sides of the bowl, add flour by the tablespoon, with the machine running.

KNEADING
I min.

When the dough cleans the sides of the bowl, process to knead for 1 minute.

Uncover the bowl; pinch the dough to determine if it is soft, smooth, elastic, and slightly sticky.

FIRST RISING
I hour

Place the dough in a greased bowl, cover tightly with plastic wrap, and set aside to double in bulk, about 1 hour.

SECOND RISING
45 mins.

Uncover the bowl and punch down the dough with the fingers. Re-cover the bowl and allow the dough to double in volume again, about 45 minutes.

SHAPING
15 mins.

Place the dough on a floured work surface and roll it into an 18"-long cylinder. With a sharp knife, cut 18 pieces from the length (at every inch on the yardstick). Shape the pieces under a cupped palm into smooth rounds. Cover and allow to relax for 5 minutes.

Flatten each roll with your hand to about ⅜" thick. Dust lightly with rye flour. Place your thumb in the center of a roll. With the forefinger of your other hand pick up a section equal to about one-fifth of the dough and fold the portion slightly over your thumb. With the side of your hand, hit the dough up against the thumb. Pick up the second section and repeat the procedure, overlapping slightly. Repeat this action a total of 5 times, but don't hit the last section, just press it into the gap made by removing the thumb. Press the last piece into place.

The entire procedure may be viewed as assembling the spokes of a wheel.

Sprinkle the baking sheet liberally with poppy seeds. As each roll is shaped, place it face down on the sheet.

THIRD RISING
40 mins.

Cover the rolls with a length of wax or parchment paper, and leave at room temperature to rise to slightly less than double in size, about 40 minutes.

PREHEAT

In the meantime, prepare the oven by placing a pan under the shelf. Preheat the oven to 450° 20 minutes before baking. Five minutes before the rolls are to go into the oven, pour 1 cup hot water into the pan to form steam and provide a moist environment for the rolls.

BAKING
450°
25 mins.

Be certain hot water is in the pan.

Uncover the rolls, carefully turn them right side up, brush them with water or spray lightly with an atomizer.

Place the pan on the middle shelf of the hot oven. Three minutes later lightly spray the interior of the oven—not directly on the rolls. Bake for 25 minutes, until crispy and brown all over. Midway during baking turn the sheet around so that the rolls are exposed equally to temperature variations in the oven.

(If using a convection oven, place the hot water in a pan on the floor before putting in the rolls. Bake at 400° for 30 minutes.)

FINAL STEP

Remove the rolls from the oven. If after the rolls have cooled, they are not as crisp and crusty as you like, put them back into a hot oven for 10 minutes. Do the same later for reheating the rolls.

These are delicious just spread with butter.

Pumpernickel with Cheese Heart   [eight large buns]

The Russians make a delicious pumpernickel bun and give it a heart—a heart of Cheddar cheese. Cornmeal, mashed potato, and rye and whole-wheat flours are the body of the buns. Moist as pumpernickel should be, it is more open-textured because of the leavening with 2 packages active dry yeast. While no white flour is among the ingredients, I liberally sprinkle it on while kneading the dough and forming the rolls. The dough is less sticky when worked with white flour.

To serve, the buns are cut into pie-shape pieces. When the dough rises it forms a small pocket above the cheese—ideal to fill with a pâté or a ham spread.

A fine home baker, David Simmons, found the cheese-filled bun on a tour of Russia, and when he returned home he created the recipe.

This dough, without the cheese, also makes a delicious loaf.

INGREDIENTS

3 cups water

³/₄ cup white or yellow cornmeal

2 teaspoons salt

1 tablespoon *each* sugar, shortening, and caraway seeds

2 packages dry yeast

¹/₄ cup instant potato flakes

2 cups rye flour

2¹/₂ cups whole-wheat flour, approximately

White flour, for dusting

1 10-ounce block sharp Cheddar cheese

1 egg, beaten, mixed with 1 teaspoon water

2 tablespoons caraway seeds (optional)

BAKING SHEET

1 baking sheet, Teflon, greased, or covered with parchment paper

BY HAND
OR MIXER
20 mins.

Caution: A mixer can be used in the early stage of preparation, but the resulting heavy dough cannot be kneaded in most electric mixers. The Bosch machine is the exception.

In a saucepan stir water into the cornmeal and cook over low heat. Stir constantly, until thick and smooth. Add the salt, sugar, shortening, and 1 tablespoon caraway seeds. Let stand until the mixture is warm (110°) to the touch.

Sprinkle the yeast and potato flakes into the warm mixture and blend in. Stir in the rye flour. This can be done with the mixer flat beater as well as by hand.

Add sufficient whole-wheat flour to form a ball. It will be sticky at the beginning. Let it stand for 5 minutes, until the flours have fully absorbed the moisture. The dough is now too dense for most mixer dough hooks.

KNEADING
10 mins.

Turn out onto a work surface that is liberally sprinkled with white flour. It will be helpful to use a spatula or wide putty knife to turn the dough and, at the same time, to keep the work surface scraped clean. The dough will become somewhat elastic and smooth. It will never achieve the elasticity of white dough. Knead for 10 minutes. Add sprinkles of white flour to control stickiness.

BY PROCESSOR
4 mins.

The processor can be used to blend together all of the ingredients including 2 or 3 cups flour. But thereafter work and knead the heavy dough by hand, as above.

FIRST RISING
1½ hours

Place the dough in a greased bowl, cover tightly with plastic wrap, and put aside at room temperature until the dough has risen to twice its original size, about 1½ hours.

While the dough is rising, cut the cheese into 1½"-x-1½"-x-1" chunks. I usually buy a stick or block of cheese wrapped in foil, about the size of a stick of butter, and divide it equally into 8 pieces. Set aside.

SHAPING
10 mins.

Punch down the dough and divide it into 8 pieces. Round each into a ball, and let rest for 5 minutes to relax the dough.

With your palm, flatten each ball of dough into a 6" round. Place a block of cheese in the center; draw up the edges to completely envelop the cheese. Pinch and press the edges tightly together. Place on the baking sheet with the seam under.

SECOND RISING
45 mins.

Place the baking sheet in a warm place, cover with wax or parchment paper, and leave until the rolls have doubled in bulk and are puffy to touch, about 45 minutes.

PREHEAT

Preheat the oven to 375° about 20 minutes before baking.

BAKING
375°
45 mins.

Uncover the rolls and brush each with the egg-water wash. Sprinkle with caraway seeds, if desired.

Bake on the middle shelf of the oven for 45 minutes until the rolls are browned and test done when tapped on the bottom with a forefinger. They will be crusty and hard.

(If using a convection oven, reduce heat 50°.)

FINAL STEP

Remove from the oven and allow the rolls (and cheese) to cool before serving.

Delicious as a snack in itself.

Grandmother's Southern Biscuits   [one dozen biscuits]

These Southern biscuits are called "touch-of-grace" biscuits, so named because the Southern grandmother who created this recipe left this notation as one of the ingredients: "Don't forget to add a touch of grace." It was her way of saying that biscuit-making should be a joy, and that the love of doing it for the family is an essential ingredient.

The search for the perfect Southern biscuit began when Nathalie Dupree, a noted Atlanta cook and cookbook author, gathered together a panel of six including Shirley Corriher, another skilled cook, whose grandmother was the one who made her biscuits with a "touch of grace." This panel of fine Georgia cooks was determined to create the best biscuit from among scores of recipes collected by their grandmothers as well as those recipes found in old cookbooks. The best biscuits, the panel members agreed, must be light, fluffy, a light golden brown on the outside and just cooked and still moist on the inside.

Here, according to these Southern cooks, are some important dos and don'ts in the art of making a true Southern biscuit:

- The less flour used, the better. Southern flours, usually labeled "made with soft winter wheat," have less gluten strength than most other flours and therefore make lighter biscuits. In the South, most home bakers use White Lily flour. Don't hesitate to use other all-purpose flours, however. The difference in baking quality is very slight.
- The leavening agent in biscuits is baking powder. Self-rising flour, widely used and popular in the South, contains baking powder. In any case, baking powder has poor keeping qualities, so store in airtight tins and use within a short period of time.
- Use shortening rather than butter for a lighter biscuit. Lard gives biscuits a pronounced flavor and is lighter than butter.
- The moister the dough, the lighter the biscuit. The dough should be as wet as possible and yet hold a shape.
- The most tender biscuits are those that are handled and kneaded just enough to mix the dry ingredients with the fat and the liquid, perhaps 5 to 10 quick kneads in all. More than that, the flour's gluten tightens up, and a tougher biscuit results.
- The amount of flour used in shaping varies with the method of shaping. A rolled dough calls for more flour than one shaped and dropped on the sheet. Therefore the lightest biscuits are dropped from a spoon; the heaviest, rolled like pie dough.
- Half-inch-thick dough is ideal for a tender, crumbly, light biscuit.
- Bake close together for soft-sided biscuits. For crusty sides, 1 inch apart.
- The hotter the oven, the better. Between 450° and 500° will make a golden biscuit that is moist on the inside.
- For a brown finish, brush the tops of the biscuits with milk or melted butter.

INGREDIENTS

2 cups all-purpose flour (after sifting)
1 teaspoon salt
1 tablespoon sugar
4 teaspoons baking powder
$^1/_3$ cup shortening (Crisco preferred)
1$^1/_4$ cups sweet milk

BAKING PAN

1 baking sheet, Teflon, greased, or lined with parchment paper

PREHEAT	Preheat the oven to 500°. This is a hot oven.
BY HAND OR MIXER 5 mins.	In a mixing or mixer bowl sift together the dry ingredients. Cut in the shortening with your fingers, a pastry blender, or 2 knives—or with the mixer flat beater. Pour in all of the milk at once. Stir with a fork or beater blade until just mixed. Add more milk if the dough is dry. The dough will be quite wet but able to retain its shape.
BY PROCESSOR 4 mins.	Use the steel blade. Measure the dry ingredients into the work bowl. Pulse to aerate. Add shortening, pulsing several times to cut the shortening into the flour until it resembles coarse meal. Add the milk and combine by quickly turning the processor on and off only 2 or 3 times, just enough to mix. Lengthy processing after adding the milk will toughen the biscuits.
SHAPING 8 mins.	Gather the dough into a ball; place on a floured surface, and sprinkle lightly with flour, if necessary, to prevent sticking. Work with your hands for a moment or so to pull all the dough pieces together. Dust again with flour if necessary. Roll with a rolling pin to ½" thickness, cut with a cookie or biscuit cutter into 3" rounds, and place the biscuits on the baking sheet. Knead any scraps gently together and cut again. If the dough is too wet to roll without sticking, for each biscuit, pinch off pieces of dough. Dust lightly with flour and pat into shape on the baking sheet.
BAKING 500° 8–10 mins.	Bake on the middle shelf of the hot oven for 8 to 10 minutes, or until golden brown. (If using a convection oven, reduce heat 50°.)
FINAL STEP	Remove the biscuits from the oven and serve right away. Pass the butter, and bless Grandmother for such a light and feathery creation.

Beaten Biscuits   [about three dozen biscuits]

The thunk, thunk of a wooden beater brought crashing down against a ball of dough was often the first sound to be heard in the early morning hours from a nineteenth-century Southern kitchen. A slave or member of the family would be hard at work at the ritual of making the small, crisp, short, and delicious beaten biscuits for breakfast.

It was not an easy chore but the results were outstanding. Flailing with a rolling pin, a flatiron, or the side of a cleaver, the beating went on for 30 minutes, if just family, or 45 minutes for guests.

Later some ingenious person developed a beaten biscuit machine with metal rollers through which the dough was squeezed time and again until it began to crackle and pop as air bubbles burst. Most of these machines are antiques, highly prized by their owners and museums. My rollers are mounted above a polished maple deck. A machine that has a top of Tennessee marble gives its owner considerable prestige in some circles.

There is yet a third way to make the biscuits—the coarse blade of a food or meat grinder. The dough is passed through a dozen or more times. The results are satisfactory to good.

A recent development in the long history of the beaten biscuit, which has changed the operation from one measured in hours to one measured in seconds, is the food processor. In some mysterious way the force of the whirling steel blade has almost the same effect on the dough as a wooden beater.

The traditional biscuit is 1½ to 2 inches in diameter and about ½-inch thick. It is fashioned with a special cutter that presses 6 prongs through the center of the biscuit as it cuts. These holes can also be made with the tines of a fork. In Virginia, it is customary to form the biscuit by squeezing the dough between the thumb and forefinger to make a ball the size of a small egg. Pinched off, it is patted or rolled flat and pricked with the fork.

There is a ritual, too, about opening the biscuit. It must be done with the tines of a fork, held in one hand, pressing against the biscuit standing on its edge on the plate. Never a knife or fingers, and never done from the horizontal position.

Note: *It is assumed that a beaten biscuit machine is not readily at hand, and that one of two ways will be used to prepare the biscuits—by beating or in a food processor.*

INGREDIENTS	3½ cups bread or all-purpose flour
	1 teaspoon salt
	1 tablespoon sugar
	1 teaspoon baking powder
	½ cup lard
	1¼ cups milk, approximately
BAKING SHEET	1 baking sheet, ungreased or Teflon
BY HAND	Into a large bowl sift the dry ingredients. Stir to mix. Cut the lard into
15 mins.	small pieces and drop into the dry ingredients. With a pastry blender or your hands (or both), work the lard into the flour.

Slowly pour 1 cup milk into the bowl and work it into the mixture. Add the balance of the milk, if it is needed, to hold the dough together. Remember, it is to be a fairly stiff dough—be sparing of the liquid.

KNEADING **2–3 mins.**	Knead the dough with your hands for 2 or 3 minutes until you are certain it will cling together in one mass and not fragment with the first blow of the blunt instrument.
REST **30–60 mins.**	Cover the dough with plastic wrap and put aside to relax, 30 minutes to 1 hour.
BEATING **30–45 mins.**	Select a place on a countertop or table that is the height most comfortable for prolonged beating. Don't beat frantically. Use measured beats. When the dough has been beaten crosswise in one direction, shift the dough or your position so that you are beating across the previous pattern. When the dough is flattened, fold it and continue beating. The dough will become silky and elastic. Bubbles will form and pop when beaten.
BY PROCESSOR **4 mins.**	Attach the steel blade. Add the dry ingredients to the work bowl. Turn the machine on and off twice to aerate the mixture. Add the shortening and process until the mixture is the consistency of cornmeal. With the machine running, pour 1 cup milk through the feed tube in a steady stream. When the milk has been absorbed, remove the cover and pinch the dough to determine its consistency. It will be soft but not sticky. If it is wet, add a small portion of flour. If it seems too dry, add a teaspoon or two of milk.
KNEADING **2 mins.**	Process until the mixture forms a ball, then process for an additional 2 minutes.
REST **30–60 mins.**	Cover the dough with plastic wrap and put aside to relax, 30 minutes to 1 hour.
BEATING **3 mins.**	Remove the dough from the work bowl and flatten with 100 whacks of a rolling pin. Turn the dough crosswise and give it another 100 blows. Not only does this let the dough know that at heart it is a *beaten* biscuit but prepares it for the next step.
PREHEAT	Preheat the oven to 400° 10 minutes before the biscuits are to be cut.
SHAPING **10 mins.**	Roll the dough into a ½" thick sheet. Use a 1½" or 2" biscuit cutter to make about 36 rounds. Pierce each round with the tines of a fork. Place on the baking sheet.

BAKING
400°
25–30 mins.

Bake in the moderately hot oven until the biscuits begin to tan or brown—but only lightly—25 to 30 minutes.

(If using a convection oven, reduce heat 50°.)

FINAL STEP

Remove the biscuits from the oven. Serve warm.

These keep for several days in a tightly closed bag. Wrap in foil to reheat. They freeze nicely for up to 6 months.

P.S. A beaten biscuit party can be a crashing success. Let the guests take turns beating on the dough for 45 minutes, then they will have a half hour to recharge their energies before *their* biscuits come out of the oven.

Ausytes   [three dozen small rolls]
(Lithuanian Bacon Buns)

A special treat in a Lithuanian home during the holiday season is a small 3-bite bun filled with a nugget of sautéed bacon and onion. It would be accompanied with the greeting Linksmu Kaledu—*"Merry Christmas!" This recipe is from a fine home baker, Mrs. Petras Dauzvardis, whose family is part of the Lithuanian community that borders the great steel mills in northern Indiana.*

INGREDIENTS

1 pound bacon, finely chopped
1 large onion, finely chopped
1 cup milk
$^1/_2$ cup (1 stick) butter
2 eggs, lightly stirred
4 cups bread or all-purpose flour, approximately
1 package dry yeast
1 teaspoon salt
$^1/_4$ cup sugar
1 egg yolk, beaten, mixed with 1 teaspoon milk

BAKING SHEET

1 baking sheet, greased or Teflon

PREPARATION
1 hour
approximately

Place the chopped bacon and onion in a heavy skillet; barely cover the mixture with water. Place the skillet over medium heat and boil off the water. When the water is gone, in about 1 hour, the mixture will have cooked into a rich brown filling. It will crackle and pop to announce that it is done. Remove from the heat. Drain the grease through a sieve and allow it to drip while it cools.

When cool, chop again under a knife or in a food processor to be certain the mixture is finely cut. Set aside.

BY HAND
OR MIXER
15 mins.

In a small saucepan heat the milk and butter until the butter is melted. Don't bring to scald, however. Remove the milk from the burner and when it has cooled to lukewarm, stir in the eggs. Set aside.

Into a mixing or mixer bowl measure the dry ingredients. Stir to blend by hand or with the flat beater and slowly pour in the liquid mixture. It will make a heavy batter. Add flour, ¼ cup at a time, to form a rough mass that can be lifted from the bowl, or left under the dough hook. Add sprinkles of flour if the dough is sticky. The dough under the hook should clean the sides of the bowl and form a ball around the hook as it revolves. If it sticks to the sides, add sprinkles of flour.

KNEADING
10 mins.

If by hand, turn the dough from the mixing bowl onto a floured work surface, and knead aggressively with a strong motion of push-turn-fold. The dough will become smooth and elastic. Or knead in the mixer bowl with the dough hook. Knead for 10 minutes.

BY PROCESSOR
6 mins.

Prepare the bacon-onion mixture, as above, and heat the milk, butter, and eggs, as above.

Attach the plastic dough blade.

Measure 3½ cups flour and the other dry ingredients into the processor work bowl. Pulse to blend. With the processor running, pour three-quarters of the liquid slowly through the feed tube, keeping some of the milk in reserve until the rest is absorbed by the flour. The dough should be kept wet yet thick so that a thin batter does not climb the inner shaft.

Add the balance of the flour and pour in the rest of the milk. Stop the machine, remove the cover, and pinch the dough to test its consistency. A slight stickiness is acceptable, but if wet, more flour should be added.

KNEADING
45 secs.

When the dough cleans the sides of the bowl and rides the blade, process for 45 seconds to knead.

FIRST RISING
45 mins.

Place the dough in a greased bowl, cover tightly with plastic wrap, and put aside to double in volume, about 45 minutes.

SECOND RISING
30 mins.

Punch down the dough with your extended fingers, cover the bowl again, and let the dough rise to double in size, about 30 minutes.

SHAPING
20 mins.

Remove the dough from the bowl, knead for a few moments to press out the bubbles, and roll until it is about ½" thick. Cut out circles with a 2¼" biscuit or cookie cutter. (They can be made smaller, of course, or larger, but the 2¼" cutter seems to do the best job.) Lay the dough circles aside as you cut them. The dough will have pulled back as the circles are cut. With your palm or fist, press back into original shape, or perhaps a bit larger.

Put about a teaspoon of cooled bacon mixture in the center of each circle of dough. Draw the sides of each circle up and over the bacon. Tightly pinch the seam together, and place each bun, seam under, on the baking sheet.

THIRD RISING I hour	Cover the buns with wax paper or parchment paper and allow to double in size, about 1 hour.
PREHEAT	Preheat the oven to 375° about 20 minutes before baking.
BAKING 375° 20 mins.	Brush the buns with the egg-milk wash. Place in the oven on the middle or bottom shelf. The glossy brown buns will bake in about 20 minutes. (If using a convection oven, reduce heat 50°. The buns may need to be baked in 2 batches in some of the smaller home convection ovens.)
FINAL STEP	The buns are best served warm from the oven. They can be frozen and reheated for 20 minutes in a 350° oven. *Linksmu Kaledu!*

Hot Cross Buns   [about two dozen buns]

Traditionally served on Good Friday, the hot cross bun is one of the season's legendary breads. This one is speckled nut-brown, rich with cloves, nutmeg, currants, and candied fruit.

A cross of confectioners' icing is the distinctive mark of this bread that is in every child's book of nursery rhymes. Despite its Christian overtone, the bun is supposed to have originated in pagan England. Even today, a hot cross bun baked and served on Good Friday is believed to have special curative powers.

Note: *The dough is refrigerated overnight, so prepare it on Maundy Thursday if you wish to serve it on Good Friday. Bake enough for Easter breakfast, too.*

INGREDIENTS

$^1/_2$ cup sugar
$^1/_4$ cup ($^1/_2$ stick) butter, melted, plus extra for brushing
2 eggs, separated
I cup hot milk (120°–130°)
$3^1/_2$ to 4 cups bread or all-purpose flour, approximately
I package dry yeast
I teaspoon salt
$^1/_2$ teaspoon grated nutmeg

$^1/_4$ teaspoon ground cloves
$^1/_2$ cup currants or raisins
$^1/_4$ cup chopped candied fruit
I egg yolk, beaten, mixed with 2 tablespoons water
I cup confectioners' sugar mixed with I tablespoon milk and I
    teaspoon lemon juice

BAKING SHEET — 1 baking sheet, greased or Teflon

**BY HAND
OR MIXER
30 mins.**

In a large bowl mix the sugar, melted butter, egg yolks, and hot milk. Stir to blend and set aside for a moment.

Into a mixing or mixer bowl measure 2½ cups flour, the yeast, salt, and spices; blend. Pour the liquid mixture into the flour with 50 strong strokes of a wooden spoon, or for 2 minutes with a mixer flat beater. Add the currants or raisins and candied fruit. Blend.

Beat the egg whites until frothy but not quite stiff, and work into the batter. Add additional flour, ½ cup at a time, with the spoon or dough hook, until it is a rough mass. Knead for 2 or 3 minutes. Don't make it a stiff dough but leave it soft and elastic.

**BY PROCESSOR
5 mins.**

Attach the short plastic dough blade.

Mix the moist ingredients, as above.

Measure 2½ cups flour, the yeast, salt, and spices into the work bowl. Pulse to blend. With the processor running, pour the liquid through the feed tube to make a batter. Uncover the bowl and scrape down the sides with the spatula. Drop in the currants or raisins and candied fruit.

With the processor on, add beaten egg whites and the flour, ¼ cup at a time, to form a rough, shaggy dough that cleans the sides of the bowl and rides on the blade.

**FIRST RISING
1½ hours**

Place the dough in a greased bowl, cover with plastic wrap, and let stand at room temperature while it rises to double in bulk, about 1½ hours.

**REFRIGERATION
Overnight**

Punch down the dough. Cover and store in the refrigerator overnight.

On the following day, remove the bowl from the refrigerator and allow to stand for about 1 hour at room temperature.

**KNEADING
10 mins.
45 secs.**

Turn the dough onto a floured work surface and knead for 10 minutes until the dough is smooth and elastic.

If using a food processor, return the dough to the work bowl and knead for 45 seconds.

SHAPING 15 mins.	Divide the dough into equal parts in successive steps—2-4-8-16-32, and shape into balls. Place the balls about 1" apart on the baking sheet.
SECOND RISING 1 hour	Brush the balls with melted butter, cover with wax or parchment paper, and put aside to rise until double in volume, 1 hour.
PREHEAT	Preheat the oven to 375° 20 minutes before baking.
BAKING 375° 25 mins.	Remove the paper covering the balls. With a razor or scissors, cut a cross on the top of each bun. Brush with the egg-water wash. Place in the oven until nicely browned, about 25 minutes. If oven space is limited, several batches may be baked. (If using a convection oven, reduce heat 50°.)
FINAL STEP	Remove the buns from the oven. Place on wire racks. When cool, form a cross in the cuts on each bun with fairly firm confectioners' icing.

Les Bagels de Jo Goldenberg   [ten large water bagels]
(*Jo Goldenberg's Bagels*)

More than half of the half-million French Jews live in Paris—and all at one time or another eat and shop at the large Jo Goldenberg restaurant-deli at 7 rue des Rosiers. It is a Paris institution in a neighborhood surrounded by four synagogues and half again as many Catholic churches (the Cathedral of Notre Dame is less than a mile away).

One should have a mission to go there, and a Goldenberg bagel is mine whenever I visit Paris.

The Goldenberg bagel can be made as varied as the imagination will allow—onion, sesame seed, poppy seed, white, rye, salted, plain, whole wheat, caraway seed, and on and on. Bagel lovers are fiercely partisan to their water or egg positions.

This recipe is for a water bagel made with white flour. It is plain, with suggestions as to how it can be glamourized.

The technique suggested here for shaping the bagel is for the occasional home baker. The professional would roll the dough into a slender length that would go completely around his open hand—plus enough to overlap. He would then roll the bagel back and forth under the palm to seal the ends. It is difficult for a tyro to maintain the same thickness over the whole length of the dough. (Mine sometimes look like a sleeping bag that has not been shaken out for several days.)

The easy way to achieve a high professional bagel is simply to push a hole through the ball of dough and gently work it into a bagel with smooth sides. Warning: Never use a cookie or doughnut cutter. Tradition frowns on it. If you do, don't mention it when someone praises your perfectly shaped bagels.

INGREDIENTS	3½ cups bread or all-purpose flour, approximately
	2 packages dry yeast
	3 tablespoons sugar
	1 tablespoon salt
	1½ cups hot water (120°–130°)
	3 quarts water
	1½ tablespoons malt syrup or sugar
	1 egg white, beaten, mixed with 1 teaspoon water
	Topping of choice (see headnote)
BAKING SHEET	1 baking sheet, greased or Teflon, sprinkled with cornmeal
SPECIAL EQUIPMENT	A 4½"-quart saucepan

BY HAND OR MIXER
12 mins.

Into a mixing or mixer bowl measure 3 cups flour and stir in the dry ingredients. Pour in the hot water, and stir vigorously with a wooden spoon, or with mixer flat beater at low speed for 2 minutes. Add the balance of the flour, a small portion at a time; stir by hand. When the batter gets thick and heavy, attach the mixer dough hook. If by hand, lift from the bowl and place on the floured work surface.

KNEADING
10 mins.

If kneading by hand, do so with a strong rhythm of push-turn-fold. Add flour if the dough is sticky or elastic. If under the dough hook, knead at medium low speed. Add flour if the dough sticks to the sides of the bowl. Bagel dough should be firm and solid when pinched with the fingers. Knead for 10 minutes.

BY PROCESSOR
5 mins.

Attach the plastic dough blade.

Measure 2½ cups flour and the dry ingredients into the work bowl. Pulse to blend. With the processor on, pour the hot water through the feed tube to form a heavy, sticky dough. With the machine running, add small portions of flour through the feed tube to make a ball of dough that will ride the blade and clean the sides of the work bowl.

KNEADING
1 min.

Process to knead for 1 minute.

Stop the machine, uncover, and pinch the dough to determine if it is wet and needs more flour. If not, turn from the bowl and dust lightly with flour (to prevent sticking).

FIRST RISING
I hour

Place the dough in a greased bowl, cover tightly with plastic wrap, and set aside at room temperature until doubled in volume, about 1 hour.

During this period bring the 3 quarts water to a boil in the large saucepan. Add the malt syrup or sugar. Reduce heat and leave at a simmer—water barely moving.

SHAPING
15 mins.

Turn the dough onto a flour-dusted work surface and punch down with extended fingers. Divide the dough into 10 pieces, 3 to 4 ounces each. Shape each into a ball. Allow to relax for a few minutes before flattening with the palm of your hand.

With your thumb, press deep into the center of the bagel and tear the depression open with your fingers. Pull the hole open, pull it down over a finger and smooth the rough edges. It should look like a bagel!

Place the bagels together on the work surface.

SECOND RISING
10 mins.

Cover the bagels with wax paper and leave at room temperature only until the dough is slightly raised, about 10 minutes. A baker calls this "half-proofed." If they go beyond half-proof, the bagels may not sink as they should when first dropped into the simmering water. If by chance the bagels do go beyond this point, no great problem. Proceed as if they sank although they are floating. Only a professional bagel maker would appreciate the nuance.

PREHEAT

Preheat the oven to 400°.

BOILING
3–4 mins.

The water should be simmering. Gently lift one bagel at a time with a large skimmer and lower into the hot water. Do not do more than 2 or 3 at a time. Don't crowd them. The bagel should sink and then rise again after a few seconds. Simmer for 1 minute, turning over once. Lift out with the skimmer, drain briefly on a towel, then place on the prepared baking sheet. Repeat with all of the bagels.

Thanks to the malt syrup or sugar, the bagels will be shiny as they come from the water.

BAKING
425°
25–30 mins.

This is the time to give the bagels glamour with different toppings—salt, onion bits or sesame, poppy or caraway seeds. Brush lightly with the egg white–water glaze and sprinkle on the topping.

Place the bagels on the baking sheet and bake on the middle oven shelf for 25 to 30 minutes. When the bagel tops are a light brown color, turn them over to complete baking. This will keep bagels in a rounded shape without the sharp flatness on one side. Remove from the oven when brown and shiny.

(If using a convection oven, reduce heat 50°.)

FINAL STEP

Place on a metal rack to cool.

Note: Bagels are versatile. In addition to all the other ways to eat bagels, try slicing into 4 thin rounds; bake until dry throughout and beginning to brown, about 20 minutes. Remove from the oven, butter and salt lightly—and return to the oven until the butter soaks into the rounds, about 5 minutes. Serve hot, or let stand until cool before serving.

Great snack.

Celery Seed Rolls/Buns
[two dozen rolls or one dozen buns)

Deep in my file I came across a recipe for small celery seed rolls that I had made big for grilled hamburgers at a lakeside picnic almost two decades ago. Not only were they big but they were delicious. My notation on the recipe card gave them an A+. I vowed then to bring them out of the retired file and put them on the active list.

Made small, they are fine for brunch or buffet; shaped large, they are ideally suited for large hamburgers. Eggs give the dough the aura of a golden richness.

INGREDIENTS

5½ cups bread or all-purpose flour, approximately
1 package dry yeast
2 cups milk
3 tablespoons butter, room temperature
3 tablespoons sugar
1 teaspoon salt
2 eggs, room temperature
1 egg yolk, beaten, mixed with 1 teaspoon water
1 tablespoon celery seeds (other seeds may be substituted)

BAKING SHEET

1 baking sheet, greased, Teflon, or sprinkled liberally with cornmeal

BY HAND
OR MIXER
8 mins.

In a large mixing or mixer bowl measure 3 cups flour and sprinkle in the yeast. Blend and set aside for the moment. Into a medium saucepan pour the milk and add small chunks of butter, the sugar, and salt. Over a low flame heat the milk until most of the butter is melted—but not long enough to scald the milk.

Pour the heated milk (not above 130°) into the flour-yeast, and stir to make a smooth batter. Lightly beat the eggs in a small bowl and add these to the dough mixture. Beat with a spoon or the mixer flat beater until the eggs are absorbed.

FERMENTING
1 hour

Cover the bowl with plastic wrap and leave to ferment and become puffy, about 1 hour.

Stir down the spongy batter. Add the balance of the flour, ¼ cup at a time, to form a heavy dense mass that can be lifted to the work surface, or left in the bowl under the dough hook. If wet, add flour.

KNEADING
10 mins.

Knead the dough with a forceful rhythm of push-turn-fold until the dough is soft and elastic. If under the dough hook, the dough should pull away from the sides of the bowl and form a ball around the revolving hook. If it sticks to the sides, add liberal sprinkles of flour. Knead for 10 minutes.

BY PROCESSOR
8 mins.

Attach the plastic dough blade.

The sequence of adding ingredients varies from above.

Measure 4 cups flour into the processor work bowl. Add the yeast, sugar, and salt. Pulse to blend. Heat the butter and milk in a small saucepan and, with the processor on, pour the liquid through the feed tube. Stop the machine. Break the eggs in a small bowl, stir to beat, and pour into the work bowl. Pulse 4 or 5 times to mix all of the ingredients together.

FERMENTING
1 hour

With the cover in place or covered with plastic wrap, leave the batter to ferment and rise, about 1 hour.

Pulse to stir down the batter. With the machine on, add flour, ¼ cup at a time, until a heavy mass has formed that will pull away from the sides of the bowl and spin with the blade. Add flour if the dough continues to be wet and sticky.

KNEADING
45 secs.

With the processor on, knead for 45 seconds.

The dough may be slightly sticky when taken from the bowl, so dust with flour and form into a ball.

FIRST RISING
45 mins.

Place the dough in a greased bowl, cover with plastic wrap, and put aside to rise until doubled in volume, about 45 minutes.

SHAPING
15 mins.

The dough, which will weigh about 3 pounds, can be shaped into 2 dozen or more smaller rolls or a dozen large (4") buns.

Push down the dough with your hands and lift to the work surface. Roll the dough into a cylinder, measure with a yardstick, and cut off pieces of equal length.

Cupping your hand, press down hard on one piece of dough, rolling it back and forth on the work surface—until a tight ball is formed. Set aside to rest, and proceed with the balance.

Starting with the first piece, knock flat with the side of your fist or press with your palms into an oval of dough about ½" thick. Place the disk of dough on the baking sheet, and continue with the other pieces.

SECOND RISING
40 mins.

Cover the sheet with wax or parchment paper, and set aside to rise until puffy and doubled in volume, about 40 minutes.

PREHEAT

Preheat the oven to 425° 20 minutes before baking.

BAKING
425°
20 mins.

Brush the buns with the egg-milk wash, and liberally sprinkle with celery seeds or seeds of choice.

Place on the middle shelf of the hot oven and bake until the crusts are golden, about 20 minutes.

(If using a convection oven, reduce heat 50°.)

FINAL STEP

Remove from the oven and cool on a metal rack before serving.

These keep well for 2 or 3 days in a plastic bag, or, if frozen at 0°, several months.

Angel Biscuits   [three dozen biscuits]

A properly made angel biscuit is as soft and fluffy and light as one might imagine an angel to be.

Recipes for angel biscuits seem to be as numerous as the number of angels said to dance on the head of a pin, but none is more inspired than this one from the country kitchen of Marilyn Kluger, my southern Indiana neighbor and friend, who cooks and bakes as well as she writes. She is a widely respected author of cookbooks, including Country Kitchens Remembered, *published recently.*

The levitation for these angels comes from 3 sources—yeast, baking powder, and baking soda.

This convenient dough can be refrigerated up to 4 or 5 days, and baked as needed. Or it can be frozen to keep for several months.

Note: *The dough needs to be refrigerated overnight, so allow the time.*

INGREDIENTS	4½ to 5 cups all-purpose flour, approximately
	1 package dry yeast
	1 tablespoon baking powder
	1 teaspoon baking soda
	3 tablespoons sugar
	1 teaspoon salt
	¾ cup shortening, lard preferred
	2 cups buttermilk

BAKING SHEET

1 baking sheet, greased or Teflon

BY HAND
OR MIXER
12 mins.

In a large mixing or mixer bowl stir together the dry ingredients. The mixer flat beater is good for this.

Drop chunks of shortening into the flour; work in the shortening either with your hands, 2 knives cutting across each other, or a pastry blender. The flour will resemble grains of rice or smaller. If using the mixer, the flat beater blade will cut the shortening into tiny pieces, almost indistinguishable.

Stir the buttermilk into the flour; mix it thoroughly but do not knead. With the mixer on, slowly pour in the liquid to form a heavy and wet batter. It will become stiff and workable when it has been chilled in the refrigerator.

BY PROCESSOR
6 mins.

Attach the plastic blade.

Measure all the dry ingredients into the work bowl. Pulse to blend. Uncover the bowl and scatter pieces of the shortening over the flour. Replace the cover; pulse 6 or 7 times to cut the shortening into the flour. Pulsing the processor on and off (rather than allowing it to run), slowly pour the buttermilk through the feed tube. The dough is not to be kneaded—only mixed.

REFRIGERATION
Overnight

Place the dough in a greased bowl, cover with plastic wrap, and leave overnight in the refrigerator.

PREHEAT

Preheat the oven to 400° 20 minutes before baking.

SHAPING
12 mins.

Pinch off only enough dough to make the desired number of biscuits—whether a half dozen, or the entire batch. Return the balance of the dough to the refrigerator or freeze.

Knead the dough under your palms for 3 or 4 minutes. Roll into a rectangle, fold into thirds, and roll again. Fold and roll one more time. The dough should be about ½" thick.

Cut the dough with a cutter of the desired size and place the biscuits on the baking sheet. Do not allow to rise.

BAKING	Place the sheet of biscuits on the middle shelf of the hot oven, and

BAKING
400°
15–17 mins.

Place the sheet of biscuits on the middle shelf of the hot oven, and bake for 15 to 17 minutes, until the tops are nicely browned.
        (If using a convection oven, reduce heat 50°.)

FINAL STEP

Take from the oven—and serve with lots of butter and other good things.

THE SCONE

Suddenly this country has discovered what the Scots have known for several centuries—scones are delicious. This Scottish tea cake is simply made. It is seldom embellished with more than raisins or currants. Occasionally, caraway seeds.

But in the United States, the scone has grown apart from its Scots cousin, just as the U.S. croissant, stuffed with everything considered edible, has grown away from the original and simple French croissant. In this country anything seems to go. Walnut, whole wheat, cheddar and dill, blueberry, chocolate chip, and cheese are just a few of the flavors.

Below is the traditional scone, or skon, which may be customized as you wish or left in its simple grandeur. The author has made one concession, however, by including a recipe for a Michigan cherry-studded scone or bannock, but it has been placed in the chapter "Special Breads."

Mrs. Macnab's Scones   [sixteen small scones]

Mrs. Macnab, who lived near Ballater, Scotland, had many customers for her celebrated scones but none more prominent than King Frederick of Prussia, who rode often from Balmoral Castle, where he was a visitor, to relish her small tea cakes.

While it is not possible to impart Mrs. Macnab's lightness of touch, her recipe in other hands does produce a delicious scone, white and soft on the inside, brown and crisp on the out.

The secret of her success, said Mrs. Macnab, was not working the dough with the hands except just once, briefly, when kneading it.

INGREDIENTS

2 cups all-purpose flour, approximately
1 teaspoon *each* salt and baking soda
2 teaspoons cream of tartar
3 tablespoons butter, room temperature
1 egg, room temperature, lightly beaten
1/2 cup buttermilk, room temperature
1/2 cup currants or raisins (more if you wish)

BAKING SHEET	1 baking sheet, greased or Teflon
PREHEAT	Preheat the oven to 375°.
BY HAND OR MIXER 10 mins.	Into a mixing or mixer bowl measure the dry ingredients. Stir with a wooden spoon or with the mixer flat beater. With your fingers or with the flat beater rub the butter into the dry ingredients. In a small bowl stir together the egg and buttermilk. Pour the liquid gradually into the flour. If it is too moist and sticks to your hands or the flat beater, add sprinkles of flour. Stir in the currants or raisins. If the mass is too thick, it may be necessary to attach the dough hook.
KNEADING 2 mins.	If by hand, turn the dough onto a lightly floured work surface but knead and work as little as possible to achieve a soft, pliable ball. If under the dough hook, knead at low speed for no more than 2 minutes.
BY PROCESSOR 2 mins.	*Note:* The food processor works almost too fast for this recipe. It may knead the dough too much before it can be turned off—but try it.
	Attach the steel blade.
	Measure the dry ingredients into the work bowl. Pulse to blend. Drop in the butter and cut into the flour with several pulses. In a small bowl stir together the egg and buttermilk. With the machine running, pour the buttermilk mixture through the feed tube. At the moment it has been absorbed stop the machine. Turn the dough onto a floured work surface and work in the currants with a kneading action. Add sprinkles of flour if the mass is sticky.
SHAPING 8 mins.	Divide the dough into 4 equal parts. Flatten each with your knuckles—not a rolling pin—into a round disk, about 6" in diameter and ½" thick. Prick each a dozen times with the tines of a fork. With the moist edge of a kitchen knife cut each into quarters. Lift the quarters onto the baking sheet.
BAKING 375° 15 mins.	Bake in the moderate oven until the scones are a lovely tan, 15 minutes. Don't scorch.
	(If using a convection oven, reduce heat 50°.)
FINAL STEP	Remove the scones from the oven. Serve while hot at breakfast, tea, or brunch.
	I have frozen these but they are much better freshly prepared.

Sour Skons   [one large scone to serve eight]

The base for this delicious caraway-flavored scone from the Orkney Islands, to the north of the Scottish mainland, is a cupful of oatmeal soaked in buttermilk for 2 or 3 days.

I copied down the spare 2-sentence recipe in a Scottish kitchen: "Soak up some oatmeal in buttermilk for a few days, then take it and beat it up with flour into which you have stirred a little baking soda, sugar to taste (don't over-sweeten), and a few caraway seeds." The second sentence said, "Lay it on the griddle." End of recipe.

I have also made this "skon" with currants rather than caraway seeds—with equally delicious results.

INGREDIENTS

1 cup oatmeal

1 cup buttermilk

1 teaspoon *each* sugar and baking soda

¹/₂ teaspoon *each* salt and caraway seeds

1¹/₄ cups all-purpose flour

GRIDDLE OR BAKING SHEET

1 heavy griddle or baking sheet

PREPARATION 2 or 3 days

Two or three days beforehand, measure the oatmeal into a small bowl and stir in the buttermilk. Cover with plastic wrap and place in the refrigerator to soak. Stir once each day.

BY HAND OR MIXER 5 mins.

On baking day, stir down the soaked oatmeal. In a separate mixing or mixer bowl stir together the dry ingredients. Pour the wet mixture into the dry ingredients. Blend by hand or with the flat beater until the oat-meal is absorbed into the flour. The dough should be firm enough to lift from the bowl. If it is wet, add sprinkles of flour. If dry, add a tea-spoon or two more buttermilk.

BY PROCESSOR 5 mins.

Soak the oatmeal, as above.

Attach the steel blade.

The dough is only to be mixed thoroughly, not kneaded at length, so pulse the processor sparingly.

Measure all of the dry ingredients into the bowl. Pulse to blend. Drop large tablespoons of the oatmeal mixture through the feed tube, pulsing after each addition. When the mixture has been absorbed by the flour, stop the processor and feel the dough. If wet, add flour. When turned from the work bowl it will be slightly sticky, so dust with flour.

SHAPING 5 mins.	Pat the dough into a circular loaf, about 8" in diameter and ¾" thick.
PREHEAT	Heat the griddle, or preheat the oven to 425° 20 minutes before baking.
BAKING Griddle: 1 hour	Test the griddle with a sprinkle of flour. If the flour turns a deep brown within 10 seconds, the griddle is ready for the scone. Lay the scone on the griddle and, with a knife, score the top into 8 wedge-shaped pieces, cutting lightly into the dough no more than ¼" deep. Bake for 5 minutes and turn to bake for 5 minutes on the other side. Reduce the heat to medium and bake for 45 to 60 minutes. During the bake period turn the scone every 10 minutes. Insert a wooden toothpick into the scone to test for doneness. When it comes out clean and dry, the scone is done. If moist particles stick to the probe, leave on the griddle for another 5 to 10 minutes and test again.
BAKING: 425° 30 mins.	If the scone is to be baked in the oven, arrange on the baking sheet, score as above, and place in the oven until it tests done, as above, about 30 minutes. (If using a convection oven, reduce heat 50°.)
FINAL STEP	Lift the scone off the griddle with a spatula, or remove from the oven. Place on a metal rack to cool somewhat before serving. Break along the scored lines—and serve.

Pogácsa   [six dozen cocktail-size scones]
(Hungarian Cheese Scones)

Pogácsa, *baked in Hungary for breakfast, lunch, and snack, is to be found in many Hungarian folk tales. Storytellers call them* hamuba sült pogácsa— *"biscuits baked in ashes." Also when a farmer returns from the fields at the end of the day, the children expect something to be left over from his midday meal, usually a* pogácsa. *This treat is called* madár láttá, *meaning "seen by the birds."*

A guest in a Hungarian home will almost certainly be offered a glass of wine and pogácsa *as a gesture of hospitality.*

My friend, Hungarian-born Judith Goldinger, is an outstanding baker and she gave me the recipe with these words—jé étvágyat! The French would translate it as bon appetit!

While these are made with cheese, the scones may be made plain and sprinkled with sugar or cracklings or spread with butter. They may also be dec-

orated with slivered almonds or sprinkled with poppy or sesame seeds. I have broken them open and laid on a tiny slice of ham or chicken or a pâté.
Note: *The dough needs to be chilled overnight, so allow time.*

INGREDIENTS

3 cups bread or all-purpose flour
1½ teaspoons salt
2 packages dry yeast
¾ cup (1½ sticks) butter, cut into 1" pieces
⅓ cup milk
½ cup sour cream
1 egg yolk
1 cup Parmesan or Romano cheese
1 egg, beaten, mixed with 1 tablespoon milk

BAKING SHEET

1 large baking sheet, greased, Teflon, or covered with parchment paper

BY HAND
OR MIXER
10 mins.

Measure 2 cups flour into the mixing or mixer bowl and add the salt and yeast. In a small saucepan stir together the butter, milk, sour cream, and egg yolk. Place over low heat to warm to the touch. Do not let simmer or it will cook the egg.

Pour the liquid into the flour and blend by hand or with the mixer flat beater for 2 minutes, to make a smooth batter. Add flour, ¼ cup at a time. Mix vigorously with a wooden spoon or dough hook. The dough will be smooth and soft.

KNEADING
12–14 mins.

Transfer the dough to a floured work surface, if by hand, or leave in the bowl under the dough hook. The dough should be soft but not sticky. If sticky, add sprinkles of flour. Knead for 8 to 10 minutes, until the dough is velvety and responsive under your hands.

Press the dough into a flat oval and spread with ½ cup cheese. Turn in the sides and knead. Again press the dough into an oval, and add ¼ cup more cheese. Knead until the cheese is spread throughout the dough, about 4 minutes.

BY PROCESSOR
5 mins.

Attach the steel blade.

The sequence differs from above.

Heat the moist ingredients in a saucepan, as above. The butter need not be completely melted. Measure 2 cups flour into the work bowl and sprinkle in the salt and yeast. Pulse to blend.

With the processor running, slowly pour the liquid in a stream through the feed tube. Add flour, ¼ cup at a time, through the feed tube until the dough becomes a ball riding on the blade and cleans the sides of the bowl.

KNEADING	Once the dough forms a ball, process for 45 seconds.
5 mins.	

If the dough is dry and hard, add water by the tablespoon. If the dough is wet and sticks to the sides of the bowl, add flour by the tablespoon and process for a few more seconds.

Turn the dough from the bowl, and knead for a few moments to be certain the dough has the proper consistency. Work in the cheese and knead, as above.

CHILL
Overnight

Press the dough into a flat oval, wrap with plastic wrap or place in a plastic bag, and chill overnight in the refrigerator.

The following day leave the dough at room temperature for 1 hour, then roll into a flat piece about ¼" thick. Fold and roll once or twice more to make it flaky.

PREHEAT

Preheat the oven to 350°.

SHAPING
15 mins.

Cut the dough with a 1" cookie cutter; turn each piece over and place bottom up on the baking sheet (this permits maximum rise). Lightly score each scone twice across the top with a sharp knife, brush with the egg wash, and sprinkle with the balance of the cheese (¼ cup).

BAKING
350°
30 mins.

Place the sheet on the middle shelf of the moderate oven and bake until the scones are a golden brown, about 30 minutes.

(If using a convection oven, reduce heat 50°. Plan to bake in 2 or more batches since most home convection ovens will not accommodate large baking sheets.)

FINAL STEP

Remove from the sheet and place on a metal rack to cool—although they are delicious still warm from the oven.

They can be frozen for months.

Jé étvágyat!

London's Cream Scones   [one dozen scones]

This recipe was not in the Complete Book of Breads *but it is so outstanding among recipes I have since collected that I have included it here.*

Wendy London and her husband, Michael, are two of the most accomplished bakers in the country. He is the master of big and hearty loaves of French and sourdough breads; she, the more delicate breads and pastries, including this cream scone. They began all this in the Rock Hill Bakehouse on the grounds of their two-hundred-year-old red-brick farmhouse near the small town of Greenwich in upstate New York, and a satellite bakery in the nearby resort city of Saratoga Springs.

This is one of the finest breads to come from the Londons' ovens. It is ten-
der, soft, and rich. Very rich. Start with thick cream, add milk, a half cup of
sugar, two sticks of butter, and speckle with currants. Unlike dough for other
scones, this dough is chilled before cutting, then returned to the refrigerator for
at least 2 hours or overnight to relax.

To give these scones the touch of elegance they deserve, cut them from
the dough with a fluted cutter that is a favorite of pastry makers. Razor sharp,
the crinkle cutter cuts cleanly without smearing the dough, and leaves a hand-
some scalloped edge. They are equally good, of course, cut with ordinary bis-
cuit or cookie cutters.

INGREDIENTS

2 cups all-purpose flour, approximately
$^1/_2$ cup cake flour (Softasilk is a good choice)
$^1/_2$ cup sugar
1 teaspoon salt (sea salt preferred)
1 tablespoon baking powder
2 sticks butter, chilled
$^1/_2$ cup heavy cream, chilled
$^1/_4$ cup milk, chilled
$^3/_4$ cup currants
1 egg beaten with 1 teaspoon cream, to glaze

BAKING SHEET

1 baking sheet, greased or Teflon

BY HAND
OR MIXER
15 mins.

In a large bowl mix the dry ingredients together by hand or in the
mixer bowl with flat beater blade. Cut the chilled butter into ½" cubes
and drop them into the flour one at a time. By hand, use a pastry
blender to chop the butter into small pieces resembling crumbs or
coarse meal. In the mixer, set at slow speed to reduce the butter to
crumbs. Don't over-mix or it will turn into a dough. It must remain dry.

Add cold cream, milk, and currants. Mix until the dough cleans the
bowl and is well blended. Do not knead. Mix only as for pie dough.
Turn out onto the floured work surface. If the mix is still cold, thanks
to the chilled ingredients, it can be rolled and cut right away. If not,
and the dough has become sticky, cover with plastic wrap and place in
the refrigerator for an hour. Push and shape the dough into a smooth
solid mass, adding sprinkles of flour to control the stickiness.

BY PROCESSOR
15 mins.

Insert metal blade.

The mixture must be done in quick, short bursts to keep the particles intact, *not* blended into a solid mass.

Measure the dry ingredients into the work bowl. Pulse to blend.

Uncover the bowl. With a sharp knife, cut the two sticks of butter into cubes and scatter them over the flour. Cover the bowl and pulse to cut the butter into small particles like bread crumbs. Pour the liquid through the feeder tube, while at the same time pulsing the processor. Stop the machine immediately when the dough forms a ball and cleans the sides of the bowl. Do not knead. The dough will be soft and quite moist when it is removed from the work bowl. Add sprinkles of flour if necessary to make it easier to work. Place the dough on the floured work surface. Spread the currants over the dough and work them into it by hand, otherwise the whirling blade would cut the currants into tiny black bits.

SHAPING
10 mins.

With a rolling pin or by hand, flatten the dough into a sheet 1" thick. Use a ruler to check the thickness to keep the scones uniform.

Dip the cutter in flour and cut out the scones. Place on the baking sheet. Work the scraps together and roll flat and cut. Brush the scones with the wash. Cover the bake tray tightly with plastic wrap or place it in a plastic bag and refrigerate for one or two hours or overnight until the dough has relaxed.

PREHEAT

Preheat oven to 400°.

BAKING
400°
20–25 mins.

Lightly brush each scone again with egg glaze. Place the baking sheet on the middle shelf of the oven and bake until light golden in color, about 25 minutes. To test, gently open one scone to be certain it has properly baked. Check the bottom which should be a deep brown.

FINAL STEP

Treat the scones gently when they first come from the oven for they are fragile when hot. Place them on a metal rack to cool. Scones keep nicely for a day or so. Freeze if for a longer period, then thaw and reheat.

Serve with butter and jam or eat plain as is. Delicious.

English Muffins   [about two dozen muffins]

Never cut an English muffin with a knife!

An English muffin must be torn apart by hand or with the help of a fork if it is ever to attain its true splendor of rough peaks and valleys bathed in butter. Even the best muffin, once violated with a knife (no matter how sharp), can never give the taste sensation of one torn apart and toasted.

This recipe is for a good English muffin ready to be torn apart—not sliced.

These may not look like the packaged English muffins, of precise size and shape. There will be irregular shapes among them, but so much the better.

INGREDIENTS	5 to 5½ cups bread or all-purpose flour, approximately
	2 packages dry yeast
	2 tablespoons sugar
	I teaspoon salt
	½ cup nonfat dry milk
	1¼ cups hot water (120°–130°)
	3 tablespoons butter, room temperature
	I egg, room temperature
	Cornmeal

GRIDDLE OR
BAKING SHEET

1 heavy metal, electric, or soapstone griddle, or heavy skillet, or baking sheet

BY HAND
OR MIXER
12 mins.

In a large mixing or mixer bowl measure 3 cups flour, and the dry ingredients. Stir to blend together. Add the butter to the hot water and pour into the dry ingredients. Beat for 2 minutes with the mixer flat beater, or 150 strokes with a wooden spoon. Add the egg. Stir in the remaining flour, ¼ cup at a time, until the dough is a rough, shaggy mass. If using a mixer, change to the dough hook.

KNEADING
10 mins.

Turn the dough onto a floured work surface and knead with a strong push-turn-fold motion until the dough is smooth, elastic, and feels alive under your hands. In the mixer, the dough will clean the sides of the bowl and form a ball around the hook and move with it. If the dough should continue to be sticky, add liberal sprinkles of flour. Knead for 10 minutes.

BY PROCESSOR
4 mins.

Attach the plastic dough blade.

Measure 3 cups flour into the work bowl and add the dry ingredients. Pulse to blend. Remove the cover and drop in the hot water, butter, and egg. Replace the cover and process for 30 seconds to blend thoroughly.

With the processor on, add flour, ¼ cup at a time, through the feed tube to form a mass that cleans the sides of the bowl and rides with the blade as it whirls. Remove the cover; pinch the dough to see if it has enough flour to make it a solid but soft ball of dough. If it is moist, add flour. If it seems stiff, add teaspoons of water and process for an additional 10 seconds.

KNEADING	When the ball has formed, knead with the processor running for
1 min.	1 minute. When turned from the bowl the dough will be sticky, but a few sprinkles of flour will leave it dry and workable.

FIRST RISING	Pat the ball of dough with lightly greased fingertips and place in a
1 hour	bowl. Cover with plastic wrap and set aside at room temperature to double in size, about 1 hour.

SHAPING	Punch down the dough, knead for 30 seconds, and set aside to rest for
20 mins.	10 minutes.

Sprinkle the work surface with cornmeal and turn the dough onto it. Roll out the dough until it is ¼" thick. If it resists the rolling pin and pulls back, let it rest for 1 or 2 minutes. Cut into 3" rounds (4" for eggs Benedict) with a cookie cutter.

SECOND RISING	Sprinkle the work surface with cornmeal and put the rounds under a
45 mins.	towel. Let rise until they are doubled in size to about ½" thick, 45 minutes.

PREHEAT	Heat the electric griddle to 325°. Or preheat the oven to 450° 20 minutes before baking.

BAKING	Bake the muffins for 2 minutes on each side. Do not cook fast, so avoid
Griddle:	the hot center of the griddle; place the muffins around the sides of the
325°	griddle. Reduce heat and bake for 6 additional minutes on each side or
16 mins.	a total of about 16 minutes. Don't scorch.

BAKING	If using the oven, place the cut muffins on the baking sheet and bake
450°	for 15 minutes, turning them over after 6 or 7 minutes. They will rise
15 mins.	and swell to look rather like puffballs.

(If using a convection oven, reduce heat 50°.)

FINAL STEP	Remove the muffins from the griddle or baking sheet. Cool on a metal rack before toasting. Pull apart with the tines of a fork, or the fingers, to toast.

These freeze well and keep for months in the deep freeze at 0°.

Buttery Rowies   [eighteen rolls]
(Aberdeen Butter Rolls)

"Buttery Rowies and Bawbee Baps!"

This was a cry once heard in the early morning hours in the streets of Aberdeen as street vendors called out the names of these two delicious breakfast rolls.

The Buttery Rowie is a flaky rectangle that has a fried taste and texture even though it is baked in the oven. A mixture of butter and lard is slathered on a thin rectangle of dough which is then folded over, rolled, folded, rolled, folded—a total of 3 times, much as is done with flaky pastry or croissants. They are best served warm from the oven.

INGREDIENTS

3 cups bread or all-purpose flour, approximately
1 package dry yeast
1 tablespoon sugar
1 teaspoon salt
1½ cups hot water (120°–130°)
¾ cup (1½ sticks) butter, room temperature
¾ cup lard, room temperature

BAKING SHEET

1 baking sheet. Be certain the sheet has a lip (or create one with foil) so the melted butter and lard do not run into the oven.

BY HAND OR MIXER 8 mins.

Into a large mixing or mixer bowl measure 1½ cups flour and stir in the yeast, sugar, salt, and hot water. Beat by hand vigorously or with the mixer flat beater for 2 minutes. Stir in the balance of the flour, ½ cup at a time, first with the spoon and then by hand, or with the flat beater and dough hook. The dough will be a rough, shaggy mass that can be lifted to the work surface or left to be processed in the mixer bowl. If the dough continues to be slack and moist, and is sticky, add sprinkles of flour.

KNEADING 10 mins.

Turn the dough onto the work surface and knead with the rhythmic motion of push-turn-fold. The dough will become smooth and elastic and bubbles will form beneath the surface. Break the kneading rhythm occasionally by throwing the dough down hard against the work surface. If using a mixer, place under the dough hook. If sticky, add small portions of flour until the dough cleans the sides of the bowl and forms a ball around the hook. Knead for 10 minutes either way.

BY PROCESSOR 5 mins.

Attach the steel blade.

Measure 2 cups flour and the other dry ingredients into the work bowl; pour in the hot water. Cover and pulse 6 or 7 times to blend to a heavy batterlike mass.

Add flour, ¼ cup at a time, through the feed tube, with the processor running, until the dough forms a rough mass and rides the blade around the bowl. Uncover the bowl and test the dough with your fingers. If wet, add more flour.

KNEADING 45 secs.	When the mass has formed, process for 45 additional seconds to thoroughly knead the dough. When turned from the bowl the dough will be somewhat sticky, so dust lightly with flour.
RISING 1 hour	Place the dough in a greased bowl, cover tightly with plastic wrap, and leave at room temperature until the dough has risen to about twice its original size, 1 hour. Or test by poking a finger into the dough; the dent will remain.
REFRIGERATION 30 mins.	When the dough has risen, punch it down, turn it out onto the work surface again, and knead for 30 seconds to press out the bubbles. Place in a clean bowl, cover with plastic wrap again, and put in the refrigerator for 30 minutes to chill. While the dough is chilling, cream together the butter and lard. Divide into 3 equal parts on a length of wax paper and set aside.
LAYERING 70 mins.: 10 mins. 20 mins. 20 mins. 20 mins.	On a lightly floured work surface roll the dough to a rectangle 3 times as long as it is wide, about 12" x 4", for example. *Turn 1:* Spread one-third of the shortening mixture over the dough, leaving a 1" margin around the edge with no butter on it. Fold the dough in three, as for a business letter. Wrap in wax paper and return to the refrigerator to chill the dough, about 15 minutes. *Turn 2:* Roll out, spread on the second portion of butter and lard, and fold in three. Chill for 15 minutes. *Turn 3:* Roll out, spread on the last portion of butter and lard, and fold in three. Chill for 15 minutes more.
PREHEAT	Preheat the oven to 400° before cutting the rowies.
SHAPING 20 mins.	Roll out the dough into a rectangle 3 times as long as it is wide. It should be about ¾" thick. With a pastry wheel or wet knife blade, cut into rectangles, about 1½" x 4½". Place on the baking sheet and leave a space of 1½" between.
BAKING 400° 25 mins.	Place the rolls in the oven and bake until raised, flaky, and light brown, about 25 minutes. (If using a convection oven, reduce heat 50°.)
FINAL STEP	Remove from the oven. Call out the old Scottish street cry (above) as you serve the rowies. Guests will love it.

Almond-Bran Muffins   [one dozen muffins]

This delicious buttermilk muffin is named for its bran and slivered almonds, but it contains other good-tasting ingredients, including shredded coconut, raisins, and brown sugar.

Note: *This recipe is so easy to mix in a bowl by hand that no instructions for a mixer or food processor are here. The latter would further shred the ingredients and the muffins would lose their interesting texture.*

INGREDIENTS

1 cup all-purpose flour
1 cup bran flakes (100% is good)
$1/2$ teaspoon baking soda
2 teaspoons baking powder
$1/2$ teaspoon salt
2 tablespoons brown sugar
1 egg
1 cup buttermilk
$1/4$ cup cooking oil
$1/2$ cup *each* slivered almonds, raisins, and shredded coconut

MUFFIN TINS

2 muffin tins with a total of 12 cups, greased

PREHEAT

Preheat the oven to 400°.

BY HAND
10 mins.

In a large bowl combine all the dry ingredients. Make a well in the center.

In a separate small bowl stir together the egg, oil, and buttermilk.

Add liquid to dry ingredients and stir only to moisten. Then fold in the almonds, raisins, and coconuts.

Pour the batter into the muffin cups two-thirds full.

BAKE
400°
18–20 mins.

Bake for 18 to 20 minutes.

(If using a convection oven, reduce heat 50°.)

FINAL STEP

Remove from the oven and cool slightly.
Serve warm with lots of butter!

Blueberry-Lemon Muffins
[eighteen large or thirty-six small muffins]

Mackinac is a jewel of an island in the Straits of Mackinac (pronounced Mack-in-aw) in Michigan, near the Canadian border, and one of its treasures is the blueberry-lemon muffin that has been served for years at the lovely turn-of-the-century Iroquois Hotel on the beach.

No autos are allowed on the streets of Mackinac. Horses and carriages clop down the streets and bicycles scurry everywhere, and in the Iroquois kitchen the pace is unhurried. The only deadline for Melanie Sullivan, the baker, is to have many baskets of warm muffins ready for guests coming down to breakfast on the terrace at water's edge.

The plump blueberries bake to become deep purple pools flavored by the lemon zest. When the muffins are done and allowed to cool for a few moments, each is dipped first in melted butter and then in granulated sugar.

The only way to reach these blueberry muffins is by ferry from the mainland, worth every nautical mile. Of course, you can bake them yourself. Melanie Sullivan sees no difference in taste or texture when using frozen blueberries instead of fresh ones.

INGREDIENTS	2⅔ cups all-purpose flour
	1 tablespoon baking powder
	1½ teaspoons salt
	½ cup sugar
	2 eggs
	1 cup milk
	⅔ cup cooking oil
	1½ cups fresh or frozen blueberries
	½ tablespoon lemon zest

Glaze:
4 tablespoons butter
½ cup sugar

MUFFIN TINS   2 medium (2½") muffin tins for 18, or 3 small (1½") muffin tins for 36, greased or coated

PREHEAT   Preheat the oven to 400°.

BY HAND
10 mins.   Into a mixing bowl sift the flour and add the other dry ingredients.

In a small bowl crack the eggs and beat with a wire whisk for 10 seconds. Add the milk and oil to the eggs and stir to blend.

Make a well in the flour and pour in the egg-milk mixture. Stir as little as possible to moisten the flour. Set the batter aside for a moment.

Combine the blueberries with the lemon zest, and fold the berry mix into the muffin mix. Again stir gently and as little as possible.

Spoon the batter into the tins to three-fourths full.

BAKING
400°
20 mins.

Put the muffins into the oven and set the timer for 20 minutes. It may take them an additional 5 minutes, however, to get golden brown. Check at 15 minutes, and if they are browning too quickly, set on the bottom shelf of the oven.

(If using a convection oven, reduce heat 40°.)

Note: In both types of ovens, the muffins on the outside may get done before those on the inside. If so, remove the ones that are brown and return the tray to the oven for an additional 5 minutes.

In the meantime, melt the butter in a small saucepan. Pour the sugar into a small bowl or pan into which the muffins will be dipped.

FINAL STEP

When the muffins are baked, cool for 5 minutes. Run a knife around the edges of each. Tilt the tray and gently lift each muffin from its tin.

Dip the top of each lightly in the melted butter and then lightly in the sugar.

The muffins can be held overnight and heated for eating the following day. They can also be frozen, but fresh baked are best.

Present the muffins in the manner prescribed on a sign in the Iroquois bake shop: "Arrange the muffins in an orderly manner and serve."

Sopaipillas   [eighteen to twenty-four puffs]

A favorite in the Southwest and Mexico to serve with highly seasoned dishes are Sopaipillas—golden puffs to be filled with honey. The dough is rolled wafer-thin ($1/8$"), cut into 2" or 3" squares, and dropped into hot oil.

Sopaipillas should be served hot from the kettle. Break off a corner of the puff, fill with honey, and it becomes a fine accompaniment for Mexican foods, or a dessert.

INGREDIENTS	2" vegetable oil
	1³/₄ cups all-purpose flour
	2 teaspoons baking powder
	1 teaspoon salt
	2 tablespoons shortening
	²/₃ cup cold water, approximately
	Honey
KETTLE OR SKILLET	1 deep kettle or skillet
PREHEAT	Preheat the oil or fat to 385° in the kettle or skillet.
BY HAND OR MIXER 8 mins.	Into a mixing or mixer bowl, sift the dry ingredients. Cut the shortening into the flour with a pastry blender, crossed knives, or your fingers. The mixer flat beater is also excellent for this chore. The mixture will resemble coarse meal. Add water by the tablespoon but only enough to make a stiff dough.
KNEADING 4 mins.	Turn onto a lightly floured work surface and knead until smooth and somewhat elastic. The dough will be responsive under your hands but not as much so as a fully developed bread dough. Or knead in the mixer bowl with the dough hook. Knead for 4 minutes.
BY PROCESSOR 5 mins.	Attach the steel blade.

Measure the dry ingredients into the work bowl and drop pieces of the shortening over the mixture. Cover and pulse 3 or 4 times to cut the shortening into tiny pieces in the flour. With the processor running, pour in the water through the feed tube to form a ball of dough that will ride on the blade and clean the sides of the bowl. |
| KNEADING 40 secs. | When the ball has formed, process to knead for 40 seconds. |
| SHAPING 15 mins. | Place the dough on the work surface, cover with a cloth or a length of wax or parchment paper, and allow to rest for 10 minutes.

Roll the dough into a rectangle about 12" x 15" and very thin— no more than ⅛" thick. With a pastry wheel or knife cut into 2" or 3" squares. |
| FRYING 1–2 mins. | Drop 2 or 3 squares of the dough into the hot oil. Turn several times with a slotted spoon so each sopaipilla puffs and browns evenly, 1 to 2 minutes. Remove and drain on paper towels. |
| FINAL STEP | Serve immediately with honey. |

Popovers   [eight to twelve popovers]

Popovers are good to eat. Popovers are unpredictable. There isn't very much to a popover. It is an ungainly looking medium for getting butter, jams, jellies, and honey into the mouth.

The popover owes its fragile puffiness to steam levitation. It is done without yeast or chemicals of any kind. Only steam raises it high, and then drops it back down into a clumsy shape.

There should be at least one popover recipe in every home baker's repertoire. This is a good one.

INGREDIENTS

1 cup bread or all-purpose flour (sift before measuring)
¹/₄ teaspoon salt
1 tablespoon sugar
1 tablespoon butter, melted, or salad oil
1 cup milk, room temperature
2 large eggs

BAKING PANS

Muffin pans, heavy cast-iron popover pans, or ovenproof custard cups, greased

PREHEAT

Preheat the oven to 375° or 400°.

BY HAND, MIXER, OR BLENDER
1–4 mins.

In a mixing or mixer bowl combine the dry ingredients. Add the butter or oil, milk, and eggs. Beat by hand or at medium-high speed with the mixer flat beater, until very smooth, for 3 minutes.

Popover batter can also be made in a blender. Combine all of the ingredients and whirl at high speed for 45 seconds. Stop the blender and scrape down the sides after the first 10 seconds.

BY PROCESSOR
2 mins.

Attach the steel blade.

Measure all of the ingredients into the work bowl; pulse 8 or 10 times to blend thoroughly.

SHAPING
3 mins.

Fill the cups half full with batter.

BAKING
400°
40 mins.
or
375°
50–55 mins.

Bake in the hot oven (400°) for a dark brown shell with a moist interior, 40 minutes. Or bake at 375° for a light popover with a drier interior, 50 to 55 minutes. Be sure to keep the door of the oven closed during baking to prevent a collapse under a draft of cold air.

(If using a convection oven, reduce heat 50° in either case.)

FINAL STEP   Remove the popovers from the oven. Turn from the pans and serve while hot. Or prick the popovers with a skewer or fork if you like a dry interior. Leave them in a turned-off oven, door slightly ajar, for 8 to 10 minutes.

Pikelets and Crumpets

[twenty-four pikelets or eight large crumpets]

In the north country of England the small, two-bite yeast-raised breads, baked on a griddle, are "pikelets." With a bit more flour to make a thicker batter, and baked in metal rings, they become "crumpets." Both are delicious served toasted, slathered with butter, and spread with a jam or jelly of choice.

Yeast is combined with baking soda with the result that pikelets and crumpets are full of myriad bubbles—so many holes and channels that one can see straight through a crumpet held to the light. These holes fill with butter and other good things to make a delicious bite.

Crumpets can probably be best described as a cross between an English muffin and a pancake. They hold as much nostalgia for the English as sourdough does for westerners.

Scots, too, love their crumpets, and this is the way one cook describes her way of making them:

"Put a griddle on a bright clear fire and rub with suet. To have light, pretty crumpets the fire must be brisk and the griddle hot, so that they will rise quickly. Before they get dry on top they should be turned. Do this quickly, and a lovely golden-brown skin as smooth as velvet will be formed, and a delightfully light crumpet produced."

The recipe below makes a batter for a pikelet. Add ½ cup flour—or a bit more—to thicken, for a crumpet.

Some kind of metal rings are needed to contain the batter while it bakes in a frying pan or on a griddle. Use 3-inch flan rings, English muffin rings, open-topped cookie cutters, or well-washed tuna cans with the tops and bottoms removed.

INGREDIENTS   1½ cups bread or all-purpose flour (½ cup flour *additional* if
    for crumpets)
1 teaspoon salt
1 package dry yeast
⅓ cup nonfat milk powder
1 cup hot water (120°–130°)

¹/₄ teaspoon baking soda
¹/₄ cup cold water
1 egg white, lightly beaten

BAKING PAN	1 griddle or heavy skillet
SPECIAL EQUIPMENT	Four or more 3" to 4" round metal rings, described above (for crumpets)

BY HAND OR MIXER 40 mins.

Into a medium bowl stir 1½ cups flour and the salt, yeast, and milk powder. Pour in the hot water and beat for 5 minutes with a wooden spoon, or for 3 minutes in the mixer with the flat beater to make a smooth batter.

Cover with cloth and leave at room temperature for about 30 minutes, or until the risen mixture starts to drop.

Mix the baking soda in the cold water and beat it into the batter. Fold in the beaten egg white thoroughly to produce a batter the consistency of thick pouring cream.

For crumpets, blend in an additional ½ cup flour to make a heavier batter. If desired, some pikelets can be made first, then the appropriate amount of flour added to thicken for crumpets.

COOKING 20–30 mins.

Lightly grease the griddle or heavy skillet and heat over medium heat until a drop of water sizzles immediately on contact.

Put a tablespoon of batter on the hot surface and cook until the top of the pikelet is almost dry, 8 to 10 minutes. Turn over with a spatula and cook until the other side is lightly browned.

To make crumpets, place greased rings on the hot surface. Half fill the rings with batter. As they cook, the crumpets will begin to fill with holes. Cook until the surface of the crumpet is almost dry, about 10 to 12 minutes. Don't scorch the bottoms. Lift one occasionally to check how it is doing.

Turn the crumpets over to brown lightly. At this point they will slip easily from the rings.

FINAL STEP

Eat the pikelets hot from the pan, or cool and then toast.

The crumpets may be eaten whole or split in half, toasted and buttered.

Both pikelets and crumpets are ideal vehicles for lots of butter and jam and jelly. They also freeze nicely. Reheat in a 350° oven before serving.

Bath Buns   [two dozen large buns]

Bakers in the English city of Bath, west of London on the river Avon, were the first to make—and make famous—this savory sweet bun, delicately browned and sparkling with three different glazes. The bun is flavored with mace, the ground outer coating of the nutmeg.

Bath has the only mineral springs in Great Britain and the Roman colonists were inspired to build a spa there, which is how it got the name.

INGREDIENTS

5 to 6 cups bread or all-purpose flour, approximately
I package dry yeast
$^1/_2$ cup sugar
I teaspoon salt
$^1/_2$ teaspoon ground mace
$^1/_3$ cup nonfat dry milk
I $^1/_2$ cups hot water (120°–130°)
3 eggs, beaten
$^1/_4$ cup ($^1/_2$ stick) butter, room temperature
I cup raisins or currants
$^1/_2$ cup water

Glazes:
I egg yolk, beaten
I tablespoon lemon juice mixed with 3 tablespoons sugar
I tablespoon milk

BAKING SHEET

1 or more baking sheets, greased or Teflon, depending on the size of the oven

BY HAND
OR MIXER
10 mins.

In a mixing or mixer bowl measure 2 cups flour and stir in the dry ingredients and hot water. Add the eggs and beat in the mixer with the flat beater at slow speed for 30 seconds. Add the butter and beat at medium speed for 3 minutes, or for an equal length of time with a wooden spoon.

Stop the mixer. Stir in the balance of flour, ½ cup at a time, first with the spoon and then by hand—or under the dough hook in the mixer. The dough will be a rough, shaggy mass that will clean the sides of the bowl. However, if the dough continues to be moist and sticky, add sprinkles of flour.

KNEADING
8 mins.

If by hand, turn the dough onto a lightly floured work surface and knead with the rhythmic motion of push-turn-fold. The dough will become smooth and elastic and bubbles will form under the surface of the dough. In the mixer, the dough will form a ball around the moving dough hook. The sides of the bowl will be wiped clean. Knead for 8 minutes.

BY PROCESSOR
8 mins.

Attach the short plastic dough blade.

The sequence for adding ingredients differs from above.

Measure 3 cups flour into the work bowl, and add the dry ingredients. Pulse to blend. Remove the cover and drop in the butter in pieces. Pulse until the butter becomes tiny rice-size bits. With the machine running, pour the hot water slowly through the feed tube. Break and drop in the eggs, one at a time, to form a thick batter.

With the machine running, add the flour, ¼ cup at a time, until the dough forms a ball. If the dough is wet and sticks to the sides of the bowl, add flour by the tablespoon. If the dough is dry, add water by the teaspoon.

KNEADING
1 min.

Once the ball of dough has formed, process for 1 minute to knead.

FIRST RISING
1½ hours

Place the dough on the floured work surface and knead into a ball. It will be soft, smooth, and slightly sticky (until dusted with flour).

Drop the dough into a greased bowl, turn to film all sides, and cover the bowl with plastic wrap. Put aside at room temperature to allow the dough to double in volume, about 1½ hours.

While the dough is rising, soak the currants or raisins in the water for 1 hour and drain.

SHAPING
15 mins.

The Bath Bun is about 4" in diameter.

Begin by punching down the dough and kneading in the currants or raisins. Shape the dough under your hands into a 24"-long roll. Cut into 24 equal-size pieces—each about the size of a large egg—one will weigh about 2 ounces. Work the pieces into balls, and flatten on top. Place them on a baking sheet, leaving 1½" between them.

Brush each with the beaten egg yolk. Dribble the lemon juice and sugar over the tops.

SECOND RISING
45 mins.

Place the baking sheet in a warm place; cover carefully with a length of wax or parchment paper. The buns will double in bulk in about 45 minutes.

PREHEAT

Preheat the oven to 350° about 20 minutes before baking.

BAKING
350°
25–30 mins.

Brush the rolls with milk before placing them in the oven.

Bake in the moderate oven until the buns test done, 25 to 30 minutes. Rap one on the bottom crust. A hard, hollow sound means the bun is baked.

(If using a convection oven, reduce heat 50°.)

FINAL STEP

Remove from the oven. Place on a metal rack to cool before serving.

These keep well for several days wrapped in plastic or foil, or for several months frozen at 0°.

Egg Shell Rolls   [two dozen large or four dozen small rolls]

Egg whites, whipped to a light peak, are used in this dough to produce a thin, crisp paper-shell crust which will keep the rolls fresh and delicious for a long period of time. Store in a bread box or paper sack. Don't place them in a plastic bag or they will quickly lose their crispness. If this should happen, reheat the rolls.

I found this recipe in a 40-year-old booklet developed by General Mills for commercial bakers. It works equally well in the home kitchen.

INGREDIENTS

4 1/2 cups bread or all-purpose flour, approximately
2 packages dry yeast
2 teaspoons salt
2 cups hot water (120°–130°)
2 tablespoons sugar
3 tablespoons shortening
1 teaspoon malt extract, if available
3 egg whites

BAKING SHEETS

Two 11"-x-17" baking sheets. (If only 1 sheet is available or if the oven will only take a single sheet, reserve half the dough for baking later.)

BY HAND
OR MIXER
13 mins.

In a large mixing bowl stir together 2 cups flour, the yeast, salt, and water. Stir to blend. Cream the sugar and shortening together and drop into the batterlike dough. Add the malt extract, if available.

Whip egg whites to a light peak and fold into mixture.

Add the balance of the flour, ½ cup at a time, until it becomes a shaggy mass, moist and stringy.

KNEADING
6–8 mins.

Turn the dough onto a floured work surface and knead with a strong push-turn-fold motion for 8 minutes, or for 6 minutes with a dough hook. The dough will be elastic and smooth.

BY PROCESSOR
5 mins.

Attach the plastic dough blade.

Place 2 cups flour and the yeast, salt, water, sugar, shortening, and malt extract, if available, in the work bowl. Pulse 3 or 4 times to blend the ingredients. Set aside for a moment. Whip the egg whites and add to the work bowl. Pulse to blend.

Add flour, ¼ cup at a time, pulsing each time to blend the ingredients. Add the last cup of flour with care so that the dough doesn't suddenly turn into a hard ball.

KNEADING
50 secs.

When the dough cleans the sides of the work bowl and rides in a ball on top of the blade, knead for 50 seconds. The dough will be soft and elastic.

FIRST RISING
1–1½ hours

Place the dough in a greased bowl, cover tightly with plastic wrap, and place in a warm spot (80°–90°) for 1 to 1½ hours.

SHAPING
10 mins.

For small rolls, cut the dough into 1-ounce pieces, about the size of a golf ball. For larger rolls, cut the dough into 2- or 3-ounce pieces. Roll each piece into a tight ball under your palm. Press down hard as the dough ball is rolled. Place the rolls on the baking sheets, taking care to allow sufficient room between each so they will not touch during rising. If they do, they will not brown overall as they should.

SECOND RISING
45 mins.

Cover the rolls and put in a warm place until double in volume, about 45 minutes.

PREHEAT

Preheat the oven to 400° 20 minutes before baking.

BAKING
400°
25–30 mins.

Place the baking sheets on the middle shelf of the oven. The baking time will be between 25 and 30 minutes depending on the size of the rolls, until they are a golden brown.

(If using a convection oven, reduce heat 50°.)

FINAL STEP

Place the crispy rolls on a rack to cool. Serve immediately or store in a paper sack to preserve the crust.

If the rolls should lose their crispness, reheat in 300° oven for 15 minutes. The rolls may be frozen. Thaw and reheat.

Chelsea Buns   [fifteen buns]

It was fashionable in London in the late seventeenth and early eighteenth centuries to visit the Chelsea Bun House for its delicious buns, characteristically square in shape, spicy, rich with fruit and crusty with sugar. King George III and Queen Charlotte were frequent teatime guests of the Hand family, who owned the Bun House. (The proprietor, a "Captain Bun," always wore a dressing gown and a fez whether serving the common man or king.)

INGREDIENTS

Sponge:
2 cups bread or all-purpose flour
I package dry yeast
I tablespoon sugar
$1/3$ cup nonfat dry milk
$1 1/2$ cups hot water (120°–130°)
2 eggs, room temperature, lightly beaten

Dough:
$1/2$ teaspoon salt
$1/4$ cup sugar
$2 1/2$ cups bread or all-purpose flour, approximately
$1/2$ cup (I stick) butter, softened at room temperature

Filling:
I tablespoon butter, melted
$1/3$ cup sugar
I tablespoon ground cinnamon
I cup light or dark raisins

Topping:
$1/2$ cup granulated sugar
   or
I cup confectioners' sugar mixed with I tablespoon milk and
   $1/8$ teaspoon vanilla extract

BAKING SHEET
AND PAN

One 13"-x-8" baking sheet, greased; 1 small pan for end pieces

PREPARATION
40–50 mins.

To make the sponge, in a large mixing or mixer bowl measure the flour and add the dry ingredients and hot water. Stir to make a batter. Add the eggs and beat until absorbed.

Cover the bowl with plastic wrap and put aside to ferment for 30 to 45 minutes.

**BY HAND
OR MIXER
10 mins.**

To make the dough, uncover the bowl and stir in the salt, sugar, and 1 cup flour. Beat with strong strokes 45 times with a wooden spoon, or for 3 minutes at medium speed with the mixer flat beater. Drop pieces of the soft butter into the mixture and thoroughly blend. Add flour, ¼ cup at a time, until the dough has become a shaggy mass that can be lifted from the bowl, or left in the mixer bowl under the dough hook.

**KNEADING
10 mins.**

If the dough is sticky under your hands or in the mixer bowl, add small portions of flour. Knead the dough with the rhythmic motion of push-turn-fold. It is to be a soft dough, so don't overload it with flour. While it may not be sticky, it will be velvety smooth and a pleasure under your hands. Knead for 10 minutes.

**BY PROCESSOR
8 mins.**

Prepare the sponge, as above.

Attach the plastic dough blade.

The mixing sequence differs from above.

Measure 1 cup flour into the work bowl and add the salt and sugar. Stir down the sponge and scrape it into the work bowl on top of the flour. Pulse to blend. Uncover and drop pieces of the soft butter into the mixture.

With the machine running, add flour, ¼ cup at a time, to form a rough mass that will ride the blade and clean the sides of the bowl. If the dough is dry and stiff, add water by teaspoons with the machine running; if it is wet, add flour by the tablespoon.

**KNEADING
1 min.**

Process the dough for 1 minute to knead.

The dough should be slightly sticky and very elastic. Pull and stretch the dough between your hands to test the consistency; if necessary, return the dough to the work bowl to process for a few seconds more.

**FIRST RISING
45 mins.**

Shape the dough into a ball, put it into a greased bowl, cover with plastic wrap, and put aside at room temperature to rise for 45 minutes.

**SHAPING
18 mins.**

Roll out the dough into a 10"-x-18" piece. Place the dough lengthwise in front of you. Brush with some of the melted butter, leaving a narrow ½" strip at the upper edge. Brush this strip with water.

Sprinkle the sugar over the surface and dust with the cinnamon. Scatter the raisins over the dough and roll up from the buttered long edge, stretching the dough slightly while rolling so that the sugar and raisins are gripped tightly. Seal the roll by pressing the moistened edge down firmly on it.

Brush the roll all over with more melted butter, then cut into slices 1" thick, to give 15-plus pieces from the roll. (The small leftover pieces

are baked in a smaller pan.) After cutting each slice, wipe the sticky blade clean. Lay the pieces about ½" apart on the prepared sheet with the cut side uppermost.

SECOND RISING
40 mins.

Cover with wax or parchment paper and put aside to rise for 40 minutes, or until the rolls have doubled in volume.

PREHEAT

Preheat the oven to 400° 20 minutes before baking.

BAKING
400°
18–20 mins.

Place the pan(s) in the oven and bake for 18 to 20 minutes. As the buns rise and are baked, they will spread together and become square.

(If using a convection oven, reduce heat 50°.)

FINAL STEP

Either sprinkle the granulated sugar liberally over the tops of the buns when they come from the oven, or drizzle with the confectioners' icing after the buns have cooled somewhat.

Separate the buns when they are nearly cold.

Captain Bun would have been delighted to know you are enjoying his creation with coffee or afternoon tea.

Oliebollen   [three dozen fritters]
(Dutch Fruit Fritters)

I have eaten the delicious fruit fritter—Oliebollen—in two Hollands. One is the Netherlands, and the other is a lovely small city on the shores of Lake Michigan. Holland, the one in Michigan, is as Dutch as it is possible to be and still be in the United States—tulip festivals, street signs in Dutch, family names like VanWieren, Beove, VandeWege, Vander Kolk, and VanDyke, wooden shoes, a working windmill, and a cookbook, Eet Smakelijk, which means "Eat Well and with Taste."

The recipe for this unusual fruit-filled fritter is adapted from one in Eet Smakelijk, a compilation of recipes handed down from one generation of Hollanders to the next, and put together by the city's Junior Welfare League.

The dough is allowed to rise to double in volume before forming the fritters.

INGREDIENTS	3¹/₂ cups all-purpose or unbleached flour, approximately
	2 packages dry yeast
	I teaspoon salt
	¹/₂ cup nonfat dry milk
	¹/₄ cup granulated sugar
	I¹/₂ cups hot water (120°–130°)
	3 eggs, room temperature
	I quart or more vegetable oil
	¹/₄ cup *each* light or dark raisins, currants, and chopped candied orange peel
	2 tablespoons grated lemon peel
	¹/₄ cup confectioners' sugar

BAKE PAN	1 deep skillet or small kettle

BY HAND OR MIXER 15 mins.	Into a large mixing or mixer bowl measure 2 cups flour and add the dry ingredients. Stir in the hot water. In a small bowl beat the eggs and pour into the flour mixture. The batter will not absorb the eggs immediately, but keep beating with vigorous strokes, by hand or with the mixer flat beater, until it does. Add more flour, a small portion at a time, to make a heavy batter that can be spooned later into the hot fat.

RISING 1 hour	Cover the mixing bowl with plastic wrap and put aside to let the batter rise to double its volume, about 1 hour.

PREHEAT 15 mins.	Heat the skillet and bring the oil to about 375°, about 15 minutes. Stir down the batter with a heavy wooden spoon and work in the raisins, currants, orange and lemon peels.

FRYING 375° 15–20 mins.	Drop rounded teaspoons of batter into the hot fat. Cook until the fritters are puffed and both sides are golden brown, about 3 minutes per side. Repeat for all.

FINAL STEP	Place the hot fritters on absorbent paper to drain.

FINAL STEP

Place the hot fritters on absorbent paper to drain.

While warm, arrange them on a serving dish and sprinkle liberally with confectioners' sugar. Delicious with coffee or tea.

Feta Biscuits

[t w o   d o z e n   o n e - i n c h   o r   o n e   d o z e n   t w o - i n c h   b i s c u i t s]

The feta biscuit—biscotakia me feta—is to the Greeks what the croissant is to the French. Feta cheese, which gives the biscuits a mild cheesy flavor, is made with sheep's, goat's, or cow's milk. Sold in most supermarkets, some feta cheese is ready-packaged in plastic and is a poor substitute for the real thing. Instead, look for the authentic feta in Middle Eastern food shops where the white, semisoft, and crumbly cheese is stored in brine. Always wash off the brine in clear running water before using.

I brought back a recipe for biscuits from Athens, but I like the one I found in the fine book Cooking and Baking the Greek Way, *by Anne Theoharous.*

INGREDIENTS

2 cups all-purpose flour
$^1/_2$ teaspoon salt
3 teaspoons baking powder
1 tablespoon sugar
6 tablespoons cold butter
$^3/_4$ cup milk
$^3/_4$ cup feta cheese, rinsed and crumbled
1 egg yolk, beaten, mixed with 1 tablespoon water

BAKING SHEET

1 baking sheet

BY HAND
OR MIXER
5 mins.

Into a large mixing or mixer bowl sift the dry ingredients. Quickly cut the butter into the mixture with a pastry blender until the mixture resembles coarse oatmeal. Pour in the milk, add the cheese, and stir by hand or flat beater for about 30 seconds to make a soft dough.

KNEADING
3 mins.

Knead the dough quickly for another 30 seconds on a lightly floured work surface. Press the dough flat and fold in half. Repeat pressing down and folding 6 or 8 times. Roll out with a rolling pin to about ½" thickness.

BY PROCESSOR
4 mins.

Attach the steel blade.

The order of ingredients varies slightly from above.

Pour the dry ingredients into the work bowl; pulse to blend. Drop the butter and cheese in the bowl. Pulse rapidly while pouring the milk through the feed tube.

When the ingredients have come together in a ball, stop the machine and turn the dough onto a floured work surface. Don't over-process; process on the short side. No kneading is necessary.

PREHEAT

Preheat the oven to 425°.

CUT ROUNDS
10 mins.

Cut the dough into 1" or 2" rounds with a cookie or biscuit cutter. Place on the ungreased baking sheet and brush with the egg-water glaze.

For trim, browned-all-over biscuits, leave a space around each on the pan. For biscuits that are high, soft, and golden in color, place in the pan touching one another.

BAKE
425°
12–15 mins.

Put the sheet in the oven and bake the biscuits until lightly browned, about 12 minutes for the small ones and 15 for the large.

(If using a convection oven, reduce heat 40°.)

FINAL STEP

Remove the biscuits from the oven. Serve hot, or if for hors d'oeuvres, cool and break open for a ham slice or a spread.

To freeze, seal in a plastic bag. To defrost, place the biscuits in a brown paper bag and heat in a 300° oven for 10 minutes, or until heated through.

The Hamburger Bun   [one dozen large buns]

The hamburger sandwich should be viewed in its totality. It is the sum of two parts, the meat and the bread. The rest—ketchup, mustard, relish, pickle, onion—is window dressing. It is more than the meat. It is more than the bread. It is togetherness at its finest.

It is almost always possible to buy good meat. It is not always possible to buy good buns. But it is possible always to bake them yourself—and of superior quality. So much so that it will be a challenge to the butcher and his meat to do equally well.

Surprisingly, this exceptional hamburger bun is made with the same basic dough used for many peasant breads, French and Italian as well as the flat Armenian and Israeli breads. The ingredients are few—flour, water, salt, and yeast, plus a small quantity of butter.

Top these with sprinkles of poppy or sesame seeds.

It is the beginning of a noteworthy sandwich.

INGREDIENTS	5 cups of bread or all-purpose flour, approximately
	2 packages dry yeast
	1 tablespoon salt
	2 tablespoons butter or margarine, softened at room temperature
	2 cups hot water (120°–130°)
	Milk
	1/4 cup poppy or sesame seeds

| BAKING SHEET | 1 baking sheet, greased, Teflon, or covered with brown sack paper |

| BY HAND OR MIXER 10 mins. | In a medium mixing or mixer bowl pour 2 cups flour and add the yeast and salt. Stir to blend. Cut the softened butter into pieces and drop into the flour. Add the hot water. Beat together with a wooden spoon or with the mixer flat beater. When the dough is a smooth batter, add additional flour, ½ cup at a time, mixing each addition vigorously until the dough has formed a rough, shaggy mass. |

| KNEADING 6–8 mins. | Turn the dough onto a floured work surface and knead with a strong push-turn-fold motion for about 6 minutes. If the dough sticks to your hands or the countertop, add sprinkles of flour. The dough will become soft, elastic, and smooth. There will be no small lumps in the dough if it has been kneaded properly. |
| | If under a dough hook in the mixer, knead for 6 to 8 minutes. If the dough clings to the sides of the bowl while the machine is running, carefully add sprinkles of flour. Don't overload the dough or it could become a hard ball. |

| BY PROCESSOR 5 mins. | Insert the plastic dough blade. |
| | Place 2 cups flour in the work bowl and sprinkle on the yeast and salt. Zap once to mix the dry ingredients. Cut in the butter and process for 10 seconds. Pour in the hot water and turn on the machine for 10 seconds to dissolve the yeast particles. Add additional flour, a small portion at a time, processing after each addition. |

| KNEADING 45 secs. | When the dough forms into a ball and is whisked around the bowl by the blade, knead for 45 seconds. |

| FIRST RISING 30–40 mins. | Place the dough in a lightly greased and warmed bowl, cover tightly with plastic wrap, and put in a warm place (80°–100°) to rise. The dough will double in bulk in about 30 to 40 minutes. |

| SHAPING 10 mins. | Turn the dough onto a floured work surface and divide into 12 pieces. Shape into balls. Cover with wax paper and let relax for 4 to 5 minutes. |

To shape, flatten a ball under your palm so that it is about 1" thick and 4" in diameter. As each bun is shaped, place it on the prepared baking sheet and cover with wax paper or a cloth.

SECOND RISING
30 mins.

Let the buns rise until they are soft and puffy, about 30 minutes.

PREHEAT

Preheat the oven to 400° 20 minutes before baking.

BAKING
400°
20 mins.

Brush each bun with milk and sprinkle with poppy and/or sesame seeds.

Place in the oven and bake for 20 minutes, or until the buns are browned. Turn a bun over. If the bottom is nicely browned, it is done. If the buns at the outer edges of the baking sheet are browning too quickly, push them into the center and move the center ones to the outside.

(A convection oven may not hold all of the buns at one time. Place half on baking sheet, and leave the remainder under wax paper. Bake at 350° for about 25 minutes, or until browned.)

FINAL STEP

Place the buns on a rack to cool before serving.

Split and toasted they are delicious. If any are left after the picnic, they may be frozen and kept for up to a year at 0°.

SPECIAL BREADS

IN A BOOK of more than three hundred bread recipes there are a few that demand special attention. They fit in no conventional category. This chapter is a collection of such recipes.

Cornell Bread   [one medium loaf]

The late Dr. Clive M. McCay of Cornell University's department of nutrition and food developed this three-way formula for a nutritionally balanced loaf of white bread. It has protein, calcium, and riboflavin (which keeps you young longer). He called it the "Triple-Rich Formula," and a true Cornell Bread must include three ingredients to boost the nutritive value of refined flour—wheat germ, soy flour, and nonfat milk.

This recipe is one of many versions of loaves made with the Cornell formula. If you wish to adapt your favorite breads to include these supplements, the proportions for 1 cup white flour are: 1 tablespoon soy flour, 1 tablespoon nonfat dry milk, and 1 teaspoon wheat germ.

The bread has a fine, soft texture and a pale golden crumb.

INGREDIENTS
3 cups bread or all-purpose flour, approximately
2 packages dry yeast
3 tablespoons soy flour
¼ cup wheat germ
½ cup nonfat dry milk
1 teaspoon salt
⅔ cup hot water (120°–130°)
2 tablespoons honey
1 egg, room temperature
2 tablespoons butter, room temperature

| BAKING PAN | 1 medium (8"-x-4") loaf pan, greased or Teflon |

BY HAND OR MIXER
8 mins.

Into a mixing or mixer bowl measure 1½ cups flour and the dry ingredients. Stir together by hand or with the mixer flat beater. Pour in the hot water and add the honey, egg, and butter. Beat vigorously 100 times with a wooden spoon, or for 2 minutes in the mixer. If by hand, add flour, ½ cup at a time, stirring with the spoon and your hands until the dough is a rough, shaggy mass that can be turned out onto the work surface. Or attach the mixer dough hook. Add flour, ¼ cup at a time, until the dough cleans the sides of the bowl and forms a soft ball around the revolving hook.

KNEADING
10 mins.

Knead by hand or with the dough hook for 10 minutes, adding sprinkles of flour to control stickiness.

BY PROCESSOR
4 mins.

Attach the steel blade.

Measure 2 cups flour into the work bowl and add the dry ingredients. Pulse to mix well. Pour the hot water into a small bowl and lightly beat in the honey, egg, and butter. With the processor running, pour the liquid through the feed tube in a slow, steady stream, taking 15 to 20 seconds to do so.

KNEADING
1½ mins.

Once the dough forms and cleans the bowl, process for 1½ minutes to knead.

If the dough is wet and sticks to the sides, add bread flour by tablespoons; if the dough is too dry, add water by the teaspoon. The dough should be soft, smooth, and elastic when kneading is completed.

FIRST RISING
1½ hours

Place the dough in a buttered bowl, cover tightly with plastic wrap, and put aside to rise until almost tripled in volume, about 1½ hours.

SHAPING
5 mins.

Turn the dough out of the bowl, punch down to press out the bubbles, and shape into a ball. Allow the dough to rest for 3 minutes.

Press the dough into an oval roughly the length of the pan. Fold lengthwise, pinch together the seam, tuck under the ends, and drop into the pan, seam down.

SECOND RISING
1½ hours

Cover the pan loosely with plastic wrap and leave until the dough has risen to 1" above the rim of the pan, about 1½ hours.

PREHEAT

Adjust the oven rack to lower-third position. Preheat the oven to 375° 20 minutes before baking.

BAKING
375°
35–40 mins.

Uncover the loaf and bake until the bread is well browned and sounds hollow when rapped on the bottom, 35 to 40 minutes. If the loaf seems to be browning too quickly, cover loosely with foil during the last 10 minutes of baking.

(If using a convection oven, reduce heat 50°.)

FINAL STEP

Turn the loaf out onto a rack to cool before slicing.

It toasts well and is excellent for sandwiches. It also freezes well.

Sausage Bread   [two round loaves]

One pound of sausage of your choice is cut into small cubes and sprinkled throughout these 2 loaves. A round flat bread, it is made with other rich ingredients including sugar, eggs, and milk.

It is a fine breakfast bread, and good served with soup or with a main-course salad for a light lunch or supper.

INGREDIENTS

I pound sausage of choice (fresh, smoked, pepperoni, or chorizo)
I tablespoon sugar
1¼ cups hot milk (120°–130°)
¼ cup (½ stick) butter, room temperature
I teaspoon salt
3 eggs, room temperature
5 cups bread or all-purpose flour, approximately
2 packages dry yeast

BAKING PANS

Two 8" cake pans, greased or Teflon

PREPARATION
25 mins.

If using a cooked or smoked sausage, remove the casing, and dice into ¼" cubes or cut with 1 or 2 pulses of the food processor. If the sausage is fresh, remove the casing, cut into small cubes, cover with water, and parboil over low heat for 8 minutes. Drain, and sauté in a skillet until cooked. Set aside to cool.

BY HAND
OR MIXER
10 mins.

In a large mixing or mixer bowl combine the sugar, hot milk, butter, and salt. Stir until the butter has melted and the mixture has cooled to lukewarm. Beat in the eggs. Stir in 3 cups flour and the yeast; beat for 3 minutes at fast speed with the mixer flat beater, or 150 strokes with a wooden spoon. The batter will be thick. Stir in the balance of the flour, ½ cup at a time, by spoon or with the dough hook. If the dough is sticky, add sprinkles of flour. The dough will be a rough, shaggy but elastic mass—not too solid—that will clean the sides of the bowl.

KNEADING
10 mins.

Turn the dough out onto a lightly floured work surface and knead until the dough is smooth and small blisters appear under the surface. If using a mixer, the dough will clean the sides of the bowl and form a ball around the dough hook. Knead for 10 minutes.

The sausage bits are not added until after the first rising.

BY PROCESSOR
5 mins.

Attach the plastic dough hook.

The order of ingredients varies from above.

Measure 3½ cups flour into the work bowl. Add the yeast, sugar, and salt. Pulse to blend. In a small bowl combine the hot milk and butter. Beat in the eggs. Turn on the processor and pour the milk mixture slowly through the feed tube. When the liquid has been absorbed, add flour, ¼ cup at a time, until the dough is a rough mass that cleans the sides of the bowl and rides with the blade.

KNEADING
50 secs.

Process to knead for 50 seconds.

FIRST RISING
1½ hours

Drop the dough into a greased bowl, cover tightly with plastic wrap, and put aside to rise about twice its original size (judged as it creeps up the sides of the bowl), 1½ hours.

SHAPING
15 mins.

Punch the dough down and turn out of the bowl. Knead briefly and flatten it down. Spread half of the sausage on the dough and fold it into the mass. Knead for 1 or 2 minutes. Flatten the dough again, and spread the balance of the sausage over it. Continue to knead the dough until the sausage bits are uniformly mixed throughout.

Divide the dough into 2 pieces and shape both into flat round loaves. Press them into the bottoms of the cake pans. They will fill the bottom of the pans and come halfway up the sides.

SECOND RISING
1 hour

Cover the pans with wax or parchment paper and leave until the dough has doubled in bulk, 1 hour.

PREHEAT

Preheat the oven to 375° 20 minutes before baking.

BAKING
375°
40 mins.

Put the pans in the oven. Bake until the loaves are a rich golden brown, 40 minutes. They are done when tapping the bottom crust yields a hard, hollow sound.

(If using a convection oven, reduce heat 50°.)

FINAL STEP

Remove the bread from the oven and place on a wire rack to cool. Slice and eat while fresh.

Serve this to a great aunt with a glass of port.

Pulled Bread   [for a dinner party of eight to ten]

Pulled bread is the ultimate crouton. Shaggy chunks are torn from a loaf that has been trimmed of its crusts; then they are buttered, and baked for 30 minutes in a slow oven.

These golden crisps should be made fresh for a party or dinner, but they will keep in the refrigerator to be heated. Fun to drop into salad or soup.

INGREDIENTS	1 (or part) loaf white bread, crusts removed 3 tablespoons butter, melted
BAKING SHEET	1 baking sheet
PREHEAT	Preheat the oven to 300°.
BY HAND 20 mins.	With 1 or 2 forks tear out chunks of bread about 1" wide and 2" long. (This is surprisingly easy to do once you get started!) Brush these jagged chunks on all sides with the melted butter and arrange on the baking sheet.
BAKING 300° 30 mins.	Place the baking sheet in the middle shelf of the oven and leave until the chunks are crisp and golden brown, about 30 minutes.
FINAL STEP	Remove the breads from the oven. Serve immediately. They can be held a day or two in the refrigerator but reheat before serving.

Hobo Bread   [two loaves]

Hobo bread is as delicious and rich-tasting when eaten indoors as it is out of doors. Baked in a 1-pound coffee can, it is great for gift-giving, as well as sending along with the family campers.

Soaked overnight, the raisins plump as big as grapes and the liquid gives the bread a dark golden color. For the more daring in the mountains or under the Christmas tree, soak the raisins in brandy or rum, or a portion thereof.

INGREDIENTS	1 cup *each* light and dark raisins, or 2 cups of either 2 cups hot water, brandy, or rum (120°–130°) 4 teaspoons baking soda 2 cups sugar 1/4 cup vegetable oil 1/2 teaspoon salt 3 1/2 to 4 cups bread or all-purpose flour, approximately 1/2 cup chopped walnuts, almonds, or pecans (optional)

TIN CANS	Two 1-pound coffee cans, greased, bottoms lined with rounds of wax or parchment paper. Keep the plastic lids to cover the breads later.
PREPARATION 6–8 hours or overnight	Place the raisins in a large bowl, cover with the hot water, brandy, or rum, and stir in the baking soda. Cover with plastic wrap and leave for 6 to 8 hours or overnight to plump. The liquid is used to make the batter, so don't drain.
PREHEAT	Preheat the oven to 350° before preparing the batter.
BY HAND 11 mins.	Uncover the raisins and measure in the sugar, oil, salt, 3 cups flour, and the nuts, if desired. Stir to blend. The batter should be thick—to spoon rather than pour. If thin, add a small amount of flour. Spoon the batter into the prepared cans. Fill between one-half and two-thirds full. Push the batter down into the bottoms with a spatula.
BAKING 350° 1 hour	Bake in the moderate oven for 1 hour, or until a deep, deep brown. (If using a convection oven, reduce heat 50°.)
FINAL STEP	Take the breads out of the oven and allow to set for 10 minutes before slipping them out of the containers. Let the breads cool completely. Return the breads to the cans and cover with plastic lids. They will keep for 3 or 4 months stored in the refrigerator. The breads also travel well in the tin cans to the picnic, the races, the lake, or to Grandma's house.

Squaw Bread   [pieces for eight]

Squaw Bread is an American Indian creation that is crispy, crusty, and fine to serve with soups, salads, and as a snack. This recipe is by Mrs. Myrtol Coe, from Hominy, Oklahoma, the center of Osage Indian culture. The recipe is from one of the few Indian cookbooks published, a project of the Indian Women's Club of Tulsa.

While the dough can be rolled and cut into precise squares or circles before frying, I like my pieces cut in random patterns guided only by whim.

INGREDIENTS	2 cups bread or all-purpose flour, approximately 1 teaspoon salt 2 teaspoons baking powder 1 tablespoon lard, melted 1 cup hot water (120°–130°) Vegetable oil

DEEP FRYER OR SKILLET	1 deep fryer or skillet
BY HAND OR MIXER **5 mins.**	Into a medium mixing or mixer bowl measure 2 cups flour, the salt, and baking powder and blend together. Form a well in the flour; pour in the lard and hot water. By hand or with the mixer flat beater, draw in the flour and mix. Add flour, if needed, to make a soft, elastic mass that can be lifted from the bowl and placed on the work surface, or left in the mixer under the dough hook.
KNEADING **3 mins.**	The kneading period is short—no longer than necessary to work the dough so that it will hold together when rolled, about 3 minutes by hand or mixer. Add sprinkles of flour if necessary to control stickiness.
BY PROCESSOR **4 mins.**	Attach the steel blade. Pour the dry ingredients into the work bowl and, with the machine running, pour the combined lard and water through the feed tube. Add flour, if needed, to form a mass that cleans the sides of the bowl and rides on the blade.
KNEADING **3–4 secs.**	Pulse the machine on and off several times to knead the dough.
PREHEAT	Heat the oil to 350° in the deep fryer or skillet.
SHAPING **4 mins.**	Divide the dough into 3 or 4 pieces and roll each as thin as possible without breaking apart. One way to assure thinness is to roll the dough out, leave it, and return a few minutes later to roll it again, once, perhaps twice. Thinner each time. Cut the dough pieces into shapes roughly measuring 4" x 6"—or smaller, as desired. Prick each piece with the tines of a fork.
FRYING **350°** **20 mins.**	Drop 1 or 2 pieces into the hot oil. Don't crowd. Watch the breads carefully. When a deep, golden brown and bubbly on one side, turn over. The breads will be fried in 3 or 4 minutes—depending on how crisp and brown you want them.
FINAL STEP	As the breads are taken from the oil, place to drain on paper towels.

Croutons   [about one cup]

Croutons for soups and salads are the delicious dividend to be declared when a few pieces of slightly stale bread are at hand.

Note: *As a garnish for delicate-tasting soups, prepare with clarified butter. For strong-flavored soups, sauté the bread cubes in olive oil. For garlic or herb croutons for salads, add minced garlic or some minced fresh herbs to the butter when you sauté or butter the bread.*

INGREDIENTS	**2 bread slices, $1/2$" thick, cut from a day-old, firm-textured white loaf** **4 tablespoons butter** **$1/4$ to $1/2$ cup vegetable oil**
BAKING SHEET OR SKILLET	1 large skillet or baking sheet
TO FRY: **6 mins.**	Remove the crusts from the bread, and cut the slices into cubes. Combine the butter and ¼ cup oil in the skillet. Melt the butter over medium heat and, as soon as the butter and oil mixture is hot, add the bread cubes and increase heat to high. Turn the cubes frequently with a metal spatula so that they brown evenly on all sides, about 6 minutes, and add more oil as necessary to keep the cubes from burning.
TO BAKE: **400°** **6 mins.**	Preheat the oven to 400°. To toast or bake the croutons, lightly butter the bread slices on both sides, trim the crusts, then cut into cubes. Place on a baking sheet and insert in the oven. Bake the cubes, turning until evenly brown, 3 minutes per side.
FINAL STEP	Remove from the skillet or oven and drain the croutons on paper towels before serving (or storing).

Pain Perdu of Louisiana   [six to eight slices]
(Lost Bread)

The Cajuns call it Pain Perdu—*a slice of stale bread that would otherwise be "lost." Pain Perdu has humble beginnings but once immersed in frothy eggs and then dropped into a skillet of hot butter emerges a proud dish. It can be served at breakfast with coffee or tea, and bacon on the side. Served with honey, jelly, and powdered sugar, it is a light dessert for a special luncheon. At dinner it's an ideal side dish with hamburgers.*

Pain Perdu made with slices of Buckwheat Bread is a marvelous brunch surprise. Warm growing-up memories of my grandmother Condon and her buckwheat cakes!

INGREDIENTS	5 eggs
	2 tablespoons orange flower water or orange juice
	3 tablespoons brandy
	$1/2$ cup granulated sugar
	Juice of 1 lemon
	Twist of lemon peel
	6 to 8 slices stale bread, crusts trimmed off
	3 tablespoons butter
	Confectioners' sugar
	Grated nutmeg
SKILLET	1 large heavy skillet
BY HAND 15 mins.	In a bowl beat the eggs until they are light and fluffy. Stir in the orange flower water or juice, brandy, and sugar and mix thoroughly. Add the lemon juice and lemon peel.
SOAK 30 mins.	Cut the bread into triangles or rounds. Soak the bread in the egg mixture for about 30 minutes.
FRYING 30–60 mins.	Melt the butter in the skillet. Remove the bread from the egg mixture and fry the pieces until lightly browned on both sides, 3 to 4 minutes per side. Remove and drain on paper towels.
FINAL STEP	Sprinkle the bread with the confectioners' sugar and nutmeg.

Bacon Batter Bread   [two medium loaves]

Bacon Batter Bread has the cold-winter-morning taste of crisp fried bacon. The loaves are big, husky, and brown-flecked with bacon pieces. A trace of coriander complements the bacon and underscores the whole wheat.

A batter bread, it will rise without kneading. The batter will probably be too thick to pour, and too wet to lift with your hands. I have found that two spoons is the easiest way to transfer the batter from the bowl to the pans.

INGREDIENTS	$1/4$ pound uncooked bacon (or enough to make $1/3$ cup crumbled fried bacon)
	1 cup whole-wheat flour
	4 cups bread or all-purpose flour
	2 packages dry yeast
	2 teaspoons salt
	$1/4$ teaspoon ground coriander
	$1/2$ cup nonfat dry milk

2 cups hot water (120°–130°)
¼ cup firmly packed brown sugar
1 egg, room temperature

BAKING PANS

2 medium (8"-x-4") loaf pans, greased or Teflon

PREPARATION
15 mins.

In a skillet cook the bacon to make ⅓ cup of crumbled bacon, and reserve it plus 2 tablespoons of the drippings.

BY MIXER
OR HAND
15 mins.

In a mixing or mixer bowl measure the whole-wheat flour, 3 cups white flour, the yeast, salt, coriander, milk, drippings, and hot water. Blend at low speed with the mixer flat beater for 30 seconds, or with a large wooden spoon. Add the brown sugar, egg, and bacon. Stir. Increase the mixer speed to high for 3 minutes, or 200 strokes with the spoon.

Stop the mixer and add the remaining flour. Blend it well.

BY PROCESSOR
5 mins.

Prepare the bacon, as above.

Use the short plastic dough blade.

Measure the whole-wheat flour, 3 cups white flour, the yeast, salt, coriander, dry milk and drippings into the work bowl; pulse to blend well. With the machine turned on, add the hot water, then the brown sugar, egg, and bacon through the feed tube. Process for 5 seconds. Add the balance of the white flour, and process for 20 seconds.

FIRST RISING
50 mins.

Scrape down the sides of the bowl, cover the batter tightly with plastic wrap, and leave at room temperature until the batter has doubled in volume, 50 minutes. If using a food processor, transfer the batter to a regular bowl, cover, and leave to rise, as above. (Batter left in the processor bowl may work its way into the drive shaft.)

SHAPING
5 mins.

Turn back the plastic covering and stir down the batter. Lift it with 2 spoons into the pans. Push into the corners of the pans with a spoon and smooth the tops.

SECOND RISING
30 mins.

Cover the pans with plastic wrap or wax paper and allow the batter to rise to the edge of the pans, 30 minutes.

PREHEAT

Preheat the oven to 375° about 20 minutes before baking.

BAKING
375°
40 mins.

Place the pans in the oven and bake until the loaves are a deep brown, about 40 minutes. The loaf is done when a metal skewer or a wooden toothpick comes out clean and dry when inserted in the center. If moist particles cling to the probe, return the loaf to the oven for an additional 10 minutes. Test again.

(If using a convection oven, reduce heat 40°.)

FINAL STEP

Remove the bread from the oven. Carefully turn the hot loaves out onto a metal rack to cool before serving or freezing.

Tea Brack   [one medium loaf]

Tea Brack, with cold tea as one of its chief ingredients, gives a double reward. Thinly sliced, the moist, dark loaf is delicious served with tea.

Early on, this recipe caught my fancy because so few things in this country cater to the devoted tea drinker, which I am, as opposed to coffee-this-and-coffee-that.

Note: Begin the preparation the night before to allow the fruit to soak in the tea.

INGREDIENTS

1 cup white raisins
$^3/_4$ cup currants
$^1/_4$ cup chopped candied peel
$1^1/_2$ cups brown sugar
$1^1/_2$ cups cold tea (orange pekoe is fine)
$^1/_4$ cup brandy or rum (optional but good)
2 cups bread or all-purpose flour
$1^1/_2$ teaspoons baking powder
$^1/_2$ teaspoon *each* ground cinnamon, grated nutmeg, and salt
1 egg, room temperature, well beaten

BAKING PAN

1 medium (8"-x-4") loaf pan, greased or Teflon, long sides and bottom lined with buttered wax paper. (Leave the paper ends sticking out about ½" so the loaf can be pulled from the pan.)

PREPARATION
overnight

In a bowl combine the raisins, currants, candied peel, brown sugar, and cold tea. Add a dollop of brandy or rum to give it a secret goodness. Cover tightly with plastic wrap so that no moisture escapes and let marinate overnight.

PREHEAT

Preheat the oven to 325° before preparing the batter.

BY HAND
15 mins.

In another bowl mix together, with your fingers or a spoon, the remaining dry ingredients. Pour the dry ingredients into the tea-fruit mixture, stir well, and add the egg. The mixture will be on the thin side.
    Pour or spoon the batter into the prepared pan.

BAKING
325°
1½ hours

Bake the loaf slowly in the moderate oven until a metal skewer or wooden toothpick comes out dry when pierced into the loaf, 1½ hours.
    (If using a convection oven, reduce heat 25°.)

FINAL STEP

Remove the bread from the oven. Place on a wire rack for about 5 minutes before removing from the pan. Let it cool completely before it is cut.

Serve with butter or cream cheese. And tea!

Cherry-Studded Scone (Bannock)
[one nine-inch scone to be divided]

In June and July the deep red sweet cherries hang from the trees in Michigan like countless tiny Christmas tree ornaments. Other states grow sweet cherries (which as a boy I knew as Bings) but none the likes of Michigan's.

A sweet cherry does not have the bite of a Montmorency, the bright red tart fruit beloved by home bakers for pies. The sweet cherry is meaty and moist but not running with juice, ideal for this two-layered scone, with the fruit sandwiched between.

To a Scot, this scone, because of its size, would be a "bannock." The terms are loosely applied. The bannock is a large plate-size scone. When the bannock is cut into wedges, the wedges become scones.

INGREDIENTS

3/4 cup to 1 cup sweet cherries
1/4 cup all-purpose flour
1/2 cup whole-wheat flour
2 tablespoons sugar
3 teaspoons baking powder
1/2 teaspoon salt
1/2 teaspoon ground cinnamon
1/3 cup shortening, butter, or margarine, chilled
1/2 cup buttermilk
2 eggs

BAKING SHEET

1 baking sheet, lightly sprinkled with flour

PREPARATION
5 mins.

Wash, pit, and finely chop the sweet cherries—enough to make ¾ cup. One pulse in a food processor does it nicely.

PREHEAT

Preheat the oven to 400°.

BY HAND
8 mins.

In a large bowl mix the dry ingredients. Cut the shortening into the flour mixture with a pastry blender or fork until rice-size.

In a small bowl stir together the buttermilk and 1 egg (the other egg will be used for glaze). Add all at once to the dry ingredients. Stir together just long enough to moisten. The less stirring and mixing the better.

BY PROCESSOR
5 secs.
	Attach the steel blade.
	
	    Process the dry ingredients and shortening until coarsely crumbled, about 5 seconds.
	    Proceed as above.

SHAPING
5 mins.
	Divide the dough in half. Pat one piece into a 9" circle on the baking sheet. Spread the chopped cherries evenly over the top. Shape the second piece and, with care, lift and cover the cherries.
	    With a knife lightly score the scone into 12 or 16 wedges.
	    Beat the remaining egg and brush the top layer.

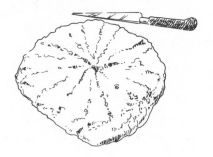

BAKING **400°** **20 mins.**	Bake for 20 minutes, or until a golden brown. (If using a convection oven, reduce heat 75°.)
FINAL STEP	Remove the scone from the oven and place on a cooling rack. When cool, cut into wedges. Delicious served with honey, butter, whipped cream cheese—or alone.

Babka   [two loaves]
(Grandmother's Loaf)

In Russia, as in this country, this lovely yeast-raised coffee cake is called Babka or "grandmother's loaf."

The dough is rich and sweet and it can be made into several shapes—ranging from twists baked in pans to twists laid in a spiral in cake tins. Or the twist can be looped into a figure "8" or shaped as a doughnutlike cruller and baked on a sheet.

Because of the richness of the dough, Babka is made in two stages. The first is as a sponge that allows the yeast to grow and to become viable before the balance of the ingredients are worked in.

INGREDIENTS

Sponge:
2 cups bread or all-purpose flour
2 packages dry yeast
$^1/_2$ cup nonfat dry milk
$1^1/_4$ cups hot water (120°–130°)

Dough:
$^1/_2$ cup sugar
1 teaspoon salt
$^1/_4$ teaspoon ground cardamom
$^1/_4$ teaspoon vanilla extract
2 eggs
2 egg yolks
$2^1/_2$ cups bread or all-purpose flour, approximately
$^1/_2$ cup (1 stick) butter, softened

Filling:
$1^1/_2$ cups almond paste (see page 591)
1 cup bittersweet chocolate, melted
1 cup raisins, plumped in brandy or water (see Note)
1 cup slivered almonds or broken walnuts

Topping:
$^1/_2$ cup (1 stick) butter, melted
2 tablespoons poppy seeds

BAKING PANS
OR SHEET

Two 8" round layer or cake pans, greased, bottom lined with wax or parchment paper; or 2 medium loaf pans (8"-x-4"), greased or Teflon, also lined as above; or 1 baking sheet, greased or Teflon.

PREPARATION
2 hours

To make the sponge, into a large mixing or mixer bowl measure all the sponge ingredients. Stir with a wooden spoon for 1 or 2 minutes to make a heavy, wet dough, or use the mixer flat beater.

While the sponge can be made in the processor work bowl, the plastic dough blade does not adequately mix this small volume. It can be done, however, by removing the processor cover one or two times and scraping the flour into the center with a spatula.

Cover the bowl tightly with plastic wrap and leave at room temperature to allow the sponge to form and ferment, about 2 hours. The sponge will double in bulk.

BY HAND
OR MIXER
15 mins.

To make the dough, remove the plastic wrap and stir down the sponge. Measure in the sugar, salt, cardamom, and vanilla. Stir vigorously to blend. Add the eggs and egg yolks, one at a time, beating each into the batter, which will begin to pull away in sheets as it is beaten—this is desirable. Add 1½ cups flour to the mixture and beat with a wooden spoon or flat beater until it has been absorbed into the batterlike dough. Drop in the butter, a small portion at a time, beating until it is mixed into the dough.

Add flour, ¼ cup at a time, to form a dough that is quite soft yet elastic. It will have had enough flour when it can be turned from the bowl and be pushed or worked without sticking to your hands or the work surface. Sprinkle lightly with flour, if necessary. The soft almost rubbery texture is unlike most bread doughs.

KNEADING
5 mins.

With the dough on the surface knead only until it is smooth, about 5 minutes. If using a mixer, attach the dough hook. The dough will leave the sides of the bowl and form a ball around the hook. Knead for 5 minutes.

BY PROCESSOR
5 mins.

In a separate bowl, make the sponge, as above.

Attach the short plastic dough blade.

Scrape the sponge into the work bowl (if it was made by hand or mixer) and add the sugar, salt, cardamom, and vanilla. Pulse to mix. Add the eggs and egg yolks, one by one, through the feed tube, pulsing after each to blend.

With the machine running, add 1 cup flour through the feed tube. Drop in the butter. Add the remaining flour, ¼ cup at a time. The dough will become a smooth, elastic mass that will clean the sides of the bowl.

KNEADING
30 secs.

With the machine running, knead for 30 seconds.

When the dough is turned from the work bowl it may be sticky under your hands, but sprinkles of flour will give it a dry surface. Shape into a ball.

FIRST RISING
1½ hours

Place the dough in a greased bowl, cover tightly with plastic wrap, and put aside to double in volume, about 1½ hours.

SHAPING
15 mins.

Punch down the dough and turn it onto the floured work surface. It is a joy to work this rich dough, and if it does seem sticky, dust lightly with flour.

Divide the dough into 2 pieces. With your hands and a rolling pin, form each dough piece into an 8"-x-14" rectangle, ¼" thick. Allow the dough to rest for a few minutes before continuing.

Spread each rectangle first with half the almond paste and then with half the melted chocolate. Sprinkle on the raisins and nuts. Lightly press these into the dough with the palms of your hands or the rolling pin. Roll up the dough, lengthwise, as for a jelly roll. Pinch the seams tightly to secure. Put the seams under and with the rolling pin roll each length of dough 2 or 3 times, lightly. Twist each length of dough 6 or 8 turns, and allow the twist to rest for a few moments to adjust to its new shape.

For the cake pan, simply lay the twist loosely in the pan in a spiral form beginning in the center and working to the sides. Don't crowd the spiral. The twist may also be baked in a loaf pan. Or it can be formed into a figure "8" and placed on a baking sheet. It may also be shaped like a cruller—the long twist folded and twisted on itself—and put on the baking sheet.

Brush the tops with melted butter and sprinkle generously with poppy seeds.

SECOND RISING 1 hour	Cover the loaves with wax or parchment paper and put aside to rise to *slightly less* than double in volume, about 1 hour. This measurement is not critical but bakers consider it as the optimum.
PREHEAT	Preheat the oven to 350° 20 minutes before baking.
BAKING 350° 45 mins.	Place the baking pans or sheet on the middle shelf of the moderate oven, and bake until each twist is a deep brown, about 45 minutes. Halfway through baking, open the oven and turn the pans around to equalize the heat. If the crusts seem to be browning too quickly, cover with a length of foil or brown sack paper. (If using a convection oven, reduce heat 50°. My oven will not accept two 8" cake pans at once. I place one in the refrigerator to hold while baking the first.)
FINAL STEP	Remove the loaves from the pans with care for they are fragile while still warm. Allow to cool before cutting.

Tip: Each time a slice is cut (filled with rich, sticky almond paste and chocolate), wet and wipe the knife blade clean.

The best way to slice the round Babka twist is to cut from the center into wedge-shaped serving pieces.

Note: To plump the raisins, place them in a small bowl and cover with brandy or water. Let them stand for 1 to 2 hours while the dough is prepared. Drain.

Pompe aux Gratons   [two medium or three small loaves]
(Crackling Bread)

This crackling bread, which I found in the heart of rural France near Gannat, is unusually rich, almost cakelike, and contains not only cracklings but butter and eggs. The Italians add 2 teaspoons freshly ground black pepper to give it a special spiciness. The American counterpart, on the other hand, is made mostly with cornmeal and is rather bland.

Cracklings are the crisp bits left over after lard has been rendered over heat from fat cut from the hog carcass during butchering. The best cracklings are made from fatback, the solid sheet of fat over the hind quarters of the animal. There should be no meat scraps or pieces of skin included.

You can make your own cracklings (see below) or you can sometimes find them in a specialty food store or in a supermarket, slaughterhouse, or frozen food plant. Be certain they are top grade, and not a mixture of meat pieces and hide, which are tough to chew.

INGREDIENTS

5 pounds ground fatback
5 cups bread or all-purpose flour, approximately
2 packages dry yeast
1 teaspoon salt
1/3 cup nonfat dry milk
1 1/2 cups hot water (120°–130°)

4 eggs, room temperature
$^{1}/_{2}$ cup (1 stick) butter, room temperature
1 egg, beaten, mixed with 1 tablespoon milk

BAKING PANS

2 medium (8"-x-4") or 3 small (7"-x-3") loaf pans, greased or Teflon

PREPARATION
2 hours

In a large saucepan or skillet over a low flame render the ground fatback slowly. The light brown cracklings will float to the top of the hot fat. Allow at least 2 hours to reduce the fat to lard and produce the cracklings. Don't let the cracklings scorch. With a slotted spoon, remove the cracklings and press through a sieve to get 2 cups or about ½ pound of high quality cracklings. After separating the cracklings, pour the lard into containers and store in the refrigerator. Fresh homemade lard is a fine shortening for many recipes.

BY HAND
OR MIXER
15 mins.

Into a mixing or mixer bowl measure 3 cups flour and sprinkle on the dry ingredients. Stir to blend. Pour in the hot water and stir with 50 strokes by hand, or for 1 minute with the mixer flat beater. Drop in the eggs, one at a time, and stir to blend after each addition. Add 1 cup flour. Cut the butter into 6 or 8 pieces and drop into the batter. Beat the butter thoroughly into the batter and add additional flour, ¼ cup at a time, to make a rough ball of dough that can be lifted from the bowl. If using a mixer, attach the dough hook and continue.

KNEADING
10 mins.

Punch the dough into a flat disk. Spread 1 cup of cracklings over the dough and fold in. Knead for a moment or two until the cracklings disappear. Push down the dough and add the remainder of the cracklings. Fold in. If the cracklings have introduced additional moisture, it may be necessary to work more flour into the dough to make it elastic again.

Knead the ball of dough on a lightly floured work surface with a rhythm of push-turn-fold. Add sprinkles of flour if the dough is unusually soft and tends to stick to the hands and work surface. If under the dough hook, the dough should clean the sides of the bowl and form a ball around the rotating hook. If it does not and continues to be sticky, add liberal sprinkles of flour. Because of the high fat content of the cracklings and butter, the dough will be soft, pliable, and a delight to work under the hands. Knead for 10 minutes.

BY PROCESSOR
5 mins.

Prepare the cracklings, as above.
Attach the short plastic dough blade.
The order of adding ingredients differs from above.
In the work bowl pour 4 cups flour and the dry ingredients. Pulse to

mix thoroughly. In a small bowl pour the hot water over the butter, and stir for a moment or two. Turn on the machine. Pour the water-butter mixture though the feed tube. Drop in the eggs, one at a time, until they have been blended into the heavy batter. Add the cracklings and flour, ¼ cup at a time, either through the feed tube or by taking the cover off the bowl, to process a dough that will clean the sides of the bowl as it whirls with the blade.

KNEADING
1 min.

With the machine running, knead the dough for 1 minute. When turned from the bowl the dough may be slightly sticky, but a dusting of flour will correct this.

FIRST RISING
1–1½ hours

Place the dough in a bowl, cover with plastic wrap, and leave at room temperature to double in volume, about 1 to 1½ hours.

SHAPING
10 mins.

Divide the dough into as many loaves as desired. Shape each piece of dough into a ball and allow to rest for 2 or 3 minutes. Press each dough piece into a circle, roughly the length of the loaf pan. Fold the dough in half, pinching the long seam closed. Tuck in the ends and place each loaf in the pan with the seam under.

SECOND RISING
1 hour

Cover with wax paper and leave undisturbed at room temperature to allow the dough to rise to the edge of the pans, 1 hour. (This rich dough is somewhat slower to rise than a plain bread dough.)

PREHEAT

Preheat the oven to 375° about 20 minutes before baking.

BAKING
375°
35–40 mins.

Remove the wax paper and brush the dough with the egg-milk glaze. If desired, cut a design on the crust before placing on the middle shelf of the oven.

The loaves will be a light golden brown when baked, 35 to 40 minutes. Turn one loaf from the pan to determine if the bottom crust is deep brown, and sounds hard and hollow when tapped with a forefinger. If the bottom crust is soft, return the bread to the oven for an additional 5 minutes.

(If using a convection oven, reduce heat 50°.)

FINAL STEP

Place loaves on metal rack to cool.

Pompe aux Gratons is delicious cool or reheated. There's a marvelous aroma of a country kitchen—in this country or in France.

Shredded Wheat and Molasses Bread

[one large or two small loaves]

When I was a boy growing up barefoot in a small Indiana town, I carried shred-ded wheat biscuits in the pockets of my bib overalls to sustain me when hunt-ing tigers and crocodiles and frogs. It won me a degree of notoriety—"Oh, you're the kid that eats shredded wheat biscuits dry!"

I was delighted, therefore, to find a recipe for bread made with whole-wheat biscuits combined with another childhood favorite, molasses. It should be a light molasses rather than the dark, which would overpower the wonder-ful new-mown-hay smell of the shredded wheat.

The recipe found its way to my kitchen from the White Lily flour people in Knoxville, Tennessee, who operate a mill famous throughout the South for its flours. This recipe was developed in the White Lily kitchen to introduce a new bread flour.

INGREDIENTS	4 large shredded wheat biscuits 2 cups boiling water I tablespoon sugar I teaspoon salt $^1/_4$ cup light molasses 3 tablespoons shortening 2 packages dry yeast 4 cups bread or all-purpose flour, approximately Butter or margarine, melted
BAKING PANS	1 large (9"-x-5") or 2 small (7"-x-3") loaf pans, greased or Teflon
PREPARATION 12 mins.	Into a large bowl crumble the whole-wheat biscuits and cover with the boiling water. Stir in the sugar, salt, molasses, and shortening. Put the mixture aside to cool to lukewarm so the yeast will not be harmed.
BY HAND OR MIXER 5 mins.	When cool, add the yeast and blend. Stir in the flour, ½ cup at a time, either by hand with a wooden spoon or in a mixer with a flat beater. When the dough becomes a rough, shaggy mass, lift from the bowl and place on the floured work surface, or leave in the mixer bowl to knead under the dough hook.
KNEADING 8 mins.	Begin to knead the dough. If it is sticky, add sprinkles of flour. It will be easier to work the dough with a dough blade in hand to lift and turn it. Knead with a push-turn-fold motion until the dough is soft, elastic, and smooth, about 8 minutes. Knead with the dough hook in the mixer for the same length of time.

BY PROCESSOR **5 mins.**	Prepare the shredded wheat mixture, as above. Attach the steel blade. When cooled, pour the mixture into the work bowl and add the yeast. Pulse. Measure in 2 cups white flour, and pulse to blend thoroughly. With the machine running, add the balance of the flour, ½ cup at a time, until the dough forms a mass that is carried around the bowl on the blade; it will clean the sides of the bowl.
KNEADING **45 secs.**	With the machine running, knead for 45 seconds before turning the dough from the bowl. It will be sticky so add sprinkles of flour as you shape it into a ball to rise.
FIRST RISING **1¼ hours**	Place the dough in a greased bowl, cover with plastic wrap, and leave at room temperature until the dough doubles in volume, about 1¼ hours.
SHAPING **5 mins.**	Divide the dough. Flatten each piece under your palms to the length of the pan. Fold the oval in two, press the seam to seal, and drop into the pan with the seam under.
SECOND RISING **1 hour**	Cover the pans with wax paper and leave to rise to the top edge of the pans, about 1 hour.
PREHEAT	Preheat the oven to 375° about 20 minutes before baking.
BAKING **375°** **45–50 mins.**	Bake in the moderate oven for 45 to 50 minutes. Cover with aluminum foil during the last 15 minutes to prevent overbrowning. Turn one loaf from the pan and check if it is done by tapping the bottom crust. It is baked if the sound is hard and hollow. If the crust is soft, return to the oven for another 5 to 10 minutes. (If using a convection oven, reduce heat 50°.)
FINAL STEP	Remove the loaves from the pans and brush the tops with melted butter. Leave on a rack to cool before slicing.

Gluten Bread   [one loaf]

Gluten, the protein in wheat flour so important to yeast-raised bread, is processed into a flour that is baked into a dietetic loaf which, when sliced and toasted, has a crisp bite and a pleasant nutlike flavor. The flour is expensive (costing almost eight times as much as bread flour), so it will probably be reserved for special diets.

To make gluten flour, white flour goes through a washing process that takes away most of the starch and leaves the gluten, which is then processed into a light brown flour. Gluten, of course, is the wonderful substance found in wheat flour, which forms an elastic network in yeast dough to trap gas bubbles and expand the dough. (Don't, however, expect the addition of gluten flour to ordinary wheat flour to give it more lift. It won't.)

INGREDIENTS	2½ to 3 cups gluten flour, approximately
	1 package dry yeast
	2 teaspoons sugar
	2 teaspoons salt
	⅓ cup nonfat dry milk
	1½ cups hot water (120°–130°)
	1 tablespoon vegetable oil

BAKING PAN

1 medium (8"-x-4") loaf pan, greased or Teflon

BY HAND OR MIXER 10 mins.

Into a large bowl pour 1½ cups gluten flour and the other dry ingredients. Stir together. Add the hot water and vegetable oil. Beat with a wooden spoon for 1 minute, or 100 strokes, or for 2 minutes with the mixer flat blade.

Unlike other yeast doughs, the gluten dough will immediately pull together into a ball and quickly clean the sides of the bowl. Gradually add flour, 1 tablespoon at a time, until the dough loses its wetness and can be worked without sticking to the hands.

KNEADING 10–18 mins.

Knead under a dough hook or by hand on a lightly floured work surface. Knead with a strong push-turn-fold motion for at least 10 minutes, or 18 minutes with a dough hook. While the dough will be fairly stiff, it will become smooth and elastic under your hands.

BY PROCESSOR 4 mins.

Attach the steel blade.

Measure 1½ cups gluten flour into the work bowl and follow with the rest of the ingredients, as above. Pulse to mix. With the machine running, add flour, ¼ cup at a time. Since the dough will quickly form a ball on the blade, process for 5 or 6 pulses, and then stop the machine. Remove the cover and feel the dough. If it is soft and sticky, add more flour.

KNEADING 1 min.

With the machine running, knead for 1 minute.

FIRST RISING 1¼ hours

Place the dough in a greased bowl, cover with plastic wrap, and leave at room temperature until the dough has doubled in bulk, about 1¼ hours.

SHAPING 10 mins.	Punch down the dough in the bowl. Turn it out onto the work surface and knead for 30 seconds to work out the bubbles. Press the ball into a flat oval, about the length of the baking pan. Fold the oval in half, pinch the seam tightly to seal, tuck in the ends, and place in the prepared pan, seam down.
SECOND RISING 1 hour	Cover the pan with wax paper and leave until the center of the dough has risen to the edge of the pan, about 1 hour.
PREHEAT	Preheat the oven to 400° 20 minutes before baking.
BAKING 400° 25 mins. 350° 20 mins.	Bake the loaf for 25 minutes; reduce the heat to 350° for an additional 20 minutes. Halfway through baking, turn the pan around. The loaf is done when it makes a hollow sound when tapped on the bottom. (If using a convection oven, reduce 50° for each bake period.)
FINAL STEP	Take the bread from the oven and place on a cooling rack. If this is to be the bread supplement for only one person in the household, you may wish to slice just enough bread for 3 days, wrap, and store; freeze the balance.

Pain de Mariage   [one large or two small loaves]
(Wedding Bread)

The quotation is English but the bread is French: "For bread are weddings made and sermons said, / Of all good things the first and best is bread."

INGREDIENTS	2 eggs $^1/_2$ cup honey $^1/_2$ cup orange juice 1 cup (2 sticks) butter, melted 2 tablespoons Cointreau or brandy $^1/_4$ teaspoon almond extract 1 tablespoon finely chopped orange peel 1 cup chopped almonds 1$^1/_2$ cups all-purpose flour 1 cup rye flour 2 teaspoons baking powder $^1/_2$ teaspoon baking soda 1 teaspoon salt $^1/_2$ teaspoon ground cardamom $^1/_2$ teaspoon ground black pepper

BAKING PANS	1 large (9"-x-5") or 2 small (7"-x-3") loaf pans, greased or Teflon
PREHEAT	Preheat the oven to 350°.
BY HAND 18 mins.	In a large bowl beat the eggs until they are thick and light in color. Add the honey and beat well. Mix in the orange juice, butter, Cointreau or brandy, almond extract, and orange peel. Fold in the almonds. In a separate mixing bowl blend together the remaining dry ingredients. Stir them gently into the egg mixture. Pour the batter into the pans, leveling with a spatula.
BAKING 350° 45 mins.	Place the pans in the lower third of the oven and bake for 45 minutes, or until the center is firm and dry when tested with a toothpick or cake testing pin. (If using a convection oven, reduce heat 50°.)
FINAL STEP	Take the pans from the oven and allow to cool for 10 minutes before turning them onto a metal cooling rack. Serve warm or cold. One needn't be a bride or groom or a member of the wedding party to appreciate its delicate goodness.

Pain au Riz   [two plump loaves]
(Rice Bread)

Pain au Riz is a brown loaf, thanks to molasses, and speckled throughout with cooked grains of rice and black currants. It is a delicious, different kind of bread that is great for sandwiches, toasted for breakfast, and for snacks in between. It is a French creation, one of Cécile Chemin's, a fine cookbook author.

INGREDIENTS	1¼ cups milk ⅓ cup molasses (see Note) 2 tablespoons butter 2 teaspoons salt 2 packages dry yeast 4 cups bread or all-purpose flour, approximately 1 egg 2 cups cooked rice, cooled ½ cup currants
BAKING PANS	2 medium (8"-x-4") loaf pans, greased or Teflon
BY HAND OR MIXER 5 mins.	In a medium saucepan warm the milk, molasses, butter, and salt. In a separate bowl sprinkle the yeast over 2 cups flour and stir to blend. Pour in the milk mixture and beat 100 strokes with a spoon, or for 2 minutes with the mixer flat beater. While beating, add the egg, rice, and currants.
KNEADING 8–10 mins.	Add the remaining flour, a little at a time, until the dough forms a solid mass and pulls away from the sides of the bowl, about 10 minutes by hand, or 8 minutes under a dough hook. The dough will be quite sticky as you begin but will become elastic and smooth as sprinkles of flour are added. Refrain from using too much flour. Keep the dough elastic and *not* a hard ball.

BY PROCESSOR
2 mins.
	Attach the plastic dough blade.
	    Add the milk, molasses, butter, salt, and yeast to the work bowl. Pulse once to mix. Add 2 cups flour. Pulse. Add the egg and then the rice and currants. Pulse to blend.
	    Add flour through the work tube, with the processor on, ½ cup at a time.

KNEADING 45 secs.	When the dough cleans the sides of the bowl and forms a ball riding on top of the blade, process for 45 seconds to knead.
FIRST RISING 1 hour	Place the dough in a greased bowl, cover with plastic wrap, and put aside at room temperature to double in volume, about 1 hour.
SHAPING 15 mins.	Remove the dough from the bowl, cover with a cloth, and allow to rest for 10 minutes. Cut the dough into 2 pieces. Form rectangular loaves the length of the pans. Place the dough in the pans and press down with your fingers to push the dough into the corners and level.

SECOND RISING
45 mins.

Cover the loaves with wax or parchment paper and leave to rise at room temperature until the dough reaches 1" above the edge of the pans, about 45 minutes.

PREHEAT

Preheat the oven to 400° 20 minutes before baking.

BAKING
400°
35 mins.

A design cut in the top of the loaf will make it more appealing. Cut with a razor blade down the length of the loaf, or make 4 or 5 cuts diagonally.

Place the loaves on the middle or lower shelf of the oven and bake for 35 minutes, or until the loaves test done when tapped on the bottom with a forefinger.

(If using a convection oven, reduce heat 50°.)

FINAL STEP

Turn out from the pans onto the metal rack to cool.

This bread's dark deliciousness may surprise you when sliced.

Note: There is a choice between unsulphured molasses (Plantation, Golden Harvest, etc.) which has a distinct and assertive flavor, or a mild molasses such as Br'er Rabbit, either light or dark.

Pain Rapide au Chocolat   [one large or two small loaves]
(Quick Chocolate Bread)

Chocolate combines with brandy, butter, eggs, honey, and potato in this loaf to delight the palate of the most ardent chocoholics. It is a quick bread as rapide suggests, leavened with baking powder.

In my search for recipes over a large part of the world I have found chocolate used in about every type of dish, including chili, but this recipe from my travels in France is the first true "chocolate bread."

INGREDIENTS

4 ounces unsweetened chocolate

$1/2$ cup (1 stick) butter

4 eggs

$2/3$ cup honey

2 cups fresh or instant mashed potatoes

$1/2$ cup brandy, rum, or orange juice

2 teaspoons *each* vanilla extract and grated orange zest

$2^1/4$ cups all-purpose flour

4 teaspoons baking powder

1 teaspoon salt

BAKING PANS

1 large (9"-x-5") or 2 small (7"-x-3") loaf pans, greased or Teflon, lined down one side and up the other with greased wax or parchment paper

PREHEAT

Preheat the oven to 350°.

BY HAND
12 mins.

In a double boiler melt the chocolate and butter. Set aside for the moment.

In a medium bowl beat the eggs until they are thick and light-colored. Fold in the honey, mashed potatoes, brandy, rum, or orange juice, vanilla extract, and orange zest. Stir in the chocolate-butter mixture.

In a separate bowl mix together the flour, baking powder, and salt. Stir 2 cups into the chocolate mixture. The mixture should be a heavy batter. If thin, add the remaining ¼ cup flour. Stir gently just until moistened.

Pour or spoon the batter into the prepared pan(s). Push the batter into the corners and smooth the loaves with a rubber spatula.

BAKING
350°
1 hour

Place the loaves on the middle shelf of the oven and bake for 1 hour. Test the loaves for doneness with a toothpick, metal skewer, or cake testing pin. If the probe comes out clean and dry, the loaves are done.

(If baked in a convection oven, reduce heat 50°.)

FINAL STEP

Place the pans on a metal rack to cool for 10 minutes before turning the pans on their sides and tugging on the paper to pull the loaves out. *Note:* For a delicious variation, add ½ cup coconut flakes to the batter.

THRILL OF DISCOVERY

COOKBOOK AUTHORS take vacations just like other people but they usually visit the resort kitchen, not the golf course. In Rome the food writer may forget details of a tour of St. Peter's but forever will hold the memory of the exquisite *gnocchi alla romana* served around the corner. And while other passengers aboard the S.S. *France* are sound asleep in their bunks, he is helping make brioche in the ship's *pâtisserie*.

It is equally rewarding to share food adventures, and this chapter is about finding bread treasures in Paris, in a bakery in a small city in western France, aboard a trans-atlantic passenger liner, and in a village in Switzerland, and then on a special tour of four U.S. towns with strong family ties to Holland, Germany, France, and Sweden.

DISCOVERY: PARIS

When I started the search for some of the best breads to be found anywhere, it made sense to begin in Paris, considered by many the gastronomic capital of the world.

The path led from an array of luxury food at Fauchon to the famous *boulangerie* of Poilâne built over the ruins of a fourteenth-century abbey. A Jewish restaurant-deli in a less-than-grand section of Paris provided delicious bagels ("Little Breads" chapter) and a sharp contrast to the elegant *boulangeries* shaded by trees in Place Victor Hugo, where I found Pain d'Épice, made with wild honey and rye flour ("Herb and Spice Breads" chapter).

The path to Fauchon is easy to find. Look for the riot of color that is the open-air flower market at Place de la Madeleine and you are very close to the two buildings that house Fauchon. It will not be difficult to spot. A dozen or more passersby will be at the windows, feasting their eyes on spectacular food displays put together by the store's two full-time decorators. A sleek limousine may be at the curb waiting for the owner to browse and buy among the hanging hams and sausages and pyramids of fresh vegetables and fruits rushed there from gardens and orchards everywhere in the world.

Fauchon is not an especially large place but everything is absolutely tops—top quality and top price. Wholesale markets hold their best for the Fauchon buyer. If he doesn't want it, then it will be released for sale to others.

Fauchon was the creation in 1886 of Monsieur Auguste Fauchon, who in the beginning refused to display or sell any food that was not a product of France. But two wars changed all that and today Fauchon, while resting its reputation solidly on French foods, has gone far afield to stock such exotic items as U.S. sweet corn, cranberry sauce, maple syrup, mincemeat, and California wines which, 3,000 miles away from home, are displayed alongside Bombay duck, Indian herbs, Maili mangoes, Spanish peppers, Scotch smoked salmon, and Israeli avocados and passion fruit.

In the main Fauchon store, midway between the vegetables and the *charcuterie,* is a counter given over to breads that are *spécialités de la maison.* One of the best is Fauchon's own creation, Pain Hawaiien (with coconut, of course).

Pain Hawaiien Fauchon   [one large or two small loaves]
(Fauchon's Hawaiian Bread)

To fully appreciate a slice of Pain Hawaiien it must be toasted, the baker at Fauchon told me. He was lyrical about it. I could not disagree, yet there is a lovely and haunting aftertaste even in an untoasted bite.

If baked in Hawaii, the nut of choice would be macadamia, but the hazelnut (noisette), highly favored in all things by the French, has much the same hard crunchiness, and a unique flavor of its own. It is an able substitute and not nearly so expensive. Nevertheless, that afternoon in Paris a pound of Fauchon's Pain Hawaiien was almost $4!

INGREDIENTS

3 cups bread or all-purpose flour, approximately
1 package dry yeast
2 teaspoons salt
1 tablespoon sugar
$^1/_4$ cup nonfat dry milk
$^3/_4$ cup hot water (120°–130°)
2 eggs, room temperature
$^1/_4$ cup ($^1/_2$ stick) butter, room temperature
$^3/_4$ cup packaged or fresh coconut flakes
$^3/_4$ cup coarsely ground hazelnuts (see Note)
1 tablespoon butter, melted

BAKING PANS

1 large (9"-x-5") or 2 small (7"-x-3") loaf pans, greased or Teflon

**BY HAND
OR MIXER
12 mins.**

In a large bowl or mixer bowl combine 1 cup flour, the yeast, salt, sugar, dry milk, and hot water to make a thick batter. By hand, with a wooden spoon, or with the mixer flat beater, stir in the eggs and blend them into the batter. Work in one more cup flour. Cut the butter into several pieces and drop into the mixture. Blend with 25 strong strokes of a wooden spoon, or for 1 minute in the mixer.

Work in the coconut flakes and ground nuts. Add the remaining flour, ½ cup at a time, to form a shaggy mass that can be lifted from the bowl—or left in the mixer bowl under the dough hook.

**KNEADING
10 mins.**

If by hand, sprinkle the work surface with flour and turn out the dough. With a rhythm of push-turn-fold, knead the dough until it becomes smooth (save for the nut and coconut particles, of course) and elastic. If using a mixer, the dough will clean the sides of the bowl (except for a small spot on the bottom of the bowl) and form a ball around the hook.

**BY PROCESSOR
5 mins.**

Attach the steel blade.

Measure 2 cups flour into the work bowl and add the yeast, salt, sugar, and dry milk. Pulse to blend. With the processor on, pour in the hot water to make a thick batter. Add the eggs. Cut the butter into pieces and add. Stop the machine to allow the mixture to rest for a moment or so.

Measure in the coconut flakes and ground nuts; pulse 5 or 6 times to blend thoroughly. Turn on the processor and add flour, ¼ cup at a time, until the dough forms a mass that cleans the sides of the bowl, and is whipped around the bowl by the blade. Add small portions of flour through the feed tube if the dough continues to be wet (slack).

**KNEADING
45 secs.**

Knead with the processor running for 45 seconds.

If the dough is slightly sticky when turned from the work bowl, dust with light sprinkles of flour as you work it into a ball.

**FIRST RISING
1 hour**

Place the dough in a greased bowl, cover with plastic wrap, and leave undisturbed at room temperature until doubled in volume, 1 hour.

**SHAPING
15 mins.**

Punch down the dough and turn it onto a floured work surface; with a knife or dough scraper divide the dough into the number of loaves desired. Roll each into a ball and let stand for 2 or 3 minutes to relax.

Press each ball into a flat oval—as wide as the pan is long—fold in half and pinch the seam together. Tuck in the ends and drop into the prepared pan, with seam under.

SECOND RISING	Cover with wax paper and leave at room temperature to rise until the
1 hour	dough has risen above the level of the pan edge, about 1 hour.

PREHEAT	Preheat the oven to 400° 20 minutes before baking.

BAKING	With a razor blade make one long slice down the center of the loaf
400°	with 4 or 5 short diagonal cuts radiating on either side, as fronds from
30–40 mins.	the trunk of a coconut palm.

Place on the middle shelf of the oven. When the loaves have been in the oven for 20 minutes, turn the pans around. The loaves are baked when golden brown with darker flakes of nuts and coconut in the crust. (Larger loaves may need an additional 10 minutes in the oven.)

Turn the baked loaves out of the pans. Brush the top crust with the melted butter and return to the oven without the pan for 5 minutes.

(If using a convection oven, reduce heat 40°.)

FINAL STEP	Remove the bread from the oven and place on a metal rack to cool.

Good toasted. Good anytime.

Note: Since much of the good taste of this bread rests on the nuts, they should be coarsely ground, preferably in a nut grinder or food processor, so that the particles are about the size of rice grains. Don't grind or process them so fine that they become like flour or they will disappear into the mixture.

DISCOVERY: BRITTANY

In a small one-man *boulangerie* in the resort town of Bénodet, in Brittany, I helped Monsieur Yves Monfort load lengths of soft dough into long black-metal baguette pans, open-ended and trough-shaped. These we stacked in a large wooden cabinet to rise.

From the moment I walked into his bakery at three o'clock in the morning until I left at eight o'clock, M. Monfort scarcely looked up from his work. The only noise in the bakery when the last loaves were resting on end in wire baskets was the sound of hard crust crackling in the cool air.

Two things were quickly apparent during my visit with M. Monfort and each contributed importantly to the making of his excellent French loaf.

Despite a gas-fired oven going full blast in the room, the air in the bakery was relatively cool—70°. In baskets, pans, and large mixing bowls the dough was slowly rising in a relaxed way to develop the full wheaty flavor characteristic of French bread. It took almost twice as long to rise as it would in a room 10° to 15° warmer.

I pinched off a small piece of dough from a batch resting in a large bowl and discovered to my surprise that it was softer than anything to which I was accustomed. I could *force* it to stick to my fingers but handled gingerly it would not. It was just one step

beyond the sticky stage, a point at which I would have been inclined to firm it up with more flour. But not M. Monfort. He sprinkled flour liberally over the work surface, but this didn't affect the consistency of the dough.

M. Monfort's recipe takes both of these factors into consideration—the temperature of the room and the consistency of the dough. Because of the extended period allowed for resting the dough at lower temperatures, 5 to 6 hours are needed to prepare, raise, shape, and bake the bread.

Monsieur Monfort's French Bread
[two medium round or four long loaves]

INGREDIENTS	3¹/₂ cups all-purpose flour, approximately
	3¹/₂ cups bread flour, approximately
	2 packages dry yeast
	4 teaspoons salt
	3 cups hot water (120°–130°)
BAKING SHEETS OR PANS	1 baking sheet for hearth loaves, greased or Teflon, or if available, 4 long (18") French bread pans, greased
PREPARATION 5 mins.	Place a dough blade or putty knife to one side before you begin. Stir the two flours together.
BY HAND OR MIXER 10 mins.	In a large mixing or mixer bowl measure 5 cups of the blended flour and stir in the yeast and salt. Form a well in the bottom of the bowl and pour in the hot water. If by hand, slowly pull the flour into the liquid with a wooden spoon—until it is fully absorbed. If using a mixer, attach the flat beater and mix at medium speed. Add more flour, ½ cup at a time, to make a shaggy mass that can be lifted from the bowl and placed on the work surface—or left in the mixer under the dough hook. The dough should be tacky but not hopelessly sticky.
KNEADING 10 mins.	If by hand, begin turning and folding the dough with the dough blade. Sprinkle flour on the work surface and hands if sticky. Continue to lift, fold, and turn for 10 minutes. Throw the dough down against the

work surface to break the lift-fold-turn rhythm. The dough will become elastic but will continue to stick to moist fingers unless powdered with flour.

If you are using a mixer, attach the dough hook. Stop the mixer occasionally to determine the development of the dough. Add flour if sticky. The soft dough will clean the sides of the mixer but will not form the compact ball as with other doughs. Knead for 10 minutes.

BY PROCESSOR
4 mins.

Prepare the flours as above.

Attach the short plastic blade.

Measure 6 cups blended flour and the yeast and salt into the work bowl. With the processor running, pour the hot water through the feed tube. The dough will be a heavy batter. Add the balance of the flour, ¼ cup at a time, to make a rough mass that spins with the blade and cleans the sides of the bowl. Stop the machine, remove the cover, and test the dough between your fingers. It should be slightly sticky but not wet. Add flour if necessary.

KNEADING
1 min.

With the processor on knead for 1 minute.

FIRST RISING
2–3 hours

Turn the dough into a greased bowl. Cover tightly with plastic wrap, and leave at room temperature until the dough has expanded fully to more than double its volume, 2 to 3 hours.

SECOND RISING
1–2 hours

Turn back the plastic, punch down the dough, and re-cover the bowl. Allow the dough to double in volume, 1 to 2 hours.

SHAPING
15 mins.

Turn the dough onto the floured work surface, punch down, and knead briefly to press out the bubbles. Divide the dough, which will weigh about 3¾ pounds, into as many loaves as you wish to make.

Form the divided dough into balls and let them rest for 5 minutes.

For a long loaf, flatten a ball into an oval. Fold over, flatten with blows with the side of the open hand, fold again, and roll under the palms of the hands. If the dough resists, let it rest while preparing the other pieces. Return to the partially formed loaf and continue to roll under the palms until it is shaped. The seam will disappear.

The long pieces of dough can be placed directly on the baking sheet to rise although they will slump somewhat because the dough lacks stiffness. They can be placed in a *banneton* (a long basket lined with a cloth and liberally sprinkled with flour—see Note). The baskets will direct the dough upwards during the rising period.

By placing the shaped dough in a *couche*—a length of canvas (18"-x-36") or pastry cloth—and pulling the cloth up between the loaves to separate them, the home baker can do as M. Monfort does with large loaves. Sprinkle the cloth liberally with flour beforehand. The dough expands upwards and puts pressure on the loaf or loaves adjoining to do the same.

A third way is to place the long loaves in half-cylindrical French-type pans.

Round loaves can be placed on the corners of the baking sheet to rise, but because of the softness of this particular dough it is often better to use cloth-lined baskets.

THIRD RISING
1 hour

Cover the loaves with a wool cloth or rest a sheet of wax or parchment paper on glasses over the dough so it doesn't touch. If it does, it may stick. (The wool will not.) Let rise for 1 hour.

PREHEAT

Preheat the oven to 425° 20 minutes before baking. Place a broiler pan or similar vessel on the lowest shelf, and 5 minutes before baking pour 1 cup hot tap water in the pan.

BAKING
425°
25–30 mins.

If the loaf was raised in a basket, tip onto your hand and lower gently onto the baking sheet. The dough raised on canvas is gently rolled onto a flat cardboard or baking sheet held in one hand and then transferred to the prepared baking sheet.

With a razor blade, slash the top of the round loaves in a tic-tac-toe design. For the long loaves, make a series of diagonal slashes.

Spray the loaves lightly with water as you place them in the hot oven; 5 minutes later spray the loaves again. Do it from the oven door. Don't pull out the loaves or the moist hot air will escape.

The loaves will be fully ovenproofed (expanded) in about 18 minutes, at which time color will begin to tinge the crusts. The pan should now be empty of water; if it is not, remove the water.

Bake in the oven until the loaves are a golden brown, a total of 25 to 30 minutes. Turn over 1 loaf and top the bottom crust with a forefinger—a hard hollow sound means the bread is baked. If not, return to the oven for an additional 5 minutes. If the loaves appear to be browning too quickly, cover with a piece of foil or brown sack paper.

Midway during baking and again near the end of it, shift the loaves to expose them equally to the temperature variations in the oven.

(If using a convection oven, reduce heat 50°.)

FINAL STEP   Remove the bread from the oven. Place the loaves on a wire rack to cool. The *boulanger* stands his loaves on end so that cool air circulates around them. For a bright, shiny crust, brush lightly with slightly salted water.

Bon appétit!

Note: For a more complete description of *banneton* and *couche,* see "Special Bread Pans" in the equipment chapter.

DISCOVERY: ANGOULÊME

It began with a glimpse of a brioche in the window while driving through the French city of Angoulême. A tremendous crush of traffic was sweeping our car past the tree-lined Place Victor Hugo when out of the corner of my eye I spotted the window—filled with a handsome display of breads, one of them Brioche Vendéenne. It was impossible to stop. We found a motel on the outskirts of the city and came back the next day.

It was the *boulangerie* of Monsieur and Madame Yves Ordonneau. She was a handsome young woman—jet black hair drawn back into a bun, sparkling white teeth. In his white smock, Yves looked more like one of television's young medics than the city's best baker.

The Ordonneaus were delighted we had found their *boulangerie,* which was jammed with customers waiting to be served. With dozens of customers coming and going, I was trying to carry on an English-French conversation as I thumbed through a French-English dictionary while at the same time looking for a place in the crowded room to put down my glasses, take photographs, flip on a tape recorder, make notes in my steno book, and, with some decorum, present a copy of a cookbook to the Ordonneaus.

It was bedlam, or so it seemed, but the young couple was not the least flustered. Each bread I admired they insisted we take with us as a gift. These I added to the stock of things precariously perched on the narrow ledge by the cash register.

The most bewildered person in the shop was a bakery equipment salesman who came into the *boulangerie* with us, an order book in one hand and a catalog in the other, to find himself ignored by the Ordonneaus for more than an hour. He even volunteered to translate but gave that up because he said my English wasn't clear and, besides, I spoke too fast.

Brioche Vendéenne   [two loaves]
(Vendéenne Brioche)

The Brioche Vendéenne takes time to make but is worth every minute of it. Allow a minimum of 7 hours to mature the dough through three risings—3, 2, and 1½ hours.

Half the dough can be made into the classic stollen while the balance can be braided. The recipe should be halved for most food processors.

INGREDIENTS	$^1/_2$ cup light or dark raisins
	$^1/_4$ cup brandy or water
	6 to 7 cups bread or all-purpose flour, approximately
	2 teaspoons salt
	2 packages dry yeast
	5 eggs, room temperature
	I cup granulated sugar
	$^3/_4$ cup (I $^1/_2$ sticks) butter, melted
	I egg, beaten, mixed with I tablespoon milk or cream
	Confectioners' sugar

BAKING PAN

1 baking sheet, greased or Teflon

PREPARATION
45 mins.

Soak the raisins in brandy, if desired, or water for 45 minutes. Drain and pat dry.

BY HAND
OR MIXER
20 mins.

In a mixing or mixer bowl measure 4 cups flour, and add the salt and yeast. In a separate bowl whip together the eggs, granulated sugar, and butter. Shape a well in the flour and slowly add the egg mixture, pulling the flour into the center with a spatula or wooden spoon or with the mixer flat beater to form a heavy batter.

Stirring with the spoon and working with the hands or with the dough hook, add flour, ¼ cup at a time, to form a mass that can be lifted from the bowl and placed on the work surface to knead, or left in the bowl under the dough hook.

KNEADING
10 mins.

This is a rich dough and will feel smooth under the hands. Knead for 10 minutes, until the dough is elastic and can be stretched between the hands without breaking up. Add sprinkles of flour if the dough seems slack or moist.

In the mixer, add flour to form a mass that will be a soft ball around the revolving dough hook. Knead for 10 minutes.

BY PROCESSOR
8 mins.

Process this large recipe in two batches if your food processor is small and can't accommodate the full recipe at one time, or cut the quantities in half to make 1 loaf. Rising times will not be affected.

Plump the raisins as above.

Attach the plastic dough blade.

The sequence of adding ingredients differs slightly from above.

In a bowl blend together the eggs, sugar, and melted butter. Measure

4 cups flour into the work bowl and add the salt and yeast. Pulse to blend. With the processor on, slowly pour the egg mixture through the feed tube to create a heavy batter.

Add flour, ¼ cup at a time, to make a mass that will clean the sides of the bowl and ride on the blade. If the dough is wet, add small quantities of flour. If it is dry, add a spoonful of water.

KNEADING
45 secs.

Process to knead the dough for 45 seconds.

The dough should be slightly sticky when turned from the bowl. Sprinkles of flour will make it easy to handle.

FIRST RISING
3 hours

Place the dough in a bowl, cover tightly with plastic wrap, and leave to rise until doubled in volume. It is a dough slow to rise—but it will, given the time, about 3 hours.

SECOND RISING
2 hours

Turn back the plastic wrap and punch down the dough with extended fingers. Turn the dough over, re-cover, and leave undisturbed. The dough will rise to double in volume, about 2 hours.

SHAPING
15 mins.

Knead the raisins into the dough. Shape the dough into 2 balls. You can create braided loaves or stollen.

To braid, divide one ball into 3 equal parts and roll into strands about 14" long. If the dough resists or draws back, go on to the other loaf and return to the braids a few moments later. Lay the 3 strands parallel and touching. Braid from the middle to one end. Turn the strands around and complete the braid. Pinch the ends tightly together. Place on the baking sheet and cover.

For stollen: pat the ball of dough into an oblong shape, about 12" long and 1" thick. Fold together. The back of the piece will be straight, while the front will make a gentle half-moon arc from one end to the other. Place on the baking sheet.

THIRD RISING
1½ hours

Place the baking sheet in an undisturbed place, cover with wax or parchment paper, and leave to double in bulk, about 1½ hours.

PREHEAT

Preheat the oven to 375° about 20 minutes before baking.

BAKING
375°
30–40 mins.

Brush the dough with the egg-milk mixture.

Although this is not a hot oven, the rich dough and egg wash will brown easily, so watch carefully after 25 minutes. If the loaves are browning too rapidly, cover with aluminum foil or brown sack paper. Turn a loaf over in 30 to 40 minutes. If it is nicely browned and sounds hard and hollow when tapped with a finger, it's done.

(If using a convection oven, reduce heat 40°.)

FINAL STEP   Remove from the oven and place on a metal rack to cool.

When cool, sprinkle liberally with confectioners' sugar.

This bread freezes nicely for 1 or 2 months. (If frozen, decorate with the confectioners' sugar later when thawed.)

It is a versatile loaf that can be served anytime, but it seems meant for greater things—brunch or a fancy luncheon or simply served with a glass of wine.

DISCOVERY: S.S. *FRANCE*

No one knew that Voyage 202 of the great passenger liner S.S. *France,* from New York City to Le Havre and return, was to be her last. Certainly not the Claytons. Actually it didn't matter—we were aboard for twelve days and nights to live a great travel experience. I purposely mention the nights because that is when I went below to learn in the *boulangerie* and the *pâtisserie.*

I was scarcely at sea and anxious to begin my quasi-apprenticeship in the galley when I discovered a curious separation between the work in the *boulangerie* and that of the *pâtisserie.* The nine *boulangers* had been together as a team for eight years, and worked in shifts around the clock every day of the week baking only breads. They wore skull-tight toques and white cotton short-sleeve pullover shirts. In the *pâtisserie* the men wore the traditional towering white chef hats and starched jackets, buttoned to the collar. Here the work was divided between men who worked through the night making brioches and croissants for breakfast and others who came later in the morning to fashion delicate petits fours, cakes, ice cream, and ices.

I had expected all three delicacies—petits pains, brioches, and croissants—to be baked in the same shop. But not so.

The dominant feature of the bakery, apart from two large electric ovens built into one bulkhead, was an 8-foot-square beechwood table (never oiled, only scrubbed) around which the nine bakers stood. Only the mixing and kneading was done by machine.

The bread dough for the *petits pains* was cut by one baker, slicing furiously with a dough blade held in one hand while tossing the small pieces of dough to his mates. Each piece landed unerringly in front of a baker who quickly rolled it into a tight little ball for the second rise. It occurred to me that perhaps this was the last large bakery left in the world—9 bakers feeding 2,500 people—that relied so heavily on hand labor.

While bread was the product of nine bakers working together at intervals around the clock, croissants and brioches were almost one man's effort between midnight and 6:00 in the morning.

He was Monsieur Marcel Gousse, small, lean, and untiring.

M. Gousse had a small team of four men assigned to help him, but he trusted no one to do the knife work involved in cutting the croissant dough into precise triangles. And it was he alone who presided over the cutting of a spectacular 6-foot-long roll of brioche dough into small pieces for the fluted pans.

The voyage had been twelve days to Le Havre and back. During those days and nights at sea I spent hours learning from those gracious men, both *boulangers* and *pâtissiers*. Again and again they applauded my clumsy efforts and I loved them for it.

Petits Pains S.S. *France*
[two dozen 5" rolls, or four 1-pound loaves]
(Rolls S.S. France)

The anchor of the cuisine aboard the S.S. France was French bread in its least complicated form—flour, yeast, salt, and water. These four basic ingredients became something special in the hands of the nine boulangers.

It is not French flour that makes the difference, said the bakers.

"American flour can be used if one understands that it must be treated with deference. Permit it to relax. Don't rush it or it will get stubborn. There is more gluten in American flour and it will fight back when it has been kneaded too aggressively. Walk away from it. Let it relax, then start again."

The bakers also cautioned not to pour hot water into flour because this, too, will toughen the dough. Use water that is baby-bottle warm—about 97°.

One surprising practice in the France bakery was the use of a piece of well-laundered wool blanket to cover the dough as it rises. The bakers had cut 6-by-3-foot strips from wonderfully soft white blankets that in earlier times had been used by stewards to tuck around passengers taking their ease in deck chairs. The names of famous French line ships were woven into many. Now they were keeping dough warm.

My one regret is that I did not ask for one of the old blankets as a memento of the voyage. I fear they were tossed out when shortly thereafter the liner was taken from French Line service.

This method can be adapted by the home baker. I have since cut up an old army blanket to use in my kitchen and have discovered that even the softer doughs will not stick to wool.

To allow the dough to grow and mature and to become more flavorful, the France recipe calls for the dough to rise three times and to rest for one 15-minute interval.

The petit pain or small bread is nothing more than an elongated roll about 5 inches in length and 1½ inches in girth. It is a golden brown and crusty on the outside, white and soft inside. The dough can be made into four 1-pound loaves if you wish.

INGREDIENTS

7 cups bread or all-purpose flour, approximately
2 packages dry yeast
3 cups warm water (80°–100°)
1 tablespoon salt

BAKING SHEET

1 baking sheet, greased or Teflon. The rolls can also be baked in the traditional French bread pan: place 3 rolls end to end where the long loaf would customarily go.

PREPARATION
20 mins.

Place 6 cups flour in a large mixer or mixing bowl and form a well or "fountain" in the center. Add the yeast and pour in ½ cup warm water. Stir a small portion of the flour, yeast, and water into a light batter. Let it bubble and grow for 15 minutes.

If using a processor, in a small bowl stir together 1 cup flour, the yeast, and ½ cup water and set aside to ferment for about 15 minutes.

BY HAND
OR MIXER
20 mins.

Dissolve the salt in 2½ cups water and pour it over the yeast mixture, slowly stirring in a portion from the sides.

If using a mixer, attach the flat beater and mix at low speed. Beat the soft batter after the addition of each portion of flour. When the dough is firm and can no longer be stirred, use the hands to blend in additional flour, if needed, or change to the dough hook in the mixer. The dough should be soft but should not stick to the hands if lightly sprinkled with flour.

KNEADING
10 mins.

If by hand, turn out on the countertop and begin kneading—push down with force with the heels of your hands, draw back, give the dough a quarter turn; fold it in half, push down with force, draw back, turn the dough again, and fold, and so continue.

This is a lean dough (no shortening) so it will have a tendency to stick. A dough scraper or broad putty knife in the hand is useful to turn the dough.

If using a dough hook, add flour, if necessary, to form a soft, elastic ball that will form around the dough hook and clean the sides of the bowl. Knead for 10 minutes, or until the dough is a velvety ball—elastic to the touch but not solid nor too firm. If the latter, work in a little water (2 tablespoons).

BY PROCESSOR
5 mins.

Attach the plastic dough blade.

Measure 4 cups flour into the work bowl. Dissolve the salt in 2½ cups water and, with the processor running, pour this mixture through the feed tube. Turn off the machine and scrape the yeast mixture into the bowl. Pulse several times to blend the yeast into the batter.

With the machine on, add flour, ¼ cup at a time, to form a heavy mass that will ride with the blade and clean the sides of the bowl. If flour should stick around the bottom edge of the bowl, scrape into the center with a spatula.

Remove the cover and press the dough between the fingers. It should be only slightly sticky. Light sprinkles of flour will make it manageable. If, however, the dough is wet or slack, add flour and continue kneading. If dry and hard, add water—a teaspoon at a time—and knead.

KNEADING 1 min.	With the processor running, knead for 1 minute.
FIRST RISING 1½ hours	Wash and rinse a large bowl in hot water. Coat lightly with shortening. Drop in the ball of dough, turning it so all of it is filmed with grease. Cover the bowl tightly with plastic wrap. Put aside to double in volume at room temperature.
REST 15 mins.	Turn back the plastic wrap and punch down the dough. Cover again and let rest for 15 minutes.
SHAPING 15 mins.	Turn the dough onto the work surface. With a sharp knife or dough scraper, cut off small pieces slightly larger than a large egg; they should weigh roughly 3 ounces. Once you have established the size, be consistent. Use a scale if necessary. These pieces are rolled into tight balls to be placed on a baking sheet or left on the work surface to rise. Form the balls by compressing the small piece of dough between the thumb and forefinger, while tucking and pinching together the cut surfaces with the fingers of the other hand—or roll between the palms. The *France* bakers formed the pieces on the workbench, pressing down hard and rolling the dough in a circular fashion with a cupped palm of the hand.
SECOND RISING 1 hour	Place the balls about 1" apart, cover with a piece of wool blanket or length of wax paper, and leave for 1 hour.
SHAPING 10 mins.	Place each ball in front of you on the work surface. Flatten and then fold in half. With the palm of the hand roll back and forth to form a *petit pain* about 5" long and 1" thick, tapered to the ends. Place on the baking sheet with seam down.

If you wish, round rolls may be shaped. Flatten the dough and reshape into balls.

The *France* bakers used this same dough to make large loaves eaten by the officers and men. To do this, divide the dough into 4 pieces; shape into loaves; place on the baking sheet. After the third rising, slash the top of the loaves diagonally 4 or 5 times with a razor blade and bake for 35 to 40 minutes at 450°.

THIRD RISING
1 hour

Cover the rolls and leave at room temperature for 1 hour.

PREHEAT

Preheat the oven to 450° 20 minutes before baking. Place a broiler pan or other container (for ½ cup hot water) on the lower oven rack, but do not pour in the water yet.

BAKING
450°
20–25 mins.

With a razor blade, make a ½"-deep cut three-quarters the length of each *petit pain*.

Carefully pour ½ cup hot water into the broiler pan. Close the door for 3 or 4 minutes, and then slip the baking sheet onto the middle rack of the oven.

Look at the bread in 20 minutes. If the rolls along the edge of the baking sheet appear golden brown, remove them and bake the balance for another 5 minutes.

(If using a convection oven, reduce heat 40°, and add hot water at the time the rolls are put into the oven rather than before.)

FINAL STEP

Remove from the oven and place on a rack to cool.

Delicious when served warm, or reheated. However, because they are made with lean dough, they will soon begin to dry out. They freeze well for a later meal.

DISCOVERY: WICHTRACH, SWITZERLAND

The reason for the visit to Switzerland was to discover what cross-pollination of breads there had been in a country so heavily influenced by several cultures. We were en route from one large Swiss city to another when we stopped overnight at a small roadside hotel in the village of Wichtrach, south of Bern. It was the beginning of a warm relationship with the town and its people that has lasted for more than a decade.

We were yet to meet Rolf and Verena Thomas when the waiter brought rolls from the Thomas *Bäckerei* to our table for breakfast. I knew right away we had made no mistake in forsaking a hotel in Bern for this charming country *Gasthaus* that served breads such as these. There were two kinds in the wicker basket—Weggliteig (which we thereafter called "button rolls") and Gipfelteig, a kind of croissant. The buttons or small peaks came from scissor cuts along the top of each roll made by Verena just before it went into the oven. It was a favorite.

The Thomases' reputation as topnotch bakers has spread far beyond the immediate neighborhood and the 120 farm families for whom they bake. There are probably another 30 customers, farm families higher up the mountain slopes, who come to the bakery twice a week on their way to the doctor or to the post office or some other errand.

The Thomas *Bäkerei* has prospered. When we first met they lived in a small apartment over the bakery and a small shop that Verena managed. Recently they tore down a 500-year-old thatched-roof chalet next door and in its stead built a modern house but in the image of the old, with overhanging roofs and balconies lined with flower boxes. ("The old building smelled like cows and the roof leaked," Verena said when I asked why they didn't restore it.)

If you visit Wichtrach turn toward the mountain at the village crossroads where you will also find the Hotel Kreuz. Then you are on your own. Roadside advertising is prohibited in Switzerland and there is not even a small arrow pointing to the *Bäckerei*. However, it is not hard to find. One block, on the left, is the imposing four-story chalet. The *Bäckerei* is on the ground floor.

Weggliteig   [about two dozen]
(Button Rolls)

A specialty of Herr Thomas's Bäckerei *is Weggliteig, a delicious breakfast roll, several of which were in our breakfast basket at the hotel. It is a long roll brushed twice with beaten egg and snipped with scissors down the top to produce a sawtooth effect. My grandson saw it differently: "Looks like the buttons on a mother pig." The description is not far afield when one considers that some of the good flavor comes from a portion of country lard.*

INGREDIENTS
2 cups hot water (120°–130°)
1 cup nonfat dry milk
2 tablespoons sugar
2 teaspoons salt
5 cups bread or all-purpose flour, approximately
2 packages dry yeast
2 tablespoons *each* lard and vegetable shortening
1 egg, beaten, mixed with pinch of salt

BAKING SHEET
1 baking sheet, greased or Teflon

**BY HAND
OR MIXER
14 mins.**

In a large mixing or mixer bowl pour the hot water and add the milk, sugar, salt, and 2 cups flour. Stir to blend. Add the yeast; stir. Measure in the shortening. (Herr Thomas insists half of it be lard if one wishes to duplicate the flavor of his rolls.) If by hand, use a wooden spoon to beat. If using a mixer, attach the flat beater. When the shortening has been blended into the heavy batter, add the balance of the flour, ½ cup at a time, until the dough is a shaggy mass and can be worked with the hands or under the dough hook.

**KNEADING
8 mins.**

If by hand, turn the dough from the bowl onto a flour-dusted work surface. Knead with a strong push-turn-fold motion. Add liberal sprinkles of flour to control the stickiness. The dough should be soft, elastic, and a pleasure to work. If using a dough hook, add flour until a soft ball forms around the revolving arm—and the sides are clean. Knead the dough for 8 minutes by hand or in the mixer.

**BY PROCESSOR
5 mins.**

Attach the plastic dough blade.

The sequence of adding ingredients differs from the above.

Measure 3 cups flour into the work bowl and add dry milk, sugar, salt, and yeast. Pour in the hot water. Pulse to blend. With the machine running, drop the 4 tablespoons shortening through the feed tube.

Add the remaining flour, ¼ cup at a time, to form a heavy mass that will spin with the blade and clean the sides of the bowl. Stop the machine; pinch the dough between the fingers to determine if the dough is wet or slack. If so, add liberal sprinkles of flour. When turned from the bowl the dough will be slightly sticky but sprinkles of flour will make it manageable.

**KNEADING
45 secs.**

Let the processor run for 45 seconds to knead the dough.

**FIRST RISING
2 hours**

Place the dough in a greased bowl, cover tightly with plastic wrap, and set aside until it has doubled in bulk, 2 hours.

**SHAPING
20 mins.**

Turn dough from the bowl and punch down.

Divide the dough into 24 pieces and roll each piece into a ball. To form a ball, the dough must be pressed down hard under your cupped palm to force the edges and folds to blend into the dough and disappear. When each ball is round and cohesive, fashion it into a long roll—4" to 5"—by pushing it back and forth under your flattened palm with considerable pressure. It should be slightly longer than the width of your hand.

Place the rolls end to end on the baking sheet with a 3" space between the parallel rows. If there is dough for more rolls than the baking sheet will accommodate, reserve it and repeat this step when the sheet and oven are available.

SECOND RISING
1 hour

Cover the rolls with wax paper and leave undisturbed for 40 minutes. Then brush each roll with the egg-salt mixture. Leave uncovered for another 20 minutes.

At the end of the hour brush again with the glaze.

PREHEAT

Preheat the oven to 375° 20 minutes before baking.

BAKING
375°
35 mins.

When the rolls have been brushed a second time, face the long side of the rolls. Hold scissors at a 45° angle and snip 5 triangular cuts across the roll, about 1" long, down the center of each roll. The points of the triangles will rise, forming the buttons. Dip the scissors in water each time you cut so the points don't stick to the glaze.

When all of the rolls have been cut, place the baking sheet on the center shelf of the oven. Halfway through baking, turn the sheet end for end to equalize the heat on the breads. The rolls are done when glossy brown, 35 minutes. Turn a roll over and tap the bottom crust to be certain the crust is firm.

FINAL STEP

Place on a metal rack to cool somewhat before serving.

Equally delicious reheated later.

DISCOVERY: USA

Finding recipes for breads has been a passion and it has taken us overseas many times. Each trip was rewarding. Having first gone far afield, we were inspired to repeat the experience closer to home. Why not spend a fortnight visiting communities near us where old ways have been kept, and where Old World recipes have changed little as they've been passed down generation to generation? Free of the hassle with languages or customs or passports, it would be unencumbered travel in the family car, with gasoline less than a quarter of the price overseas. Over a period of several months we sought Sweden, Holland, Germany, and France—in America.

Sweden would be Batavia, Illinois, on the bank of the Fox River near Chicago in eastern Illinois (Germans were on the other bank and often the young bucks of both sides fought on the bridge connecting the two). Our choice for Holland was Pella, a town of 10,000—almost all of Dutch descent—in the heart of Iowa.

Farther south would be Hermann, Missouri, on the river of the same name, and as German as Pella is Dutch. A small town of less than 3,000, it is an important contributor to the state's growing reputation for quality wines.

Early on, the French considered the Mississippi River to be *theirs* so I looked for a community along its banks that had held fast to French traditions and cuisine. I found it south of St. Louis in Ste. Genevieve county, at a place where a ferry crosses into Illinois. Population: 4,400. The weather was gray and filled with rain on our visit yet the spirit of the town was upbeat.

The trip was made during harvest time. The autumn display of brilliant leaf colors was ending, and bare limbs were silhouetted against the sky. Across the flat fields of northern Indiana, my home state, giant farm machines ran in straight (and highly unimaginative) lines from horizon to horizon, stripping corn and soybeans from the dry brown stalks. In the hilly farmlands of southern Iowa and Missouri, artistic patterns were everywhere as the combines cut grand designs that contoured the fields in graceful curves.

The trip, beginning in my small Indiana city of Bloomington, across three states, and back again, covered about 1,300 miles and a variety of cultures—and baking.

The rewards of the trip were many—meeting friendly, helpful people all along the way, and receiving from them recipes that went back generations to old European kitchens.

Here is a recipe from each of the communities I visited. There are, of course, a number of other recipes from this trip and these have been placed in appropriate chapters. Only a delicious sample of each is here.

DISCOVERY: PELLA, IOWA

To enter the Jaarsma Bakery in Pella, Iowa, is to go back to an earlier era in America when the baker baked for the whole community, and there were no semi-trailers from big cities trucking in vast quantities of impersonally produced goods. In the Jaarsma Bakery every piece—a loaf, a cookie, a doughnut, a cake—has at some time in its short life been touched by hand.

"A loving hand, I might add," said Ralph Jaarsma, one of two brothers whose grandfather was born in Holland, emigrated to Pella, and founded the bakery in his home.

Today the Jaarsma Bakery, located prominently on the town square, is a long, narrow building of distinctively Dutch design, with a steep tiled roof and a high, stair-stepped gable front enlivened by a painted decorative panel. There is a stained-glass fanlight over the door with the legend BROOD EN BANKET BAKKERIJ—"Bread and Pastry Bakery."

In autumn, when the leaves are falling and there is early morning frost on the grass, Pella looks like any other small Midwest city, until you reach the parklike square in the center of town; there it becomes another place. Towering dramatically above the trees and shrubs and a small windmill are two great white columns surmounted by bells and heraldic lions holding a gold crown. It is the *Tulpen Toren* but most in town call it simply the Tulip Tower, a gift from a Pella citizen. It is the anchor for the town's big tulip festival in the spring when streets and sidewalks are bordered with 100,000 Dutch tulips in bloom. In addition, every home has a gardenful.

Dutchness is evident everywhere in Pella but no more so than in the bakeries. Every two years the Jaarsma brothers visit the Netherlands to bring back new recipes and to make certain their Pella recipes have not strayed too far from the originals.

"We like to keep in touch," Howard Jaarsma said. "There are only two things in which we and the Dutch part company. Our pastries are sweeter. The Dutch would say too much sugar. Also we slice most of our bread. The Dutch don't."

Pella (the name means "City of Refuge") was founded in 1847 by a dissenting pastor of the Dutch Reformed Church, Dominie H. P. Scholte, who was born in Amsterdam in 1805. In the beginning, the town was little more than a cluster of log shanties and huts roofed with prairie grass, and often called "Strawtown." Wyatt Earp (of Scottish descent) grew up here from 1850 to 1866 and today the house where he lived is part of the Pella Museum.

But it is a bakery like the Jaarsmas' at three o'clock in the morning, when the town is asleep and only the bakers are up and about, that excites a cookbook author.

Fat mixing bowls filled with rich, eggy dough churn and grind while a baker pinches off samples the size of golf balls and stretches the dough thinly against the light to test its elasticity and its readiness to be shaped into loaves. Another cuts triangles of layered dough with strokes of a pizza cutter, rolls each tightly from the broad end to the apex, tucks the point under, shapes the dough to become a croissant, and places it on a big tray to rise before baking. Dough, earlier put aside to rise overnight, has been shaped into loaves and now is coming hot from the oven to be stacked (by hand) on big metal racks and wheeled up front to the sales counters.

The bakery is filled with the wonderful and unmistakable aroma of hot bread. Heaven!

The recipe for the delicious Currant Bread with its core of almond paste is below. Other Jaarsma breads are Chopped Apple Bread in the "Fruit and Nut Breads" chapter and Sprouted Wheat Bread in the "Whole-Wheat Breads" chapter.

Currant Bread with Almonds   [two medium loaves]

Currant Bread begins as a golden egg-and-butter-rich dough speckled with currants. The dough is rolled into a flat rectangle—and a length of almond paste is laid down the center. The dough is folded over so the dark almond paste becomes the center of the loaf.

When the bread is baked and cut, each slice has a core of delicious almond paste.

Almond paste, whether store-bought or homemade, is expensive. Odense Pure Almond Paste, manufactured in Denmark, can be purchased in 7-ounce plastic tubes in most supermarkets and specialty food shops. Marzipan, which can also be used, is less expensive.

But the best almond paste for this bread is homemade. It has the right consistency, and becomes better integrated into the loaf in the baking.

INGREDIENTS

Almond Paste:
1½ cups whole blanched almonds
1½ cups sifted confectioners' sugar
1 egg white
1 teaspoon almond extract
¼ teaspoon salt
    or
¾ cup (7 ounces) store-bought almond paste
1 egg white
1 tablespoon butter

Dough:
5½ cups bread or all-purpose flour, approximately
¼ cup nonfat dry milk
1 package dry yeast
1 tablespoon salt
2 tablespoons sugar
1¾ cups hot water (120°–130°)
2 eggs, room temperature
½ cup (1 stick) butter, room temperature
2 cups currants

BAKING PANS

2 medium (8"-x-4") loaf pans, greased or Teflon

PREPARATION
2 hours

To make the paste, grind the almonds, a portion at a time, in a food processor or blender. Combine with the confectioners' sugar, egg white, almond extract, and salt. Work into a stiff paste. Refrigerate (or freeze) in an airtight container or plastic bag. The paste must be thoroughly chilled before it can be rolled under your palms—about 2 hours.

If using a store-bought paste, mash and work it with a fork, adding the egg white and butter. Chill.

BY HAND
OR MIXER
20 mins.

To make the dough, measure 2 cups flour into a bowl and stir in the dry milk, yeast, salt, and sugar. Pour in the hot water and stir vigorously by hand with a wooden spoon or the mixer flat beater until the batter is smooth. Drop in the eggs and butter. Continue to stir until they are absorbed. Measure in the currants.

Add flour, ½ cup at a time, blending each addition into the batter, until the dough becomes a rough, shaggy mass that can be lifted from the bowl and placed on the work surface. If using a mixer, continue to work and knead with the dough hook.

KNEADING
8 mins.

If by hand, knead with a strong push-turn-fold motion, adding sprinkles of flour if sticky. Continue kneading for 8 minutes.

If the dough sticks to the sides of the mixer bowl, sprinkle liberally with flour until it cleans the bowl and rotates freely under the dough hook. Knead for 8 minutes.

BY PROCESSOR
5 mins.

Prepare the paste, as above.

Attach the short plastic dough blade (which will not shred the currants).

Measure 2 cups flour into the work bowl and add the dry ingredients. Pulse to blend. Pour in the hot water and pulse several times to form a smooth batter. Drop in the eggs and butter. Leave the processor running until the eggs and butter have been absorbed. Measure in the currants.

Add flour, ¼ cup at a time, through the feed tube. When the mass begins to form, carefully add small portions of flour. Don't make the dough a hard ball with the flour or it may stall the machine.

KNEADING
45 secs.

When the dough is fully formed and riding the blade around the bowl—and the bowl is cleaned by the spinning dough—leave the machine on for 45 seconds to knead. As the kneading continues, the blade may have a difficult time, and the machine may slow. Stand by to turn it off if this happens, and continue by hand.

Turn the dough from the work bowl. Sprinkle liberally with flour to control the stickiness that is always evident when the dough is first turned from the processor.

FIRST RISING
I hour

Place the dough in a buttered bowl, cover tightly with plastic wrap, and put aside to double in volume, about 1 hour.

While the dough is rising, divide the chilled almond paste into 2 pieces.

Roll each into a length 1" shorter than the dough when shaped as a loaf—use the pan you plan to bake in as a guide. The dough must overlap to seal the ends. Keep chilled until the dough is ready to shape.

If the commercial almond paste has been prepared (with egg and butter) it may be too soft to fashion into a roll. If so, a spoon can be used to lay it down the center of the loaf oval.

SHAPING **8 mins.**	Take the dough from the bowl, divide into 2 pieces, and push and roll each into a flat oval the length of the bread pan. Lay the roll of almond paste down the center of the oval. Encase it with the dough as one would a hot dog in a bun. Pinch the seam tightly. If necessary, roll under the palms to lengthen and fit the pan. Repeat for the second loaf.
SECOND RISING **45 mins.**	Cover the loaves with plastic wrap or brown sack paper and leave to rise at room temperature until puffy and doubled in bulk, about 45 minutes.
PREHEAT	Preheat the oven to 375° about 20 minutes before baking.
BAKING **375°** **40 mins.**	Place the loaves on the middle shelf of the oven, and bake until a deep brown, about 40 minutes. (If using a convection oven, reduce heat 50°.)
FINAL STEP	Remove the loaves from the oven and allow to cool before slicing or the almond center may be sticky.

Discovery: Batavia, Illinois

Ethel Cristina Wiberg was ten years old, stranded with her parents in Sweden during World War I while visiting relatives, when her father told her that from that day on she would be the cook for the family that included an ailing mother and five brothers and sisters.

She learned well, and when she returned home to Illinois she brought with her a growing reputation as a cook and home baker.

Batavia, on the Fox River west of Chicago, is Swedish on the west bank, and German on the east. It is a small city, with impressively big houses built in the early part of this century. Until the last generation or so, Swedish was spoken throughout the community; when a child was confirmed in church, the ceremony was in Swedish.

Ethel Wiberg has been baking limpa for almost three-quarters of a century. She presses the dough flat, dimples it with the tips of her fingers or with a fork, and bakes it as a flat bread. After her mother baked the Christmas limpa it was buried in grain stored in the attic to keep the loaves fresh, but Ethel bakes her limpa several days ahead and lets it dry out somewhat in preparation for the *doppi grryta*—dipping the pieces of limpa into the broth in which the meats for the Christmas meal have been cooked. It is a family tradition that the limpa be dipped and eaten while the tree is being decorated, and this is to be done while standing or walking around the tree.

When I stood in her kitchen and ate limpa I held it on a napkin inscribed:

I Jesu namn	In Jesus' name
till bords vi ga	to the table we go
valsigna Gud	bless God
den mat vi fa	the food we receive

A devout woman, the cadence to which Ethel Wiberg kneads her bread is the Lord's Prayer.

Limpa   [two large round loaves]
(Swedish Limpa Rye)

Limpa has long been one of the author's favorite loaves, a romance that began in Göteborg, Sweden, a lifetime ago (or so it seems). Limpa has the chililike flavor of crushed cuminseed, the unmistakable fragrance of fennel, and the pleasant goodness of orange.

Mrs. Wiberg's recipe does not include raisins, but they add something special to the loaf so I have included them below.

The loaves may be baked flat in a large baking pan, with sides, as Mrs. Wiberg does for the Christmas meal, or as round loaves on a baking sheet. For delicious sandwiches of cold meats or cheese, Mrs. Wiberg cuts the flat loaf into 3"-x-6"-inch pieces, and then slices each horizontally to serve.

INGREDIENTS	2¹/₂ cups medium rye flour
	2 packages dry yeast
	2 cups hot water (120°–130°)
	¹/₄ cup *each* sugar and molasses
	1 teaspoon *each* crushed or ground cumin, fennel, and caraway seeds
	Rind of 2 oranges, grated
	1 cup light or dark raisins
	4 cups bread or all-purpose flour, approximately
	3 tablespoons shortening, room temperature
	2 teaspoons salt

BAKING SHEET OR PAN

1 large baking sheet or rectangular or circular pan with sides, Teflon, or greased and/or sprinkled with cornmeal

BY HAND OR MIXER
15 mins.

In a large mixing bowl measure the rye flour and blend in the yeast. Pour in the hot water, and mix into a light batter.

With a large wooden spoon or mixer flat beater stir in the sugar, molasses, ground seeds, orange rind, raisins, and about 1½ cups white flour. Beat until smooth, about 2 minutes by hand or with the flat beater. Add the shortening and salt. Continue beating for an additional 2 minutes.

By hand or with the mixer flat beater, add more flour, a little at a time, until the dough cleans the sides of the bowl and is stiff. If a raisin works its way out, push it back into the dough. The slight discoloration that sometimes comes with working the fruit into the light dough will not be noticed in the finished dark loaf.

KNEADING
10 mins.

Turn the dough onto a lightly floured work surface or leave in the mixer bowl under the dough hook. Add liberal sprinkles of flour if the dough continues to be sticky. Knead until the dough is smooth and is soft and elastic under the hands.

BY PROCESSOR
8 mins.

Attach the plastic blade. (If the short blade does not pull in all the flour when it spins, stop the processor and scrape the flour toward the center with a rubber spatula.)

The order for adding the ingredients varies from the list above. The raisins are added last to prevent them from being cut too fine by the blade.

Measure the rye flour into the work bowl, add the yeast, and pulse to combine them. Pour in the water, and pulse to mix into a thin batter. Add the sugar, molasses, seeds, orange rind, shortening, salt, and

2 cups white flour. Pulse several times to thoroughly mix all the ingredients. Add the raisins.

Measure in additional flour, ¼ cup at a time, and process until the dough becomes a mass that will ride with the blade, and clean the sides of the bowl as it spins.

KNEADING
45 secs.

Let the machine run for 45 seconds to knead the dough.

When the dough is turned from the work bowl it may seem sticky—dust with flour to form a protective coating around the ball of dough.

FIRST RISING
1 hour

Place the dough in a greased large bowl, cover tightly with plastic wrap, and leave at room temperature until it doubles in bulk, about 1 hour.

SHAPING
12 mins.

Take the dough from the bowl and knead briefly to press out the bubbles. Divide the dough into 2 pieces.

For Mrs. Wiberg's flat bread, flatten the dough under your palms, and place in the pan. Press the dough against the sides of the pan.

For a round loaf, cup the dough tightly between the hands and place on the baking sheet. Flatten the ball slightly.

SECOND RISING
45 mins.

Cover the dough with wax paper or foil and leave to double in volume, about 45 minutes.

PREHEAT

Preheat the oven to 375° 20 minutes before baking.

BAKING
375°
45 mins.

Uncover the loaves.

For the flat loaf, dimple the dough with your fingertips or pierce at intervals with the tines of a large fork.

For the round loaf, slash a cross on the top of each loaf with a razor blade or sharp knife.

Place in the oven, and bake for about 45 minutes. When the loaves are crusty and tapping the bottom yields a hard and hollow sound, they are done. If not, return to the oven for an additional 5 to 10 minutes. If the loaves appear to be browning too quickly, cover with a piece of foil or brown sack paper.

(If using a convection oven, reduce heat 50°.)

FINAL STEP

Remove from the oven and place the loaves on a wire cooling rack.

This limpa makes exceptionally good toast.

DISCOVERY: HERMANN, MISSOURI

The approach to Hermann from the north is over a narrow two-lane bridge high above the Missouri River. It is an impressively long bridge over an impressively wide river. The bridge is old, built in an era when engineers took pride in exposing all of the iron trussing. It sets the appropriate mood. A modern, sleek structure would have destroyed the illusion of driving back into the past century.

The river was turbulent and muddy. The bridge, after crossing over train tracks that run along at water's edge, is anchored to a high bluff. This surprised me. I had expected to see the town spread out along the water's edge, looking *toward* the water, not beyond in a sheltered valley where the river could not be seen.

Nonetheless, Hermann (named for a German folk hero) is a river town but access to the water, wharfs, piers, and fish-for-sale shacks is in another part of town, away from the bridge. The main thoroughfare is Market Street, a broad but short avenue (five blocks) that slopes steeply away from the river. It drops down the bluff, into the valley pocket, where the town was founded as well as where grapes for local wineries have been grown for more than a century.

At first glance Hermann does not appear to have the kind of personality that would draw people from all over the country to stop by for a visit. But it has, and the tradition took root a long time ago.

In 1837, the German Settlement Society of Philadelphia (Deutsche Ansiedlungs Gesellschaft zu Philadelphia), an organization created by a group of German-Americans of that city for the purpose of establishing a settlement that would perpetuate German culture and the German language on the frontier, chose Hermann because it reminded the first settlers of the Rhine Valley. The charter also stipulated that it should be "characteristically German in every particular."

Hermann has aged gracefully through the years with little change in spirit or in looks, still solidly and determinedly German while at the same time possessing all the elements of small-town America. Its population has held steady for generations at about 2,500.

We stayed at the German Haus and had lunch at the Burger Haus and a cup of coffee at Hillebrand's. We walked past the Sausage Shop with "Fifty Different Types of Cheeses and Sausages," and read the sale bill tacked to a wall by Kallmeyer-Schroff, auctioneers, offering for sale the estate of Hermann Eickermann. Street-corner trash cans were labeled SCHUND.

The good things I had heard about two aspects of life in the small town were the spur to make the trip across three states to get there.

One was the reputation of Schulte's Bakery, noted for its *lebkuchen, springerli, stollen, pfeffernuesse, schnitzbrot,* and *streusel.*

The other destination was to an outstanding restaurant—Vintage 1847—atop one of the high surrounding hills, and part of Stone Hill Winery, which has been in and out of the business of making fine wines since 1847. Production had ceased only during Prohibition when its enormous underground vaulted cellars proved ideal for mushroom production.

The wines are good, but Vintage 1847, the restaurant, is choice.

It is in an old carriage house and horse barn, next to the winery, that were converted several years ago at the suggestion of Gary Buckler, who had come from California vineyards to manage Stone Hill. He is now Chef Buckler, with impressive credentials.

Vintage 1847 draws a steady stream of visitors from St. Louis and Kansas City, and many places beyond.

And one thing these diners seek is the baking of Ethel Scheer, whose great-great-grandfather Schawmberg emigrated from Germany. Ethel, who speaks German so well that on her first visit to Germany she was mistaken by the locals as a local, is a gentle, quiet-spoken woman whose skills are professional.

One of her best creations, adapted from a family recipe, is Kaffee Kuchen, a coffee bread spread thinly with sour cream, sprinkled liberally with sugar and cinnamon, and baked.

Her unusual technique for developing the dough for a peasant loaf is in the "French Breads" chapter.

Kaffee Kuchen   [two round 9" loaves]
(German Coffee Cake)

The rich risen dough is dimpled by the fingertips, spread lightly with sour cream, and sprinkled with cinnamon and sugar just before it goes into the oven. It comes from the oven plump with streaks of brown and pools of sour cream across the top.

Ethel Scheer uses this same dough to fashion delicious dinner rolls.

I was delighted to discover that this recipe closely paralleled my mother's old German recipe for her famous (certainly to family and friends) dinner rolls (see the "Little Breads" chapter, Lenora's Yeast Rolls). My mother added a small portion of mashed potato to the dough.

Another simple yet delicious topping for the coffee cake is melted butter sprinkled with the sugar and cinnamon.

Marje Clayton, who loves coffee as she does life, insists Kaffee Kuchen was created to be dunked, preferably a dry, slightly stale slice.

INGREDIENTS   *Dough:*
1 package dry yeast
2 tablespoons sugar
$^1/_2$ teaspoon salt

2½ to 3 cups all-purpose or bread flour, approximately
⅔ cup hot milk (120°–130°)
5 tablespoons butter, room temperature
1 egg

Topping:
½ cup sugar
1 teaspoon ground cinnamon
⅛ teaspoon salt
⅔ cup sour cream

BAKING PANS

Two 9" round baking pans, buttered or Teflon

BY HAND
OR MIXER
8 mins.

Place the yeast, sugar, salt, and 1½ cups flour in a mixing bowl. Pour in the hot milk, stir vigorously, and add the butter and egg. This stage is an easy one for the electric mixer.

When the ingredients are thoroughly blended, add flour, ½ cup at a time, and stir by hand or with the mixer to make a soft mass that can be lifted from the bowl and placed on the work surface, or left in the mixer bowl to knead under the dough hook. If the dough is sticky, add liberal sprinkles of flour. It helps to work the dough with a metal spatula or dough blade.

KNEADING
10 mins.

If by hand, knead the dough with a strong push-turn-fold motion to develop a dough that is soft and elastic. Add small sprinkles of flour if the moisture breaks through and the dough seems sticky.

If using a mixer dough hook, knead at medium/low speed (no. 2 on my KitchenAid), dropping in sprinkles of flour if the dough continues to stick to the edge of the bowl. When sufficient flour has been added, the dough will remain a mass around the hook as it revolves.

By hand or in the mixer, knead for a total of 10 minutes, or until the dough is smooth and elastic and feels alive and warm to the touch.

BY PROCESSOR
5 mins.

Attach the steel blade.

Add the yeast, sugar, salt, and 2 cups flour to the work bowl. Pulse to blend. Pour in the milk, pulse, and add the butter and egg. Pulse several times to thoroughly blend all of the ingredients.

(I find it more satisfactory to stop the machine each time to add a portion of the flour rather than attempt to pour it down the feed tube. It gives me an opportunity to touch and feel the dough so that I know how it is developing.)

Measure additional flour into the work bowl, ¼ cup at a time, until the dough becomes a mass and is spun around on the blade. At the same time, the dough will clean (but not perfectly) the sides of the bowl.

KNEADING
45 secs.

With the machine running, knead the dough for 45 seconds.

FIRST RISING
1 hour

Place the dough in a greased bowl, cover tightly with plastic wrap, and leave at room temperature to double in volume, about 1 hour.

SHAPING
10 mins.

Divide the dough into 2 pieces. Shape each into a ball. Press flat and roll to shape the dough to fit the baking pan. The dough should be about ½" to ¾" thick.

SECOND RISING
1 hour

Cover with plastic wrap or cloth, and leave to rise until doubled in volume—not quite to the top of the pan.

Meanwhile, in a small bowl mix together the sugar, cinnamon, and salt, and put aside.

PREHEAT

Preheat the oven to 375° about 20 minutes before baking.

BAKING
375°
25 mins.

Uncover the pans. Dimple the dough in a pattern of choice, and spread thinly with sour cream. Liberally sprinkle the sugar mixture over the sour cream.

Place the pans in the middle shelf of the oven and bake until the breads are deep brown, and with a hard bottom crust, about 25 minutes.

(If using a convection oven, reduce heat 50°).

FINAL STEP

Allow the breads to cool for 10 minutes before turning them from the pans onto a rack.

My mother always cut her coffee bread in wedges; I cut mine across the loaf into thin slices—easier to toast later.

DISCOVERY: STE. GENEVIEVE, MISSOURI

The natives of Ste. Genevieve like to point out that shortly after the French founded New Orleans they hurried up the Mississippi River to be the first to raise the flag over the settlement, the first west of the great river. German immigrants followed but the community never lost its essentially French ambience.

It was a wet, soggy day when we drove down along the Mississippi from St. Louis. I was anxious to stay as close to the river as possible for it is in this region that several hundred eagles fly down each year from the north to winter near the open water. We found the open water but not the birds. It was too early.

The town was just ending its summer-long fete celebrating its 250th birthday when we arrived. There were few celebrants on the rainy streets but there were enough banners and flags still in place to show the town had gone full-out to mark the historic occasion.

For their part, home bakers and cooks up and down the river had pooled their considerable talents to write a semiquincentennial cookbook, *Missouri History on the Table—250 Years of Good Cooking and Good Eating*, which is where I found the recipe for Black Walnut Bread.

Black Walnut Bread   [two round loaves]

Black Walnut Bread, one of those in the semiquincentennial recipe collection, is as delicious as it is unusual—a combination of black walnuts, with their dark, smoky taste, and onions. The recipe came from Burgundy in France many generations ago.

The taste is so different that it will take a moment or so to realize, yes, it is delicious. If black walnuts are not at hand, make the loaf with English walnuts. The taste will not be the same, of course, but good nevertheless.

While the bread is baking, the kitchen will be scented with the unmistakable fragrance of onion.

INGREDIENTS	I package dry yeast
	I teaspoon salt
	5 to 6 cups bread flour, approximately
	2 cups hot milk (120°–130°)
	$\frac{1}{2}$ cup (1 stick) butter, room temperature
	$\frac{3}{4}$ cup minced onions
	I cup chopped black walnuts (or English walnuts)
	I egg, beaten, mixed with 1 tablespoon milk

BAKING SHEET   1 baking sheet, Teflon, or greased and sprinkled with cornmeal

BY HAND OR MIXER 12 mins.   In a large mixing or mixer bowl blend together the yeast, salt, and 2 cups flour. Pour in the hot milk and stir to make a light batter. Add the butter. Stir vigorously with a wooden spoon—or with the mixer flat beater—until the butter has been absorbed into the batter. Add flour, ½ cup at a time, stirring all the while with a wooden spoon until the dough forms a mass that can be lifted from the bowl and placed on the floured work surface. (The dough may be left in the mixer bowl if the kneading is to be done with the dough hook.)

KNEADING 8 mins.   If by hand, knead the dough with a strong push-turn-fold motion. If using a mixer knead with the mixer dough hook. If the dough is sticky, sprinkle liberally with flour. As it is kneaded it will become smooth and elastic. Break the kneading rhythm occasionally by lifting the dough above the work surface and throwing it crashing down. Good for the formation of the gluten. Knead by hand or with the dough hook for 8 minutes.

BY PROCESSOR
8 mins.

Attach the short plastic blade.

Measure the yeast, salt, and 2 cups flour into the work bowl, and pulse to blend. Pour in the milk. Pulse to make a thin batter. The short blade may not reach the flour along the outer edge. If it does not, pull the flour into the center of the bowl with a rubber scraper.

Cut the butter into several pieces and drop them into the work bowl. Pulse on and off several times until the butter has been blended into the mixture.

The balance of the flour can be poured, ¼ cup at a time, through the feed tube, but I like to stop the machine, remove the cover, and add a portion of the flour. This gives me the opportunity to inspect and feel the developing dough—and to sense when it is reaching the optimum.

KNEADING
45 secs.

When the dough forms a mass that rides with the blade—and cleans the sides of the bowl—allow the machine to run for 45 seconds to knead it.

Even though well kneaded, the dough may be sticky when first taken from the bowl. Dust lightly with flour to form a dry surface around the ball of dough.

FIRST RISING
I hour

Drop the dough into a greased bowl, cover with plastic wrap, and set aside at room temperature to double in volume, about 1 hour.

SHAPING
20–30 mins.

While the dough is rising, prepare the onions and walnuts. Mix together in a small bowl and sprinkle with flour to keep the bits separate.

Place the dough on the work surface and knead for a moment or so to collapse the dough. Push the dough level. Place half the onion-nut mixture over the surface of the dough, and turn in the edges to completely cover the onion and nut pieces. Knead and work the dough until the onion and nuts disappear. Flatten the dough again and spread the balance of the mixture over it. Knead and work the dough until the pieces are scattered evenly throughout the dough.

Cover the dough with a towel or plastic wrap and let rest for 10 or 15 minutes to relax the dough.

Cut the dough into 2 equal pieces. Shape each into a ball and place on the prepared baking sheet. Press to flatten slightly, and cut a design on the top with a sharp knife or razor blade.

SECOND RISING
45 mins.

Cover the loaves with plastic wrap or a towel and let rise for about 45 minutes, or until the dough has nearly doubled in volume.

PREHEAT

Preheat the oven to 375° 15 or 20 minutes before baking.

BAKING
375°
40 mins.

Remove the covering from the dough and brush with the egg glaze.

Place in the moderately hot oven and bake until the crust is a golden brown, and the loaf sounds hard and hollow when it is turned over and thumped with a forefinger, 40 minutes.

(If using a convection oven, reduce heat 50°.)

FINAL STEP

The aroma of the nuts and onions baking in the loaves will have aroused appetites, but fend them off until the bread has cooled.

Delicious toasted.

THE ELEGANT
CROISSANT AND BRIOCHE

THE CROISSANT AND BRIOCHE—two outstanding and delicious examples of the art of the French baker—have a chapter of their own in this book. Together they represent the finest of French baking, the apex of the *boulanger's* art. But to make these recipes is not difficult if basic rules and techniques are followed.

The French follow prescribed rules to create the croissant, in the singular, and the brioche in a number of forms—*à Tête* (a topknot), *Mousseline* (tall and elegant), *aux Pruneaux* (a braid), *Nanterre* (small rounds of dough rising in the pan), *au Fromage* (cheese), to mention but a few.

THE FRENCH CROISSANT

While the croissant today in the United States is received with the enthusiasm and, at times, adoration that it has enjoyed in France for more than half a century, there is a concern that the American deli may have stuffed it with so many odd and unusual fillings that in time it will be difficult to recall what the *true* croissant was really like.

The French croissant, as it should be remembered, is a flaky masterpiece, crescent in shape, that stands proudly alone with nothing in or on it. To the eye, it is beautiful in its golden simplicity. To the palate, it is a myriad of layers crushed into buttery goodness.

To achieve this miracle of baking, the French *boulanger* attends to several aspects of croissant-making:

• Kneading, to assure tender dough, should be less than for a loaf of bread. It will have been kneaded sufficiently when all of the ingredients are blended and the dough is smooth, usually about 5 minutes.

• Butter for layering produces the best croissant—finer, softer, and with greater keeping ability than one made with margarine. However, a croissant made with margarine is usually more flaky. There is a mid-path—half butter and half margarine—which will give excellent results. Margarine alone becomes soft and oily when layered into the dough.

• Both the dough and the butter (and/or margarine) should be chilled to between 60° and 65°. If it is too cold, the butter will break into rough pieces and tear the dough. If the butter is warm and oily, it will be absorbed into the dough instead of remaining intact in layers. A small Taylor dial thermometer is handy to check the temperatures of both the butter and dough.

• If, during the rolling process, the butter oozes out from between the layers, chill the dough again. "The cold will correct many mistakes," a *boulanger* aboard the S.S. *France* explained. "Cold," he said, "is indispensable for the making of a quality croissant."

• Place a moist cloth over the dough during rests both in and out of the refrigerator so it will not crust. Wrap it in a damp towel before placing it in the refrigerator overnight after the third and final turn.

• After the dough is cut into triangles, shape them with care so that the layers are not broken down and forced together.

• When the rolled dough is bent into the shape of a horseshoe, the tip of the triangle or tongue is placed low on the side of the croissant, not completely under.

• Steam is not necessary if the croissants are glazed with egg yolks or a mixture of milk and egg. Croissants brushed only with water should also have a broiler pan of water in the oven for additional moisture.

French Croissant   [twenty-four to thirty pieces]

This recipe is for the feathery light (1-ounce) croissant served aboard the Atlantic passenger liner the S.S. France *before she was retired from service by the French. On a round-trip voyage of the ship, the author spent several memorable days with her boulangers and pâtissiers working and observing.*

I have found that a combination of flours—3 parts all-purpose and 1 part cake flour—makes a fine croissant. Mix the flours beforehand, of course.

Note: *Plan to allow a total of 18 to 22 hours for making this recipe.*

INGREDIENTS

1½ cups (3 sticks) butter or butter and margarine, equally divided, softened at room temperature (see Note)
3 tablespoons flour

Dough:
3 cups all-purpose flour, approximately
1 cup cake flour, approximately
2 teaspoons salt
2 tablespoons sugar

2 packages dry yeast
1²/₃ cups hot milk (120°–130°)
¹/₃ cup cream, warmed
I egg plus I yolk, beaten

BAKING SHEETS

1 or more baking sheets or trays. Do not use a flat baking sheet or one with open corners unless you form a liner of aluminum foil with ½" sides to retain butter should it run.

PREPARATION
2–3 hours

Sprinkle the 3 tablespoons flour over the butter and blend together on the work surface. On a length of foil fashion a 6" square of soft butter; fold over the sides of the foil to enclose. Place in the refrigerator to chill for 2 to 3 hours.

BY HAND
OR MIXER
5 mins.

While the butter is chilling, prepare the dough. Both can be done several hours or even a day or two in advance of actually layering the two together.

Combine the 2 flours.

In a large mixing or mixer bowl blend 2 cups of the 2 flours with the dry ingredients. Add the hot milk and cream and stir with a wooden spoon or the mixer flat beater to thoroughly blend the batterlike dough, about 2 minutes.

KNEADING
5 mins.

Stir in additional flour, ¼ cup at a time, to make a soft dough. (It will stiffen considerably when chilled.) Knead by hand or under a dough hook for 5 minutes to form a solid mass. There is no lengthy kneading, which would toughen the otherwise tender dough.

BY PROCESSOR
4 mins.

Prepare the butter as above.

Attach the steel blade.

Place 2 cups of mixed flours in the work bowl and add the dry ingredients. Pulse to mix. Pour the hot milk and cream through the feed tube. Pulse once or twice to be certain that all the dry ingredients are moistened.

Add the balance of the flour, ½ cup at a time, turning the machine on briefly after each addition. When the mixture forms a mass and begins to clean the sides of the bowl, stop the machine. The dough has been sufficiently mixed and kneaded. Don't overknead!

REFRIGERATION
I hour or more

This begins the process of cooling the dough and at the same time allowing it to rise. Cover the bowl with plastic wrap and place in the refrigerator for at least 1 hour.

SHAPING
10 mins.

Determine that both the butter and dough are about the same temperature—65° is ideal. The block of butter should bend but not break (too cold) nor be oily (too warm) when bent slightly. This may mean taking the butter out of the refrigerator an hour or so early to reach workable temperature. Likewise for the dough.

Place the dough on a floured work surface and with your hands press it into a 10" square. Unwrap the block of butter and lay the block diagonally on the dough. Bring each point of dough into the center, overlapping the edges at least 1". Press the dough into a neat package. With a heavy rolling pin, roll the dough into a rectangle approximately 8"-x-18". This dimension is not critical.

Caution: If the butter seems to be breaking into small pieces under the dough rather than remaining solid, allow the dough/butter to warm a few minutes. But if the butter softens, becomes sticky, and oozes while making the turns, put the dough back into the refrigerator for several minutes.

First and second turns: Fold the length of dough into three, as for a letter. Turn so that the open ends are at 12 and 6 o'clock. Roll again into a rectangle. This time fold both ends into the middle and then close, as one would a book. The dough will now be in 4 layers.

Wrap the package of dough in a cloth (an old tea towel is fine) that has been soaked in cold water and wrung dry.

REFRIGERATION
1–2 hours

Place the wrapped dough in the refrigerator to relax and chill for 1–2 hours.

Third turn: Remove the dough from the refrigerator and place on the floured work surface. Unwrap, roll out, and fold in three, as for a letter. This is the final turn before it is rolled out and cut into croissants.

REFRIGERATION
6–8 hours or
overnight

Dampen the cloth again and wrap loosely around the dough. Place the package in a plastic bag so moisture will not be pulled out of the cloth. Leave in the refrigerator for 6 to 8 hours or overnight.

SHAPING
40 mins.

Have ready a knife or pastry cutter and a wooden yardstick if you wish the pieces to be cut precisely—otherwise plan to cut them freehand. You may have or be able to borrow a French-made croissant cutter that cuts the dough into triangles.

Sprinkle the work surface with flour.

Roll the dough until it is a generous 10"-x-38" rectangle, and, most importantly, about ⅛" thick. This is a crucial dimension since it determines the size and texture of the croissants.

Trim irregularities to make the rectangle uniform in width. Cut the rectangle lengthwise to make two 5" strips. Mark each strip into triangles, 5" wide on the bottom. Using a yardstick as a guide, cut through the dough with a pastry or pizza cutter or knife.

Separate the triangles, place them on a baking sheet, and chill for 15 to 20 minutes. Any time the butter softens and sticks, place the triangles in the refrigerator until they are chilled again.

Place the first triangle on the work surface, point away. Pull the point gently out about ¾". Roll the triangle from the bottom to the point, slightly stretching the dough sideways with your fingers as you roll. Place the croissant on the baking sheet. Touch the tip of the point to the pan but do not place underneath the body of the croissant. Bend into a crescent or half-moon shape. Repeat until the sheet is filled. Cover lightly with wax paper or a sheet of nonstick Teflon.

If there are more croissants to bake than there are pans or oven space, cover the triangles before shaping and reserve in the refrigerator.

RISING
1–2 hours

The covered croissants will double in volume at room temperature in 1 to 2 hours.

When the croissants are two-thirds raised, remove the wax paper and brush with the egg wash. Leave uncovered for the remaining rising time.

PREHEAT	Preheat the oven to 425° 15 minutes before baking.
BAKING 425° 22–25 mins.	Place the sheet on the bottom shelf. After 10 minutes move to the middle or top shelf for an additional 12 to 15 minutes. (Parisians like their croissants a deep brown, almost burned. Or you may wish to take the croissants out early if you plan to freeze, reheat, and brown additionally later.) Croissants at the edge of the pan will brown quicker than those inside, so remove them early from the oven and shuffle those remaining. Return to the oven for a few additional minutes. (If using a convection oven, reduce heat 50° and bake as above.)
FINAL STEP	Place the croissants on a rack to cool. Admire—and then take the first delicious flaky bite. Delicious departure: slice an older croissant horizontally and toast. *Note:* While cold butter can be worked into a pliable mass with a metal dough blade or spatula, it is much easier to leave butter at room temperature for 1 or 2 hours to soften and shape. Not necessary with margarine alone. If not done in advance, make butter pliable by beating and pressing it with a rolling pin until it can be worked into a square.

BRIOCHE

Brioche is deliciously adaptable to many shapes and forms, and to many uses. It can be rolled into the shape of a croissant, given a small topknot to become Brioche à Tête; raised high into a dramatic Mousseline; or wrapped around a sausage, a fish, or prunes (Brioche aux Pruneaux).

The possibilities for brioche are endless.

The eight recipes for using the three different brioche doughs, one of which is made in a food processor, cut across those possibilities. The quantity of dough in each recipe is modest—usually sufficient for 4 or 6 persons. All can be doubled, but be forewarned that twice as much dough may be twice as much as you want to handle. At least for the first time around.

All of these recipes demand chilled dough. Don't attempt brioche unless there is room for chilling. After it is shaped it will soon come to room temperature, and begin to rise.

Brioche Dough with Starter   [three pounds]

The classic brioche is made in 2 steps. It begins with the preparation of a starter or levain *which grows active and puffy in 2 or 3 hours. Meanwhile, the dough is prepared separately. The two come together when the starter is spread over the dough and folded in. Together they are kneaded into a light golden mass.*

This recipe comes from the famous boulangerie of Monsieur Andre David in the small Normandy fishing port of Honfleur at the mouth of the Seine on the English Channel.

INGREDIENTS

Starter:

1 package dry yeast

^{1}/$_2$ cup warm milk

1 cup all-purpose flour, approximately

Dough:

4 cups all-purpose flour, approximately

6 eggs, room temperature

^{1}/$_4$ cup warm water (105°–115°)

3 tablespoons sugar

2 teaspoons salt

1^1/$_2$ cups (3 sticks) butter, room temperature

PREPARATION

2 hours

To make the starter, in a small bowl dissolve the yeast in warm milk. Stir in the flour to make a shaggy mass of dough, and blend for 3 minutes. It will not be a pretty ball, but it doesn't matter. Cover with plastic wrap and leave at room temperature for at least 2 hours. It may be left overnight if more convenient.

BY HAND
OR MIXER
15 mins.

Shortly before the starter is done proofing, prepare the dough. In a large mixing or mixer bowl measure 2 cups flour and make a well to receive 4 of the 6 eggs. Break in one egg at a time, stirring with a wooden spoon or spatula or with a mixer flat beater to pull in the flour from the sides. Add the warm water, sugar, and salt, and blend to make a thick batter.

On the work surface, press and work the butter with a dough scraper or spatula to make it pliable and soft. Blend the butter into the batter either with a wooden spoon or in the mixer. Add the remaining 2 eggs and beat into the thick mixture.

Stir the rest of the flour into the batter, ½ cup at a time, until the dough is a soft elastic ball and can be worked with your hands or that pulls away from the work bowl in a mixer. *Do not make it a hard ball of dough.* Lift from the bowl.

KNEADING
10 mins.

Place the dough on the work surface, press it into a flat oval, and place the starter in the center. Fold the edge of the larger dough over the starter and knead to incorporate the starter dough with the yellow egg-

and-butter dough. Knead by hand or under the dough hook until the 2 doughs have blended into a light yellow mass, with no contrasting dough distinguishable, 10 minutes. If the dough is sticky, work it with the help of a dough scraper. Light sprinkles of flour will make the dough more manageable. It may seem soft and tacky even when thoroughly blended. It will become stiff when chilled.

BY PROCESSOR	To make brioche dough in the food processor, see Processor Brioche Dough, below.
RISING 2 hours	Place the dough in a greased bowl, cover with plastic wrap, and leave at room temperature until the dough has doubled, about 2 hours. Under the plastic the dough will be light and puffy.
REFRIGERATION 2 hours or overnight	Remove the plastic wrap, punch down, and turn the dough with your hands. Return the cover and place the dough in the refrigerator to chill for at least 2 hours. It can be left overnight, but it will require a somewhat longer rising time when shaped.

Brioche Dough without Starter   [three pounds]

This recipe is for the traditional French brioche, with one exception—it does not begin with a separate starter. Some may find mixing all of the ingredients together at one time more attractive than in two stages. Plus this method does offer the opportunity to make it the old-fashioned way—by hand, crashing it down into the bowl.

INGREDIENTS	5 cups all-purpose flour, approximately 1 package dry yeast 1/4 cup nonfat dry milk 1 tablespoon sugar 2 teaspoons salt 1 cup hot water (120°–130°) 1 cup (2 sticks) butter, room temperature 5 eggs, room temperature
BY HAND OR MIXER 15 mins.	Into a large mixing or mixer bowl pour 2 cups flour, the dry ingredients, and hot water. Beat in the mixer for 2 minutes at medium speed, or for an equal length of time with a large wooden spoon or spatula. Add the butter and continue beating for 1 minute. Add the eggs, one at a time, and the remaining flour, ½ cup at a time, beating thoroughly with each addition.

The dough will be soft and sticky, and it must be beaten until it is shiny, elastic, and pulls from your hands.

KNEADING
10–20 mins.

If by hand, grab the dough in one hand, steadying the bowl with the other, and pull a large handful of it out of the bowl, about 14" aloft, and throw it back—with considerable force. Continue pulling and slapping back the dough for about 18 to 20 minutes. Don't despair. It is sticky. It is a mess. But it will slowly begin to stretch and pull away as you work it.

A heavy-duty mixer, at medium speed, can do this in about 10 minutes. The flat beater is better than a dough hook for this kneading.

BY PROCESSOR

To make brioche dough in a food processor, see Processor Brioche Dough, below.

RISING
2–3 hours

Cover the bowl with plastic wrap and put in a warm place (80° to 85°) until the dough has doubled in volume, 2 to 3 hours.
Note: If cheese, nuts, or fruit are to be added to the dough, do so at this point *before* the dough is chilled.

REFRIGERATION
4 hours or
overnight

Stir down the dough (and add other ingredients, if wanted). Place the covered bowl in the refrigerator. The rich dough must be thoroughly chilled before it can be shaped, 4 hours or overnight.

Processor Brioche Dough   [one pound]

If sticky brioche dough (though delicious) is not for you, then the food processor is. While this dough takes about 24 hours to fully develop, there is only about 15 minutes of actual working time.

INGREDIENTS

¼ cup warm water
1 package dry yeast
1¾ cups all-purpose flour
3 tablespoons sugar
¼ teaspoon salt
2 large eggs, room temperature
6 tablespoons butter, melted

BY PROCESSOR
6 mins.

Attach the steel blade of the food processor.

In a cup dissolve dry yeast in ¼ cup warm water. Measure the flour into the work bowl and add the yeast, sugar, and salt. Turn the machine on and off several times to aerate. Drop in the eggs and process until mixed, about 5 seconds.

Start the processor and pour the melted butter through the feed tube in a steady stream. Stop processing after 20 seconds. The dough will be very sticky, like batter.

RISING
3 hours

With a spatula, scrape the dough into a buttered mixing bowl. Cover tightly with plastic wrap and put aside at room temperature until the dough has almost tripled, about 3 hours.

Punch down the sticky dough in the bowl with floured hands.

REFRIGERATION
Overnight

Cover tightly again with plastic wrap and place in the refrigerator overnight to chill and make firm before using.

Le Havre Brioches: Parisienne and Nanterre
[one loaf each of two shapes]

Le Havre, the great French maritime port at the mouth of the Seine River, is noted—at least by me—for brioche in all of its forms, flavors, and textures. Whenever I go to Le Havre (the first time on the S.S. France), I press my nose against the windows of all the boulangeries in the vicinity of the big city market, Halles Centrales, and sigh in anticipation of the feast to come.

Two favorites, made with the same dough, are Brioche Nanterre and Brioche Parisienne. They are full-size loaves shaped in different ways.

The Nanterre is made by placing 6 or 8 balls of brioche dough in a zigzag pattern along the bottom of a loaf pan. They rise to fill out the pan in the same overall pattern. The Parisienne is made by placing 9 or 10 short lengths of brioche dough side by side across the pan. They rise in identical sections as do the Nanterre.

INGREDIENTS

3 pounds Brioche Dough, chilled (pages 609–13)
1 egg, beaten, mixed with 1 tablespoon milk

BAKING PANS

2 medium (8"-x-4") loaf pans, greased or Teflon

SHAPING
30 mins.

Place the chilled dough on the floured work surface and divide into 2 pieces.

Nanterre: Cut off 6 to 8 pieces of dough, each weighing about 2 ounces or about 2½" in diameter when rolled into a ball. Shape each into a ball and place in the bottom of the prepared pan in a zigzag pattern. They can be pressed together, if necessary, to fit.

Parisienne: Cut off 9 or 10 pieces of dough, each weighing about 2 ounces. Fashion each into a roll or cylinder 4" long (the width of the pan) and about 1" in diameter. Lay parallel and tightly together across the bottom of the pan.

RISING 2¹/₂–3 hours	Cover the pans with wax paper and leave at room temperature until the pieces have doubled in volume, about 2½ hours.
PREHEAT	Preheat the oven to 375° 20 minutes before baking.

BAKING
375°
35 mins.
	Brush the tops with the egg-milk glaze.
	    Place the pans on the middle shelf of the oven and bake until the loaves are light brown, 35 minutes. Turn the pans around midway during the baking period. Handle the loaves with care because they may break along the lines where the dough pieces were joined. They will become firm when cool. Since the loaves are fragile test for doneness with a cake testing pin rather than turning them out of their pans to check the bottom crust.
	    (If using a convection oven, reduce heat 30°.)

FINAL STEP	Place the pans on the metal rack and turn on the side to loosen the loaves. Gently turn out the loaves, remembering to handle the hot loaves with care until they cool.

Cheese/Raisin Brioches   [one braided loaf of each]

These 2 loaves are made by dividing the dough into 2 pieces—adding diced cheese in one portion, and ½ cup currants or raisins in the other. One becomes Brioche au Fromage and the other Brioche aux Raisins Secs, both favorites in Le Havre, France, where I got the recipes. Each is braided, and given an egg-milk glaze to produce a rich, deep brown crust.

There is no commandment that dictates one each cheese and raisins. Both cheese or both raisin. Your choice.

INGREDIENTS	3 pounds Brioche Dough, before chilling (pages 609–13) ³/₄ cup diced Gruyère or Swiss cheese ¹/₂ cup currants or raisins 1 egg, beaten, mixed with 1 tablespoon milk
BAKING SHEET	1 large baking sheet, greased or Teflon
PREPARATION 10 mins.	Divide the dough into 2 portions—one for the cheese and the other for raisins—*after* the mixing but *before* kneading. Stir the cheese into one and raisins into the other portion. Let the dough rise, as per instructions, then chill for several hours.
SHAPING 15 mins.	Take one of the two doughs from the refrigerator. It will be cold and hard but will become more workable after it has been rolled and stretched under your palms for a few moments. Divide the dough into

3 pieces and roll each into a 12" to 16" strand. Don't rush or the dough may tear. When the strands are completed, place them parallel and braid from the middle, carefully pinching the ends together. Turn the dough around and complete the braid.

Place the braid on the baking sheet and repeat for the second dough.

RISING
1–2 hours

Brush the completed braids with the egg-milk wash. Set the braids aside, uncovered, until they have doubled in volume. The dough will be cold and will take at least 1 to 2 hours to rise.

PREHEAT

Preheat the oven to 400° 20 minutes before baking.

BAKING
400°
50 mins.

Brush the loaves again and place them on the middle shelf of the oven for 50 minutes, until a deep golden brown. Halfway through baking, turn the baking sheet around. The braids are fragile when just out of the oven. Rather than attempt to tap the bottom of a loaf to test for doneness, use a cake testing pin or metal skewer.

(If using a convection oven, reduce heat 75°. It is unlikely that most home convection ovens will accept more than one loaf at a time. Cover the second loaf with wax paper and reserve in the refrigerator until it can be baked.)

FINAL STEP

With the aid of a spatula slide the loaves off the baking sheet onto the cooling rack. They will become firm when cool.

Brioche à Tête   [about three dozen pieces]

The lovely Brioche à Tête, with its golden topknot, is as much a fixture on the French table as the Eiffel Tower is on the Paris skyline. While the tower has become a favorite because of its dramatic presence, the tiny brioche has done so with butter and eggs.

While Brioche à Tête is now equally at home en table in this country, one of the finest examples of this bread I found aboard the S.S. France. Not only was it delicious in taste, it was also easy to make, thanks to the talent of the chief pâtissier aboard, Monsieur Gousse. He thought it was unnecessary to make the small bread in 2 pieces—to roll a piece of dough for the body and a smaller one for the head and then attach them—when it could be done more simply.

Note: *Because brioche dough must be well chilled, plan to make the dough in the afternoon or evening to bake the following day.*

INGREDIENTS

3 pounds Brioche Dough, chilled (pages 609–13)
1 egg, beaten, mixed with 1 tablespoon milk or cream

BAKING TINS AND SHEET	Small fluted brioche or muffin tins, buttered, and 1 baking sheet on which to place the small tins for the oven
SHAPING 25 mins.	Remove the dough from the refrigerator and divide into 2 or 3 pieces to make work easier. Return all but one to the refrigerator. Slowly work one piece into an 18" roll, 1½" in diameter. Use a yardstick and press a mark at 1" intervals. With a knife or scraper, cut the 1" pieces from the long roll. Each will weigh about 2 ounces.

Roll each piece into a ball under your palm. Each will be about the size of a large egg.

Gently rest the side of your palm on one of the balls, not midway, but at the edge so that about a quarter of the dough is on one side of your palm and three-quarters on the other side. Press down and roll the dough back and forth (perhaps 3 times) until there is a small neck (about ¾") connecting the 2 pieces. Lift the dough by the small end and lower it into the bottom of the fluted tin.

With your fingers still grasping the small piece, force the smaller piece of dough into the larger one, with your fingertips pushing to the bottom of the tin. The top of the small piece should now be about even with the top of the larger piece of dough forced up the sides. If the dough becomes sticky, place the balls in the refrigerator to chill.

The brioche can also be shaped by pinching off one-quarter of each piece of dough, rolling each into a ball—one large and one small. Deeply indent the large ball with your finger. Place the small ball in the indentation, and press down to seal the two together.

If brioches are to be made over a period of time because of a shortage either of tins or oven space, cover the unused dough and leave in the refrigerator until the tins and/or oven space are forthcoming.

RISING 1½ hours	Carefully brush each piece with the egg-milk wash. This will keep the dough moist during the rise as well as give it its golden color when baked. Do not cover the brioches as they rise at room temperature, 1½ hours.

When the topknot has risen and the finger marks on the body have disappeared, brush again with the egg-milk wash. The brioches are now ready to be baked.

PREHEAT	Preheat the oven to 450° 20 minutes before baking. Also preheat the baking sheet on which the brioche tins will be placed in the oven. The heat underneath will give the dough an extra push in the oven.

BAKING	Fill the hot *plaque* or baking sheet with the tins and place in the oven. The brioches will be done when the topknots are well raised, and they are a rich deep brown in color, about 20 minutes.
450°	
20 mins.	

(If using a convection oven, reduce heat 50°.)

| FINAL STEP | Ideally, the Brioche à Tête should be served warm from the oven, but they may be reheated later or frozen. They are delicious whenever served. |

Note: The finished topknot can be cut off and the center of the brioche cut out—to be filled with an egg, baked, and sauced with béarnaise. Cover with the topknot. (I make these by the dozens for family when we vacation in Hawaii.) Also fill with chicken or tuna salad or something similar of choice. Delicious!

Camembert Brioche   [one cheese-filled packet for six]

At the heart of this golden package of brioche created by a young chef, Jeremy Ungar, is a Camembert cheese. Brioche dough is wrapped around the cheese, sealed, and then placed in a hot oven for 20 minutes. The brioche bakes and the cheese melts. Together they blend into a delicious dish, ideal to serve with a soup or salad.

| INGREDIENTS | ³/₄ pound Brioche Dough, chilled (pages 609–13) 6 to 8 ounces not-too-ripe Camembert cheese, crust removed 1 egg, beaten, mixed with 1 tablespoon milk |

| BAKING DISH AND SHEET | 1 shallow 8"-wide baking dish, lightly buttered, plus 1 baking sheet |

| SHAPING | Roll the chilled dough on a floured work surface to make a 12" round or square. Place the cheese in the center and bring the sides up and around to cover. Overlap the edges and seal with the egg glaze. Pinch the dough together to enclose securely. |
| 15 mins. | |

| RISING | Invert the package onto the baking dish. Cover with wax paper and leave at room temperature until it has become light and springy, 1½ to 2 hours. |
| 1½–2 hours | |

| PREHEAT | Preheat the oven to 425° 20 minutes before baking. Place a baking sheet on the middle shelf of the oven so that it will get hot and give a boost to the lower crust. |

BAKING 425° 10 mins. 350° 10 mins.	Place the dish on the hot sheet and bake for 10 minutes. Lower oven heat to 350° and bake for 10 minutes longer. (If using a convection oven, reduce heat 50° for each bake period.)
FINAL STEP	Remove the brioche from the oven. Cut into wedges. Serve warm.

Brioche aux Pruneaux   [one large braided loaf]
(Brioche with Prune Filling)

The lovely yellow-white braids of Brioche aux Pruneaux are wrapped around lengths of a soft prune puree. The result is not only delicious but it is dramatic when cut—the black prune core contrasting with the brioche.

Brioche aux Pruneaux is a different coffeecake-style of bread. It goes well with coffee, tea, or a glass of wine.

I found the brioche (and its recipe) on a bicycle trip through France at a small boulangerie at the junction of three country roads near Villesavin, a seldom-visited château near Bracieux.

INGREDIENTS	36 prunes, preferably pitted 1¹/₂ pounds Brioche Dough, chilled (pages 609–13) 1 egg, beaten, mixed with 1 tablespoon milk
BAKING SHEET	1 baking sheet (to fit the oven), greased or Teflon
PREPARATION Overnight	The day before baking place the prunes in a medium bowl and pour boiling water to cover them. Leave to cool overnight. When cooled, seed the prunes if they are not pitted. Put the prunes through the medium blade of a grinder, food mill, or blender. Reserve the puree.
REST 20 mins.	Remove the dough from the refrigerator 20 minutes before the braids are to be shaped to allow it to soften somewhat.
SHAPING 30 mins.	Roll the dough and stretch it with your fingers into a rectangle 24" to 28" long and about 10" wide. The dough should be about ¼" thick. Allow the dough to relax for 5 minutes before further shaping or the dough will pull back when cut. The prune filling will be wrapped in the dough before the dough is cut from the larger piece: place a line of prune filling (about 3 table-spoons) across the width of the dough, leaving a 1" margin at the bottom and ½" on either side. Carefully lift the bottom edge over the

filling and press into the dough on the other side. Roll the dough so there will be a 1" overlap. Cut off the rolled piece with a knife or pastry cutter. Pinch the seam and ends tightly.

Roll the length of dough gently back and forth to shape a strand. Leave with the seam down while proceeding with the other 2 braids.

When the 3 strands are completed, lay parallel, with seams down. Braid from the center. Turn the braids around and finish from the middle. Don't tighten the braids as you work them. They need freedom when they rise. Pinch the ends of the braids together. Place on the baking sheet.

RISING **30 mins.**	Cover with wax paper and leave at room temperature for 30 minutes.
PREHEAT	Preheat the oven to 400° 20 minutes before baking.
BAKING **400°** **25 mins.**	Brush the loaf with the egg-milk glaze. 　　Place the brioche in the oven for about 25 minutes. Watch carefully during the last 10 minutes of baking—if the loaf browns too rapidly, cover with foil or brown sack paper. The braid is fragile when hot so don't turn it over to check for doneness. If the braids are a deep brown and strands feel solid under your finger, the loaf is done. 　　(If using a convection oven, reduce heat 50°.)
FINAL STEP	Allow the braid to cool on the baking sheet for 15 minutes before transferring to a metal rack. Handle with care while warm, as it is fragile.

Croissant Brioches　[two dozen crescent-shaped brioches]

The Croissant Brioche is a croissant in shape only. It is brioche dough rolled into a crescent shape to become a fine breakfast roll. The dough is rolled quite thin—the thinner the more delicate.

This recipe was created by Monsieur Raymond Calvel, an outstanding French boulanger, a professor in the Française de Meunerie in Paris, and a friend.

INGREDIENTS	**3 pounds Brioche Dough, chilled (pages 609–13)** **1 egg, beaten, mixed with 1 tablespoon milk**
BAKING SHEETS	1 or 2 baking sheets, Teflon or lined with parchment paper
SHAPING **25 mins.**	Remove the dough from the refrigerator. If the full recipe is more than can be shaped and baked at one time, divide the dough and return a portion to the refrigerator to keep chilled.

Roll the dough into a rectangle 24" long by 10" wide, and about ⅛" thick, the thickness of a wooden yardstick. Don't rush the rolling. Allow the dough to relax or it will continue to draw back. When the sheet of dough is at least 10" wide, and thin, let rest for a few minutes before cutting.

Trim the sides of the rectangle with a pastry wheel or sharp knife, and cut the sheet lengthwise into 2 pieces. With a yardstick or ruler, mark a series of 5" triangles down the length of each piece and cut.

Roll each triangle from the bottom edge toward the point. Stretch the dough slightly as you begin to roll. Stop when the point is toward you and tipped down. Place each on a baking sheet and bend the ends to form a crescent. Place the pieces 1" apart.

RISING
25–30 mins.

Brush with the egg-milk glaze and leave uncovered at room temperature for about 25 to 30 minutes, until raised and slightly puffy.

PREHEAT

Preheat the oven to 425° 20 minutes before baking.

BAKING
425°
20 mins.

Brush with the glaze again before the pieces go into the oven.

The croissants will be baked when a deep golden brown, about 20 minutes. If using a large oven, the croissants may be baked on the lower and middle shelves. However, midway during baking exchange the baking sheets so each will have been exposed to the same temperature variations.

(If using a convection oven, reduce heat 70°.)

FINAL STEP

Remove from the oven and place on a rack to cool.

Delicious warm or rewarmed. These freeze well.

Brioche Mousseline   [two loaves—tall and elegant]

An uncommon dough—brioche—baked in a common coffee can to create a spectacular loaf that rises to a golden height. The dough is allowed to rise to the edge of a cylindrical container, and then a paper collar is tied around the can. The dough rises higher. In the oven it rises even higher—to about double the height of the coffee can (the most readily available baking tin for this).

This is one of the breads that caught my eye when I walked past M. Andre David's boulangerie in Honfleur, on the coast of Normandy. The Mousseline took me through the door and to a friendship with M. David that, over time, has been responsible for many of the outstanding French bread recipes in the book.

INGREDIENTS   **3 pounds Brioche Dough, chilled (pages 609–13)**

COFFEE CANS
AND TINS

Two 1-pound coffee cans, or a combination of other size cans, if you desire. The containers should be printed. Shiny containers reflect the heat and will not bake nor brown as well. Cut and grease 2 strips of heavy brown or parchment paper, long enough to encircle cans, to tie on as collars after the dough is partially risen. If there is more dough than needed for the containers, the excess can be baked in buttered small brioche tins.

SHAPING
10 mins.

Determine by experimenting with one can, how much dough is needed to fill a 1-pound coffee can exactly two-thirds full—usually 1½ pounds.

Turn out the dough after determining how much is needed. Butter each can, and place a round of wax or parchment paper in the bottom (to prevent sticking). Fill the buttered cans two-thirds full.

The collars will be tied on later when the dough reaches the edge of the can during the rise.

RISING
1–2 hours

Cover the cans and leave at room temperature until the dough rises to the edge of the container. The time will vary depending on how long the dough was chilling in the refrigerator. If left overnight, rising may take 1 to 2 hours.

PREHEAT

Preheat the oven to 375° about 20 minutes before the dough reaches the edge of the can.

BAKING
375°
1 hour

Tie a paper collar on each coffee can with a length of string. The dough will rise 4 to 5 inches in the collar so make allowances.

A tall coffee can will dictate the bottom shelf of a small oven—or the dough may try to push its way through the roof. Midway during baking, turn the coffee cans around to expose them to temperature variations in the oven. The brioche is done when the crust is a deep brown, about 1 hour. To be sure, thrust a cake-testing pin or metal skewer into the bread. If it comes out clean, the bread is done.

(If using a convection oven, it is not possible to bake a tall Mousseline loaf, since most home convection ovens are too small. However, smaller tins can be used. Just be certain there is enough head room for the bread when it rises in the oven. Bake for about 50 minutes at 300°, or until the loaves test done, as above.

FINAL STEP

Untie and remove the collars but let the bread stand for 10 minutes before removing. If the bread is difficult to remove, hold the can firmly in one hand, grasp the top of the brioche with a hot pad, and slowly work back and forth to twist the loaf out. Place on a metal rack to cool.

While this loaf is a handsome upright piece, most often it is turned on its side to slice.

Petits Pains au Chocolat   [one dozen rolls]
(Chocolate-Filled Rolls)

Only recently has America discovered Petits Pains au Chocolat—a bar of chocolate in the center of a soft and delicate roll. French children have known about it for years. Clutched in a hot little hand, the warmth can soften the totally protected chocolate and make it even more desirable. Schoolboys often sit on them for a few minutes to hasten the melting process.

French boulangers wrap the dough around a slender stick of chocolate made expressly for these rolls. A spoonful of chocolate bits is an excellent substitute.

INGREDIENTS

1½ pounds Brioche Dough, chilled (pages 609–13)
2 cups semisweet chocolate bits
1 egg, beaten, mixed with 1 tablespoon milk

BAKING SHEET

1 baking sheet, greased, Teflon, or lined with parchment paper

SHAPING
20 mins.

Turn the chilled dough onto a floured work surface. Press and roll the dough into a narrow rectangle, about 24" long. Cut the length into 2 pieces. Return one piece to the refrigerator while working with the other.

With a rolling pin and your fingers, shape the piece into a length about 36" long and 4" wide. Keep a sprinkle of flour on the work surface so the dough can move freely. If the dough becomes sticky, return it to the refrigerator for a brief respite.

When the dough has been rolled about ¼" thick, place 1 or 2 tablespoons chocolate bits in a line 1" below the top edge. Leave a ½" margin at both ends. Lift the front edge of the dough sheet and place over the row of chocolate. Gently roll the length of dough forward until the chocolate center is surrounded with about 2 thicknesses of the dough.

Cut the roll into 6" lengths with a knife or dough scraper. Pinch the seam and ends tightly together, pushing back chocolate bits if they intrude. Place on the baking sheet, seam down.

Repeat cutting and shaping *petits pains* from the length of dough. When finished with the first length, repeat with the second piece of dough.

RISING
45 mins.

Cover the *petits pains* and allow to rest at room temperature until risen to about double in size, about 45 minutes.

PREHEAT

Preheat the oven to 375° 20 minutes before baking and glaze the *petits pains* with the egg-milk wash. Leave uncovered until they are placed in the oven.

BAKING
375°
25 mins.

Place the baking sheet on the middle shelf of the oven. The bread is done when a deep golden brown and firm to the touch, 25 minutes. Look at the *petits pains* after 20 minutes: if those on the outer perimeter are browning too fast while those on the inside are not, gently shift them around.

(If using a convection oven, reduce heat 40°.)

FINAL STEP

Place on a metal rack to cool. Delicious when a bit warm and the chocolate is soft and runny.

Great to place one in the inside pocket of a ski jacket to have warm at the top of the mountain.

FLAT AND POCKET BREADS

THINK OF THE CUISINE of the Middle East and India and their breads come immediately to mind. Here are five of the best flatbreads plus one from Norway. Two of them are Lavash—one crisp and one soft.

Pita [eight 6-inch pieces]

At the heart of the Middle East cuisine is a flat disk of bread known as pita in some countries and peda in others. As it bakes, the dough puffs to leave the center hollow. Not surprisingly it is also known as pocket bread. The pita can be torn or cut open and filled with meat or other delicacies, or a bit of it can be used as a spoon.

The pieces of dough must be rolled flat before they are placed in a hot (500°) oven. The dough should be rolled to a thickness of no more than 3/16 inch. This is the thickness of a wooden yardstick, the kind given away at fairs and by auto dealers and paint stores. It can be used as a gauge. The oven heat generates steam inside the pita and immediately the dough puffs into a ball. Later, as it cools, the bread will collapse. The oven must be hot. If it is not, the piece of dough will think it is meant to be a bun, and will rise slowly but without the all-important pocket in the center.

While this is a yeast dough, it puffs up because of steam. The yeast adds only flavor and texture. Don't overpower the dough with flour or it will be too dry to allow sufficient steam to be generated. Leave the dough on the soft side. Sprinkles of flour will take care of stickiness.

INGREDIENTS	2¹/₂ cups bread flour, approximately
	2 teaspoons salt
	1 tablespoon sugar
	1 package dry yeast
	2 tablespoons oil, olive oil preferred
	1 cup hot water (120°–130°)

SPECIAL
EQUIPMENT

Eight 7" squares of aluminum foil

BY HAND
OR MIXER
5 mins.

Into a large mixing or mixer bowl measure 1 cup flour and stir in the dry ingredients. Add the oil and hot water. Blend at low speed with a mixer flat beater for 30 seconds, increase to high for 3 minutes, or beat vigorously with a wooden spoon for an equal length of time. Stop the mixer. Stir in the balance of the flour, ½ cup at a time. The dough should be a rough, shaggy mass that will clean the sides of the bowl. If the dough is moist, add a small amount of additional flour.

KNEADING
6 mins.

Turn the dough onto a lightly floured work surface—counter top or bread board—and knead with a rhythmic motion of push-turn-fold. Knead for about 6 minutes, or an equal length of time with a dough hook in the mixer.

BY PROCESSOR
5 mins.

Attach the steel blade.
   Place 1 cup flour and the other dry ingredients in the work bowl. Pulse once or twice to blend the ingredients. Mix the oil with the hot water and pour through the feed tube. Process for 15 seconds. Remove the cover and add flour, ½ cup at a time, until the dough forms a ball and rides on the blade.

KNEADING
45 secs.

With the processor on, knead for 45 seconds.
   The dough should be soft and perhaps slightly sticky. Use sprinkles of flour to control stickiness. Turn from the bowl and knead by hand for a moment or two to be certain the dough is of the right consistency.

PREHEAT
20 mins.

Preheat the oven to 500°.
   Divide the dough into 8 pieces. Roll into balls, cover with a towel or wax paper, and let rest for 20 minutes.

SHAPING
5 mins.

With the palm of your hand flatten each ball into a disk. Finish with a rolling pin, flattening the dough into a disk about 6" in diameter and ³/₁₆" thick. Their thinness is more important than making them perfectly round. Irregularity adds charm.
   Place each round on a prepared piece of foil. Placing the rounds on

the foil rather than on a baking sheet or stone allows a softer heat to surround the dough. A direct thrust of heat from a baking sheet would form a crust difficult to puff.

BAKING
500°
8 mins.

Carefully place 2 or 3 of the breads directly on the oven shelf. Bake for about 8 minutes, or until they are puffed. Repeat with the remaining disks. Place the pitas under the broiler for 2 minutes if browner crusts are desired.

(If using a convection oven, reduce heat 50°.)

FINAL STEP

Remove the breads from the oven and wrap in a large piece of foil. The tops will fall and there will be a pocket in the center. Serve warm, or let cool and freeze.

Thaw before using. To reheat, stack several in a pile, wrap with foil, and place in a 375° oven for 10 to 15 minutes.

Lavash (Crisp)   [ten crackers]
(Cracker Bread)

Ideal to serve with soups or broken into small pieces at the buffet table by guests for spreads and dips, Lavash is thin, crisp, and crackly. It can be made almost any size, but Armenians like it the shape and size of a dinner plate.

A rolling pin will press this dough thinly. Then the piece should be spread across the backs of your hands and stretched ever so gently. Don't be tempted to grab the edges with your fingers and pull because the dough will tear.

INGREDIENTS

2 cups bread or all-purpose flour
2 cups whole-wheat flour
1 package dry yeast
1 tablespoon salt
1½ cups hot water (120°–130°)
¼ cup milk
¼ cup toasted sesame and/or poppy seeds (see Note)

BAKING SHEETS

1 or more baking sheets, lightly greased (usually only 2 breads fit on 1 sheet but they bake so quickly one sheet can be used repeatedly)

BY HAND
OR MIXER
15 mins.

In a mixing or mixer bowl place 1 cup each of the 2 flours and add the yeast and salt. Stir well to blend. Pour in the hot water and beat with a wooden spoon to thoroughly mix for 3 minutes, or for 2 minutes with a mixer flat beater. Add the remaining cup whole-wheat flour and stir vigorously to blend. Add the remaining white flour, ¼ cup at a time. Don't overload the dough with flour. It should be soft and elastic.

KNEADING
6–8 mins.

Turn the dough onto the work space and knead with a brisk rhythm of push-turn-fold. If the dough is sticky, add sprinkles of flour. Knead by hand for 6 to 8 minutes. If using a dough hook, knead for 8 minutes at medium speed. If the dough does not clean the bowl but sticks to the sides, add sprinkles of flour.

BY PROCESSOR
6 mins.

Attach the steel blade.

Place all of the 2 flours in the work bowl. Add the yeast and salt. Process for a few seconds to blend. Pour the hot water through the tube as the machine is running. Stop the processor, remove the top, and check the consistency of the dough. If too dry, add a small amount of additional water. If wet, add flour. When in balance, the dough will form a ball and spin around the bowl on top of the blade.

KNEADING
45 secs.

With the machine running, knead for 45 seconds.

FIRST RISING
1 hour

Lightly grease a bowl. Drop in the dough and turn to coat all sides. Cover with plastic wrap and put in a warm place (80° to 100°) until the dough has doubled in bulk, about 1 hour.

SECOND RISING
30 mins.

Turn back the plastic wrap and punch down the dough with your fingers. It will collapse. Cover again and let rise for an additional 30 minutes.

PREHEAT

Preheat the oven to 400° just before shaping the dough.

SHAPING
12 mins.

With a knife or dough blade divide the dough into 10 pieces. Roll each into a ball, cover with wax paper, and let rest for 5 minutes.

On a lightly floured work surface, press down the first ball of dough under your palm. Next, roll the dough as thin as possible. Under pressure it may stick to the work surface, but leave it there for a moment until the dough relaxes. With a spatula or dough blade, work the piece loose from the table. Keep the dough dusted with flour as it is rolled.

When the dough has been rolled as thinly as possible, lift it in your hands and drape it carefully over the backs of your hands. Slowly stretch the dough, turning it as you stretch. When it is paper-thin and stretched to its thinnest point without tearing, lay it carefully on the work surface. Cover with wax paper and proceed to the next piece. When the second one has been prepared, brush both with milk, and sprinkle with your choice of seeds—sesame or poppy. These 2 crackers will be in the oven while the others are prepared.

BAKING
400°
10 mins.

Place the dough pieces on a prepared baking sheet and place in the hot oven. The baking period will be short so be attentive! Bake for 10 minutes, or until the breads have pulled away from the baking sheet and are beginning to brown.

(If using a convection oven, reduce heat 50° and bake for 8 minutes or until golden brown [in places]. The pieces will not brown uniformly.)

FINAL STEP

Put the baked Lavash on racks to cool. They will do so quickly because they are so thin.

Store those not eaten immediately in a dry place. Watch for crumbs as they are very crispy. Stored in a sealed carton or bag, the pieces of crackerlike bread will keep indefinitely.

Note: To toast seeds, place them on a baking sheet and put into a 300° oven for 20 minutes.

Lavash (Soft)   [six to eight sheets]

Flatbreads—some crisp, some soft, some puffed, some not—are a delicious staple baked throughout the Middle East and on into the Indian subcontinent. They range from pita in Greece and khubz mar'ook in Lebanon to naan and chapatti in India.

One bread common to all is a large soft disk—nan-e lavash (Persia), tonir lavash (Armenia), and tandoor (India). It is often referred to as a sheet rather than as a loaf.

An easy way to bake soft bread sheets is to borrow a cooking implement from another culture, a Chinese wok. Invert the wok over a burner, brush the metal with a thin coat of oil, and drop the dough on the wok. This technique came from a fine cookbook, Middle Eastern Cooking, *by Rose Dosti.*

INGREDIENTS	4 cups bread or all-purpose flour
	1 package dry yeast
	2 teaspoons salt
	1 tablespoon olive or vegetable oil, plus enough for baking
	1½ cups hot water (120°–130°)

SPECIAL EQUIPMENT

1 wok, scoured clean on the outside; an inverted bowl (with gently sloping sides) covered with a cloth over which to rest the bread before it is baked

BY HAND OR MIXER
15 mins.

In a mixing or mixer bowl place 2 cups flour, the yeast, and salt. Mix the tablespoon oil with the hot water and pour into the flour. Stir with a wooden spoon or the mixer flat beater to blend well. Add additional flour, ½ cup at a time, to form a shaggy mass of dough.

KNEADING
5–8 mins.

Turn from the bowl onto the work counter and knead with a firm push-turn-fold motion until the dough is soft and elastic, about 8 minutes. If under a dough hook, knead for 5 minutes.

BY PROCESSOR
5 mins.

Attach the steel blade.

The order of ingredients varies from above.

Pour hot water and oil into the work bowl and add the yeast and salt. Pulse on/off to mix. Remove the cover and add 2 cups flour. Process 10 seconds. Add the balance of flour, ¼ cup at a time, processing each time to blend.

KNEADING
50 secs.

When the dough forms into a ball and rides on the blade, knead for 50 seconds.

RISING
40 mins.

Place the dough in a greased bowl, cover tightly with plastic wrap, and put in a warm place (80° to 100°) until doubled in bulk, about 40 minutes.

SHAPING
20 mins.

Turn the dough onto a floured work surface and divide into 6 or 8 pieces. First under your palm and then with a rolling pin, shape each ball of dough into a 10" circle. Place the flattened dough on the back of your hands and carefully stretch the diameter to 15" or 16". (The back of the hands are used rather than the fingers, which can tear the dough.)

After shaping the dough, dust each with flour and drape them together over the cloth-covered bowl (inverted) to rest for 10 minutes.

PREHEAT

Preheat the inverted wok over a medium-high flame while the dough is resting. The wok is hot enough for the dough when a drop of water sizzles and bounces off the metal. Lightly brush oil over the surface.

BAKING
18–32 mins.

Place the dough circles, one at a time, on the hot wok. Bake until the dough is browned underneath, about 3 or 4 minutes. Don't bake until it is crisp (then it becomes a cracker bread!). Turn the dough over and brown the other side. The bread should be soft and floppy. Reduce baking time or lower the heat if the bread is hard.

Lift the bread off the wok and fold into quarters while still hot. Place in a plastic bag to keep soft. Continue baking the balance of the breads.

FINAL STEP

The breads may be served warm. After they have cooled, refrigerate or freeze.

This is a marvelous bread to take on a picnic and wrap around meats and other delicacies. It is truly an edible napkin!

Italian Country Flatbread

[one large or two small flatbreads]
(Pizza Rustica)

Two delicious Italian foods—prosciutto and Pecorino cheese—give this golden and flecked loaf a fragrance and taste that is as happily eaten in the city as it is in the country.

Pecorino cheese is Italian sheep's-milk cheese that can be found in most cheese specialty stores. If it is not available, a sharp Cheddar is a good substitute. Prosciutto ham is expensive. I have used Smithfield and other quality hams with excellent results.

INGREDIENTS

2^1/$_3$ cups bread or all-purpose flour, approximately
1 package dry yeast
1 teaspoon salt
1^1/$_4$ cups hot water (120°–130°)
^{1}/$_4$ pound prosciutto, diced
^{1}/$_4$ cup finely diced Pecorino cheese
1 cup freshly grated Parmesan cheese
2 eggs, room temperature
^{1}/$_4$ cup olive oil
Salt and pepper to taste

BAKING PANS

The dough will make one 18" round or a 12"-x-16" rectangle so choose pans accordingly. The dough can also be divided into smaller rounds if oven space is a consideration. Bake on parchment paper or greased pans.

BY HAND
OR MIXER
6 mins.

Into a mixing or mixer bowl measure 2 cups flour and add the yeast and salt. Stir to blend. Slowly pour in the hot water. If by hand, stir the heavy batter 100 strokes with a wooden spoon, or for 2 minutes with the mixer flat beater.

Remove the flat beater and attach the dough hook. Add flour to make a rough, shaggy dough that will clean the bowl. Add sprinkles of flour if the dough continues to be sticky. The dough under the hook should form a soft ball around the revolving arm.

KNEADING
10 mins.

If by hand, turn the dough onto a floured work surface and knead with a strong push-turn-fold motion, bearing down heavily on the dough, until the dough is soft and elastic. Add flour if the dough is wet. If under the dough hook the dough clings to the sides of the bowl, add flour until it cleans the sides. Knead for 10 minutes.

BY PROCESSOR
5 mins.

Attach the steel blade.

Measure 2 cups flour into the work bowl and add the yeast and salt. Pulse to blend. With the processor on, pour the water through the feed tube to make a heavy batter.

Add small portions of flour through the feed tube to make a dough that will ride with the blade and clean the sides of the bowl. When turned from the bowl the dough will be slightly sticky, so dust lightly with flour.

KNEADING
1 min.

Knead with the processor for 1 minute.

FIRST RISING
45 mins.

Place the dough in a greased bowl, cover tightly with plastic wrap, and set aside to double in bulk, about 45 minutes.

In a bowl mix the ham and 2 cheeses and stir in the eggs, olive oil, salt and pepper. The mixture will be moist and quite thick. Set aside.

SHAPING
18 mins.

Punch down the dough; work small portions of the ham and cheese mixture into the dough. This can be done also with the dough hook and processor. The dough will become quite sticky, due to the oil, so add several tablespoons of flour. Knead until the flour is fully absorbed and the dough is again soft and elastic, about 8 minutes. Put the ball of dough aside to relax for 5 minutes.

Although it can be done with a rolling pin, I prefer to use my hands to press the dough into a round or rectangle that is about ½" or less thick. The hands give the loaf a country look. Shape the dough to fit the pan.

SECOND RISING
45 mins.

Cover the pan(s) with wax or parchment paper and set aside until light and puffy, about 45 minutes.

PREHEAT

Preheat the oven to 425° about 15 minutes before baking.

BAKING
425°
25 mins.

Uncover and prick the surface of the dough with a fork to give a uniform pattern over the loaf.

Bake on the middle shelf of the oven for about 25 minutes, or until the loaf is a light golden brown, flecked with bits of cheese and ham. (If using a convection oven, reduce heat 50°.)

FINAL STEP

Remove from the oven and allow the bread to cool in the pan for 3 or 4 minutes before removing to a metal rack to cool thoroughly before serving.

Naan   [eight pieces]

A delicious unleavened flatbread from the steppes of Central Asia, Naan is rolled as thin as the thickness of the freshly chopped onions in the dough will allow.

The recipe can easily be doubled or trebled for a large buffet or barbecue, where it will find an enthusiastic reception. Or serve at breakfast with a sharp cheese or at a luncheon with fruit and tea.

INGREDIENTS

3 tablespoons butter, room temperature
1 cup finely chopped or grated onions
½ cup warm water (105°–115°)
1 teaspoon salt
1½ to 2 cups bread or all-purpose flour, approximately

BAKING PAN
OR GRIDDLE

1 heavy 10" to 12" pan or griddle to place over high heat

PREPARATION
15 mins.

In a heavy skillet set over medium-high heat melt 1 tablespoon butter. Add the onions, reduce heat to low, and cook, covered, for 3 to 5 minutes, or until the onions are soft but not brown. Place them in a small bowl and cool to room temperature.

BY HAND
OR MIXER
10 mins.

Melt the remaining butter in the skillet and pour into a large mixing bowl. Add the warm water, onions, salt, and 1½ cups flour, ½ cup at a time. Work the dough into a ball by hand or under a dough hook. If it continues to be sticky add 1 or 2 teaspoons flour.

KNEADING
1–2 mins.

Turn the dough out onto a lightly floured work surface and work the dough with your fingers and under your palms until the dough is slightly firm, 1 to 2 minutes. (This short interval is not kneading in the truest sense.)

BY PROCESSOR
5 mins.

Sauté the onions, as above, and set aside.

Attach the steel blade.

Melt the remaining butter in the skillet and pour into the work bowl. Add the warm water, onions, salt, and 1½ cups of flour. Pulse 7 or 8 times to blend and to work the dough into a slightly firm ball that will clean the bowl and ride on the blade. If it is too moist, add sprinkles of flour.

Do not knead as for a yeast-raised dough.

SHAPING
15 mins.

Divide the dough into 8 pieces and roll each into a ball. Cluster them on the floured work surface and let rest for 3 minutes.

Roll each ball into an 8" round about ½" thick. If the dough resists, move on to another round and return to the first one later. In the meantime, it will have relaxed and it will flatten and stretch with less effort so that it can be rolled as thin as possible. Set the rounds aside and cover with a towel as you complete them.

BAKING
6–8 mins.

Use either an ungreased pan, a metal griddle, or a soapstone griddle. Place it over a high heat. When a drop of water vaporizes the moment it hits the hot surface, place a round in the pan's center. Brown for 3 to 4 minutes on each side. Don't be concerned if the rounds brown unevenly.

FINAL STEP

Place the breads on a rack to dry as you remove them from the heat.

Serve the bread in a basket or other container that will allow air to get to the breads (and not steamed as under a cloth).

If the bread should become limp in a day or so, place the rounds in a single layer on a baking sheet and bake in a 250° oven for 5 to 10 minutes, or until they crisp again.

Flatbrød   [two thick eight-inch circles]
(Norwegian Flatbread)

Unlike many Scandinavian flatbreads, which are paper-thin and crisp, this Norwegian flatbrød, made with whole-wheat and rye flours, is soft, plump, and more easily torn than broken to serve.

We discovered this flatbrød in Oslo when we arrived by train. Even though we had just cycled more than 1,000 miles through France and into Scandinavia and were in top physical shape, we could not make it to Norway and back on the bikes in time to catch a Swedish freighter for home. The train ride was spectacular and, at the end of it, we found this loaf in a small bake shop near the Oslo train station.

Delicious dividend.

INGREDIENTS	1¹/₂ cups rye flour
	1¹/₂ cups whole-wheat flour
	1 tablespoon dark brown sugar
	2 teaspoons baking powder
	1 teaspoon salt
	¹/₂ teaspoon baking soda
	1 egg, room temperature
	1 cup buttermilk
	¹/₄ cup (¹/₂ stick) butter, melted

BAKING SHEET   1 baking sheet, Teflon, sprinkled with cornmeal, or buttered

PREHEAT   Preheat the oven to 425°.

BY HAND
OR MIXER
12 mins.

Into a mixing or mixer bowl measure the rye and whole-wheat flours and add the dry ingredients. In a small bowl lightly beat the egg into the buttermilk. Add the melted butter. With a wooden spoon or a flat beater, blend the buttermilk mixture into the dry ingredients. The flours will gradually accept all of the liquid. Turn onto the floured work surface and work the dough with a dough blade or your hands (or both) until the mixture is smooth, about 3 minutes.

BY PROCESSOR
5 mins.

Attach the steel blade.

Measure the rye and whole-wheat flours into the work bowl and add the dry ingredients. Pulse to blend. In a separate bowl lightly beat the egg into the buttermilk. Stir in the melted butter. With the processor on, pour the buttermilk-butter mixture through the feed tube. When the ingredients are blended together, stop the processor. Don't knead.

SHAPING
4 mins.

The dough may be slightly sticky so dust lightly with sprinkles of flour. Divide the dough into 2 pieces. With your hands and a rolling pin, roll each piece into an 8" to 10" circle, about ½" thick. It need not be perfectly round; a rough shape adds interest.

Place the rounds on the baking sheet and pierce the tops with a fork in a simple design of choice.

BAKING
425°
20 mins.

Bake in the hot oven until browned, about 20 minutes. Turn one loaf over and tap the bottom with a forefinger. It should be crusty, not soft.

(If using a convection oven, reduce heat 50°.)

FINAL STEP

When the loaves are baked, carefully place them on a metal rack. Lift them with a metal spatula because they are fragile while hot.

Serve the breads warm. Tear off pieces to serve. Spread with lots of butter. Also can be used as a pusher or, if no one is looking, dipped into the soup or dunked into coffee.

While it can be frozen, it is best eaten fresh. It can be refrigerated and warmed in the oven before serving.

Middle Eastern Flatbread   [six small loaves]

It is traditional for home bakers in the Middle East to draw the edge of the thumb down the face of the flat loaf to form a series of ridges and sprinkle with toasted sesame or poppy seeds. Others dimple the dough with fingertips just before it goes into the oven. A length of ½-inch dowel pressed against the dough in furrows or the smooth handle of a knife will make a better pattern. It will also allow the finished loaf to be broken into sticks.

There is no substitute for fingers, however, so dimple some of the loaves traditionally and furrow others.

INGREDIENTS

5 cups bread or all-purpose flour, approximately
1 package dry yeast
2 teaspoons salt
3 tablespoons sugar
3 tablespoons olive oil or melted butter
2 cups hot water (120°–130°)
Milk
¼ cup toasted sesame or poppy seeds (see Note)

BAKING SHEETS

1 or more baking sheets, greased or Teflon

BY HAND
OR MIXER
15 mins.

In a large mixing or mixer bowl place 2 cups flour and the dry ingredients. Stir well to mix. Mix the olive oil or butter with the hot water and pour into the flour mixture. Beat with a wooden spoon about 100 strokes, or with a mixer flat beater for 3 minutes. Add flour, ½ cup at a time, working with the wooden spoon and then your hands, to form a rough ball of dough.

KNEADING
6–8 mins.

Turn the dough out onto the work counter, or place under the mixer's dough hook, and knead for 6 to 8 minutes. Add sprinkles of flour if the dough is sticky under your hands or sticks to the sides of the mixer work bowl.

BY PROCESSOR
4 mins.

Attach the plastic blade.

Add 3 cups flour and the dry ingredients to the work bowl. Pour the olive oil or melted butter and hot water through the feed tube. Mix for 10 seconds. Stop the machine and add flour, ½ cup at a time, processing after each addition.

KNEADING
45 secs.

When the ball of dough forms on the blade, knead for 45 seconds.

RISING
30 mins.

Be certain the dough is smooth and elastic before placing it into a greased bowl. Cover tightly with plastic wrap and put in a warm place (80° to 100°) until the dough has doubled in volume, about 30 minutes.

SHAPING
20 mins.

On a floured work surface divide the ball of dough into 6 pieces. With your hands fashion each piece of dough into roughly shaped rectangles. With a rolling pin, roll out the dough to 4"-x-8" and about 1" thick. Use sprinkles of flour if the dough sticks to your hands or the rolling pin.

To make a furrowed bread, press an oiled wooden dowel hard against the dough (lengthwise) at 1" intervals.

For a dimpled loaf, press the fingertips into the dough in a pattern.

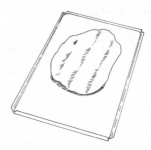

PREHEAT

Preheat the oven to 375°.

When the loaves have been shaped, assemble on the work surface and cover with wax paper. Let rest for 20 minutes.

BAKING
375°
25–30 mins.

Gently but firmly redefine the furrows and dimples with the dowel and your fingers before carefully lifting the dough pieces onto the baking sheet. Not all may go on one sheet, so reserve other pieces under wax paper. Brush each loaf with milk and sprinkle with sesame or poppy seeds.

Place the loaves in the oven and bake until a light golden brown, about 25 to 30 minutes.

(If using a convection oven, reduce heat 50°.)

FINAL STEP

Remove from the baking sheet and cool on racks.

Serve warm or wrap cooled bread in plastic and freeze.

Note: To toast seeds, spread them over a baking sheet and place in a 300° oven for 15 minutes, until lightly browned. Watch carefully so that they don't scorch or burn.

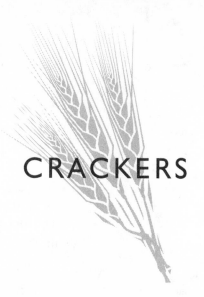

CRACKERS

WHETHER ON A RIVER RAFT or in a balloon, offer me a common soda cracker and I am ecstatic. I am a dedicated crackerphile. I slip across the kitchen and steal them when my wife isn't looking. Waitresses rush the crackers to safety when I come in the door. The romance began alongside a freshly opened barrel of crackers at Knox's Grocery. I was seven years old and just able to peek over the top of the barrel. Mr. Knox offered me the pick of the barrel. It was the beginning of an affair that has lasted more than half a century.

Here are seven cracker recipes, including the common soda cracker. There are dozens of possible variations—some with cheese, some without; some with seeds, some without; some are light, and others dark.

All are good.

The trick in all cracker-making is to get the dough rolled so thin that when it puffs in the oven it will look like a slender cracker and not a fat little wafer. The dough can be rolled directly on the baking surface to achieve a thinness not possible if rolled on the work surface and transferred.

If the dough should draw back as it is being rolled, walk away from it for a few minutes, then come back and roll again. Eventually the sheet of dough will be properly thin—thin to the point that it appears fragile.

An even simpler way is to use a pasta machine, which easily cranks out a perfectly uniform, wafer-thin strip of dough. I also use my hand-cranked beaten biscuit machine with the same uniform results.

The baking time will vary slightly for each cracker on the baking tin: faster along the outside edges and slower in the center. Remove crackers around the perimeter as they brown and crisp.

Crackers are more attractive when they are cut into uniform squares or rounds. Measure off parallel lines on the dough and cut with a pizza cutter, which will not pull the dough as will a knife. Or use a pastry jagger—a wheel that leaves a border not unlike the cut of pinking shears.

Folding the dough—ends into the middle—helps produce tender crackers. Pricking the rolled-out dough with the tines of a fork will keep the crackers from excess blistering during baking. The closer the marks, the flatter the crackers.

Sprinkle salt about 12 inches above the crackers. Toss the salt quickly, moving from side to side. You will use less salt and it will be distributed evenly. Brushing the crackers with melted butter or vegetable shortening immediately upon removing them from the oven will keep them crisper longer and create a golden sheen.

Note: While a good cracker can be baked with all-purpose flour, a better cracker can be made with a mixture of 3 cups all-purpose flour and 1 cup cake flour. The combination of these two flours in a 3 to 1 ratio is very close to the kind of flour used for crackers by commercial bakers.

Plain Soda Crackers   [one hundred crackers]

The baking soda in this cracker has the help of yeast and cream of tartar to puff it up and make it delicious and crisp. The crackers can be cut into squares and rectangles or fanciful shapes with a knife or with a cookie cutter. The dough is kneaded only briefly.

This recipe is adapted from one that came to my kitchen in The Pleasures of Cooking, *an outstanding magazine for home cooks and bakers. It is a fine basic recipe that can easily be used to make a number of other kinds of crackers with the addition of seeds, herbs, and spices. Cheese, too.*

INGREDIENTS	1 1/2 cups bread or all-purpose flour, approximately
	1 package dry yeast
	1/4 teaspoon salt, plus extra for sprinkling
	1/4 teaspoon baking soda
	1/4 teaspoon cream of tartar
	2/3 cup hot water (120°–130°)
	1/2 teaspoon malt syrup
	2 tablespoons solid vegetable shortening
	2 tablespoons butter, melted
BAKING SHEET	1 baking sheet to fit the oven, lightly greased or lined with parchment paper
BY HAND OR MIXER 6 mins.	Into the mixing or mixer bowl measure 1 cup flour and the dry ingredients. In a small bowl combine the hot water, malt syrup, and shortening. Stir to blend and pour the liquid into the bowl; stir vigorously

to blend with a wooden spoon or with the mixer flat beater. Add the balance of the flour to make a rough mass that can be worked under your hands or with the dough hook. If the dough is sticky, add liberal sprinkles of flour.

KNEADING
4 mins.

If by hand, knead with a rhythmic push-turn-fold motion until the dough is soft and elastic. Add sprinkles of flour to control stickiness. If using a mixer, the dough will form a soft ball around the revolving dough hook and clean the sides of the bowl. Add flour if necessary to firm up the dough. Knead only until smooth, about 4 minutes.

BY PROCESSOR
4 mins.

Attach the steel blade.

Measure 1 cup flour and the dry ingredients into the work bowl. Pulse. Combine the hot water, malt syrup, and shortening, as above. With the processor on, pour the liquid through the feed tube.

Add flour, ¼ cup at a time, until the dough becomes a soft, elastic mass that will ride on the blade and clean the sides of the bowl.

KNEADING
30 secs.

Process to knead the dough for 30 seconds.

REFRIGERATION
1 hour–
overnight

Drop the dough into a buttered bowl, cover with plastic wrap, and place in the refrigerator to relax for 1 hour or overnight. The longer the better, up to 18 hours.

PREHEAT

Preheat the oven to 425° 20 minutes before baking.

SHAPING
10 mins.

With a heavy rolling pin, roll the dough into a rectangle about 18"-x-6" and no thicker than ¹⁄₁₆". Fold the dough from the short ends, brushing off excess flour, to make 3 layers. Roll again—with the rolling pin or put through a pasta machine. The dough should be no more than ¹⁄₁₆" thick.

Prick the dough evenly with the tines of a fork; this is called "docking." Cut the dough along the edge of a ruler with a pizza or cookie cutter into desired shapes.

Place the crackers close together on the prepared baking sheet; sprinkle lightly with salt.

BAKING
425°
10–20 mins.

Bake in the center of the oven until lightly browned and crisp, 10 to 20 minutes, depending on the thickness of the crackers. Inspect the crackers several times during baking to make certain they are getting browned, not burned.

(If using a convection oven, reduce heat 50°.)

FINAL STEP	Brush the crackers with the melted butter before removing them from the tray to cool on a metal rack.
VARIATIONS	For sesame-onion crackers, add to the dough 4 teaspoons *each* sesame seeds and grated onion; for an herb cracker, 4 teaspoons *each* chopped fresh parsley and chives, and ½ teaspoon dried dillweed; also try 4 teaspoons caraway seeds or 2 teaspoons poppy seeds.

Onion Crackers   [five dozen tiny crackers]

Onions, poppy seeds, and just a touch of black pepper give these crackers a wonderful aroma while baking and delicious taste when eating. Fine for cocktails and buffets.

INGREDIENTS	2 cups all-purpose flour, approximately 1 teaspoon baking powder 1 tablespoon sugar 2 teaspoons salt ¼ teaspoon freshly ground black pepper 2 tablespoons poppy seeds 1 egg, room temperature ⅓ cup vegetable oil 1 cup finely chopped onions (see Note) 2 tablespoons water, if needed
BAKING SHEET	Baking sheet or sheets to fit the oven, lightly greased or lined with parchment paper
BY HAND OR MIXER 6 mins.	Into the mixing or mixer bowl measure the dry ingredients. In a separate bowl stir together the egg, oil, and chopped onions. Slowly pour the onion mixture into the flour, stirring vigorously with a wooden spoon to blend well, or with the mixer flat beater. The dough should be firm. Add more flour if needed.
KNEADING 4 mins.	If by hand, turn the dough onto a floured work surface and knead briefly—only enough to make a smooth dough. Add sprinkles of flour if the dough is sticky. If using a mixer, attach the dough hook and knead until the dough forms a soft mass around the revolving hook. If the dough does not clean the bowl, add a small amount of flour. Knead for 4 minutes.
BY PROCESSOR	Attach the steel blade. Measure the dry ingredients into the work bowl. Pulse. Prepare the

egg, oil, and onion, as above. With the processor on, pour the liquid mixture through the feed tube. If the dough is dry and crumbly, add 1 or 2 tablespoons water. If the dough is wet, add tablespoons of flour. *Note:* More flour may be needed since the onions will continue to release juice as the processor runs. Add the final portion of flour by hand rather than in the machine to better judge the texture of the dough.

KNEADING
20 secs.

Process to knead in the machine for 20 seconds and then transfer the dough to the work surface to complete the kneading.

REFRIGERATION
30 mins.

Place the dough in a buttered bowl, cover with plastic wrap, and put in the refrigerator to relax for 30 minutes.

PREHEAT

Preheat the oven to 375° just before shaping.

SHAPING
12 mins.

Divide the dough into 2 pieces. Cover one piece with plastic wrap while shaping the first batch of crackers. Press and roll the dough into a rectangle about the length of the baking sheet. Roll the dough as thin as possible without tearing it apart. With the help of the rolling pin, lift and transfer the thin sheet of dough to the baking sheet.

With a rolling pizza cutter or jagger cut the dough into as many crackers as you desire. I do mine freehand because I like the design irregularity, while a ruler or yardstick will give it a professional touch. Prick (dock) each cracker with the tines of a fork.

Repeat for the second piece of dough.

About sixty 1" crackers can be cut from the dough.

BAKING
375°
10–20 mins.

Place the baking sheet on the middle or lower shelf of the oven. Bake until a light golden brown, about 10 minutes, but this depends on the thickness of the dough, and can take as long as 20 minutes. After 8 minutes, check the crackers to be certain they are baking as you want them. (I like mine crispy and deep brown, which takes longer.)

(If using a convection oven, reduce heat 50°.)

FINAL STEP

Remove the baking sheet and lift off the crackers with a spatula to cool on a metal rack.

Note: The food processor is ideal for the chore of onion chopping. The more finely the onions are chopped, the more juice they will release, and thus the more flour they will need. If you don't enjoy chopping by hand or in the processor, substitute dehydrated onion flakes and add a little more water.

Sesame Crackers   [eight eighteen-inch-long strips]

As popular in today's kitchen as it was in those of the ancient Greeks and Hebrews, the Egyptians and Persians, sesame seeds and oil are used in these crackers—enriched further with honey and butter.

If sesame oil—which has a strong flavor and must be used with care—is not available, substitute more butter.

INGREDIENTS

1 cup whole-wheat flour
2 cups all-purpose flour, approximately
1 package dry yeast
1 tablespoon salt
1 cup hot water (120°–130°)
1 tablespoon honey
3 tablespoons butter, melted and cooled to lukewarm, plus extra for brushing
1½ teaspoons Oriental or "dark" sesame oil
½ cup sesame seeds

BAKING SHEET

1 baking sheet to fit the oven, greased lightly or lined with parchment paper

BY HAND OR MIXER
6 mins.

Into a mixing or mixer bowl measure 1 cup each white and whole-wheat flours and add the yeast and salt. In a separate bowl stir together the hot water, honey, melted butter, and sesame oil. Pour the liquid slowly into the flour, beating with strong strokes for 3 minutes with a wooden spoon or at medium speed with a mixer flat beater. Add white flour, ¼ cup at a time, to make a soft dough that can be lifted to the work space, or left in the mixer bowl under the dough hook.

KNEADING
4 mins.

If by hand, knead with an aggressive push-turn-fold rhythm, adding sprinkles of flour if the dough is sticky. Knead only until the dough is smooth. If using the mixer, knead with the dough hook and add flour, if needed, to form a soft ball around the revolving arm. It will clean the sides of the bowl at the same time. Knead for 4 minutes.

BY PROCESSOR
4 mins.

Attach the steel blade.

The order of ingredients varies from above.

Measure ½ cup white flour into the work bowl and add the yeast and salt. Pulse to blend. Prepare the liquids in a separate bowl, as above. With the processor running, pour the liquid through the feed tube. The dough will be a heavy batter.

Add whole-wheat and white flours, ¼ cup at a time, through the feed tube to form a mass that will ride the blade and clean the sides of the bowl. Turn off the machine and allow to stand for 1 minute so the liquid is fully absorbed into the whole-wheat flour. If the dough is dry and crumbly, add water by the teaspoon, with the machine running; if it is too wet, add either white or whole-wheat flour by the tablespoon. The dough should be slightly sticky.

KNEADING
30 secs.

Process to knead for 30 seconds.

RISING
1 hour

Butter a bowl, drop in the dough, and cover the bowl with plastic wrap. Set aside to rise for 1 hour.

PREHEAT

Preheat the oven to 375° before shaping.

SHAPING
12 mins.

Divide the dough into 2 pieces. Cover one piece with plastic wrap while pressing the other by hand into a rough rectangle. In a pasta machine or with a rolling pin, roll the dough into a thin rectangle the length of the baking sheet and about 6" to 8" wide, as thin as it can be rolled. Be concerned more about its thickness than its length or width. If the dough pulls back as it is being rolled, step aside for a few moments while it relaxes.

Place the length of dough on the baking sheet and with a rolling pizza blade or jagger cut into strips about 1½" wide. Prick (dock) each cracker with the tines of a fork. Brush with melted butter, and sprinkle with sesame seeds.

Repeat for the second piece. If the dough is to be held for a second baking, cover with plastic wrap and leave on the work surface.

BAKING
375°
10–20 mins.

Place the baking sheet on the middle shelf of the oven. Bake until golden brown and dry. The baking time will depend on the thickness of the crackers, and may range from 10 to 20 minutes. Test for doneness by pressing with a finger. Watch the crackers carefully.

(If using a convection oven, reduce heat 35°.)

FINAL STEP

Remove from the oven. With a spatula, lift the sheet of crackers from the pan and place on a rack to cool. Break off the long strips, and then break the strips into one- or two-bite pieces of whatever length desired.

These crackers will keep well for 2 or 3 weeks in a tightly covered container.

Knäckerbröd   [about one hundred crackers]
(Swedish Oatmeal Crackers)

This favorite Swedish cracker, Knäckerbröd, is rich and decidedly oatmeal-flavored with 2 full cups uncooked rolled oats in the ingredients. The original Scandinavian recipe called for ½ cup sugar. I thought it was too sweet and cut it back to 3 tablespoons.

These are delicious served with cheese and soup and fruit.

Note: *This recipe is so easy to do by hand that I have not included instructions for the mixer or food processor. Although either can be used it is hardly worth the extra clean-up time.*

INGREDIENTS	½ cup **vegetable shortening** ¼ cup **butter, room temperature** 3 tablespoons **sugar** 2 cups **uncooked rolled oats** 3 cups **all-purpose flour** 2 teaspoons **salt** 1 teaspoon **baking soda** 1½ cups **buttermilk**
BAKING SHEET	1 large baking sheet (the largest the oven will accommodate), greased and sprinkled lightly with rolled oats
BY HAND 8 mins.	In a large bowl cream the shortening, butter, and sugar until smooth. In another bowl combine the oats, flour, salt, and baking soda. Alternately add flour and buttermilk to the creamed mixture, blending until stiff like cookie dough.
REFRIGERATION 1 hour	Refrigerate the dough for at least 1 hour or more to stiffen.
PREHEAT	Preheat the oven to 375° before shaping.
SHAPING 10 mins. for each sheet	Divide the dough into 4, 6, or 8 portions, depending on the size of the baking sheet. Shape each portion into a ball. Return all but one ball to the refrigerator to keep chilled. Place the ball of dough on the prepared baking sheet. Flatten as much as possible with your hands, then use a rolling pin to roll the dough to the edges of the baking sheet—as thinly as possible, no more than ⅛". Prick the sheet evenly with the tines of a fork. Using a pastry wheel, knife, or pizza cutter, score the dough into 2" squares.

BAKING	Bake for 10 to 20 minutes, or until nicely browned and crisp. As they
375°	bake, remove those crackers along the edges of the pan that are brown-
10–20 mins.	ing faster than the others.

          (If using a convection oven, reduce heat 40°.)

FINAL STEP

Allow the crackers to cool for 3 minutes on the baking sheet before placing them on a rack.

      When cooled, break the crackers where scored. Repeat with the remaining dough.

      Store in a container with a tight-fitting lid.

A Rich Cracker   [about three dozen crackers]

Milk, butter, and 1 egg go into this dough to make a rich but crispy cracker.

INGREDIENTS

2 cups all-purpose flour, approximately
1 teaspoon salt
$1/2$ teaspoon baking powder
$1/4$ cup ($1/2$ stick) butter, room temperature
$3/4$ cup milk
1 large egg
Coarse or kosher salt (optional)

BAKING SHEET

1 sheet to fit the oven, lightly buttered or lined with parchment paper

PREHEAT

Preheat the oven to 400°.

**BY HAND
OR MIXER
8 mins.**

Into a mixing or mixer bowl measure 1 cup flour and add the salt and baking powder. Cut the butter into the flour with a pastry blender or 2 knives, or use the mixer flat beater. Stir the milk and egg together and pour into the flour. Beat the batter with vigorous strokes of a wooden spoon or at medium speed in the mixer. Add the balance of the flour, ¼ cup at a time, to make a dough that is a soft mass that can be lifted to the work surface or left in the mixer under the dough hook.

**KNEADING
4 mins.**

Knead for a short period, no more than 4 minutes, with your hands or under the dough hook.

**BY PROCESSOR
5 mins.**

Attach the steel blade.

      Measure 1 cup flour, the salt, and baking powder into the work bowl. Pulse. With the processor on, drop in the butter and follow this with the milk and egg. Add the balance of the flour. The dough will form a ball and clean the sides of the bowl. Add sprinkles of flour if the dough is wet.

KNEADING
30 secs.

Process to knead for 30 seconds.

SHAPING
10 mins.

Divide the dough into 2 pieces. Reserve one piece under plastic wrap as you work with the other. Roll the dough as thin as possible and yet be able to move to the baking sheet. Place on the sheet, dock or prick the dough with the tines of a fork, and cut into squares or rounds. It is better to do the cutting on the baking sheet rather than to cut on the work surface and then try to move the crackers one by one.

BAKING
400°
10–20 mins.

If desired, lightly sprinkle the crackers with coarse (kosher) salt.

Place the baking sheet in the middle of the oven and bake until a rich brown, 10 to 20 minutes. The bake time will vary according to the thickness of the crackers so check the crackers every 5 minutes.

(If using a convection oven, reduce heat 25°.)

When the first batch of crackers is baked repeat with the remainder.

FINAL STEP

When the crackers are a golden brown and crispy, take from the oven and place on a rack to cool.

Stored in a closed container, the crackers will stay fresh for several weeks. They also freeze very well.

Cheddar Cheese Crackers [four dozen tiny crackers]

There is just a hint of cayenne pepper to accent the Cheddar cheese in this recipe. It makes a great cracker for snacks, the cocktail tray, or a buffet. Or just to eat out of hand.

INGREDIENTS

1 1/2 ounces Cheddar cheese
1 1/2 cups all-purpose flour
1/4 teaspoon salt, plus extra for sprinkling
1/4 teaspoon cream of tartar
1/4 teaspoon baking soda
1/8 teaspoon cayenne pepper
1/3 cup plus 2 tablespoons tepid water (90°–100°)
1/2 teaspoon malt syrup
2 tablespoons solid vegetable shortening, room temperature
Butter, melted

BAKING SHEET

1 or 2 baking sheets, depending on the size of the oven, greased or lined with parchment paper

PREPARATION 3 mins.	Shred the cheese or, if using a food processor for the recipe, cut the cheese into chunks.
BY HAND OR MIXER 8 mins.	Into a mixing or mixer bowl measure 1 cup flour and add the dry ingredients and cheese. Stir to mix well. In a separate bowl dissolve the malt in the water and add the shortening. Form a well in the center of the flour; pour in the liquid shortening. If by hand, stir with a wooden spoon to blend. The mixture will be quite heavy. If using a mixer, use the flat beater and mix for 2 minutes. Add flour, a few tablespoons at a time, to form a dough that can be lifted from the bowl to knead, or left in the mixer bowl under the dough hook.
KNEADING 4 mins.	On a work surface knead briefly by hand, adding sprinkles of flour if the dough is wet. In the mixer the dough will form a soft ball around the revolving dough hook. If the dough clings to the sides of the mixer bowl, add light sprinkles of flour. Knead by hand or with the mixer for 4 minutes, until the dough is smooth.
BY PROCESSOR 4 mins.	Attach the steel blade. Measure all of the flour into the work bowl and add the dry ingredients and the cheese chunks. Pulse until the cheese pieces are small granules in the flour. In a small bowl dissolve the malt in the water and add the shortening. Turn on the processor and pour the liquid through the feed tube. If the dough does not form a ball, add water by the teaspoon.
KNEADING 25 secs.	When the dough forms a ball and rides with the blade, process to knead for 25 seconds.
REFRIGERATION 1 hour	Place the dough in a small bowl, cover tightly with plastic wrap, and place in the refrigerator to relax for at least 1 hour. The dough can be used immediately or it can be kept, tightly wrapped, for up to 2 days in the refrigerator.
PREHEAT	Preheat the oven to 400° 20 minutes before baking.
SHAPING 12 mins.	Divide the dough in half. Keep one half covered. With your hands and a heavy rolling pin, press and roll the dough into a rectangle no longer than the length of the baking pan, usually about 18", and 7" wide. The dough should be no thicker than 1⁄16". Fold the dough from the ends to make 3 layers. Turn the dough and roll it again into a 1⁄16" rectangle. Lift the dough from the work surface and lay on the prepared bak-

ing sheet. Prick (dock) the entire surface with the tines of a fork. With a rolling pizza cutter, cookie cutter, or a sharp knife cut the dough into crackers of the desired size. The crackers will be broken apart after baking.

Sprinkle the crackers lightly with salt.

BAKING
400°
8–15 mins.

Bake in the center of the oven until lightly browned and crisp, 8 to 15 minutes, depending on the thickness of the dough. Check the crackers frequently so they are not baked beyond where you want them. I like mine well baked and crisp, which means that often my crackers are almost scorched along the fringes.

(If using a convection oven, reduce heat 50°.)

FINAL STEP

Remove from the oven and immediately brush with melted butter. Cool on wire racks. Repeat with the remaining dough.

The crackers will stay fresh for 3 to 4 weeks if stored in an airtight container.

Lil's Ice-Water Crackers [two dozen crackers]

While it is hard to beat a store-bought saltine for crispness and pleasant good taste, it is possible to give that same saltine a different and delicious personality by dipping it in ice water, spreading with melted butter, and baking again. Puffy, buttery, and done to a deep golden brown, the cracker is especially good with soups and chowders.

Lillian Marshall, an outstanding Kentucky cook and author, does imaginative things with food, and this is one of them.

INGREDIENTS

24 plain saltine crackers
2 quarts ice water
$^1/_2$ cup (1 stick) butter or margarine, melted

BAKING PAN

1 shallow pan in which to soak crackers and later in which to bake them

PREHEAT

Preheat the oven to 475°.

PREPARATION
15 mins.

Lay a single layer of saltines in the shallow pan and pour ice water over them. Let stand for about 3 minutes.

Carefully remove the crackers with a slotted spoon and place on a double layer of paper towels (laid over a linen towel) to drain for 5 to 8 minutes.

Dry the pan and pour half the melted butter over the bottom; spread with your fingers. Arrange the crackers on the pan and drizzle the remaining butter over them.

BAKING
475°
15–20 mins.

Place in the hot oven and bake for 15 to 20 minutes. Check frequently: don't let the crackers burn.

(If using a convection oven, reduce heat 50°.)

FINAL STEP

Serve hot. Enjoy.

STORING AND FREEZING

BREAD TO BE EATEN within the next day or two should be kept in a paper bag, bread box, or bread drawer. Don't wrap it in plastic unless you want an especially soft crust. If the bread is to be used for toast, it doesn't matter. The toaster will crisp the slice.

Bread will not go stale as quickly at room temperature as it will in the refrigerator. However, if you fear the loaf may mold, refrigerate it.

Bread will freshen simply by heating it unwrapped in a 350° oven for 15 minutes.

If you are concerned that a whole loaf will stale before it can be eaten, freeze part of it to serve fresh at a later date.

Frozen bread keeps and freshens so well that I freeze all bread to be held, even though I may plan to use it within the next few days.

To freeze, allow the loaf to cool before placing it in two medium or heavy plastic bags, one inside the other. Tie securely with a wire wrap. Freeze. After taking the bread out of the freezer, allow it to thaw inside the unopened bags. Frost particles and ice crystals inside the bag represent moisture from the bread and should be allowed to be absorbed back. Keep the bread in the plastic bag until the crystals have disappeared, then remove the bread from the bag, place on a baking sheet, and put it in a 350° oven for 15 minutes.

Freezing dough is less than satisfactory. It can be done, of course, but you must watch it for hours as it thaws so that when it doubles in volume it can be shaped into loaves and placed in pans or on a baking sheet. Then it must be allowed to double or triple in volume before putting it in the oven. Considering the amount of time devoted to waiting for things to happen, it is hardly worth the bother.

WHAT WENT WRONG—AND HOW TO MAKE IT RIGHT

WHILE THERE ARE SEVERAL things that can go wrong in bread-making, there are far more things that can go right. Bread-making is a forgiving art. Expect good things to come out of the oven, and they usually will.

Here are some of the things that can go wrong and what can be done about them.

TOO-SOFT DOUGH

If the dough for the freestanding hearth loaf that you formed on the baking sheet spreads and slouches when it is supposed to rise, work a small quantity of flour into the slack dough and knead it aggressively. The combination of flour and kneading will give the dough sufficient body to stand alone on the baking sheet. Test it by slapping your open hand against the ball of dough. Leave it there for a count of ten. If your hand comes away clean, the dough has enough flour.

CANNONBALL

It happens to all bakers, especially new ones. There it is—a solid ball of dough that has neither elasticity nor suppleness. It can best be described as a cannonball. Too much flour has been forced into the dough. If you attempt to knead or punch it down, there's no give. Solid. Add water to soften it. This is a sticky process, but the dough *can* be salvaged. Knead again.

SALT?

When the loaf is baked and the slice tastes flat, you probably have forgotten the salt. It happens. Taste a bit of dough during the kneading to make certain you salted it. Also, if made without salt, the dough will be stringy, unresponsive, and pull away in strands as it is being kneaded. If you realize you forgot the salt, dissolve some in a little water and add to the dough. Or brush salt water on the crust before and after it is baked.

Won't Rise

If the dough refuses to rise, you may have forgotten the yeast or the yeast may have been outdated and dead. Don't throw the dough away. Start a new batch of dough but make certain the yeast—in the amount specified in the recipe—is among the ingredients. After the dough is mixed, blend the two doughs. There will be more than enough healthy yeast cells to go around. Or dissolve the yeast in a small amount of water and work this into the dough. It will be a sticky mess in the beginning, but the yeast will be absorbed.

Loaf Too High

If it is obvious that the dough rising in the pan is pushing too high, it will probably collapse when the heat of the oven forces it to stretch even further (oven-spring). Punch down the dough, reshape the loaves, and don't allow the dough to rise beyond the recommended volume, usually double.

Pans Too Big; Pans Too Small

When the dough has risen in the pans, it may be obvious that the dough and the pans are mismatched—too much dough in pans too small, or too little dough in pans too large. Either way, the loaves will be less than attractive.

Turn the dough out of the pans, knead briefly again, reshape, and match to the proper size pans according to the Dough Volume chart on page 16. Let rise in the pans again. Most doughs in conventional rectangular bread pans should rise about a half inch above the edge before they go into the oven. Cylindrical pans, such as coffee cans, are filled two-thirds and dough is allowed to rise to the edge before baking.

Pale Bottom, Pale Sides

The top crust is golden brown but the side and bottom crusts are pale and appear not done when the loaves are turned out of their pans. Shiny aluminum pans are the worst offenders since they reflect rather than transmit heat. Return the loaves to the oven out of the pans for 5 to 10 minutes. They will get a lovely overall tan.

Crust Too Hard

If the crust is too hard and crisp, next time bake with less steam in the oven. A hard crust softens overnight if left in a plastic bag.

CRUST TOO SOFT

If the crust for French-type bread is not thick or crusty enough, place more water in the broiler pan to generate more steam, or give it an additional spray of water with an atomizer. A swipe with a wet pastry brush will also help a hard crust to develop.

UNEVEN CRUST COLOR

Once or twice during baking open the oven door and change the positions of the pans so the loaves are exposed evenly to the temperature variations that occur in most ovens.

POORLY BAKED

The dough was beautifully risen when it went into the oven but it came out a disappointment. Bread must be baked at the recommended temperature. Test the oven with a thermometer. Never trust the oven thermostat to deliver the temperature it promises. An oven 100° too cool will not bake bread. An oven 100° too hot may burn it to a crisp.

SHELLING

When the bread under the top crust separates to form a tunnel the length of the loaf, it is probably caused by one of two things. The top surface of the dough may have been partially dried out during the rising and later, in the oven, the heat could not uniformly penetrate the thick surface of the "shell." Or the oven heat may have been too low and the dough expanded unevenly. For the next bake session, cover the dough with wax or parchment paper or foil during rising to prevent loss of moisture. Preheat the oven so the dough will get the full benefit of all heat at the outset. Use a thermometer beforehand to make certain the oven temperature is correct.

LAYERED EFFECT

If there is a layer of dough in the loaf just below the crust that is different in texture and color when baked, it may be that you added too much flour too late in the kneading process and it didn't get absorbed into the dough. Sprinkles of flour are no problem, but substantial amounts can be, unless followed by additional kneading.

STANDARD WEIGHTS
AND MEASURES

Make certain all measurements are level.

Dash	= 8 drops
1 tablespoon	= 3 teaspoons
4 tablespoons	= ¼ cup
5 ⅓ tablespoons	= ⅓ cup
8 tablespoons	= ½ cup
16 tablespoons	= 1 cup (dry)
1 fluid ounce	= 2 tablespoons
1 cup (liquid)	= ½ pint
2 cups (16 ounces)	= 1 pint
2 pints (4 cups)	= 1 quart
4 quarts	= 1 gallon
8 quarts	= 1 peck (dry)
4 pecks	= 1 bushel
16 ounces (dry measure)	= 1 pound

OTHER MEASUREMENTS

1 lemon	= 2–3 tablespoons juice and 2 teaspoons zest
1 orange	= 6–8 tablespoons juice and 2–3 tablespoons zest
1 cup heavy cream	= 2 cups whipped cream
2 cups water	= 1 pound

5 large whole eggs
6 medium   } = 1 cup, approximately
7 small

8 large egg whites
10–11 medium   } = 1 cup, approximately
11–12 small

12 large egg yolks
13–14 medium   } = 1 cup, approximately
15–16 small

FLUID MEASURE EQUIVALENTS

METRIC	UNITED STATES	BRITISH
1 liter	4½ cups *or* 1 quart 2 ounces	1¾ pints
1 demiliter (½ liter)	2 cups (generous) *or* 1 pint (generous)	¾ pint (generous)
1 deciliter (¹/₁₀ liter)	½ cup (scant) *or* ¼ pint (scant)	3–4 ounces

MEASURE EQUIVALENTS

METRIC	UNITED STATES	BRITISH
1.00 gram	.035 ounce	.035 ounce
28.35 grams	1 ounce	1 ounce
100.00 grams	3.5 ounces	3.5 ounces
114.00 grams	4 ounces (approximately)	4 ounces (approximately)
226.78 grams	8 ounces	8 ounces
500.00 grams	1 pound 1.5 ounces	1 pound 1.5 ounces
1.00 kilogram	2.21 pounds	2.21 pounds

Comparative U.S., British and Metric Weights and Measures for Ingredients Important to Pastry Makers

INGREDIENT	UNITED STATES	BRITISH	METRIC
Almond paste	1¾ cups	16 ounces	450 grams
Apples, pared/sliced	1 cup	4 ounces	125 grams
Berries	1¾ cups	6 ounces	190 grams
Butter	1 tablespoon	½ ounce	15 grams
	½ cup	4 ounces	125 grams
	2 cups	1 pound (generous)	450 grams
Cheese	1 pound (generous)	1 pound (generous)	450 grams
Cheese, grated hard type	1 cup (scant)	4 ounces (scant)	100 grams
Cheese, cottage	1 cup	16 ounces	450 grams
Cheese, cream	6 tablespoons	3 ounces	80 grams
Cornstarch	1 tablespoon	⅓ ounce	10 grams
Flour (unsifted)	¼ cup	1¼ ounces	35 grams
	½ cup	2½ ounces	70 grams
	1 cup	4 ¾ ounces	142 grams
	3½ cups	1 pound	450 grams
Herbs, fresh/chopped	1 tablespoon	½ ounce	15 grams
Nuts, chopped	1 cup	5½ ounces	155 grams
Raisins (seedless)	1 tablespoon	⅓ ounce	10 grams
	1 cup	5 ⅓ ounces	160 grams
	3 cups	1 pound	450 grams
Spices, ground	1 teaspoon	¹/₁₂ ounce	2.5 grams
	2 tablespoons	½ ounce	15 grams
Sugar, granulated	1 teaspoon	¹/₆ ounce	15 grams
	1 tablespoon	½ ounce	15 grams
	¼ cup	2 ounces	60 grams
	1 cup	8 ounces	226 grams
Sugar, confectioners'	¼ cup	1 ounce (generous)	35 grams
	½ cup	2¼ ounces (scant)	70 grams
	1 cup	4½ ounces (scant)	140 grams
Sugar, brown	1 tablespoon	⅓ ounce	10 grams
	½ cup	2 ⅔ ounces	80 grams
	1 cup	5 ⅓ ounces	160 grams

BAKING FOR DOGS

AFTER WATCHING TELEVISION commercials in which dogs seemed to be eating better than I, I tried a sampling of dog food and found the biscuits for dogs hard, dry, and with little taste, and I was turned off by the odor of "moist and chunky bits."

This was the second time in recent years I had looked into canine cuisine, and I found it no better now than it was ten years ago when I visited the neighbors and begged for leftovers from the dog's dinner to conduct my research. They thought I was slightly daft then and they still do, a decade later.

It all began when a woman in California wrote that she was tired of mounting food bills for a growing dog, and since she baked a week's supply of bread for the family at one time, why not mix up a batch of something savory for the family dog at the same time?

At the termination of this study I can report that 1) the taste of dog food has not improved at all, and 2) it sells for whatever price the manufacturer thinks it can get at the moment. At this writing dry dog food is about 50 cents a pound, slightly higher for "nutritious tender biscuits especially for puppies," and biscuits that give your dog "cleaner, whiter teeth in three weeks—or your money back."

The ingredients for all are much the same—wheat flour, cornmeal, wheat germ meal, meat meal, poultry by-products, condensed fish solubles, and on and on through a dozen more ingredients. "Glandular meat" is not my idea of haute cuisine, and one is inclined to ask "where is the beef?"

My creation, I decided, must be palatable to beast and man alike, for who knows how many dog biscuits have been eaten by human two-year-olds?

Dog Biscuits   [about 200 biscuits]

Here is the recipe: no sugar, no shortening. The cracked wheat gives an inter-esting speckled texture to the dough. In the refrigerator I found chicken stock made a week before with chicken necks, wings, backs, and giblets. About ¹/₂ inch of fat had congealed on the surface; I scraped this off, and warmed it in a pan.

3¹/₂ cups all-purpose flour, approximately
2 cups whole-wheat flour
I cup rye flour
I cup cornmeal
2 cups cracked wheat (bulgur)
¹/₂ cup nonfat dry milk
I tablespoon salt (or less)
I package dry yeast dissolved in ¹/₄ cup warm water (105°–115°)
I pint chicken stock or other liquid, approximately, warmed
I egg, beaten, mixed with I tablespoon milk

In a large bowl combine the dry ingredients. Add the dissolved yeast and the chicken stock or other liquid and egg. Mix together.

Knead for about 3 minutes into a stiff dough.

Roll the dough into ¼" sheets. Cut with cookie cutters into stars, circles, trees, bears, cats, and rabbits, any one of which should pleaure your dog. Place on a baking sheet.

Since there is no need to let them rise beforehand, I put the biscuits directly into a 300° oven for 45 minutes, turn off the heat, and leave them overnight. In the morning they are bone-hard, guaranteed to clean a dog's teeth in hours.

When I created this recipe the only problem that developed was that my homemade dog biscuits were so tasty I could hardly bring myself to feed them to my test animal, Timothy, a Cairn terrier. He loved them and bit into them with a satisfying crunch— and begged for more. But there were none. I had eaten them.

It is a wonderfully versatile food.

It can be nutritionally tailored any way you and the dog want. If he (or she) has a sweet tooth, add sugar or honey or molasses. If he is on a salt-free diet, omit the sodium. If his diet requires vitamins, include them. I could have used butter, mar-garine, or cooking oil, as well as the more economical lard, suet, or bacon drippings. If eggs had been cheap, I might have included a half dozen or so for a rich golden batch.

A veterinarian could suggest other ingredients that only a dog's doctor can prescribe, but personally I will stick with the original recipe since neither Timothy nor I can get enough of them.

And the price is roughly 25 cents a pound, about half the cost of inferior store-bought biscuits.

This recipe, revised only slightly, was first published in 1975, and since then I have received scores of thank-you cards and letters, especially at Christmastime, from dogs all across the country who have received presents of these biscuits from the dog next door or down the street.

HOMEMADE OVEN

 N THE "Equipment" chapter of this book I described a homemade adobe oven for the
backyard. I have received letters from hundreds of readers asking for the adobe oven plans.

Here are those plans.

Have a great time.

ADOBE OVEN—TO BUILD AND USE

MATERIALS

16 6"-x-8"-x-16" concrete blocks

129 ordinary building bricks

1 28-gallon paper drum or barrel (can usually be obtained from
    lumberyard)

1 3'-x-4' piece of 4" concrete reinforcing wire

1 3'-x-4' piece chicken wire or mesh

1 1-pound can (juice or fruit, not coffee), ends removed, for use as
    draft chimney

1 2"-x-6" board for oven door (you'll probably need 8')

1 1"-x-3" board, about 6' long

3 98-pound bags cement

Garden soil (equivalent to 10 or 12 bags), preferably dry and sifted
    through ¼" hardware cloth for better blend

Water

1 crosscut saw

1 saber saw

1 pair rubber gloves

1 plastic sheet

1 pint exterior paint

1 3"-x-5" metal sheet

1. Arrange 12 concrete blocks in a level 32" wide by 48" deep rectangle. (See Fig. A.)

2. Top the blocks with 2 layers of building bricks (96 bricks). (See Fig. A.)

FIGURE A

3. Place the remaining 4 concrete blocks in front to serve as a hearth. Set in 2 layers perpendicular to the other blocks. (See Fig. B.)

4. Cut the paper drum in half lengthwise with a hacksaw or saber saw. (See Fig. B.) Cut the draft hole in the drum end to fit the tin can.

5. Stack the bricks on the sides and back 3 bricks high and 4" in. Set the paper drum on them. (See Fig. B.)

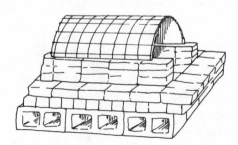

FIGURE B

6. Shape the concrete reinforcing wire over the drum, tucking the excess under the drum front. (See Fig. B.) Mold the chicken wire over the top, back of the drum, and around the front opening. Cut out the draft hole in the chicken wire and fit the can into it. (See Fig. C.)

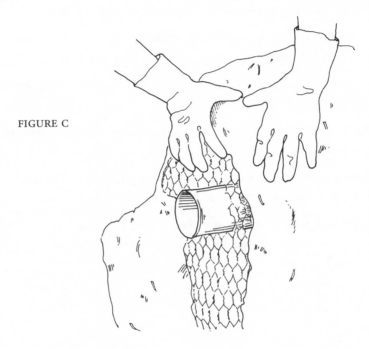

FIGURE C

7. Estimate the door size. Make the door using the 2" board for the door and 1" board for the cross pieces and handle—if desired—(see Fig. D). The adobe will be molded while the door is in place to achieve a close-fitting opening. (See Fig. D.)

FIGURE D

8. The mud or adobe is a blend of 1 shovelful of cement with 3 shovelsful of garden soil mixed with water to a consistency that can be forced between the wires by hand yet is firm enough not to run or slump. Make the walls about 4" thick. My recommendations for a workable batch of adobe would be one made from 3 shovelsful of cement to 9 shovelsful of garden soil. Cover the floor bricks with a 1" layer.

9. Put the door in place and mold a close-fitting oven opening. Remove the door when the adobe is slightly firm.

10. If desired, place 2 large metal hook-eyes in wet mud on top of the oven to secure a metal sheet for winter protection.

11. Smooth the surface with a gloved hand dipped in water. Cover with wet cloths, a plastic sheet, and allow to cure for 1 week. Keep the cloths damp.

12. Later, when the oven is thoroughly dry, paint with exterior latex. After frequent use, repaint to help conceal harmless heat cracks and smoke marks.

13. To protect the oven against snow or heavy freezing, bend a sheet of galvanized metal over the crown of the oven, cut slits for the 2 eyes, and secure the cover in place with wires through the eyes.

14. If the heat of the oven scorches or burns the wood door, it can be faced with a sheet of metal or asbestos shingles.

To Use the Oven

TOOLS
Long-handled shovel
Broom (push-broom is best)
Mop
Bucket of water
Large galvanized rubbish can with lid, or other metal receptacle
Thermometer
Baker's peel or long-handled paddle
Razor blade
Meat baster

To improvise a baker's peel, fasten a broom or other long handle to a smooth, thin board large enough to hold at least 1 loaf of bread.

Remove the door and open the draft hole.

Build and maintain a fire for at least 2 hours at the end of which time hot, glowing embers and ashes will cover the floor to a depth of 4" to 6". The outside of the oven will be hot to the touch.

The fruit woods (apple, cherry, etc.) or any of the hard woods, such as oak or ash, are best. I prefer not to use pine or fir because of the high resin content.

With the shovel, scoop out the embers and drop into the metal rubbish can. Don't leave the can on the unprotected lawn or it will scorch the grass. Elevate it on bricks. (Put the lid on the can. Later toss the ashes back into the oven so they will burn away.)

Insert a plug of wet rags or a can lid over the draft hole to prevent heat from escaping.

Dip the broom into water and sweep the ashes forward. Lift out with the shovel. Quickly mop the floor.

Set the thermometer in the center of the floor. Place the door in position. After 5 minutes, check the temperature. It may be around 600°—far too hot for bread but ideal for a standing rib roast. Leave the door off and allow the oven to cool to about 400°.

Place the first loaf onto a peel or paddle that has been sprinkled liberally with cornmeal. Slash the top of the loaf with a sharp knife or razor blade. Brush with an egg mixture.

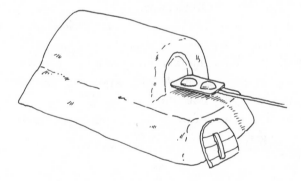

When the oven has cooled to between 325° and 300°, slip the first loaf onto the clean oven floor. (A quick jerk will drop the loaf onto the floor.) When all the loaves are in the oven, set the door in place. Check the temperature in 5 minutes. If it has risen to above 400°, remove the door until the temperature drops, then close. The oven will be considerably hotter in the back portion, so be prepared to shuffle loaves during the bake period. While the loaves can be moved around with the peel, I often use a gloved hand.

Spray or squirt water from a meat baster onto the floor alongside the loaves twice (at 5-minute intervals) to create a cloud of steam.

Continue baking for about 45 minutes, or until the loaves are a rich golden brown. Remove from the oven and allow to cool. Break or slice to serve.

A RECIPE FOR BAKER'S CLAY

Eᴠᴇʀʏ ʙᴀᴋᴇʀ ᴄʀᴇᴀᴛᴇꜱ a bread—a wreath, a braid, an animal, or just a handsome loaf—of which he (or she) is especially proud, and wishes he could keep it forever as a decorative piece. With baker's clay, it can be done.

Baker's clay, too, is excellent for original work far afield from the kitchen. If a figure can be done in modeling clay, it can be done in baker's clay.

The dough should be used within four hours or it may become too dry to shape. For upright designs, use an armature made with wire or chicken wire. Preferably, build pieces horizontally, or they may not fit into the oven.

There is no leavening power in this dough to make it rise, so what you see as you shape it is what you'll get.

Final note: Don't eat!

Baker's Clay   [one pound inedible dough]

INGREDIENTS	4 cups all-purpose flour
	1 cup salt
	1½ cups water
BAKING SHEET	1 baking sheet, ungreased
PREHEAT	Preheat the oven to 350°.
BY HAND OR MIXER 10 mins.	In a medium bowl combine the ingredients. Mix thoroughly with a wooden spoon and your hands or in an electric mixer with a flat beater. If the dough is too stiff to handle, add more water, a little at a time. If the dough is wet and sticky, add sprinkles of flour.

KNEADING **4 mins.**	Knead for 4 minutes by hand or with the mixer dough hook.
BY PROCESSOR **3 mins.**	Attach the plastic blade. Measure all of the ingredients into the work bowl, and pulse to blend. Add sprinkles of flour if wet.
KNEADING **30 secs.**	Process for 30 seconds, or until the dough forms a ball and rides on the blade.
SHAPING	Shape the dough into desired pieces, and place on the baking sheet.
BAKING **350°** **1 hour or** **longer**	Bake for 1 hour or more depending on the size and thickness of the pieces. Some may take 2 hours or longer. Test for doneness with a fork or toothpick in the thickest part of the piece. If still soft, bake a little longer.
FINAL STEP	Lift the pieces from the sheet with a spatula. Cool on racks. When thoroughly cooled, paint or decorate, if desired. Spray finished pieces with a clear fixative to prevent softening. *Don't eat!*

GLOSSARY

ATOMIZER	Small water-filled bottle with spray head used to create steam in the oven. I use a glass-cleaner bottle, well rinsed.
CUT IN	To mix fat and flour with a wire pastry blender, tips of the fingers, crossed knives, or machine, so that fat particles are flour covered but discrete, not smeared.
DOUGH KNIFE OR BLADE	A metal rectangle about 4" by 5", with a handhold to lift and work dough. It is also called a "bench knife." French call it a *coupe-pâte*. It becomes an extension of the hand.
DUST	Sprinkle lightly or brush with flour, sugar, and so on.
FERMENTATION	The chemical reaction of the ingredients in dough that causes the forming of a gas, carbon dioxide which, in turn, causes the dough to expand.
FOLD	To gently incorporate or blend flour and other ingredients into a mixture with a spatula or mixer at low speed so as not to destroy the texture of the mixture.
GLAZE	To create a glossy finish with a thin coating of sugar, icing, fruit syrups, jellies, and other liquids.
GLUTEN	The rubbery, elastic substance found in most flours when water is added.
GREASE	To rub lightly with butter, margarine, shortening, lard, or salad oil.
KNEAD	To work into a mass or to develop dough while mixing.

LEAVENING	A substance that will produce gas to cause aeration within a product, found in bread yeast and chemicals, such as baking powder and baking soda.
LIGHT	Dough that has risen and is puffy with gas is spoken of as light.
MIX	Blend into one mass.
PARCHMENT PAPER	Specially treated paper used to line baking sheets and tins without sticking. Sold in rolls in gourmet cookware shops, and some well-stocked supermarkets.
PEEL	A flat board used for placing bakery products in the oven and taking them out again.
PINCH	Approximately ⅛ teaspoon, or an amount that can be held between the thumb and forefinger.
PREHEAT	Turn on and heat oven to desired temperature before putting in breads, usually 25 to 20 minutes.
PROOF	The stages of fermentation before baking.
SCALE	Weigh materials.
SIMMER	To cook just below the boiling point. There are no bubbles, but the surface moves slightly.
STIR	To blend with a circular motion, with a spoon, widening circles until all ingredients are well mixed. Used in dissolving.
STEAM	Inject water into the oven to create steam while baking.
DOCK, STIPPLE	Pierce dough with tines of a fork or a straight piece of heavy wire before baking to let gas escape during baking.
WASH	To brush the surface, before or after baking, with a mixture, usually of whole egg lightly beaten and thinned with milk or cream. If deeper color is desired, use yolks instead of whole eggs.
ZEST	Finely grated peel of orange, lemon, or lime.

INDEX

ABOUT THE AUTHOR

BERNARD CLAYTON began his career as a reporter and foreign correspondent. Baking was his hobby. As a result, he has experimented with various modern techniques, developing his craft. He has been writing cookbooks for thirty years, beginning with *The Complete Book of Breads*. When he travels, Mr. Clayton investigates historical and regional recipes, conversing with bakers around the world. He lives with his wife in Bloomington, Indiana.